The Process of Research and Statistical Analysis in Psychology

For my family

Sara Miller McCune founded SAGE Publishing in 1965 to support the dissemination of usable knowledge and educate a global community. SAGE publishes more than 1000 journals and over 600 new books each year, spanning a wide range of subject areas. Our growing selection of library products includes archives, data, case studies and video. SAGE remains majority owned by our founder and after her lifetime will become owned by a charitable trust that secures the company's continued independence.

Los Angeles | London | New Delhi | Singapore | Washington DC | Melbourne

The Process of Research and Statistical Analysis in Psychology

Dawn M. McBride

Illinois State University

Los Angeles | London | New Delhi
Singapore | Washington DC | Melbourne

FOR INFORMATION:

SAGE Publications, Inc.
2455 Teller Road
Thousand Oaks, California 91320
E-mail: order@sagepub.com

SAGE Publications Ltd.
1 Oliver's Yard
55 City Road
London EC1Y 1SP
United Kingdom

SAGE Publications India Pvt. Ltd.
B 1/I 1 Mohan Cooperative Industrial Area
Mathura Road, New Delhi 110 044
India

SAGE Publications Asia-Pacific Pte. Ltd.
18 Cross Street #10-10/11/12
China Square Central
Singapore 048423

Acquisitions Editor: Abbie Rickard
Editorial Assistant: Elizabeth Cruz
Content Development Editor: Emma Newsom
Production Editor: Andrew Olson
Copy Editor: Megan Markanich
Typesetter: C&M Digitals (P) Ltd.
Proofreader: Scott Oney
Indexer: Karen Wiley
Cover Designer: Candice Harman
Marketing Manager: Katherine Hepburn

Printed in the United States of America

Library of Congress Cataloging-in-Publication Data

Names: McBride, Dawn M., author.

Title: The process of research and statistical analysis in psychology / Dawn M. McBride, Illinois State University.

Description: First Edition. | Thousand Oaks, California : SAGE Publications, [2019] | Includes bibliographical references and index.

Identifiers: LCCN 2019007217 | ISBN 9781544361994 (pbk. : alk. paper)

Subjects: LCSH: Psychology—Research. | Psychology—Research—Methodology. | Analysis of variance. | Statistics.

Classification: LCC BF76.5 .M3757 2019 | DDC 150.72—dc23
LC record available at https://lccn.loc.gov/2019007217

This book is printed on acid-free paper.

SFI label applies to text stock

19 20 21 22 23 10 9 8 7 6 5 4 3 2 1

BRIEF CONTENTS

DETAILED CONTENTS

PREFACE

My goal in writing this text is to provide a clearly written, student-friendly introduction to conducting research and using statistics in psychological studies. In organizing the text, I have drawn on my experiences over the past 20 plus years teaching methods courses and the hands-on, step-by-step approach I take with this topic in my courses. The text covers topics in the order they arise in the research process to help students understand how to develop, conduct, and present a research study. The coverage also focuses on using knowledge of research and statistics in everyday life to inform students in their decision making. To this end, concepts important for developing research ideas, subject sampling, and ethics are covered in early chapters of the text along with a brief overview of data collection techniques and research designs and data distributions. In addition, concepts and skills relevant to more than one stage of the research process are covered in multiple contexts. This approach allows students repeated exposure to the topics that are most important in learning research skills and to the topics in methods and statistics courses that I have found students have the most difficulty learning. For example, internal validity is covered in multiple chapters and discussed as it relates to different designs such as experiments and correlational studies. Chapters describing statistical tests also provide specific connections to the steps of hypothesis testing introduced in earlier chapters. Thus, important and difficult concepts are repeated in different scenarios to aid students' learning with spaced repetition of concepts so that knowledge and skills are more easily gained over time. Using findings from memory research, I present material in ways that will optimize student learning. Most research in memory shows that spaced repetition of information leads to better long-term memory. Thus, reading about difficult topics in multiple contexts will use these principles to students' advantage. I also include opportunities for students to practice recalling the information both within the text of the chapters in Stop and Think sections and in the end-of-chapter quizzes to strengthen their retention of the material.

The text also includes numerous research examples from published studies and activities in each chapter that come from a wide range of areas in psychology, giving students a useful overview of real research. Additional exercises with research examples are available online at edge.sagepub.com/mcbridermstats. Thinking About Research sections at the end of each chapter provide students with condensed summaries of published research studies to help practice reading and understanding empirical articles. Critical thinking questions help students tie the research they read about to the topics covered in the chapters.

This book mirrors the steps in the research process and creates logical scaffolding upon which students can build their knowledge. I hope students will find this text to be a readable and practical guide to conducting psychological research.

With J. Cooper Cutting, I have also written the *Lab Manual for Psychological Research and Statistical Analysis,* which can serve as a hands-on supplement to this book by providing students with additional practice of research methods skills and activities related to conducting their own research projects.

ACKNOWLEDGMENTS

Many important people in my life have helped shape the writing of this text. First is Jeff Wagman, who supports me in all my endeavors and talks me out of all my bad ideas. In addition, my family, friends, and colleagues provided support and helpful feedback during the writing process. Most especially, Cooper Cutting, Corinne Zimmerman, and Marla Reese-Weber provided useful feedback and helpful discussion. Steve Croker provided invaluable feedback and proofreading.

The helpful folks at SAGE provided much appreciated support during the production of this text: Abbie Rickard, Emma Newsom, and Liz Cruz. My thanks also go to the students at Illinois State University who have taken my courses and influenced my teaching of this material.

The author and SAGE gratefully acknowledge the contributions of the following reviewers:

Kristin Anderson, University of Houston-Downtown

Emily F. Coyle, Saint Martin's University

Tifani Fletcher, West Liberty University

Stephani M. Foraker, SUNY Buffalo State

Steven J. Haase, Shippensburg University

Maria Maust-Mohl, Manhattan College

Stephanie S. Pierce, Louisiana State University Health Sciences Center at New Orleans School of Nursing

Eric C. Stephens, University of the Cumberlands

Stephen A. Truhon, Austin Peay State University

ABOUT THE AUTHOR

Dawn M. McBride is a professor of psychology at Illinois State University, where she has taught research methods since 1998. Her research interests include automatic forms of memory, false memory, prospective memory, and forgetting. In addition to research methods, she teaches courses in introductory psychology, cognition and learning, and human memory, and a graduate course in experimental design. She is a recipient of the Illinois State University Teaching Initiative Award and the Illinois State University SPA/Psi Chi Jim Johnson Award for commitment to undergraduate mentorship, involvement, and achievement. Her nonacademic interests include spending time with her family, traveling, watching Philadelphia Sports teams (Yay Eagles!), and reading British murder mysteries. She earned her PhD in cognitive psychology from the University of California, Irvine, and her BA from the University of California, Los Angeles.

PSYCHOLOGICAL RESEARCH

The Whys and Hows of the Scientific Method and Data

CONSIDER THE FOLLOWING QUESTIONS AS YOU READ CHAPTER 1

- What is the value of research in psychology?
- Why do psychologists conduct research?
- What is the difference between a population and a sample?
- What kinds of data are collected in psychological studies?
- What is a distribution, and how does its shape affect our analysis of the data?

LEARNING OBJECTIVES FOR CHAPTER 1

- Understand that knowledge of research in psychology has value beyond careers in research.
- Understand what it means to learn about behavior through observation.
- Identify different measurement scales.
- Examine data using frequency distributions.

As an instructor of an introductory psychology course for psychology majors, I have asked my first-semester freshman students this question: What is a psychologist? At the beginning of the semester, students typically say that a psychologist listens to other people's problems to help them live happier lives. By the end of the semester and their first college course in psychology, these same students will respond that a psychologist studies behavior through research. These students have learned that psychology is a science that investigates behaviors, mental processes, and their causes. That is what this book is about: how psychologists use the scientific method to observe and understand behaviors and mental processes and how they understand those data using statistics.

The goal of this text is to give you a step-by-step approach to designing research in psychology—from the purpose of research (discussed in this chapter) and the types of questions psychologists ask about behavior; to the methods used by psychologists to observe and understand behavior as well as the statistical tools they use to interpret the data collected about behavior; and finally, how psychologists describe their findings to others in the field.

WHY SHOULD I CARE ABOUT RESEARCH IF I DON'T WANT TO DO RESEARCH IN MY CAREER?

Through my years of teaching psychology methods courses, this question is often asked by students who don't think they want to conduct research in their careers. A few of you might be bitten by the "research bug," as I was as an undergraduate, and find research to be an exciting way to answer questions you have about behavior. Knowing the process of research can help you better understand the topics presented in other psychology courses you may take because you will better understand how this information was gained. However, a majority of students majoring in psychology are interested in working as a practitioner of psychology or may be completing a psychology minor that is related to another career they want to pursue (education, social work, criminal justice, etc.) and do not understand why research methods courses are part of their curriculum. In fact, the majority of individuals who hold a degree in psychology do not conduct research in their jobs. Instead, the majority of individuals working in psychological areas are in helping or other applied professions. However, what we know about behavior in everyday settings comes from research findings. For example, effective treatments and counseling techniques come from research in these areas. When a new treatment technique is tested, its effectiveness is determined by the research conducted on it. Thus, just as medical doctors do, clinicians and counselors must evaluate the latest research in psychology to determine whether a new treatment is one they should adopt. Knowledge of how research is conducted can help them evaluate this research more effectively to aid their practice. In addition, other popular applied areas, such as industrial–organizational psychology and human factors, use research findings to help address issues in everyday life. Industrial–organizational psychologists help organizations hire effective employees, prevent job dissatisfaction, and explore the best training methods for new employees using research findings on these topics (see Photo 1.1). Human factors professionals use research to help understand the best way to design products and interfaces (such as an airplane cockpit—see Photo 1.2) to make them easier to use and prevent errors. Finally, it is important that we as individuals understand how to interpret the vast amounts of information we take in each day through media sources. Research findings are reported by the media every day. Knowing the basics of how research is conducted can help you decide which of those reports you should listen to and which are best ignored. Understanding research can also help you figure out how to decide whether you believe something you read about on social media or not. Learning how to investigate what people know about a topic is part of the research process.

Photos 1.1 and 1.2 Knowledge of research can aid in applied areas of psychology, such as industrial–organizational psychology and human factors.

To give you a recent example, in debates about climate change and the seriousness of the problem, many opponents of climate change solutions point out that there is disagreement among scientists about the cause. My own father once told me that this is the reason that he doesn't believe global warming is caused by human activities—some scientists have stated that there isn't enough evidence. As voters and consumers, it is important that we understand which evidence from research is the most valid (i.e., accurate) and that there will almost always be disagreement among researchers in an area because no single study can fully answer a research question. In order to understand what answers research provides on a question, we must consider the accumulation of data in many research studies (and this is what I told my father when he stated his reasoning to me about his beliefs). We must also understand that new knowledge is always being discovered, and we must be flexible in our conclusions about an issue when new data suggest a different answer. Remember, there was a time when most humans believed the sun revolved around the earth. Scientific study revealed this idea to be false, and over time, humans adapted their beliefs to the new knowledge. We must do the same when we learn new findings about the best everyday behaviors, such as how to prevent Alzheimer's disease or how to keep our hearts healthy and live longer.

Understanding research methods can also help you better interpret research study results that are reported in the media. In almost all cases, media sources present concise and simplified reports of a research study and its results, leaving many questions about the quality of the study still to be answered. When one encounters reports of research in the media, some important questions should come to mind. Who were the research subjects? Was an appropriate sample tested? Was an appropriate method used to investigate the question? Were the results published in a high-quality source where other researchers were able to critique the work? How do the results correspond to past studies on this topic? The topics covered in this text and in your methods course will help you ask and answer these questions as you evaluate reports in the media that you can use to make decisions about your life.

Finally, the new knowledge you gain from your study of research methods can help you decide how to evaluate claims made by others in general. When you see an ad on television for a new miracle diet pill that the ad claims has helped people lose weight in studies, should you buy the pill? When your friends tell you that drinking energy drinks helps you study better and achieve higher scores on exams, should you follow their advice? Should you believe claims that vaccines cause autism? (You shouldn't: There's no valid research evidence that vaccinations cause autism.) Hopefully, one of the things you will consider as you learn about research is to be skeptical about claims that seem too good to be true. A good researcher uses the data to decide what is the best thing to do rather than use unsubstantiated advice from others who just sound knowledgeable about a topic but who cannot provide evidence beyond an anecdote or two. Examples of how to evaluate claims and research reported in the media are given in some of the Applying Your Knowledge sections found at the ends of the chapters in this text.

WHY PSYCHOLOGISTS CONDUCT RESEARCH

Think about how you know the things you know. How do you know the earth is round? How do you know it is September? How do you know that reading over your notes will help you prepare for an exam? How do you know that terrorist threats are increasing around the world? There are probably many ways that you know these things. In some cases, you may know things because you used your **intuition** or previous knowledge that led to **deduction** of these facts. For example, you may know from past experience that where you live, in the month of September, days tend to be warm but start to get cooler, especially at night. Therefore, remembering the characteristics of the weather you are experiencing and knowing you are still living in the same location as past years, you can deduce that the month is September from your knowledge base. You can also consult a calendar online, using technology as an authoritative information source. You may have first learned that the earth is round from an **authority** figure such as your parents, teachers, or text authors. You may have also observed that the earth is round by viewing photographs of the earth taken from space. You may know that terrorist threats are increasing from authority figures as well (e.g., magazine and newspaper reporters, your country's leaders' statements). These are the primary ways that we learn new facts: intuition, deduction, authority, and observation.

intuition: Relying on common sense as a means of knowing about the world

deduction: Using logical reasoning and current knowledge as a means of knowing about the world

authority: Relying on a knowledgeable person or group as a means of knowing about the world

Suppose something occurred that caused you to suspect that the authority figures you have learned these facts from are not reliable sources of information. Perhaps they have been caught lying about other facts. You might also consider a situation where you do not have enough previous experience with a topic to deduce the information for yourself. In these situations, what is the best way for you to find the facts? The answer is **observation.** If you had reason to believe, for example, that an increase in terrorist threats is not being represented accurately, you could examine the incidence of terrorist attacks (e.g., from public records) over a period of time to find out if people are representing the true conditions. Observing the world directly is going to give you the most accurate information because you are directly gaining the knowledge yourself—you are not relying on possibly faulty reasoning on your part or information someone may be giving you that is false or misleading. See Table 1.1 for some examples of the different ways of knowing information.

observation: Relying on what one observes as a means of knowing about the world

This is why psychologists conduct behavioral research; it is the best way to make certain that the information they have about behavior is accurate. By conducting careful and systematic observations, they can be certain that they are getting the most accurate knowledge they can about behavior. This does not mean that every study conducted will yield accurate results. There are many cases where the observations collected by different researchers conflict, but this is an important part of the process. Different ways of observing a behavior may yield different observations, and these different observations help us to better understand how behaviors occur. Over time, with enough observations, a clearer answer to the question can be found. But no single research study can "prove" that something is true. Researchers are not able to "prove" facts with a study; the best they can do is support an idea about behavior with their data. Despite the limits of observation as a way of knowing, it is superior to the other methods because it allows for a more objective way of gaining knowledge. Relying on the other ways of gaining knowledge can be misleading because they can be more easily influenced by biases that people have.

TABLE 1.1 ■ Examples of Ways of Knowing Information

Way of knowing	Example
Intuition	I'm trying to go someplace I've never been, but I do not know the way. I decide to turn left because it just "feels like" that's the right way to go.
Deduction	I want to know which direction I am facing. The sun is setting to my right, and I know the sun sets in the west, so I know that south is the direction I am facing.
Authority	I want to know what my pancreas does. I know that my pancreas produces hormones important for digestion because that is what my high school biology teacher told me.
Observation	I want to know how much sleep on average Americans get per night. I determine this by conducting a survey of Americans to learn that most Americans get an average of 6 to 8 hr of sleep per night (e.g., Moore, 2004).

Photo 1.3
If we want to know how much sleep people get, we can use scientific methods to measure this directly or ask people to report this behavior on a survey.

Using Science to Understand and Explain Behavior

Observation is really what sets scientific fields apart from other fields of study. Someone who wants to know about the political situation during the Civil War may read historical documents and use his or her intuition to describe the situation based on these documents. He or she might also read books by experts (authority figures) on the Civil War period or books on important figures who lived during that time. However, historians typically cannot observe the historical event they are studying. Psychologists have an advantage in that the behavior they want to learn about is happening in humans and other animals in the world around them. The best way to learn about it is to just observe it (see Photo 1.3).

Some behaviors, such as mental processes, cannot be directly observed (e.g., attitudes, thoughts, or memories). Thus, psychologists have developed techniques for inferring information about mental processes through observation of specific behaviors that are affected by these mental processes. Psychologists then attempt to understand mental processes through observation of these behaviors and the investigation of the factors that influence those behaviors. That is what this book (and the course you are taking) is all about—understanding the methods psychologists use to observe, measure, and understand behavior and mental processes.

Research is the foundation of the field of psychology. Many people think of the *helping* professions when they think about what psychologists do. This is because most people with a graduate degree in psychology work in these helping (or related) professions (American Psychological Association [APA], 2003). However, to do their jobs well, helping professionals, such as clinicians and counselors, need to understand the findings from research about behavior so that they know what types of treatments and therapies can best help their clients. The research studies conducted in psychology also help clinicians and counselors understand what constitutes "normal" behavior and what behaviors might be considered "abnormal." Psychological research also informs society about issues related to these behaviors. How do we know when to trust eyewitness testimony based on one's memory and when it is likely to be inaccurate? What is the best way to set up a course to help students remember the information over the long term? What are some daily activities that older adults can engage in that make them less likely to develop dementia? These are some of the applied questions that can be answered with research in psychology. Knowing the results of studies in different areas can help us, as a society, work out some answers to these questions that will be helpful in different realistic situations.

Thinking about the field of biology may help you understand how influential research is in the field of psychology. In the biological field, there are researchers who investigate the way our bodies react physically to the world around us (e.g., after being exposed to a virus). This knowledge helps other researchers determine which drugs may be effective in helping us improve these physical reactions (e.g., reduce our symptoms as we fight the virus). Finally, the knowledge gained in biological research helps doctors correctly diagnose and treat their patients (e.g., what symptoms indicate the presence of a particular virus and which drugs are most effective in treating these symptoms). The field of psychology works a lot like the field of biology (although the term *psychologist* applies to both scientists and practitioners in psychology, sometimes causing confusion). Some researchers investigate what causes certain types of behaviors (e.g., distraction in people with attention deficit hyperactivity disorder [ADHD]). Other researchers investigate what treatments are effective in reducing these behaviors (e.g., rewarding someone for staying on task). Finally, some psychologists work with clients to help them deal with problem behaviors. For example, school psychologists work with teachers and parents to develop a reward system for students with ADHD who have difficulty completing work in class because they become easily distracted. The research that investigated the behaviors associated with ADHD and the factors that can reduce those behaviors was necessary in order for the school psychologist to be able to develop an effective treatment plan for the student.

In the next section, we will begin to examine how observations of behavior occur in research studies.

STOP AND THINK

1.1. Think about some things you know are true about the world. For each of these facts, try to determine the way you know that information (intuition, deduction, authority, or observation).

1.2. Suppose you wanted to know about the factors that cause college students to become anxious. Describe how you might learn about these factors by using observation.

1.3. Explain how the fields of psychology and biology are similar.

POPULATIONS AND SAMPLES

Have you ever wondered about the opinion polls presented by media news sources and how accurate they are? Consider a poll done on global warming by ABC News/*Washington Post* taken in November 2015 (http://www.pollingreport.com/enviro.htm). People were asked if they considered global warming a serious problem facing the country (see Photo 1.4). From those polled, 63% said yes, it was a serious problem (the highest response on this measure). We can compare this with a poll conducted in May and June of 2015 by the Pew Research Center (http://www.pollingreport.com/enviro.htm). In this poll, people were asked if global warming was a serious problem, and only 46% said it was very serious (the highest response on this measure). Why is there such a large difference between the reported percentages? Did many people suddenly decide that global warming was a big problem between June and November? This is one possible explanation,

Photo 1.4
How many people believe that global warming is a serious problem? Polls can provide some information about this, but it is important to consider the sample and population for the poll to determine its validity.

but it is not very likely. Another possible explanation could be that different people answered the question in the two polls. One way to determine this is to look at the information provided about the polls. The ABC News/*Washington Post* poll describes that it was from 1,004 adults nationwide (in the United States) with a margin of error of plus or minus 3.5. The Pew Research Center poll describes that it was from 5,122 adults nationwide with a margin of error of plus or minus 1.6. Is this information important? What does it tell us about the **validity** of the polls?

In fact, the information provided about the polls can be important in deciding whether the information from the poll is accurate (i.e., valid). The Pew Research Center poll surveyed more people, which allowed for a smaller margin of error. This means we can be more certain that the percentage of all adults in the United States who would report global warming as a very serious problem is close to 46%. What we're looking at here is the difference between a **population** and a **sample**, and the information provided helps us determine how well the sample represents the whole population (see Figure 1.1). The *population* in this case is all adults in the United States. This is the group of individuals we are trying to learn about with the poll. The *sample* is the set of people who answered the question in the poll. They were selected from the population in an attempt to represent the opinions of the whole population without having to ask the whole population (which would be impossible, given the population's size). How well the sample represents the population of interest is a function of the sample size, the way in which the sample was chosen, how many people chosen actually responded or chose to participate, and a few other factors that researchers must consider when conducting any type of research study. Differences between the sample and the population contribute to **sampling error**. Sampling error exists any time we collect data from a sample of the population because we will never be able to get the exact population data from a sample of the population. Each sample is a different subset of the population and will provide different scores, resulting in different means across samples. We're trying to estimate the population mean using the sample mean, so with each sample, we will be at least a little bit wrong about the population mean. This difference between the sample mean and the population mean is the sampling error.

validity: The accuracy of the results of a study

population: A group of individuals a researcher seeks to learn about from a research study

sample: The group of individuals chosen from the population to represent it in a research study

sampling error: The difference between the observations in the population and in the sample that represents that population in a study

One way to think about this is to imagine someone trying to figure out what picture is on a puzzle with only a small part of the puzzle put together. We're not likely to understand the whole picture from just one part of the puzzle; however, the more of the puzzle we have together (i.e., the larger the sample size), the better we'll be at guessing the picture. But putting the whole puzzle together would be difficult and time-consuming if there were thousands or millions of pieces. So instead, we make our best guess from the part of the puzzle we can put together in our study (the sample). With only a small part of the puzzle put together, though, we're not going to get the whole picture exactly

FIGURE 1.1 ■ The Sample Is Chosen to Represent the Population in a Study

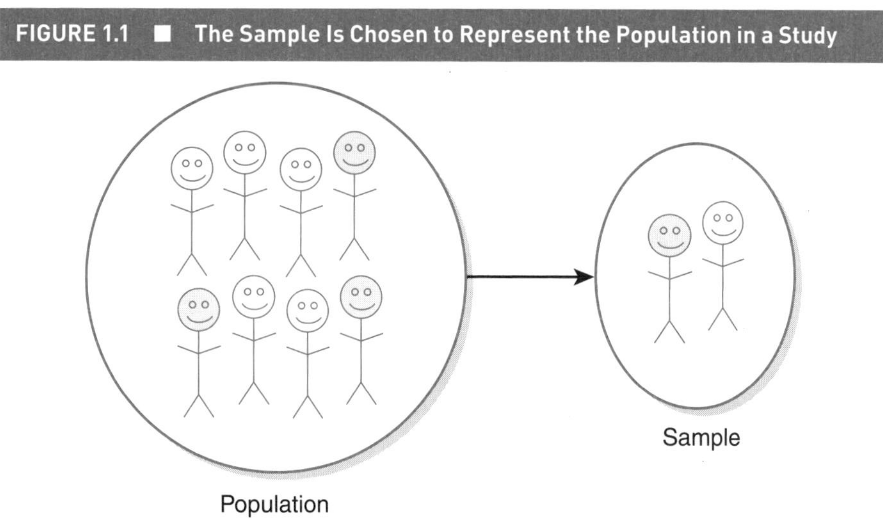

right. Thus, there is some error in our estimate of the population data from our sample data (sampling error). The margin of error reported for polls (such as those described here) provides an estimate of the sampling error. This is an estimate of how far off the reported percentage in our data is likely to be from the population percentage. Thus, knowing the sample size and margin of error for opinion polls can help you decide if the poll is useful in telling you how people really think about an issue.

It is very rare that a researcher will observe the entire population in a research study, so samples are almost always used in order to represent the population in the study by collecting data from a realistic number of individuals. This is due to the size of most populations; they tend to be very large because researchers want to be able to learn about the behavior of large groups of individuals, not just a small set of people—as in our survey examples where we wanted to know about how Americans felt about global warming. Thus, a smaller sample was chosen to collect data from. If you have ever participated in a research study, then you have been a member of a sample selected from a population. Many research studies in psychology use samples selected from the population of college students because it is a sample that is fairly easy to obtain. However, *college students* is too narrow a population for some studies because college students tend to be fairly educated, higher income, and young, giving us a biased sample for these characteristics from the whole population of adults. Because of this possible bias, researchers have begun to sample from larger populations of individuals using online technologies to deliver surveys and experimental tasks to a larger population. For example, a fairly recent study by Brown-Iannuzzi, Lundberg, Kay, and Payne (2015) sampled their participants from a large population of adults using the Amazon site Mechanical Turk (MTurk). This site rewards people with small amounts of money in their account for completing research studies. Brown-Iannuzzi et al. sampled individuals from this site to learn how one's sense of one's own wealth, relative to others' wealth, influences one's political ideas about the redistribution of wealth in society (their research suggested that relative wealth does

FIGURE 1.2 ■ Results From Brown-Iannuzzi et al.'s (2015) Study Comparing Support for Redistribution of Wealth Based on Experimental Conditions of Relative Wealth Compared With Others' Wealth; Greater Support for Redistribution Was Found for Low-Status Participants Than for High-Status Participants

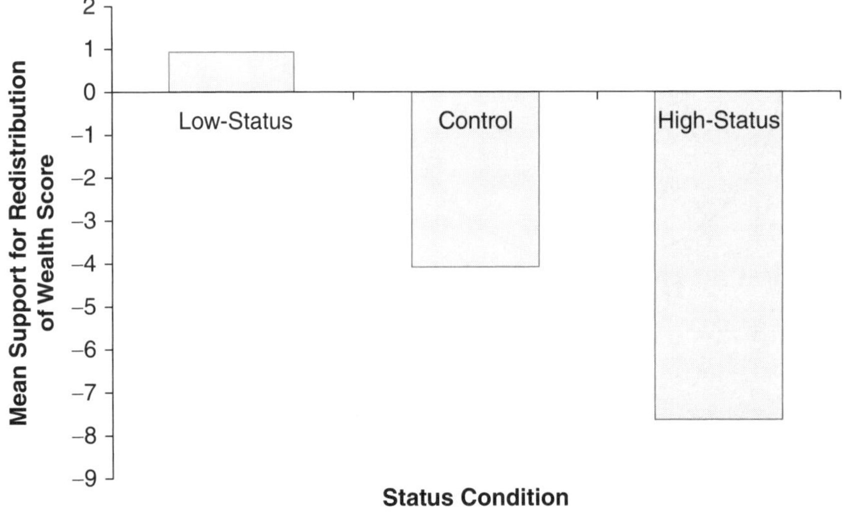

Source: Brown-Iannuzzi et al. (2015).

affect one's political ideas on this issue; see Figure 1.2). MTurk is becoming a popular method for selecting a large sample from the very large population of adults in the world. We will consider more issues of sampling in Chapter 4.

The population and sample of a research study are important for choosing the statistical tools researchers use to better understand data. As you will see in Chapter 4, the way that you choose a sample from a population can affect the validity of your study. Discussions in the later chapters of this text will show you how hypotheses are made about populations before a sample is chosen. Finally, the type of data collected from the sample will influence the statistics we choose to summarize the data (i.e., **descriptive statistics**) and to test our hypotheses about the population (i.e., inferential statistics).

descriptive statistics: Statistics that help researchers summarize or describe data

TYPES OF DATA

operational definition: The way a behavior is defined in a research study to allow for its measurement

There are many different types of data that can be collected in psychological research studies. Researchers attempt to choose the best measure for the behavior they want to observe. This choice is important because it can affect the internal validity of the study—a poor choice can mean that the data do not actually measure the behavior of interest. In other words, researchers try to determine a good **operational definition** of the behavior they are interested in. An operational definition is the way a behavior is measured in a particular study. It also provides a way for a researcher to measure a behavior that is not directly observable. Operational definitions are a necessary part of the research process because many behaviors can be defined in multiple ways, and researchers need to know what to measure from the individuals in the sample when they collect their data. For example, what behaviors should be measured to learn about one's level of depression (see Photo 1.5)? There are many ways we could operationally define depression: how often someone smiles in an hour (fewer smiles = more depression), observers' ratings of how lethargic someone seems (lower ratings of energy level = more depression), or a score on a questionnaire of self-reported thoughts and behaviors that we think are present in someone who is depressed (more sleep than is typical, loss of appetite, feelings of sadness, etc.). Thus, researchers have many choices when they want to measure depression, and they try to come up with the most valid measure (within the practical limitations of the research study) for the behavior they want to learn about.

Photo 1.5
There are many ways to measure depression; a researcher operationally defines the behavior to allow its measurement.

Scales of Measurement

Observations of behavior (i.e., data) in a study constitute what is called a **dependent or response variable**. Dependent variables are measured in every research study. For some designs, only a single dependent variable is measured, and the behavior is examined descriptively or causally (if the researcher is interested in a causal relationship and uses an experiment to study this relationship). Other designs examine relationships between multiple dependent variables. As a result, how a dependent variable is measured depends on the data collection technique used, and what is learned about a dependent variable depends on the type of research design used. One choice that is made by the researcher in operationally defining a behavior for a research study is the scale of measurement he or she uses. The scale of measurement will be important in determining which statistics are used to describe the data and test hypotheses about the data. Table 1.2 presents an overview of the different scales of measurement and an example of each type.

dependent or response variable: A variable that is measured or observed from an individual

Nominal Scales

Many measurements categorize observed behavior or behavior that is reported by the participants. For example, if you ask someone to indicate their current mood, you might give them response choices such as happy, sad, excited, anxious, and so on. This type of measurement is called a **nominal scale** because it involves nonordered categories that are nonnumerical in nature. You cannot order these moods from highest to lowest—they are simply different. Some types of demographic information collected in research studies are measured on a nominal scale. Questions about someone's gender or major in college are good examples of these types of nominal scales.

nominal scale: A scale of data measurement that involves nonordered categorical responses

TABLE 1.2 ■ Scales of Measurement

Scale	Definition	Example
Nominal	Unordered categories	University where degree was earned
Ordinal	Categorical, ordered categories	Letter grades earned in a course (A, B, C, D, F)
Interval	Numerical categories without a true zero point	Ratings on personality surveys with values from 1 to 5
Ratio	Numerical categories with a true zero point	Age measured in days since birth

Ordinal Scales

ordinal scale: A scale of data measurement that involves ordered categorical responses

Anytime you rank order your preferences for different things, you are using an **ordinal scale**. Rankings in a competition (1st, 2nd, 3rd, etc.) also measure individuals on an ordinal scale. Ordinal scales are measures that involve categories that can be ordered from highest to lowest. However, the ordered categories are not necessarily equally spaced on an ordinal scale. Imagine you are asked to report your level of anxiety today on a scale that includes response choices of *not at all anxious, a little anxious, fairly anxious*, and *very anxious*. On this scale, the difference between *a little anxious* and *fairly anxious* may be smaller than the difference between *fairly anxious* and *very anxious*. Thus, this is considered an ordinal scale because the categories can be ordered from highest to lowest level of anxiety, but the categories are not always equally spaced across the scale.

Interval Scales

interval scale: A scale of data measurement that involves numerical responses that are equally spaced, but the scores are not ratios of each other

If the ordered categories on a scale are equally spaced, then the scale is known as an **interval scale**. Interval scales are used when the researcher wants to know that the difference between any two values on the scale is the same across all values of the scale. Typically, this involves numerical responses. Many rating scales on questionnaires are interval scales because they ask participants to rate their agreement with statements or their likelihood of performing specific behaviors on a numerical rating scale. An example of such a scale might be to rate how much you agree with the statement "Global warming is a serious issue facing society today" on a scale of 1 to 10, where a higher number indicates higher agreement. Such scales do not have a true zero point, because the values cannot be considered ratios of one another. For example, because there is a minimum and maximum score on a 1 to 10 scale, there is no way to determine the ratio function between scores—a score of 4 is not twice that of a score of 2 (2 is only one value higher than the minimum, whereas 4 is three values higher than the minimum). The scores on the scale are not distributed in this way.

ratio scale: A scale of data measurement that involves numerical responses in which scores are ratios of each other

Ratio Scales

A numerical scale with a true zero point allows for values that are ratios of one another. This is known as a **ratio scale**. On ratio scales, you can determine what score would be twice as high as another score. Some examples of ratio scales are accuracy on a task, speed to complete a task, and age. A score of 50% accuracy is twice as high as a score of 25% accuracy. Ratio scales are often used in systematic and controlled measures of behavior, a topic we will discuss later in this chapter. Note that interval and ratio scales are often grouped together because data from these scales are typically analyzed in the same way, and there are cases where it is difficult to determine if a scale is truly an interval scale. The important difference to note for the scales of measurement and how they are analyzed is whether they involve numbers or categories as responses on the scale.

STOP AND THINK

1.4. For each study description that follows, identify the population and the sample.
   a. A researcher recruits students from a fifth-grade class at an elementary school to examine math abilities on a standardized test in children who are 9 to 10 years old.
   b. A researcher recruits college students from the university subject pool to test the effect of time pressure on accuracy in completing a task.
   c. Older adults are recruited from a retirement center to examine sources of anxiety in retirees. Anxiety is measured using survey items in which the participants rate their level of anxiety on a 1 to 7 scale for different issues that might be anxiety inducing (e.g., financial security, failing health).
   d. Patients who have suffered a traumatic brain injury (TBI) are included (with their consent) in a study of how one's diet after the injury affects recovery time (measured in number of days they stay in the hospital after their injury) from a local hospital.

1.5. For each study described in 1.4, identify the most likely scale of measurement used in the study.

Survey Data

We have already discussed some issues with sampling from populations to collect survey data in this chapter. Using surveys to measure behavior can also limit the types of measures that a researcher can use to observe those behaviors. Although any of the scales of measurement described in this chapter can be used in surveys, the measures are limited to an individual's report of their thoughts and behaviors. In other words, surveys indirectly measure the behavior of interest in a study. They rely on responses to items that together provide information about the behavior. The survey score is an operational definition of that behavior. However, the way survey responses are presented can greatly affect the results. Consider the surveys on global warming described at the beginning of this chapter. Do you notice any differences in the types of responses used in the polls? In fact, the difference in survey response options is likely the reason for the differences in the percentage of people who agreed with the survey statement. In the first survey, people stated that global warming was a *serious problem*. In the second survey, the percentage reported was for people who *very strongly agreed* with this statement. It may be that a fair

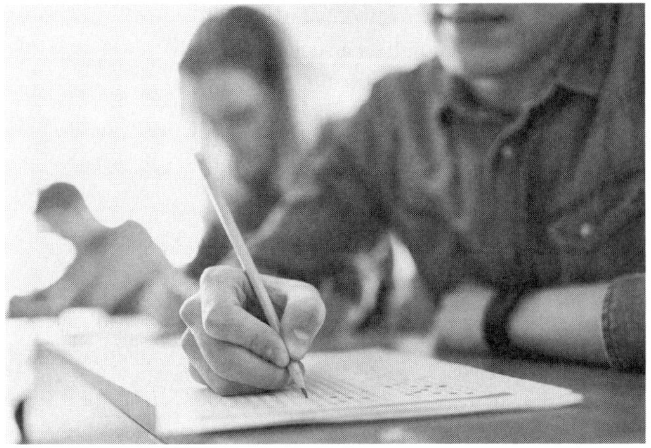

Photo 1.6 Survey responses can be prone to social desirability bias in which participants try to respond in a way that makes them look more positive.

percentage of people in the second survey chose a response of *strongly agree* instead of *very strongly agree*. In the first survey, there was no *very strongly agree* option, so some of the people who chose the *serious problem* response may in fact have felt very strongly about their agreement. Because the response choices are different in the two surveys, it can appear as if they obtained different results.

In addition, there are some issues related to the self-report nature of survey data that can influence the validity of the data. Because surveys rely on reports of the behavior from the participants themselves, the validity of the measurement may not be as high as when the researcher directly observes those behaviors. Participants may not have an accurate perception of their own behaviors, making the reports subjective. Further, participants may wish to portray their behaviors more positively than they actually are—an issue known as **social desirability bias**. If participants respond to survey items in a way that makes them appear more positive, they are reducing the validity of the behavioral measure (see Photo 1.6).

social desirability bias: Bias created in survey responses from respondents' desire to be viewed more favorably by others, typically resulting in overreporting of positive behaviors and underreporting of negative behaviors

construct validity: The degree to which a survey is an accurate measure of interest

reliability: The degree to which the results of a study can be replicated under similar conditions

Because survey data have some issues that can affect their validity, researchers are careful in checking the **construct validity** of surveys and questionnaires when they are first used to make sure that they accurately measure the behaviors of interest. **Reliability** of surveys and questionnaires is also examined before they are used as measures of a behavior to ensure that they will produce consistent results when they are used in research studies.

Systematic and Controlled Measures

Another type of data collected in many research studies is more systematic and controlled. In experimental studies, where internal validity is increased through control of the measurement of the behaviors and the situations in which they are observed, researchers often employ more systematic and controlled measures (see Photo 1.7). These measures are more direct observations of behavior than the self-reports collected on surveys (e.g., accuracy or speed in performing a task), which can provide more internally valid measures of behavior, but they can also have lower external validity than the behaviors measured in surveys because the control imposed during the observations can influence the behaviors observed. When someone knows they are participating in a research study, they may try harder in completing a task (or may perform worse due to lack of motivation because they know they will get research credit regardless of their performance), changing their accuracy and speed in performing the task compared with a more naturalistic setting.

Consider the experiment conducted by Metcalfe, Casal-Roscum, Radin, and Friedman (2015) to compare older and younger adults' memories for facts. Both young and older adults were asked to answer a series of general knowledge questions (e.g., "In what ancient city were the Hanging Gardens located?" Correct answer: Babylon). For each answer, they provided a rating of their confidence in their response on a 1 to 7 scale. Feedback was then given for their answer (correct or incorrect with the correct answer given as feedback). After a short delay, they were then tested on 20 of the questions for which they made high-confidence errors (i.e., they answered incorrectly but were highly confident in their incorrect response) and 20 questions where they made low-confidence errors (i.e., they answered incorrectly but were not very confident in their incorrect response) to determine final test accuracy on these questions. The mean accuracy for each group and type of question is shown in Figure 1.3. Older adults showed better memory on the final test—an atypical finding—especially when they had low confidence in their original response. The researchers measured memory accuracy as a controlled measure: They carefully chose the items presented to the participants and tested their memory in a lab, where they could control other factors that contribute to memory other than the age group and the participants' confidence in their responses. This control increased the internal validity of the study in providing a good test of the comparison of younger and older adults. However, this control of the measure and the situation may have reduced the realism of the memory being tested. For example, because the participants knew that the researchers were interested in their memory performance, they may have tried harder on the task (especially the older participants, for whom research participation may be a less-common experience) and raised their memory levels compared with how they would perform in a less-controlled setting. This shows how controlled observations of behavior can have high internal validity but may also have lower external validity.

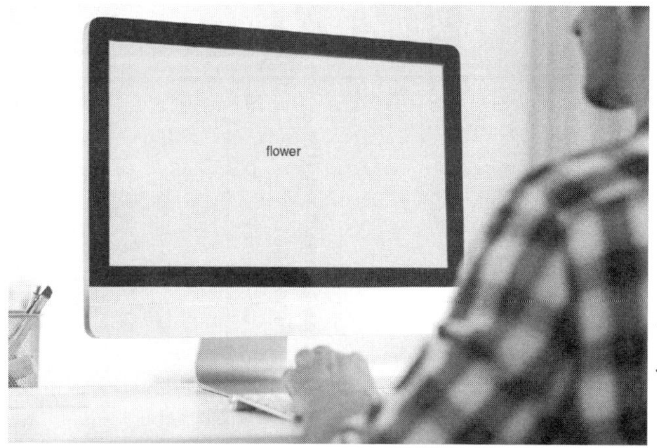

Photo 1.7 Systematic measures of behavior sometimes involve collecting responses on a computer to allow for direct measures of behavior in terms of speed or accuracy in completing a task.

FREQUENCY DISTRIBUTIONS

Let's now consider what the data we collect in a study might look like. When we collect a set of data, we have a **distribution** of scores to consider. This distribution might range over the entire scale of measurement (e.g., participants have used all of the values on a 1 to 7 rating scale in their responses), or it might be restricted to just a small range of scores (e.g., participants have used only the values between 3 and 6 on the 1 to 7 rating scale). In addition, the scores might cluster close to one value on the scale with very few values at the high and low ends of the scale. Or the scores could be equally spaced along the values of the scale. Thus, different distributions can have different characteristics depending on the variability seen in the scores. A good way to examine the distribution and see what it looks like is to create a **frequency distribution** table or graph. The frequency distribution will indicate how often each value in the scale was used by the participants in their responses or in measurements of their behavior.

distribution: A set of scores

frequency distribution: A graph or table of a distribution showing the frequency of each score in the distribution

FIGURE 1.3 ■ Memory Accuracy Data From Metcalfe et al.'s (2015) Study

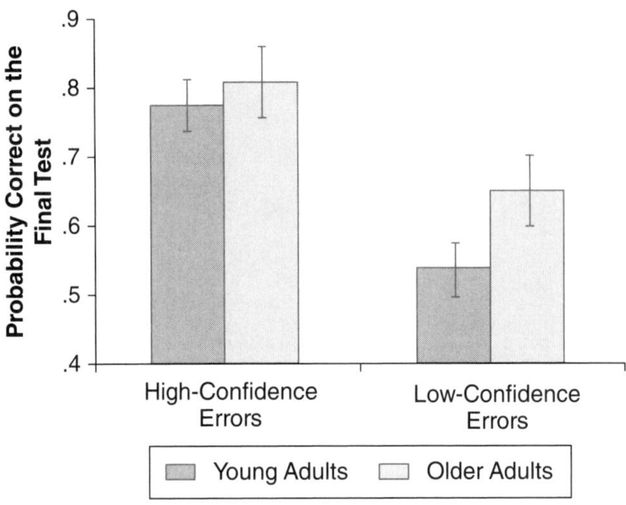

Source: Metcalfe et al. (2015).

To create a frequency distribution graph by hand, you place the scores on the x-axis of the graph and then indicate the number of times each of those scores appears in a set of data with the bar height along the y-axis. Figure 1.4 shows a frequency distribution graph for responses on a 1 to 7 scale that might be present from a survey question asking how likely someone is to watch a new show on television after watching an ad for that show. The graph shows that the respondents used all the scores on the scale, but most of the scores were clustered around the values of 5 and 6 (these were the most frequent scores in the distribution). Table 1.3 shows a frequency distribution table of the same set of scores. To create the table, the scores are listed in one column, and the frequency count of each of the scores in the distribution is listed in the second column. For example, 16 respondents rated their likelihood of watching the new show at a 6 on the 1 to 7 scale. The other columns in the table show the percentage of all the scores in the distribution at that value and the cumulative percentage from lowest to highest that adds in all previous percentages as you move from one score to the next.

Shape of a Distribution

inferential statistics: A set of statistical procedures used by researchers to test hypotheses about populations

One thing we can see more easily using a frequency distribution graph is the shape of the distribution. The shape of the distribution can affect the choices a researcher makes in analyzing the data with **inferential statistics**. Look at the frequency distribution in Figure 1.4. What do you notice about its shape? Is the distribution symmetrical, with the half of the distribution above the most frequent score (a score of 6) the mirror image of the other? Or are the scores clustered more toward one end of the distribution than the other? If the distribution shows a mirror image across the most frequent score, then it is

FIGURE 1.4 ■ A Frequency Distribution Graph for Ratings on a 1 to 7 Scale of How Likely One Is to Watch a New Television Show

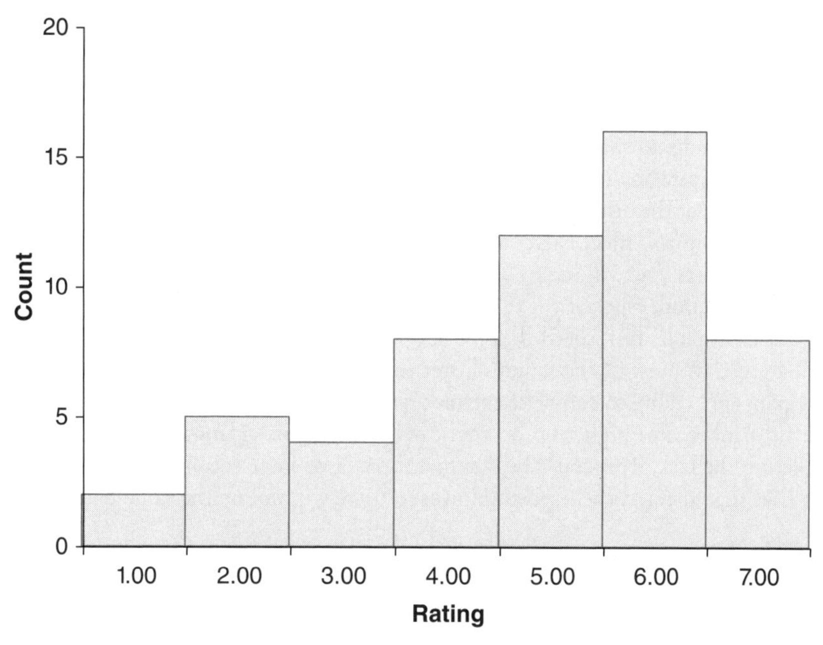

TABLE 1.3 ■ A Frequency Distribution Table for Ratings on a 1 to 7 Scale of How Likely One Is to Watch a New Television Show

Score	Frequency	Percentage	Cumulative percentage
1	2	3.6	3.6
2	5	9.1	12.7
3	4	7.3	20.0
4	8	14.5	34.5
5	12	21.8	56.4
6	16	29.1	85.5
7	8	14.5	100.0

symmetrical distribution: A distribution of scores where the shape of the distribution shows a mirror image on either side of the middle score

a **symmetrical distribution**. Symmetrical distributions occur naturally in some types of data. For example, standardized test scores typically show symmetrical distributions with an average score in the center and each half of the distribution around the average showing fewer scores at each end of the scale in a similar pattern (i.e., a typical bell shape). Figure 1.5 shows a fairly symmetrical distribution of data in a frequency distribution graph. These data represent the distribution of letter grades in a college course where the instructor has "curved" the grade distribution around an average grade of C (i.e., made it symmetrical around the C grade).

Many distributions, however, show clustering of scores toward the top or bottom end of the scale. In fact, without curving, grade distributions in many college courses show a clustering of grades toward the high end of the grade scale—often because there are more people in a course who do well than who do very poorly. When scores are clustered at one end of the scale or the other in a distribution, it is known as a **skewed distribution**. Skew in a distribution can affect the comparison of different measures of what is considered a typical score (as you will see in Chapter 6). Speed in completing a task often shows a skewed distribution, especially if the research participants complete multiple trials of the task. For example, a task speed distribution is shown in Figure 1.6. You can see in this distribution that most of the scores cluster toward the low end of the scale because the participants are trying to complete the task quickly, based on the instructions. However, there are a few scores higher up on the scale where a participant was especially slow in completing the task. This could be due to a short lapse in attention or a particularly difficult trial that affected their speed. However, there will not be the same pattern of very

skewed distribution: A distribution of scores where the shape of the distribution shows a clustering of scores at the low or high end of the scale

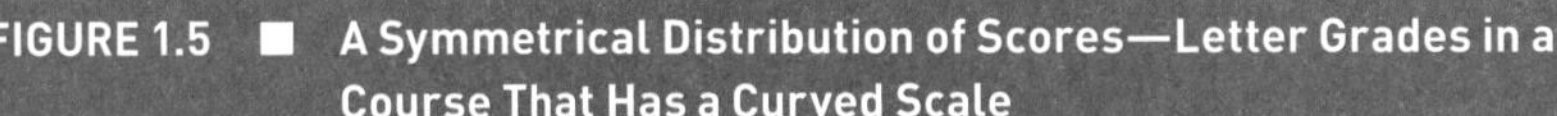

FIGURE 1.5 ■ A Symmetrical Distribution of Scores—Letter Grades in a Course That Has a Curved Scale

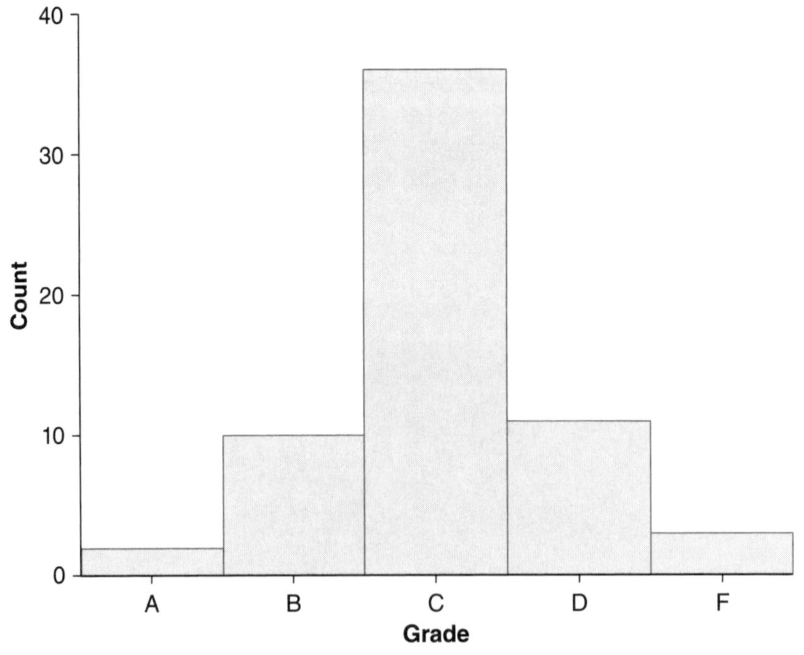

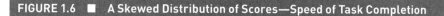

FIGURE 1.6 ■ A Skewed Distribution of Scores—Speed of Task Completion

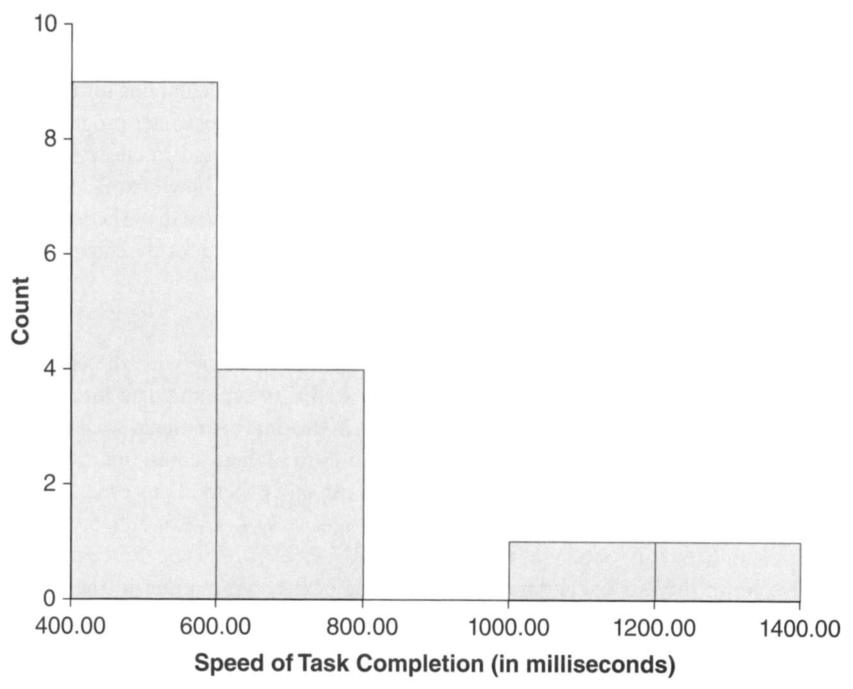

fast trials at the low end of the scale because the lowest the scores can go is 0 on the scale, keeping the fast scores from spreading out at the low end. This is why most distributions of data that measure task speed are skewed. This distribution represents a *positive skew*, where the tail of infrequent scores is at the high end of the scale. A *negative skew* shows the opposite pattern—the tail of the distribution is on the low end of the scale.

STOP AND THINK

1.6. Explain how internal validity is increased in a study using systematic and controlled measures of behavior.

1.7. Create a frequency distribution table or graph for the following set of data using ranges of scores by 10 (i.e., frequency for 51–60, 61–70):

77, 75, 78, 56, 90, 68, 65, 63, 73, 77, 74, 78, 72, 79, 82, 85, 88, 52, 96, 71

Does this distribution appear to be symmetrical or skewed in shape? Explain your answer.

Frequency Distributions in Excel

In this text, we will discuss two ways to use computer programs to produce statistics. Although it is important for you to understand what is contributing to the statistics being produced by the programs, most researchers use computer programs to calculate statistics for their data. Therefore, in this text you will see both the formulas and calculations for the statistics and the instructions for producing those statistics using the computer programs. The first program we will consider is Microsoft Excel. Excel can be used to create frequency distribution tables and graphs. Let's work through an example of how it works using the distribution of data shown in Figure 1.4 and Table 1.3. These data are hypothetical ratings for likelihood of watching a new television show after viewing an ad for the show.

Tables

We will begin by entering the rating scores. You can follow along with the example if you have Excel to work with as you read. The first step is to type the data into the data window. This is the first column shown in Figure 1.7. The data are entered with one score per row. They are presented in order from lowest scores to highest scores, but the order of the data entry in this column is not important; you can enter them in any order. Here are the data to enter: 1, 1, 2, 2, 2, 2, 2, 3, 3, 3, 3, 4, 4, 4, 4, 4, 4, 4, 4, 5, 5, 5, 5, 5, 5, 5, 5, 5, 5, 5, 5, 6, 6, 6, 6, 6, 6, 6, 6, 6, 6, 6, 6, 6, 6, 6, 6, 7, 7, 7, 7, 7, 7, 7, 7. Type these ratings into the first column in your Excel data window. In the next column, enter in the response

FIGURE 1.7 ■ Excel Data Window Showing a Frequency Distribution Table

	A	B	C	D	E
1	DATA	SCORES	COUNTS	PERCENTAGE	CUMULATIVE PERCENTAGE
2	1	1	2	3.636363636	3.636363636
3	1	2	5	9.090909091	12.72727273
4	2	3	4	7.272727273	20
5	2	4	8	14.54545455	34.54545455
6	2	5	12	21.81818182	56.36363636
7	2	6	16	29.09090909	85.45454545
8	2	7	8	14.54545455	100
9	3				
10	3				
11	3				
12	3				
13	4				
14	4				

Note: Excel is a registered trademark of Microsoft Corporation.

choices—the values from 1 to 7. In some cases, you may not have exact scores to enter here, but because these data are from a survey with a rating scale, we can enter the exact scores that are in the distribution.

The third column will include our counts for each score. You could count these by hand from the list of data that was just given, but for large data sets, this would be time-consuming, and you might make a mistake. Instead, we can use the formulas in Excel to calculate the counts. We will use the COUNTIF command here. To use a command in Excel, type = and then the command; so in the COUNTS column's first cell, you can type =COUNTIF. The COUNTIF command will include the **range** of scores you want to count (all the scores in the DATA column) and the specific score you want to count. Your COUNTIF command will be =COUNTIF(range,score). To calculate the counts, type a (, then highlight all of the scores in the DATA column to enter the range (by dragging the cursor over the whole column), and then type ,"="& (comma, quotation mark, equal sign, quotation mark, ampersand). Then highlight the score in the SCORES column you want to count (or you can just type in the score you want). This will then add the score you are looking at. If you want a range of scores here, you can use COUNTIFS (instead of COUNTIF) and include sets of < or > before the & and score to indicate a range. Close the) and then hit Enter. If you included labels at the top of the columns as in Figure 1.7, your first cell should look like this before you hit Enter (you can see the formula by clicking on a cell to show it in the bar at the top):

range: The difference between the highest and lowest scores in a distribution

=COUNTIF(A2:A56,"="&1) or =COUNTIF(A2:A56,"="&B3)

You should see a count of 2 in the COUNTS column for a score of 1 (see Figure 1.7). Repeat this formula for each score to calculate counts in your COUNTS column.

The next column in our frequency distribution table is the percentage of the total that each count represents in the data set. To calculate this value, type =, highlight the value in the COUNTS column, then /COUNT(. Then highlight the scores in the DATA column and type). Then type *100 and hit Enter. Your first cell should look like this (again, if you have a column header):

=C2/COUNT(A2:A56)*100

You should see the percentage of scores that had a value of 1 in the data set in the PERCENTAGE column (see Figure 1.7).

The last column in our table is the cumulative percentage of values for each score. This will tell us what percentage of the scores is at a certain value or lower. To calculate this value, again begin by typing = to indicate a formula, then highlight the next value in the PERCENTAGE column, type +, and then highlight the previous value on the CUMULATIVE PERCENTAGE column (if there is one) before hitting Enter. For the first score, the cumulative percentage will simply be the percentage value. Your completed table should look similar to the one shown in Figure 1.7.

SUMMARY OF STEPS

- Type the data into a data window in Excel (1st column).
- Type in response choices (2nd column).
- Type in =COUNTIF(range, scores) command (3rd column).
- Repeat COUNTIF command for each score or range of scores to complete third column.
- Calculate percentages for each score using =score cell/COUNT(range)*100 (4th column).
- Calculate cumulative percentages by successively adding up the percentages for each score (5th column).

Graphs

Excel can also create a frequency distribution graph of these data for us. To create the graph, highlight the SCORES and COUNTS columns of values. Then click the Charts function window. Excel's default is typically a bar graph for these types of data, but your settings may be different, so you may need to choose the Column Graph option. To show the distribution shape, choose the option under Chart Layouts that shows the bars adjacent in the graph. You should then have a graph that looks like the one in Figure 1.8. You can type in axis labels and change the fill color of the bars to format as you like.

FIGURE 1.8 ■ Excel Chart Showing a Frequency Distribution Graph

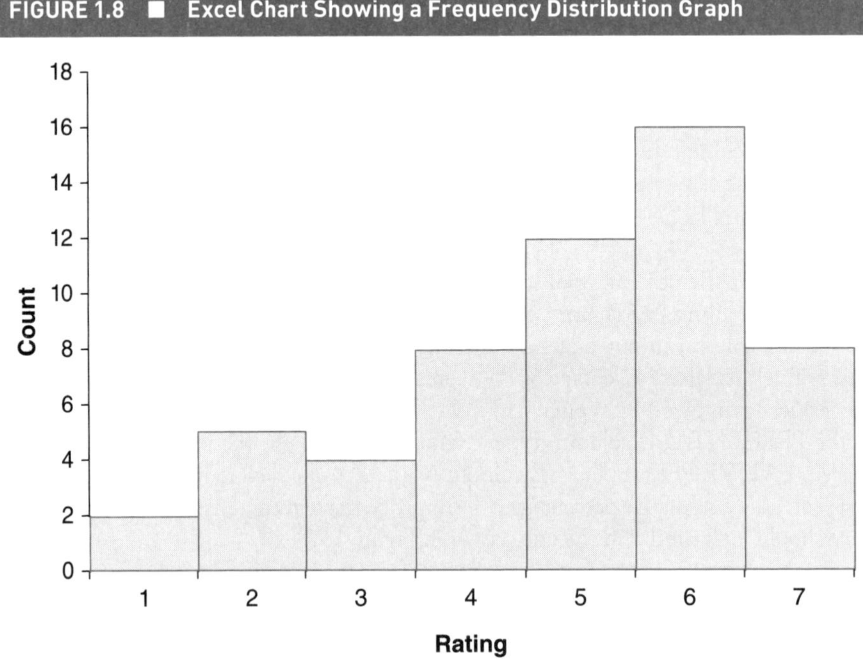

Frequency Distributions in SPSS

The second computer program I will describe in this text is IBM® SPSS® Statistics.[1] SPSS is a common program used by researchers for descriptive and inferential statistics in psychology. You may be asked to use this program in some of your psychology courses to analyze data from research studies. In many cases, it will produce the statistics you want more easily than Excel. However, this program is not as commonly available as Excel, which is why there is instruction for both programs provided in this text.

Note: SPSS is a registered trademark of International Business Machines Corporation.

Tables

As with Excel, the first step in using SPSS is to enter the data you wish to examine. The data window in SPSS has a similar setup to the one in Excel. However, you will define the variable names and details in a separate tab of the window. An example of the data window in SPSS is shown in Figure 1.9. As in Excel, each row contains data from a different participant, and each column indicates a different variable. Thus, the first column contains the ratings for desire to watch the television show for each participant from our earlier example as in the Excel window. However, to label this variable, you need to choose the Variable View tab at the bottom of the window. This view will allow you to name the variable (as I have done here with the label *Rating*). See Figure 1.10 for the Variable View in SPSS.

Once your data are entered and labeled, you are ready to create your frequency distribution table. To create a table, you will choose the Frequencies function in the Descriptive Statistics menu under the Analyze menu at the top. Different versions of SPSS look a bit different for these menus, so first find the Analyze menu (or tab) at the top of the window; then choose Descriptive Statistics and then Frequencies. You should see a small window pop up that looks like Figure 1.11. To create the table for the ratings, make sure the Rating variable is highlighted (if not, click on it), and then click the arrow to move it into the Variable(s) box. Be sure to keep the Display frequency tables box

FIGURE 1.9 ■ Data Window for SPSS

	Rating	var	var	var
1	1.00			
2	1.00			
3	2.00			
4	2.00			
5	2.00			
6	2.00			
7	2.00			
8	3.00			
9	3.00			
10	3.00			
11	3.00			
12	4.00			
13	4.00			
14	4.00			
15	4.00			
16	4.00			
17	4.00			
18	4.00			
19	4.00			
20	5.00			
21	5.00			
22	5.00			
23	5.00			
24	5.00			
25	5.00			
26	5.00			
27	5.00			
28	5.00			
29	5.00			
30	5.00			
31	5.00			
32	6.00			
33	6.00			
34	6.00			

[1]SPSS is a registered trademark of International Business Machines Corporation.

FIGURE 1.10 ■ Variable View Window for SPSS

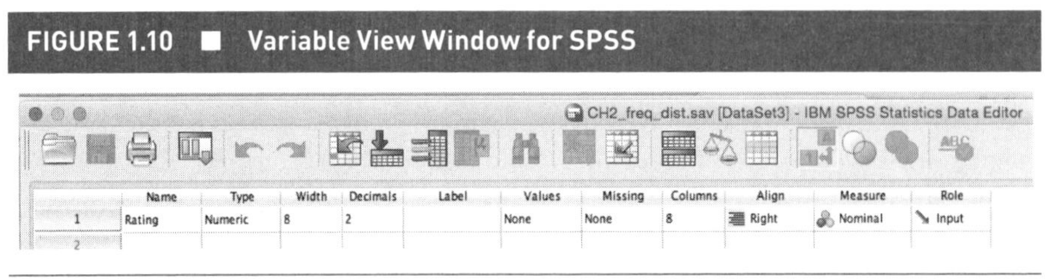

FIGURE 1.11 ■ Frequencies Window in SPSS

FIGURE 1.12 ■ Frequency Distribution Table in SPSS, Seen in the Output Window

Rating

		Frequency	Percent	Valid Percent	Cumulative Percent
Valid	1.00	2	3.6	3.6	3.6
	2.00	5	9.1	9.1	12.7
	3.00	4	7.3	7.3	20.0
	4.00	8	14.5	14.5	34.5
	5.00	12	21.8	21.8	56.4
	6.00	16	29.1	29.1	85.5
	7.00	8	14.5	14.5	100.0
	Total	55	100.0	100.0	

checked. The OK button should then be available. When you click OK or hit Enter, a new Output window will appear. Your table will be displayed as shown in Figure 1.12. The Valid column shows the scores in the distribution, the Frequency column shows the counts for each score (including a total count), the Percent and Valid Percent columns show the percentage of scores in the distribution that are at that score, and the Cumulative Percent column shows the cumulative percentage for each score. You can compare this table with those shown in Table 1.3 and Figure 1.7 to see the similarities across the different program versions of the same table.

SUMMARY OF STEPS

- Type the data into a data window.
- Label the variable in Variable View tab.
- Choose Descriptive Statistics in the Analyze menu at the top.
- Choose Frequencies from the Descriptive Statistics choices.
- In the Frequencies window, choose the variable(s) you are interested in by highlighting the variable(s) and using the arrow in the center of the window.
- Make sure the Display Frequency Tables box is checked.
- Click OK; your table will be shown in the Output window.

Graphs

A frequency distribution graph can also be created using the Frequencies function. If you click on the Charts option in the Frequencies window (see Figure 1.11), a new window will open with chart options. Choose the Histograms option and click Continue. Then when you click OK, both your Table and your Graph will appear in the Output window. The graph will look like Figure 1.13. Notice that some additional descriptive statistics are also provided alongside the graph. We will discuss these statistics in the upcoming chapters.

SUMMARY OF FREQUENCY DISTRIBUTIONS

Frequency distribution tables and graphs are useful in helping summarize a distribution of scores. They allow you to see the shape of the distribution and clustering of scores in a particular part of the distribution. They can be created by hand, but Excel and SPSS can create them more easily for you, reducing the chance of error if your data have been entered into the program correctly. As we continue to discuss additional descriptive statistics in the next few chapters, you will see that these programs are quite useful in calculating your statistics.

STOP AND THINK

Create a frequency distribution graph in both Excel and SPSS for the following final exam scores according to letter grade groupings with 90%–100% = A, 80%–89% = B, 70%–79% = C, 60%–69% = D, below 60% = F:

83, 92, 100, 90, 74, 58, 84, 78, 85, 78, 72, 60, 67, 92, 92, 88, 88, 66, 60, 80, 88, 58, 92, 84, 84, 59, 80, 68, 78, 86, 76, 80, 64, 84, 68, 58, 72, 88, 89, 72, 88, 65, 80, 84, 68, 73, 92

1.8. Does this distribution appear to be symmetrical or skewed? If the shape is skewed, describe the skew (i.e., positive or negative skew).

1.9. About how many students received an A on the final? How many received a D or F?

FIGURE 1.13 ■ Frequency Distribution Graph in SPSS, Seen in the Output Window

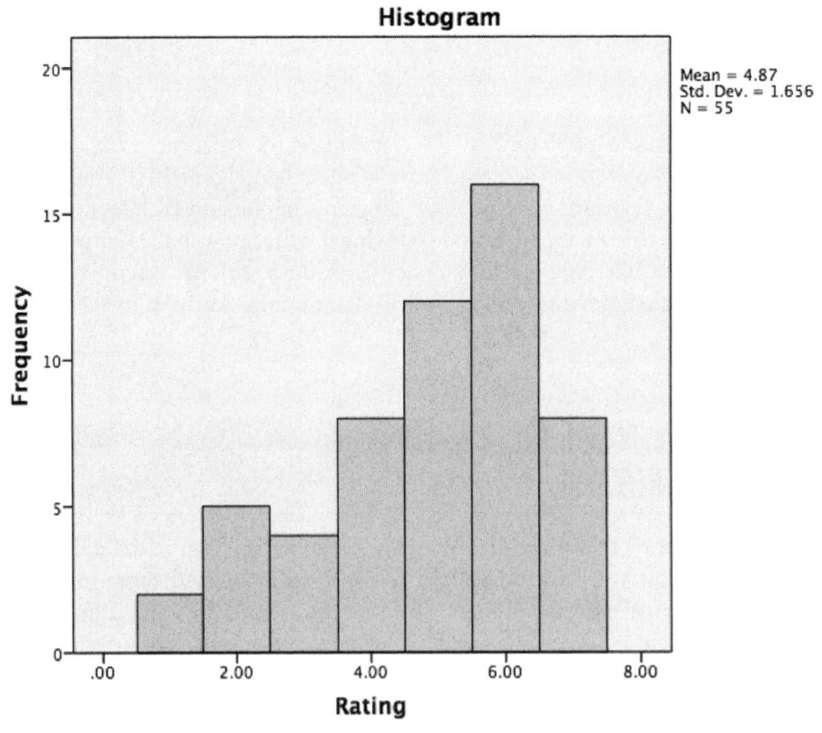

THINKING ABOUT RESEARCH

A summary of a research study in psychology is given here. As you read the summary, think about the following questions:

1. What behaviors have the researchers observed?
2. How were the observations recorded by the researchers?
3. Were the researchers able to answer their research questions with the observations they collected? How?
4. Consider the graphs in Figure 1.14. Explain how these results address the researchers' question about behavior.
5. What are some examples of real-world behaviors that the results of this study might apply to?

©istockphoto.com/goldy

Photo 1.8
Strayer and Johnston's (2001) study examined whether talking on a cell phone while driving decreases driving performance.

Research Study. Strayer, D. L., & Johnston, W. A. (2001). Driven to distraction: Dual-task studies of simulated driving and conversing on a cellular phone. *Psychological Science, 12*, 462–466. [Note: Only Experiment 1 of this study is described.]

Purpose of the Study. The researchers were interested in how use of a cell phone while driving influences driving performance (see Photo 1.8). They describe previous studies that have shown that devices that require one's hands while driving (e.g., the radio, temperature controls) can reduce driving performance. In this study, they predicted that cell phone use would reduce driving performance. They tested two ideas about how cell phone use could decrease driving: (1) that the handheld use of the phone would interfere with driving and (2) that the attention requirements of a phone conversation would interfere with driving.

Method of the Study. Forty-eight undergraduates (half male, half female) participated in the experiment. Each of the students was randomly assigned to one of three cell phone conditions: handheld phone, hands-free phone, and no phone (radio control only). The participants performed a computer-simulated driving task where they moved the cursor on the screen to match a moving target as closely as possible, using a joystick. Red and green lights flashed periodically during the task, and subjects were instructed to press the "brake" button as quickly as possible when the red light flashed. They performed this task on its own in a practice segment and two test segments; a dual-task segment was placed between the two test segments. In the dual-task segment, they were given an additional task that included one of the following to match the conditions listed previously: handheld phone conversation with another person (who was part of the research team) about a current news story, hands-free phone conversation with another person about a current news story, or controlling a radio to listen to a broadcast of their choice. The frequency of missing red lights and the reaction time to hit the brake button when a red light appeared were measured and compared for the three phone conditions.

(Continued)

(Continued)

Results of the Study. The two cell phone use conditions did not differ in their results, suggesting that driving performance in response to red lights is similar for handheld and hands-free phone use. Figure 1.14 shows a graph for each of the measures according to the phone (combined for handheld and hands-free conditions) and no-phone conditions. The data are shown in each graph separately for driving performance in the driving only segments (single task) and for the phone or radio task while driving (dual-task) segment. The graphs show that more red lights were missed and time to press the brake button was longer when subjects were talking on the phone (compared with when only driving), but there was no difference in driving performance when subjects listened to the radio while driving and when they just performed the driving task on its own.

Conclusions of the Study. The authors concluded that phone use, regardless of whether it requires one's hands, interferes with driving performance more than just listening to the radio. This suggests that the attention component of phone use is the key factor in the driving performance interference.

FIGURE 1.14 ■ Driving Performance as Measured by Responses to Red Lights in the Driving Task While Performing the Driving Task on Its Own (Single Task) or While Also Performing the Phone or Radio Task (Dual Task)

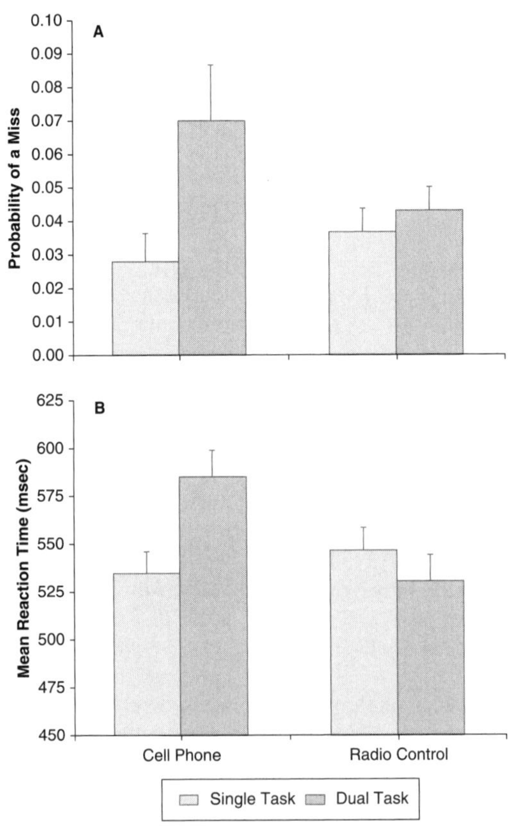

Source: Strayer and Johnston (2001, Figure 1).

Chapter Summary

- **What is the value of research in psychology?**
  Research provides psychologists with new knowledge about behavior, regardless of the type of behavior of interest.
- **Why do psychologists conduct research?**
  Psychologists conduct research because it provides the best way to gain new knowledge about behavior.
- **What is the difference between a population and a sample?**
  A population is the group of individuals a researcher wants to learn about. The sample is the portion of the population that participates in the research study. This is the group of individuals observed by the researcher.
- **What kinds of data are collected in psychological studies?**
  Many different kinds of data are collected in research studies. Survey responses and systematic and controlled responses on a task are two common examples of the types of data researchers collect. Four measurement scales define the type of measurements used in the data collected: nominal, ordinal, interval, and ratio scales.
- **What is a distribution, and how does its shape affect our analysis of the data?**
  A distribution is a set of scores collected as data. The shape of a distribution can take many forms, but two common shapes are symmetrical and skewed shapes. These shapes will affect our choice of both descriptive and inferential statistics, as we will see in the coming chapters.

Applying Your Knowledge

On Facebook one day, you see a post from one of your friends that they have found the most amazing vitamin supplement. They claim that they have taken the vitamin once a day for the past few weeks, and they have more energy and feel great. They are passing on the information to their friends (including you) and urging you to try the vitamin for yourself.

- Why should you be skeptical of the claim you read from your friend?
- What other information would you want to have before deciding if you should try the new vitamin your friend is so excited about?
- Suppose you came across a news item reporting that thousands of people have been trying the new vitamin (they include interviews with some of these people) and that overall, these people have reported positive results. Would this convince you to try the new vitamin? Why or why not?

Test Yourself

1. Freud hypothesized that many of our personality traits are controlled by an unconscious conflict between aspects of ourselves—the id, ego, and superego—that we are not consciously aware of (Nairne, 2009). Using what you know about conducting research, explain why this hypothesis is difficult to support with observations of behavior.

2. The scientific method relies on which way of knowing information about the world?

3. If I am concerned about whether the survey I am using in my study accurately measures the behavior I am interested in, I am considering the ________________ of my study.

4. For each study description that follows, identify the most likely population of interest, identify the operational definition of the behavior of interest, and identify the scale of measurement of the dependent variable.

    a. College student participants were asked to play a virtual ball-tossing game during which some participants are systematically excluded from the game a short time after they began. The study tested the effects of social exclusion on the participants' mood. The researchers then asked the students to complete a mood survey in which they rated their mood on a 1 to 7 scale—higher numbers indicating a more positive mood.

    b. To examine the effect of diet on cognitive abilities, researchers taught rats to navigate a maze to reach a food reward. Half of the rats in the study were fed a special diet high in sugar; the other group of rats was fed the standard rat chow. The rats were then tested in the maze after being fed the assigned diet for 2 weeks. The amount of time it took the rats to reach the food reward in the maze was measured. Rats on the high-sugar diet took longer to run the maze on average than the normal diet rats.

    c. A study was conducted to examine the effects of violence on social behaviors in young children. Five-year-olds were asked to play a superhero video game with mild violence (e.g., punching, throwing). Two researchers who were not aware of the purpose of the study observed the children's behavior at recess. The number of social behaviors seen (e.g., helping another child, playing cooperatively with another child) was recorded on a school day both before and after they played the video game.

5. Providing responses on a survey to make yourself look better is called _________.

    a. symmetrical bias
    b. skewed bias
    c. social desirability bias
    d. ratio bias

6. In a research study on navigation, participants were asked to judge the distance of a landmark in the environment from their current location. This dependent variable was measured on a(n) _____________ measurement scale.

    a. nominal
    b. ordinal
    c. interval
    d. ratio

7. In a research study, you are asked to indicate your college major on a survey. This dependent variable was measured on a(n) _______________ measurement scale.
   a. nominal
   b. ordinal
   c. interval
   d. ratio
8. You are conducting a study that uses IQ tests. On these tests, the participants score an average of 100. All other scores are evenly distributed above and below this average. What type of distribution is this?
   a. Skewed distribution
   b. Symmetrical distribution
   c. Hypothetical distribution
   d. Faulty distribution
9. _____________ scales typically involve numerical scores, whereas _______________ scales do not.
   a. Interval, ratio
   b. Ratio, nominal
   c. Nominal, ordinal
   d. Ordinal, nominal
10. Survey data are always accurate.
    a. True
    b. False
11. A frequency distribution graph can show you the shape of a distribution.
    a. True
    b. False
12. Systematic and controlled measures are more direct observations of behavior than the self-reports collected on surveys.
    a. True
    b. False
13. Of the following choices, which are good operational definitions of anxiety?
    a. Scores on an anxiety scale
    b. Score on an exam
    c. A general feeling of helplessness
    d. Both a and c

SAGE edge™

Visit **edge.sagepub.com/mcbridermstats** to find the answers to the Test Yourself questions above, as well as quizzes, flashcards, and other resources to help you accomplish your coursework goals.

DEVELOPING A RESEARCH QUESTION AND UNDERSTANDING RESEARCH REPORTS

Where Research Questions Come From

CONSIDER THE FOLLOWING QUESTIONS AS YOU READ CHAPTER 2

- How do researchers develop a research question?
- How do researchers conduct a literature review?
- What are the different types of research articles, and how are they organized?
- How do we use a literature review to make hypotheses?
- What are the different ways that psychologists present research?
- How do we write an American Psychological Association (APA)-style article? What information goes into each section of the article? How do we format the article?

LEARNING OBJECTIVES FOR CHAPTER 2

- Generate appropriate research questions for a psychological study.
- Demonstrate how to conduct a literature review for a research question.
- Locate relevant information in an empirical journal article.
- Demonstrate scientific writing in APA style.
- Compare different methods of communicating research findings.

A number of years ago, I was playing the game Catch Phrase with some friends. In this game, a handheld device displays a target phrase (e.g., a name or object) while ticking down a timer. The players with the device must provide clues to the target phrase (without saying it) to get their teammates to say the phrase. Meanwhile, the timer ticks faster and faster until it runs out and buzzes. When the time runs out, the player who ends up with the device loses a point for their team. The game moves swiftly; teammates are constantly calling out phrases to guess the target phrase.

After the game ended, we discussed the sequence of guessing of a particularly difficult phrase. Two players, Joel and Renée, claimed to have guessed the phrase, but only one had actually done so. Everyone agreed that Renée had actually guessed the phrase, but Joel claimed to have a clear memory of guessing it. It was determined that although Joel believed that he had guessed the correct phrase, he actually did not accurately recall (had an inaccurate memory of) the events of the game. He had a *false memory* in remembering who had actually guessed correctly. Perplexed by his error, Joel suggested that "someone should study this." As a memory researcher, I became interested in this phenomenon and conducted experiments to investigate false memories like the one that Joel had during the game (e.g., Coane & McBride, 2006; Coane, McBride, Termonen, & Cutting, 2016; McBride, Coane, & Raulerson, 2006). This story illustrates how everyday events such as these can spark psychological research questions (e.g., Why do false memories occur?).

DEVELOPING A RESEARCH QUESTION

Choosing a research question is the first step in the research process (see Figure 2.1). Answering a research question is the researcher's primary motivation for designing and conducting a study. These questions come from many sources. Primarily, they come from what the researcher is interested in learning about. Think about what topics in psychology interest you the most. Can you think of questions about behavior that you would like to have answered? Have you ever asked yourself a "what if . . ." question about a behavior? That is often where research questions begin—from the questions a researcher is interested in. In the situation described at the start of the chapter, a research question was sparked by an everyday event (e.g., Why do false memories occur?). In other cases, research questions are developed to solve a real-world problem (e.g., How does the use of a cellular phone affect driving performance?). Finally, explanations of behavior that need to be tested (theories) can guide research questions (e.g., Do negative thoughts cause depression?).

descriptive research question: A research question that asks about the presence of behavior, how frequently it is exhibited, or whether there is a relationship between different behaviors

There can be a **descriptive research question**, such as whether a specific behavior occurs (Are college students anxious?), what the nature of the behavior is (How does anxiety manifest itself in college students?), or whether behaviors occur together (Do college students

FIGURE 2.1 ■ Steps in the Research Process: Choosing a Research Question

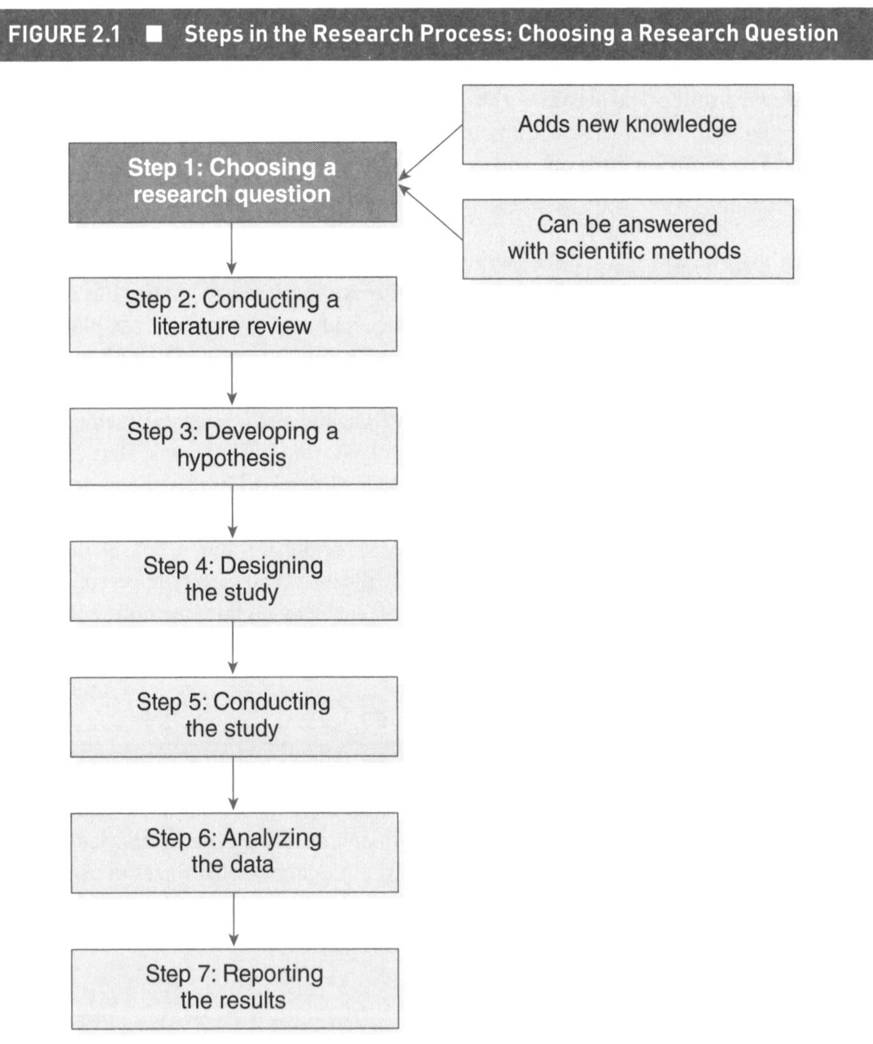

who smoke also tend to be anxious?). There can also be a **causal research question**—about causes of behavior (What types of events cause college students to become anxious?). Many causal research questions are also designed to test a **theory** about the cause of a behavior (Is anxiety in college students caused by a lack of confidence in their abilities?) or to compare theories about behavior to see which theory has more support (Is anxiety in college students caused by a lack of confidence in their abilities or a lack of social support?). Research questions can answer fundamental questions about behavior (What are the causes of anxiety among college students?) or questions about how to solve real-world problems (What kinds of student-oriented programs can a college or university initiate that will reduce anxiety in college students?). This is the difference between **basic research** questions and **applied research** questions. The type of question a researcher pursues is based on whether the researcher is interested in basic questions about a behavior or applications of the behavior in daily life. However, even though researcher interest is often a starting place for choosing a question to study, researchers should consider how appropriate their question is for both scientific methods and the specific field of study before moving on to designing a study.

causal research question: A research question that asks what causes specific behaviors to occur

theory: An explanation of behavior that can be tested through research studies

basic research: Research conducted with the goal of understanding fundamental processes of phenomena

applied research: Research conducted with the goal of solving everyday problems

One important issue in choosing a research question is whether the question can be answered with scientific methods. Can observations of behavior provide an answer to the question? Some questions that would be difficult to test with scientific methods are "Does God exist?" and "Was the Iraq War a moral war?" If specific observations of behavior can be made to help answer the question, then it might be an appropriate question for psychological research. Table 2.1 provides some examples of research questions that have been examined in different areas of psychological research to give you some examples of questions that can be answered by observing behavior.

TABLE 2.1 ■ Examples of Research Questions in Different Areas of Psychology

Area of psychological research	Examples of research questions
Social psychology	How does an authority figure influence behavior (Milgram, 1963)?
	What types of faces are considered attractive (Corneille, Monin, & Pleyers, 2005)?
Cognitive psychology	What types of memory decline as people age (Lipman & Caplan, 1992)?
	How does our knowledge of the world influence our perception (Ban, Lee, & Yang, 2004)?
Industrial–organizational psychology	How does work environment affect job stress (Pal & Saksvik, 2008)?
	How does perception of power in the workplace affect perceptions of sexual harassment (DeSouza & Fansler, 2003)?
Clinical psychology	What types of people benefit most from cognitive behavioral therapy (Green, Hadjistavropoulos, & Sharpe, 2008)?
	What are the causes of schizophrenia (Compton, Goulding, & Walker, 2007)?
Biological psychology	What are the effects of amphetamine on brain activity (Heidenreich, 1993)?
	What are the neurological causes of Parkinson's disease (Olzmann, 2007)?

We all develop research questions about behavior every day—"Why did that person just scowl at me? Was it in response to something I did?" "Why did I score well on this exam but score poorly on my other exam when I studied equally hard for both of them?" "How can I get my dogs to tell me they need to go outside?" The human brain is designed to look for explanations of things that happen in the world. But not all research questions are causal, as these examples are. "How many other people are feeling as anxious as I am about the upcoming exam?" "How did the way I studied differ for the two exams on which I got different scores?" These questions simply ask about a description of behavior or how different behaviors are related instead of what causes the behavior. Either type of research question is appropriate for a psychological study. The key is the research question should be as specific as possible. A question like "Does listening to music help me study?" is not specific enough to directly study. We would need to first make the question more specific, such as "Will I get a lower exam score if I study while listening to rock music than studying in silence?" In this question, the concepts of interest are clearer: the background while studying (music and silence) and exam score. This is the type of research question you should try to come up with. Take a minute now to jot down some research questions you have about behavior, and try to make them as specific as possible.

Another important consideration in choosing a research question is how much is already known about the question. In other words, what has been learned from previous studies about the question? To investigate what is known about a research question from previous studies, a thorough **literature review** should be conducted. A literature review involves searching research databases or other sources to find relevant research that has been done in an area of the field. Reading about what other researchers have done will help you to determine what is already known about a research question, determine what methods have been used to investigate the question, and find information that can help you make a prediction about what the answer to the research question will be. (Making predictions will be discussed in a later section of this chapter.) Conducting a literature review ensures that a new study will add to the knowledge in an area without duplicating what is already known. However, it can take many studies with the same research question before the answer to the research question is supported by enough evidence to provide confidence in the answer. Thus, replication of results is an important part of the scientific process. Just because a study had been done before on a specific research question does not mean more studies are not needed to fully answer the question. A research question does not need to be wholly original to contribute to psychological science (see Figure 2.2).

literature review: A process of searching for and reviewing previous studies related to a study being developed to add to the knowledge in an area and make appropriate predictions about the data

STOP AND THINK

2.1. For each of the following research questions, identify whether it is a descriptive or causal question:

a. How often does operant conditioning occur in daily life?

b. Does jet lag affect one's mood?

c. Can cognitive training decrease dementia?

2.2. Explain why a researcher should conduct a literature review before conducting a study.

FIGURE 2.2 ■ A Literature Review Can Help a Researcher Determine What Is Already Known About a Topic

Source: Copyright by S. Harris, http://www.sciencecartoonsplus.com/scimags.html.

HOW TO CONDUCT A LITERATURE REVIEW

©istockphoto.com/bearinmind

Photo 2.1 Conducting a literature review involves a search for published studies that others have already done on a topic.

There are many sources researchers use to conduct a literature review. Searching through databases helps identify studies relevant to a research question (see Photo 2.1). Databases may also hold references to helpful reviews of research in an area. However, if you want to learn about the most recent studies in an area, databases may not be the best source because these databases typically reference published works, and the publication process can take a year or more from the time an article or a book chapter is written to when it is published and cataloged in the database. Therefore, to conduct the most up-to-date literature review, it can be helpful to attend a psychological conference in an area where researchers often present studies that have not yet been published. More information about the sources for conducting a literature review is provided in the rest of this chapter (see Figure 2.3).

FIGURE 2.3 ■ Steps in the Research Process: Conducting a Literature Review

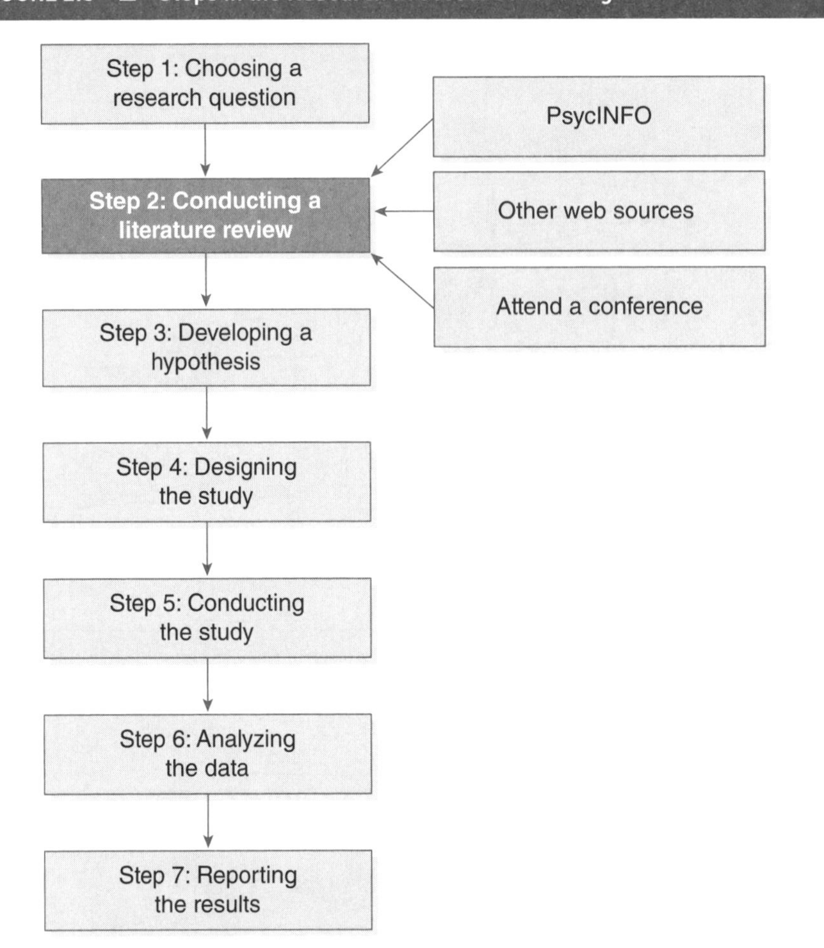

variable: An attribute that can vary across individuals

One thing to think about as you begin a literature review is which variables are of most interest to you for the topic you wish to study. A **variable** is something that can change across individuals in a study (see Photo 2.2). It could be something you want to measure, such as anxiety, math skill, or feelings of belonging. Or it could be something you want to compare in a study, such as whether people are given time pressure for a task, whether people get a full night's sleep, or it could also be taking different types of drugs. In the research question example described earlier in the chapter—"Will I get a lower exam score if I study while listening to rock music than studying in silence?"—the variables were the background while studying (either music or silence) and exam score. Performance on the exam is the behavior we want to measure (using exam score as the measure), and the background while studying is the causal variable we want to examine to see if it affects the behavior of performance on the exam. Identifying the variables that are of interest to you (e.g., which type of drug—causal variable—best helps reduce anxiety—behavior) is an important step to take before you begin your literature review. For the research questions you jotted down in the last section, try to identify the variables in each question.

Photo 2.2
Age can be a variable of interest to allow comparisons for a specific behavior.

PsycINFO

A very useful database for a literature review of psychological research is PsycINFO. PsycINFO is a searchable database that contains records of articles, books, and book chapters written by researchers about research studies in an area of psychology. Although each version may have a different appearance, all versions of PsycINFO can be searched by topic words, words that appear in the citation information for the article (including the title, authors, abstract, and topic words), author names, journal in which the article was published, and so on. In other words, there are many ways to find articles and book chapters about a research question by using PsycINFO. Searching by topic words (called keywords in PsycINFO) is a good way to start a search for a literature review. Note that PsycINFO is not the same as PsycTESTS. PsycTESTS is a database of survey and questionnaire measures that have been developed for use in psychological research and applied settings.

There are two primary ways to search for articles and chapters by keywords. One is to map the term to a subject heading. The APA has designated specific subject headings as general topics of study in psychology. Each article or chapter has been coded by the subject headings that best describe the topic of the article. In PsycINFO, you click a box or a button to turn on the mapping to subject headings, and various subject headings appear that correspond to the keywords you have typed in (you do not have to know the exact subject heading—PsycINFO searches for subject headings similar to what you type in). You can also choose to search just the keywords you entered, which allows PsycINFO to search for articles and chapters that contain those words in the title or abstract. You can also combine searches that focus on different keywords.

An example helps explain how this works (you can follow along by trying this out in PsycINFO if it is available at your college or university—if you have a different database available to you, such as PsycARTICLES, you may be able to follow this process, as most databases allow you to search in similar ways—see also http://www.apa.org/pubs/databases/training/search-guides.aspx for information on searching different databases). Suppose that you are interested in conducting a literature search for the relationship between depression and bullying behaviors in children. A good place to start is a keyword search in PsycINFO. You can start by typing *depression* into the keyword window and mapping it onto the subject headings if such an option is shown. Without selecting additional heading phrases, PsycINFO will execute a search of articles that have *depression* anywhere in the full reference of the article (e.g., title, abstract, topic words). You should find that PsycINFO yields a large number of records that fit these keywords (I found 304,994 sources when I last conducted this search using the keyword *depression—see* Figure 2.4). Depending on which subject terms you choose, different sets of articles are found. Obviously, there are far too many for us to search through one by one, so we need to narrow the search further and include the bullying portion of our topic. See Figure 2.4 for what a keyword search on *depression* might look like in PsycINFO.

We can conduct a second keyword search for *bullying* using the same search procedure described previously for *depression*. This search should find a large number of records as well but fewer records than the search for *depression,* as there have been fewer studies conducted on the topic of bullying. Finally, to narrow our search to the specific topic (we started with depression and bullying), we can combine our two searches. Your version of PsycINFO may have a Combine function for this purpose. Or it may have an AND option that automatically combines the search. If you combine your searches, you should find a more reasonable number of records to look at (when I conducted this search in December 2018, I found 194 records, but you may find more if your search terms include more choices or if additional articles have been published on these topics since that time).

Before we look at the results of the search, consider a possible outcome of our *bullying* search. Suppose that *bullying* was not the proper term, and we find no subject headings that are relevant. One thing we can do to be certain that we get the right subject headings is to use a shorter form of our term and search for truncations. We can do this by shortening our term to *bully* and adding a * or $ to the end of it in the search window. This

FIGURE 2.4 ■ A Keyword Search in PsycINFO on the Topic of Depression

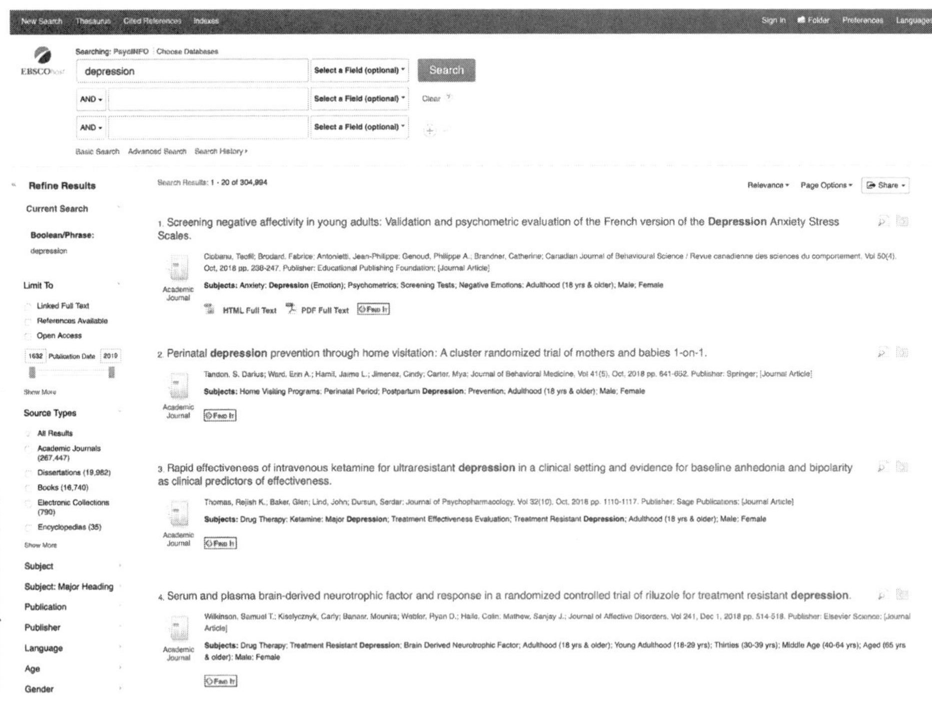

addition searches for all words that begin with bully and finds any variations that might get us closer to our search objective. Be sure to use the truncation symbols if you are not certain that you have the right term or if you do not find appropriate subject headings with a given search term.

What will you get from the PsycINFO search? If you view the results of the search I described previously, you will see a list of articles (probably the most recently published articles first) that indicates the names of the authors, the title of the article, the type of article (journal article, book chapter, dissertation, etc.), and where and when the article was published. You should pay attention to the type of article because some of these may not have gone through **peer review**, meaning that they have not been carefully reviewed by experts in the field and revised by the author(s) based on the review. For example, although dissertations have been approved by a committee before being published in PsycINFO, they are not considered peer-reviewed articles in the way a journal article has been reviewed.

peer review: A process that takes place prior to publication of an article in many journals where experts make suggestions for improving an article and make recommendations about whether an article should be published in a journal

For each article, you can choose to view the *abstract* of the article. The abstract is a short paragraph that summarizes the content of the article (abstracts are discussed in detail later in this chapter when the structure of journal articles is presented). You can then read through the abstracts of articles that might be relevant to your topic. You might also see a link to the article available online in PDF format or a link to search your library for the journal or book in which the article was published to assist you in locating any articles you find relevant to your literature review. Finally, the reference sections of the articles you find may also lead you to other relevant articles on your topic. Note that the entire article you find on a topic may not be relevant to your topic. It may be that their theoretical description of behavior is most relevant or that their research method is one you want to model in your study. Be sure to focus on the most relevant parts of the articles from your literature review when you summarize the background studies in developing the rationale for your study. Summarizing the entire article will not be appropriate in many cases.

Suppose that you find an article that is especially relevant to your topic and that you would like to know if the same author has published other articles relevant to your topic. You can find articles by a particular author by conducting an author search in PsycINFO (you could also just click on the reference for the article, and the author name will appear as a link that will give you a list of all articles in the database by that author). Simply type the author's last name and first initial into PsycINFO, and you will see either a list of sources by that author or choices, in alphabetical order, that match what you typed. You can choose any that seem relevant (sometimes the same author will be listed in a few different ways—with or without middle initial). You can also limit keyword and author searches by year if you are just interested in the most recent articles that have been published. Finally, articles in a particular psychology journal can be searched in PsycINFO. For more information on PsycINFO searches, go to http://www.apa.org/pubs/databases/training/search-guides.aspx for APA guides on how to use PsycINFO.

Let's consider another example of how to search PsycINFO for articles you might want in your literature review. The first step is to state your research question and to identify the variables in your question. Imagine that you are designing a research study for your class on how use of social media affects one's self-image. What are the variables in your research question? The causal variable is "use of social media," and the behavior variable is "one's self-image." What terms should we use in PsycINFO to find relevant articles? The first one is "social media," so we can type this one into the search box as a keyword. The other term is "self-image," so we can use the AND (or another combine) command to search for articles that include both terms. This search comes up with only a few articles—looking at the abstracts of these articles can help you decide if they are relevant to your study. But if only a couple of articles come up with these terms, you can look at the reference list from one of the relevant articles (look for this link in PsycINFO) to see if any of the sources cited by those authors are also relevant to your study.

PubMed and ERIC

Although most articles published in psychology journals can be found in PsycINFO or similar psychology databases, some journals publish articles in other topic areas that overlap with psychology, and you will find them only in other databases. For example, journals that publish research in biological and medical areas can be found by searching the PubMed (also called MEDLINE) database. If you are interested in conducting a literature review on topics in biological psychology or about psychological disorders or specific conditions such as autism, you may want to search PubMed in addition to PsycINFO to complete a thorough literature review. Articles in areas related to education can be found in the ERIC (Education Resources Information Center) database. Thus, if you are conducting a literature review on topics such as standardized testing, you may also want to search for articles in ERIC. Like PsycINFO, PubMed and ERIC can be searched by topic, author, and journal with advanced search capabilities that can include year of publication, language of publication, and so on. The search screen will have a different layout, depending on the version of the database that you are viewing, but many versions of both PubMed and ERIC have drop-down menus for choosing a search by these features of an article. A database dealing with more general topics, called Web of Science, is also available for searching for journal articles in different areas of research.

Other Sources

In addition to PsycINFO and similar databases, there are search engines that can be accessed to obtain articles relevant to your topic. The first is a sub-engine of Google called Google Scholar. You can access Google Scholar at https://scholar.google.com. Google Scholar searches the web for academic journals and books to find articles relevant to a defined topic or specific author. As with PsycINFO, you may not always find links to copies of the articles on Google Scholar, but you may find articles that were not found in a search of PsycINFO. Because Google Scholar will search for articles on many different topics, you are not limited to what is categorized in a particular database (e.g., you can find articles that are in both PsycINFO and PubMed in Google Scholar). With search engines, though, you are also more likely to come across articles that have not been peer reviewed (see the next section for more discussion of peer review). Articles that have not been peer reviewed are typically less reliable sources of information because they have not been evaluated by experts in the field who verify the quality of the study.

Other search engines may yield information on a topic, but the veracity of that information may vary. Whereas PsycINFO and Google Scholar yield articles published in journals and books, most search engines produce other sources of information, such as popular press articles that may or may not report research findings accurately. Thus, a search of a database such as PsycINFO or Google Scholar is a necessary step in any literature review. Simply typing your topic into Google or Wikipedia will not provide an adequate search for a literature review. The sources that are represented in such searches are not reliable enough to use to design a study or to write a research report of a study. Wikipedia provides unverified information on a topic that is too general for use in a literature review, and a normal Google search of the web will not provide a thorough search of the articles on your topic, as many are not freely available on the web. You will also likely find sources that are not reliable with a Google search. In other words, Google web searches and Wikipedia searches are how *not* to do a literature review.

Finally, psychology conferences can provide a way to get the most up-to-date information about research conducted in an area (often so new that it has not been published yet). If you are unable to attend such a conference yourself, you can often search the programs of these conferences online to view titles, authors, and abstracts or research studies that will be or have been presented at the conference. Some of the larger conferences in the United States that cover many areas of psychology are the APA Convention (typically held in August each year) and the Association for Psychological Science Convention (typically held in May each year). International meetings on specific topics in psychology are also periodically held. In addition, there are many area-wide psychological association conferences for all areas of psychology (the Midwestern Psychological Association, the Southeastern Psychological Association, the Western Psychological Association, etc.) that can be found on the APA webpage (https://www.apa.org) under News & Events. Many areas of psychology also hold annual conventions (a quick web search will yield some of these meetings and sites).

WHAT YOU FIND IN A LITERATURE REVIEW

As described in the previous section, a PsycINFO search (or a search with one of the other sources) provides you with a list of journal articles and/or book chapters that are relevant to your topic. How can these sources help you as you attempt to make a prediction about your research question? As you read the articles, you may find important information for your literature review in different sections of the articles. Before you conduct your literature review, it is a good idea to become familiar with the structure of different types of articles and what type of information you can expect to get from the different sections of an article. The next section will discuss the structure of some of the different article types. We will begin with journal articles.

What Is a Journal Article?

An empirical journal article is written by a researcher, or multiple researchers in many cases, to describe a research study to others who might be interested in knowing what the researcher did (someone like you if you are conducting a literature review on the researcher's topic). The researcher's article may describe a single study (e.g., one experiment), or it may describe multiple studies, all of which relate to the same research question. After the researcher has written the article, the researcher submits it to a psychological journal to attempt to get it published. If the article is published, it will be cataloged in PsycINFO, PsycARTICLES, and other databases. The article is typically sent out to several reviewers who are experts on the general topic of the article (they are typically researchers who have done studies on the topic in the past). This is the process known as peer review. These reviewers make recommendations about revisions to the article to improve it and indicate whether or not they think the journal should publish the article. The editor of the journal uses these reviews to decide if the article can be published in the journal and which revisions are most important. The author of the article then revises the article or may attempt to submit it to a different journal if the editor has decided not to publish the article in that particular journal. If the revised article is submitted to the same journal, it may then be reviewed again, or it may be accepted by the editor for publication. The review process can be lengthy (sometimes taking many months or even a year), but it is important in verifying the quality of the study before it is published. Thus, articles that are not peer reviewed may describe studies of lower quality. If you conduct only a simple Google search of the web for your literature review, you may find some of these unpublished articles. After the article is accepted for publication, it can then take a few more months before the article appears in the journal, but many journals now publish an online version as soon as it is ready, which gives readers earlier access to the article. Despite this, articles are rarely published very soon after they are written, which means that research is typically a year or more old before it is published.

Empirical journal articles are considered primary sources for research information because they are written by the researchers who conducted the research, and details of the study are provided. Journal articles differ from popular magazine articles. Popular magazine articles often contain short summaries of the study written by an author other than the primary source (i.e., they are secondary sources) and may not provide an accurate account of the study in all cases. Thus, popular magazine articles are considered secondary sources. An accurate and thorough literature review requires review of primary sources (i.e., journal articles).

Many areas of psychology have journals devoted to research on a particular topic, but there are also journals that publish research in all areas of psychology. Table 2.2 provides a list of some general psychology journals as well as journals that specialize in a particular area. In most cases, you can figure out what types of studies are published in the journal from the title of the journal.

Structure of an Empirical Journal Article

Journal articles are organized into sections. Each section provides specific information about a study. Each major section of a journal article is described here.

abstract: A summary of an article that appears at the beginning of the article and in searchable databases of journal articles

Abstract

As described earlier, an **abstract** is a short summary of the study that allows readers to decide if the article is relevant to their literature review without their reading the entire article. Abstracts of articles are catalogued in PsycINFO. They are typically 150 to 250 words long and include a sentence or two summarizing each of the major sections of the article. Thus, the abstract usually includes (a) the general topic of the study, (b) a

TABLE 2.2 ■ A List of Psychological Journals by Type of Article Published

General Psychology Journals: These journals publish studies from various areas of psychology.
Psychological Science
Journal of Experimental Psychology: General
Journal of Experimental Psychology: Applied
American Psychologist
Canadian Journal of Experimental Psychology
Experimental Psychology
Acta Psychologica
Personality and Social Psychology Journals
Journal of Personality and Social Psychology
Journal of Experimental Social Psychology
Personality and Social Psychology Bulletin
Personality and Individual Differences
Journal of Research in Personality
Cognitive Psychology Journals
Journal of Experimental Psychology: Learning, Memory, and Cognition
Journal of Experimental Psychology: Human Perception and Performance
Cognition
Journal of Memory and Language
Memory & Cognition
Applied Cognitive Psychology
Attention, Perception, & Psychophysics
Developmental Psychology Journals
Journal of Experimental Child Psychology
Child Development
Psychology and Aging
Developmental Psychology
British Journal of Developmental Psychology
Biological Psychology Journals
Neuropsychology
Neuropsychologia
Applied Neuropsychology
Review and Theoretical Journals: These journals publish review articles and/or articles describing new or revised theories about behavior (some of these journals publish empirical studies as well).
Psychological Review
Psychological Bulletin
Psychonomic Bulletin & Review
Developmental Review
Best Practices in School Psychology
Behavioral and Brain Sciences

brief description of the methodology, (c) the major results of the study, and (d) what was learned from the study.

Introduction

introduction: A section of an APA-style article that introduces the topic of the study, reviews relevant background studies, and presents predictions for the data

As the title implies, the **introduction** section of the article introduces the topic, research question, and other relevant information for the study. If an introduction is written well, it should contain the following information:

- Introduction to the general topic of the study (e.g., the bystander effect)
- General problem that the study addressed (e.g., factors that affect the bystander effect)
- Discussion of relevant background studies that inform the reader about what is known about the problem and how these studies are related to the present study the researchers described in their article (e.g., studies that were found in a literature review of factors that affect the bystander effect)
- Justification of the present study (i.e., what aspect of the research question the present study answered that has not been determined from past studies)
- Brief description of how the current study addressed the relevant aspect of the research question (may include variables that were studied and a short outline of the method of the study)
- Predictions (i.e., hypotheses) that the researchers made about the outcome of the present study

The introduction should essentially make an argument about what the present study contributes to knowledge in the selected area of psychology and why the researchers made their hypotheses. If you can identify the points of support for the authors' argument, then you probably have a reasonable understanding of the important information in the introduction.

Method

method: Section of an APA-style article that describes the participants, design, stimuli, apparatus, and procedure used in the study

The purpose of the **method** section is to provide enough information about how a study was conducted so that others can evaluate and (if they wish) reproduce the study to see if the results replicate. There are four subsections of the method that may be seen in empirical articles: (1) participants (also called subjects in non-APA-style journals or if animal subjects are used), (2) design, (3) materials (or apparatus), and (4) procedure. The participants subsection describes who the participants in the study were (How many were there? Were they college students? How many males and females participated? If they were animal subjects, what species were they?). How the participants for the study were obtained is also described (Did they volunteer from a participant pool? Were they recruited on a website? If they were animal subjects, were they bred by the researcher?). The design subsection describes the design of the study (What were the variables studied? How were they studied?). The materials (or apparatus) subsection describes the various materials and apparatus that were used in the study (If there were stimuli shown to the participants, what were the stimuli? If a survey was used, what kinds of items did it include?). The procedure subsection provides a chronological description of what the participants did in the study (What did they do from start to finish? What were their tasks? What instructions were they given? How many trials did the participants complete?). Sometimes authors will combine some of these subsections (e.g., design and materials) as the information in these sections can overlap. In very short empirical articles (e.g., *Psychological Science* short reports), the subsections will all be combined into one large method section.

Results

The **results** section provides a summary of the data (often in tables or figures) and information about the statistical tests that were performed to analyze the data. The findings are described in the text; statistical values are given as support for the findings. The specific types of values given depend on the type of tests the researchers conducted. Thus, if the tests themselves are not familiar to you, focus on the description the authors provide of the findings. Were there group differences? Was there a relationship between the behaviors measured? Look back at what the authors expected to find to see if you can match their findings to their predictions. Tables and figures are typically organized by the most important variables of interest, so consider the organization of tables and figures as you work on understanding the design of a study. The graph in Figure 2.5 shows an example of this organization from a study by Russell, Ickes, and Ta (2018) that investigated women's comfort level interacting with gay and straight men. The behavior variable the researchers measured (participants' rating of how comfortable they would be talking to a male described in a scenario) is shown on the y-axis, and one of the causal variables (whether the participant knew the sexual orientation of the male described in the scenario when they made their ratings) is shown on the x-axis. The bars are grouped according to the other causal variable (sexual orientation—gay or straight—of the male described in the scenario).

results: Section of an APA-style article that presents a summary of the results and the statistical tests of the predictions

Discussion

The last section of the article is the **discussion** section. The authors go back to their predictions and discuss their findings in reference to their predictions. If the findings support their predictions, the authors indicate what they learned about the research question and perhaps where researchers should go next in this area. If the findings do not support their predictions, they should describe some possible explanations for why they did not support the predictions. A discussion of the results in the context of previous findings is also included. Finally, a summary of what was learned from the study should be included in the discussion section, including possible limitations of these conclusions based on strengths and weaknesses of the study conducted. Researchers may also suggest a direction for future research in that area.

discussion: Section of an APA-style article that compares the results of a study with the predictions and the results of previous studies

Review Articles and Book Chapters

Most of the articles you come across in a literature review are empirical journal articles, as described in the previous section. However, you may find a smaller number of articles that fit into the categories of review article or book chapter. The purpose of these

FIGURE 2.5 ■ Results From Russell et al.'s (2018) Study Showed That Women Were More Comfortable Interacting With Gay Men Than Straight Men When They Knew the Man's Sexual Orientation

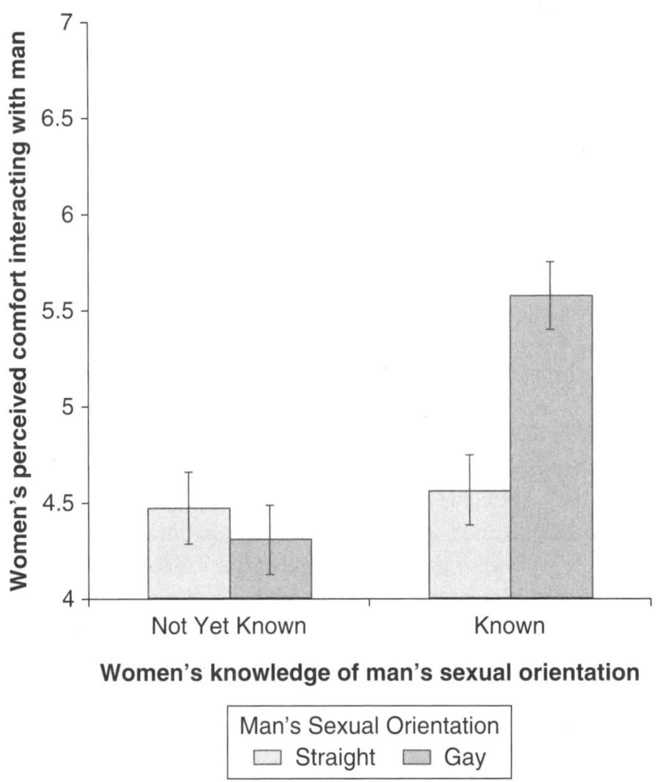

Source: Russell et al. (2018).

articles is to organize and summarize research in a particular area of psychology to give researchers a review of the research to date. Accordingly, these sorts of articles can be very useful in a literature review because they allow a researcher to find a lot of information about a topic in a single article. These reviews also provide a list of references that can be helpful in searching for empirical articles about specific studies that may be important for developing a prediction for the researcher's study. The main difference between review articles and book chapters is where they are published. Some psychological journals are devoted entirely to review articles (see Table 2.2 for some examples). There are also journals that reserve a small portion of space for review articles (e.g., *Psychonomic Bulletin & Review*). Review articles go through the same rigorous review process as that for empirical journal articles, which were described earlier. Book chapters are typically published in a book that is entirely written by a set of authors (i.e., every chapter is written by the authors) or is in an edited book where editors compile chapters on a similar topic from

STOP AND THINK

2.3. What is the purpose of a journal article?

2.4. How can reading journal articles aid in a literature review?

2.5. In what way(s) can peer review affect the quality of a journal article?

2.6. Briefly describe the major sections of a journal article.

multiple authors. The review process for book chapters is variable and may not be as rigorous as that for journal articles but does typically involve some peer review.

USING THE LITERATURE REVIEW TO MAKE HYPOTHESES

The primary goals of a literature review are to (a) determine what research has been done on a research question to avoid duplicating previous research and (b) review previous findings and theories to make a **hypothesis** about the outcome of a study. A hypothesis is the prediction for the findings of the study. For example, a researcher might hypothesize that a relationship exists between two measures of behavior. For a different type of study, a researcher might predict that one group of participants will have average scores that are higher than the average scores of another group. There are two primary types of information that researchers use to make hypotheses from a literature review: theories and previous results. From these types of information, researchers can make a **theory-driven hypothesis** or a **data-driven hypothesis**, respectively. However, regardless of the types of hypotheses that are developed, hypotheses should be stated as specifically as possible in terms of how behaviors and conditions are related (see Figure 2.6).

hypothesis: Prediction regarding the results of a research study

theory-driven hypothesis: Hypothesis for a study that is based on a theory about the behavior of interest

data-driven hypothesis: Hypothesis for a study that is based on the results of previous, related studies

Theory-Driven Hypotheses

Theory-driven hypotheses are made from the predictions of a theory. These are typically made in studies designed to test a theory (i.e., look for data that support or falsify a theory). For example, suppose a theory has been proposed that anxiety causes insomnia. A researcher conducting a study to test this theory might then predict that if two groups of participants are compared—one that is put in an anxiety-provoking situation and one that is put in a relaxing situation—the anxious group will report more problems sleeping than the relaxed group. In other words, the researcher might predict that the anxious group, on average, will report fewer hours of sleep per night than the relaxed group. This hypothesis would be consistent with the theory that anxiety causes insomnia and is therefore a theory-driven hypothesis. A theory-driven hypothesis involves a researcher taking a general statement about behavior (the theory) and making a specific prediction (the hypothesis) about the study from this general statement.

FIGURE 2.6 ■ Steps in the Research Process: Developing a Hypothesis

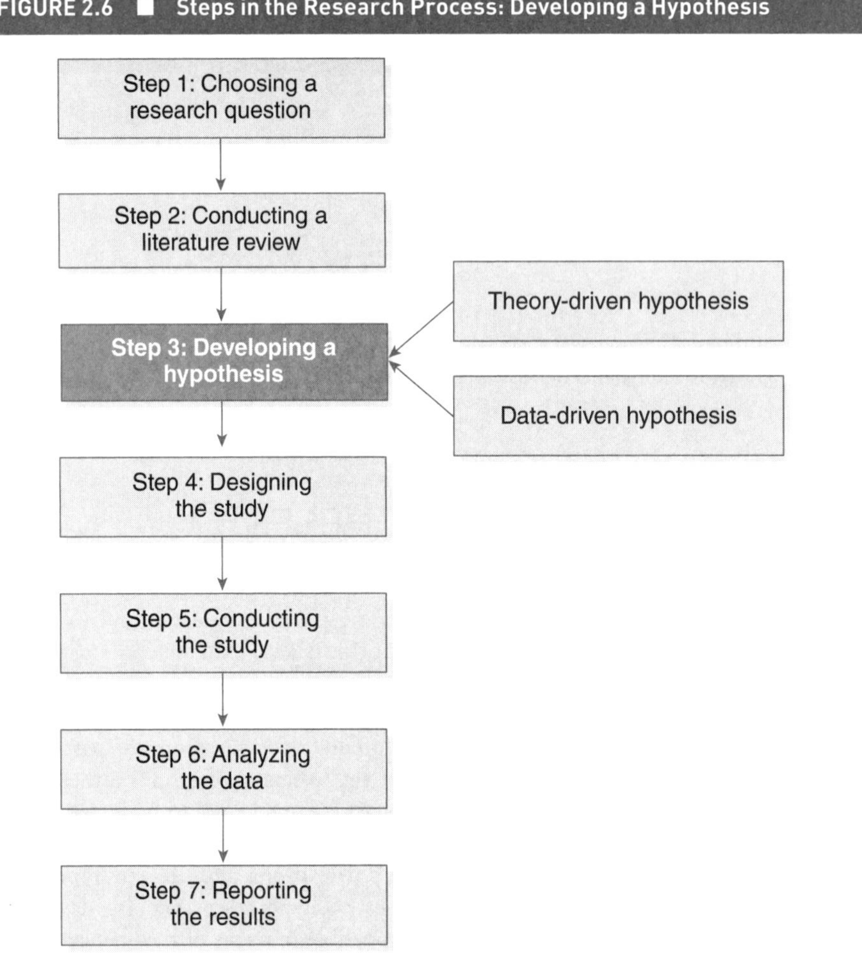

Another example of a theory-driven hypothesis can be seen in a recent study on face perception (see Photo 2.3). Sofer, Dotsch, Wigboldus, and Todorov (2015, Experiment 1) tested a theory that the typicality of a face is important in social evaluations of a person. From this theory, the researchers hypothesized that more typical faces would be judged as more trustworthy because trustworthiness is an important part of social interaction. To test their hypothesis, they conducted a study where female students were presented with female faces created from composites of two faces: an attractive female face and a typical female face (see Figure 2.7 for the two types of faces used in composites). Thus, the faces ranged from highly typical to highly attractive depending on the amount of each of the two original faces present in the composite. Subjects in the study were asked to judge both the attractiveness and the trustworthiness of each face. The results were consistent with their hypothesis: The more typical the face was, the higher the ratings of trustworthiness from the participants. The attractiveness ratings supported their prediction as well, as the less typical faces were judged as more attractive and less trustworthy than the more typical faces. Thus, their study supported the hypothesis that typical faces are judged as more trustworthy, which provided support for the theory that the typicality of a face is important in social evaluations.

Now, consider how the process of a literature review can aid you in developing research questions and hypotheses for your studies. Suppose you are interested in the origin of math abilities and you are conducting a literature review on the development of mathematical concepts. You find that a researcher has suggested the theory that understanding of mathematical operations (e.g., addition, subtraction) is innate (something children are born with). Can you think of a way to make a theory-driven hypothesis for a study that tests this theory? Think about how a study would be conducted to test this theory, and then use the theory to make a hypothesis about the outcome of the study (see the following box for an example of how you could do this).

CanStockPhoto/photography33

Photo 2.3 Sofer et al. (2015) found that attractive faces are judged as less trustworthy because they are less typical.

FIGURE 2.7 ■ Faces Used to Create Stimuli in the Sofer et al. (2015) Study. Photo a Shows a Typical Face, and Photo b Shows an Attractive Face

a

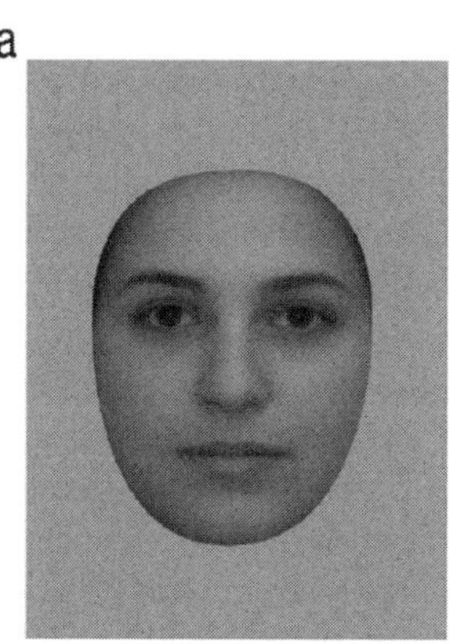

b

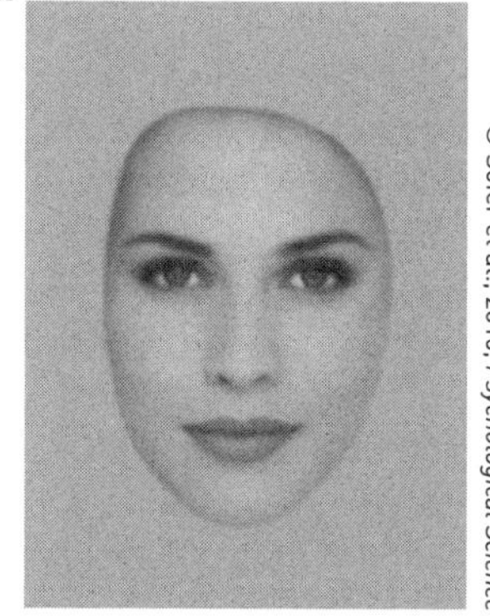

© Sofer et al., 2015, *Psychological Science*

Source: Sofer et al. (2015, Figure 1).

Example of Theory-Driven Hypothesis for Innateness of Mathematical Operations

To determine that something is innate, you would need to test infants who are very young and have not had enough experience with objects to develop an understanding of mathematical operations such as addition and subtraction. You could then test these infants in a study where you show them objects of a set number that they are habituated to (no longer show interest in), occlude the objects with a screen, and then either add an object or remove an object behind the screen so that the infant can see the object being added or subtracted. You then remove the screen and show them the objects but show them an incorrect number of objects based on the operation. If the infants show interest (indicating something that was not expected by the infants) in what they are shown, this can be seen as evidence that the infants understand what they should have seen after the operation was performed. Thus, the theory-driven hypothesis for this study is that infants will look longer when the number of objects does not match the operation than when the number of objects does match the operation.

A study like this was performed by Wynn (1992), where her findings indicated that infants as young as 5 months looked longer when the number of objects did not match the operation than when the number of objects shown was correct based on the operation. Wynn argued that these results support the theory that understanding of addition and subtraction operations is innate.

CanStockPhoto/lzf

Photo 2.4 Schnall, Benton, and Harvey (2008) found that priming the concept of cleanliness led to less harsh judgments of moral situations, such as keeping money in a found wallet.

Data-Driven Hypotheses

Another way in which researchers can make hypotheses about a study is by examining the specific findings of previous studies that are similar and generalizing the findings to their study. Hypotheses made in this way are considered data-driven hypotheses because they are made based on data from previous studies. For this type of hypothesis, a researcher takes a specific result from another study and uses it to make a more general prediction for the research question of interest. For example, suppose researchers are interested in causes of insomnia. In their literature review, they come across a study that found that people who report high levels of anxiety also report getting less sleep per night. From this study's results, they may conclude that anxiety is related to insomnia and make the hypothesis for their study that a relationship between level of anxiety and number of hours of sleep will be found.

A study by Schnall, Benton, and Harvey (2008) provides an example of a hypothesis based on data from previous studies. These researchers were interested in the connection between emotions and moral judgments. Previous studies (Schnall, Haidt, Clore, & Jordan, 2008) had shown that when participants were induced to feel disgust (e.g., exposed to a bad smell), they judged an action as more immoral than control participants who did not experience the disgusting situation. Schnall, Benton, and Harvey (2008) hypothesized from these results that if feelings of cleanliness were induced, the opposite effect should occur: Participants should judge actions less harshly (see Photo 2.4). They conducted two experiments to test this data-driven hypothesis.

In both experiments, one group of participants was primed with the concept of cleanliness, whereas another group was not primed with this concept. Participants then judged the actions of others in a set of moral dilemmas (e.g., keeping money in a found wallet). Results indicated that participants who experienced the concept of cleanliness in the study rated the actions in the dilemmas less harshly than participants who were not primed with the concept. Schnall, Benton, and Harvey (2008) supported their data-driven hypothesis with the results of their study.

Descriptive and Causal Hypotheses

descriptive hypothesis: A prediction about the results of a study that describes the behavior or the relationship between behaviors

causal hypothesis: A prediction about the results of a study that includes the causes of a behavior

Regardless of where the information comes from, hypotheses will either attempt to describe behavior or make a causal prediction about behavior. This distinction maps onto the different types of research questions described above: descriptive and causal. Which type of research question is being asked will also dictate which type of hypothesis is made: a **descriptive hypothesis** or a **causal hypothesis**. If researchers are interested in the causes of behavior, they state a prediction about a particular cause of that behavior—typically as a difference in groups or conditions based on the causal factor they studied. For example, if researchers have the research question "Does drinking caffeine on the day of an exam cause an improvement in test performance in college students?," then their hypothesis may be that students who drink caffeine the day of an exam will have higher test performance than students who do not drink caffeine. If, however, the researchers are interested only in whether certain behaviors occur together or wish to document the occurrence of a particular behavior, they are likely to have a descriptive research question and a descriptive hypothesis. For example, if researchers have the research question "Do students who score low on an exam also have high levels of anxiety?," then their hypothesis may be descriptive, such that a relationship between these behaviors is predicted (i.e., when these behaviors are measured together, students with lower test performance will have higher anxiety scores; see Photo 2.5). Descriptive and causal hypotheses are typically tested with different types of research designs, which are discussed in later chapters of this text.

©istockphoto.com/PeopleImages

Photo 2.5
The research question "Do students who score low on an exam also have high levels of anxiety?" leads to a descriptive hypothesis about the relationship between these variables.

Here is one important thing to note about testing hypotheses and theories: We can never *prove* a hypothesis or theory is correct in our research studies. The best we can do is to support or not support the hypothesis or theory from the data we observe in our study. This is due to the limitations of the research process (e.g., we are testing a small sample, our statistical tests are based on the probabilities of outcomes). We will discuss these limitations throughout the text but know that they are part of any scientific process. The goal is not to prove facts but to support predictions and explanations of the phenomena through the observations we make in our studies.

STOP AND THINK

2.7. Explain the difference between a theory-driven and a data-driven hypothesis.

2.8. How does a literature review help researchers make hypotheses about their study?

2.9. Describe the difference between a theory and a hypothesis.

APA-STYLE ARTICLE WRITING

Because this chapter covers the structure of empirical articles and how research is reported, we'll take a look at the last step in the research process here so that you can keep this step in mind as you continue through the process of conducting research (see Figure 2.8). As you have seen in the journal articles you have read and from the description of these articles earlier in this chapter, APA-style articles follow a particular organizational style. APA style refers to the writing style proposed by the APA (2010) for research articles in psychology and related fields. There are other formatting styles for research articles, but APA style is the most commonly used style in psychology, and most psychological journals require submissions of articles for publication to be written in APA style. Appendix A illustrates an APA-style article that has been typed in by a researcher to give you an example of the format you should use in typing up your own APA-style research report. This section discusses each section of the APA-style article and the information that should be included in each section. Some important APA-style rules are also covered to help you format your own research articles. All information described in the following section is also covered in the *Publication Manual of the American Psychological Association* (APA, 2010).

Before You Write

Citations. There are a couple of issues to consider before you begin writing a research report—how to cite sources and how to avoid plagiarism. In your research reports, it is important to cite the sources where you obtain information. You should cite sources for definitions of concepts, review of previous studies, sources for stimuli or questionnaires, and so on. By citing these sources, you are giving credit to the authors for the information you got from their publications. This could be the definition of a concept, a description of their study, use of their methodology, and so forth. This is different from quoting their words—in psychological writing, very few quotes tend to be used, and these are reserved for times when the authors' specific wording is important to preserve. In most cases, you will just be summarizing the authors' ideas in your own words in your paper: This is the expected writing style in reports of psychological research. Quoting without quotation marks and a citation is plagiarism (see the next section) and will likely have serious negative consequences.

FIGURE 2.8 ■ Steps in the Research Process: Reporting Results

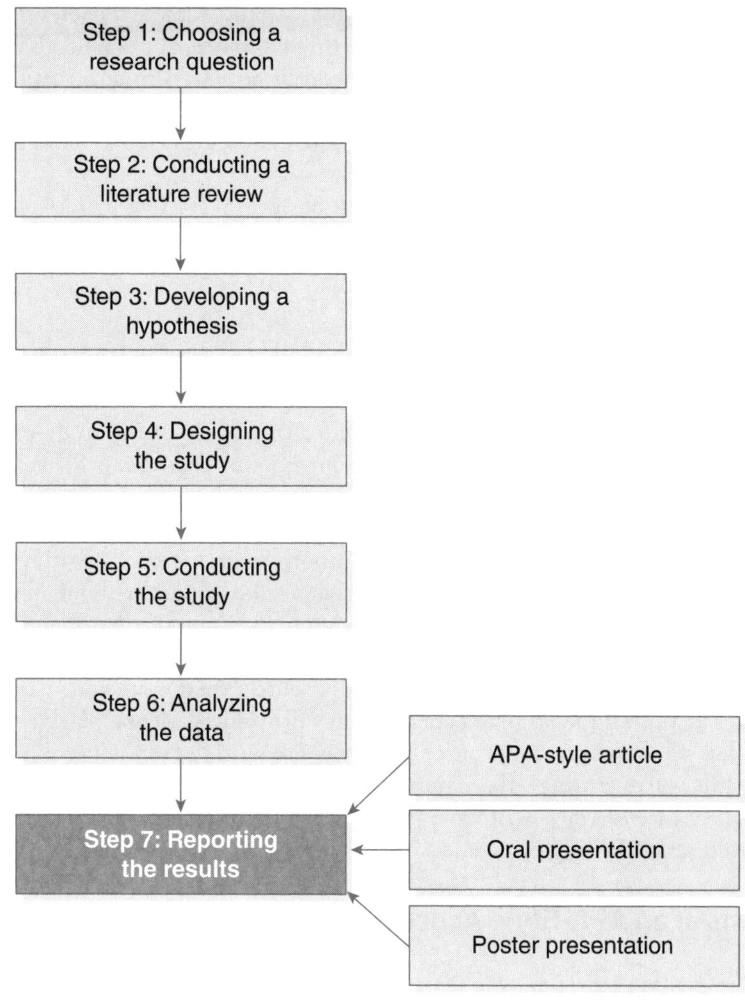

APA-style citation format includes the last names of the authors in the order they appear in the publication and then the year of publication. For articles with five or fewer authors, list all authors the first time you cite the article. If you cite a source with three or more authors a second time or more than five authors at any time, include just the last name of the first author and et al. to indicate there are other authors. For single- or double-author articles, continue to cite the authors' last names.

Sources can be cited by naming the authors in the text and including the publication year in parentheses. An example of a citation of this type is this: Hamilton and Mayes (2006) stated that. . . . Alternatively, the entire citation can be provided in parentheses to indicate the source of a statement. An example of a citation of this type is this: Prospective memory (PM) is defined as remembering to perform a task at a future time (Einstein & McDaniel, 2005). Note that this statement is not a quote from the Einstein and McDaniel article. It is a summarization of the definition in my words. Although quotes should be used sparingly, if you do include a direct quote from a source, you should also include the page number on which you found the quote in the article. Also note that the word *and* is used for citations where the authors are directly referred to in the text, whereas an ampersand (&) is used for citations enclosed in parentheses. Remember to include a full reference for each citation in the reference section.

An important consideration for creating citations is to preserve the order of authors listed for the source. The order of authors on a paper typically denotes the amount of work each author contributed to the paper, so it should not be rearranged when you create a citation or reference of the source.

plagiarism: Claiming another's work or ideas as one's own

Plagiarism. Proper citation of sources is an important part of avoiding **plagiarism**—taking credit for someone else's work or ideas. Any description of another study or of someone's theory must include the citation of the source of the study or theory to give proper credit to the author(s) of the source. Note that this is different from quoting. You may not use another author's words unless you use quotation marks, and direct quotes should be rare in your writing (and your instructor may forbid them in your papers). Presenting another author's written work verbatim or in a manner similar to the written form produced by the author without quotations also constitutes plagiarism. You should not simply take one of their sentences and rearrange the words—this is still plagiarism. The advice I give my students is to first take notes in your own words when you read a source, then write your paper from your notes instead of the original paper to help you avoid accidental plagiarism. The further you get away from this source while you are writing (i.e., not looking at the source while you're writing), the easier it will be to use your own words. You should be extremely careful when writing from sources to ensure that quotation marks or your own original writing is included.

Sections of an APA-Style Article

Title Page

The first page of your article is the title page. It includes the title of the article, the authors' names, and the authors' affiliations centered on the page (see Appendix A). Your title should be concise and informative. Someone should be able to determine the general topic of your study from the title you choose. The title page also contains a running head that is a shortened version of the title (50 or fewer characters including spaces). The purpose of the running head is to include a shortened version of your title that runs along the top of every other page of a published article to identify the article within the journal. Take a look at an article published in APA style, and you will see the running head in the top margin of every other page. The running head is typed in all capital letters and appears in the header on each page, left margin justified. Finally, the page number appears in the header, right margin justified, of every page in the article (including the title page, which is page 1). Figure 2.9 provides an example title page with each part explained in a bubble.

FIGURE 2.9 ■ Sample APA-Style Title Page

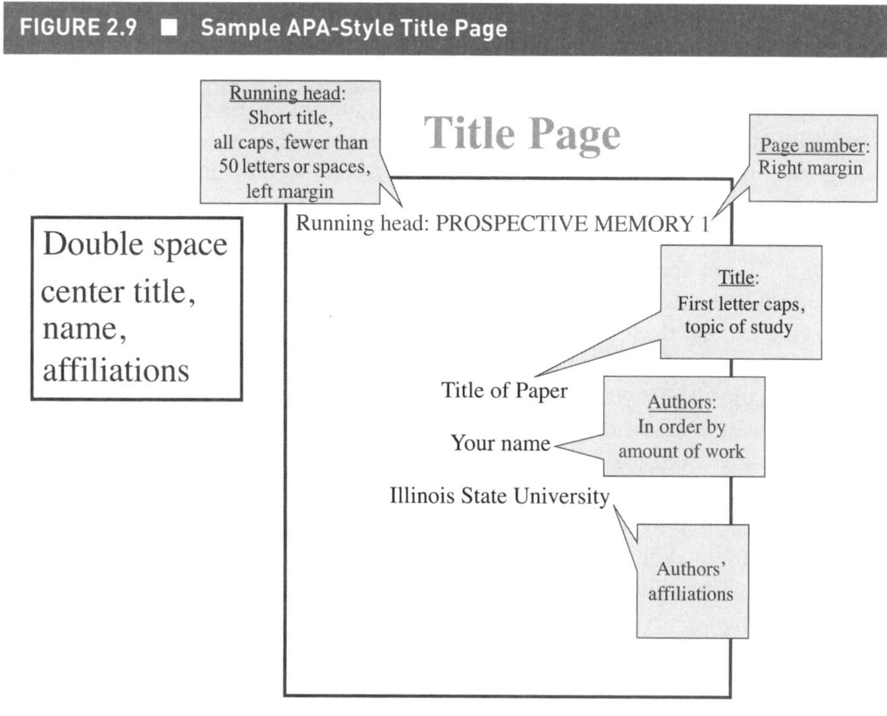

Abstract

The second page of your article contains your abstract. The abstract is a short paragraph (first line not indented) that describes the important aspects of your article. In other words, your abstract contains a sentence or two for each of the four major sections of your article: introduction, method, results, and discussion. For example, a sentence or two that explains the purpose of your article begins your abstract. A sentence or two that describes the method follows. Be sure to describe the primary variables in your study. The primary result(s) are described in a sentence or two, and your abstract ends with the primary conclusion of the study. However, the length of your abstract is limited (in most cases, to 150 to 250 words), so you must be selective in what you discuss. Do not include too many details of the method, and do not include all results. If you use numbers in your abstract, they are typed in numerical form. Finally, the heading Abstract is centered in bold at the top of the page.

Introduction

Your introduction begins on the third page of your article. Your full title (not the heading Introduction) is centered at the top of the page. Your introduction should cover several things. It should inform your reader about the general topic of your study (e.g., the bystander effect, visual short-term memory, therapeutic treatments for depression). Be careful not to begin your introduction too generally. Your introduction should not begin with statements about all of psychology or all human behavior. Begin by explaining what behavior your study addresses and which aspects of that behavior are most relevant to your study. Be sure to indicate what your research question is. You should also review the parts of relevant background studies that tell your reader what is already known about your research question and how it has been studied previously. Be careful not to simply summarize each background article. Instead, you should discuss only the aspects of these studies that are particularly relevant for the development of your study.

Your introduction should become more specific as it progresses; some details about your study's design should be discussed (e.g., briefly describing the variables that were studied) to inform the reader how your study addresses your stated research question. State your hypotheses toward the end of your introduction. Be sure to explain (briefly) why you are making those hypotheses, tying them to the background literature you discussed earlier in your introduction. One of the main purposes of your introduction is to make the argument that your study contributes important knowledge to the topic area you have chosen to study and that you are justified in making the hypotheses you are making. In other words, if you have written a good introduction, your readers should have a good idea of what your hypotheses are before you state them and be convinced that they are the best hypotheses to make for your study. By the time readers reach the end of your introduction, they should also be convinced that the study you are describing is important and worthy of reading. Be sure to keep your argument in mind as you write your introduction.

Method

The method section begins on the next line after your introduction ends. To begin the method, type the heading Method in bold, centered on the page. Do not begin a new page for the method section. A general rule of thumb to use in deciding what information to include in your method section is enough information that researchers could replicate your study if they wanted to. For example, your method section should contain a description of your stimuli or survey but should not include the type of writing instrument used by your participants (unless it is relevant to the design of your study). The method section has four subsections: (1) participants, (2) design, (3) materials or apparatus, and (4) procedure. Each subsection should begin with the subsection heading left justified and in bold. You may not need to include each subsection in every method section you write. If you take a look at some different journal articles published in APA style, you will see that some authors chose to combine some of these subsections, and in very short articles (e.g., Short Reports of the journal *Psychological Science*), the subsections are all combined into one method section that contains the relevant details of all the subsections. In addition, in many articles, you may see that the design section has been omitted or combined with the materials section.

Participants

In the participants subsection, describe the relevant details of the participants or subjects in your study (humans are typically referred to as "participants" and nonhuman animals as "subjects"). For example, how many participants took part in the study? How were the participants recruited? How were they compensated? Who were the participants? Were they college students or individuals living in retirement communities? Or did the researcher use Sprague Dawley rats as subjects? Also include demographic information about the participants that is relevant to your study, such as gender breakdown, socioeconomic status, education level, and age. How many participants were assigned to study conditions is also typically indicated in this section.

Design

Although not explicitly listed in the *Publication Manual of the American Psychological Association* (APA, 2010), the design subsection is often included by authors for studies with more complex designs (e.g., experiments) to improve the clarity of the method. The design subsection describes the variables in your study and how they were measured and manipulated. Be sure to indicate any independent and dependent variables included in your study. Describe levels of any independent variables. In other words, provide operational definitions of the variables in the method section. In many cases, the materials used in the study (e.g., stimuli, questionnaires) are too closely tied to the design to separate them, and the author combines these two sections.

Materials or Apparatus

The materials or apparatus subsection contains information about what was used to run the study. Any stimuli or questionnaires presented in the study are described in this subsection, including the origin of these materials and number of items. Assignment of stimuli to conditions is also described in this section. If complex equipment is used in a study, this section may be labeled *Apparatus*, or the author may include a separate apparatus section.

Procedure

The procedure subsection describes what the participants or subjects experience in the study in chronological order. Information about the instructions they were given in the study and the tasks they performed is included. Timing of any stimulus presentations is described in the procedure subsection. In addition, how the participants or subjects were assigned to conditions is included for studies that are experiments, and debriefing is described for studies that involve deception. A statement indicating that participants or subjects were treated according to ethical standards is often included in this section or in the participants section.

Results

The results section begins on the next line after the end of the method section. Do not begin a new page for the results section. This section begins with the heading Results centered on the page in bold. The results section states the dependent variables that were analyzed and the tests used to analyze them. The alpha level for the statistical tests is given, and the tests that were run are described. You should make statements about the results, indicating what differences or relationships were found, with support for the statements provided by the statistical values. For example, your results section may contain a statement such as "The difference between the two age groups was significant: $t(65) = 4.56$, $p = .002$; older participants scored higher ($M = 85.00$, $SD = 7.89$) than younger participants ($M = 67.00$, $SD = 7.32$)." Notice that the statistics are not the focus of the sentence. The difference is the focus—with support provided by the t and p values and the mean values for each condition. Also note that statistical values are generally rounded to two decimal places. Be sure to format statistics according to APA style—italics for statistics, degrees of freedom provided, and spaces surrounding equal signs. Consult the *Publication Manual of the American Psychological Association* (APA, 2010) for APA style for specific statistics.

The results section also includes any tables or figures that help illustrate the important results of the study. Choose one or the other for any set of results. Do not provide both a table and a figure for the same results. Figures may take the form of a graph (e.g., line graph of means, bar graph of means, scatterplot). Be sure to refer to the table or figure in the text of the results section. However, tables and figures are positioned near the end of the typed article. They are not embedded in the text of the results section. All figures have a figure caption that is typed above the figure. See Appendix A for examples of formatted tables and figures in APA style.

Discussion

The last section of text in your article is the discussion section. Begin the section with the heading Discussion on the next line after your results section ends. The discussion section continues where your introduction left off, beginning with a review of the hypotheses, some statements about whether these hypotheses were supported, and which results provide that support. The discussion section also contains a comparison of your results with those from past studies—especially the studies you described in the introduction section. For example, are your results consistent with those from similar studies? If not, why not? Limitations of the study are also discussed in this section of the article. However, be careful not to argue that the study was conducted poorly. You are still making an argument (as you did in the introduction) that the study contributes to scientific knowledge. As part of that argument, you can point out, based on the results you found, issues your study does not address or limitations of the research method chosen for the study, and you may also wish to suggest directions for future studies in your area of research. Your discussion section ends with a summary paragraph, describing what you learned overall from the study.

References

The references section provides a complete listing of all the sources cited in the article. The references are listed in alphabetical order by the last name of the first author. All subsequent authors are listed in the reference in the order in which they appear in the publication. You should also provide the publication year, title of the source, where the source was published, and additional information about the publication source. For example, a reference for a journal article should appear as follows:

Geraerts, E., Bernstein, D. M., Merekelbach, H., Linders, C., Raymaekers, L., & Loftus, E. F. (2008). Lasting false beliefs and their behavioral consequences. *Psychological Science, 19*, 749–753. doi:10.1111/j.1467-9280.2008.02151.x

See the references section of Appendix A for some additional examples of reference formatting. Figure 2.10 also provides a breakdown of how to format a reference. Begin a new page for the references section. Reference organization packages, such as RefWorks and EndNote, can help you format source references into APA style.

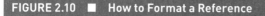

FIGURE 2.10 ■ How to Format a Reference

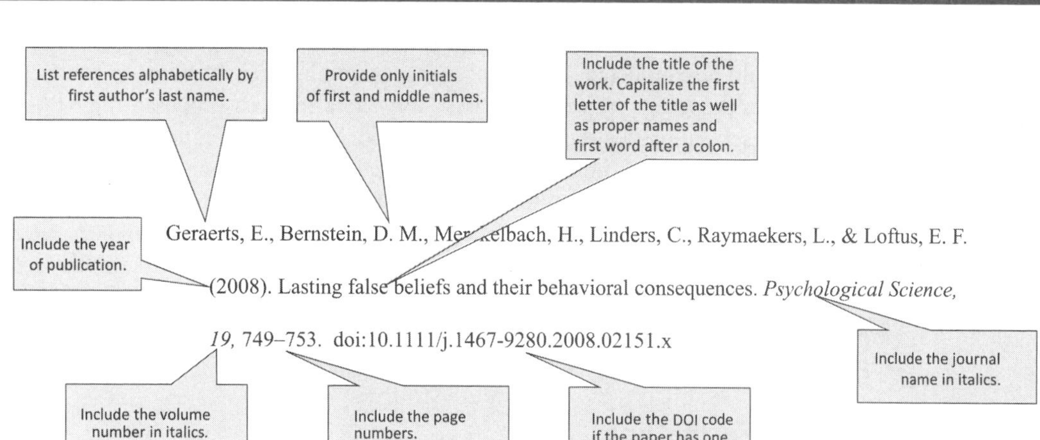

STOP AND THINK

2.10. For each of the following pieces of information that follow, identify the appropriate section(s) of an APA-style paper it should be placed in:

a. Reference to a figure
b. Description of the stimuli shown to subjects
c. A statement of the hypothesis
d. Suggestions for future studies
e. Mean scores

2.11. Explain why the method of a study is described in detail in an APA-style paper.

Multiple-Study Articles

For some APA-style articles, you may be describing multiple related studies in one article. For multiple-study articles, you should include one introduction section that provides background for all your studies, a method for each study, a results section for each study, and a general discussion section that describes conclusions for all the studies combined. The method and results sections of each study are preceded by headings that indicate the study number, such as Study 1 or Experiment 1, centered on the page. A new hierarchy of headings follows for the method, results, and subsections of the method. In multiple-study articles, method and results headings are left justified in bold, and the subsections of the method are indented with the paragraph and end with a period. See the *Publication Manual of the American Psychological Association* (APA, 2010) for additional information about formatting multiple-study articles.

Research Proposals

In some situations, researchers must write a proposal for a research project before they conduct the study. Proposals are typically written to convince someone else that a research project should be conducted. The purpose may be to obtain grant funds to conduct the project or to propose a project for a class. To write a research proposal, the APA-style structure described previously is generally followed, but a few modifications are made to account for the fact that the study has not yet been completed. For example, the results section typically contains a plan for the analysis of the data and predicted results for the study. Likewise, the discussion section contains a discussion of what may be learned in the cases where the hypotheses are supported and not supported. In addition, the details of the study (method details, etc.) are described in the future tense (e.g., "The participants will be recruited from a population of university students") because the study will take place in the future.

General Formatting

When you type your APA-style article, you should format it according to the following APA-style guidelines. The entire article should be double-spaced. Use 1-in. margins all around the pages. Type the running head in the top left header and the page number in the top right header of each page. Use past tense when you describe any study (including yours) that has already been completed. For example, state, "The participants volunteered . . ." rather than "The participants will volunteer . . ." or "The participants are volunteering. . . ." The only exception to this rule is if you are writing a proposal for a research study that has not yet been conducted. In this case, use future tense to describe the study. Always use past tense to describe details of published studies. Minimize use of the passive voice in your writing. Instead, use the active voice. For example, state, "Williams and Jones (2006) manipulated the stimulus presentation" instead of "The stimulus presentation was manipulated by Williams and Jones (2006)."

When you present numbers in your article, use words for numbers one through nine, and numerals for values 10 and above, unless the number is a measurement, a statistical value, or a value representing the sample, for which you should always use numbers. In addition, all numbers in the abstract should be in numerical form. Any number that begins a sentence should be presented as a word. Numbers that are used in lists (Study 1, Study 2, Group 1, Group 2, etc.) should be given in numerical form. Check the *Publication Manual of the American Psychological Association* (APA, 2010) for more rules regarding use of numbers. If you use abbreviations in your article, you must define the abbreviation the first time you use it. For example, earlier in this chapter, I defined the APA and then used this abbreviation throughout the chapter. APA style provides for a few exceptions for some abbreviations that do not need to be defined, such as *M* for mean, min for minute, and so on, when they are presented with a value.

ORAL PRESENTATIONS

The most common venue for oral presentations of psychological research is a psychological conference. While you may not experience psychology conferences as an undergraduate student, there are many conferences held each year to showcase research conducted by undergraduate students. Your college or university may hold one of these conferences. There are also regional conferences, such as the Mid-America Undergraduate Psychology Research Conference (MAUPRC), and undergraduate psychology conferences in many U.S. states (e.g., Illinois–Iowa Undergraduate Psychology Empirical Research Conference [ILLOWA]) that may be of interest to you. Compared with poster presentations, oral presentations of research studies are less likely to be given by undergraduate students at conferences although the class in which you were assigned this text may have such an assignment.

Preparing an oral presentation of a research study is not very different from writing an APA-style article. The primary differences are that you present the information orally to an audience, and there is usually a time limit, so you must work out ahead of time how much information you can reasonably include in the presentation. The type of information you present, however, is very similar but in an abbreviated form. You begin an oral presentation by introducing the main concepts (e.g., the bystander effect, visual short-term memory, therapeutic treatments for depression) and then present your research question and review what is already known about the research question. You present hypotheses for your study. You then explain the method of the study and review the results, typically using tables or figures to illustrate the main results. Finally, you state conclusions of the study, including whether the hypotheses were supported (or not) by the results and what you learned from the study. Throughout the presentation, you cite sources for your information, just as you would in an APA-style article. However, slides should not contain a lot of text. It is better to use a bulleted outline form to help your audience follow what you are saying rather than do a lot of reading during your presentation (see Figure 2.11 for some example slides from an oral presentation of research).

Organization is very important for an oral presentation, just as it is for a paper presentation of research. You must present a coherent argument for your study and your hypotheses. In fact, it can be more difficult to organize an oral presentation because you must choose carefully what information to present to fit into the time limit you are given. For example, many conference-style oral presentations are limited to 10 or 15 min. Thus, presenters must be very clear in what they present to make themselves understood by their audience in such a short time. A good oral presentation is accompanied by visual aids, typically presented as PowerPoint slides. Because audience members must absorb the information quickly, visual displays of information are more important in oral and poster presentations than in written papers.

POSTER PRESENTATIONS

As with oral presentations, you are most likely to encounter a poster presentation of psychology research at a psychology conference. You may have been assigned a poster presentation in the course you are taking that assigned this text. Poster presentations are essentially mini-APA-style articles that are condensed to allow a visual presentation rather than a text presentation. They contain the same information as an oral presentation but may be even further condensed according to the space allowed for the poster. See Figure 2.12 for an example of a poster presentation of research. Notice that each of the

FIGURE 2.11 ■ Example Slides From an Oral Presentation of Research

TYPES OF PROSPECTIVE MEMORY

- Prospective Memory (PM): remembering to perform a future task
  - Respond to an email from a colleague during the day
  - Take medication after dinner or at 6 p.m.
- Event-based PM: Perform task after an event occurs (eat dinner)
- Time-based PM: Perform task at a set time (6 p.m.) or after a period of time (in 20 min)

EVENT-BASED COGNITIVE COST

- No cost shown for focal PM task, but significant cost found for non-focal PM task

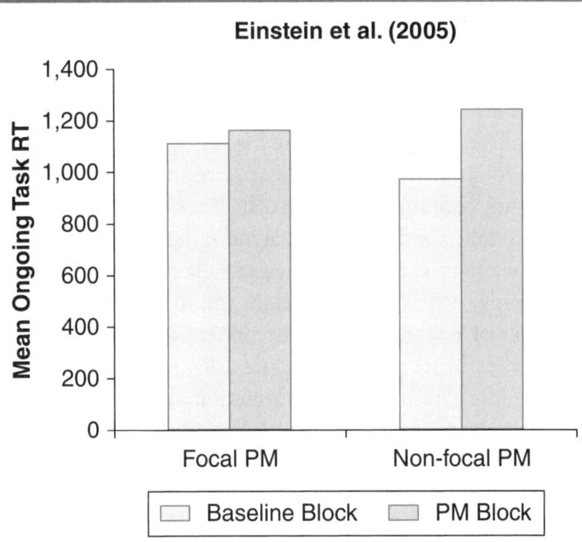

main APA-style sections is included as well as visual presentations of stimuli and results. Bullet points are used in many places instead of full sentences to make the poster more easily read and to save space.

The organization of a poster presentation should be as visual as possible. Include examples of sample stimuli and organize sections so that they flow. Include a title and authors at the top of the poster. The body of the poster is often organized into segments to make information easier to find and comprehend. Place the introductory information at the left of the poster, and then direct the flow of information down each segment with new segments placed to the right. See the sample poster in Figure 2.12 for the organization style used in a poster.

FIGURE 2.12 ■ Poster Presentation of Research

Pre-crastination Effects in a Prospective Memory Task

Rachel L. VonderHaar[1], Dawn M. McBride[1], and David A. Rosenbaum[2]

Illinois State University[1]

University of California, Riverside[2]

Introduction

Prospective memory (PM) is remembering to perform a future task (Einstein & McDaniel, 2005). In the "real world" there are often delays between receiving the PM cue and completing the PM response, which causes a decrease in PM accuracy (Einstein et al., 2000). In lab settings, some participants respond before the delay is over to avoid forgetting the task (McDaniel et al., 2003), thus, they *pre-crastinate*. Pre-crastination is the phenomenon of completing tasks earlier rather than later to "get it out of the way" (Rosenbaum et al., 2014). Rosenbaum et al. found that participants pre-crastinated in a motor task. In the current study, we applied this phenomenon to a PM task in which participants were given a choice of when to complete the PM task. We also manipulated the difficulty of the PM task to determine its effect on pre-crastination. Thus, the purpose of the current study was to investigate pre-crastination using PM tasks of easy, medium, and hard difficulties, within an ongoing motor task. The primary question was whether participants complete a more difficult cognitive PM task later than an easy PM task in ongoing motor task trials.

Hypotheses

H1: Pre-crastination tendencies will decrease with an increase in difficulty of PM task

H2: There will be more cognitive cost for the difficult PM task than the easy task

Method

Participants

- Experiment 1: 92 Illinois State University students
- Experiment 2: 122 Illinois State University students

Method

Experiments 1 & 2 Procedure

Ongoing task (continuous computerized motor task): Move the 10 boxes one at a time in numerical order to the corresponding ending table. Blue boxes still need to be moved. Purple boxes have already been moved.

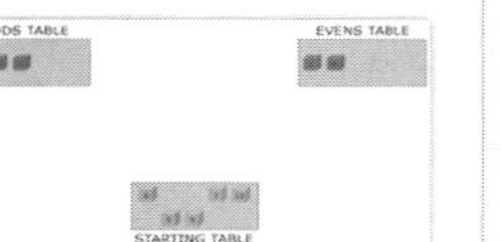

PM task (cognitive task):
Generate *n* items aloud at one time during the motor task. Subjects choose when to say items,

- n = 3, 7, and 15 in Experiment 1 for a total of 3 blocks (musical instruments, countries, insects)
- n = 5, 10, and 15 in Experiment 2 (2 blocks of each for body parts, 4-footed animals, sports, kitchen items, clothing items, fruits)

Experiments 1 & 2 Design

- Within-subjects design for category difficulty factor
- Counterbalanced category order and assignment between-participants

Results

Experiment 1:

- Manipulation check: Percentage of items correctly generated significantly affected by number of items to be generated, $p < .001$.
- Reaction times: not significantly affected by number of items to be generated, $p = .62$
- Pre-crastination: Generation time chosen significantly affected by number of items to be generated, $p < 001$.

Results

Experiment 1:

Box Number: 10, 8, 6, 4, 2, 0
3 items, 7 items, 15 items
Number of Items Needed

- Consistency and reaction times: Difference in reaction times (RTs) Before completion of PM task and After completion of PM task.
  Consistent = same box # (completion time) for each block.
  Not consistent = different box # (completion time) for each block.
  Overall, RTs were longer in the ongoing task before completing the PM task and shorter after completing the PM task.

Consistency: Reaction Times
Average RT (ms): 5000, 4000, 3000, 2000, 1000, 0
3, 7, 15 (All Consistent); 3, 7, 15 (Not Consistent)
■ Before ■ After

Experiment 2:

- Manipulation check: Percentage of items correctly generated significantly affected by number of items to be generated, $p < .001$.
- Reaction times: not significantly affected by number of items to be generated, $p = .17$.
- Pre-crastination: Box number when generation occurred significantly affected by number of items to be generated, $p = .01$

Box Number: 8, 6, 4, 2, 0
5 items, 10 items, 15 items
Number of Items Needed

Results

Consistency: Reaction Times
Average RT (ms): 3000, 2000, 1000, 0
5, 10, 15 (All Consistent); 5, 10, 15 (Not Consistent)
■ Before ■ After

- Consistency and reaction times: Experiment 2 data found the same general trend as Experiment 1 data

Conclusions

- Rosenbaum et al. (2014) found that participants pre-crastinated less when the earlier choice was more difficult.
- Our study supports this finding because our participants also pre-crastinated less when the task was more difficult.
- Unexpectedly, participants' reaction times were not affected by task difficulty.
- However, participants reaction times were longer before completion of the PM task, especially if they were not consistent in when they generated items, suggesting that the cognitive load of the PM task affected the cost to the motor task.

References

- Einstein, G. O., & McDaniel, M. A. (2005). Prospective memory: Multiple retrieval processes. *Current Directions in Psychological Science, 14*, 286-290.
- Einstein, G. O., McDaniel, M. A., Manzi, M., Cochran, B., & Baker, M. (2000). Prospective memory and aging: Forgetting intentions over short delays. *Psychology and Aging, 15*, 671 - 683.
- McDaniel, M. A., Einstein, G. O., Stout, A. A., & Morgan, Z. (2003). Aging and maintaining intentions over delays: Do it or lose it. *Psychology and Aging, 18*, 823-835.
- Rosenbaum, D. A., Gong, L., & Potts, C. A. (2014). Pre-crastination: Hastening of subglobal completion at the expense of extra physical effort. *Psychological Science, 25*, 1487-1496.
- Zhang, L., Wininger, M., & Rosenbaum, D. A. (2014). Word generation affects continuous hand movements. *Journal of Motor Behavior, 46*, 115-123.

FIGURE 2.13 ■ Presenting at a Conference for the First Time—Rachel VonderHaar

Rachel VonderHaar

The first poster I brought to a conference was on the survival processing effect, studied intensely by Dr. James Nairne. I was nervous because I was told that he would be at the conference, and I wanted to impress him with my work. To prepare, I created an "elevator speech" of my work to present to individuals who were less familiar with the topic, making sure to hit the most important parts of the background, the methods, results, and discussion. Dr. Nairne did stop by my poster, and I did not need to say my speech to him since my work was trying to replicate his results. Thus, he had a couple of questions and we ended up having a great discussion about my results and reasons I may have found the results I did. It was awesome getting to discuss my work with Dr. Nairne and with other cognitive psychologists who cared about my topic of interest. I was afraid to mistakenly explain my data and I was afraid to talk too much, or not enough, about my work. I was also afraid that I would be asked a question that I did not know the answer to. I learned that it's okay to say, "I'm not sure" to a question I did not know how to answer. I also learned that the people who stop by your poster are doing so to have a simple, and usually exciting, conversation about your work, not to make you feel bad if you don't have the correct answer to a question.

During a poster presentation, the authors typically stand by their poster, prepared to offer a short summary to interested viewers and answer questions viewers may have as they read the poster. If you are preparing to give a poster presentation, it is a good idea to think through what you will say ahead of time, so you give clear and concise descriptions of the research study described in the poster. See Figure 2.13 for a description of what it was like to present at a conference for the first time from one of my students.

STOP AND THINK

2.12. In what ways do paper presentations of a study differ from poster and oral presentations of a study? In what ways are they similar?

THINKING ABOUT RESEARCH

A summary of a research study in psychology is given here. As you read the summary, think about the following questions:

1. What type of hypothesis (theory-driven or data-driven) did the authors make?
2. Do you think this is a causal or a descriptive hypothesis? How do you know?
3. Can you state the authors' research question? From the description of the study, how do you think they developed this research question?

4. If you were to conduct a literature review for their research question on PsycINFO, how would you proceed? Describe the steps you would take.
5. Write an abstract for the study in your own words that adheres to APA guidelines.
6. If you were to read an APA-style article describing this study (which you can do by finding the reference that follows), in which section would you find information about the paragraphs the participants read during the study? In which section would the authors report what statistical test they conducted? In which section would they indicate if their hypothesis was supported?

Research Study. Vohs, K. D., & Schooler, J. W. (2008). The value of believing in free will: Encouraging a belief in determinism increases cheating. *Psychological Science, 19*, 49–54.

Purpose of the Study. Vohs and Schooler (2008) were interested in the effects of a belief in determinism (i.e., believing that events in a person's life are not under their control) on moral behaviors. Their interest stemmed from recent findings from neuroscientists that our behaviors may be caused by factors out of our control (e.g., our genes, the functioning of our brain, our environments). They reported that a previous study (Mueller & Dweck, 1998) had found that children exert less effort in a task if they are told that their failure, in a difficult task they had previously completed, was due to their intelligence level rather than their level of effort. From this finding, Vohs and Schooler reasoned that a belief in determinism may negatively affect behavior. Thus, in their study, they predicted that exposure to a deterministic argument would result in more cheating behaviors than if this belief was not promoted.

Method of the Study. Thirty college students participated in the study. Participants were randomly assigned to read one of two paragraphs taken from the same book. One of the paragraphs suggested that scientists believe that free will is an illusion. The other paragraph discussed consciousness and did not mention the topic of free

FIGURE 2.14 ■ Mean Number of Space Bar Presses for Each Group

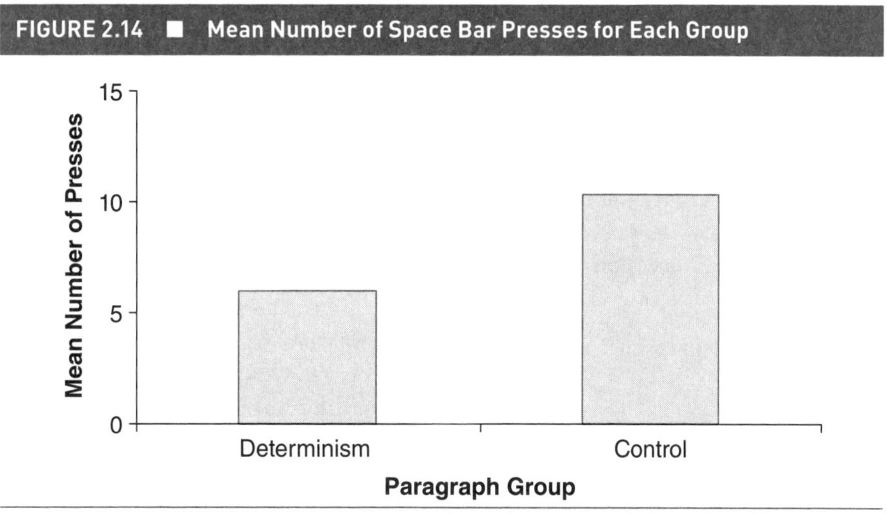

Source: Results from Vohs and Schooler's (2008) study.

(Continued)

(Continued)

will. All participants were then asked to complete a set of math problems, presented one at a time on a computer screen. Participants were asked to complete each problem. They were also told that the computer program had an error such that the answers to some of the problems may appear with the problem and that they should try to solve the problems on their own (they could make the answer disappear by pressing the space bar when the problem appeared). The researchers measured the number of times the participants pressed the space bar as a measure of cheating behavior (more presses means less cheating).

Results of the Study. The results indicated that the group that read the determinism paragraph pressed the space bar less often (about 5 times during the study) than the control group (about 10 times during the study) that read the consciousness paragraph. Figure 2.14 displays the mean space bar presses for each group.

Conclusions of the Study. From their results, Vohs and Schooler (2008) concluded that a belief in determinism (i.e., free will is an illusion) causes more immoral behavior (e.g., cheating) to be exhibited by individuals.

Chapter Summary

Reconsider the questions from the beginning of the chapter:

- **How do researchers develop a research question?**
  Research questions come from many sources, including researchers' curiosity. However, research questions should be relevant to current knowledge in the field of study and answerable using scientific methods. A literature review helps researchers know if their research question fulfills these criteria.
- **How do researchers conduct a literature review?**
  A literature review is a thorough review of research done in an area of study. Searchable databases, such as PsycINFO and PsycARTICLES, are useful for conducting a literature review. Conducting a Google web search or using Wikipedia is *not* a good way to conduct a literature review.
- **What are the different types of research articles, and how are they organized?**
  Research articles are empirical, review, or theoretical. Empirical articles describe a study conducted by the authors of the article. Review articles summarize results and methods from a particular area of study. Theoretical articles discuss new or revised theories of behavior in an area of study.
- **How do we use a literature review to make hypotheses?**
  Researchers can use theories described in journal articles to develop hypotheses, or researchers can use past studies' results to develop a hypothesis about the outcome of their study.
- **What are the different ways that psychologists present research?**
  Psychologists present research as written reports, oral presentations, and poster presentations.

- **How do we write an APA-style article? What information goes in each section of the article? How do we format the article?** An APA-style article is organized into sections that present the background and purpose of the study (Introduction), method of the study, results of the study, and conclusions of the study (Discussion). Additional format information is described in this chapter and in the *Publication Manual of the American Psychological Association* (APA, 2010).

Applying Your Knowledge

Shark attacks are often reported in the news, making it seem as though the chance of an attack is higher than it actually is.

- Suppose you wanted to determine how likely a shark attack is. What are some good research questions to study this?
- What kinds of sources would be appropriate to answer your research questions? Explain how you would go about finding these sources.

Test Yourself

1. For the information in the list that follows, indicate in which section(s) of a journal article it should be found:
   a. Average scores for different groups in a study
   b. Number of participants in the study
   c. Researchers' hypotheses
   d. Comparison of results of present study with results of previous studies
   e. Summary of the instructions given to the participants
2. Describe how theory-driven and data-driven hypotheses are made.
3. Explain why the following research question is not an appropriate research question for psychological research: Does every human being have a soul?
4. What is a peer-reviewed journal article, and how does it differ from an article you might find in a popular magazine?
5. What is a literature review, and why is it an important part of the research process?
6. For each research question that follows, identify the behavior variable and the causal variable:
   a. Do men and women differ in conscientiousness?
   b. Does waking up at the same time (i.e., setting an alarm) every day improve sleep quality?

(Continued)

(Continued)

c. Does ostracism increase violent behavior?
d. Is eyewitness memory in children worse than in adults?
e. Does using crutches change the way you perceive the size of an opening?

7. Explain the differences between a database such as PsycINFO and a search engine such as Google.
8. A short summary of a journal article that appears at the beginning of the article and in databases such as PsycINFO is called a(n) ____________________.
9. A hypothesis that proposes a link between exercise and memory would be classified as a ____________________ hypothesis.
10. What is the difference between an empirical journal article and a book chapter or review article?
11. In which section of an APA-style article would you include the following information about your study?
    a. Statements of hypotheses
    b. Graphs of the means for each condition
    c. A description of the questionnaire the participants completed
    d. The number of participants or subjects in the study
    e. A citation for a published source
    f. Instructions that were given to the participants
12. Which of the following is true about formatting an APA-style article? (Choose all that apply.)
    a. Two-inch margins should be used.
    b. The entire article should be double-spaced.
    c. Tables and figures should be embedded into the results section.
    d. You need to provide citations only when you quote from a source.
    e. You should begin a new page for the references section.
13. For the citation examples that follow, indicate which ones display correct APA style:
    a. Regia-Corte and Wagman (2008) reported that participants perceived a slope to be more difficult to stand on when wearing a weighted backpack.
    b. In a review of how scientific thinking skills develop, Corinne Zimmerman reported many studies that support this theory.
    c. The list-strength effect is exhibited when stronger items (studied for a longer time, studied to a deeper level, etc.) in a list produce better memory than weaker items (Verde, 2009).
    d. The method used in the current study is based on the method described by Garrison (Feb, 2009).
14. Place the following APA-style sections into the correct order in which they should appear in a manuscript: results, introduction, procedure, discussion, abstract, references, title page, participants.
15. Which of the following illustrates correct APA style for references of journal articles?
    a. Reese-Weber, Marla (2008). A new experimental method assessing attitudes toward adolescent dating and sibling violence using observations of violent interactions. *Journal of Adolescence, 31*, 857–876.
    b. Reese-Weber, M. (2008). A new experimental method assessing attitudes

toward adolescent dating and sibling violence using observations of violent interactions. *Journal of Adolescence, 31*, 857–876.

c. Marla Reese-Weber (2008). A New Experimental Method Assessing Attitudes Toward Adolescent Dating and Sibling Violence Using Observations of Violent Interactions. *Journal of Adolescence, 31*, 857–876.

d. Reese-Weber, M. (March, 2008). A new experimental method assessing attitudes toward adolescent dating and sibling violence using observations of violent interactions. *Journal of Adolescence, Vol. 31*, pp. 857–876.

16. Explain how an oral presentation differs from a poster presentation.

17. In APA style, the participants section is a subsection of the ____________________ section.

18. Figures and tables will most likely be referred to in the ____________________ section of an APA-style paper.

SAGE edge™

Visit **edge.sagepub.com/mcbridermstats** to find the answers to the Test Yourself questions above, as well as quizzes, flashcards, and other resources to help you accomplish your coursework goals.

ETHICAL GUIDELINES FOR PSYCHOLOGICAL RESEARCH

CONSIDER THE FOLLOWING QUESTIONS AS YOU READ CHAPTER 3

- Why do we need ethical guidelines for research?
- How were ethical guidelines for psychological research developed?
- Were the Milgram (1963) and Zimbardo (1974) studies ethical? Why or why not?
- What are the current ethical guidelines for human participants?
- What is an institutional review board (IRB), and what purpose does it serve?
- How do ethics influence the way we report research?

LEARNING OBJECTIVES FOR CHAPTER 3

- Understand the purpose of ethics in psychological research.
- Understand how ethical guidelines were developed.
- Evaluate research studies for their adherence to ethical guidelines.

In 1932, in Tuskegee, Alabama, the U.S. Public Health Service began a research study to investigate the course of syphilis in the human male. The researchers recruited 399 African American men who had previously contracted syphilis (see Photo 3.1). The men were told that they had "bad blood" and that they could receive free health care by coming to the clinic where they were studied. None of the men were informed that they had syphilis by the researchers, and none of the men were treated for the disease (Brandt, 2000).

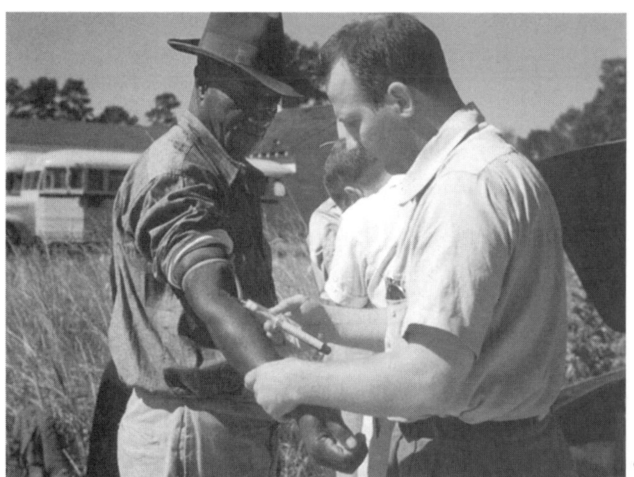

Photo 3.1
The U.S. Public Health Service studied the course of syphilis in African American men without their knowledge or consent in Tuskegee, Alabama.

At the time the study started, the treatment for syphilis was dangerous and was not always effective. Thus, the researchers of the Tuskegee syphilis study were interested in better understanding the damage that the disease did to the men as it progressed to help determine if treating the disease was better than not treating it. By 1947, however, penicillin had become available as a safe and effective treatment for syphilis. Yet the researchers of the Tuskegee syphilis study did not end their study until 1972 and did not make penicillin available to the participants to treat the disease.

Through this study, the researchers learned a good deal about the progression of the syphilis disease. They learned about the different stages of the disease and about the many symptoms that accompany the disease. These symptoms include rashes, warts on the genitalia, and pus-filled skin pox. Later stages involve damage to the internal organs, including dementia when the brain deteriorates in some patients.

The researchers who were responsible for the Tuskegee syphilis study believed, for the most part, that their study was ethical (Brandt, 2000). They thought the medical knowledge about syphilis that would be gained was an important contribution to science. In addition, they argued that the men in the study were not being harmed by the study. The participants had already contracted syphilis, so the researchers believed that they were not doing anything to worsen the disease. The participants were also receiving free medical examinations that they could not have afforded on their own. In addition, in 1969, the Communicable Disease Center (now the Centers for Disease Control and Prevention [CDC]) reaffirmed the need for the study after concerns about the ethics of the study were raised. They also won the approval of the American Medical Association (AMA) for the study.

Do you agree with the attitudes of the researchers of the Tuskegee syphilis study that their study was not harmful to the participants in the study? If you answered no and believe it was harmful, *why* do you think it was harmful? In what way did the study harm the research participants? The answers to these questions have been a major point of discussion among psychologists and medical researchers for the past 50 years or so, as changes in the way society views the ethics of research on human participants have taken place. These changes in ethical guidelines for research have been motivated in large part by the discussion of studies such as the Tuskegee syphilis study, where it is clear to many people that the researchers did not meet their ethical obligations. In this chapter, we discuss the historical context for ethical guidelines that provides the motivation for current ethical standards, the current guidelines for research with humans and animals, and the role of an IRB in the research process. See Figure 3.1 for an indication of the steps in the research process to which ethics are relevant.

FIGURE 3.1 ■ Steps in the Research Process: Ethical Guidelines

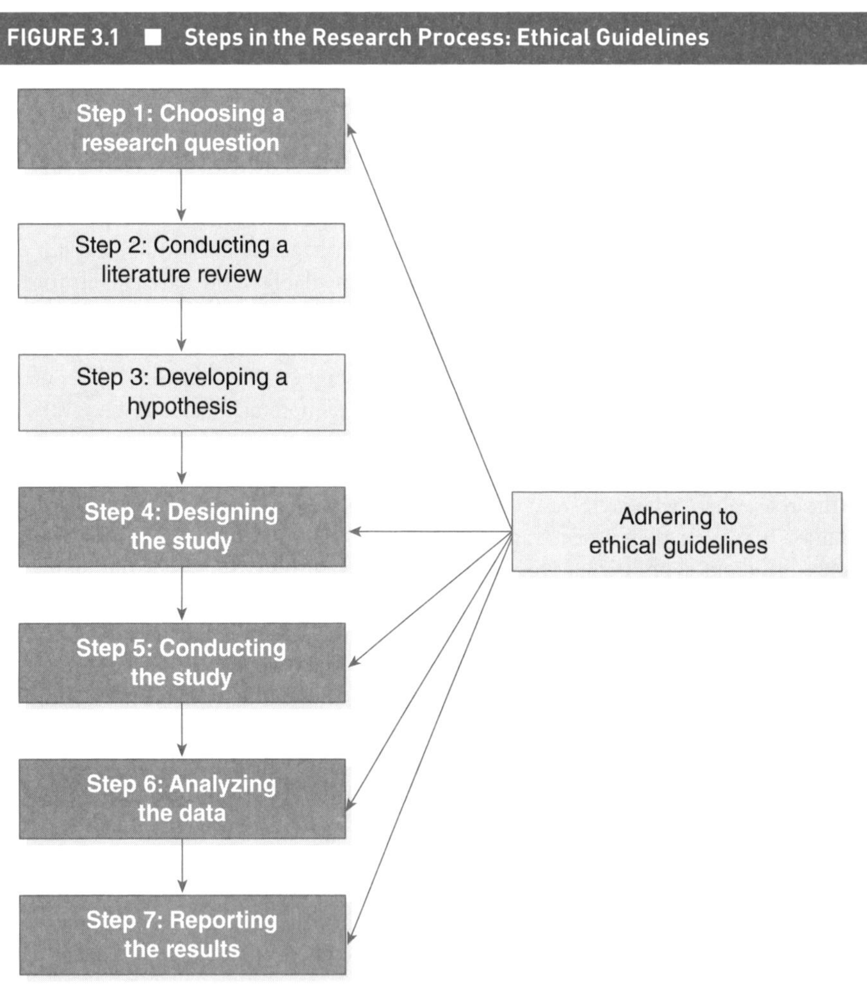

Note: Ethical guidelines must be followed at several steps in the research process.

HISTORICAL CONTEXT FOR ETHICAL GUIDELINES

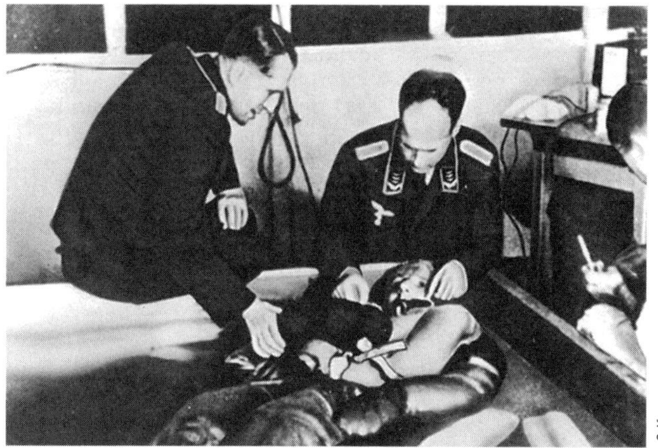

http://wikipedia.org/wiki/File:Dachau_cold_water_immersion.jpg.

Photo 3.2 Experiments conducted on Nazi concentration camp prisoners during World War II prompted the development of the Nuremberg Code.

Note: Photo from Dachau during World War II.

Why do we need ethical guidelines for research in psychology? There are several reasons that researchers are held to ethical standards, but the most important one is that researchers are not always able to be objective about the effects of a study on the participants and whether or not a study will be harmful to the participants. In addition to the Tuskegee syphilis study, there are a few other important examples of studies that were conducted to advance scientific knowledge but may have also harmed the research participants in the process. Some particularly heinous examples are the experiments conducted by the Nazis on World War II concentration camp prisoners.

Nuremberg Code

At the end of World War II, the world learned of the atrocities the Nazis had committed during the war. Among their horrific acts were experiments conducted on concentration camp inmates. These experiments were conducted by scientists interested in learning about the limits of the human body and mind. Many of the experiments were designed to better understand the conditions soldiers are able to endure in war and involved subject exposure to extreme temperatures, infections, and noxious chemicals (Schuler, 1982). The subjects of these experiments were forced to participate as prisoners in the Nazi concentration camps. The details of the experiments became public during the Nuremberg trials held between 1945 and 1949, when Nazi officers and officials were tried for war crimes (see Photo 3.2). The **Nuremberg Code** was developed by officials involved in the trials (judges, medical experts) as a result of what was learned about the Nazi experiments and was an early attempt to specify ethical standards for any research involving human participants.

Nuremberg Code: Set of ethical guidelines developed for research with human participants based on information gained during the Nuremberg trials after World War II

The Nuremberg Code focuses on the issues of **informed consent**, which is informing participants about the study and then gaining their consent for participation, and **coercion**, where the participants' right to refuse or end participation in a study is taken away. The code also includes other important ethical guidelines that remain part of the current ethical guidelines for psychologists. The Nuremberg Code states the following (Schuler, 1982):

informed consent: Obtaining consent from participants for participation in research after the participants have been informed about the purpose, procedure, and risks of the research

coercion: Forcing participants to participate in research without their consent

1. Participation in research is voluntary, and participants must be given information about the risks involved in the research (i.e., informed consent and freedom from coercion).

2. The research must contribute to scientific knowledge and be conducted by qualified researchers.

3. The researchers must avoid unnecessary harm, take precautions against risk, ensure that benefits outweigh the risks of the study, and terminate the study if unforeseen harm comes to the participants.

4. The participants have the right to discontinue their participation in the study (i.e., freedom from coercion).

APA Code

In 1953, the American Psychological Association (APA) codified its own ethical standards for the field of psychology, including psychological research (Schuler, 1982). The European Federation of Psychologists' Association, www.efpa.eu, and several other international psychologists' associations have developed similar ethics codes that have been adopted by other countries. Many of the elements in the APA code overlapped with the main elements of the Nuremberg Code described earlier. Two additional elements were included in the guidelines for research: (1) the researchers must reduce harm due to **deception**, which is misleading the participants about the study's purpose or procedures, and (2) the researchers must ensure the confidentiality of participant data. However, the original APA code left the responsibility for overseeing research studies to the researchers, and several researchers used the element of weighing benefits against risk to justify harmful studies by claiming that the studies were highly beneficial. In some psychological studies, the researchers have argued that the important knowledge gained in the study justified the risk to the participants. Two well-known examples of research conducted by psychologists that many have argued stretched the APA ethical standards are described in the next sections: the Milgram (1963) obedience study and the Zimbardo (1973) prison study.

deception: Misleading participants about the purpose or procedures of a research study

Milgram (1963) Obedience Study

During the Nuremberg trials, several defendants argued that they were not responsible for their wartime actions because their actions were carried out to follow orders of their superiors. This defense argument led social psychologists to some interesting research questions. How strong is the power of authority? Does a person need to have sadistic tendencies in order to harm another person, or is an order from an authority figure enough to cause someone to commit these actions? Stanley Milgram became interested in these questions and wondered how many people would harm another person simply because an authority figure told them to do so. Milgram designed a study to investigate these research questions that examined the effect of an authority figure on participants' behavior. In his study, participants were recruited to administer a memory task to a second participant. The second participant was actually a **confederate** in the study. In other words, the second participant was not an actual participant; instead, the confederate acted a part in the study to make the participants believe that he was just another participant in the study.

confederate: A person who is part of a research study but acts as though he or she is not to deceive the participant about the study's purpose

The confederate was placed behind a screen and attached to electrodes in the participants' presence. After that point, the participants could hear the confederate but could not see him during the study. The participants were then asked to read word pairs to the confederate for a later memory test. The participants administered the memory test by reading a word and asking the confederate to choose from four choices the word it was paired with in the study list. Each time the confederate answered incorrectly, the participants were instructed to deliver an electric shock to the confederate by pressing a button on a console placed in front of them. For each wrong answer, the participants were told to increase the level of shock delivered. Shocks were not actually delivered to the confederate, but participants were led to believe that they were actually shocking the confederate. The confederate cried out after some of the shocks as if in pain and was silent for the more severe shock levels. The buttons on the participants' console were labeled such that the shocks appeared to increase in intensity with each incorrect answer. If participants resisted (verbally or nonverbally), an experimenter in a white lab coat (i.e., an authority figure) encouraged them to continue; those statements increased in strength as more resistance was displayed (see Photo 3.3).

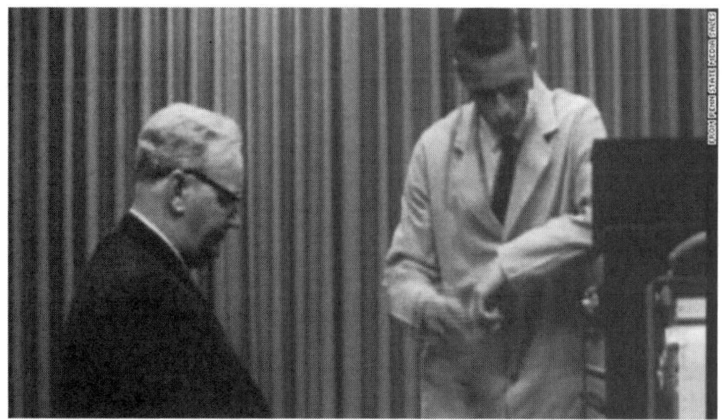

Photo 3.3
Here is an experimenter and participant in the Milgram (1963) study.

Note: The photograph shows that an experimenter in a lab coat served as the authority figure and encouraged the participants to continue the study if they were hesitant to administer electric shocks to the "learner" confederate.

At the start of the study, Milgram asked other social psychologists how many participants they thought would continue the experiment to the end, where the shocks were labeled *danger* and *XXX*. Most predicted that only the very cruelest participants (less than 2%) would administer all the shocks. However, the results of Milgram's study showed that almost two thirds of the participants administered all the shocks, and none of the participants checked on the confederate without asking permission first. This study showed that the presence of an authority figure greatly influences people's behavior—to the point where people may harm another person when ordered to do so.

Milgram justified his study by arguing that, although the participants were deceived in the study, they did not experience long-term harm from the study. The participants were fully debriefed after the study to show that no harm had been done to the confederate. In addition, vital knowledge about human behavior was learned. The social psychologists Milgram had surveyed at the start of the study had been unable to predict the results of the study. Thus, new knowledge was gained about the effect of authority figures on behavior. However, critics of the study argued that the stress of the situation and deception of the participants were too great and were psychologically harmful (Schuler, 1982). Furthermore, it is unclear whether the participants felt they could withdraw from the study if they wished, given that every time they protested the experimenter told them that they were required to continue. There is also some evidence that the procedures were inconsistent across participants, suggesting that ethical research practices were not followed in the study (Griggs & Whitehead, 2015).

Imagine how you would feel if you were a participant in the Milgram study and learned that you were willing to shock another person simply because a stranger in a lab coat told you to. How would that knowledge change the way you felt about yourself? Milgram countered the criticisms with a survey of the participants after the study that showed that a large majority of them were "glad" or "very glad" to have participated, despite

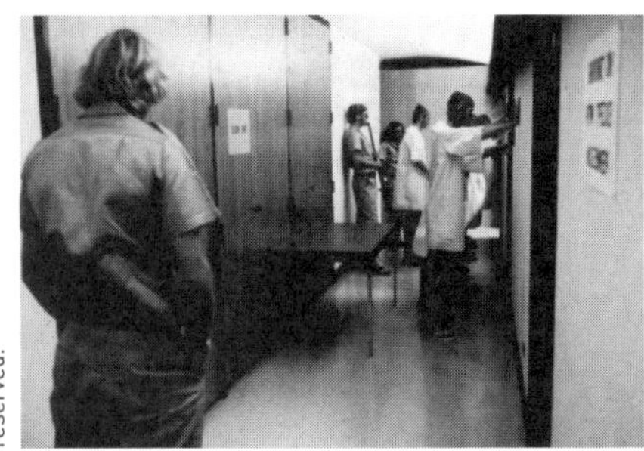

Photo 3.4 Philip Zimbardo and his colleagues studied the effect of social roles in a mock prison at Stanford University.

the stressful situation they experienced in the study. Despite Milgram's arguments, an exact replication of the Milgram study is unlikely to meet the ethical standards for research currently in use in psychology (but see Burger, 2009, for a description of a recent modified replication that was also covered on the ABC News show *Primetime*).

Zimbardo (1973) Prison Experiment

Another famous study that was criticized for stretching ethical standards for research was conducted by Philip Zimbardo and his colleagues at Stanford University in the early 1970s. Zimbardo was interested in how the roles we are given in a society affect our behavior toward others. He created a mock prison in the basement of the psychology building at Stanford and randomly assigned students to play the role of prisoner or guard in the mock prison (see Photo 3.4). He carefully screened the participants to ensure that they were all similar in terms of intelligence and personality characteristics. Thus, the only difference between the prisoner and guard groups was the role they were randomly assigned to play in the prison experiment.

Zimbardo created conditions for the prison that were as realistic as possible. He had the participants assigned as prisoners publicly arrested by campus police before they were placed in the prison. They were given prison clothes to wear and assigned a number. They remained in the prison 24 hr a day for the length of the experiment. Small cells were built in the prison area to confine the prisoners for much of their time. The guards were given uniforms and worked set shifts at the prison, returning to their student lives during their off hours.

Zimbardo had planned for the prison experiment to take place over 2 weeks but stopped the study after only a few days when he realized that the study had become harmful to the participants. Some of the prisoners had extreme stress reactions and had to be released. Several of the guards became cruel and forced the prisoners to engage in embarrassing behaviors. However, none of the participants ever asked to stop the experiment. Both groups of participants, prisoners and guards, had lost the reality that they were participants in an experiment and were greatly affected by the situation they were placed in during the experiment.

Zimbardo followed ethical guidelines in designing the experiment. He considered alternate ways of studying the effects of the prisoner and guard roles, received informed consent from all the participants before beginning the study, and discussed the purpose of the study and its benefits (a process called **debriefing**) with the participants after the study ended (Zimbardo, 1973). He also stopped the experiment earlier than planned to avoid further harming the participants (see https://www.prisonexp.org for more information on this study provided by Zimbardo). However, critics of the study claimed that the participants should not have been placed in such a stressful situation in the study. Furthermore, given the powerful influence of the prison context, it was difficult for those involved in the study to be objective about the effects of the study. Zimbardo himself admitted to being influenced by the context of the prison study, feeling like a prison warden at times when the study was taking place (Reiniger, 2001).

debriefing: Discussing the purpose and benefits of a research study with participants—often done at the end of the study

STOP AND THINK

3.1. Describe the elements of the Nuremberg Code that are still present in ethical guidelines for researchers.

3.2. Explain what is involved in obtaining informed consent.

3.3. Which ethical guidelines (if any) do you think the Milgram and Zimbardo studies may have violated?

CURRENT ETHICAL GUIDELINES FOR HUMAN PARTICIPANTS RESEARCH

Due to the criticism leveled at studies such as Milgram's and Zimbardo's, the APA Ethics Code has been revised several times to ensure that researchers include a thorough debriefing of the participants, more clearly define the conditions under which deception may be used, and include specific guidelines for research with animal subjects. See Table 3.1 for a summary of the current APA Ethics Code guidelines for research.

In addition to the APA Ethics Code, federal ethical guidelines exist that must be adhered to by all institutions that receive public funds. After the Tuskegee syphilis study became public, the U.S. government formed a committee to discuss appropriate ethical guidelines for medical and psychological research. The committee produced the *Belmont Report* (National Commission for the Protection of Human Subjects of Biomedical and Behavioral Research, 1979, p. 200), which lists the responsibilities of researchers as they conduct research with human participants and the rights of those participants before, during, and after a study (a copy of the full report can be viewed at https://www.hhs.gov/ohrp/regulations-and-policy/belmont-report/index.html). The *Belmont Report* provides the set of ethical guidelines that researchers in psychology must adhere to. Three major principles described in the report outline the responsibilities of researchers: (1) *respect for persons*, (2) *beneficence*, and (3) *justice*. We will consider how these principles translate to ethical guidelines for psychological research in the sections that follow. Table 3.2 also provides an overview of the application of these principles to psychological research.

Respect for Persons

The first principle of the *Belmont Report*, respect for persons, refers to the treatment of participants in research studies. Informed consent is an important element of this principle, and it includes informing the participants about the nature of their participation in a study, including what the participants will do in the study, the purpose of the study, any risks associated with the study, benefits of the study, information about alternative treatments (if applicable), and the participants' rights during the study (especially their right to withdraw from the study and their right to ask questions about the study). It is the researchers' responsibility to ensure that the participants have the ability to understand the information they are given during the informed consent process. Often, researchers

TABLE 3.1 ■ Summary of the APA Ethics Code for Research

APA Ethics Code	Ethics issues addressed
1. Research should be approved by the researcher's IRB where applicable.	IRB approval
2. Research must include an informed consent process, including the following:	Informed consent
a. Purpose of the research	
b. Expected duration of participation	
c. Procedures used in the research	
d. Participants' rights to decline to participate and withdraw participation at any time and the consequences of withdrawal	
e. Foreseeable risks of the research to the participants	
f. Benefits of the research	
g. Confidentiality rights of the participants	
h. Incentives for participation	
i. Whom to contact for questions or concerns	
3. In addition to 2, if the research involves an experimental treatment, the participants must be informed that it is experimental, how participants will be assigned to groups, the available alternative treatments, and the compensation they will receive for participation.	Informed consent; Reduce harm
4. In addition to 2, if the research involves recording of the participants, they must be informed ahead of time if it does not compromise the research to do so.	Informed consent; Confidentiality
5. Incentives for participation must be reasonable so as not to be coercive.	Coercion
6. If the research involves deception, the researchers must determine that the deception is necessary and justified and explain any use of deception to participants as soon as possible at the completion of the study. Researchers may not use deception that is expected to cause physical pain or severe distress.	Deception; Reduce harm
7. Thorough debriefing must be given for the study. If it is not possible to give debriefing immediately, researchers must protect against participants' harm.	Reduce harm
8. If researchers become aware of unexpected harm to participants, they must take reasonable measures to reduce harm, including termination of the study if necessary.	Reduce harm
9. The following are rules to be remembered while doing research with animals:	Animal research ethics

APA Ethics Code	Ethics issues addressed
a. Adhere to federal and local guidelines for care and treatment of animals.	
b. Involve trained personnel.	
c. Minimize discomfort to the animals.	
d. Justify painful or stressful procedures and only use them when alternative procedures cannot be used.	
e. Use anesthesia and prevent infection when surgical procedures are used.	
f. Terminate animals quickly with minimal pain if termination is necessary.	
10. Researchers must report data accurately and correct errors if they are discovered.	Ethics in reporting research
11. Researchers must properly cite others' ideas and work when reporting research.	Ethics in reporting research
12. Publication credit can be taken only for work the authors have performed, and credit order should be determined according to the contribution of each author.	Ethics in reporting research
13. Data should be shared with other researchers to allow verification of results.	Ethics in reporting research

Source: Adapted from APA (2017).

TABLE 3.2 ■ Applications of the *Belmont Report* Principles

Principle	Application
Respect for persons	Information about the study must be provided before it begins (nature of participation, purpose, risks, benefits).
	Voluntary consent from participants must be given after they are informed (i.e., informed consent).
	Participants should have the opportunity to ask questions.
	Participants should be informed of right to withdraw.
Beneficence	There should be a reduced risk of harm to participants.
	Potential benefits of the study must outweigh risks.
	Inhumane treatment of participants is never justified.
Justice	Selection of participants must be fair.
	All participant groups must have opportunity to receive benefits of research.
	No participant groups may be unfairly selected for harmful research.

Source: "Belmont Report" (1979), US Department of Health and Human Services.

© Thierry Berrod, Mona Lisa Production/Science Source

Photo 3.5
The *Belmont Report* specifies that special protections are required for participants who may not be able to fully comprehend the consent process.

provide a **consent form** that includes the information just listed about the study that the participants need to read and sign before their participation in the study. Special protections must be provided for participants who may not have the ability to fully comprehend the information (e.g., children, persons with certain types of disabilities or illnesses). The amount of protection needed depends on the risk of harm to those individuals and the benefits of their participation (see Photo 3.5).

As part of the informed consent process, research participants must volunteer to participate in the study after they are informed about the study as described previously. This creates a dilemma for participants who may feel coerced to participate in the study. For example, the rights of participants who are prisoners must be carefully considered to reduce any implied coercion the participants may feel to participate. This may also be an issue when students are included in a research study where the instructor is a researcher for the study. In this case, the instructor needs to make it clear in the informed consent process that the participants have the right to refuse to participate without it affecting their evaluation in the course. If non-English-speaking participants are included, a translated version of the informed consent information must be provided. If children or other individuals with legal guardianship are included as participants, informed consent must be obtained from the legal guardian and assent for their participation must be obtained from the participants. The assent process must explain what the participation will entail and must be explained in a way that the participants can understand what they are being asked to do.

consent form: A form provided to the participants at the beginning of a research study to obtain their consent for the study and to explain the study's purpose and risks and the participants' rights as participants

Beneficence

Beneficence refers to the reduction of risk of harm to the participants as compared with the benefit of the study. In other words, a **risk–benefit analysis** should be conducted to ensure that the benefits of a study outweigh the risks to the participants. In addition, the risk of harm to the participants should be reduced as much as possible when designing a study. There are many types of risks that must be considered in psychological research. Physical risk is an obvious factor but is an issue in only a small number of studies. More common are risks to a participant's psychological health, reputation, and social standing. Some studies can be emotionally upsetting to participants or cause them stress (as the 1963 Milgram study did). If they are asked to consider difficult or traumatic experiences during an interview or in answering a questionnaire, participants can experience psychological harm in a study. In some studies, negative mood induction may occur to compare mood states. Thus, altering participants' moods may also psychologically harm them. Risk to participants' social standing may occur if their **confidentiality** is breached in disseminating a research study. Consequently, it is the researcher's responsibility to maintain the participants' confidentiality at all times during the research process.

risk–benefit analysis: Weighing the risks against the benefits of a research study to ensure that the benefits outweigh the risks

confidentiality: The researcher's responsibility to protect the participants' identity and right to privacy (including participant responses) during and after the research study

The risks described previously are weighed by the researcher against the benefits of the study to society to ensure that the benefits outweigh the risks. The researcher must determine what the likely benefit of the study is, determine the likely risks to the participants—often by reviewing past studies conducted in a similar manner to determine their effect on the participants—and describe the study in terms of its potential benefits to justify whatever risks might befall the participants during the study. Hence, studies with the potential to gain important knowledge may have increased risks as compared with studies with lesser potential benefits. However, inhumane treatment of participants is never justified, and the researcher is responsible for determining what conditions may be too harmful to participants to include in a study.

Justice

Fair selection of participants is covered by the justice principle. Researchers are responsible for ensuring that all participants have a fair chance of receiving potentially beneficial treatments in research (e.g., treatments for specific mental illnesses or conditions) as well as ensuring that potentially harmful conditions are not exclusively administered to a specific group (as it was when treatment was withheld from African American men with syphilis in the Tuskegee study). Special considerations must be provided for groups that may be easier to manipulate (e.g., individuals with illnesses, low-income individuals). For example, suppose that you are a researcher conducting a study in a geographical area where there are many economically disadvantaged individuals (e.g., a low-income area of a large city, a developing country). As compensation, you plan to offer the participants $50 to participate in your extensive study (e.g., you plan to interview the participants extensively and observe them for a period of time). Compensation of $50 is a reasonable amount to offer U.S. students for this type of participation, so you offer the same amount to the low-income participants in your study. However, $50 has a different value to low-income individuals than it has to middle-class individuals. Even if the participants did not want to participate in your study, they may feel compelled to participate to earn the $50, which may feed their family for a period of time. Thus, many would consider this type of compensation coercive to the low-income participants. These individuals may feel that they have less choice in participating because they are in greater need of the compensation than higher income individuals. These issues must be considered by researchers to ensure that the selection of their participants is fair. If a participant group is to be excluded from a research study, there must be a scientific justification for the exclusion.

An Example

Consider a study by Mihai et al. (2007). These researchers were interested in testing a possible treatment for alcohol abuse. After long-term alcohol abuse, individuals may experience delirium tremens. These episodes can include hallucinations, disorientation, motor tremors, and severe anxiety. In the Mihai et al. study, the treatment involved recording patients with severe alcohol dependence while they were experiencing a delirium tremens episode.

Patients who were hospitalized with delirium tremens were recruited for inclusion in the study. To be eligible, patients had to have severe alcohol dependence for at least three years and consume a large quantity of alcohol per day. Consent to videotape the patients

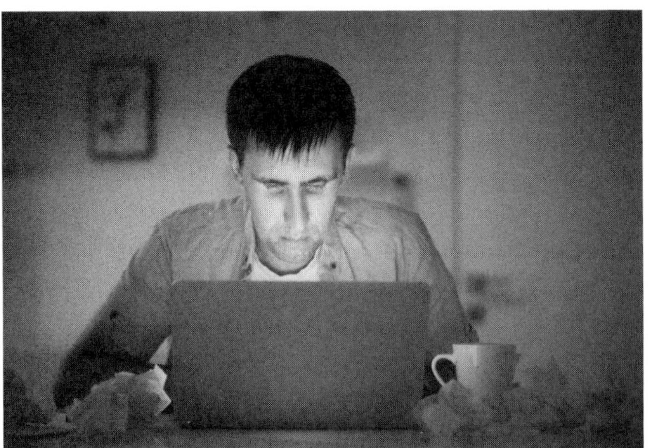

Photo 3.6
Mihai et al. (2007) found that patients with delirium tremens from alcohol abuse who viewed a video of themselves in this state were less likely to relapse than those who did not view the video.

was obtained from the patients' families. Patients were recorded during their delirium tremens episode with a psychiatrist and a medical assistant present. Consent for the study was obtained from the patients themselves at some point after recording. After the patients had recovered from their delirium tremens episode (9 to 27 days later), they were randomly assigned to one of two groups. One group of patients (the experimental group) was shown the recordings of their episodes with a psychiatrist explaining the symptoms and their connection to the alcohol abuse (see Photo 3.6). The other group (the control group) was given the choice to erase their tapes or to view them after 6 months had passed and the follow-up measures had been completed (the majority chose the latter option).

Each month for 6 months after the beginning of the study, the patients were tested for relapse rates, number of days per week they drank, and number of drinks they had on each day they drank. Results (see Figure 3.2) indicated that the group that viewed their recordings showed lower relapse rates, fewer drinking days per week, and fewer drinks per drinking day than the group that did not view their recordings. Mihai et al. (2007) concluded that the recording treatment was effective in reducing relapse in patients with alcohol dependency.

FIGURE 3.2 ■ Results From Mihai et al.'s (2007) Study Showed That Participants Who Viewed the Videos of Their Delirium Tremens Episodes (Group A) Had Lower Rates of Relapse Over Time Than the Participants Who Did Not View the Videos (Group B)

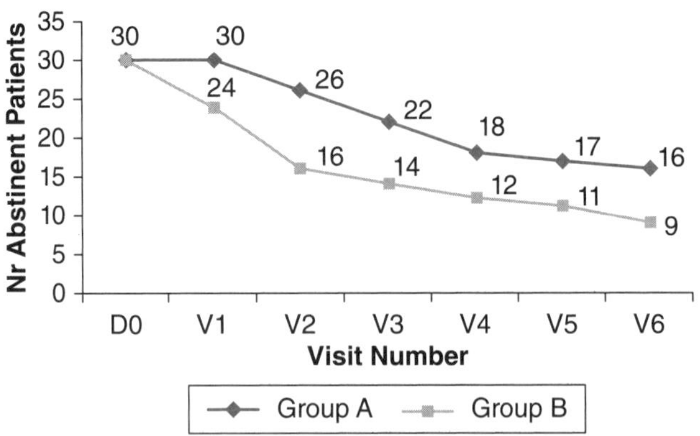

Source: Results from Mihai et al.'s (2006) study. © Society for the Study of Addiction.

Based on the ethical guidelines described in Tables 3.1 and 3.2, what are the ethical issues involved in this study? What issues should the researchers consider before they conduct this study? One issue you may consider is the coercion of the participants. Initial consent for the study was obtained from the patients' families instead of from the patients themselves. Consent was not obtained from the patients before recording took place. However, the researchers may have felt that the patients were not in a position to provide consent during their delirium tremens episode. Instead, they destroyed the videos of any patient who refused to consent after the recording took place. Another issue is the participants' confidentiality. The recordings of the participants' delirium tremens episodes provide a lasting record of a difficult and potentially defaming episode in the participants' lives (see Broyles, Tate, & Happ, 2008, for a more thorough discussion of ethical issues involved in recordings collected in research). Where the recordings are stored, who is allowed access to them, and what happens to them when the study is concluded are all important issues in this study. In fact, the researchers reported destroying the recordings at the conclusion of the study (if they had not already been destroyed prior to this time at the participants' request) to protect the confidentiality of the participants. A third issue is the harm the study procedures may bring to the participant and whether the risk of harm outweighs the benefit of the study. The participants in the study may have experienced stress, anxiety, or other negative emotions while viewing the recordings of their delirium tremens episodes. However, the researchers may have argued that the possible benefit of finding an effective treatment for alcohol abuse may outweigh the negative emotions experienced by the participants in the study. This is a difficult question best answered by society at large: When is the discomfort of a few worth knowledge that may aid many?

INSTITUTIONAL REVIEW BOARDS

In response to reported abuses of research ethics, the U.S. Department of Health and Human Services (HHS) currently requires that all institutions where research is conducted (universities and colleges, hospitals, companies, etc.) have an **institutional review board (IRB)** to oversee the research conducted at that site or the research done by researchers affiliated with that institution in order to ensure that ethical guidelines are adhered to in research with human participants (U.S. Department of HHS, 2005). This policy applies to all institutions that are subject to federal regulations. The IRB reviews all research proposed at the institution to provide a more objective evaluation of the ethics of a study. The IRB is made up of at least five members with backgrounds sufficient to ensure qualified review of the research proposals. If the IRB finds ethical problems with a proposed study, the board can instruct the researcher to revise the study or simply disapprove the study. In other words, before researchers can conduct a study, they must first receive approval from their IRB.

institutional review board (IRB): A committee of knowledgeable individuals who oversee the ethics of research with human participants conducted at an institution

There are three categories of review by IRBs. The category for a study is determined by the amount of risk there is to the participants in the study. Riskier studies require more careful and thorough review. The three categories of IRB review are (1) *exempt*, (2) *expedited*, and (3) *full review*.

Exempt Studies

Exempt studies are those studies that have the smallest amount of risk involved. They are typically studies that involve educational or cognitive testing of participants, where there is no physical or psychological risk and no risk of loss of social standing if confidentiality were to be breached. Archival studies where the individuals cannot be identified in the data also fall into the exempt category. Research conducted in educational settings for educational purposes also qualifies for exempt review. Studies that fit into this category are typically given a brief review and then assigned exempt status, which means that they are exempt from further review as long as the procedures of the study do not change in the future.

Expedited Studies

U.S. Department of HHS (2005) identified a category of expedited review for studies that involve minimal risk. Expedited studies need to be reviewed by only one member of the IRB, which speeds the process of review. Expedited studies may involve a small amount of physical or psychological risk. For example, studies involving noninvasive medical procedures (measurements of heart rate, galvanic skin response, brain-wave activity, etc.), collection of blood by normal means (finger stick, venipuncture, etc.), video- or audiotaping of observations, and survey or questionnaire studies with minimal emotional impact are typically given expedited review.

Full-Review Studies

Studies with the highest amount of risk receive full review by the IRB, meaning that each member of the IRB reviews the research proposal. Studies requiring full review are often studies where a special population has a risk of harm, such as studies with particular risk to children or other individuals who may not be capable of providing informed consent on their own. Studies involving invasive medical procedures or high psychological risk, as with deception that could cause stress or questionnaires about behaviors that could cause emotional distress, typically require full IRB review.

Criteria for Institutional Review Board Approval

IRB members use a set of criteria to evaluate research proposals and ensure that the research meets the ethical guidelines described in the *Belmont Report* (U.S. Department of HHS, 2005). The criteria are as follows:

1. The researcher minimizes unnecessary risk to the participants.
2. The risk in the study is justified by the potential benefits of the study.
3. The selection of the participants is fair and appropriate for the study.
4. An informed consent process is included in the study and can be documented by the researcher.
5. The researcher monitors collection of the data to ensure the safety of the participants during the course of the study.
6. The privacy and confidentiality of the participants is protected by the researcher.
7. If a special participant group is included in the study, procedures must be included to protect the rights of these participants.

A research proposal sent to the IRB for review must address each of these elements. Individual IRBs may have their own proposal form that researchers must complete to allow all elements of the criteria to be addressed clearly in the proposal.

Deception and Debriefing

In addition to the criteria listed previously, the APA Ethics Code (APA, 2017) requires sufficient justification for studies involving deception and a debriefing process in all studies. If a study makes use of deception, the researcher must justify why the deception is necessary and why alternative procedures that do not use deception cannot be employed. The deception cannot be used if it will cause physical or severe psychological harm. Note, however, that there is a difference between deception and not fully disclosing the study's purpose. In many cases, researchers do not fully disclose the purpose of the study to reduce **demand characteristics**, where the participants may alter their behavior based on their perception of the study's purpose or hypothesis. For example, in research testing a type of memory called indirect or implicit memory, researchers may not call the test a memory test because they do not want the participants to intentionally retrieve studied items during this test. In other words, indirect memory tests involve a form of memory that is used unintentionally. In studies of indirect memory (e.g., Roediger & McDermott, 1993), participants are given a study session and then a task that they are to complete as quickly as possible (e.g., identify a word flashed very quickly on the computer screen); studied items are included in the task. No mention is made of the study episode, however, when the indirect memory test is given, and participants are often told that it is an unrelated task. This is done to discourage participants from using direct memory in the test (i.e., intentionally retrieving studied items). Indirect memory can be measured in these tests by the faster speed with which participants identify words they have studied versus items not studied. This is a procedure commonly used in research I have conducted on indirect or implicit memory (e.g., McBride, Coane, & Raulerson, 2006). Describing the indirect memory test in general or alternative terms that reduce demand characteristics is not the same as deceiving the participants, and the IRB will view these situations differently when reviewing a study for approval.

demand characteristics: A source of bias that can occur in a study due to participants changing their behavior based on their perception of the study and its purpose

Photo 3.7 In the debriefing process, the purpose and hypotheses are fully disclosed to the participants in a research study.

Most studies involve a debriefing process to fully explain the purpose of the study to the participants and the knowledge that the study will contribute, including expected results of the study (see Photo 3.7). However, if the study uses deception, the debriefing process must thoroughly explain the nature of the study and the deception used, including the purpose of the deception in the study. The goal of the debriefing process is to allow the participant to leave the study with a positive attitude toward the research. Thus, if the participant has been stressed during the study, part of the debriefing process should attempt to reduce this stress. If the participant's mood has been negatively altered by the study, an attempt should be made during the debriefing process to restore the participant's mood to its state before the study began. The participants are also provided with an opportunity to gain new knowledge about their behavior in the debriefing through the explanation of the study provided by the researcher and through questions they may wish to ask about the study.

An Example

Consider the ethics of the following social psychology study: To investigate the effects on physiological behaviors of personal-space invasions, Middlemist, Knowles, and Matter (1976) arranged an interesting field experiment of urination behaviors in college males. They conducted their experiment in a men's restroom at a university, such that men using the restroom were selected as participants, and a **field experiment** was conducted. Three urinals in the restroom were arranged so that men entering the restroom were forced to use (1) the end urinal with a confederate next to them (the urinal at the other end had a "being cleaned" sign and a bucket and sponge placed on it), (2) the end urinal with a confederate two urinals away (the middle urinal had the sign), or (3) the end urinal with no confederate nearby (both of the other urinals had signs). An experimenter in a stall measured the time it took for the participant to begin urination and the length of time he urinated. Participants were never informed that they were participating in a research study. The researchers found that the participants in the condition with the confederate at the urinal next to them took longer to begin urination and urinated for a shorter duration than the other two conditions, indicating that invasion of personal space affects physiological behaviors.

field experiment: An experiment conducted in the participants' natural environment

Imagine that you are a member of the IRB reviewing this study before it is conducted. What issues might you have with the research? What are the risks to the participants in this study? Do you feel that the risk to the participants outweighed the benefit of the knowledge gained? Why or why not? Can you think of any other way that this study could be designed to reduce the risks to the participants? One issue that you may have noticed is that no informed consent process or debriefing took place because the participants were never informed that they were involved in a research study. The informed consent process would likely have affected the participants' behavior, but a debriefing process may have alleviated any psychological discomfort caused by the presence of the confederate, especially in the condition with a confederate at the next urinal. However, the researchers may have argued that the process of debriefing the participants may have embarrassed them, thus causing harm. These are the sorts of issues that are considered by the members of an IRB as they review research.

Collaborative Institutional Training Initiative

Many IRBs now require researchers (faculty and students) to complete the Collaborative Institutional Training Initiative (CITI) ethics training modules. The CITI website (https://about.citiprogram.org/en/homepage) allows researchers to register and then complete modules that cover ethical guidelines for different types of research. Many universities, colleges, and other institutions are linked to CITI so that you can complete modules designated by your institution as required to work on research with human subjects. For example, the Social–Behavioral–Educational Basic course in CITI required of principle investigators at my university covers ethical guidelines and U.S. federal regulations for protecting research subjects, learning the informed consent process, assessing risk in research, conducting research with children and in schools, conducting international research, and conducting research with protected or at-risk populations. However, a shorter module covers the most important ethical guidelines for research with minimal risk, and the students who work on most of my research projects on human memory take this shorter course before being approved by the IRB for these projects. Completing CITI modules is also a good way for students to review the ethical guideline concepts covered in this section.

STOP AND THINK

3.4. Explain the purpose of the IRB.

3.5. New drugs are sometimes tested just in male research participants for side effects. Explain how this practice violates the ethical guideline of justice as described in the *Belmont Report*.

3.6. Explain why a debriefing typically takes place at the end of a research study. Include both ethical and reduction of bias purposes.

ETHICS IN REPORTING RESEARCH

In addition to the treatment of participants or subjects in a study, the APA Ethics Code (APA, 2017) contains sections outlining ethical guidelines for reporting research in an ethical manner. Two primary issues are addressed in these sections: (1) errors in the data that are reported (either intended or unintended) and (2) plagiarism. These issues are just as important to the scientific process as the treatment of participants or subjects.

As you have seen, the scientific method relies on reports of previous studies for developing a hypothesis, designing valid methods, and anticipating negative consequences of study procedures on participants. Thus, the reports of psychological research must be accurate, or future research decreases in validity—an effect that can ripple through the literature for many years. Researchers are ethically bound to report data accurately. If an error is discovered in the report, the researcher must correct the error or make it known if correction is not possible.

Credit must also be given for information contained in the reports of research. Thus, researchers must properly cite the source of information they give in research reports. This includes both word-for-word reports from others (your university or college likely has a student code of conduct that forbids and punishes this type of plagiarism) and summarized representation of another's ideas. You have seen such citations throughout this text that provide sources for the information it contains. Research reports (even those that may not be published) must always cite sources for theories, methods, data, and other topics an author describes that came from another source. Even oral and poster presentations must include source information for material that is not original to the reporting author. Figures and pictures taken from previous studies or items posted on the web are included. Regardless of the form, the original source must be credited (e.g., see the source credits with the photos in this text).

When I teach scientific writing to students, my suggestion is to be especially careful when summarizing previous studies. If you are writing directly from the source, inadvertent plagiarism can easily occur. Thus, a better strategy is to first read the original source and take notes in your own words about the important information you want to use in your own writing. Then write using your notes, instead of the original source, to ensure that your writing is in your own summarized words. This strategy can help you avoid accidentally plagiarizing the words of the article's authors.

Violation of either of the previously stated ethical guidelines (data errors or plagiarism) can seriously damage one's career. There have been several famous examples of such violations that damaged the standing of researchers in the scientific community. One such recent example was reported in 2011, when it was discovered that Diederik Stapel, a Dutch social psychologist, had falsified data in many of his published papers (Shea, 2011). All of his research has fallen under suspicion, including two particularly publicized findings: a paper published in *Psychological Science* titled "Power Increases Infidelity Among Men and Women" and a paper published in *Science* titled "Coping With Chaos: How Disordered Contexts Promote Stereotyping and Discrimination." The *Science* paper has been retracted (along with many of his other papers), and Stapel was criminally prosecuted. One reason such cases occur is the pressure on researchers to publish surprising and statistically significant results. Often, there is a bias in publishing research studies for such findings (i.e., findings that are not surprising and/or and not statistically significant are less likely to be published), resulting in pressure on researchers to produce data that fit this description. However, this also creates another problem that you should be aware of: There may be many studies that have failed to find an effect that have never been published, meaning most researchers are unaware of them. This is also why it is important to replicate research findings that are new and surprising. If they can't be replicated, then it's possible they were due to chance factors in the studies that first reported them. This is how the falsified data are typically discovered—they cannot be replicated by other researchers.

From this example, you can see that false data reports can have very serious consequences—not just to the individual who falsified the data but to the field of psychology as well in leading researchers in pursuit of findings that are not real as they attempt to replicate and expand on the falsified data. Publicizing of such cases also make the general public skeptical of all research despite their infrequent occurrence. Researchers have an ethical duty to accurately report their methods and data in their research reports and to alert others to errors in their work if they are found (e.g., by having an erratum correcting a research article if the researcher finds an error after it is published). You are probably more likely, however, to be concerned about the second issue discussed here: plagiarism. Plagiarism can be intentional or unintentional; however, both are serious ethical violations, as they both involve taking credit for someone's work or ideas. Students should exercise caution when writing about psychological research in their own reports to ensure that their own words are used and that information is properly cited. If you have any doubts about your own writing, it is always a good idea to check with your instructor to make sure your writing does not contain plagiarism.

STOP AND THINK

3.7. Describe some ethical issues in reporting research.

THINKING ABOUT RESEARCH

A summary of a research study in psychology is given here. As you read the summary, think about the following questions:

1. What are some ethical issues for this study regarding informed consent?
2. How do you think informed consent was obtained in this study?
3. What steps should the researchers take to protect the confidentiality of the child participants in this study?
4. Ethically, what role is appropriate for parents or guardians to play in the participation of children in research studies? What role do you think they played in this particular study?
5. What are the possible risks to the child participants?
6. If you were an IRB member reviewing this study, what information would you ask the researchers to provide to allow you to determine the risk–benefit analysis for this study?

Research Study. Adolph, K. E., Cole, W. C., Komati, M., Garciaguirre, J. S., Badaly, D., Lingeman, J. M., . . . Sotsky, R. B. (2012). How do you learn to walk? Thousands of steps and dozens of falls per day. *Psychological Science, 23,* 1387–1394. doi: 10.1177/0956797612446346

Purpose of the Study. The researchers investigated naturalistic infant movements, including number of steps, variety of paths, distance moved, and falls over time, during playtime. Their primary research questions were why infants chose to walk instead of crawl, whether measures such as number of steps and falls change with age, and whether different measures of walking skill are related.

Method of the Study. Infants, between 11 and 19 months old, were recorded while playing with caregivers in a lab or home setting. Infants were observed for 15- to 60-min periods while crawling or walking. A total of 151 infants were observed. A number of measures were coded from the videos, including number of falls, time in motion, number of steps per hour, and distance traveled per hour. See Figure 3.3 for the laboratory playroom setup used in the study.

Results of the Study. Comparisons of crawlers and walkers revealed that walkers had more falls, traveled more distance, and spent more time in motion than crawlers, all *ps* $< .05$. Further, even infants who crawled fell, indicating that falls were not exclusive to infants who walked. Results also showed that falls decrease and distance traveled increases with age. Finally, correlational analyses showed that various measures of movement skill were related.

Conclusions of the Study. The researchers concluded from their results that walking provides greater locomotion without increased risk of falls

(Continued)

(Continued)

in infants. They also found that locomotor skills develop with age as measured in natural play movements and that several standard measures of movement used in previous studies are related to functional measures of movement in naturalistic environments.

FIGURE 3.3 ■ Laboratory Playroom Setup

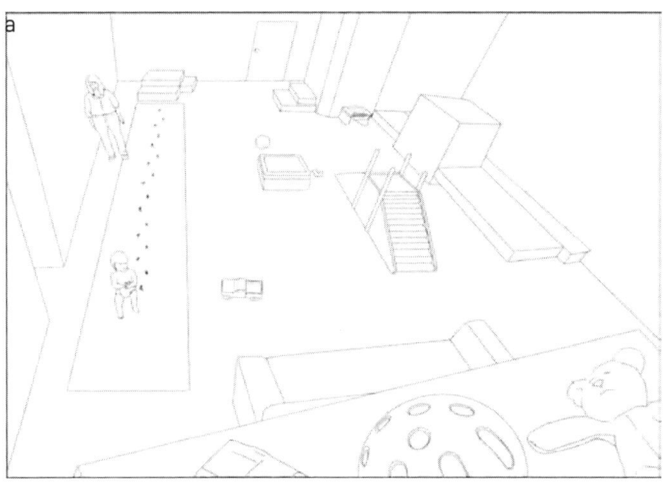

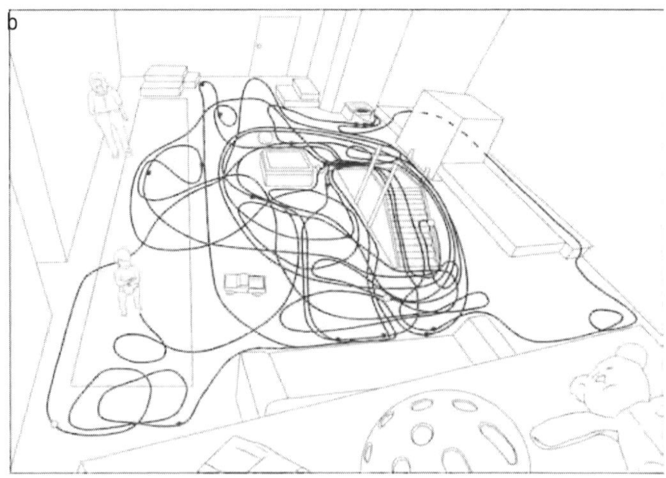

Source: Adolph et al. (2012), Figure 1.

a. a child is shown in a scale drawing of the playroom

b. a typical walking path of a 13-month-old child during 10 min of play superimposed on the drawing

Chapter Summary

Reconsider the questions from the beginning of the chapter:

- **Why do we need ethical guidelines for research?**
  As described in this chapter, ethical guidelines are needed to define the appropriate treatment of subjects in psychological research.
- **How were ethical guidelines for psychological research developed?**
  Current ethical guidelines were derived over the years as the original Nuremberg Code was revised and adopted by the APA and the U.S. government in the *Belmont Report*.
- **Were the Milgram (1963) and Zimbardo (1974) studies ethical? Why or why not?**
  Due to the level of deception and stress caused by both the situation and the participants' experience in the Milgram study and the level of stress experienced by the "prisoners" in the Zimbardo study, many researchers believe that these studies were not ethical.
- **What are the current ethical guidelines for human participants?**
  Current ethical guidelines for psychological research are summarized in Table 3.1.
- **What is an IRB, and what purpose does it serve?**
  The IRB oversees research conducted at each institution. In cases where the researchers may not be the most objective judges of the ethics of their study, the IRB provides a more objective review of the ethics of psychological research.
- **How do ethics influence the way we report research?**
  Ethical guidelines for reporting research necessitate accurate reports of results and proper citation of sources.

Applying Your Knowledge

An instructor wants to better understand how often her students are off task during class time. She sets up a video camera to record the class without their knowledge and then has undergraduate students working in a lab code the videos for time off task and what other things her students were doing during class time (e.g., looking at their phone, sleeping).

- Why do you think the instructor chose to film the students without their knowledge?
- Imagine you were a student in this course. How would you feel about this study? What kinds of things would you be concerned about?
- How could the instructor design her study to be more in line with ethical guidelines?

Test Yourself

1. Suppose you wanted to replicate the Milgram (1963) study to adhere to ethical guidelines currently in place for psychological research. What changes would you need to make to the procedures (described in this chapter) in order to conduct the study ethically?
2. Given what is described in this chapter regarding the informed consent process, make a list of information that should be provided on a consent form for participants in your modified Milgram (1963) study (see Question 1).
3. Why is the debriefing process especially important in studies that involve deception?
4. Write a debriefing statement that you think might be appropriate for the Middlemist et al. (1976) study on male urination described in the chapter.
5. Which of the following is part of the ethical guidelines for research with human participants?
   a. No identifying information may be collected from the participants during the study.
   b. Participants can withdraw from the study at any point before the study begins but not after that point.
   c. Participants must be informed about the study's procedures before they are asked to give consent for their participation.
   d. All of the above.
6. Which of the following is part of the ethical guidelines for research with animal subjects?
   a. Only trained personnel may be involved with the research.
   b. Discomfort of the animals must be minimized as much as possible.
   c. Use of animals and the particular species of animal used must be strongly justified for the study.
   d. All of the above.
7. The ________ provides a set of ethical guidelines provided by the U.S. government that must be adhered to by all researchers conducting studies with human participants.
   a. Nuremberg Code
   b. APA Ethics Code
   c. *Belmont Report*
   d. Institutional Animal Care and Use Committee (IACUC)
8. Informed consent involves ______________.
   a. informing participants about the study and its risks
   b. obtaining participants' consent to run them in the study
   c. explaining all of the researchers' hypotheses before the participant consents
   d. a and b only
9. The *Belmont Report* principle of __________________ involves making certain that harm to the subjects in a research study is reduced such that the benefit of the study is greater than the risk.
10. If I were to discuss a research study without citing the source or authors of the study, I would be guilty of ______________.

SAGE edge™

Visit **edge.sagepub.com/mcbridermstats** to find the answers to the Test Yourself questions above, as well as quizzes, flashcards, and other resources to help you accomplish your coursework goals.

PROBABILITY AND SAMPLING

CONSIDER THE FOLLOWING QUESTIONS AS YOU READ CHAPTER 4

- What role does probability play in selecting a sample and the results obtained from the sample?
- What are the different ways we can sample from a population?
- What is the distribution of sample means?
- What is the difference between probability and convenience samples?
- How accurately can we estimate the population values from a sample?
- What are the advantages of using Internet samples?

LEARNING OBJECTIVES FOR CHAPTER 4

- Compare different methods for creating a sample from a population.
- Evaluate how well a sample represents a population.
- Understand how sampling error occurs.

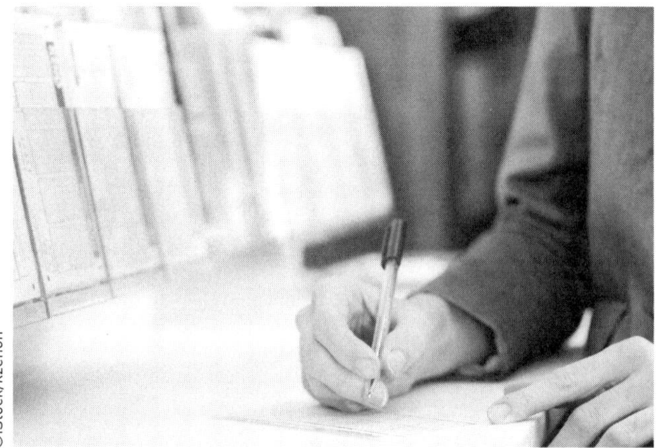

©iStock/kzenon

Photo 4.1
The probability of winning the lottery is very, very low.

PROBABILITY CONCEPTS

What are the odds of winning the lottery (see Photo 4.1)? What do they depend on? Most people do not have a very accurate sense of their chance of winning the lottery—if they did, there would probably be fewer people playing the lottery. How about something easier to imagine—what are the odds of tossing a coin and getting three heads in a row? You may be able to estimate the chance of three heads in a row more easily than the odds of winning the lottery (see Figure 4.1). Okay, how about something more practical—what is the chance it's going to rain today? Although this value is much harder to determine than the odds of winning the lottery or getting three heads in a row, it is typically much more valuable in our everyday lives.

Probability comes into play in many situations in our lives. Collecting data is no exception—we use concepts of probability whenever we collect data from a sample to learn about a population. We also use probability in testing hypotheses by using the data we collect. Therefore, it is important to understand how probability works and how we can use that knowledge to conduct research on behavior and understand the statistics we use to analyze our data.

FIGURE 4.1 ■ Probability of Getting Three Heads in Three Coin Tosses

©iStock/rusm

Possible outcomes from three coin tosses
(H = Heads, T = Tails):

H H H
T H H
H T H
H H T
T T H
H T T
T H T
T T T

8 possible outcomes

1 of the 8 possible outcomes has three heads—chance of this outcome = 1 divided by 8 (proportion of this outcome out of the total number of outcomes) = .125 or 12.5%

Sample Outcomes

Let's consider again our example of tossing a coin and getting three heads in a row (see Figure 4.1). Each time we toss the coin, we are, in fact, sampling the coin with possible outcomes of heads or tails. Our result of three heads in a row is a combination of the outcomes of each of these tosses. If we consider all the possible outcomes of three coin tosses, we can determine the probability of getting three heads in a row. In Figure 4.1, all possible outcomes are shown. How many possible outcomes are there in total? If we consider all possible ways that three coin tosses could play out, we have eight possible outcomes. Only one of these eight outcomes contains three heads (the first one listed in Figure 4.1). We can calculate the proportion out of the total possible outcomes for our result of three heads in a row to determine its probability. From the figure, you can see that each outcome is 0.125 of all of the outcomes of three coin tosses, which is the same as a 12.5% chance of getting this result. This is how we can determine the probability of any result in our data: by considering the total number of possible outcomes and calculating the proportion of those outcomes that correspond with our result of interest. You could calculate the odds of winning the lottery this same way, but there are many more possible outcomes of the number sequence for the lottery than of three coin tosses, so this would be a much more complicated process. However, you can imagine that the proportion of those outcomes for just one number sequence (i.e., the winning number) would be very, very small.

This process using probability can also be used to consider the likelihood of obtaining a specific sample mean from a sample selected from the population we are interested in. In fact, this is how we test hypotheses for our research studies: by considering the likelihood of obtaining the sample mean we got for our sample given what we know about the population we want to learn about.

Sampling From a Population

When we collect data from a sample in a research study, we are doing something quite similar to tossing a coin. When we choose an individual from the population to observe his or her behavior, we are choosing them (and their data) from the population with a certain probability—just as we obtain the outcome of the coin toss. The behavior we observe from that individual is the outcome of the toss, but there are typically more than two possible outcomes. In fact, the outcomes are partly determined by the scale of measurement we use in our study. If we choose a nominal or ordinal scale, then the response choices on those scales will determine the possible measurement outcomes from an individual. A similar constraint occurs with some interval scales—rating scales typically restrict the responses to whole numbers between two values, making the possible outcomes one of those values. Ratio scale values are constrained by a range at the bottom end but can be broken down into smaller and smaller increments (e.g., hours, minutes, seconds, milliseconds), constraining the number of possible outcomes according to the unit of measure. But with ratio scales, there is often a large number of possible outcomes (e.g., any value from zero and up).

Probability will also help us determine how likely it is our sample data came from the population we want to learn about. In fact, probability is a very important part of the hypothesis testing procedure. We will consider how likely it is that we obtained our sample mean from all the possible sample means that could be obtained from samples from our population of interest. This is similar to how we determined the chance of obtaining all heads in three coin tosses using the probability for this outcome relative to all the possible outcomes for three coin tosses. These concepts will be further discussed in later sections of this chapter.

Another way to think about sampling from a population is using a dartboard analogy. You can consider the entire dartboard the population of interest; each location represents a score from someone in that population (see Figure 4.2). The individuals in the sample are the darts. We select an individual (and their score on our measure) by hitting a spot on the dartboard with a dart. A collection of darts is our sample. We are not measuring all the scores in the population. For most populations, this would be too difficult, given their large size. Instead, we choose individuals from the population to measure their behavior (in our analogy, the darts on the board). Then we attempt to estimate the actual population's average score from the average score in our sample. If we assume that the actual population's average score is at the center of the dartboard, you can imagine from the placement of the darts on the board that with different samples, our accuracy in determining the population's average score may differ with each sample we select. With each sample we select, we get a different sample mean. How far off from the center—the population mean—is the sampling error. Remember that sampling error is the difference between the population mean score and the mean score in our sample. Our goal is to reduce sampling error as much as possible. But how can we do that in our study? One way is to use a good sampling technique to choose the individuals from the population for our sample.

FIGURE 4.2 ■ Dartboard Analogy for Sampling From a Population. The Board Represents the Whole Population of Scores; the Darts Represent Scores From Individuals in the Sample

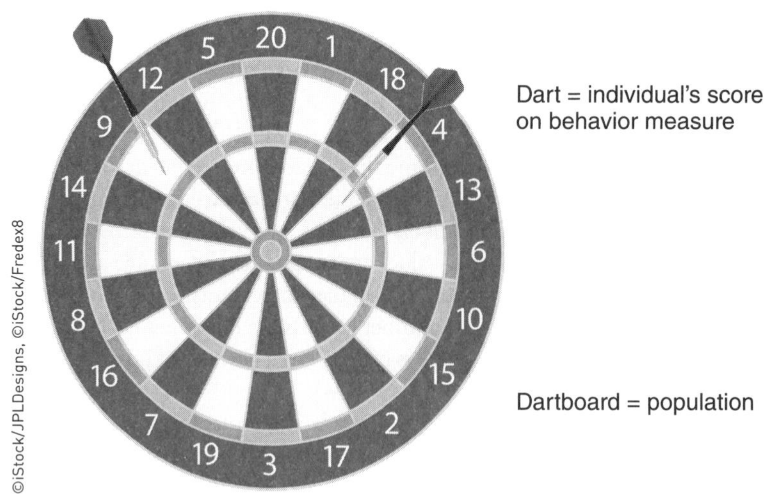

STOP AND THINK

Try sampling on your own by using a pair of dice.

4.1. How many different outcomes are there for a roll of a pair of dice? If you add together the values on each die, what is the most common value outcome from a roll of the two dice? What is the probability of obtaining the most common value on a roll?

4.2. Roll the dice 20 times, and record the total score on each roll. Was the most common outcome your most frequent outcome? Why do you think this result occurred?

4.3. Make a frequency distribution graph of your roll outcomes by using any of the procedures discussed in Chapter 1. Does the distribution of scores appear to be symmetrical or skewed? Explain your answer.

SAMPLING TECHNIQUES

Sampling from a population is a two-step process: (1) select individuals from the population for the sample and (2) observe the behaviors you are interested in (i.e., collect the data) from the individuals in the sample. We will look here at the first step: the different ways we can select the individuals for our sample (see Figure 4.3). This can be an important decision in the research process, because the way a researcher samples from a population for their study can influence the amount of sampling error present in their data. The closer the sample data come to the data that exist in the whole population, the less sampling error you will have. However, making sure that the sample is chosen so that the population is represented well in the sample (e.g., has similar demographics) can be difficult with large samples. Thus, researchers often attempt to balance the desire to reduce sampling error and select a representative sample within the practical limits of selecting individuals from very large populations. This balance plays out in the choice between a **probability sample** and a **convenience or purposive sample**. With both types of sampling techniques, though, the goal is to select a representative sample from the population that will minimize any bias that will cause your sample data to differ from the data that the entire population would provide.

probability sample: A sample chosen such that individuals are chosen with a specific probability

convenience or purposive sample: A sample chosen such that the probability of an individual being chosen cannot be determined

Probability samples are chosen such that everyone in the population has a specific, predetermined chance of being selected at random for the sample. In other words, probability determines how likely any one individual is to be chosen for the sample. A convenience sample, on the contrary, does not allow individuals to be chosen with a known probability from the population. Instead, individuals are chosen from the population based on the convenience of their availability for the sample. Thus, probability samples are more likely to be representative of the population, but convenience samples are much easier to select and are often used in cases where researchers want to learn about a very large population (e.g., all adults, all children ages 5 and 6). This means that sampling error will typically

FIGURE 4.3 ■ Sampling Is the Process of Choosing Individuals From the Population for a Sample in a Study

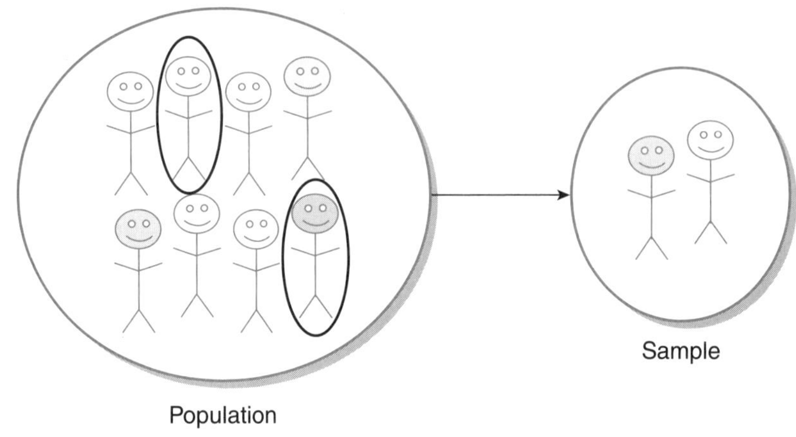

be smaller with probability samples. However, for some behaviors of interest that do not differ much across individuals (e.g., some types of biological or cognitive behaviors), sampling error can be small with either type of sample, meaning that convenience samples can be used without too much concern that the sample is not representative. We will discuss these issues as we look at some different kinds of samples of each type. Table 4.1 provides an overview of the different sampling techniques discussed in the next sections.

Probability Samples

simple random sample: A sample chosen randomly from the population such that each individual has an equal chance of being selected

There are a few different kinds of probability samples that can be used to provide a good representation of the population. In all these samples, the researcher determines the probability of selecting an individual from the population for the sample. However, this can be done in a few different ways. In a **simple random sample**, all individuals in the population have an equal chance of being selected for the sample. Thus, the chance of any one person being selected at the start of the selection process is the number in the sample divided by the total number of people in the population (see Figure 4.4). In the case of a simple random sample, the outcome of interest is that a specific individual is selected for the sample and the total number of outcomes is the total number of individuals in the population. Simple random samples use the random selection process to create a representative sample, but this requires that a researcher first identify all the individuals in the population in order to randomly select some of them. This may be a difficult process for some very large populations. Opinion surveys, such as the one on global warming described in Chapter 1, typically identify individuals in the population through their phone numbers and select them by randomly dialing a phone number to call the individuals selected. This allows everyone with a phone in the population an equal chance of

TABLE 4.1 ■ Overview of Sampling Techniques

Technique	Characteristics	Example	Advantages	Disadvantages
Simple random	Each member of the population has an equal probability of being selected using random sampling.	Students are chosen randomly from a list of all students at a university.	It reduces sampling error by choosing from all members of the population to best represent the population.	It is difficult to ensure that each member of a large population can be chosen in a sample.
Cluster	Clusters of individuals are identified and then a subset of clusters is randomly chosen to sample from.	Doctors who work at hospitals are chosen for a sample by identifying all hospitals in different areas of the United States and then randomly choosing 10 hospitals in each area of the United States to sample from.	It makes it easier to choose members randomly from smaller clusters to better represent the population.	It can ignore segments of the population that are not in the clusters chosen for the sample.
Stratified random	Members of a population are selected such that the proportion of a group in the sample is equal to the proportion of that group in the population using random sampling.	Registered voters are randomly selected from lists of Democrats and Republicans to equal the proportion of registered Democrats and Republicans in the United States.	It reduces bias due to an identified characteristic of the population by equating proportions in the sample and the population for that characteristic to better represent the population.	It is similar to simple random sampling—can be difficult to ensure equal probability of being chosen from a large population.
Convenience	Members of population are chosen based on convenience and on who volunteers.	The sample is chosen from students who volunteer to complete an extra-credit assignment in their psychology course.	It is easier to obtain than probability samples.	It may not represent the population properly due to selection bias because random sampling is not used.

being selected. However, this process might still provide a sample that is biased in some way with more individuals from a certain geographic area, racial or ethnic group, gender, or income bracket. Thus, there are other types of probability samples that can be used to attempt to reduce these sources of bias in the sample.

FIGURE 4.4 ■ Simple Random Sample

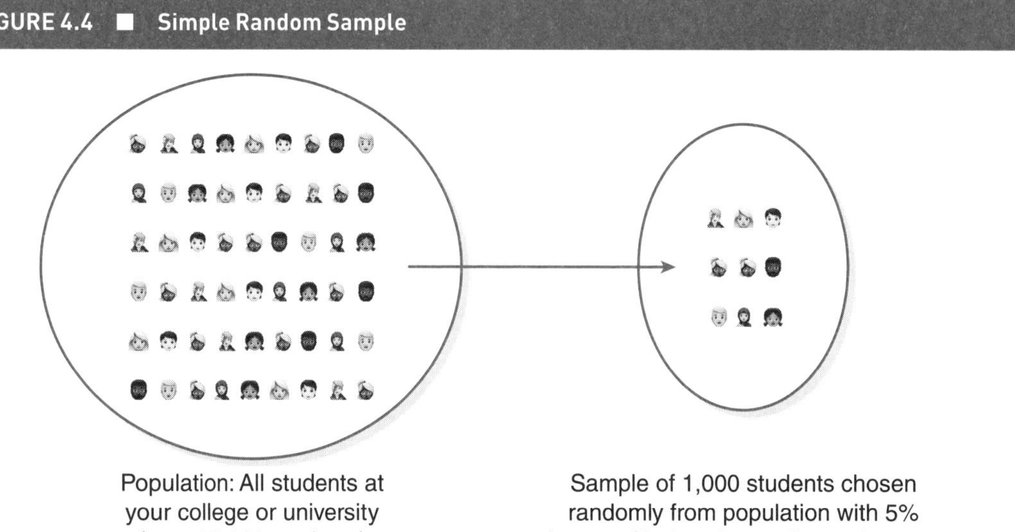

Note: Each individual in the population has an equal chance of being chosen.

cluster sample: A sample chosen randomly from clusters identified in the population

Another type of probability sample is a **cluster sample**. Cluster samples help reduce bias due to oversampling from a group or cluster within the population. These clusters can exist based on being in a certain geographic location, being a member of a club or an institution (such as a college or university), or being a student in a class. For example, imagine you wanted to survey the opinions of college students on the current cost of tuition at their university from a population of all students in your country. Depending on the selection process you choose, a simple random sample might accidentally select more students from cheaper or more costly schools than the average school and bias your sample. A simple random sample might also be difficult to use because you would need to identify all students at all colleges and universities in order to use an unbiased process for selecting your sample. Instead, a cluster sample can allow you to select a sample with a better balance of the cost of tuition at different schools by first identifying a small cluster of schools within each price range you have predetermined and then randomly selecting students from each cluster to ensure that you get students from each tuition cost range in your sample (see Figure 4.5). This will reduce the bias in your sample from the different tuition costs across schools and give you a more representative sample from your population. This cluster sample also allows you to more easily identify the individuals you will sample from the population because you can more easily obtain a list of students from a small set of schools than from all the schools in your country.

stratified random sample: A sample chosen from the population such that the proportion of individuals with a particular characteristic is equivalent in the population and sample

Another method of reducing bias in a sample is to use a **stratified random sample**. Stratified random samples allow researchers to control the percentage of their sample that falls into a specific category. For example, if the population of interest is unequal in gender and men and women differ on the behavior of interest, a researcher might wish to match the percentage of men and women in their sample to the percentage of men and women in

FIGURE 4.5 ■ Cluster Sample: Clusters Randomly Chosen From a Population

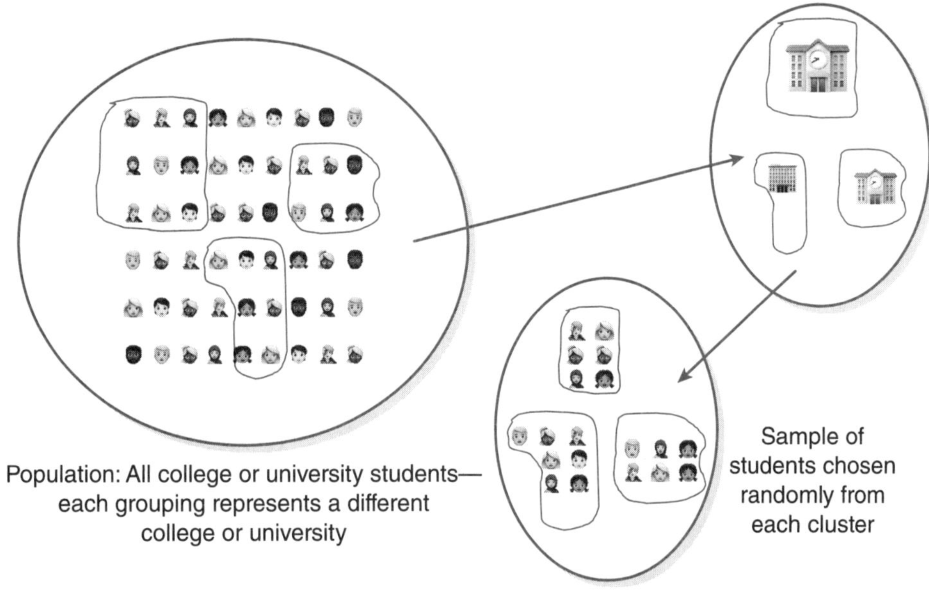

the population to make sure that gender is represented the same way as in the population. This type of stratified sample could be used to select students at your university or college for a study. Suppose you wanted to survey students at your university or college on their use of social media to connect with their friends. If you do not want differences across gender to influence the study results, you could use a stratified random sample to select the same percentage of men and women for your sample as exists in your student population (e.g., 40% men, 60% women). Figure 4.6 illustrates how the selection of this sample might work. Stratified random samples help reduce bias by keeping the representation of different population characteristics equal across the sample and the population. You just need to identify these characteristics ahead of time and select participants in a way that retains the breakdown of those characteristics in your sample. This will ensure that your sample represents the population on these characteristics (e.g., gender, location of residence, income level).

volunteer sample: A sample chosen from the population such that available individuals are chosen based on who volunteers to participate

quota sample: A sample chosen from the population such that available individuals are chosen with equivalent proportions of individuals for a specific characteristic in the population and sample

Convenience Samples

In many cases, the issue of identifying all the individuals in a large population to allow for random sampling is too difficult to overcome. For these situations, researchers often use convenience samples to select a sample from the population. Instead of randomly sampling individuals from the population, convenience samples rely on samples that are convenient to obtain, such as from a university subject pool or from users of the Amazon website Mechanical Turk (MTurk). Convenience samples can take the form of a **volunteer sample**, in which volunteers from a group of individuals make up the sample (see Figure 4.7), or of a **quota sample**, in which the sample is selected from available individuals with equivalent

FIGURE 4.6 ■ Stratified Random Sample

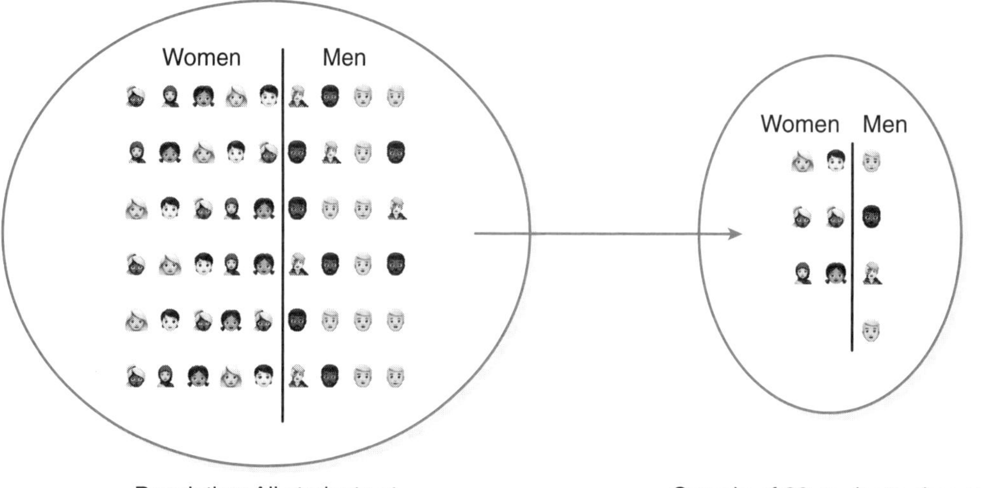

FIGURE 4.7 ■ Convenience Sample

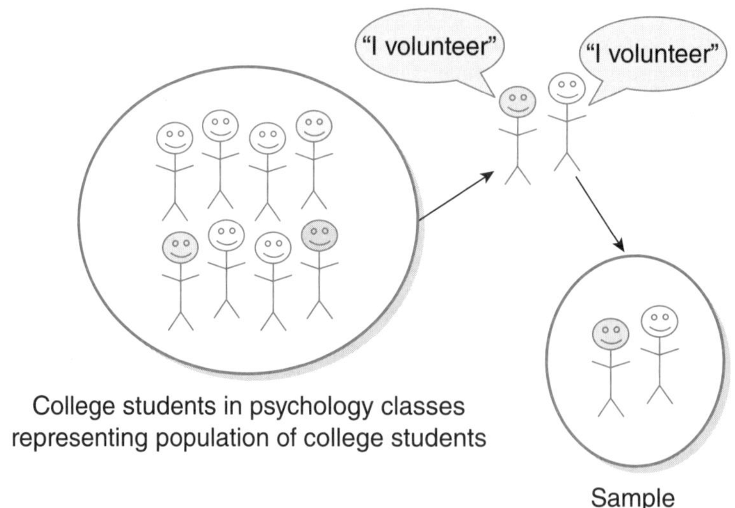

Note: Individuals are chosen from the population based on whom the researcher has easy access to and who volunteers from this group.

proportions to the population on some characteristic (similar to a stratified random sample but without the random selection).

Convenience samples are much easier to obtain than probability samples but can sacrifice some internal validity of the study due to an increase in sampling error. The more biased the sample (i.e., different from the overall population), the more sampling error there is. The more sampling error there is, the harder it is for a researcher to test their hypothesis. This process will become clearer as we go deeper into our discussion of how hypothesis testing and inferential statistics work in later chapters. However, you should be aware that a study conducted with a convenience sample might reduce the researchers' ability to generalize their results to the population of interest due to the possibility of a nonrepresentative sample.

STOP AND THINK

4.4. For each of the following study descriptions, identify both the population of interest and the sampling technique used:

   a. University administrators want to determine the frequency of underage drinking at their school. They randomly select students from the registration records to send an anonymous survey to—with the percentages of men and women in the sample equal to the percentage of men and women at that university.

   b. A researcher is interested in mimicking behaviors that affect cooperation in a task. Psychology students from the participant pool are recruited to answer questions in the presence of a confederate (a researcher pretending to be a participant) who mimics the participants' body postures during the questioning. Then the participants are asked to work with the confederate to complete a task that requires that they work together. The amount of time taken to complete the task is measured.

4.5. Imagine you are designing a study to test whether people with more money are happier than people with less money. Identify the population of interest for your study, and describe how you would select a sample from this population.

DISTRIBUTION OF SAMPLE MEANS INTRODUCTION

The previous section of this chapter described how we conduct the first step of sampling—how to select our sample from the population. This section will focus more on the second step—collecting the data from the individuals in a sample and discovering how probability plays a role in connecting our sample data to our population.

Connecting Samples to Populations

Each time we select a sample from a population (regardless of the sampling technique we use), we are likely to have some amount of sampling error because we are not testing the entire population in our study. One goal we have in sampling is to minimize the sampling error as much as possible. We can do that by using a large sample. Think about how the sample size can influence sampling error. If we have the largest sample possible, we would be testing the entire population. In that case, there would be no sampling error. But the largest sample possible is typically too large to include in our study. Therefore, we reduce the size of the sample to make it more reasonable to conduct our study. But the more we reduce the sample size, the fewer people we have from the whole population to collect our data from, which will increase our chance of collecting data that differ from the entire population. Each time we reduce our sample size, we increase the risk that our sample data differs from the entire population because we are removing people that are in the population from our sample. If we decrease the sample size all the way down to one person, we would maximize our sampling error (not what we want) because we are basing our data on just one individual, who is most likely to differ from the mean of the population.

Look back at Figure 4.2. Testing just one individual from the population (a sample size of one) is like estimating the population mean from just one dart throw. But if we make more and more dart throws, we're more likely to average those dart throws to a value closer to the center of the dartboard, where the population average is. Thus, we want to choose a sample size that is big enough to reduce sampling error but small enough that we will be able to test that sample in our study. A large-enough sample will reduce the error in the data and give us a better estimate of the actual population average. In other words, it will be a more valid (i.e., accurate) measure of the population data. When we estimate sampling error to calculate inferential statistics for our data, we will use the sample size in our calculations.

variability: The spread of scores in a distribution

How much the scores differ from each other in the sample is also an important factor in connecting our sample to the population. The larger the difference between scores (called **variability**) in the sample data, the less reliable it is as an estimate of the population data. If you consider the dartboard again, you can imagine how the darts would look for two players—one with good aim and one with poor aim (see Figure 4.8). Both samples (sets of darts) are centered on the population average at the center of the dartboard, but the top sample is clustered closer to that average and the bottom sample is clustered farther from that average. The top sample (with good aim) has lower variability in where the darts landed, so we can trust that sample as more likely to be closer to the population data than the highly variable sample at the bottom. If the same people threw those darts again (or we collected new samples in the same way from the population), we are more likely to get a similar set of data from the player in the top panel than from the player in the bottom panel, making the "good aim" samples more reliable in their measure of the population average that we want to learn about. When we estimate sampling error to calculate inferential statistics for our data, we will use the variability in our data in our measure of the reliability of our estimate of the population data. Thus, both the sample size and the sample variability will be used in our estimate of the sampling error in our data.

The Distribution of Sample Means

Something else that is important when we want to learn about a behavior of interest for a population is to conduct multiple studies to test different samples from the population.

FIGURE 4.8 ■ Samples of Darts on a Dartboard, One With Low Variability (Panel A) and One With High Variability (Panel B)

Why is this important? Well, just as the scores within a sample can differ from one another, the average scores we get from different samples can also differ from each other. This means that with just one sample, we can be very close to the population average or very far from the population average. That is why we do not assume that we have *proven* something about a behavior from a single study. A single study (with a single sample) provides support for knowledge about behavior but does not provide definitive knowledge about behavior.

With just one sample, we might not have measured the population data accurately. Often, researchers will conduct multiple studies (sometimes published together in one article, sometimes in separate articles) to investigate a behavior so that they can be sure the results they have are both valid and reliable. They want to be able to make accurate conclusions from the data, and that often means showing the same (or similar) results with different samples.

distribution of sample means: The distribution of all possible sample means for all possible samples of a particular size from a population

Let's consider how the mean scores from different samples might look relative to the actual population average. Figure 4.9 shows a distribution of possible sample means (i.e., the **distribution of sample means**) for samples pulled from a population with a mean score of 100 on some measure of interest. The mean score from each sample for a large number of samples selected from this population is plotted on the graph; the mean scores from the samples are shown on the x-axis, and the number of samples show that mean on the y-axis (you can review frequency distribution graphs in Chapter 1 if you do not remember how this works). You can see that most of the sample means cluster around the population mean of 100, but there are sample means as high as 115 and as low as 85 for the different samples. If we choose just one sample from this distribution (as we would by selecting one sample from the population and collecting data from this sample), the sample mean might be close to the population mean or it could be far from the population mean. It's more likely (than not) that we will get a sample mean near the population mean, but we could still by chance select a sample with a mean that is very different from the population mean. Thus, probability plays a role in how well we estimate the data for the population with the data from our sample.

The differences you see in the sample means in Figure 4.9 provide one explanation for the flip-flopping of research findings we sometimes see reported in the media. You may have seen reports stating that "red wine drinkers had better levels of HDL cholesterol" (Oaklander, 2015) along with statements in other reports saying, "It turns out that there's

FIGURE 4.9 ■ Distribution of Sample Means From a Population With an Actual Mean of 100

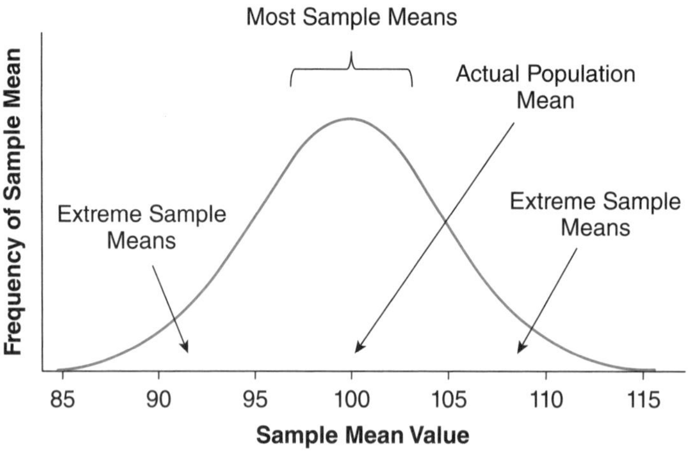

no information to suggest that red wine is better than any other form of alcohol for your heart" (Kane, 2012). Which one should you believe? The problem is that each of these reports may be based on just one study that contains a single sample from the population. One of these samples might be closer to the actual population mean for the measure than the other. But we do not know where in the distribution of sample means we are in these studies without the inferential statistics. In fact, inferential statistics rely on the distribution of sample means to provide some probability that our hypothesis about the population is supported by our data. We will discuss how this works further in later chapters when we talk about hypothesis testing. For now, keep in mind that data from one sample will not tell us everything we need to know about the research questions we are asking with our study because, by chance, we may not have collected data from our sample that does a good job of representing the population data.

RECRUITING PARTICIPANTS

Regardless of the type of sampling technique chosen, researchers must consider how to actually recruit the participants for a study. In other words, how are the participants contacted to let them know about the study, and what incentives are offered for their participation? The issue of how to contact the participants to recruit them is related to the selection mechanism in some types of studies. For example, if you are randomly choosing participants from the phone book, it may make sense to contact them by phone. If you are randomly choosing participants from a list of students at a university, you may only be provided with certain types of contact information (e.g., campus or permanent addresses, e-mail addresses) that will limit the means available for contacting the participants. Many university and college psychology departments have participant pools available to researchers that provide a standard means of contacting participants for volunteer samples (e.g., participant sign-up board or website). The means of contacting participants is an important issue, as it may affect the sample size obtained for a study. Researchers should carefully consider recruitment techniques that may be most effective for their population. For example, younger participants may be more likely to respond to e-mail contacts, whereas older participants may be more likely to respond to phone contacts. If you are considering recruiting acquaintances for a research study, the ethics of such recruitment should also be considered. For example, what is the best way to approach an acquaintance about participating in a study to maximize sample size but also to reduce coercion?

Incentives can also have an impact on the sample size obtained. For established institution participant pools, there may be incentives built into the recruitment process, such as completion of an assignment or extra credit in psychology courses. In these cases, an alternative assignment must also be available to students in the course to reduce coercion. Other incentives, such as payment or entrance in a drawing, may be possibilities available to researchers if the resources are available. Again, coercion issues should be considered for these incentives as well. Not all studies require incentives; individuals may be willing to participate in short studies without such incentives (e.g., completing a short survey on the street). Longer and more arduous studies may require an incentive to recruit a sufficient sample size. However, as described previously, this may also create a situation where the incentive or lack of incentive adds bias to the study.

One question you may be thinking about (especially if you are working on your own research project for your methods course) is how many subjects is enough. The answer to this question depends on several factors, including the type of study you are conducting, the type of data you are collecting, the type of population you are sampling, and the practicality of your sampling technique. In some cases, you may be collecting several measurements for each dependent variable from each subject (e.g., as in cognitive studies). For this type of study, you may not need many subjects per condition. If you take a look at some studies on perception and memory, you will see that they include sample sizes of between 20 and 50 subjects per condition. However, if you are only collecting one measurement per subject or are asking subjects to complete surveys and questionnaires, you may need to include a larger sample. Many such studies include sample sizes in the hundreds. If you are sampling from a small population (e.g., children with autism), you may need to use a small sample of only 10 to 20 subjects due to lack of availability of individuals in this population and the difficulty you may have in recruiting such subjects. Thus, researchers must consider a number of factors when they decide how large a sample is sufficient for their study.

USING THE INTERNET TO SAMPLE

Internet sample: A sample chosen from the population by recruiting on the Internet

Samples obtained using the Internet are becoming more frequent in recent psychological research. Many types of observation techniques can be used with an **Internet sample**, including surveys and systematic observations. Experiments that require systematic presentation of stimuli can be reproduced for presentation on the Internet to individual participants. See http://psych.hanover.edu/research/exponnet.html for a list of current psychological studies being conducted on the Internet ("Retrospection," 2008).

One popular source of Internet samples is MTurk. MTurk has a database of "workers" who are paid a small amount of money for completing online research studies and surveys. MTurk even has an option to select participants who have certain characteristics (e.g., only men or women, people who smoke, individuals who identify with a specific ethnicity). Another online option for researchers is to use the technology at their college or university to recruit students by sending out a recruitment e-mail with a link to the study to an e-mail list of the students (see Photo 4.2).

PeopleImages/istockphoto

Photo 4.2 Many current studies, especially those involving surveys, are administered over the Internet.

According to Birnbaum (2001), advantages of Internet samples over laboratory studies include use of larger and more diverse samples, fewer opportunities for bias due to experimenter interactions with participants, fewer constraints on the time and location of data collection, less time needed to collect a sample, and fewer researchers needed to supervise the study procedures. Many researchers have also shown that data collected with Internet samples produced similar effects to samples collected in the laboratory (Birnbaum, 2001; Krantz & Dalal, 2000).

The studies comparing lab and Internet samples show that Internet samples tend to be more demographically diverse (Birnbaum, 2001). Thus, Internet sampling may yield samples that are a better representation of large, general populations. However, there are some issues that researchers should be aware of when they choose to use an Internet sample (Birnbaum, 2001). For example, some smaller subgroups in the population may require extra work to include in the sample because the number with access to the Internet may be too small to allow for adequate sampling. Researchers may need to contact special interest groups to recruit them for the study to achieve the best representation possible. In addition, it may be difficult to control who completes a study on the Internet, making stratified random and quota samples more difficult to obtain and making it difficult to monitor repeat participation from the same individuals. It may also be difficult to balance group size in between-subjects designs. Finally, it is more difficult to monitor participants during the study procedure to rule out sources of bias (such as distractions) for Internet samples. Nonetheless, Internet samples show great promise in making sampling easier for some types of psychological studies.

Also, providing incentives is important in recruiting Internet samples. The type of incentive a researcher offers may affect the sample size obtained in an Internet sample more often than in studies where data collection is done in a laboratory or in other in-person environments because it may be harder to gain a participant's attention with an Internet study. On the other hand, the feeling of anonymity that comes with completing a study on the Internet may also be a benefit in recruiting Internet samples. Finally, Internet samples may be larger than samples obtained by other means; thus, researchers must also consider available resources when choosing an incentive for an Internet study.

THINKING ABOUT RESEARCH

A summary of a research study in psychology is given here. As you read the summary, think about the following questions:

1. What behavior(s) were the researchers observing in this study?
2. Which sampling technique do you think the researchers used in this study? What are some disadvantages of this sampling technique?
3. What was the population of individuals they sampled from?
4. What sources of bias do you think exist for samples obtained from the Internet?
5. Why do you think the researchers obtained two separate samples in this study? What advantage is there for obtaining two separate samples?

(Continued)

(Continued)

Research Study. Seli, P., Carriere, J. S. A., Wammes, J. D., Risko, E. F., Schacter, D. L., & Smilek, D. (2018). On the clock: Evidence for the rapid and strategic modulation of mind wandering. *Psychological Science, 29,* 1247–1256. doi:10.1177/0956797618761039

Purpose of the Study. This study examined how mind wandering works. Previous studies have shown that mind wandering differs depending on the difficulty of a task. The researchers tested the hypothesis that people can control their mind wandering during a task when they know their attention will be needed in the task.

FIGURE 4.10 ■ Clock Face Used in the Task in the Seli et al. (2018) Study

Source: Seli et al. (2018).

FIGURE 4.11 ■ Mind Wandering Results From Each Sample in the Seli et al. (2018) Study—Clock Quarters Are Shown on the x-axis—Overall, Mind Wandering Was Lower in the Last Quarter Than in the Second Quarter

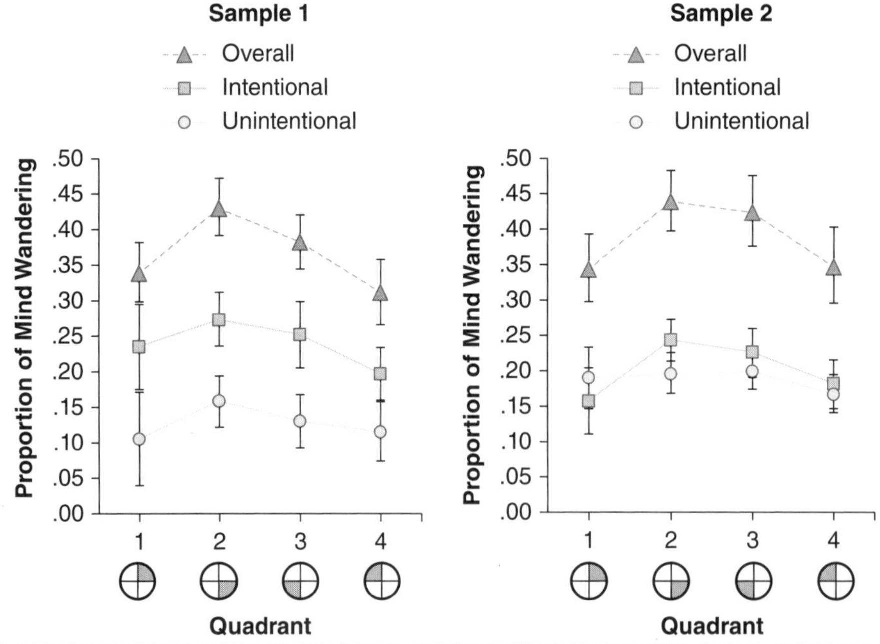

Source: Seli et al. (2018).

Method of the Study. Participants were recruited in two separate samples of 60 people from MTurk and were compensated for completing the study. Participants were asked to complete a task where they viewed a clock face with no numbers and a single tick hand that rotated around the clock face (see Figure 4.10). They were asked to press the space bar each time the clock hand reached the 12:00 position as accurately as possible. Each revolution of the tick hand took 20 s. Thought probes occurred throughout this task; five probes were presented during each quarter segment of the clock. Thought probes asked participants to indicate if their thoughts were on or off task at the moment the probe appeared. Off-task responses were separated into "intentional" and "unintentional" mind wandering.

Results of the Study. Error rates for pressing the space bar at the correct time were measured along with rates of mind wandering in the four different segments of the clock task (i.e., each quarter of the clock). The researchers compared mind wandering responses across the different clock segments and found that mind wandering (intentional and unintentional combined) in the last segment (the quarter just before 12:00) was lower than earlier segments of the clock (see Figure 4.11). The result was found in both of the samples. Overall, error rates were low and were not related to mind wandering rates.

Conclusions of the Study. From the results showing that mind wandering decreased as the time to respond neared, the researchers concluded that mind wandering can be controlled by focusing attention on a task when it is needed. The researchers suggest that a question to be explored in future research is the role working memory abilities might play in control of mind wandering.

Chapter Summary

- **What role does probability play in selecting a sample and the results obtained from the sample?**
  Probability plays an important role in both selecting a sample and how well the sample data estimate the population data and also in obtaining samples that provide the best representative sample. In probability samples, the chance of any individual being selected for the sample is known and can be determined ahead of time. The sample mean also has a particular probability of estimating the population mean that may not be known while collecting the sample.
- **What are the different ways we can sample from a population?**
  Probability samples can be created with a particular chance for each member of the population to be selected. Convenience samples do not select individuals based on chance but instead select a sample based on an individual's availability for the study.
- **What is the distribution of sample means?**
  The distribution of sample means is a frequency distribution containing the sample means from all possible samples selected from a population. It is a useful distribution (as we will see in later chapters) in

(Continued)

(Continued)

determining the probability that a hypothesis is true.

- **What is the difference between probability and convenience samples?**
  In probability samples, the probability of an individual being chosen from the population is known, and participants are chosen randomly from the population or a subset of the population. For convenience samples, the probability of an individual being chosen is not known, and the participants are chosen in a nonrandom manner.
- **How accurately can we estimate the population values from a sample?**
  The accuracy of our estimate of the population data depends on several factors, including the sample size and the variability of the scores in the sample. However, for any sample, with a set probability that we choose, we can calculate a range of values that the population mean likely falls within.
- **What are the advantages of using Internet samples?**
  The Internet is a useful tool for recruiting a representative sample that may be larger than a sample that is recruited in person. Using the Internet can help a researcher access a subject sample that is more varied in age and ethnicity than convenience samples from college student populations.

Applying Your Knowledge

The other day I was looking for a hotel to book for an upcoming trip using Hotels.com. I looked over the reviews for a few hotels in the area I wanted to stay in and saw that responses to the "Would Recommend This Hotel" banner ranged from 85% to 98%. Many products now offer this kind of information on the web, and I have contributed to such information myself in the past. I wanted to make sure I chose a hotel I would be happy with, so I began to wonder how valid the percentages were judging the quality of the hotel. Consider the following questions, which are relevant to deciding how valid this kind of information is for consumer products you may be choosing for yourself:

- What sort of differences might exist in the sample from the overall population based on how this information is obtained?
- How much does the sample size contribute to the validity of this information?
- How large a sample size would you feel comfortable with to offset sampling error in the reported percentage?

Test Yourself

1. For each of the following study descriptions, describe how you would select a sample from the population using one of the techniques described in this chapter:

a. You want to know how adults in your country feel about the issue of immigration.
b. You want to know how anxious college seniors are about their job prospects.
c. You want to learn about how people remember information based on their mood.

2. The distribution of sample means shows __________.
   a. the frequency of scores in a sample
   b. the frequency of means from all samples from a population
   c. the sampling error that exists in a sample
   d. the sampling error that exists in a population
3. Sampling error will only be present in convenience samples, not in probability samples.
   a. True
   b. False
4. Our measure of sampling error is affected by __________.
   a. sample size
   b. population size
   c. variability in the data
   d. both a and b
   e. both a and c
5. Probability plays a role in __________.
   a. selecting a representative sample
   b. estimating sampling error
   c. determining the mean of our sample
   d. all of the above
6. A probability sample typically has less sampling error than a convenience sample.
   a. True
   b. False
7. In a simple random sample, __________.
   a. the sample matches the proportions in the population on some characteristic (e.g., gender)
   b. each individual in the population has an equal chance of being selected
   c. individuals are selected at random from preexisting groups in the population
8. In what ways are probability samples preferable to convenience samples?
9. Despite the superiority of probability samples, why do many psychological studies use convenience samples?
10. Suppose you were conducting a survey study to learn about drinking behaviors for the population of students at your school with a quota sample. In your sample, you want to be sure that you represent the population according to year in school and gender. Describe how you might choose your sample for this study and how your survey would be administered.
11. What are some advantages of collecting samples by using the Internet?
12. In a __________ sample, individuals are chosen at random from the population but are chosen in proportions equivalent to proportions that exist in the population (e.g., 90% right-handed, 10% left-handed).
    a. simple random
    b. haphazard
    c. quota
    d. stratified random

(Continued)

(Continued)

13. In a __________ sample, individuals who volunteer from the population are chosen for the sample.
    a. simple random
    b. convenience
    c. quota
    d. stratified random
14. Sampling error is __________.
    a. a type of sampling technique
    b. the difference in observations between the population and the sample
    c. an error introduced into a study by the researcher's bias
    d. none of the above
15. The __________ is the group of individuals a researcher wants to learn about, whereas a __________ is the group of individuals who serve as subjects in a study.
16. In a __________ sample, all members of the population have an equal chance of being selected.

SAGE edge™

Visit **edge.sagepub.com/mcbridermstats** to find the answers to the Test Yourself questions above, as well as quizzes, flashcards, and other resources to help you accomplish your coursework goals.

5

HOW PSYCHOLOGISTS USE THE SCIENTIFIC METHOD

Data Collection Techniques and Research Designs

CONSIDER THE FOLLOWING QUESTIONS AS YOU READ CHAPTER 5

- How do psychologists observe behavior?
- What are some common techniques for observing and recording behavior (i.e., collecting data) in different situations?
- How do psychologists use observations to learn about behavior?
- What questions about behavior do the different research methods allow psychologists to answer?
- Which research method is best when asking about the cause of behavior?

LEARNING OBJECTIVES FOR CHAPTER 5

- Compare different ways to observe behavior in a research study.
- Understand the goals of different research designs.
- Connect ways to observe behavior with research designs they can be used with.
- Evaluate internal and external validity of different research designs.

external validity: The degree to which the results of a study apply to individuals and realistic behaviors outside the study

Imagine that you work in a busy corporate office. One day your boss comes to you for advice. A report found that productivity in the office tends to decline later in the afternoon, and he or she wants to find a way to increase productivity during this time period. Your boss's suggestion is that having a cappuccino machine in the office break room may influence workers to drink more coffee after lunch, in turn giving them more energy and productivity in the afternoon (see Photo 5.1). You are asked to use your knowledge of research methods to find out if the suggestion is a good one. How would you conduct a study to provide the advice your boss is looking for?

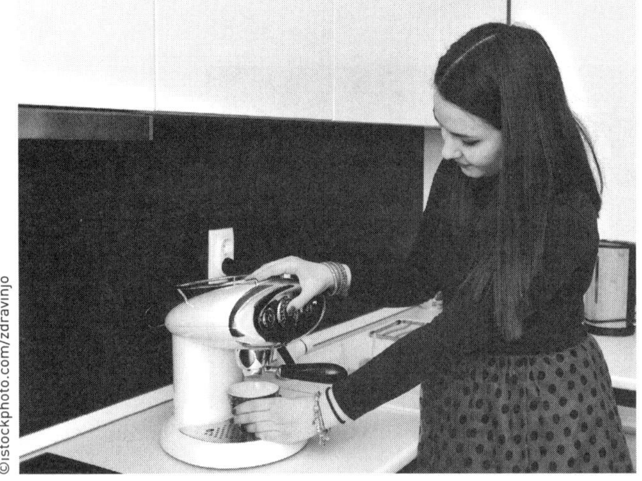

Photo 5.1 Your boss wants you to use your research knowledge to investigate whether adding a cappuccino machine to the break room at work would increase afternoon work productivity.

In this chapter, the methods psychologists use to learn about behavior are briefly introduced to provide an overview of some of the main data collection techniques and research designs used in psychological research. The goal is to illustrate some ways psychologists apply the scientific methods described in Chapter 1 to the study of behavior. Figure 5.1 illustrates where we are in the steps involved in the research process when we focus on the design of the study. The choices of data collection techniques and research design are made by the researcher. These choices depend on the type of behavior that is of interest and what kinds of questions one wants to answer about the behavior. Validity also plays a role in these choices. **External validity** is the degree to which the behavior observed in the study is realistic, would occur naturally, and can be generalized beyond the boundaries of the study to other individuals and situations. How much external validity a study has is important because the goal of research is to gain knowledge about behavior that applies to a large group of individuals in their everyday lives, not just to the individual study participants with any situational restrictions the study included. In other words, the conclusions need to generalize beyond the study itself. Some of the observation techniques and research designs that psychologists use tend to allow for higher external validity than others. However, in many cases, the higher the external validity in a study, the lower the **internal validity**. The study you would describe for your boss would likely have good external validity because it is designed to look at your coworkers' typical workplace behaviors.

internal validity: The degree to which a study provides causal information about behavior

Internal validity is the degree to which a study provides a good test of a causal hypothesis, where alternative explanations of the data can be ruled out. A study with high internal validity provides causal information about behavior. To increase the internal validity of a study, a researcher controls for extraneous factors that can affect the observations. With more control over the factors in a study, internal validity increases, but behavior may become more artificial and lower the external validity of that study. The study you design for your boss likely has lower internal than external validity because it would be difficult to control for many of the additional factors that could influence your coworkers' afternoon work productivity. For example, word about your study might get out to your

FIGURE 5.1 ■ Steps in the Research Process: Designing the Study

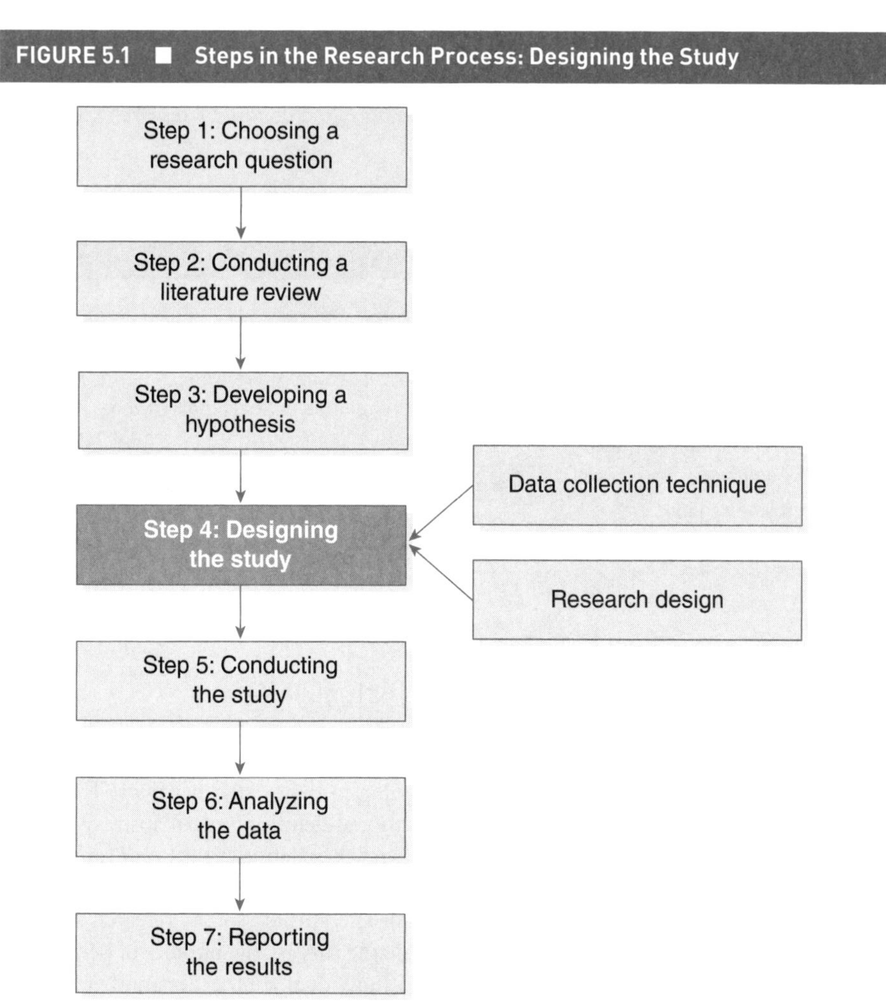

coworkers, and they might change their behavior as a result of their knowledge of the study, not as a result of the new cappuccino machine. This means there is an alternative explanation of the productivity, making it difficult for you to conclude that the cappuccino machine had an effect on its own. As we discuss the different types of studies that can be conducted by psychologists, you will see that internal and external validities are important concepts in research.

Another important issue in observing behavior is making certain that the observations are *reliable*. For some observation techniques, this means making sure that observers are categorizing behaviors the same way. For other techniques, this means making certain that different items on a survey or questionnaire designed to measure a specific behavior all provoke similar responses from the research participants. In other words, reliability in a survey means that the participants' responses are similar from item to item or from one time they complete the survey to the next. Thus, reliability is important to consider when you design a study and choose an observation technique, but how you increase reliability depends on the observation technique you are using.

Internal validity, external validity, and reliability are important concepts to consider in every research design. We will come back to these topics throughout this and additional chapters as we consider different ways to design and conduct a research study.

STOP AND THINK

5.1. For each of the following descriptions, indicate if it is an issue with internal validity, external validity, or reliability:

a. Subjects in a study complete a task in the lab in a different way than they would ordinarily do it.

b. Subjects' scores on a mood questionnaire differ each time they complete the questionnaire.

c. Different groups of subjects receive different teaching techniques to compare the effectiveness of the techniques on learning. However, the subjects in the different groups also differ in their preexisting knowledge of the topic being taught.

DATA COLLECTION TECHNIQUES

How do psychologists observe behavior? When researchers are planning to observe a behavior, they must first decide how they are going to define that behavior. This is the operational definition of the behavior. An operational definition of an abstract concept (depression, memory ability, etc.) allows the researcher to define the concept for the purpose of measurement and data collection. Thus, an operational definition is a definition of an abstract concept that makes it concrete for the purpose of the research study. If *social behavior* is of interest, the researcher may define this as "the number of people who spend time in groups," "the number of times an individual approaches another individual to interact with him or her," or "the score on a questionnaire that asks about social behaviors." There are clearly many ways to define a particular behavior for data collection. Researchers choose an operational definition for behavior that they expect will provide the best (i.e., accurate and reliable) method of learning about the behavior they are interested in. In other words, they define the concept so that it can be measured by a specific behavior (or set of behaviors). See Table 5.1 for some examples of operational definitions of different concepts. The goal in creating an operational definition for your study is to be as specific as possible so that the way you are measuring behavior is clear to and consistent across everyone involved in the study. The techniques described in the following sections are different ways in which psychologists collect data about behavior. As you will see, the choice of technique is linked to the operational definition the researcher is using. Table 5.2 provides an overview and comparison of these techniques in terms of the most common research designs that employ these techniques.

TABLE 5.1 ■ Examples of Operational Definitions

Concept	Possible operational definitions
Depression	Score on a mood questionnaire
	Number of times someone has thought about suicide in the past month
	Measure of certain neurotransmitters in areas of the brain
Problem-solving ability	Amount of time it takes to complete a puzzle
	Number of problems solved correctly
	Score on a standardized test
Learning	Difference in score from pretest to posttest
	Change in time to complete a problem or test
	Change in confidence ratings to perform a skill

TABLE 5.2 ■ Comparing Data Collection Techniques

Technique	Definition	Common research methods
Naturalistic observation	Observing individuals' behavior in their normal environments	Correlational, quasi-experiment
Surveys and questionnaires	Individuals responding to items in written form or on the Internet	Correlational, quasi-experiment, experiment
Systematic observation	Collecting systematic behaviors in controlled tasks	Experiment, quasi-experiment, correlational, case study
Archival data	Using available records to collect observations	Correlational, case study

©istockphoto.com/Mila Landau

Photo 5.2 Studying animal behavior in the animals' natural habitat often involves naturalistic observation.

Naturalistic Observation

A once-popular show on the Animal Planet cable network called *Meerkat Manor* followed packs of meerkats as they interacted with each other within the pack, with other packs of meerkats, and with the environment they live in. The show was narrated to make it more entertaining, but the animals' natural behaviors displayed on the show were observed and exhibited as they occurred in their normal environment. In other words, the researchers for the show used **naturalistic observation** to learn about meerkat behaviors. Naturalistic observation is used when a researcher wants to learn about behavior that naturally occurs for an individual without influencing the behavior. The goal of naturalistic observation is to be unobtrusive so that the researcher does not affect the observed individuals' behavior. Naturalistic observation is often used by researchers interested in observing the behavior of animals in their natural environment or children who are in specific environments (both natural and contrived).

naturalistic observation: A data collection technique involving noninvasive observation of individuals in their natural environments

To understand observed behaviors using naturalistic observation, a researcher must develop a coding scheme to categorize the exhibited behaviors of the participants. This allows the researcher to quantify (i.e., count) and summarize the behaviors for the group of individuals observed. The coding scheme depends on the operational definition of the behavior the researcher is using. In other words, the behaviors the researcher indicates are part of the operational definition become categories of behaviors in the coding scheme. For example, if researchers are studying *helping* behaviors with naturalistic observations, they may define helping behavior as approaching someone who appears to need help (e.g., has dropped something, has a broken-down car, is unable to open a door) and offering help or acting to help the person. Thus, observers may sit on a university quad and count behaviors they observe that fit into categories such as "asking someone if he or she needs help," "helping someone pick something up," "giving someone directions when asked." This allows researchers to quantify the different behaviors they see. The researchers can then describe helping behaviors according to their coding scheme to indicate the frequency of helping behaviors overall for this situation and group of individuals and which types of behaviors occur more often than others.

Developing a coding scheme generally involves defining categories of behavior that fit the type of behavior being observed. The operational definition of the behavior should guide the selection of categories of behaviors that qualify. It is important to clearly define these categories so that observers are clear about what behaviors they are looking for when they observe the individuals of interest in a study. Clear categories also help multiple observers be more consistent in how they classify the behaviors they are looking for (more on this issue in the next paragraph). Finally, the coding scheme can involve counting the number of certain types of behaviors and/or the amount of time individuals engage in the defined behaviors either in set time intervals or across the entire span of the observation period.

The primary advantage in using naturalistic observation to study behavior is that the behavior is likely to be more realistic compared with some of the other techniques. This can increase the external validity of a study. However, this technique has its disadvantages. It can sometimes be difficult to be unobtrusive. The presence of an observer can easily change the behavior of the individuals being observed. This is an issue that came up for the *Meerkat Manor* show. Camera crews followed the meerkats closely all the time to record their behaviors for the show, and their presence may have affected the behaviors they observed. Thus, researchers using this technique must take great care to ensure that they are not influencing the behavior they are observing simply by being present in an individual's environment. Another drawback to naturalistic observation is that it can be very time-consuming. The observers must wait for the behavior they are interested in to be exhibited by the participants. Thus, this technique can be more time intensive and consume more resources than other observation techniques. A third disadvantage is that multiple observers (observing the same or different individuals) may not be recording the behaviors they observe in the same way. To deal with this problem, most studies that involve naturalistic observations include training of the observers to ensure that they are collecting the data in the same way. In fact, the similarity in coding of the data is typically measured and reported in such studies. This is known as **interobserver or interrater reliability** (how similarly the observers are observing or coding the data). A measure of interobserver or interrater reliability is usually reported based on the percentage overlap in the way the observations are classified across multiple observers. To illustrate this concept, consider the previously described study that looked at helping behaviors. In this study, it is likely that more than one person would observe on the quad (either at the same time or at different times) to allow enough helping behaviors to occur and be observed. If the observers code the behaviors differently (e.g., one observer counts bending over to help as "helping someone pick something up," whereas another observer only counts this behavior if someone actually picks up something someone dropped), the internal validity of the study decreases because the observers will have different operational definitions of the behaviors.

interobserver or interrater reliability: A measure of the degree to which different observers rate behaviors in similar ways

Chiang (2008) provides an example of a study that used naturalistic observations. In this study, 32 children with autism were observed to investigate aspects of their spontaneous communication. The children were videotaped in their natural environments (classrooms at their school), while they completed normal, everyday activities (lunch, free time, academic activities, etc.). In the article reporting the study (published in the journal *Autism*), Chiang described the coding schemes developed to summarize and understand the communication behaviors that were seen in the tapes viewed by the observers coding those behaviors (speech or writing; vocalizations that were not identified as words; eye contact; common gestures such as hugging, waving, or nodding; etc.). Figure 5.2 shows the proportions of these behaviors recorded by the observers for different levels of prompting by the participants' teachers or caregivers (highest prompt level [HPL]). The interobserver or interrater reliability (above 80%) was also reported to provide evidence that the observers were coding the data in a similar manner. Chiang concluded that children with autism exhibit a range of communicative behaviors across the different settings and suggested a model for future studies of spontaneous communication in individuals with autism. The issue of intrusiveness can be considered for this study. How much did the presence of the video camera affect the participants' behavior? Were participants aware of the video camera? If so, were they more self-conscious or uncomfortable about their behavior because of its presence? The issue of obtrusiveness should be considered whenever naturalistic observations are used in a study.

FIGURE 5.2 ■ Results From the Chiang (2008) Study Showing the Proportions of Different Behaviors Coded by the Observers for Different Prompting Levels (Highest Prompt Levels [HPL]) by the Participants' Teachers or Caregivers

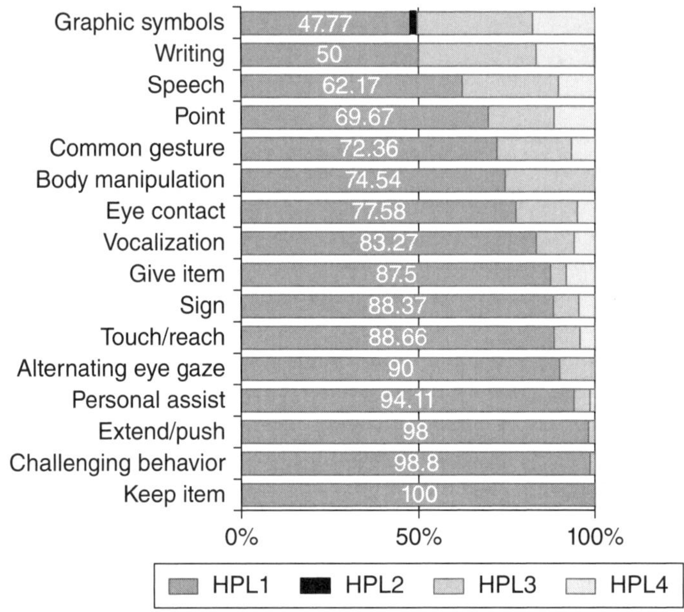

Surveys and Questionnaires

The other data collection techniques we will discuss are more obtrusive than the naturalistic observation technique because they involve some type of interaction with the research participants. One of these techniques commonly used in psychological research is a survey in which individuals are asked about specific behaviors. (Although the terms *survey* and *questionnaire* are sometimes used in different contexts in research, in this text I will use these terms interchangeably.) **Survey research** is often conducted to measure mood, attitudes about a topic, or frequency of certain behaviors through self-reports from the participants. Typically, surveys contain a number of questions that ask the research participant to rate the presence or frequency of his or her own thoughts or behaviors. When surveys are used, participants are often asked to use a response scale (e.g., 1 to 5 or 1 to 7) or response category (e.g., *often, sometimes, not very often, never*) that matches how they feel about a behavior or how likely they are to exhibit the behavior. This means that the participants are limited in the types of responses they can make to the survey items. In other words, the survey uses a **closed-ended response scale** because only certain responses are valid responses to the items. The scale in Table 5.3 was designed to assess how likely one is to discuss one's emotions and disclose personal problems to others. Scores on this scale have been shown to be related to self-esteem and general

survey research: A research study that uses the survey observational technique to measure behavior

closed-ended response scale: Participants' responses to survey questions according to the response options provided by the researcher

TABLE 5.3 ■ Distress Disclosure Index

1. When I feel upset, I usually confide in my friends.	1 Strongly disagree	2	3	4	5 Strongly agree
2. I prefer not to talk about my problems.	1 Strongly disagree	2	3	4	5 Strongly agree
3. When something unpleasant happens to me, I often look for someone to talk to.	1 Strongly disagree	2	3	4	5 Strongly agree
4. I typically don't discuss things that upset me.	1 Strongly disagree	2	3	4	5 Strongly agree
5. When I feel depressed or sad, I tend to keep those feelings to myself.	1 Strongly disagree	2	3	4	5 Strongly agree
6. I try to find people to talk with about my problems.	1 Strongly disagree	2	3	4	5 Strongly agree
7. When I am in a bad mood, I talk about it with my friends.	1 Strongly disagree	2	3	4	5 Strongly agree
8. If I have a bad day, the last thing I want to do is talk about it.	1 Strongly disagree	2	3	4	5 Strongly agree
9. I rarely look for people to talk with when I am having a problem.	1 Strongly disagree	2	3	4	5 Strongly agree
10. When I am distressed, I don't tell anyone.	1 Strongly disagree	2	3	4	5 Strongly agree
11. I usually seek out someone to talk to when I am in a bad mood.	1 Strongly disagree	2	3	4	5 Strongly agree
12. I am willing to tell others my distressing thoughts.	1 Strongly disagree	2	3	4	5 Strongly agree

Source: Kahn and Hessling (2001).

satisfaction with one's life (Kahn & Hessling, 2001). The Distress Disclosure Index provides an example of a closed-ended response scale, as a 5-point scale is given for responses.

open-ended response scale: Participants respond to survey questions in any manner they feel appropriate for the question

qualitative: Nonnumerical participant responses

quantitative: Numerical data

Another way to design a survey is to ask participants to respond to questions on an **open-ended response scale**. In other words, they can respond in whatever way they wish to the questions you asked them. Analyzing the data from an open-ended response scale also requires the development of a coding scheme because the responses are **qualitative** rather than **quantitative**. Such coding schemes are developed by researchers for some validated surveys used frequently in certain types of research. Using a closed-ended response scale allows the researcher to collect quantitative responses (i.e., numerical responses), so no coding scheme is needed for closed-ended scales. Surveys are often administered using pencil and paper or (as is becoming more frequent) over the Internet via website.

Researchers are often interested in testing the validity and reliability of the surveys and questionnaires they use. Checking the validity of a survey means making sure that the questions asked are really about the behavior the researcher is interested in. If a survey is designed to measure someone's level of anxiety, the questions have to be written to ask about behaviors that are related to anxiety, or the survey is not measuring what it is designed to measure. In other words, does the survey actually measure the construct it was designed to measure? Checking the reliability of a survey means making certain that the responses you get from an individual are similar either at different points in time or to similar items on the questionnaire. If an individual's responses change drastically from time to time or across similar items, even though the attitude or behavior being measured by the survey does not change, you will not get an accurate measure of that attitude or behavior.

Typically, using a validated survey puts a researcher a step ahead of the other techniques discussed because the validity and reliability of a survey will already have been tested and the survey revised (if necessary) to maximize its accuracy. The primary disadvantage of using surveys to collect data, however, is that the observations are based on self-reports, which means that they may not be correct representations of a person's behavior. Individuals do not always view their behavior accurately and may report who they think they are on a survey, not who they actually are. Participants may also want to portray themselves more positively to the researcher and intentionally respond in a way that achieves that goal (i.e., they self-monitor). This is called *social desirability,* and it can bias the results of a survey or questionnaire. Thus, researchers must be careful in interpreting behaviors observed with this technique, as they may not be accurate representations of individuals' behaviors.

The Beck Depression Inventory–II (BDI–II; Beck, Steer, & Brown, 1996) and Beck Anxiety Inventory (BAI; Beck & Steer, 1993) are two commonly used surveys in psychological research on mood. These respective surveys contain items that ask individuals about the intensity of certain feelings and the intensity of specific behaviors related to depression and anxiety. For example, the BDI–II contains 21 items and asks respondents about feelings of sadness, punishment, and lack of interest in sex and behaviors such as difficulty in sleeping and changes in eating habits. Many studies use the BDI–II to measure depression or the BAI to measure anxiety, and the reliability and validity of these surveys have been frequently tested.

Interviews. Surveys can also be administered as **interviews** such that individuals respond to questions orally. Interviews can be done face-to-face, over the phone, or in focus groups. Like naturalistic observations, observing behaviors with interview data requires the researcher to develop a coding scheme to understand the behaviors described or exhibited in the interview. One advantage of using interviews is that you can ask about a specific behavior instead of waiting for the individual to exhibit the behavior spontaneously (as in naturalistic observations). Another advantage is that if the interview is structured to allow flexibility, different questions can be asked depending on the response that is given. For example, if a participant responds that a question particularly applies to him or her, the interviewer can follow up that response with additional questions on the topic tailored to the type of response made.

interviews: A data collection technique that involves direct questioning of individuals about their behaviors and attitudes

Focus groups are becoming a popular way to conduct interviews to learn about individuals' attitudes toward a societal issue, political candidate, or consumer product. Interviewing people in groups uses fewer resources and can sometimes elicit responses from individuals who may be more reluctant to voice an opinion when they are asked on their own. When reluctant individuals hear that others have an opinion similar to their own, they may be more likely to voice their opinion. However, this can also be a limitation to the use of interviews: If they are conducted in groups, individuals may go along with the group rather than voice an opinion that differs from others' (Ashe, 1955). In other words, conformity of responses occurs. Interviewees may also self-monitor during interviews, meaning that they can respond according to how they wish to appear to others instead of how they actually are (i.e., the social desirability bias can occur). Another drawback to the use of interviews is that the way a question is asked can affect the response that is given. Thus, great care must be taken in writing questions for interviews.

Systematic Observation

Systematic observations are typically used when the researchers want to exert the highest amount of control over behavior. This is typically done using a controlled task to indicate the behavior of interest (e.g., speed or accuracy for completing a task). Thus, **systematic observation** is often used to study behaviors that are least likely to be affected by the process of measuring them. Examples of these behaviors are often cognitive or biological in nature (e.g., memory accuracy, problem-solving speed, firing of a neuron, activity in a particular brain area). However, systematic observation can be used to study behaviors in other areas of psychology as well. Consider an example from research on prospective memory about how we remember the things we intend to do in the future. In our everyday lives, prospective memory tasks include remembering to stop at the store on the way home to pick up milk, remembering to pay a bill on time, remembering to submit an assignment before the due date, and remembering to pick up our child at 3:00 p.m. However, people differ in how they remember to complete these tasks and whether they use reminders to help them remember. Therefore, if researchers want to study the cognitive processes people use to complete these tasks, they need to control for these differences and the use of external reminders. Thus, many research studies model everyday prospective memory tasks in the lab using systematic observations of how quickly and accurately people complete simple cognitive tasks (e.g., decide if a string of letters forms a word or not) while remembering to complete a

systematic observation: Data collection technique where control is exerted over the conditions under which the behavior is observed prospective memory task (e.g., press the *Q* key anytime you see the word *tiger* in the task, or press the *Q* key after 3 min have passed). Using computer presentation of the letter strings and keyboard presses for responses, researchers can record how often participants in a study remember to press the *Q* key whenever *tiger* appears or after 3 min has passed and whether completing this task slows them down or makes them less accurate in deciding if the letter strings are words or not. This technique for measuring prospective memory controls for factors that influence the measure by removing the use of external reminders for completing the task and other sources, such as environmental cues that might prompt someone to remember a task (e.g., seeing a child cross the street, prompting remembering that you need to pick up your son from school soon). Researchers can then determine if their causal variable of interest affects the measure. In a study I completed recently, my student and I looked at how accurate people are at completing two kinds of prospective memory tasks: one where they responded when a certain kind of word appeared in the word judgment task and one where they had to respond after 3 min in the word judgment task (Conte & McBride, 2018). Figure 5.3 shows the results for the two kinds of tasks in terms of accuracy in completing the task.

Because a high degree of control can be exerted on the measurements of behaviors observed using systematic observations (i.e., controlling the situations under which behavior is measured), they typically add to the internal validity of a study. The situation in which the behaviors are measured is typically controlled to eliminate influences on

FIGURE 5.3 ■ Results From the Conte and McBride (2018) Study Showing Higher Prospective Memory Performance for a Task to Respond to a Cue Word Compared With a Task to Respond After a Set Amount of Time

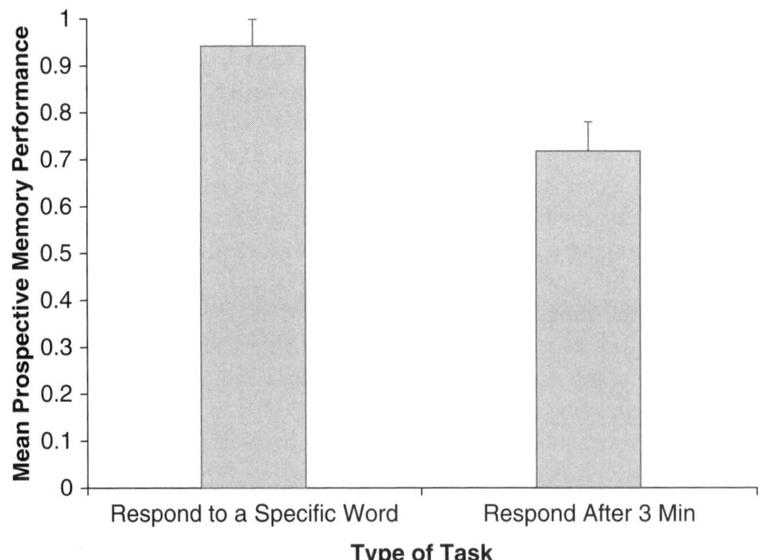

the behaviors that are not the focus of the study. Thus, systematic observations are often collected in a laboratory setting, where distractions of normal life are minimized and tasks are presented and completed on a computer to maximize accuracy. The drawback of this level of control is that the behaviors being studied may be artificial. In other words, external validity can be lower for systematic observations than other data collection methods, though these observations may have better internal validity.

Using Archival Data

Sometimes when researchers have questions about behavior, they find that those behaviors they are interested in have already been observed. In other words, the data they wish to analyze to answer their research question already exist. Someone else has collected them. For example, if researchers are interested in health-related behaviors, they may wish to use existing hospital records as their observations. An example of this type of study was done in Pueblo, Colorado, a few years ago (Bartecchi et al., 2006). Pueblo is a small town with two hospitals where residents of the town and surrounding area receive medical care. After the town passed a smoking ban, researchers decided to look at hospital records to compare the number of hospitalizations for heart attacks during the year and a half before the smoking ban began (as a way to determine the number of heart-related illnesses that occurred when people were allowed to smoke in public places) with the number of hospitalizations for heart attacks that occurred during the year and a half after the smoking ban started. They found that the number of hospitalizations for heart attacks (see Figure 5.4) decreased significantly during the year and a half after the smoking ban and concluded that the decrease in public smoking was related to this decrease (by comparing heart attack hospitalization rate change for comparable areas without a smoking ban over the same period of time). The use of hospital records in this study is an example of how researchers use **archival data** as an observation technique.

archival data: Data collection technique that involves analysis of preexisting data

Many archival data sets are collected by agencies on a periodic basis. A quick web search will show summary results for many of these observations. For example, one can find data related to presidential approval ratings, consumer confidence, consumer spending, and opinion polls. Figure 5.5 shows approval ratings (percentage of people who approve of the job the president is doing) for U.S. president Trump over his first year in office. A web search will yield periodic ratings for the current president because presidential approval ratings are collected and published frequently every few weeks by many news agencies. Many of these data sets are collected by governmental agencies and are available to researchers who wish to analyze the data on their own. Corporations may also make archival data sets available to researchers who wish to study workplace behaviors such as work productivity and absenteeism.

Archival data offer researchers a means of collecting data quickly. Few resources are needed, as the data are collected by another agency or institution. However, archival data offer the researcher no control over the circumstances under which the data are collected, the sampling technique used, or the measures used to observe behavior. Researchers using archival data also have no control over how the data are coded, which can make comparisons difficult across groups or areas if data are coded differently by different organizations.

FIGURE 5.4 ■ Results From the Bartecchi et al. (2006) Study Showing the Number of Acute Myocardial Infarctions (i.e., Heart Attacks) for Pueblo, Colorado, and Nearby Areas Both Before and After a Smoking Ban Law Was Passed

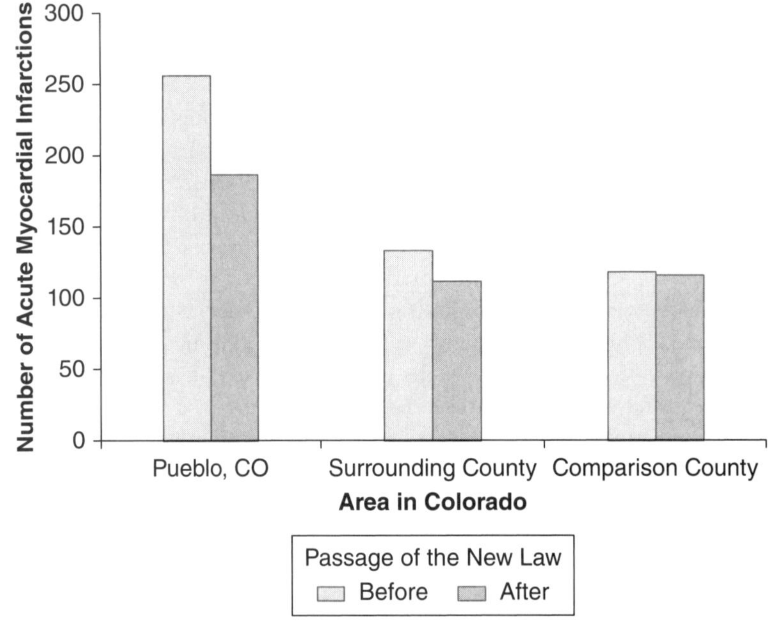

FIGURE 5.5 ■ Approval Ratings for President Donald Trump's First Year in Office

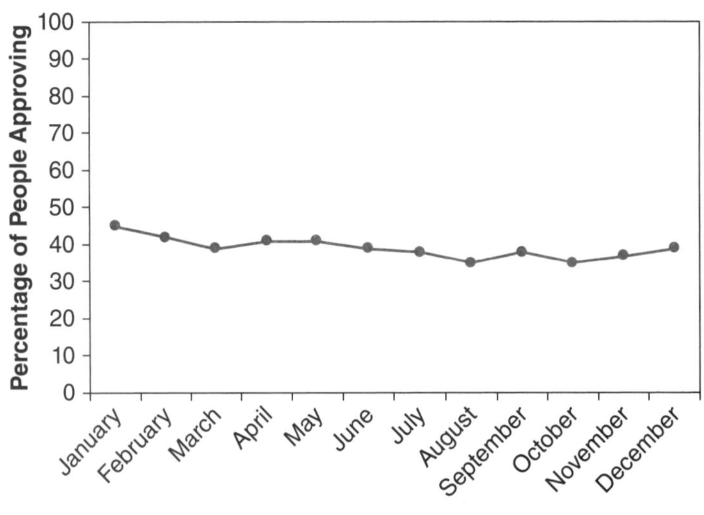

Content Analysis

Content analysis is a specific type of archival data observation technique that involves analysis of what someone has said (as in a speech or interview) or written (as in a book or article). This may involve analyzing the transcript of a speech someone gave, a written document, or a recorded statement. In content analysis, a researcher is analyzing a record of what someone has said or written in the past; thus, no interaction takes place between the research participant and the researcher. A coding scheme must be developed by the researcher to determine which behaviors will be considered in the analysis. This type of analysis can be resource intensive and time-consuming.

content analysis: An archival data collection technique that involves analysis of the content of an individual's spoken or written record

Validity and Reliability

I will end this section on data collection techniques by revisiting the issues of validity and reliability to compare the different techniques on these concepts. As described previously, naturalistic observations have the highest level of external validity among the data collection techniques because they involve observation of natural behaviors that are very realistic in the participants' everyday lives. Systematic observations often have the highest level of internal validity because they involve control of the situations under which the behavior is observed. But the high external validity of naturalistic observations comes with low internal validity because the researcher exerts no influence over the behavior, limiting the control of sources of bias on the measures. Likewise, the high internal validity of systematic observations often results in low external validity because the control the researchers impose on the situations in which the behaviors are measured can make them unrealistic for the participants' everyday lives. In this way, internal and external validity often trade off in research studies. Reliability is often high in systematic observations because they are typically collected using technology that ensures the reliability of the measures. However, reliability must be considered for naturalistic observations because it can be easily reduced if the observers are not well trained to code behaviors in the same way (i.e., low interrater or interobserver reliability).

Surveys and questionnaires have their own issues with both validity and reliability. Construct validity is important to consider in designing surveys because the researchers want to ensure they measure specific constructs accurately with their survey. If the survey they design does not tell them much about the concept they want to measure, then they have a poor operational definition for that concept and low construct validity in their survey. In addition, the responses on the survey must be reliable to provide an unbiased measure. If participants do not respond consistently to different items in a survey or to repeated completions of the survey over time, the reliability of the survey will be low and the results will be difficult to interpret.

Table 5.4 contains some examples of behaviors that psychologists might want to observe. For each behavior, consider how psychologists might use each of the data collection techniques described in this chapter to measure the behavior. In the next section, we will consider how these techniques are used to answer different kinds of research questions.

TABLE 5.4 ■ Thinking About Observations
For each question that follows, consider how you might observe the behavior using (a) naturalistic observation, (b) surveys and questionnaires, or (c) systematic observation. Be sure to operationally define the behavior before you describe how the observations would be collected. Also consider the limitations of each observation method as you choose one for each behavior.
1. How do humans (or animals) solve a problem?
2. How do people react to bad news?
3. What types of people are most likely to disclose personal problems to others?
4. How do groups of children organize themselves to complete a task?
5. What behaviors characterize people with attention deficit hyperactivity disorder (ADHD)?
6. What types of brain activity result when one consumes caffeine?

STOP AND THINK

5.2. Describe a disadvantage of using closed-ended responses on a survey or questionnaire.

5.3. For each of the following descriptions, indicate which data collection technique would be best to use:

a. You want to measure someone's ability to complete a task while controlling for sources of bias and increasing internal validity as much as possible.

b. You want to know about how subjects judge their own behavior.

c. You want to measure the most realistic behaviors possible to increase external validity.

d. You want to know how Americans' confidence in the economy has changed across four decades of time.

5.4. Reread the description at the beginning of the chapter for the study your boss asked you to design. Which data collection technique would you use to measure work productivity of your coworkers? Why would you choose this technique?

TYPES OF RESEARCH DESIGNS

Research design types differ based on the type of question the researcher wants to answer. Each of the data collection techniques described earlier can be used in any of the major research designs; however, practically speaking, some techniques are more common in certain designs than in others. As each design is discussed, examples of the most common techniques used in that design will be described. Note also that you may see the term *research design* applied to many aspects of a design. Here the term applies to the major categories of research designs that are used by psychologists to answer different types of research questions. What follows is a description of the major research designs used in psychological research with some examples of these designs.

Case Studies

In 1970, a woman walked into a welfare office in Southern California with her daughter Genie. After the woman was interviewed, it became clear that although Genie appeared to be about 6 or 7 years old, she was in fact 13 years old and had no language abilities. Her parents had kept her locked in her bedroom every day since she was very young. Genie did not attend school and had not been exposed to enough language from her family to learn how to speak. After Genie's situation was discovered, psychologists became interested in her case and hoped to learn from her about the development of language and whether it can occur at such a late age in a child (Fromkin, Krashen, Curtiss, Rigler, & Rigler, 1974). Genie became the subject of intensive study by a number of individuals. From the case study of Genie, evidence was gained for a critical period of language development because Genie was raised with little language interaction with others and had difficulty learning language after she was rescued.

The goal of a **case study** is to gain insight into and understanding of a single individual's (or just a couple of individuals') behavior. Case studies can also be conducted for a group of individuals, such as an agency or institution. Typically, a case study involves intensive observation of an individual's naturalistic behavior or set of behaviors. Thus, researchers often use naturalistic observations, interviews, or archival data (especially in the case of a famous individual) to learn about the individual's behavior, although some case studies have also included systematic observations and surveys to learn about an individual. Case studies are often exploratory studies, wherein a researcher can learn about a behavior when little is known about it (e.g., unusual symptoms of a new disorder). When a researcher is interested in testing theories about how behavior works or attempting to find a treatment that will help an individual or small set of individuals with a problem behavior, a small-*n* design is typically used instead of a case study. The primary difference between case studies and **small-*n* designs** is the goal of the researcher. In addition, small-*n* designs are often conducted as experiments (see Experiments section later in this chapter).

case study: A research design that involves intensive study of particular individuals and their behaviors

small-*n* design: An experiment conducted with one or a few participants to better understand the behavior of those individuals

Some of the more well-known case studies conducted by psychologists have been with individuals who suffered a brain injury. Researchers study such individuals after their brain injury both while they are still alive (if possible) and after their death. Behaviors these individuals exhibit are then connected to the brain injury they suffered, which can be explored more extensively after their death. Physiological psychologists have gained a lot of important knowledge about brain functions through case studies of these individuals. A famous case is that of H. M. (typically these patients are identified by initials only or a pseudonym to keep the findings confidential for these individuals). H. M. (see Photo 5.3) suffered damage to a brain area known as the hippocampus during a surgery in 1953 that was done to help reduce his epileptic seizures (Hilts, 1996). As a result of the surgery, H. M. could no longer remember new experiences for longer than a few minutes. Through extensive study of this subject, psychologists learned that the hippocampus is an important structure for encoding or retrieving memories of events because H. M. lost

Department of Brain and Cognitive Sciences, MIT, via Wikipedia

Photo 5.3
Henry Molaison (known simply as H. M. in research reports) was a famous patient who participated in many case studies that investigated the neurological functions associated with memory.

the ability to retrieve memories of things that happened after his surgery (even though he still had access to memories of events he experienced before his surgery). From case studies of H. M. came a new set of questions about the hippocampus and exactly what function it serves in memory. In addition, researchers found that H. M. could improve on tasks over time, indicating that certain types of new memories were still available to him. For example, a study of H. M. (Bohbot & Corkin, 2007) found that his ability to learn a spatial memory task was quite good despite having severe amnesia (his memory for things he experienced lasts only a few minutes). Case studies of H. M. are still conducted today. Although he died in 2008, H. M.'s brain will continue to be studied to further our understanding of the importance of specific brain areas in cognitive functioning.

Other case studies have used archival data or content analysis of a document to better understand an individual's behavior. For example, Lester (2006) recently examined the diaries of a man who committed suicide, in an attempt to identify specific events in his life that may have been connected to his choice to kill himself. Abramson (1984) conducted a case study of the sexual behaviors of a woman who called herself Sarah, after receiving a letter from her. Sarah had been abused (physically and sexually) as a child and was recovering from those traumas at the time she wrote to Abramson, a psychologist at the University of California, Los Angeles. Abramson then conducted interviews with Sarah to better understand how individuals recover from such traumatic experiences. Abramson learned a good deal about psychological resilience and recovery in an individual despite traumatic childhood events.

Case studies can also be done after a person has died, as they are with H. M.'s brain. When Albert Einstein died in 1955, portions of his brain were preserved to allow it to be studied. Since then, scientists have examined these brain sections to look for ways in which Einstein's brain may differ from brains of other people. One difference that has been found is that Einstein's brain contains many more neuron cells in a section of his brain's cortex than in the brains of control participants that were used as a comparison (Anderson & Harvey, 1996). In addition, a section of Einstein's brain appears to have been improperly formed, allowing connections between areas of the brain that are not connected in other people's brains (Witelson, Kigar, & Harvey, 1999). These differences may account for the intellectual abilities Einstein possessed, but simply examining Einstein's brain does not allow researchers to make such strong conclusions. Instead, these studies allow researchers to start hypothesizing about which brain areas or characteristics may be important for advanced intellectual abilities, and these hypotheses can then be tested in further studies (see Figure 5.6).

Due to their exploratory nature, case studies often focus on rare or unusual cases to gain some information about a behavior that is not exhibited by all individuals. This

FIGURE 5.6 ■ Case Studies Can Provide a Unique View of an Individual

Source: Copyright by S. Harris, www.sciencecartoonsplus.com/galpsych2.htm.

means that the behaviors examined in case studies often cannot be generalized to all individuals. Because of the reduced generality of the behaviors, case studies do not allow for strong tests of the cause of the behavior (experiments are best for that—as explained in a later section), and researchers must be careful about drawing conclusions about the causes of the behaviors they are studying. However, case studies can give researchers a *starting place* for investigations of a behavior or a set of behaviors. Thus, they serve an important purpose in psychological research, drawing attention to new research questions that can be further explored with additional studies.

correlational study: A type of research design that examines the relationships between multiple dependent variables without manipulating any of the variables

predictor variable: The dependent variable in a correlational study that is used to predict the score on another variable

outcome variable: The dependent variable in a correlational study that is being predicted by the predictor variable

positive relationship: Relationship between variables characterized by an increase in one variable that occurs with an increase in the other variable

negative relationship: Relationship between variables characterized by an increase in one variable that occurs with a decrease in the other variable

scatterplot: A graph showing the relationship between two dependent variables for a group of individuals

third-variable problem: The presence of extraneous factors in a study that affect the dependent variable and can decrease the internal validity of the study

Correlational Studies

Is insomnia related to depression? Do students who watch more TV have lower grade point averages (GPAs)? Do children who play violent video games behave more violently? Each of these questions can be explored in a **correlational study** (correlation means relationship). Correlational studies allow a researcher to examine relationships between variables and, if a relationship is found, predict values for one variable from values on the other variable(s). If a predictive relationship is examined, the variable that is used to make the prediction is called the **predictor variable**, and the variable that is being predicted is called the **outcome variable**. Therefore, the goal of a correlational study is to determine if different behaviors are connected and occur together. This type of study, however, still does not allow us to determine if one variable *causes* another to occur (again, only well-designed experiments allow researchers to test causal relationships). All we can learn from a correlational study is if two variables covary (i.e., change together—up, down, or in opposite directions from each other). Then researchers may be able to predict one variable from another.

If a relationship is found in a correlational study between two variables, it can take one of two forms: a **positive relationship** or a **negative relationship**. A positive relationship means that the values on the variables change in the same direction (up or down) at the same time. A negative relationship indicates that as values on one variable increase, the values on the other variable decrease. Figure 5.7 illustrates each type of relationship that might exist between GPA and the number of hours an individuals watch TV per week. The graphs in Figure 5.7 are called scatterplots. In a **scatterplot**, one variable is placed on the x-axis, and the other variable is placed on the y-axis. The data points in the graph represent the scores on the two variables for each individual (horizontally for the first variable and vertically for the second variable). Thus, the data point that is circled in Panel B shows that one individual in this study reported watching 25 hr of TV per week and had a GPA of 3.25. You may also notice that there are very few data points below 2.0 on the GPA scale in the graph. This may be because very few students in college have GPAs lower than 2.0 (if they do, they do not remain in college very long).

Remember that a relationship between these variables does not mean that watching TV will *cause* one to have a higher or lower GPA or that having a higher or lower GPA will *cause* one to watch more TV. It is quite possible that a third variable (e.g., lack of interest in academic topics, a poor academic environment while growing up, knowledge of topics that are covered in TV shows) is causing the number of hours of TV watched and GPA to change. This is called the **third-variable problem**, and it is the reason that researchers cannot determine causation from correlational studies.

Experiments

Have you ever wondered why it took so long for scientists to learn that smoking causes cancer? People have been smoking for hundreds of years, and medical science has been studying the effects of smoking on health for many decades. Yet warnings on cigarette packages did not appear until 1966, and claims about smoking causing lung cancer were tentative for many years. Scientists could show that smoking and cancer were linked but could not show that smoking caused cancer in humans in a definitive way. The reason these findings were tentative for so long is that ethically it is very difficult (if not

FIGURE 5.7 ■ Positive Relationship (A), Negative Relationship (B), and No Relationship (C) Between Number of Hours of TV Watched and GPA

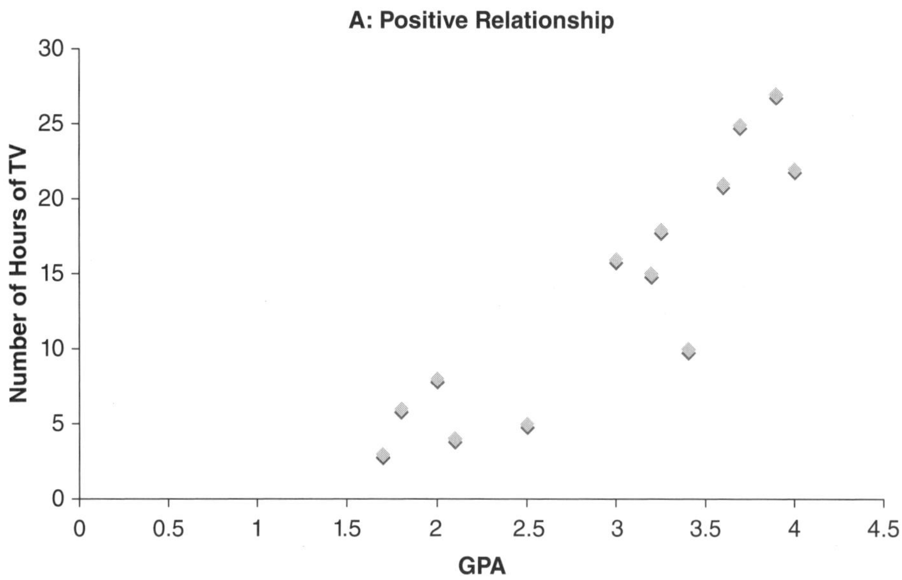

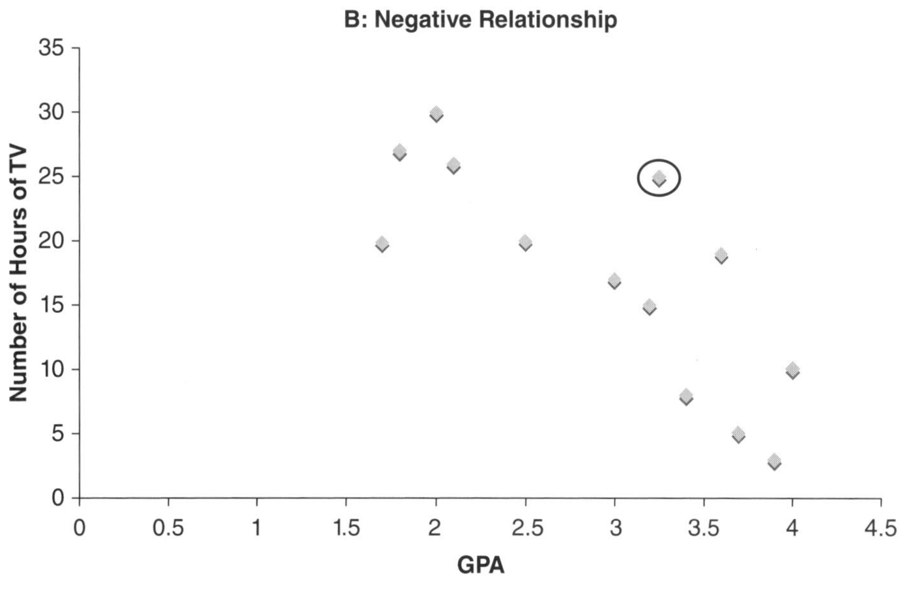

(Continued)

FIGURE 5.7 ■ (Continued)

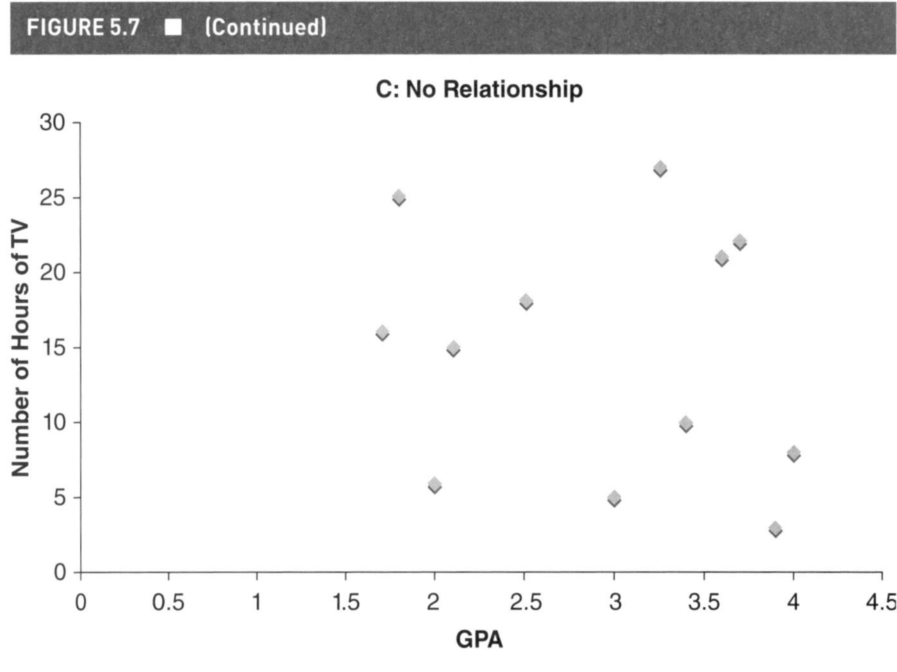

experiment: A type of research design that involves manipulation of an independent variable, allowing control of extraneous variables that could affect the results

independent variable: A variable in an experiment that is manipulated by the researcher such that the levels of the variable change across or within subjects in the experiment

impossible) to conduct an **experiment** to examine whether smoking *causes* cancer in humans. An experiment involves manipulating the presumed causal variable known as the **independent variable**. This means that in the smoking experiment, one group of people would be assigned to smoke, and a similar group of people (similar in age, weight, health, diet, etc.) would not be allowed to smoke. Obviously, researchers cannot force people to smoke (especially if they have a hypothesis that it is harmful to them) or force people to never smoke. Thus, it has been very difficult (and has taken many correlational studies and animal experiments) to show that smoking is a cause of lung cancer, but this example illustrates what is required to test causal hypotheses: experiments.

As mentioned previously, a key aspect of experiments that allows tests of causal relationships is the manipulation of the independent variable (or independent variables—an experiment can contain more than one independent variable). The independent variable is the factor that the researcher thinks may affect the observed behavior. Thus, data are collected from the participants in an experiment under at least two different conditions. The data from these conditions are then compared with one another to see if there are differences caused by the independent variable manipulation. These different conditions created from the independent variable make up the **levels of the independent variable**. For example, an experiment may involve subjecting one group of participants (randomly assigned) to treatment for depression, while another group receives no treatment. In this case, the treated group is the **experimental group**, because they receive the treatment condition, whereas the nontreated group is the **control group** because they receive no treatment. Comparison of depression scores (the dependent variable in this experiment) for the two groups would allow the researcher to determine if the treatment was helpful (scores for the treatment group are higher than the control group's), harmful (scores for the treatment group are lower than the control group's), or makes no difference (scores for the treatment and control groups are similar). Another way to conduct this experiment would be to use two different treatments (e.g., talk therapy vs. drug therapy) for the two groups. In this case, there is no control group; both groups of participants receive some type of treatment. Comparison of the scores for the two groups in this experiment would indicate which of the two therapies was more helpful or if they are similar. In fact, this comparison is a key feature of an experiment. The goal in an experiment is to examine the effect of the independent variable on the dependent variable. We do that by comparing the data observed in the different levels of the independent variable; this comparison tells us if the independent variable has an effect. In other words, the comparison across the levels of the independent variable provides the test of the hypothesis.

levels of the independent variable: Different situations or conditions that participants experience in an experiment because of the manipulation of the independent variable

experimental group: The group of participants in an experiment that experience the treatment level of the independent variable

control group: The group of participants in an experiment that do not experience the treatment level of the independent variable

confounding variable: An extraneous factor present in a study that may affect the results

placebo: A sugar pill given to the control group in a drug study to allow all groups to believe that they are receiving a treatment

Another key feature of experiments is the control of factors that could affect the results but are not part of the manipulation of the independent variable(s). These extraneous factors are called confounding variables. If confounding variables are not controlled, the causal relationship between the independent and dependent variables will be unclear. For example, in the depression examples discussed earlier, the severity of the depression the participants have before the experiment could be a **confounding variable** because participants with more severe depression may show less improvement with therapy than participants with less severe depression. If the participants with more severe depression are inadvertently assigned to the therapy group in the first example or to one of the therapy groups in the second example, they may show no effect of therapy, even if an effect does exist. In other words, the severity of the depression may mask the causal relationship between therapy group and depression at the end of the study. Thus, the researcher should control for this factor in the experiment, perhaps by using random assignment of participants to groups.

Another example of control used in experiments with a treatment as the independent variable is the use of a **placebo** for the control group. A placebo is typically given as a sugar pill in a study testing a drug treatment to the control group so that the subjects do not know whether they receive a treatment or not. This controls for the effects of the belief that one is being treated that can have an influence on the results of the study. People who believe they are receiving a treatment can improve from the belief alone, so a placebo is often used to give both the experimental and control groups the belief that they may be receiving the treatment.

Systematic observations and surveys are the most common observation techniques used in experiments. These observation techniques allow for more control over the measurement of behavior than the other techniques (see Table 5.2). The prospective memory procedure described earlier provides an example of the use of systematic observation in an experiment, where prospective memory performance was measured under controlled conditions to compare two kinds of tasks.

Quasi-Experiments

In some cases, researchers want to compare the behavior of groups of individuals but are unable to manipulate the characteristic on which the groups differ. For example,

quasi-experiment: A type of research design where a comparison is made, as in an experiment, but no random assignment of participants to groups occurs

random assignment: Participants are randomly assigned to levels of the independent variable in an experiment to control for individual differences as an extraneous variable

ex post facto design: Quasi-experiment where subjects are grouped based on a characteristic they already possess (e.g., age or gender)

pretest–posttest design: A type of research design (often a quasi-experiment) where behavior is measured both before and after a treatment or condition is implemented

suppose you wanted to compare the behavior for older and younger adults. You cannot randomly assign individuals to be of a specific age, so age cannot be a manipulated variable. This means that you lose some control over alternative explanations of the data because participants are not randomly assigned to the groups. In this example, if younger and older adults differ on the measured behavior, age may have caused the difference, or something that varies with age (e.g., experiences of different generations with technology) may have caused the difference. Thus, conclusions from a **quasi-experiment** must be more tentative than conclusions from an experiment, where a true independent variable is manipulated. However, quasi-experiments involve group comparisons just as experiments do, and data from quasi-experiments are often analyzed the same way they are analyzed in experiments. The key difference between experiments and quasi-experiments is that the **random assignment** of participants to groups is missing in a quasi-experiment (Shadish, Cook, & Campbell, 2002).

One type of quasi-experiment design is called an **ex post facto design** because the comparison of interest is based on a grouping that already exists instead of one the researcher assigns in the study. In other words, the grouping is based on something that already happened in the past (e.g., a subject decided to be a smoker or not; a subject was in an automobile accident in the last year or not). Based on these preexisting characteristics of the subjects, a researcher can create groups of subjects to compare on a particular behavior (e.g., anxiety level, impulsivity). However, a design can be a quasi-experiment even if the researcher assigns subjects to groups if that assignment is not done randomly. Researchers might decide to assign subjects to groups based on their availability for participation in the study (e.g., morning or afternoon session). If the assignment is not random, then there could be additional factors (other than the grouping factor) that are responsible for the results found (e.g., people who sign up for the morning session are more alert and perform better on the task because of their energy levels).

Some studies also have less control over conditions under which data are collected in a repeated-measures design. For example, suppose a researcher is interested in the change in attitude regarding trust of politicians after taking a political science class. In this study, attitude is measured before and after the class in what is called a **pretest–posttest design**. If attitude changes from pretest to posttest (getting either better or worse), this change may be either because of the class or because of other events that occurred in the time between the tests (e.g., a political scandal may have occurred in this time). Thus, the causal relationship between the political science class and attitude change is less clear. For this reason, pretest–posttest designs (that do not include a control group) are considered quasi-experiments.

STOP AND THINK

5.5. For each of the following descriptions, indicate what research design is being used:

a. To determine if there is a relationship between mood and weather, researchers measure subjects' moods and the temperature on the day that they complete the mood questionnaire.

b. To examine the effect of temperature on mood, subjects are randomly assigned to a room at 86 degrees or a room at 72 degrees to complete their mood questionnaire.

c. To determine if mood differs by room temperature, a researcher asks two of her classes to fill out a mood questionnaire at the end of class after adjusting the thermostat between classes. She then groups subjects by class and compares their mood scores.

5.6. Explain why the results from a case study might be difficult to generalize to a large population of people.

5.7. Consider again the study your boss asked you to design regarding work productivity. Which research design would you use to test the research question? Describe the variables in your study.

5.8. Imagine you wanted to learn about the factors that contribute to people quitting their jobs. Describe a study to examine this topic, and identify the data collection technique and research design you would use.

THINKING ABOUT RESEARCH

A summary of a research study in psychology is given here. As you read the summary, think about the following questions:

1. Two studies from a research article are described in this section. For each study, identify the data collection technique and the research design type.
2. Does Study 2 contain an independent variable? If so, what is it and what are its levels?
3. What controls did the researchers use in Study 2 to increase the internal validity of the study?
4. Would you consider Study 1 or Study 2 to have higher internal validity? Explain your answer.
5. How would you judge the external validity of this study?

Research Study. Nairne, J. S., VanArsdall, J. E., Pandeirada, J. N. S., Cogdill, M., & LeBreton, J. M. (2013). Adaptive memory: The mnemonic value of animacy. *Psychological Science, 24,* 2099–2105.

Purpose of the Study. The researchers conducted two studies to investigate whether living things have a memory advantage over nonliving things (see Photos 5.4 to 5.7). Their research was motivated by an evolutionary perspective on the development of memory in that being able to distinguish between living and nonliving things is essential for survival. In their first study, they analyzed the relationship between the living and nonliving characteristic of words used in a past study (Rubin & Friendly, 1986) and recall of the words. They predicted a positive relationship between this living and nonliving status and recall. In their second study, they tested the hypothesis that subjects would recall more words of living objects than nonliving objects.

Method of the Study. *Study 1:* The researchers examined words from the Rubin and Friendly (1986) study. Three individuals separately coded the words according to whether they represented living or nonliving objects.

(Continued)

(Continued)

Photos 5.4, 5.5, 5.6, and 5.7
Nairne, VanArsdall, Pandeirada, Cogdill, and LeBreton (2013) compared participants' memory for animate and inanimate objects to show that there is an animacy advantage in memory.

Study 2: Undergraduate students were asked to remember 24 words presented to them in random order. Twelve of the words represented living things, and 12 of the words represented nonliving things. The word sets were matched on several other characteristics (e.g., familiarity, how well an image could be brought to mind by the word, number of letters in the word). After studying the words, subjects completed a short task to categorize presented numbers as odd or even. Subjects were then asked to recall the words in any order for 4 min. This entire procedure was repeated a total of three times (i.e., they studied and recalled the words three times).

FIGURE 5.8 ■ Results of Nairne et al.'s (2013) Study 2 With Recall From Each of the Three Recall Trials and Then Average Recall for All Trials

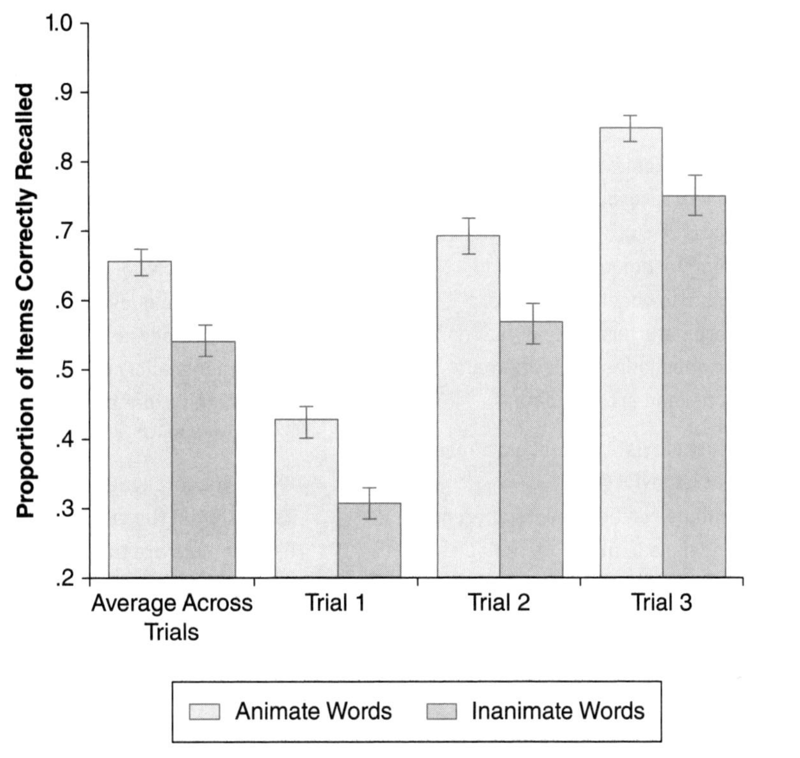

Source: Nairne et al. (2013, Study 2).

Results of the Study. In Study 1, a strong positive relationship was found between the living and nonliving aspect of the words and recall of the words. In Study 2, subjects recalled more of the words for living objects than nonliving objects. Figure 5.8 presents the recall results from Study 2.

Conclusions of the Study. The researchers concluded that the living objects hold a memorial advantage, such that memory is attuned to this characteristic of objects. They suggest that this conclusion is consistent with an evolutionary perspective on the development of memory.

Chapter Summary

Reconsider the questions from the beginning of the chapter:

- **How do psychologists observe behavior?**
  There are some common techniques used by psychologists to observe behavior described in this chapter.
- **What are some common techniques for observing and recording behavior (i.e., collecting data) in different situations?**
  The common techniques used by psychologists to observe and record behavior are naturalistic observations, surveys or questionnaires, systematic observations, and archival data.
- **How do psychologists use observations to learn about behavior?**
  Each technique can be used in different research designs to allow psychologists to answer different types of questions about behavior.
- **What questions about behavior do the different research methods allow psychologists to answer?**
  Different research designs (e.g., case studies, correlational studies, experiments, and quasi-experiments) allow researchers to ask different questions about behavior. Case studies allow descriptive questions to be answered for a single individual or institution. Correlational studies allow descriptive and predictive questions to be answered about behavior. Quasi-experiments and experiments allow comparisons among groups, and experiments answer causal questions about behavior.
- **Which research method is best when asking about the cause of behavior?**
  Experiments are the best method to use when asking causal questions about behavior.

Applying Your Knowledge

In 1998, a group of British doctors published a paper suggesting that there may be a link between vaccines for measles, mumps, and rubella diseases and incidence of autism (Wakefield et al., 1998). This means the researchers were suggesting there is a positive relationship between these vaccinations and occurrence of autism in children that were tested. Their findings started a controversy over the causes of autism. Media sources in the United Kingdom reported the findings of this paper, suggesting that having children vaccinated can cause them to develop autism. As a result, many parents in the United Kingdom and the United States refused to have their children vaccinated out of fear of their children becoming autistic, and the incidence of childhood diseases, such as measles, increased in the United Kingdom in the years after the paper was published.

- Based on the information you read in this chapter, why should parents hesitate to conclude from the findings of this paper that vaccinations can cause autism? What error did the media sources make in publicizing the study's findings?
- Why should the public refrain from making important decisions (such as refusing

vaccinations) based on the findings of a single study? If this question is a bit difficult to answer, consider what has happened more recently in this story: In February 2010, the journal that published the original paper describing this study retracted the paper because the study was found to have serious methodological flaws that were not evident in the original report of the research.

- Consider what type of study would be necessary to show that vaccinations cause autism in children. How would such a study need to be done? Is this a realistic study to conduct? Why or why not?

Test Yourself

Match each of the following research designs with its appropriate description.

1. Experiment	a. Design that focuses on observing just one or a few individuals
2. Case study	b. Design that will allow one to look for relationships between measured variables
3. Correlational study	c. Best design for testing a causal relationship
4. Quasi-experiment	d. Design that allows comparison of groups but does not contain a true independent variable

5. Reread the scenario described at the beginning of the chapter about increasing work productivity. Use the concepts you read about in this chapter to design a study to test the boss's suggestion. Be sure to operationally define *work productivity,* and decide what technique you will use to observe this behavior. Choose the research design that best fits the question you are trying to answer.
6. Suppose you are interested in testing the following hypothesis: "The herb ginkgo biloba causes one to have better memory."
   a. What is the best research design to test this hypothesis? Why?
   b. Describe the study you would conduct to test this hypothesis.
7. _________ validity indicates that a study's results can be generalized to other individuals and real-life situations. ___________ validity indicates that a study's results provide causal information about the variables tested.
8. For each of the following descriptions, indicate which data collection technique was used:
   a. Medical records of patients with depression are examined to determine how often these patients attempt suicide based on what type of treatment they received.
   b. Participants are asked to perform a task on a computer where they must unscramble sentences as quickly as possible—the

(Continued)

(Continued)

amount of time it takes to complete the task on each trial is recorded.

c. A series of statements regarding their alcohol consumption behaviors is presented to participants—they are asked to rate their agreement with each statement on a scale from 1 to 5.

d. Students in a college class are observed to record the number of times they exhibit behaviors indicating lack of attention to the lecture.

9. If a study finds that as self-esteem goes up, symptoms of depression decrease, this study has found a ____________________ relationship.

10. ____________ research designs are typically used when a researcher wants to explore the behavior of an individual or group of individuals to better understand unusual or atypical behaviors.

11. A researcher wants to study factors that cause people to become anxious. She randomly assigns groups of students to one of two conditions: (1) performing a timed task with a clock running on the screen while they perform the task or (2) performing an untimed task while someone watches them complete the task. She compares accuracy on the task for the two groups. This study used a(n) ____________ research design.

   a. case study
   b. correlational
   c. experimental
   d. quasi-experimental

12. An instructor of a statistics course is interested in the relationship between how long it takes students to take an exam and their exam score. He times the students on their exam while they take it on a computer and then looks at the relationship between time for the exam and the exam scores for the students. This study used a(n) ____________ research design.

   a. case study
   b. correlational
   c. experimental
   d. quasi-experimental

13. You arrive at a study you signed up to participate in. The researchers ask you to write down the time you spent asleep the night before. Then they ask you to perform a task categorizing items into living and nonliving categories. At the end of the study, you are told that the purpose of the study was to see if people who slept 7 hr or more the night before performed the task faster than people who slept less than 7 hr. This study used a(n) ____________ research design.

   a. case study
   b. correlational
   c. experimental
   d. quasi-experimental

SAGE edge™

Visit **edge.sagepub.com/mcbridermstats** to find the answers to the Test Yourself questions above, as well as quizzes, flashcards, and other resources to help you accomplish your coursework goals.

6

DESCRIPTIVE STATISTICS

CONSIDER THE FOLLOWING QUESTIONS AS YOU READ CHAPTER 6

- What can we learn about a distribution from measures of central tendency?
- How are the mean, median, and mode used as measures of central tendency?
- How do the mean, median, and mode compare for different distributions?
- Which measure of central tendency should I use when describing a distribution?
- What can we learn about a distribution from measures of variability?
- How is the standard deviation used as a measure of variability?
- Why does the standard deviation calculation differ for samples and populations?

LEARNING OBJECTIVES FOR CHAPTER 6

- Compare measures of central tendency.
- Compare measures of variability.
- Summarize samples based on central tendency and variability.
- Calculate measures of central tendency and variability.

©iStock/PeopleImages

Photo 6.1
In your research study, you want to learn how much students like the current food court choices at your school.

Imagine that you are a member of the student government board at your college or university. The board is trying to decide whether they should lobby the school's administration for new choices at the food court in your student center (see Photo 6.1). Knowing that you have learned some things about research and statistics, the board has tasked you with the job of determining how much the students at your school like the current food court choices. To figure this out, you are conducting a research study to survey the students at your school. You have selected a sample of 150 students who eat at the food court and asked them to complete your survey to rate how much they like the current food court choices on a scale of 1 to 7. Now you have to figure out how to turn all these survey responses into a summary that you can report to the student board. How can you do this?

In this chapter, we will begin to consider some descriptive statistics that will help you summarize your set of data to better understand your scores (see Figure 6.1 for an overview of using descriptive statistics). The three main types of descriptive statistics are **central tendency**, variability, and visual representations (i.e., tables and graphs) of the data. Chapter 1 already covered how to create frequency distributions. This chapter will introduce graphs incorporating central tendency and variability. Each of these types of descriptive statistics will help you better understand the distributions of data you are looking at. Figure 6.1 shows you how to decide which measures are best for reporting your data set. We will begin with measures of central tendency.

central tendency: Representation of a typical score in a distribution

CENTRAL TENDENCY IN DISTRIBUTIONS

Central tendency measures describe what is a *typical* score in a distribution. These measures summarize data as single values to help researchers better understand what the data look like overall. You can think of central tendency as a value that represents the entire distribution that will fall somewhere in the middle of most distributions. There are three main measures of central tendency: **mean**, **median**, and **mode**. The mean is the average score in a distribution, and it is the measure you are probably most familiar with. It is also the measure most often reported for distributions of data. However, the median and mode are useful when distributions are skewed or bimodal in shape (i.e., there are two common scores that may not fall in the middle of the distribution) or are in some way affected by extreme scores that will influence the mean to a greater degree than the median and mode. Thus, it is important to understand all these measures and in which situations you should use each one (see Photo 6.2). For each of these measures, we will consider how to calculate it by hand, using Excel, and using SPSS. This model will be followed for most of the statistics we will discuss in the rest of the chapters of the text.

mean: The calculated average of the scores in a distribution

median: The middle score in a distribution, such that half of the scores are above and half are below that value

mode: The most common score in a distribution

FIGURE 6.1 ■ Overview of Descriptive Statistics

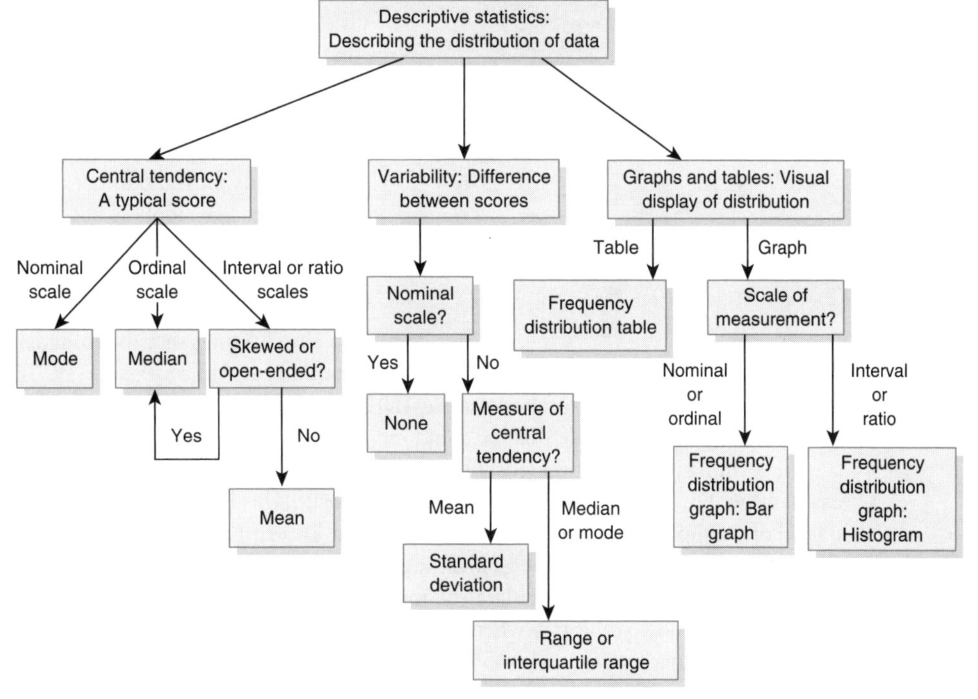

MEAN

As I mentioned, the mean is the most commonly reported measure of central tendency, and it is a good one to start with because it is fairly intuitive as the average score. You have likely calculated a mean before for a set of scores, but I will cover how to calculate the mean by hand while introducing the symbols I will use for later calculations of other statistics to help you become familiar with these symbols. We will then look at how to calculate the mean using Excel and SPSS software.

Calculating the Mean by Hand

Because the mean is simply the average of the scores, to calculate the mean, you simply need to add up all the scores and then divide by the number of scores. I'll represent this calculation for our sample of data as a simple formula:

$$\text{Mean} = \bar{X} = \frac{\Sigma X}{n}$$

©iStock/eternalcreative

Photo 6.2
It is important to understand how the measures of central tendency compare and how to calculate each one in different ways.

This is a commonly used formula for calculating a sample mean. The $\overline{X}$ is a symbol that stands for the sample mean. The $\sum$ symbol (called a *sigma*) indicates that you should add up whatever comes after this symbol. In this case, you are adding the *X*s, which means you should add up all the scores in the set of data. The *n* stands for the number of scores in the sample. Let's look at how we would do this to calculate the mean of our food court survey scores. To calculate the mean for those data, we add up all the 1 to 7 ratings that the students in the sample provided on the survey. Then we divide this number by the number of scores in the sample ($n = 150$). That gives us an average rating on the 1 to 7 scale that we could report back to the student board.

The formula presented previously is the one used to calculate a sample mean. In some cases, we will be looking at a known population mean. This is possible for some kinds of data. For example, many standardized tests have a known population mean because all the students in the population (e.g., all students taking the test that year) take the test and their scores can be used to calculate the mean for the population of students who took the test. This is how you know where your score on a test such at the SAT or ACT falls relative to all other students who took the test: It can be compared with the population mean for the test. The population mean is calculated in the same way—you add up all the scores in the population and divide by the number of scores—but we use different symbols to represent population values in our statistics. Using different symbols (and therefore, different formulas) helps us keep track of which type of mean we are looking at: one for the sample or one from the whole population. The formula for the population mean is as follows:

$$\text{Population mean} = \mu = \frac{\Sigma X}{N}$$

In this formula, the population mean is represented by a μ symbol and the total number of scores by *N*, but the calculation is the same in that you are adding up (i.e., $\sum$) the scores (the *X*s) and then dividing by the number of scores. You will encounter this formula for the population mean again in later chapters.

One way to think of the mean of a distribution is as the balancing point of the distribution. The mean score is the tipping point in the center. Figure 6.2 illustrates how this works. Suppose you have a balancing scale where blocks represent each score in the sample. The size of the block represents the frequency of a score. For the top scale in Figure 6.2, the blocks add up to three on each side because there are three standard blocks on the right and one standard block and one double block (two of that score in the data set) on the left. The mean is in the middle of the distribution for this set of scores.

FIGURE 6.2 ■ The Mean Is the Balancing Point of a Scale—for Symmetrical Distributions, It Will Be in the Middle, but for Skewed Distributions, It Will Be Adjusted Toward the High or Low Scores

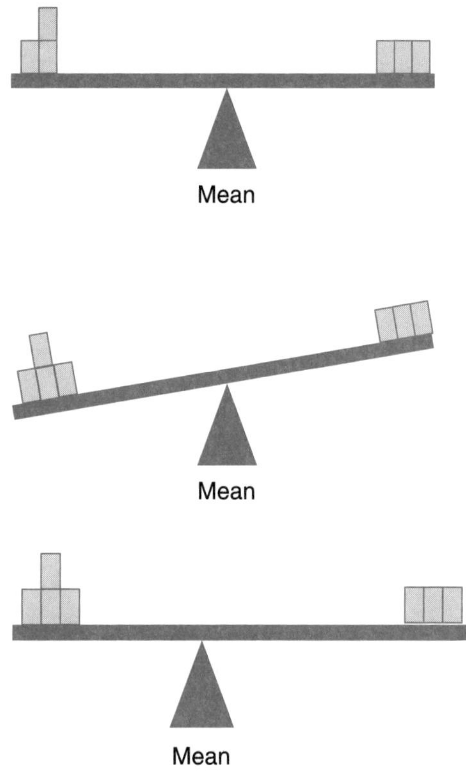

This is what will happen when we have a symmetrical distribution—the mean will be the middle score.

However, what would happen if we added another standard block to the left side (see the bottom two scales in Figure 6.2)? The added block or score would tip the scale to the left, requiring an adjustment to the mean. Now, the mean is no longer at the center of the scale—it is pushed toward the left to account for the new score. This is like adding a low score to our data set—it will adjust the mean to a lower value. This is also what happens when an extreme score, called an **outlier**, is present in our data set. Outliers bias the mean toward the high or low end of the scale, depending on whether they are extremely high or extremely low. These distributions are then positively skewed (toward high scores) or negatively skewed (toward low scores). The smaller our sample size and the more extreme the outlier score is, the more these extreme scores will affect the mean in

outlier: An extreme high or low score in a distribution

a skewed distribution. We will consider the effects of extreme scores in skewed distributions again as we discuss the median of a distribution.

Calculating the Mean Using Excel

Excel is a useful software program for calculating measures of central tendency, especially for large data sets in which hand calculation could be time-consuming and lead to errors. As with the creation of frequency distribution tables and charts, the first step in using Excel to calculate the mean is to enter the scores into the data window. It is important to double-check the entering of the scores, as this step is where errors could occur in the calculations.

To see how to use Excel to calculate the mean of a distribution, let's consider a data set introduced in Chapter 1 (see Figure 1.4 and Table 1.3): ratings of how much people want to watch a new TV show on a 1 to 7 scale. The ratings for this distribution were 1, 1, 2, 2, 2, 2, 2, 3, 3, 3, 3, 4, 4, 4, 4, 4, 4, 4, 4, 5, 5, 5, 5, 5, 5, 5, 5, 5, 5, 5, 5, 6, 6, 6, 6, 6, 6, 6, 6, 6, 6, 6, 6, 6, 6, 6, 6, 7, 7, 7, 7, 7, 7, 7, 7. We can enter these ratings into the Excel data window. To calculate the mean of these scores, we will use the AVERAGE function in Excel. In a blank cell in the window, type =AVERAGE(. You can then click on the first cell for the scores and drag your mouse down the last cell for the scores. This should automatically fill in the first and last cells you want to include in the calculation with a colon between them and an end). You could also simply type in the cells if you wish, and then close the function with an end). Your finished formula should look like this:

=AVERAGE(A2:A56)

When you hit enter, the mean of the scores (4.87) should appear in the cell containing your formula. This is the mean rating of the food court choices at your school from your sample on the 7-point scale.

SUMMARY OF STEPS

- Enter the data into a column in the data window.
- In an empty cell, type =AVERAGE(.
- Highlight the scores you want to include, or type in the cell letters or numbers.
- Close with an end parenthesis, and hit Enter.

Calculating the Mean Using SPSS

SPSS can also be used for calculating measures of central tendency. Using our same ratings scores that we used previously, we can begin with these data entered into our data window as in Figure 1.9. To calculate the mean for these scores, we will use the Descriptives function under Descriptive Statistics in the Analyze menu at the top. A Descriptives window will appear as shown in Figure 6.3. Click on your ratings variable in the left box and then the arrow to move it into the Variable(s) box on the right. Then choose Options and ensure that the Mean box is checked. Then click Continue and then OK to open an Output window. The Output box containing your mean will appear in the Output window as shown in Figure 6.4. This box also contains the number of scores in the data set, the highest (maximum) and lowest (minimum) scores in the data set, and the standard deviation—a measure of variability that we will discuss later in this chapter.

FIGURE 6.3 ■ The Descriptives Window in SPSS

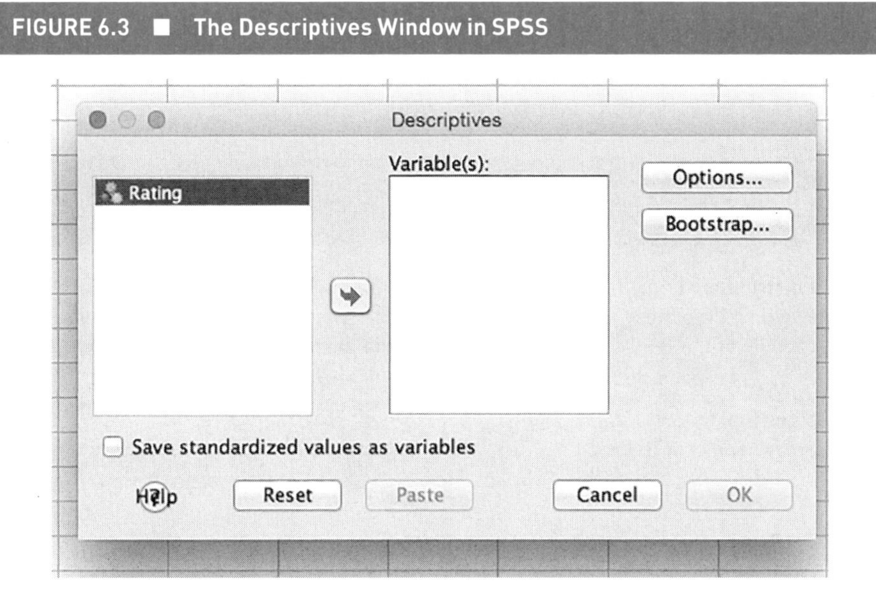

FIGURE 6.4 ■ The Output Box in SPSS Showing the Calculated Mean for the Ratings Data

➡ Descriptives

```
[DataSet1] /Stats Text/CH2_freq_dist.sav
```

Descriptive Statistics

	N	Minimum	Maximum	Mean	Std. Deviation
Rating	55	1.00	7.00	4.8727	1.65613
Valid *N* (listwise)	55				

SUMMARY OF STEPS

- Enter the data into a column in the data window.
- Label the data in the Variable View tab.
- Find Descriptive Statistics in the Analyze menu at the top.
- Choose the Descriptives function in the Descriptive Statistics options.
- Move the data column into the Variable box by highlighting it and clicking on the arrow (see Figure 6.3).
- Under Options, make sure the Mean box is clicked.
- Click Continue and OK; your mean will appear in the Output window (see Figure 6.4).

STOP AND THINK

6.1. For which type of distribution (e.g., symmetrical, skewed) will the mean be a score in the middle of the distribution?

6.2. For each set of scores that follow, calculate the mean by hand or with Excel or SPSS. How does the mean compare for these two sets of scores? Why do you think the mean is different for the two distributions?

a. 50, 58, 63, 55, 52, 60, 54, 53, 61, 50
b. 50, 58, 63, 55, 52, 60, 54, 53, 61, 96

MEDIAN

As described earlier in this chapter, the median is a score in the middle of the distribution. Another way to describe the median is that it is a value at which 50% of the scores in the distribution are at that value or lower. The median is reported less often than the mean as a measure of central tendency, but it is an important measure for skewed distributions, where the mean is influenced by extreme scores in the distribution. As we saw in the last section, an extreme score in a data set will pull the mean toward that score. The more extreme the score, the stronger its influence on the mean. The median, however, is less influenced by extreme scores, because it is a measure of the middle score in the distribution.

Calculating the Median by Hand

For a data set with an odd number of scores, the median is simply the middle score when the scores are listed from lowest to highest. Counting into the distribution to the middle score will give you the median score. For example, if your data set includes the scores 50, 52, 53, 54, 55, 58, 60, 61, 63, the median score is 55, because it is the fifth score out of nine total scores. Compare this with the mean of 56.22, and you will see that the mean is pulled more toward the larger scores in the top end of the distribution, as the scores cover a range of eight values on the scale, whereas the lower scores only cover a range of five values on the scale. For a set of data with an even number of scores, the median is the average of the two middle scores. For this data set—50, 50, 52, 53, 54, 55, 58, 60, 61, 63—the median is the average of 54 and 55, or 54.5. Notice that the scores are ordered from lowest to highest. That is important in finding the middle score. If they are not ordered in this way, you will not easily find the median.

Calculating the Median Using Excel

Excel can also be used to calculate the median of a distribution. Let's look again at our ratings for desire to watch the new TV show that we considered for Excel and SPSS in the previous section. To calculate the median for these scores, we will use the MEDIAN function. It works in a similar way to the AVERAGE function we used to calculate the mean for these data. To calculate the median, in an empty cell type =MEDIAN(. Then drag the cursor over the data in the column or type in the cells (A1:A56) with a colon separating the cell markers. End the function with a) if it is not automatically filled in. Your completed function statement should look like this:

=MEDIAN(A2:A56)

Then hit Enter. The median of 5 (on our 7-point rating scale) will appear in the cell.

SUMMARY OF STEPS

- Enter the data into a column in the data window.
- In an empty cell, type =MEDIAN(.
- Highlight the scores you want to include or type in the cell letters or numbers.
- Close with an end parenthesis, and hit Enter.

Calculating the Median Using SPSS

Calculating the median using SPSS is similar to the method used to calculate the mean with this software. However, to calculate the median, we must use the Frequencies function under Descriptive Statistics in the Analyze menu, as the median is not listed as a choice in the Options for the Statistics function. Once again, you will need to click on the ratings in the left window and then the arrow to move it into the Variable(s) window. Then click on the Statistics button to choose the Median box. Figure 6.5 shows this box with the Median chosen. You may also notice that there is a box for the Mean and one for the Mode (we will discuss the mode in the next section). Thus, using the Frequencies function, you can calculate any of the measures of central tendency discussed in this chapter using SPSS. Once you click Continue in the Statistics window, it will take you back to the Frequencies window, where you can then choose OK to calculate the Median. The output will contain the median in the top box with the frequency distribution table we created for these data (see Figure 6.6). The same median given in Excel (a score of 5) is shown in the figure.

SUMMARY OF STEPS

- Enter the data into a column in the data window.
- Label the data in the Variable View tab.
- Find Descriptive Statistics in the Analyze menu at the top.
- Choose the Frequencies function in the Descriptive Statistics options.
- Move the data column into the Variable box by highlighting it and clicking on the arrow.
- Under Statistics, click the Median box (see Figure 6.5).
- Click Continue and OK; your median will appear in the Output window (see Figure 6.6).

FIGURE 6.5 ■ The Frequencies: Statistics Window in SPSS

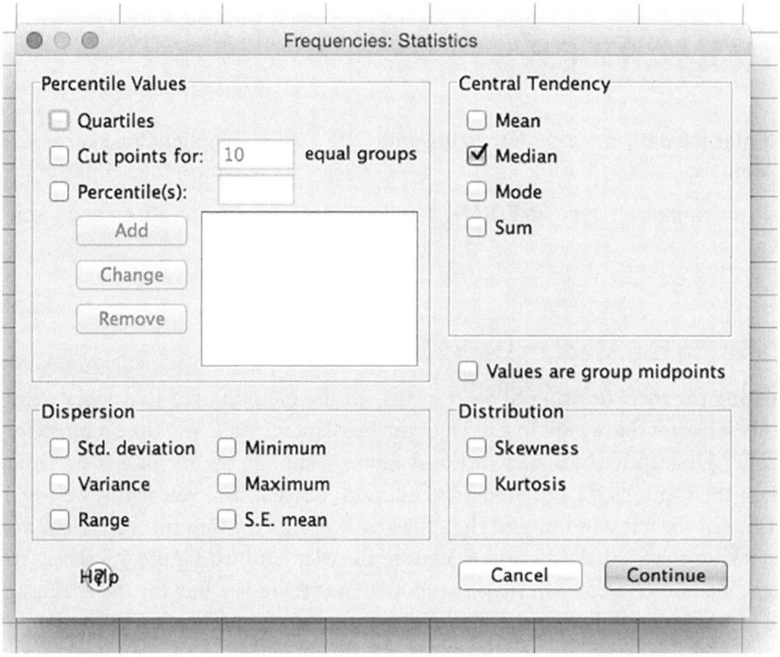

FIGURE 6.6 ■ The Output in SPSS Showing the Calculated Median for the Ratings Data

Frequencies

```
[DataSet1] /Stats Text/CH2_freq_dist.sav
```

Statistics

Rating

N	Valid	55
	Missing	0
Median		5.0000

MODE

Our third measure of central tendency is the mode. The mode is simply the most common score in the distribution. In fact, we can easily determine the mode from a frequency distribution table of a data set by looking at the score that occurs most often in the frequency column. The mode is useful to report when it differs from the mean and median. For example, if you have a data set that contains many scores at the top and bottom of the scale (e.g., a data set with 1 to 5 ratings with many *1*s and *5*s), the mode will give you a better measure of a typical score than the mean or median, which will fall between these values. Another use of the mode is for data from a nominal scale (look back at Figure 6.1 and the choice for the nominal measurement scale), where there are no numbers that can be used to calculate the mean or median. For example, if you have asked students to report their major on a demographic scale, you would likely report the frequencies of different majors listed with the mode as the most common major for the people in your sample. Although the mode is the simplest of the measures of central tendency to calculate, we will still discuss how to obtain the mode using the different methods we have covered for the other measures. Excel and SPSS can be especially useful for obtaining the mode when your data set is large so that you do not need to count the scores in your distribution.

Calculating the Mode by Hand

As described in the previous paragraph, the mode is the most common score in a distribution. Thus, if your data set contains the values 1, 2, 3, 5, 5, 1, 5, 5, 3, 5, 5, 2, 5, 4, 3, 5, 5, 2, 1, 5, the mode is fairly easy to determine. There are 10 scores of value 5 in this data set, which is easily seen as the most frequent score in the data set. There are far fewer than 10 of each of the other scores on the 1 to 5 rating scale here (the next most frequent are the scores of 1, 2, and 3, all with three scores at each of these values).

Calculating the Mode Using Excel

The MODE function in Excel will determine the mode of the distribution for you. This is useful with large data sets, such as our television show ratings distribution. To calculate the mode for this data set, type =MODE(into an empty cell in the data window. Then highlight the ratings or type in the A2:A56 range for these data and end with a). Thus, your function for calculating the mode will look like this:

=MODE(A2:A56)

When you hit Enter, the mode of 6 will be shown, as this is the most frequent rating used by the individuals in this data set. There were 16 scores of 6 in this data set, which is about 29% of the scores.

SUMMARY OF STEPS

- Enter the data into a column in the data window.
- In an empty cell, type =MODE(.
- Highlight the scores you want to include or type in the cell letter or numbers.
- Close with an end parenthesis, and hit Enter.

Calculating the Mode Using SPSS

As described in the previous section on calculating the median, to calculate the mode in SPSS, we will also use the Frequencies function under the Descriptive Statistics menu in the Analyze menu. In the Frequencies: Statistics window shown in Figure 6.5, check the box for Mode. The output box will then include the mode as shown in Figure 6.7. I have included the mean, median, and mode in the output of Figure 6.7 so that you can see how they compare for this distribution. The mean is the lowest value (4.87), followed by the median (5.00), and then the mode (6.00). This ordering shows how the mean is pulled toward the lower scores in this distribution, which are far less frequent than the higher scores of 4, 5, 6, and 7. Thus, the median and mode do a better job than the mean of capturing the typical scores in this distribution because the mean is more greatly influenced by the fewer low scores in the distribution. We will discuss how these values compare a bit more in the next section.

FIGURE 6.7 ■ The Output in SPSS Showing the Calculated Mean, Median, and Mode for the Ratings Data

Frequencies

[DataSet1] /Stats Text/CH2_freq_dist.sav

Statistics

Rating

N	Valid	55
	Missing	0
Mean		4.8727
Median		5.0000
Mode		6.00

SUMMARY OF STEPS

- Enter the data into a column in the data window.
- Label the data in the Variable View tab.
- Find Descriptive Statistics in the Analyze menu at the top.
- Choose the Frequencies function in the Descriptive Statistics options.
- Move the data column into the Variable box by highlighting it and clicking on the arrow.
- Under Statistics, click the Mode box (see Figure 6.5).
- Click Continue and OK; your mode will appear in the Output window (see Figure 6.7).

STOP AND THINK

6.3. For each data set that follows, calculate the median and mode. (*Hint:* Don't forget to put the scores in order from lowest to highest before you calculate the median.) How do these values compare for each data set? Which one seems to be more representative of the scores in the data set? Explain your answer.

a. 1 to 5 Ratings on Satisfaction With Courses in One's Chosen Major: 4, 2, 4, 3, 4, 4, 5, 4, 1, 4, 3, 3, 4, 5, 4, 5, 1

b. Accuracy on a Categorization Task (Percentage Correct): 78, 87, 90, 91, 75, 76, 88, 87, 77, 75, 92, 95, 78, 92, 87

6.4. In your own words, explain why the median is a better measure of central tendency than the mean for distributions that contain extreme scores.

WHICH MEASURE OF CENTRAL TENDENCY SHOULD I USE?

Throughout this chapter, we have discussed some differences across the mean, median, and mode as measures of central tendency of a distribution. But how do we choose which measure of central tendency to report for a specific distribution? The answer will depend on different aspects of the distribution—some of which we have already discussed.

Shape of the Distribution

As I already mentioned, the mean is the most commonly reported measure of central tendency. It is also the measure that people are most familiar with. It provides a good representative value that uses all the scores in the distribution in its calculation. In addition, as you will see in our discussion of variability in the next section, the mean is involved in the calculation of the standard deviation and variance measures of variability. It will also provide a value near the middle of the distribution when the distribution is symmetrical (or close to it) in shape. However, the disadvantage of the mean as a measure of central tendency is that by using all the scores in the distribution for its calculation, it is influenced more by extreme scores than the median or mode.

Skewed distributions with extreme scores at the high or low end of the distribution are often better represented by the median. The median will give you the middle score (or average of the two middle scores) in a distribution, resulting in a fairly representative value for distributions that are skewed. Consider the distribution shown in Figure 6.8. This frequency distribution graph shows the scores from a final exam. What do you notice about the scores? Most of the scores are clustered between the values of 80% and 82%, but there are two very low scores down at 56% and 61%, likely from students who did not study well for the exam. If we calculate the mean for these scores, we get a value of 78.67%, which is lower than where most of the scores are. However, the median is 80%, which is a more representative value for these exam scores, because it is closer to where most of the scores actually are. The mean is being pulled toward the two extremely low scores in the distribution.

FIGURE 6.8 ■ Distribution of Exam Scores Comparing Mean and Median

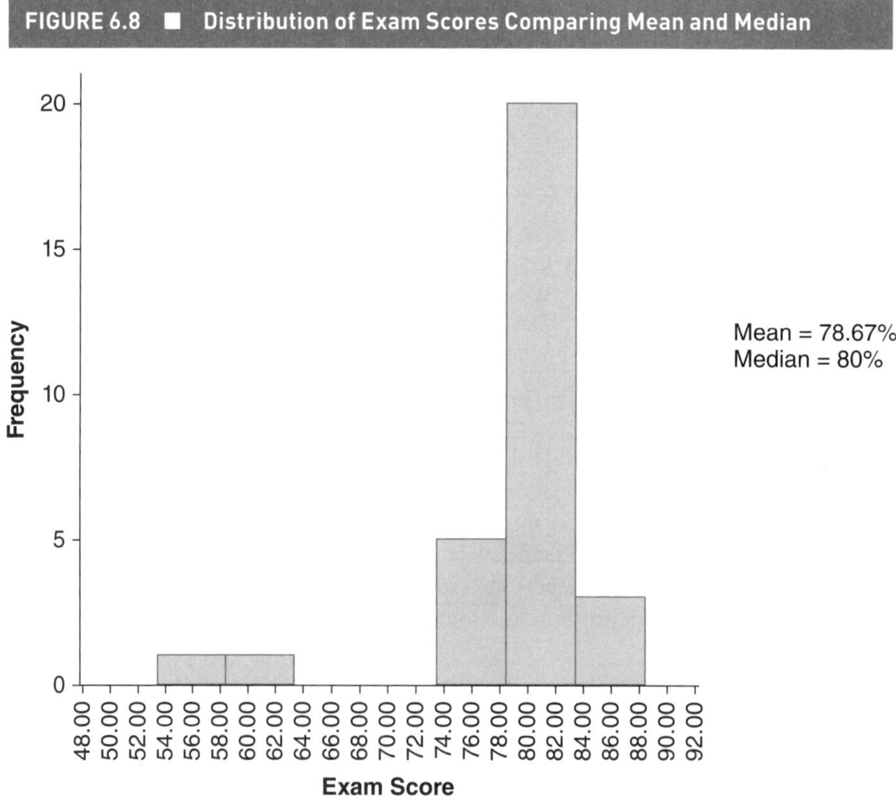

Another common distribution that is positively skewed is **reaction time** in a task. There are some scores in this distribution that are much higher than where the rest of the scores are, giving the distribution a tail on the high end of the scale. These much higher reaction times pull the mean toward the high end, making the mean response time seem much higher than it would be without these outliers. The median provides a better measure for this type of distribution because it gives us the middle score for reaction times that better represents the speed on the task for an individual.

reaction time: Measurement of the length of time to complete a task

Type of Data

Another good use of the median as a measure of central tendency is for ordinal data. When data are measured using an ordinal scale, the mean does not provide a good representation of the scores because the values on the scale are categories rather than values with equal distance between them. On such scales, there isn't a clear balance point for the scale (which is what the mean provides), but there is often a middle value. Thus, the median can provide a representative score on the scale. Consider a data set that contains responses regarding class rank: freshman, sophomore, junior, or senior. These are ordinal data because they can be ordered from lowest to highest, but how would you calculate a mean for these data? It would be difficult to do—our formula to add up the scores and divide by the total number of scores would not work. However, there would be a middle value on this scale if all the responses were ordered from highest to lowest. For example, if our sample contained 10 freshmen, 25 sophomores, 8 juniors, and 2 seniors, the median would be the sophomore level, because half of the people in the sample are at the sophomore level or lower. However, reporting a mode for these data would also be appropriate, as the mode would indicate the class rank for the majority of students in the sample.

Another example where the median would be a better measure of central tendency because the mean is difficult to calculate is an open-ended response category in our data set. For example, suppose you were responding to a survey that asked how many hours a week you study for your statistics course. The responses you are given are 2 hr, 3 hr, 4 hr, 5 hr, and 6 or more hr. The last category of 6 or more hr is open-ended; it does not define the highest value in the category. Thus, our mean formula would not work here either. But our median calculation for the middle score (e.g., 5 hr) would work because we could find the score where 50% of the responses are at that score or lower.

Nominal scales, where categories cannot even be ordered from highest to lowest, create another problem for central tendency calculations. For nominal data, we cannot apply our formula for calculating the mean (there aren't any numbered scores to add up), and we cannot find the middle scores because we cannot order our scores from highest to lowest. Thus, for nominal data, the mode is our only option for reporting central tendency. For example, if your food court survey asked students to list their favorite food court option, the most commonly listed response would be the only measure of central tendency you could report.

Another case where the mode is a good measure to use is when the response scale only has two possible values. This type of distribution is a *bimodal* distribution. You may be able to order the values in terms of which one is higher (e.g., 0 or 1), but calculating the mean and median will not provide a good representation of this distribution. Both the mean and median will come out somewhere between the two values, which does not represent the scores very well. Thus, the mode is a better measure (e.g., most values were at a 1) than the mean or median.

Figure 6.9 presents a flowchart to help you decide which measure of central tendency to use in a specific situation. If you look back at Figure 6.1, you will see that it is an enlargement of the central tendency portion of that flowchart. To use the flowchart in Figure 6.9, answer each question as you go through the chart and follow the links for your answers to determine which measure is best for your distribution of data.

FIGURE 6.9 ■ Flowchart for Deciding Which Measure of Central Tendency to Use (Expansion of Central Tendency Section of Figure 6.1)

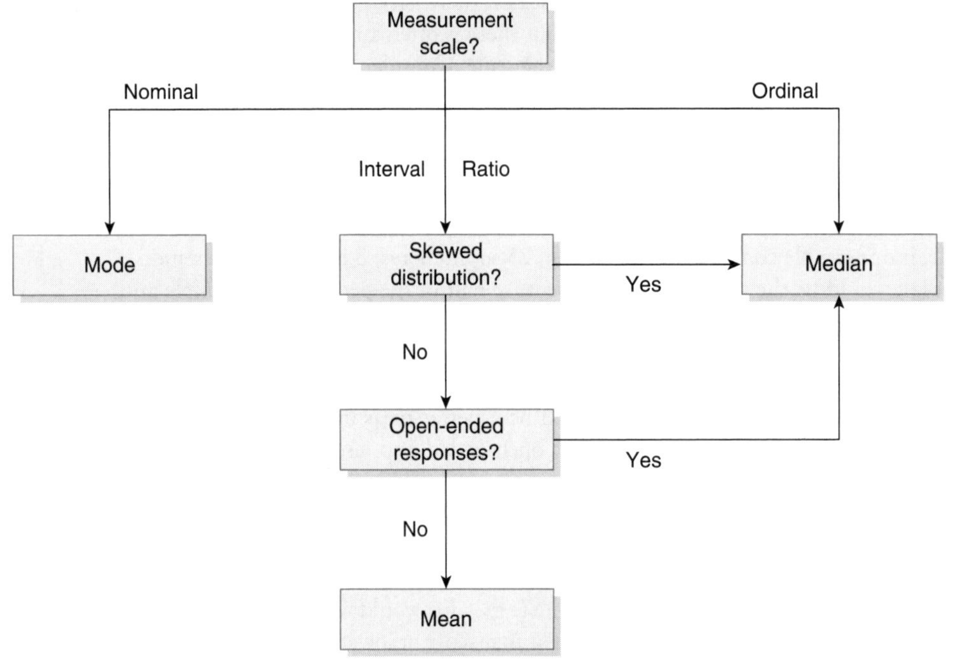

STOP AND THINK

6.5. For each of the following measures described here, indicate which measure of central tendency you would choose and why. Figure 6.9 may help you decide.

a. Speed to complete a Sudoku puzzle, measured in seconds

b. Responses indicating which time of day (morning or afternoon) someone prefers to study for an exam

c. Rating on a 1 to 5 scale indicating how pleasant someone found a social experience he or she is asked to participate in during a study

6.6. You have designed a survey for a research study you are conducting as part of a course. You are interested in how many children people are interested in having in the future to see if this is related to how many siblings one grew up with. For each item, you ask people to respond with one of the following choices: zero children or siblings, one child or sibling, two children or siblings, three children or siblings, and four or more children or siblings. Explain why the median or mode would be a better measure of central tendency for these data than the mean.

Calculation Summary

mean: Adding up the scores in the data set and dividing by the total number of scores

median: For data sets with an odd number of scores, putting the scores in order from lowest to highest and then finding the middle score; for data sets with an even number of scores, putting the scores in order from lowest to highest and then averaging the two middle scores

mode: Counting the frequencies (i.e., how often each score appears) of the scores—the mode is the score(s) with the highest frequency in the data set

VARIABILITY IN DISTRIBUTIONS

Let's once again consider our example from the beginning of the chapter: You are conducting a survey for the student government board at your school to examine the students' satisfaction with the current food court options at the student union. You've conducted your survey asking people to rate how much they like the current food court choices on a scale of 1 to 7. You have survey responses from 150 students. Let's assume you've calculated the mean rating from the sample and found that mean rating is 5. You are getting ready to report back to the student board that, overall, people are fairly satisfied with the food choices. However, you start to wonder just how often the ratings were close to a rating of 5. In other words, did most students choose a rating close to 5 (i.e., between 4 and 6), or did the ratings cover the entire scale with some students very dissatisfied (i.e., ratings of 1 or 2) and more students fairly satisfied (i.e., with ratings of 5, 6, and 7)? One way to answer this question is to consider the variability of the scores in the sample.

Variability is simply a description of how different the scores are from one another in the distribution. If something varies, it means that it differs from other things in some way (see Photo 6.3) such that high variability in a distribution means that the scores are widely spread out across the scale. Low variability means the opposite—that the scores are very similar and clustered around a middle value. If the students in our

Photo 6.3 Variability means that things (e.g., cars, scores) differ in some way (e.g., style, their value).

sample used the entire 1 to 7 scale (i.e., there were scores in the data set for all values from 1 to 7), then the variability in our sample data would be higher than if the ratings all had values of 4, 5, and 6 on the scale. However, both of these situations could yield a mean of 5, as in our survey data.

Figure 6.10 shows the difference between these two possible distributions. In the high variability graph, the scores are spread out across the whole 1 to 7 rating scale, but in the low variability graph, the scores are clustered between the values of 4 and 6. In both cases, the mean is 5, showing that variability can be high or low, regardless of what the mean of a distribution is. Although extreme scores affect the mean, the extreme scores in the high variability graph are at both the high and low end of the scale, so this data set gives you the same mean of 5 that you get from the distribution in the low variability graph, where there are no extreme scores.

You may also notice in these graphs that the high variability distribution has a negative skew (i.e., more extreme scores in the low end of the distribution, showing a tail at the low end of the scale in the shape of the distribution). In this case, the median would be a better measure of central tendency to report (look back at Figure 6.9 for an overview of the measures of central tendency), as it would better reflect the majority of the ratings that are on the high end of the scale. However, the median in this distribution is also 5 because the two middle scores are 5s in the distribution. This is the same as the median in the low variability graph (also 5), so the variability is not affecting the mean or the median for these distributions (although in some skewed distributions, the median will be a different value from the mean). Thus, the variability of a distribution can be seen in frequency distribution graphs such as those shown in Figure 6.10. Let's now consider ways to measure the variability of a distribution.

standard deviation: A measure representing the average difference between the scores and the mean of a distribution

STANDARD DEVIATION

A common measure of variability is the **standard deviation**. Simply put, you can think of the standard deviation as representing the average distance between the scores and the mean (see Figure 6.11). However, you will shortly see that we can't simply calculate the average distance because in all distributions that value would be zero. The positive and negative differences between the scores and the mean will balance out and give us a value of zero, because the mean is the balance point of the

FIGURE 6.10 ■ High and Low Variability Distributions of Satisfaction Ratings

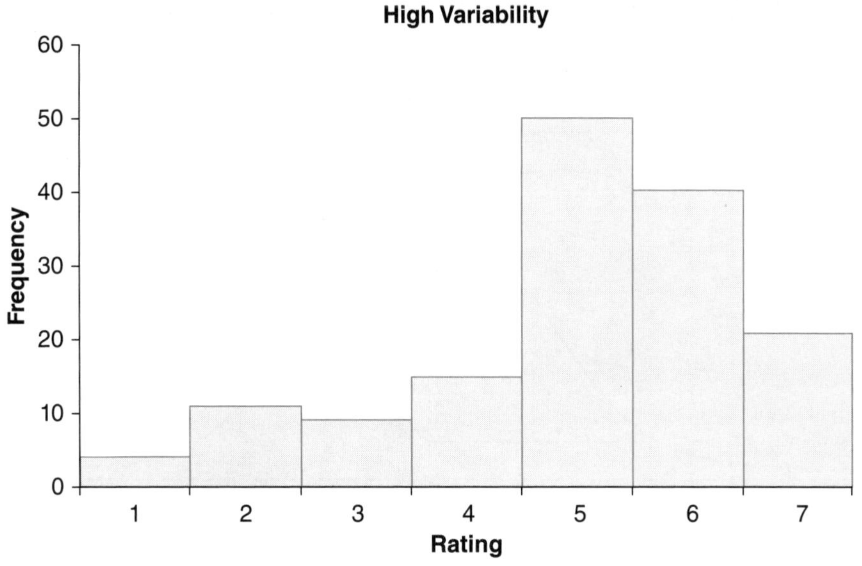

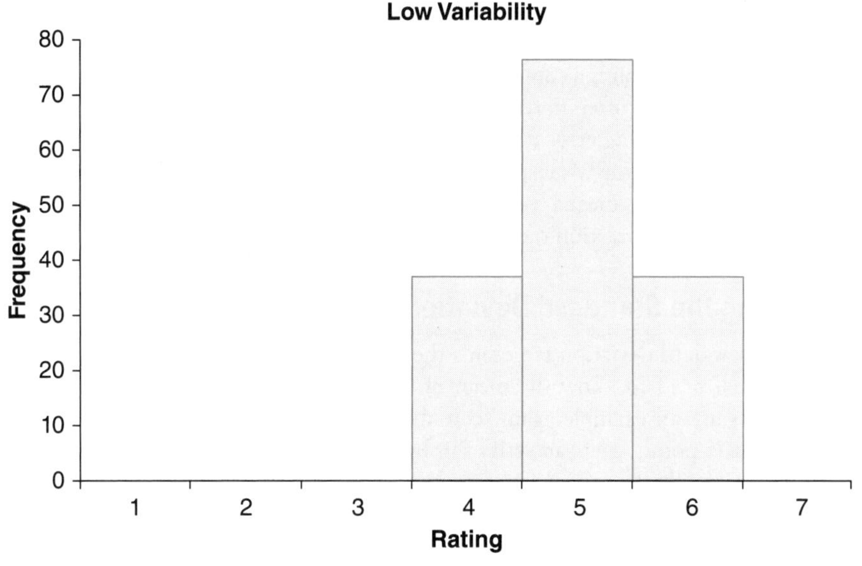

distribution. Instead, we will have to remove the direction of the differences from the mean by squaring the differences between the scores and the mean in our calculation and taking the average of the sum of those squared differences. This will give us a measure known as the **variance**, which in itself is a measure of variability that we will use in some calculations of inferential statistics in later chapters. But when we

variance: The standard deviation of a distribution squared

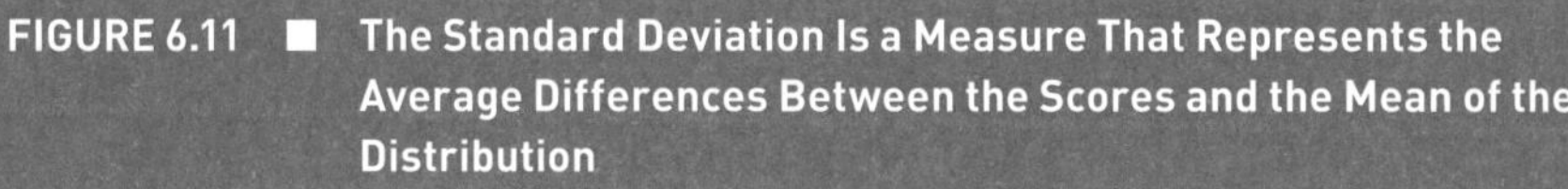
FIGURE 6.11 ■ The Standard Deviation Is a Measure That Represents the Average Differences Between the Scores and the Mean of the Distribution

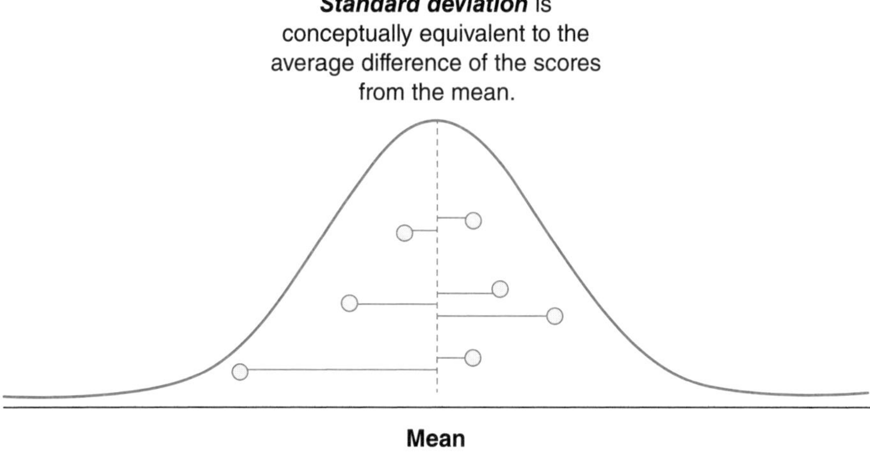

take the square root of the variance to reverse our squaring transformation, we get the standard deviation.

Standard deviation is conceptually equivalent to the average difference of the scores from the mean.
Mean

The standard deviation is a common measure of variability for a set of scores, and you will see it reported more often in research than the range or interquartile range. It is used as an estimate of sampling error (the difference between our sample statistics and those that we would get from the whole population) for our data when we calculate inferential statistics comparing the means for two samples or conditions or comparing a sample mean with a known population mean covered in later chapters of this text.

Calculating the Standard Deviation by Hand

Because the standard deviation represents the average difference between the scores and the mean, we'll need to know the mean of our distribution before we begin our calculation. Let's use an example exam score distribution shown below. The mean of the distribution is 75 points. You can verify this by calculating the mean for the scores. We'll use this mean to calculate the differences between the scores and the mean. That's our first step: Calculate the difference between each score and the mean. For our exam scores, we'll have the following:

$55 - 75 = -20$

$60 - 75 = -15$

$65 - 75 = -10$

$70 - 75 = -5$

$70 - 75 = -5$

$75 - 75 = 0$

$75 - 75 = 0$

$80 - 75 = 5$

$80 - 75 = 5$

$85 - 75 = 10$

$90 - 75 = 15$

$95 - 75 = 20$

These are our differences, also called *deviations*, from the mean. Because we are calculating the average, the next step would be to add the deviations up and divide by the number of scores. But what happens when you add these up? You get zero. This will happen every time we add up the deviations because the mean is the balancing point of the distribution. The deviations for scores above the mean balance with the deviations for scores below the mean to give us zero when we add them up. To get around this issue, we need to add an important part to Step 1: Square the deviations. If we transform the deviations by squaring them, we take away the sign (positive or negative) and we will no longer get zero when we add them up.

Step 1: Calculate the difference between each score and the mean and square the differences.

If we square the deviations we just calculated, we get the following:

$(-20)^2 = 400$

$(-15)^2 = 225$

$(-10)^2 = 100$

$(-5)^2 = 25$

$(-5)^2 = 25$

$(0)^2 = 0$

$(0)^2 = 0$

$(5)^2 = 25$

$(5)^2 = 25$

$(10)^2 = 100$

$(15)^2 = 225$

$(20)^2 = 400$

Now, we're ready for Step 2: adding up the squared deviations. Adding up these squared deviations will give us a value known as the *sum of squared deviations* or just *sum of squares*. This is often abbreviated with *SS* in equations (as you will see shortly).

Step 2: Add up the squared deviations to get the sum of squares (*SS*).

Adding these up will give us the following:

$$400 + 225 + 100 + 25 + 25 + 0 + 0 + 25 + 25 + 100 + 225 + 400 = 1550$$

Now, for Step 3, we need to take the average of the squared deviations by dividing by the total number of scores. Our distribution includes all the students in the class, so it is actually a population distribution instead of a sample (you will see why this is important in the next section). For Step 3, then, we can just divide by the total number of scores to get the average sum of squares. This is a value known as the *variance*, and it is indicated by the symbol σ^2 for a population and s^2 for a sample.

Step 3: Divide by N for a population to get the variance (σ^2).

For Step 3, we will divide the sum of squares (1550) by the number of scores (12) to get the following:

$$\textit{Population variance} = \frac{1550}{12} = 129.17$$

This is the variance of our exam score distribution. We just have one step left now: to reverse the squaring transformation we did earlier for the deviations. Step 4 is to take the square root of the variance:

Step 4: Take the square root of the variance.

$$\textit{Population standard deviation} = \sqrt{129.16667} = 11.37$$

This means that the average difference between the exam scores and the mean of 75 is 11.37 points. This value represents the average difference between the scores and the mean in the distribution. A large standard deviation indicates that the scores in the distribution are spread out across the measurement scale. A small standard deviation indicates that the scores in the distribution are packed close to the mean.

Now, let's put all these steps together into formulas for the population standard deviation:

$$\sigma = \sqrt{\frac{\Sigma\left(X - \bar{X}\right)^2}{N}} \text{ or } \sigma = \sqrt{\frac{SS}{N}}$$

Thus, our formulas contain our four steps:

Step 1: Calculate the difference between each score and the mean and then square the difference: $\left(X-\bar{X}\right)^2$

Step 2: Add up the squared deviations to get the sum of squares: $\Sigma(X-\bar{X})^2$

Step 3: Divide by N for a population to get the variance $\left(\sigma^2\right)$: $\dfrac{\Sigma(X-\bar{X})^2}{N}$

Step 4: Find the square root of the variance: $\sqrt{\dfrac{\Sigma\left(X-\bar{X}\right)^2}{N}}$ *or* $\sqrt{\dfrac{SS}{N}}$

Populations Versus Samples

The calculation that was just described is how we would determine the standard deviation for a population distribution of scores (i.e., if the entire population was tested). However, with a sample, we have fewer scores contributing to our variability. This means that the variability of a sample will be lower than the variability of the population the sample represents. Because of this difference, we have to correct for the fact that there are fewer scores in our sample using a term known as the **degrees of freedom**. The degrees of freedom are the number of scores that can vary in a set of scores with a known mean (which we have already calculated to determine the deviations). Once we know the mean, all the scores, except one, can be any value (i.e., they are "free to vary"). Thus, degrees of freedom for a sample are one less than the number of scores. We'll use this term ($n-1$) instead of N to calculate the average of the sum of squares for a sample.

degrees of freedom: The number of scores that can vary in the calculation of a statistic

To show you how this calculation is different, let's assume that instead of 12 people in the course, there are 100, but we only have a sample of exam scores from 12 of the students in the class. Now our data set in Figure 6.4 is from a sample instead of from the population. This will change our calculation of the standard deviation a bit as described previously to include the degrees of freedom. Our formula for the sample standard deviation is as follows:

$$s=\sqrt{\frac{\Sigma\left(X-\bar{X}\right)^2}{n-1}} \quad \text{or} \quad s=\sqrt{\frac{SS}{n-1}}$$

Using this formula, the standard deviation for the sample of exam scores is as follows:

$$s=\sqrt{\frac{1550}{12-1}}=\sqrt{140.91}=11.87$$

The standard deviation for this sample is higher for a sample than for all 12 scores as a population because this sample is meant to represent the population of scores from all 100 students, which should be higher because it contains more scores. Whenever we calculate the standard deviation, we will need to first determine if we are working with a sample or a population so that we can choose the correct formula.

Calculating the Standard Deviation Using Excel

In many cases, we will have a lot of scores in our distribution, making it time-consuming to calculate the standard deviation by hand. Excel can be used to calculate the standard deviation of a set of scores for us to save time and reduce the chance of a calculation error. However, it is still important that you understand the hand calculations of the statistics you are using so that you know what the values mean when they are calculated with a software program.

Excel contains formulas for the standard deviation. The STDEV function is for samples and will use the formula with the degrees of freedom ($n - 1$) in its calculation. You can verify this by typing in the formula below into an empty cell of a data window in Excel containing the exam score data:

=STDEV(A1:A12)

This formula will give you a standard deviation of 11.87 (when rounded to two significant digits) that matches our hand calculation for the sample standard deviation (s). To calculate the standard deviation for a population, you need to use the STDEVP function (P for population). Thus, for the same scores as a population, your standard deviation function would be this:

=STDEVP(A1:A12)

This formula will give you a standard deviation of 11.37 (when rounded to two significant digits) that matches our hand calculation for the population standard deviation (σ) we calculated in the previous section.

Calculating the Standard Deviation Using SPSS

SPSS will also easily calculate the standard deviation of a set of scores. In the Analyze menu, under Descriptives, you can choose the Standard deviation box under Options in this window (Analyze → Descriptive Statistics → Descriptives → Options; see Figure 6.12 for the Descriptives: Options window view). However, if you run this function in SPSS, you will see that it is for a sample standard deviation (see Figure 6.13 for the Output for the exam scores distribution). For a population of scores, the value provided by SPSS for the standard deviation would need to be transformed by multiplying it by $\sqrt{\frac{(n-1)}{n}}$. For most software packages, including Excel and SPSS, the default calculation for the standard deviation is for a sample rather than a population because the entire population is rarely tested in research studies.

FIGURE 6.12 ■ Descriptives Options Window in SPSS

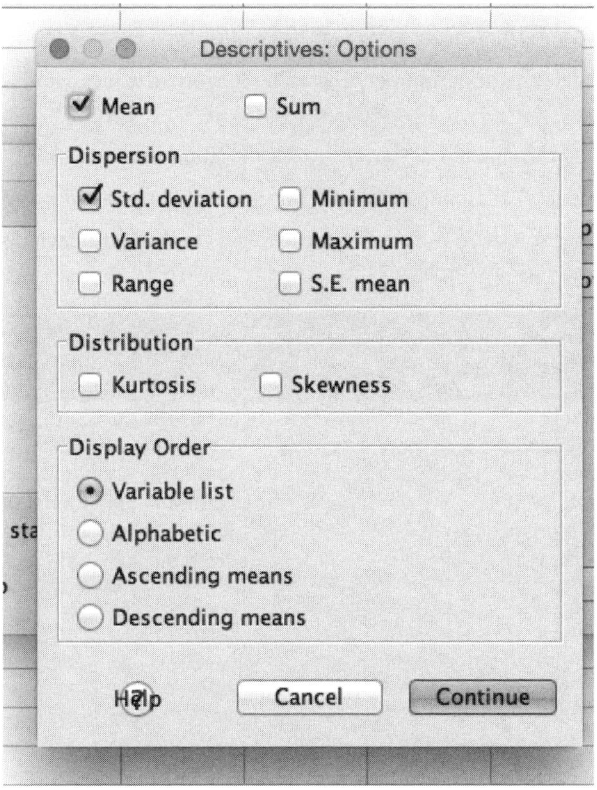

Descriptives: Options

☑ Mean ☐ Sum

Dispersion

☑ Std. deviation ☐ Minimum

☐ Variance ☐ Maximum

☐ Range ☐ S.E. mean

Distribution

☐ Kurtosis ☐ Skewness

Display Order

◉ Variable list

○ Alphabetic

○ Ascending means

○ Descending means

Help Cancel Continue

FIGURE 6.13 ■ SPSS Output Window Showing the Sample Standard Deviation (s) for the Exam Scores Distribution

Descriptives

```
[DataSet1] /Stats Text/SPSS_Excel_files/5_5.sav
```

Descriptive Statistics

	N	Mean	Std. Deviation
Exam Scores	12	75.0000	11.87051
Valid *N* (listwise)	12		

Calculation Summary

standard deviation: Have the mean calculated already in order to calculate the standard deviation.

Step 1: Calculate the deviation between each score and the mean and square the difference.

Step 2: Add up the squared deviations to get the sum of squares (*SS*).

Step 3: Divide by N for a population (σ^2) or $n - 1$ for a sample (s^2) to get the variance.

Step 4: Take the square root of the variance to get the standard deviation (σ for a population and s for a sample).

STOP AND THINK

6.7. Calculate the standard deviation for the two sets of data (from populations) that follow. In what way are the data sets related? How does this relationship influence the standard deviation for the data?

a. 1, 3, 2, 5, 1, 3, 4, 5, 1

b. 2, 6, 4, 10, 2, 6, 8, 10, 2

6.8. For the sets of data that were just given, now assume they are data from samples (instead of from populations). How will the standard deviations of the distributions change from those in 6.4?

categorical variables: Measures with responses as categories that cannot be divided into smaller units

bar graphs: Graphs of data for categorical variables where the bar height represents the size of the value (e.g., mean)

continuous variables: Measures with number scores that can be divided into smaller units

line graphs: Graphs of data for continuous variables where each value is graphed as a point and the points are connected to show differences between scores (e.g., means)

DESCRIPTIVE STATISTICS IN GRAPHS

Graphs can present a visual display of the descriptive statistics you have calculated for a set of data. However, the type of graph you choose to present your data will partially depend on the type of data you have collected. Generally, data for **categorical variables** (i.e., categories as in nominal and ordinal scales of measurement or whole numbers that cannot be divided into smaller units as in rating scales) are presented in **bar graphs**, whereas data for **continuous variables** (i.e., numerical scores that can be subdivided into smaller units) are presented in **line graphs**. You will also need to consider which variables you will include in your graph because you may have a categorical independent variable for your x-axis and a continuous variable as your dependent variable for your y-axis. In this case, you must consider what type of variable is being placed on the x-axis of the graph to determine which type of graph you will use.

Bar Graphs

Categorical variables can be represented in bar graphs. Bar graphs show the value of a variable with the height of a bar for each category of the variable. Figure 6.14 shows a bar graph

FIGURE 6.14 ■ Bar Graph of Grades on a Class Exam

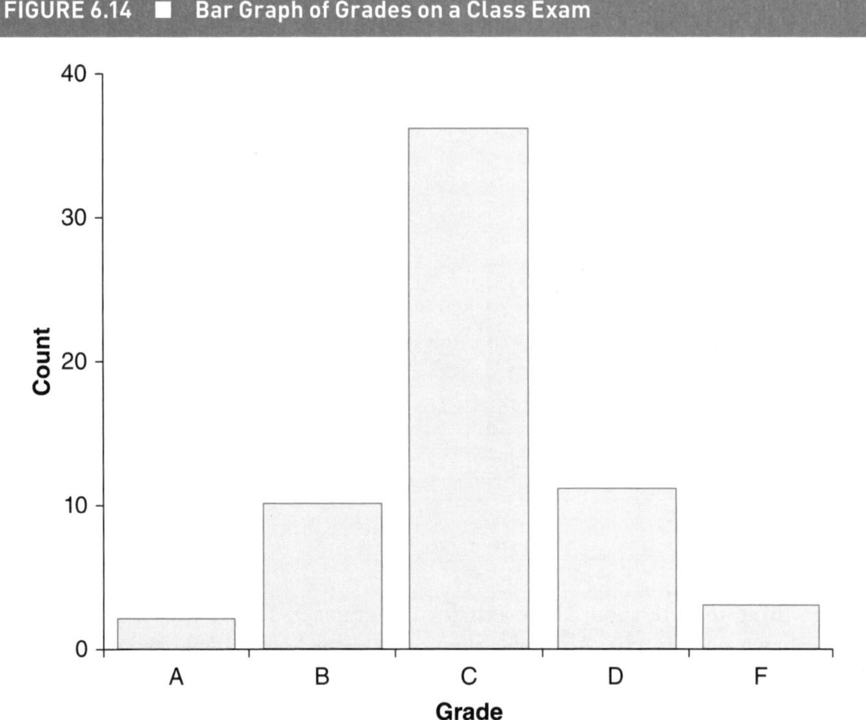

of an exam grade distribution. The bar heights indicate the proportions of students in the course that earned each letter grade on the exam. It is clear from the graph that the largest proportion of students in the course earned a grade of C on the exam.

Consider another example: Figure 6.15 shows data from a decision-making study conducted by Worthy, Gorlick, Pacheco, Schnyer, and Maddox (2011), comparing performance on a strategy task for younger and older adults. The categorical variable of *age group* is shown on the x-axis with *mean number of points earned* as the continuous performance measure on the y-axis. Bar height indicates the performance level for each age group and shows the higher number of points earned by the younger adults than the older adults in the task. Also notice the lines extending from the bars. These are the 95% **confidence intervals** (i.e., the range of the estimated population means with a specific level of probability). You will typically see these lines presented in bar graphs that show measures of central tendency (most often the mean) by group or categorical condition in research studies. The lines will show the confidence intervals for the means or another measure of variability, such as the standard deviations or the standard errors (discussed further in a later chapter of this text) to illustrate some of the information that is important for testing for differences between the means in inferential statistics. We will discuss the logic of hypothesis testing in Chapter 9 of this text.

confidence intervals: Ranges of values that the population mean likely falls in with a specific level of certainty

FIGURE 6.15 ■ Data From the Worthy et al. (2011) Study Shown in a Bar Graph

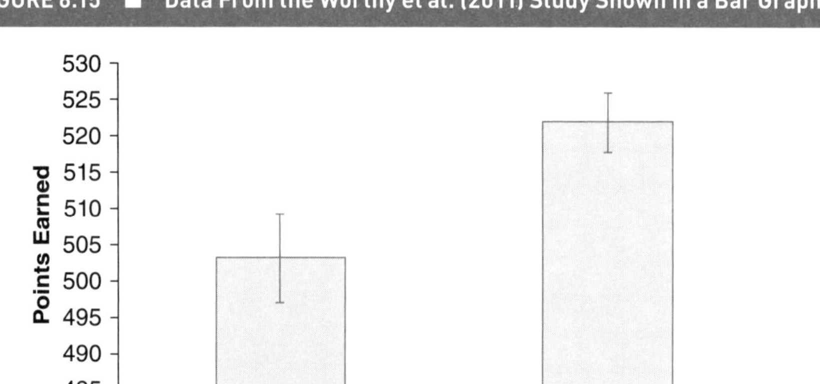

Source: Worthy et al. (2011).

One thing to note about the y-axis for the graph in Figure 6.15 is the range of values shown on this axis. Although the points earned scale likely extends down to a low point of zero for this measure, the researchers chose to present the values as extending from 480 to 530 total points in this graph. Different factors might have contributed to this choice. For example, the researchers might have chosen the lowest value of 480 on this axis based on the lowest score earned by any one participant in their study; this might then show the actual range of point values relevant for their study. However, imagine that they had used zero as the lowest value on the y-axis—how would the group difference appear in this graph? Because of the large range in values on the axis, the groups would look much more similar in their scores, although the error bars would be smaller as well, highlighting the score difference needed for a significant difference. You can also imagine what the graph might look like if the range of values on the y-axis was smaller (e.g., 490 to 530). In this case, the group differences would look much larger than they do in Figure 6.15. The error bars would be the only indication of the size of the difference needed to support a difference in the population. You can see from these examples that manipulation of the scale on a graph can be misleading. Beware of graphs that are presented to make an argument and look for error bars to help you determine if the differences shown are important or not.

Line Graphs

When presenting descriptive statistics for continuous variables such as an amount (e.g., dosage of a drug prescribed, amount of time between tasks), line graphs are more appropriate than bar graphs. In a line graph, you graph the values (e.g., means)

for each group or condition as points on the y-axis centered above the appropriate value of the continuous variable on the x-axis. The points are then connected with a line. For example, if you conducted a study comparing memory for information after two delay times, 5 min and 20 min, the line graph shown in Figure 6.16 could be used to display the mean memory performance by delay time. In this graph, the typical result of better memory for the shorter delay is clearly seen by the declining slope of the line connecting the means for the 5- and 20-min conditions. There may also be separate lines in a line graph for different levels of a categorical variable for study designs with multiple causal factors (e.g., different study tasks in the memory study).

Figure 6.17 shows bar and line graphs from another hypothetical memory study comparing two groups of subjects on two types of variables: the categorical variable of age group (Panel A) and the continuous variable of years of education (Panel B). These graphs show the difference between the construction of bar and line graphs and their uses. Both graphs show the difference in memory performance across the groups, but this difference is shown as a discrete mean difference for the groups in the bar graph and as the continuous difference based on the number of years of education for the subjects in the line graph. This figure shows the difference in the kinds of variables that these two graph types are used for in displaying descriptive statistics (e.g., mean performance on a task) from data distributions.

FIGURE 6.16 ■ Memory Data for Two Delay Times in a Line Graph

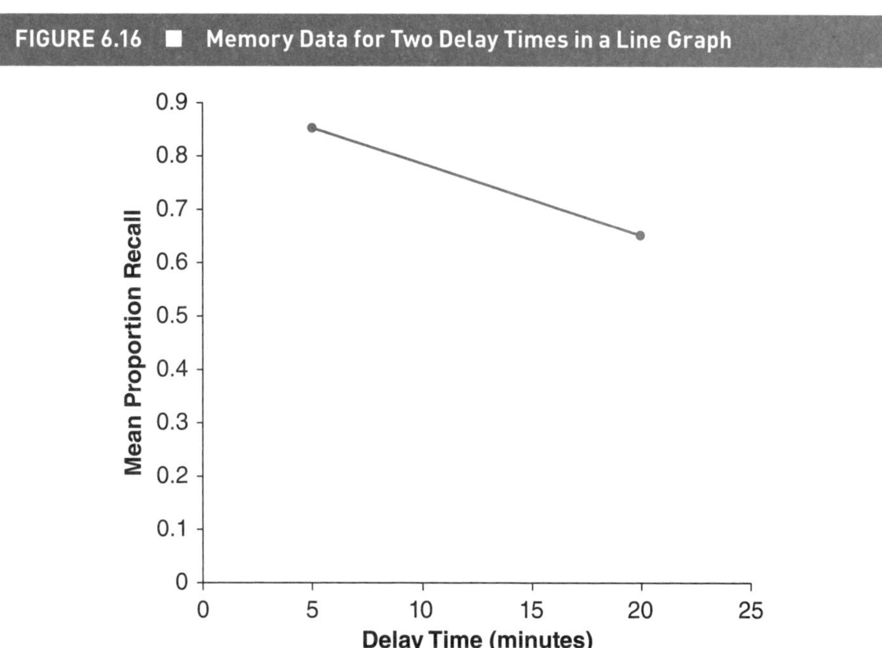

FIGURE 6.17 ■ Bar Graph Showing the Comparison of Mean Memory Scores for Children and Adults (Panel A) Line Graph Showing the Comparison of Mean Memory Scores Based on Years of Education (Panel B)

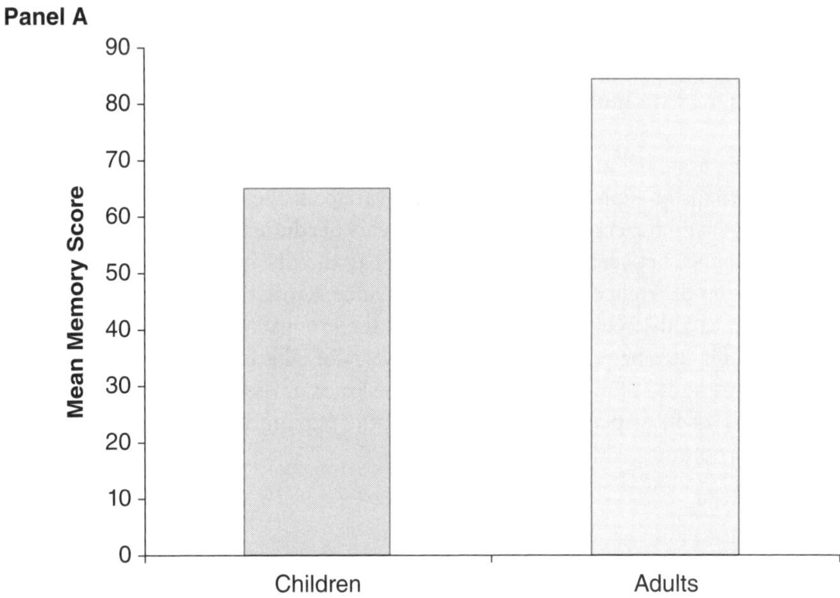

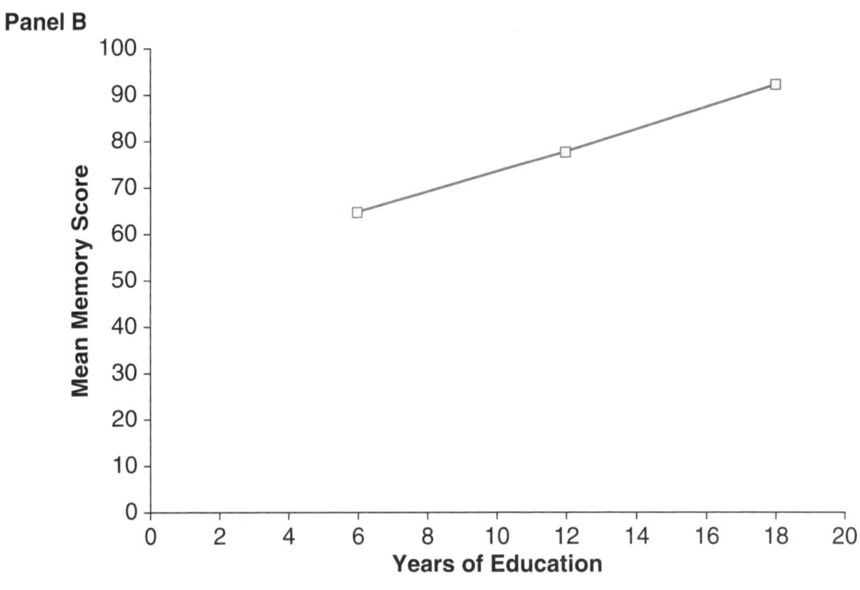

Scatterplots

A **scatterplot** is another type of graph you might see in a published paper or need to create for a correlational study. Unlike the graphs described in the previous sections, scatterplots display a data point for each individual in the data set with one measured variable on the x-axis and another measured variable on the y-axis. Scatterplots are typically used to show the relationship in scores between two continuous variables measured from a sample. They are useful in illustrating the strength and type (positive or negative) of relationship between the variables. Figure 6.18 shows a scatterplot for a hypothetical data set showing the negative relationship between hours of television watched per week and grade point average (GPA).

scatterplot: A graph showing the relationship between two dependent variables for a group of individuals

Creating Graphs Using Excel

In Chapter 1, I covered the procedure for creating frequency distribution graphs in Excel. As you saw there, we cannot easily create graphs from raw data in Excel. The data must first be transformed into descriptive statistics (e.g., frequency counts, means). This will also be the case for creating pie charts, bar graphs, and line graphs in Excel. Let's go through the process for creating the graphs in Figures 6.14 and 6.16 in Excel.

Once we have the proportions from our frequency distribution table (see the data in Figure 6.19), our Excel data window will include the values shown in Figure 6.19. To create a bar graph, we would choose the BAR option in the CHART function from the INSERT menu at the top of the window (INSERT → CHART → BAR). This will create the bar graph shown in Figure 6.20.

FIGURE 6.18 ■ Scatterplot Showing the Negative Relationship Between Hours of Television Watched per Week and GPA

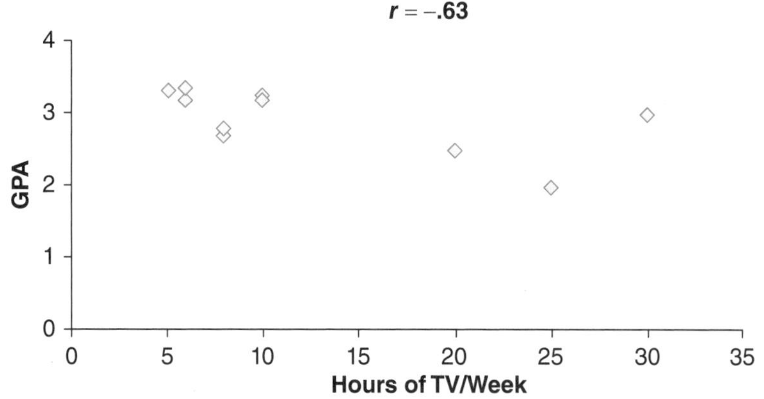

STOP AND THINK

6.9. For each of the following variable descriptions, indicate if it is a categorical or continuous variable:

a. The judged distance between two landmarks in an environment

b. Time to reach a destination using a map

c. Number of males and females in your sample

d. Grade level of the students in your sample

6.10. For each set of the following data descriptions, indicate which type of graph (bar graph or line graph) you would choose to illustrate the data and why you would choose that type of graph:

a. Number of students in each major at your university or college

b. Amount of time it took to solve different kinds of puzzles

c. Mean performance on a task by age in years

To create a line graph in Excel, you will use a similar procedure but use the scatterplot graphing function to ensure that your x-axis shows the continuous variable with appropriate spacing between the values. The scatterplot graph option will place the continuous variable on the x-axis. Figure 6.21 shows the mean memory performance

FIGURE 6.19 ■ Excel Data Window Showing Proportion of Students Earning Each Grade

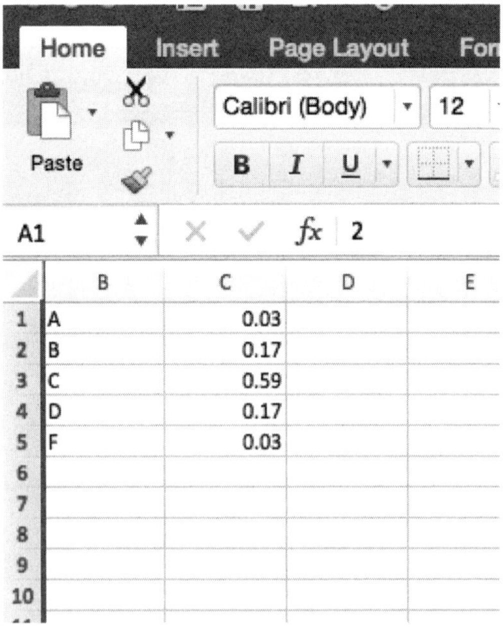

Home Insert Page Layout For

Paste Calibri (Body) 12

B I U

A1 fx 2

	B	C	D	E
1	A	0.03		
2	B	0.17		
3	C	0.59		
4	D	0.17		
5	F	0.03		
6				
7				
8				
9				
10				

FIGURE 6.20 ■ Bar Graph From Excel for Letter Grades Earned on a Class Exam

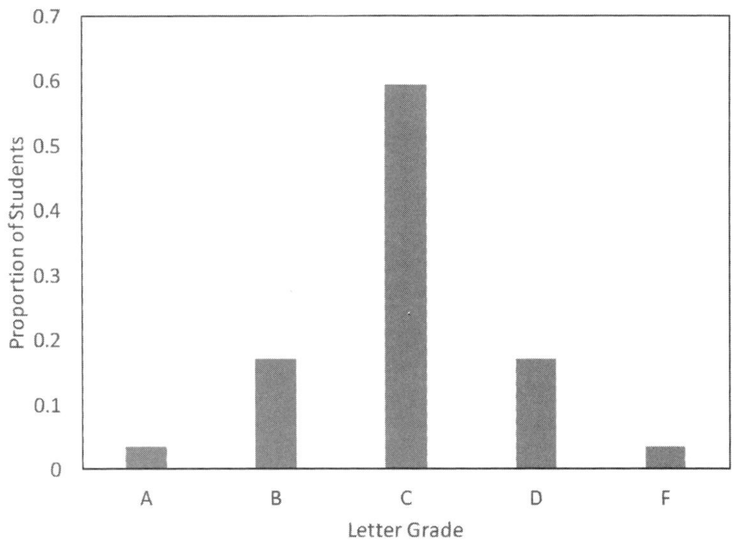

FIGURE 6.21 ■ Data Window From Excel Showing Mean Memory Performance Data by Delay Condition

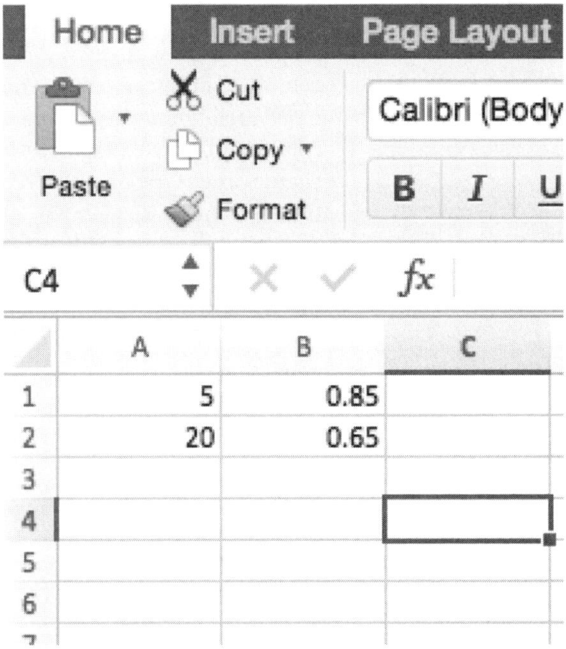

Home Insert Page Layout
Paste Cut Copy Format Calibri (Body B I U
C4 fx

	A	B	C
1	5	0.85	
2	20	0.65	
3			
4			
5			
6			

FIGURE 6.22 ■ SPSS Data Window Showing Data From the Likelihood to Watch a New TV Show

	ting	AgeGroup	var	var
1	1.00	18-24		
2	1.00	25-35		
3	2.00	36-50		
4	2.00	Over 50		
5	2.00	18-24		
6	2.00	25-35		
7	2.00	36-50		
8	3.00	Over 50		
9	3.00	Over 50		
10	3.00	Over 50		
11	3.00	Over 50		
12	4.00	Over 50		
13	4.00	36-50		
14	4.00	36-50		
15	4.00	36-50		
16	4.00	Over 50		
17	4.00	Over 50		
18	4.00	25-35		
19	4.00	18-24		
20	5.00	Over 50		
21	5.00	36-50		
22	5.00	Over 50		

for the two delay times from Figure 6.16 in an Excel data window. If you highlight these cells and choose XY SCATTER from the CHART options in the INSERT menu (INSERT → CHART → XY SCATTER), you will see a graph with the two means as points. To connect them with the lines for the line graph, click on Change Chart Type at the top of the window and then choose Scatter with Lines under the XY Scatter graphs options. This will connect the lines. You will also need to click the button to Switch Row/Column to put the Delay times on the x-axis and the memory performance means on the y-axis. This will create the graph shown in Figure 6.16.

Creating Graphs Using SPSS

Creating graphs from raw data is easier in SPSS than Excel. The data do not need to first be transformed—you can simply choose the graphing options you want for the variables in your data set. Let's consider once again the example concerning the likelihood of watching a new television show after viewing an ad for the show. Figure 6.22 shows the data window for these data with survey ratings in the first column and age group of the participant (a new variable for this example) in the second column. To create graphs with these variables, choose the Graphboard Template Chooser function from the Graphs menu at the top of the window. You will see the variables you have named in the data set on the left side of the window that opens. Choose the variables you want to graph and then choose the type of graph you wish to make.

You could choose to display the mean ratings given by each age group in a bar graph. To create this graph, choose the Legacy Dialogs function under the Graph menu at the top of the window and then the Bar option for the bar graph (see Figure 6.23). A small window will appear with graph options. With only one categorical variable to place on the x-axis, you can choose the

Simple option and then click on Define in this window. In the next window that appears, click on the Age Group variable and the corresponding arrow to move it into the Category Axis box. Then click the Other Statistic option in the list at the top. Clicking this button will allow you to then click over the Rating variable into the Variable box. It should show the mean of this variable (you can change to another measure of central tendency using the Change Statistic tab beneath the box if you wish). Then click OK. The graph in Figure 6.24 will be shown in the Output window.

FIGURE 6.23 ■ Variable Definition Window for the Legacy Dialogs Graphs Function in SPSS

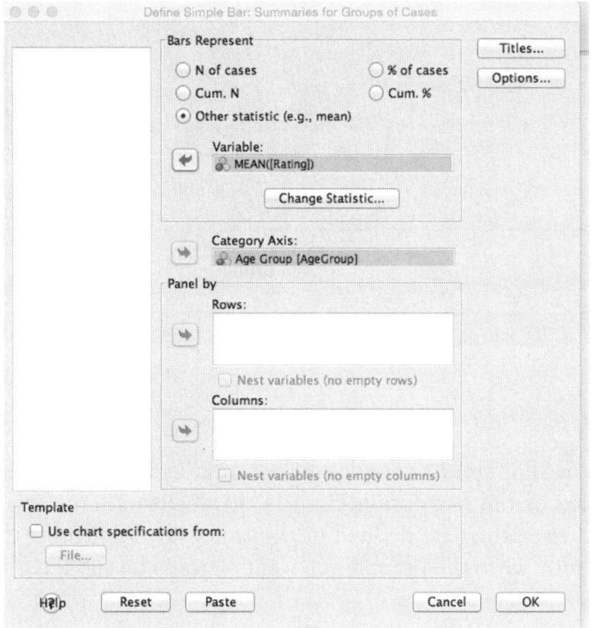

SUMMARY OF STEPS

- Type data into the data window.
- From the Graph menu at the top, choose Legacy Dialogs.
- Choose the Bar option from this list.
- Choose Simple and click Define.
- In the Define Simple Bar window, click your x-axis variable into the Category Axis box using the arrow.
- Click on Other Statistic, and place your y-axis variable into the Variable box using the arrow, and click OK to display your bar graph in the Output window.

FIGURE 6.24 ■ Bar Graph of the Mean Rating in the Data by Age Group

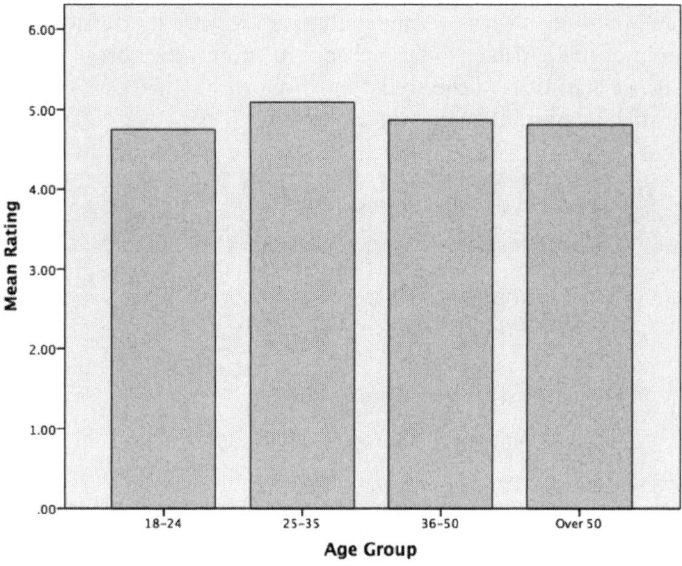

Source: *The Process of Statistical Analysis in Psychology*, Dawn McBride, SAGE Publications, 2018.

Line graphs in SPSS follow a similar procedure to that used to create Figure 6.24. However, instead of the Bar option in the Legacy Dialogs, you would choose the Line option. The variables are defined in the same way. Remember that line graphs should be used only when the variable you want to graph on the x-axis is a continuous variable.

APA STYLE FOR GRAPHS AND TABLES

One thing you may notice as you begin to read empirical research articles (i.e., published reports of a study that collected data) is that there is a fairly common structure to these articles with the sections in the same order in each article. Depending on the length of the article and the design or topic of the study, some sections may be omitted, renamed, or combined with other sections, but the general structure and purpose of each section are consistent from article to article. This structure comes from the style rules of the American Psychological Association (APA; 2010), also known as APA style. The main sections of an APA-style research report or article are Abstract, Introduction, Method, Results, and Discussion. The Abstract provides a paragraph summary of the study. The Introduction provides a description of the topic of the study, relevant background research, purpose of the study, and hypotheses for the results. The Method section provides the details of the participants; design; materials, stimuli, or apparatus; and procedure for the study. The Results section provides descriptive and inferential statistics and a description of the analyses performed on the data. Finally, the Discussion section provides a review of the results with reference to the hypotheses stated in the Introduction section and relevant past findings, along with possible future directions and general conclusions from the study.

The graphs and tables described in this chapter are typically referred to in the Results section of a research report. However, when an author types up the manuscript (i.e., before it is published), these graphs and tables are placed on their own pages at the end of the manuscript in accordance with APA-style rules. Graphs are referred to as *figures* in APA style. Each figure and table is given a title (see Appendix A for an example) that describes what is presented in the figure or table and typically includes the relevant variables. However, a description of the figure or table is also provided in the Results section, where the author refers the reader to the figure or table as they describe the data. Although these rules may, in some cases, seem arbitrary and difficult to follow, they provide a consistent organization to help readers follow the report of the study and know where to look in a research report for specific information about a study. You will likely encounter APA-style structure many times as you learn the process of conducting research and using statistics to understand data. The Thinking About Research sections at the end of each chapter in this text are organized by the major sections of an APA-style article to help you get used to this structure.

STOP AND THINK

6.11. For the following data set, create a graph in Excel or SPSS that is appropriate for the variables described:

Mean Percentage Accuracy on a Category Judgment Task by Task Instruction Condition (Completing the Tasks as Quickly as Possible Versus Completing the Tasks as Accurately as Possible)

Speed Instruction: 76, 52, 89, 75, 70, 61, 90, 88, 75, 81

Accuracy Instruction: 90, 85, 87, 66, 82, 77, 95, 90, 99, 79

6.12. Which of the following is consistent with APA style for figures and tables?

a. Embed the figure or table within the Results section.
b. Embed the figure or table within the Method section.
c. Do not duplicate data in both a figure and table.
d. Provide a single title that describes all figures or tables at once.

6.13. In which section of an APA-style report should you refer to the figures or tables of descriptive statistics?

a. Abstract
b. Introduction
c. Method
d. Results

THINKING ABOUT RESEARCH

A summary of a research study in psychology is given here. As you read the summary, think about the following questions:

1. Was this study an experiment or a correlational study?
2. Identify the dependent variables. Describe how these variables were measured in the study.
3. For the mental speed and friends' ratings variables, what scale of measurement do you think was used?
4. For mental speed, which measure of central tendency do you think would be best to report? Why?
5. For social skills and charisma ratings, which measure of central tendency do you think would be best to report? Why?
6. What kind of graph do you think would best display the main results of the study? Why is this is the best type of graph?

Research Study. von Hippel, W., Ronay, R., Baker, E., Kjelsaas, K., & Murphy, S. C. (2016). Quick thinkers are smooth talkers: Mental speed facilitates charisma. *Psychological Science, 27,* 119–122.

Purpose of the Study. In this study, the researchers explored possible cognitive abilities that are related to social skills and one's charisma. Specifically, they examined whether one's mental speed could predict social skills related to social comfort, conflict, and interpreting others' feelings. They also tested whether one's mental speed could predict how charismatic, funny, and quick-witted one was.

Method of the Study. Two studies were conducted. Each study included 200 participants that included groups of friends. In Study 1, participants completed an intelligence test (control measure), a five-factor personality survey (control measure), and 30 general knowledge questions (e.g., "Name a precious gem."). General knowledge questions provided the measure of mental speed, as participants were asked to answer the questions aloud as quickly as possible and their time to answer was measured on each question. Participants also completed three-item surveys for both social skills and charisma, rating each person in their friend group on a 1 to 7 scale. In Study 2, the participants completed the same general knowledge questions, social skills and charisma ratings, and personality survey as in Study 1. In addition, participants in Study 2 also completed speeded left–right dot detection and pattern-matching tasks as measures of mental speed and surveys for self-control, self-efficacy (i.e., self-esteem), narcissism, social values, and self-confidence as control measures.

Results of the Study. Analyses of the data tested whether participants' mental speed (time to complete cognitive tasks) predicted their friends' ratings of their social skills and charisma with control measure (e.g., intelligence, personality) removed. For both studies, faster mental speed predicted higher charisma ratings from friends but did not predict social skills ratings from friends.

Conclusions of the Study. This study supported the researchers' prediction that mental speed is predictive of charisma but did not support their hypothesis that mental speed is predictive of social skills. They suggest that future research should examine how mental speed is involved in charismatic social functioning.

Chapter Summary

- **What can we learn about a distribution from measures of central tendency?**
  Central tendency measures provide a description of the typical score in a distribution.

- **How are the mean, median, and mode used as measures of central tendency?**
  The mean is the average, the median is the middle score, and the mode is the most common score. Each of these measures gives us a summary value for the scores in a distribution but in different ways.

- **How do the mean, median, and mode compare for different distributions?**
  Because the mean is the average of the scores, it will be more influenced by extreme scores than the other measures. Thus, for a skewed distribution, the mean will be closest to the extreme scores, followed by the median and the mode, which will be closer to the middle of the distribution. For symmetrical distributions, however, the three measures will provide the same value that is in the middle of the distribution.

- **Which measure of central tendency should I use when describing a distribution?**
  The mean is the most commonly used measure of central tendency; thus, it is often reported for comparison with other data sets. However, with skewed distributions, it is best to provide the median in addition to or instead of the mean. The mode is useful when describing data sets with many scores at the high and low ends of the scale or when reporting data on a nominal scale.

- **What can we learn about a distribution from measures of variability?**
  Measures of variability provide some information about how much the scores in a distribution differ from one another.

- **How is the standard deviation used as a measure of variability?**
  The standard deviation measures the average distance between the scores and the mean of the distribution. This measure provides you with a measure of how much the scores differ from the center of the distribution.

- **Why does the standard deviation calculation differ for samples and populations?**
  The standard deviation represents the average of the differences between the scores and the mean. For a population, this value is calculated using *N* to determine the average. However, the sample, as a representative of the population, will have lower variability than the whole population because you are not obtaining scores from every member, only a subset of the population. Thus, we adjust the standard deviation calculation for a sample to account for its lower variability and still provide a good estimate of the variability in the population the sample represents. We do this using n – 1 (which are the degrees of freedom) in our calculation of the average of the deviations between the scores and the mean.

Test Yourself

1. For each of the data sets that follow, calculate the mean, median, and mode.
   a. 1, 3, 4, 4, 4, 5, 7
   b. 1, 1, 1, 1, 1, 2, 2, 7
   c. 1, 2, 3, 2, 2, 5, 7, 7, 7, 2, 7, 2, 7, 7, 2
2. For each data set in Question 1, which measure of central tendency would you choose as the most representative of the data set? Explain why you chose that measure.
3. How do the mean, median, and mode compare for symmetrical and skewed distributions (i.e., which is highest and lowest in value)?
4. Which measure of central tendency is most commonly reported?
   a. Mean
   b. Median
   c. Mode
   d. None of the above
5. Which measure of central tendency is most affected by extreme scores?
   a. Mean
   b. Median
   c. Mode
   d. None of the above
6. Which measure of central tendency is most appropriate to report for skewed distributions?
   a. Mean
   b. Median
   c. Mode
   d. None of the above
7. Which measure of central tendency is most appropriate for nominal data?
   a. Mean
   b. Median
   c. Mode
   d. None of the above
8. Which measure of central tendency will provide the middle score in a symmetrical distribution?
   a. Mean
   b. Median
   c. Mode
   d. All of the above
9. The purpose of reporting a measure of central tendency is to indicate the spread of the scores in the distribution.
   a. True
   b. False
10. The mean of a distribution is a descriptive statistic.
    a. True
    b. False
11. In a positively skewed distribution, the mean will be lower than the median.
    a. True
    b. False
12. The mean is the best measure of central tendency to report when there are open-

ended responses on the measurement scale.

a. True

b. False

13. For each of the following data sets, which appears to have the highest variability? Explain your answer.

a. 3, 3, 4, 4, 4, 2, 3

b. 1, 1, 1, 1, 1, 2, 2, 7

c. 4, 2, 3, 2, 3, 5, 7, 7, 7, 4, 7, 2, 7, 7, 3

14. For each data set in Question 13, calculate the standard deviation.

15. Compare the standard deviations you calculated in the previous question. Do these values match your guess in Question 1?

16. Which measure of variability is most commonly reported?

a. Standard deviation

b. Variance

17. Degrees of freedom are used in calculating the standard deviation for a population.

a. True

b. False

18. The variability of scores for a sample will be lower than the variability in the population it represents.

a. True

b. False

19. Explain why we need to square the deviations from the mean in our calculation of the standard deviation.

20. Where should you place tables and figures of data in an APA-style research report?

a. Embedded within the Results section

b. On a separate page at the beginning of the paper

c. On a separate page at the end of the paper

d. Embedded within the Introduction

21. Which graph is most appropriate for data with categorical variables?

a. Bar graph

b. Line graph

c. Both a and b

22. Which graph is most appropriate for data with continuous variables?

a. Bar graph

b. Line graph

c. Both a and b

23. Whenever you present data in a graph, you should always also include the exact values from the graph in a table.

a. True

b. False

24. Creating graphs in SPSS usually requires calculation of descriptive statistics before you begin.

a. True

b. False

25. Inferential statistics are typically presented in graphs in a research report.

a. True

b. False

Visit **edge.sagepub.com/mcbridermstats** to find the answers to the Test Yourself questions above, as well as quizzes, flashcards, and other resources to help you accomplish your coursework goals.

7

INDEPENDENT VARIABLES AND VALIDITY IN RESEARCH

CONSIDER THE FOLLOWING QUESTIONS AS YOU READ CHAPTER 7

- How do independent and dependent variables differ?
- Which type of research method contains an independent variable? Why?
- How does validity affect the results of a study?
- What are some factors that affect the validity of a study, and how can a researcher control these factors?

LEARNING OBJECTIVES FOR CHAPTER 7

- Determine if a research study contains an independent variable.
- Compare different types of independent variables.
- Evaluate study designs and measures for internal and external validity.

In July 2016, an 18-year-old German teen shot and killed nine people in Munich, Germany. Reports surfaced that the gunman "was a fan of first-person shooter video games" (Scutti, 2018). This information led to suggestions that violent video game playing can cause someone to become violent. In fact, CNN.com reported that U.S. president Donald Trump had recently said, "I'm hearing more and more people saying the level of violence on video games is really shaping young people's thoughts," suggesting a causal link between video game violence and violent behavior. Numerous research studies on this topic have reported that there is a significant relation between violent video game play and aggressive behavior (e.g., Anderson et al., 2010). But do these findings mean that playing video games *causes* aggressive behavior in those who play them? The answer to this question is "maybe not." The research findings reported here suggest several possibilities. One possibility is the causal relationship suggested by the media and President Trump: Playing violent video game causes violent behavior. Another possibility, however, is that individuals with violent tendencies tend to play violent video games more often than individuals who are less violent. Finally, a third possibility is that a third variable causes both violent video game playing and aggressive behavior. How can we determine which one of these relationships is accurate? One way is to conduct an experiment containing an independent variable that compares people randomly assigned to play either violent video games or nonviolent games. We can then give both groups a task where they can choose to be violent or not in their solving of a social problem (e.g., deciding which of two groups gets to settle a piece of land under dispute). The number of violent solutions the participants suggest could be measured. This comparison allows us to test whether playing violent video games *causes* violent behavior. In this example study, violent behavior is operationally defined as the number of violent solutions suggested (the dependent variable) and the group participants are assigned to is the independent variable. By comparing the two groups on the dependent variable in this experiment, we can test the causal relationship suggested previously. If we simply recruited participants for the study who reported playing violent video games to compare with participants who reported not playing violent video games, we would not have a true independent variable because the groups would be based on preexisting characteristics of the participants, not random assignment. Random assignment to groups allows us to control for individual differences that might come along with the type of video game people choose to play, such as violent tendencies.

Photo 7.1
Does playing violent video games cause one to be violent? Or does being an aggressive person cause one to play more violent video games? Correlational studies cannot distinguish between these possibilities.

In this chapter, we will consider how independent variables are manipulated in experiments, how they differ from quasi-independent variables, how manipulations allow for control of internal validity, some common sources of bias that threaten internal validity in research studies, and how control of these sources of bias can lower external validity (see Figure 7.1).

FIGURE 7.1 ■ Steps in the Research Process: Designing the Study

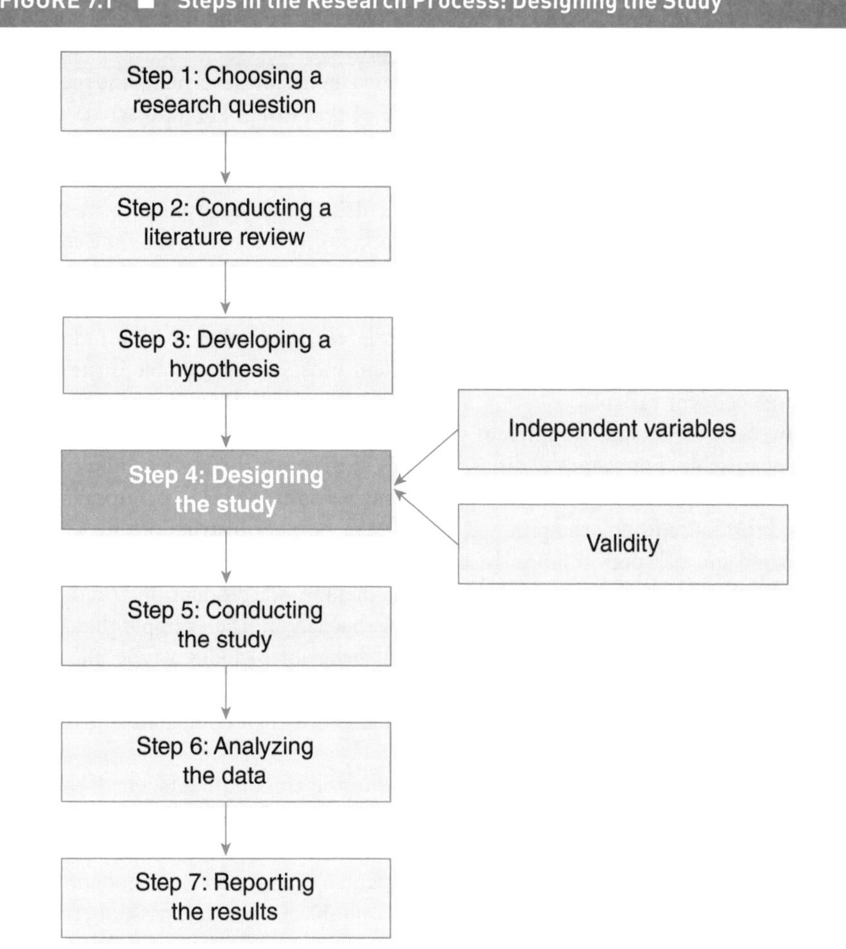

INDEPENDENT VARIABLES

All research studies include at least one dependent variable because the dependent variable is the measure of the behavior that is being observed. However, a subset of studies, classified as experiments, also includes an independent variable. Here, we discuss some different ways that independent variables can be manipulated in a study and how the manipulation of independent variables can affect the validity of a study.

Types of Manipulations

There are a few ways in which an independent variable can be manipulated to create levels of the independent variable (i.e., different situations on which to compare the dependent

presence–absence variable: A variable that involves a manipulation with a level that involves the treatment and a level that does not involve the treatment

bivalent independent variable: An independent variable with two levels—a design is considered bivalent if it contains only one bivalent independent variable

type variable: A variable that involves a manipulation of types of a treatment

amount variable: A variable that includes levels with a different amount of the treatment changing from level to level

multivalent variable: An independent variable that includes three or more levels—a design is considered multivalent if there is only one independent variable that contains three or more levels

quasi-independent or subject variable: Variable that allows comparison of groups of participants without manipulation (i.e., no random assignment)

variable). Some common ways to manipulate independent variables are (a) as the presence and absence of a treatment or situation, (b) as a type of treatment or situation, and (c) as the amount of a factor in a treatment or situation.

Presence–absence variables typically include two levels: one level being the presence of something and the other level being the absence of that thing. For a **presence–absence variable**, the presence group is also called the experimental group, and the absence group is called the control group. The "something" that is manipulated could be a therapy (presence of therapy and absence of therapy), a drug treatment (presence of the drug and absence of the drug), or a time constraint for a task (presence of the time constraint and absence of the time constraint), depending on the type of study being conducted. A presence–absence variable is also called a **bivalent independent variable** because it is an independent variable that contains only two levels. Remember that an independent variable must have at least two levels, so a bivalent independent variable is the simplest type of independent variable.

A **type variable** includes a different type of the "something" being compared on the dependent variable. For example, different types of drugs or therapies can be compared for score on a depression questionnaire, different versions of an ad or product can be compared for desire to buy the product, or different types of instructions for a task can be compared for task performance. In each of these independent variables, all the levels include the factor being manipulated (drug, therapy, ad, product, instructions), but each level involves a different type or version of that factor. The example that I started the chapter with about video games and violent behavior includes a type independent variable—type of video game with violent and nonviolent levels. The dependent variable measured (number of violent problem solutions given) is then compared across the different types.

An **amount variable** involves a manipulation of the amount of a factor in each level. For example, an experiment can investigate the amount of a drug (i.e., dosage) that is optimal for relieving symptoms such that each level of a variable includes a different amount of the same drug given to the participants. A common independent variable in memory research is the manipulation of the amount of time that passes between the study of material and the test on that material (i.e., a study–test delay) such that each level involves a different time delay (e.g., 5 min, 30 min, 2 hr, 1 day, 1 month). Whenever an independent variable contains three or more levels, it is considered a **multivalent variable** (i.e., multiple levels, more than two). See Figure 7.2 for a comparison of different independent variable manipulations.

Quasi-Independent Variables

So far in this chapter, we have been discussing true independent variables—variables that are manipulated by the researcher. Participants can also be separated into groups based on characteristics they already have. These groups create levels of a **quasi-independent or subject variable** based on characteristics that a researcher is unable to manipulate. The groups can then be compared in the same way as groups that are randomly assigned are compared. Some examples of common quasi-independent variables used in psychological research include gender, age, personality types (e.g., introverts and extroverts), and ethnicity (see Photos 7.2, 7.3, and 7.4). Any characteristic that you can measure or

FIGURE 7.2 ■ Types of Independent Variable Manipulations

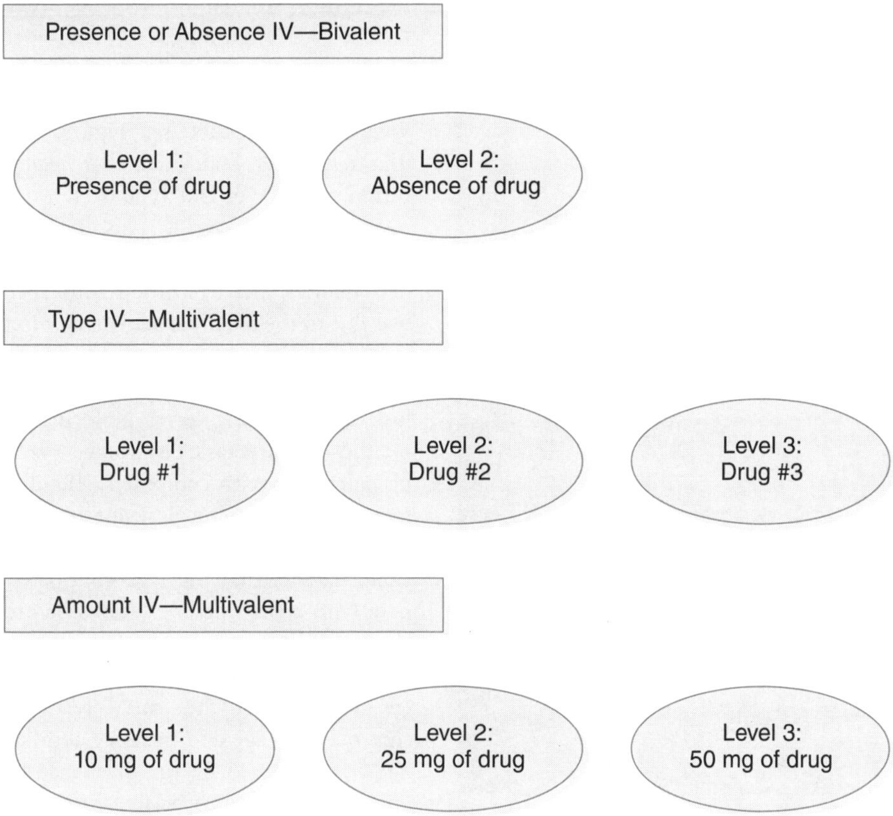

observe from the participants can be used to group those participants and create a quasi-independent variable in a study.

The use of quasi-independent variables is very common in psychological research studies. However, researchers must be cautious when including these variables because the causal relationship between the quasi-independent and dependent variables is not always as clear as it is with true independent variables. Without the manipulation by the researcher, it is always possible that additional factors (that are not part of the quasi-independent variable) are causing differences (or lack of differences) to occur between the groups. Thus, a researcher must always consider these additional factors when drawing conclusions from these factors.

For example, consider a study that compares different age groups on completion of a memory task to determine if memory declines as people age. Suppose the researcher for this study presented the items the participants were to study on a computer screen

©istockphoto.com/RealPeopleGroup

©PeopleImages/iStockPhoto

©webphotographeer/iStockPhoto

Photos 7.2, 7.3, and 7.4
Quasi-independent or subject variables allow a researcher to categorize participants to compare behaviors for different categories of individuals but are typically variables that the researcher cannot randomly assign the participants to. Can you think of additional subject variables appropriate for psychological research beyond the ones shown in the photos?

and then asked them to judge items presented on the computer screen as items they studied or not (i.e., they received a recognition test). The older participants in this study perform worse on the memory task than the younger participants (see Figure 7.3). The researcher concludes that recognition memory of this type declines as people age. However, it is also possible that instead of having a deficit in memory abilities, the age group difference was due to the older participants having less familiarity with computers, making more errors in completing the computer task, and showing lower performance on the memory task due to their lack of experience with computers. The difference in computer experience between the two groups is one of those additional factors that must be considered here (and ruled out, if possible) before the researcher can conclude that the older participants had worse memory. In other words, the causal relationship between age and memory abilities has been clouded by the difference in computer experience between the two groups. Had the researcher been able to randomly assign the participants to the different age groups (or matched the participants based on previous experience with computers), this additional explanation of the results could have been more easily ruled out. Therefore, it is important to remember that the causal information gained from quasi-independent variables is not as clear as it is from true independent variables, and the researcher must be more cautious when interpreting differences across groups that were not manipulated (i.e., assigned) by the researcher. See Figure 7.4 for a comparison of true independent and quasi-independent variables.

FIGURE 7.3 ■ Consider Possible Explanations for the Data Shown in This Graph—Are There Other Explanations Besides the Conclusion That Memory Declines With Age?

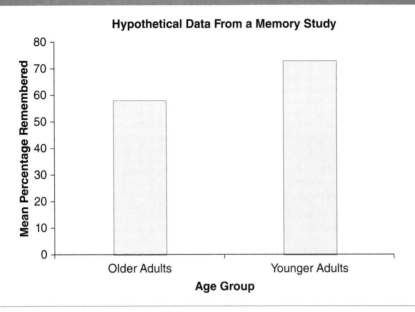

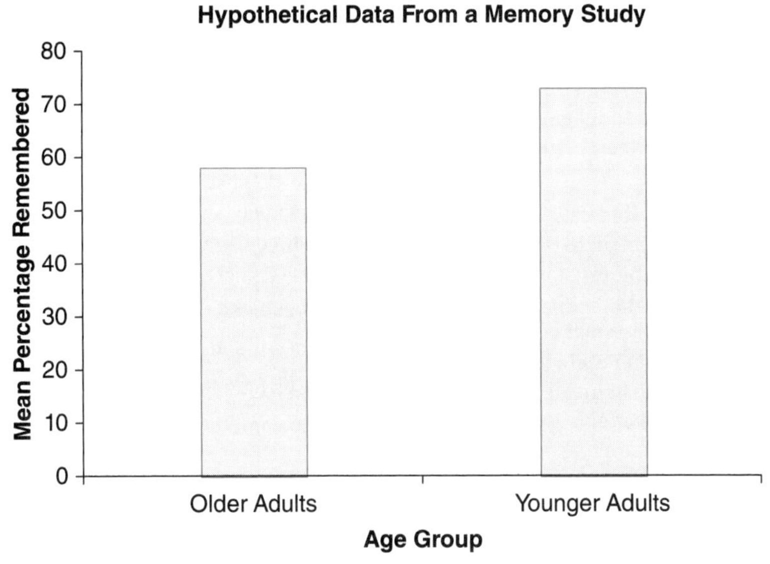

FIGURE 7.4 ■ Independent and Quasi-Independent Variables

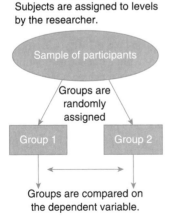

True Independent Variables:
Subjects are assigned to levels by the researcher.

Sample of participants

Groups are randomly assigned

Group 1

Group 2

Groups are compared on the dependent variable.

Quasi-Independent Variables:
Subjects are assigned to groups based on their characteristics.

Sample of participants

Observe or measure characteristics

Assignment to groups are based on characteristics.

Group 1

Group 2

Groups are compared on the dependent variable.

STOP AND THINK

7.1. For each of the following descriptions, identify the independent variable(s):

a. Subjects are randomly assigned to one of three rooms of different size (small, medium, large) to complete a puzzle. Time to complete the puzzle is measured.

b. Subjects play a computerized ball tossing game where a random half of the subjects are led to believe they are being included in the game by other subjects and the other half are led to believe they are being excluded by other subjects. Change in mood (before versus after the game) is measured by a questionnaire.

c. Subjects seeking treatment for depression are randomly assigned to either a new treatment technique or the current treatment technique. Change in score on a depression questionnaire before and after treatment is measured for the two groups.

7.2. In the following list, identify which factors can be used only as a quasi-independent variable (not a true independent variable) in a study:

- Age of subject
- Subject's mood
- Subject's height
- Time to complete a task

VALIDITY AND SOURCES OF BIAS

In this chapter, we have been discussing how the variables we examine in a study, as well as how we choose to measure or manipulate them, can affect the validity of the study. In fact, there are several different types of validity to consider when designing a study, and each has different implications.

face validity: A study or scale appearing to be intuitively valid on the surface

We have already considered choosing variables based on **face validity** (i.e., Intuitively, does the variable seem to do what it should?) and how a poor operational definition of a concept can lower the construct validity of a measure, but there are a few other types of validity that researchers should consider when designing a study. Some of the more common forms of validity and sources of bias that threaten these forms of validity are discussed in the next sections. Examples of these sources are provided in Table 7.1.

Internal Validity

Much of our discussion of validity has focused on internal validity. A study with good internal validity provides a good test of a causal hypothesis and controls for those extraneous factors that could affect the data but are not of interest in the study. In other words, a study with good internal validity provides a good test of a causal relationship by removing alternative explanations of the data (besides the independent variable). The discussion of different research designs in Chapter 5 indicated that the best way to test a causal relationship is to use the experimental method. Thus, well-designed experiments

TABLE 7.1 ■ A Summary of Sources of Bias

Bias	Definition	Examples	Type of validity threatened
Group differences	Participant groups are not equated on characteristics that can affect the data.	Group differences based on gender, previous knowledge or experience with the task, or current mood state affect the scores.	Internal
Order effects	Order of conditions in a within-subjects design can affect data collected in different conditions.	Order effects can occur when easy tasks precede difficult tasks or positive experiences precede negative experiences.	Internal
Testing effects	There are multiple testing sessions—first testing affects subsequent testing.	Scores are changed based on practice effects, fatigue effects, or accumulated knowledge of the task.	Internal
Regression toward the mean	Extreme scores are unlikely to recur.	A student earns a high score on a test in class but has a low average course grade; a professional athlete has a high-performing year compared with his or her average performance.	Internal
Experimenter bias	The researcher treats different groups of participants in different ways based on knowledge of the study.	The instructor spends more time discussing material in a class he knows is not receiving a new teaching technique designed to improve learning.	Internal
Social desirability	Participants provide survey responses to present themselves in a more positive way.	A participant responds to items on an anxiety survey with lower values than his or her actual level of anxiety.	Internal
Attrition or mortality	Some participants choose not to or are unable to complete a study, biasing the sample.	Less conscientious participants do not complete all sessions of a multisession study.	Internal and external
Hawthorne effect	Studying participants can change their behavior.	Workers' productivity improves when they know they are being studied; participants perform better in a memory study than they would outside the study.	External

typically have higher internal validity than other research designs. The best way to design a good experiment (or even a good quasi-experiment) is to control for sources of bias that can make the causal relationship less clear (i.e., other factors besides the independent variable that might affect the dependent variable). These sources of bias are often called confounding variables.

For example, suppose you were conducting a study on the effects of video game playing on spatial abilities. You ask a group of people to play a video game where they have to navigate around in a fantasy world for an hour. You ask a separate group of people to complete Sudoku math puzzles for the same amount of time. You then ask both groups to navigate to different locations on a map from written directions, measuring how long it takes each person to find the correct locations. When you compare the two groups, the group that was playing the video game found the locations faster than the group that completed the Sudoku puzzles. What can explain these results? One possibility is that *playing the video games* improved navigation skills compared with completing Sudoku puzzles. But another possible explanation for the results is that the people who were randomly assigned to play video games happen to have better navigation skills to begin with than the people assigned to complete Sudoku puzzles. In other words, a preexisting group difference caused the difference you found in navigation performance across groups. Thus, it is unclear which of these two factors caused the difference in navigation performance. The preexisting group difference might be a confounding variable in this study.

There are several common sources of bias that can lower the internal validity of a study. As they apply to many different types of studies, it is a wise researcher who keeps these bias sources in mind when designing a study in order to control for or minimize these threats to internal validity.

experimenter bias: A source of bias in a study created when a researcher treats groups differently (often unknowingly) based on knowledge of the hypothesis

Experimenter Bias. The first source of bias we discuss is one that can be caused by the researcher. **Experimenter bias** occurs when a researcher inadvertently treats groups differently in the study based on their knowledge of the hypothesis for the study. For example, suppose an instructor is trying out a new type of assignment in a class that she thinks will help students learn a topic better than her old method. To test the effectiveness of the new assignment, she gives the assignment to one section of her class and the old assignment to another section of her class. She then compares the test scores of the two groups, with each section receiving the same exam. If the section with the new assignment scores higher than the section with the old assignment, there are several possible reasons that this may have occurred. One explanation is that the new assignment is more effective than the old assignment in helping students learn the material. Another explanation is that there may be group differences (e.g., better students in the new assignment section) that caused the results because the students were not randomly assigned to the two sections. A third explanation is that there may be experimenter bias in the study. In other words, because the instructor expected the new assignment section to perform better, she may have unknowingly been more enthusiastic with these students or encouraged them more than the other section. Alternatively, the instructor may have exhibited experimenter bias in the opposite manner by spending more time teaching the material to the old assignment section because she expected them to have more trouble learning the material. Either situation represents experimenter bias in the study.

To counter experimenter bias, a blind procedure is used in a study to hide the group assignment from the researcher and prevent inadvertent bias from occurring. A **single-blind design** is used to combat effects of subjects' knowledge of their group assignment. For example, when the effectiveness of a drug is tested, the control group typically receives a placebo to equate beliefs of effectiveness of treatment across groups (see Photo 7.5). In a **double-blind design**, both the participants and the researchers who interact with the participants do not know which participants are assigned to the different groups. Thus, the instructor from the earlier assignment study could have used a double-blind design by trying out her assignment in a colleague's class or having a guest lecturer who is unaware of her hypothesis teach the material of interest. With this alternate procedure, the researcher who made the hypothesis does not interact with the participants during the course of the study.

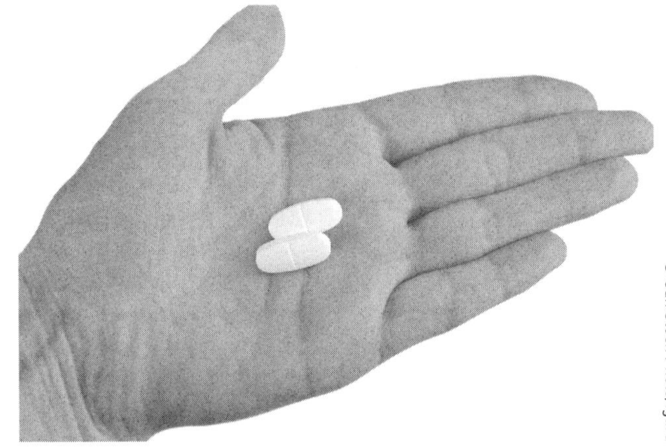

© Can Stock Photo/Iglira

Photo 7.5
Placebos are used as a control condition in research studies testing treatment effectiveness to rule out the effects of treatment knowledge on improvement of symptoms.

Testing Effects. **Testing effects** can be an issue when multiple testing sessions occur in a study. They are more likely to occur in studies where participants are tested more than once or complete a task over a series of trials. Thus, testing effects are more likely to occur for a **within-subjects variable** than a **between-subjects variable**, as participants' behavior is measured under all levels of the independent variable(s) in within-subjects experiments. Testing effects occur when an initial test affects data collected on subsequent tests. For example, in many tasks, participants improve over time due to practice effects. The more time participants spend completing a task (either across multiple levels of an independent variable or across many trials in a study), the more easily they complete the task due to experience with the task. Of course, the opposite can occur with extreme numbers of trials or many repeated testing sessions in a study. Participants can become fatigued over time, and their performance on a task declines over many repeated exposures to a task. Testing effects can be avoided in a study by minimizing the number of trials of a task as much as possible and **counterbalancing** levels of a within-subjects independent variable. When questionnaires are used in a study, different items may be used on different versions of the measure to minimize testing effects over repeated completions of a questionnaire.

Regression Toward the Mean. **Regression toward the mean** occurs when participants obtain an extreme score (high or low) on a questionnaire or task at one testing session but regress toward their mean score at another testing session. In other words, regression toward the mean signifies that extreme scores are not likely to recur (see Photo 7.6). Regression toward the mean can be problematic in studies where a test or questionnaire is given more than once. If participants score very high or very low on the test the first time it is taken but obtain a more average score the next time the test is taken, it can make

single-blind design: Procedure used to hide the group assignment from the participants in a study to prevent their beliefs about the effectiveness of a treatment from affecting the results

double-blind design: Procedure used to control for experimenter bias by keeping the knowledge of the group assignments from both the participants and the researchers who interact with the participants

testing effects: Occur when participants are tested more than once in a study—with early testing affecting later testing

Photo 7.6 Regression toward the mean is often seen in the performance of professional athletes. A record-breaking year can be followed by one where the stats are just average for that person.

comparison of scores across conditions of a study difficult. Is the change in score due to the independent variable, or is it due to regression toward the mean? This can be a difficult question for a researcher to answer, but the more times the participants are tested, the more information a researcher will have to answer this question.

Consider your academic performance. Have you ever been performing very well in a class but, for one reason or another, you do poorly on one of the exams? Given that this is not your typical performance, this low score is not likely to reoccur. Now imagine that an instructor is trying out a new way of teaching material in a course. She gives the first exam with the old teaching technique and the second exam with the new teaching technique. If several people score unusually poorly on the first exam but then regress to their more typical (and better) performance on the second exam, it may look like the new teaching technique was effective. But in reality, the difference in scores was simply due to several people regressing toward their mean performance.

Regression toward the mean can also hide an effect of a variable. If some people score unusually low on the first exam and more typically on the second exam while other people score typically on the first exam and unusually low on the second exam, it may look like the exam scores are similar for the two teaching techniques because of this regression toward the mean on both exams.

within-subjects variable: Participant experiences all levels of the independent variable

between-subjects variable: Participant experiences only one level of the independent variable

counterbalancing: A control used in within-subjects experiments where equal numbers of participants are randomly assigned to different orders of the conditions

Regression toward the mean is a difficult source of bias to remove from a research study. The best way to minimize its effects is to use random assignment to conditions for between-subjects variables and to use several repetitions of the test for within-subjects variables (i.e., use more than two exams to compare teaching techniques). Random assignment should help spread any regression toward the mean that occurs in the study across the different groups so that it does not cause group differences. Using several repetitions of the test (e.g., having participants complete the test more than once for each level of the independent variable) will allow scores closer to each participant's true mean to occur in each condition. With a single testing for each level, you may end up with an extreme score for one of those levels. Trimming extreme scores from the data (when possible) also helps minimize regression toward the mean as a source of bias. Splitting a group in half, based on high and low scores, can also control for regression toward the mean. Finally, using a large number of participants in a study (exactly how many depends on the type of study and the types of variables being tested) can help minimize the effect of a single extreme score on the data.

External Validity

External validity is the degree to which a study measures realistic behaviors and a study's results can be generalized beyond the study (i.e., to other individuals and situations).

In other words, if participants behave in a research study the way they would in their everyday lives, then the study has good external validity. The results of the study can be generalized to behaviors, conditions, and individuals who were not specifically tested in the study. External validity can be reduced by **attrition or mortality**, where subjects decide not to complete a study, reducing the representativeness of the sample. There are also other factors that can reduce the external validity of a study. For example, as more control is imposed over sources of bias that reduce internal validity, the more external validity tends to suffer. When researchers include controls for internal sources of bias, they are typically restricting the situation under which the behavior of interest is expressed. Thus, the behavior may become more artificial and specific to the study being conducted. In other words, the behavior observed in the study becomes less like behavior that occurs in the participants' everyday lives.

regression toward the mean: Can occur when participants score higher or lower than their personal average—the next time they are tested, they are more likely to score near their personal average, making scores unreliable

attrition or mortality: Occurs when participants choose not to complete a study

For example, suppose a researcher was interested in the effects of work environment on work productivity. In the study, room size and the presence or absence of a window in the room are manipulated (i.e., these are the independent variables). The participants are asked to perform a task where they have to insert blocks of varying shapes into slots in a box for a 30-min time period. At the end of the 30-min period, the number of blocks correctly inserted is counted for each participant as a measure of work productivity (i.e., number correct on the block task is the operational definition of work productivity). The mean number of blocks correctly inserted is compared for the different room types. The study is conducted as a typical laboratory experiment such that the independent variables of interest are manipulated across room type, but the rooms are the same in all other ways.

Think about the internal and external validity of this study for a moment. The study appears to be fairly high in internal validity because the work environment is kept constant except for the manipulation of the two independent variables. The task is simple enough not to be affected by individual differences in ability. In other words, the study provides a good test of the hypothesis that room size and presence or absence of a window affect work productivity. However, one might question the external validity of the study. The block task might be a realistic type of task for a factory worker but may not be a good example of a daily task for an office worker (see Photo 7.7). Thus, the results of the study may only generalize to a portion of all workers. In addition, the participants in the study know that they are participating in a study and may adjust their behavior accordingly. They may, for example, work harder than they would in their job because they know that they are being observed. Or, alternatively, they may not work as hard as they do in their job because they know that the task is just for a research study and their performance does not affect them personally as it might in a job environment. This is known as the **Hawthorne effect** (see discussion in the next section).

Hawthorne effect: A source of bias that can occur in a study due to participants changing their behavior because they are aware that they are being observed

Now consider a similar study conducted in a factory by the factory's manager. Employees are placed in the different working environments as in the study described previously (the rooms vary by size and whether or not a window is present). They complete their normal factory line task as usual. After a 30-min period in the new environment, the factory manager counts up the number of assemblies completed by each employee to compare the different environments. The study described here is considered a field experiment because the experiment (independent variables are still manipulated, as in the laboratory experiment described previously) is conducted in a naturalistic environment (i.e., in the "field").

Photo 7.7 Conducting a field experiment, where an experiment is done in a naturalistic setting, can increase the external validity of the results.

Consider the internal and external validity of this experiment compared with the one described previously. The external validity seems to be higher in the field experiment because the factory workers' normal job task is used as the operational definition of work productivity. The behavior observed is more naturalistic for these workers. In addition, they are in their normal environment with other workers and normal factory sounds, making it more likely that they will exhibit more naturalistic work behaviors. However, several sources of bias have now been introduced into the experiment that might threaten the internal validity. Interactions with other coworkers are no longer controlled and could be different for different individuals across the experimental conditions. Noise is also a factor that might contribute to work productivity. It is not controlled across the room conditions in the field experiment as it is in the laboratory experiment. Thus, in this example with comparable laboratory and field experiments, the more controls there are that increase the internal validity in these experiments, the lower the external validity of the behaviors observed in the experiments.

Note that both studies described previously are experiments. While experiments are typically higher in internal validity (and lower in external validity) than other research designs, this is not always the case, and different types of experiments can vary greatly in internal validity based on the number of sources of bias controlled by the researcher. For example, in each of the previously given experiments, changes could be made in the method or design to increase internal or external validity as needed. How carefully a study is designed can make a big difference in how high the internal and external validity are, regardless of the research design employed. The design of the study can alter a participant's perception of the study, leading to a change in behavior that is less realistic simply because the participant knows that he or she is being observed. This issue will be discussed further next.

The Hawthorne Effect. The *Hawthorne effect* is a term coined by Landsberger (1955) as he was analyzing a set of studies conducted at the Hawthorne plant, a factory that produced products for the Western Electric Company in the 1920s and 1930s in Chicago. Researchers conducted studies in the factory to determine the effects of different lighting conditions on worker productivity. The researchers found that all the lighting conditions they tried increased the workers' productivity. In other words, by the simple virtue of being studied, the workers' behavior changed. Other possible explanations have been offered for the results of this study (see Adair, 1984; Bramel & Friend, 1981), but the idea that studying individuals can change their behavior is now known as the Hawthorne effect. The act of studying individuals can alter their behavior and affect the results of a study, reducing its validity.

A related concept known as demand characteristics can also affect the validity of a study. Demand characteristics occur when participants in a study attempt to "figure out" the purpose of the study and change their behavior based on their view of the purpose of the study. The participants' understanding of the study's purpose can be correct or incorrect, but they change their behavior based on whatever notion they have of the purpose (either to exhibit behavior that is consistent with what they think the researcher expects or to exhibit behavior different from what they think the researcher expects). This is a concept related to the Hawthorne effect, as demand characteristics occur as a result of a participant's involvement in a study.

One way to deal with the Hawthorne effect (and demand characteristics) is to observe the participants unobtrusively. This can be done using the naturalistic observation technique. However, this is not always possible for all behaviors. Another way to deal with the Hawthorne effect is to make the participants' responses in a study anonymous (or confidential). This may alleviate some of the effects of this source of bias. Deception may also be used to hide the purpose of the study. These issues are also addressed in the context of ethical standards for research with human participants in Chapter 3.

Sources of Bias Specific to a Field of Study

Some sources of bias are specific to a field of study. As a researcher becomes more familiar with an area of psychological study, these sources of bias become clearer, and ways to control for these biases can be built into the design of the studies—for example, in some memory research where study–test time delay is not an independent variable of interest, as in the example given earlier in this chapter. Instead, it can become a source of bias if different individuals are tested after different delays and delay is not a variable of interest in the study. Suppose that a researcher is interested in comparing two study conditions for their effect on memory ability. If one condition takes longer to complete, it is possible that the study–test delay will be longer in this condition than the study condition that can be completed in a shorter amount of time. Thus, memory researchers must consider the delay time in designing studies to ensure that different conditions are matched on this factor. Visual acuity is often controlled for in visual perception experiments by requiring participants to have normal or corrected-to-normal vision. Survey responses can be affected by social desirability bias, where participants respond in ways that are more socially acceptable than they normally would. Many surveys include items to measure social desirability to help researchers exclude participants who are prone to this bias in their responses. Each area of research has its own sources of bias. As you become more familiar with a particular area of research, you can often learn about these sources of bias by examining the methods of other researchers to identify controls they have used to remove this bias.

STOP AND THINK

7.3. Describe the difference between a single-blind and double-blind design. Explain when each of these designs should be used.

7.4. An instructor wants to measure the amount of learning for students in his class. To measure learning, he gives subjects the final exam on the first day of class and then gives the same final exam at the end of the semester. Explain how testing effects could be a source of bias in this study.

THINKING ABOUT RESEARCH

A summary of a research study in psychology is given here. As you read the summary, think about the following questions:

1. Identify the independent variable. Was this independent variable manipulated between subjects or within subjects?
2. Consider the internal validity of this study. What aspects of the experiments increased the internal validity?
3. Consider the external validity of this study. Are the behaviors exhibited in the study realistic? Why or why not?
4. Would you characterize this study as higher on internal validity, higher on external validity, or equal on each?
5. Why do you think the researchers used a confederate as the subjects' partner in the studies? What sources of bias does the use of a confederate allow them to control?

Research Study. Boothby, E. J., Clark, M. S., & Bargh, J. A. (2014). Shared experiences are amplified. *Psychological Science, 25,* 2209–2216.

Purpose of the Study. The researchers conducted two studies to examine the social effect on one's subjective experiences, based on past studies showing that shared experiences are psychologically stronger than unshared experiences. In their studies, they had subjects participate in both pleasant (Study 1) and unpleasant (Study 2) experiences (see Photo 7.8). They predicted that when another person present was sharing the experience, the ratings of the experience would be stronger than when the other person present was engaged in a different activity.

Method of the Study. In both studies, participants completed both the shared experience and unshared experience conditions in a random order. In both studies, subjects and a research confederate were asked to complete some tasks based on a card draw. Subjects tasted the same chocolate in both conditions but were led to believe that the chocolate was different in the two tasks. In Study 1, the chocolate was pleasant tasting (pleasant experience), and in Study 2, the chocolate was bitter tasting (unpleasant experience). In the shared condition, the confederate tasted the same chocolate as the subject. In the unshared experience, the confederate appeared to be tasting a different chocolate. The subjects were not allowed to communicate during the tasks. After tasting the chocolate, the subjects completed a survey about their rating of the chocolate (e.g., "How much do you like the chocolate? How flavorful is the chocolate?") and a survey about their impressions of the confederate. For both surveys, responses were made by checking a box on a 0 to 10 scale, with higher numbers indicating higher ratings.

Results of the Study. In both studies, ratings for the chocolate were stronger (higher for pleasant and lower for unpleasant) in the shared experience conditions. Figure 7.5 shows the ratings for liking of chocolate for both studies based on the social condition.

Photo 7.8
In the Boothby et al. (2014) study, participants were asked to eat pleasant- or bitter-tasting chocolate in either a shared or unshared experience condition to examine the effect of shared experiences on the intensity of those experiences.

FIGURE 7.5 ■ Mean Liking of Chocolate in Studies 1 and 2

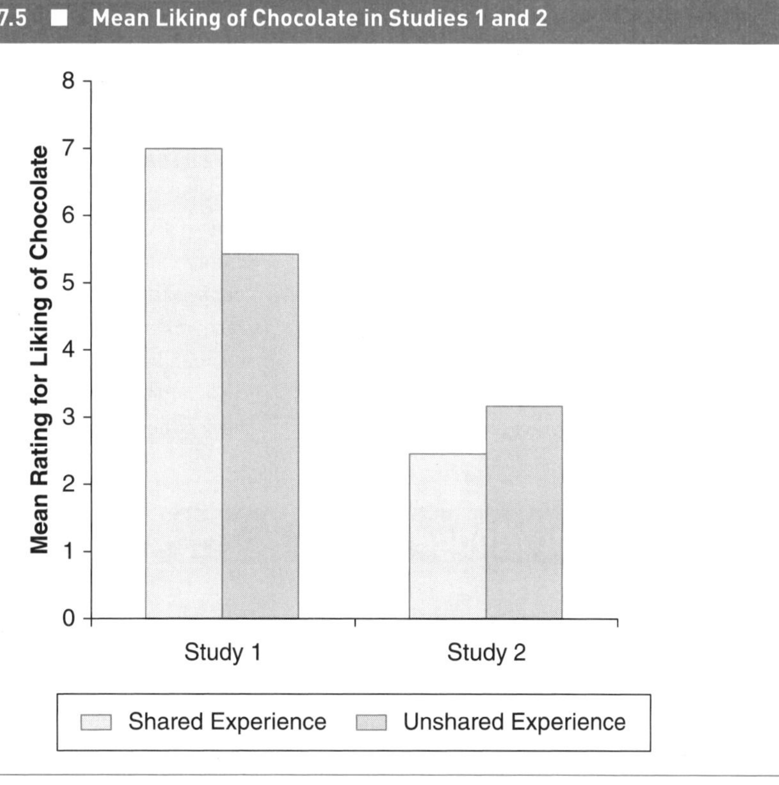

Source: Boothby et al. (2014).

Conclusions of the Study. The results of the study showed that shared experiences are more intense than unshared experiences—even when one does not communicate with someone else. This effect was present for both pleasant and unpleasant experiences, showing that the sharing of an experience does not simply make it more pleasurable but makes it stronger overall.

Chapter Summary

Reconsider the questions from the beginning of the chapter:

- **How do independent and dependent variables differ?**

Dependent variables are the behavior measures, and independent variables are the groups or situations across which the behavior is compared.

(Continued)

(Continued)

- **Which type of research method contains an independent variable? Why?**
  Experiments contain independent variables because experiments involve the manipulation of a variable that allows for additional control of confounding variables.
- **How does validity affect the results of a study?**
  Having good internal validity in a study means reducing bias that can affect the results and providing a good test of the hypothesis. Having good external validity means studying behaviors and obtaining results that generalize to individuals beyond the study in their everyday lives.
- **What are some factors that affect the validity of a study, and how can a researcher control these factors?**
  Several common sources of bias have been discussed in the chapter. Some are common to particular types of designs or behaviors. To control these sources of bias, researchers should first identify possible confounding variables in a study and then design the study in the best way to avoid having these variables bias the results.

Applying Your Knowledge

Consider the example study described at the beginning of the chapter on video games and violent behaviors.

- Explain why we cannot know that violent video games cause violent behavior based on an event of a mass shooting committed by someone who liked playing violent video games.
- Now, imagine that you want to test a causal relationship between violent video games and violent behavior in an experiment. What possible sources of bias would you need to be concerned about in this study?

Test Yourself

1. For the following study, indicate all the information you can about how the independent variable was manipulated.

   A psychologist conducted a study to compare the effect of different types of displays on participants' interest in a task. All participants in the study were asked to complete a set of math problems in the laboratory. Half of the participants just saw the text of the problem presented on the screen in black and white and typed in their answer on the computer keyboard. The other half of the participants saw the text of the problem in different colors, and small pictures that helped illustrate the problem were included. At the end of the task, all participants rated their interest in completing the task on a 1 to 10 scale.

2. For the study described in Question 1, list any possible sources of bias you can think of that might threaten the internal validity of the study, and explain how the bias could affect the results of the study.

3. For the study described in Question 1, evaluate the external validity of the study. How could this study be redesigned as a field experiment?
4. If a score on a midterm is unusually high for a student and far above his or her mean grade in the class to date, this would represent ________________ as a source of bias in using the midterm score to measure his or her learning in the course.
5. A ________________ design is often used to prevent experimenter bias, such that neither the researcher nor the subject is aware of the condition the subject has been assigned to in the study.
6. Suppose a researcher wants to study work productivity in a factory. Video cameras are installed to see how much time workers spend on task during a workday. The workers are more productive on the day after the cameras are installed than on the day before. A possible cause of the increase in productivity that would represent a source of bias in the study is ____________________.
7. A researcher is interested in studying face recognition abilities. Subjects are tested in the lab on their recognition of photos of unknown faces presented on a computer screen. If the subjects process the photos of the faces in a way that is different from how they typically process faces in their daily lives, this study would suffer from low ________________ validity.
8. Explain why attrition or mortality is a possible source of bias when it occurs in a research study.
9. Causal relationships are best tested with ________________.
   a. correlational studies
   b. a manipulated independent variable
   c. quasi-independent variables
   d. confounding variables
10. Experimenter bias is best controlled by a ________________ design.
    a. single-blind
    b. double-blind
    c. regression
    d. demand characteristic
11. As a researcher controls sources of bias in a study, ________________ will increase.
    a. internal validity
    b. external validity
    c. demand characteristics
    d. regression toward the mean
12. As confounding variables are controlled more in a study, ________________ often will decrease.
    a. internal validity
    b. external validity
    c. counterbalancing
    d. placebos

SAGE edge™

Visit **edge.sagepub.com/mcbridermstats** to find the answers to the Test Yourself questions above, as well as quizzes, flashcards, and other resources to help you accomplish your coursework goals.

8

ONE-FACTOR EXPERIMENTS

CONSIDER THE FOLLOWING QUESTIONS AS YOU READ CHAPTER 8

- What aspects of an experiment make it different from other research designs?
- What aspects of experiments allow for greater internal validity than other research designs?
- What are the different ways that independent variables can be manipulated to allow comparisons of conditions?
- What are the limitations of testing a single factor in an experiment?

LEARNING OBJECTIVES FOR CHAPTER 8

- Identify an independent variable in an experiment.
- Understand how independent variables allow for tests of causal relationships.
- Design a simple one-factor experiment.

When our dog Daphne (see Photo 8.1) became a member of our family, she did not like to be left in the house without us. Whenever we went out, even for short periods of time, she would have "accidents" on the rug and engage in destructive chewing behaviors. She ruined a few small items of furniture, many DVD cases, and more than a few pairs of my husband's shoes. In an attempt to improve her behavior, we researched the issue and found several suggested "treatments." We bought her a toy that held treats, accessed by chewing, that we could give her while we were away from home. We gave her some objects that we had used recently and smelled like us (e.g., an old T-shirt) to help her feel that we were nearby. We confined her to one room in the house to help her feel less anxious by being in a smaller space. Because we did not know which of these options would best improve her behavior, we decided to try these treatments one at a time, five times each to make sure that the treatments were tested under different conditions (different days of the week, different times of day, etc.). After each trip away from home when one of these treatments was applied, we counted the number of "bad" behaviors there was evidence of in the house. We operationally defined bad behaviors as soiling the floor or rug and chewing anything in the house that she was not supposed to chew. In other words, we used our knowledge of research methods to conduct an experiment to determine which treatment was most effective at stopping Daphne's bad behaviors while we were away from home. In most cases, an experiment involves several individuals being tested (e.g., several dogs in a study), but as we were only interested in how the treatments affected Daphne, we used a small-*n* experiment (called a small-*n* design) to test the treatments. In this experiment, Daphne experienced all the treatments, each at different times. We controlled for other possible explanations of her behavior by keeping her environment the same except for changing the treatment. We tested the treatments each time we went out until we had tested each treatment five times, but we randomly chose a treatment each time to make sure we did not accidentally test one treatment for several days while she was feeling less anxious about being on her own. Finally, we tested each treatment condition multiple times because we wanted to make sure that extreme behaviors that occurred during any single trip away from home would not bias the results. We wished to learn which treatment for Daphne would be most effective by comparing the treatments in terms of their effect on the dependent variable: her bad behavior. Through this experiment, we determined that the chew toy was the most effective in reducing Daphne's undesirable behaviors.

Photo 8.1
We conducted an experiment on Daphne. This experiment helped determine the best treatment to stop her bad behaviors.

If the example that was just given sounds like something you have tried in your life for yourself or a pet, then you may have already conducted your own experiment to learn something about your own or someone else's behavior. Perhaps you ran an experiment to determine which study techniques work best in improving your exam scores (see Photo 8.2). The experiments conducted by psychologists in their research follow the same principles as the example. Different treatments or conditions of an independent variable are compared to determine whether those treatments or conditions differ in their effects on behavior and

Photo 8.2
Have you ever considered comparing your exam scores after you've studied with music playing and after you've studied without music? If so, you've thought about conducting an experiment.

which of those treatments or conditions has the greatest effect on the behavior of interest.

Experiments as a research design was first introduced in Chapter 5. In this chapter, we will further consider some additional aspects of experiments (see Figure 8.1): how within- and between-subjects experiments differ and what we can learn from simple experiments that include one independent variable. In later chapters, we will consider more complex experiments that contain more than one independent variable.

FIGURE 8.1 ■ Steps in the Research Process: Designing the Study

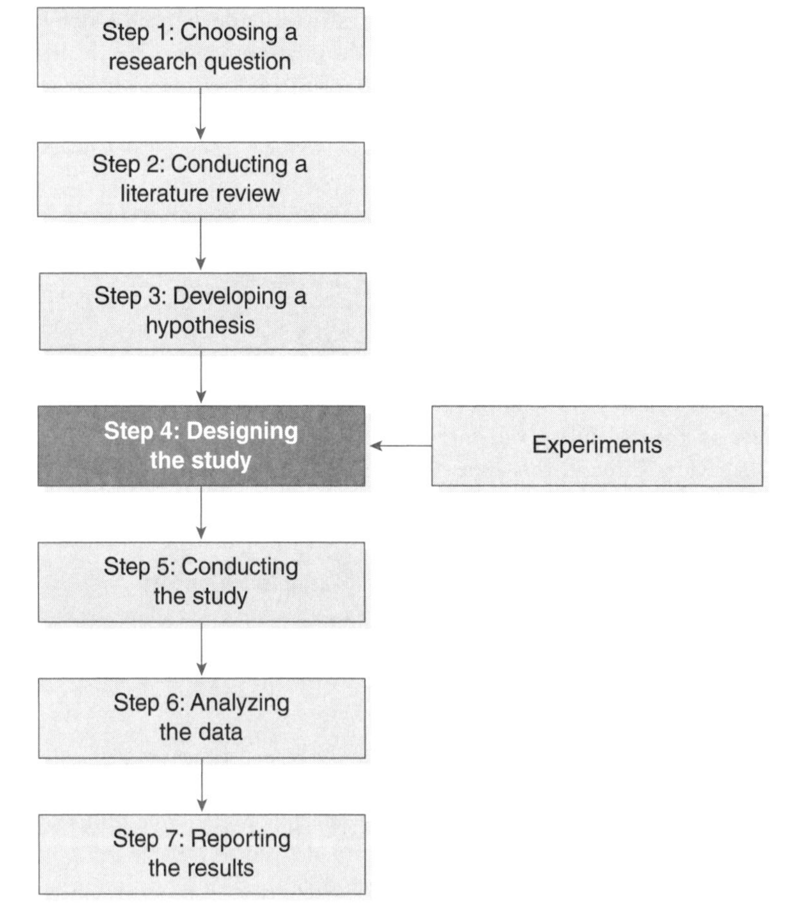

MANIPULATION OF INDEPENDENT VARIABLES

One aspect of an experiment that can seem confusing is the concept of manipulation. What does it mean to *manipulate* an independent variable? Generally, a manipulation of an independent variable involves researcher control of the administration of the levels of the independent variable to the participants. In other words, an independent variable is manipulated such that participants are randomly assigned to levels; the assignment is not based on any characteristic of the participants themselves. For example, as was discussed in the last chapter, a participant's gender, personality, and smoking status cannot be independent variables because these characteristics are not randomly assigned to a participant by the researcher. Instead, the participant comes to the study with these factors already determined.

The manipulation of an independent variable in an experiment allows the researcher to learn about the causal relationship between the independent and dependent variables. In other words, manipulation of an independent variable in a study increases the internal validity of the study. Recall from the last chapter that a study with good internal validity is one that provides a good test of a causal hypothesis. Without the manipulation of an independent variable, it is very difficult to rule out other possible factors as causes of changes in the dependent variable. When researchers design an experiment, they already are controlling for extraneous factors that can affect the results of the study through the use of a manipulated independent variable. One way is in how the independent variable is manipulated in the experiment, which can occur in two ways: The variable can be manipulated between subjects or within subjects. In between-subjects experiments, each participant receives only one level of the independent variable. Participants are typically randomly assigned to the different levels of between-subjects variables. For example, a researcher interested in the effects of text format on learning can manipulate text format as a between-subjects variable by randomly assigning different students in a class to a hard copy version of the text and an online version of the text. Random assignment of participants to levels allows random distribution of participant differences (study habits, academic achievement, etc.) across the levels, making it less likely that the participants' differences cause a difference across groups for the dependent variable being measured. This also means the researcher can be more certain that when a difference across conditions is found, it is due to the independent variable and not some other factor. In other words, random assignment means that subjects are assigned to groups according to chance, not according to any characteristic they possess or any choice made by the researcher. Each subject has an equal chance of being in any of the conditions in the experiment. Another common between-subjects example is comparing a treatment and a placebo. A researcher conducting this type of experiment would randomly assign participants to the treatment (e.g., new drug treatment) and placebo (e.g., sugar pill that looks like the drug) conditions to compare their symptoms. Using a placebo group controls for the knowledge of receiving a treatment (the participants do not know which one they received) that could also affect the symptoms the researcher is measuring. Random assignment is accomplished by chance; chance factors determine which participants will be in the different groups in the study. In this way, random assignment is a means of controlling for participant differences across groups and increases the internal validity of the experiment.

In within-subjects experiments, each participant receives all levels of the independent variable. Thus, each subject serves as his or her own comparison, and this even better controls individual differences because it removes subject differences from the comparison across conditions. Participants' scores in one condition are compared with their scores in the other condition. The researcher in the preceding example, who is interested in the effects of text format on learning, could manipulate text format within subjects by having each participant use each type of text for different chapters in the text. Random assignment is important for within-subjects variables in terms of the order in which participants receive the levels of the variable to control for possible **order effects** of the different levels of the variable. Consider a simple example: A researcher is comparing easy and difficult conditions of a task to determine the effect of task condition on task performance. To ensure that individual differences in task ability do not affect her results, she uses a within-subjects experiment. However, in this experiment, order effects could occur, where participants who receive the hard condition first perform worse overall than participants who receive the easy condition first due to discouragement in starting the task in its most difficult form. Thus, order effects are a disadvantage of using within-subjects designs. In the next section, we will consider how we can control for such effects.

order effects: Occur when the order in which the participants experience conditions in an experiment affects the results of the study

CONTROL IN WITHIN-SUBJECTS AND BETWEEN-SUBJECTS EXPERIMENTS

Random assignment is an important means of control in an experiment for between-subjects experiments. It is also useful for controlling order effects in within-subjects experiments. But there are also cases where random assignment may not be sufficient to control for extraneous factors and additional controls may be needed. Thus, researchers must consider the types of extraneous factors that may be present in an experiment when they decide whether to use a between-subjects or within-subjects independent variable. These issues are discussed here as they apply to each type of manipulation.

Between-Subjects Experiments

As described previously, in a between-subjects manipulation, randomly assigning participants to different groups controls for individual differences across the groups that might affect the data. For example, suppose you wanted to examine the effects of background music on memory for course material. You might design an experiment in a course to compare test scores on an exam for three groups of students: one group that studies for 5 hr with classical music in the background, one group that studies for 5 hr with pop music in the background, and one group that studies for 5 hr with no music. In an attempt to equate the groups, you might randomly assign the students to one of these groups, such that all students have an equal chance of being in any of the groups (i.e., they do not get to choose which group they are in based on their preference). This experiment involves the between-subjects independent variable of type of background music (classical, pop, none) because different students are randomly assigned to the groups—the students completed the study with only one type of the three background conditions.

Consider another example experiment from a study conducted by Russell, Ickes, and Ta (2018). These researchers investigated women's comfort level in interacting with a male stranger based on their sexual orientation. Female participants completed the experiment online. They were asked to read a scenario describing a situation where they were in a waiting room with a male stranger who started talking with them. Some of the participants were told that in the conversation the male stranger indicated that he was heterosexual, and other participants were told that the stranger indicated he was homosexual. The participants then rated their comfort level on a scale from 1 to 7 with higher ratings indicating more comfort in talking to the male stranger. Figure 8.2 shows the results from these two conditions in the study. The female participants rated their comfort level higher when they knew the stranger was homosexual than when they knew he was heterosexual. This study illustrates a between-subjects independent variable: sexual orientation of a male stranger. This independent variable affected the dependent variable of comfort rating in the female participants. This study is considered an experiment because the assignment of the participants to the heterosexual and homosexual male stranger conditions was determined randomly.

However, random assignment might not always be sufficient to control for group differences that can be confounding variables in your experiment. Consider the first example again about effects of background music on memory. If you have mostly good students in your sample and the few poor students all end up in the pop music group, it

FIGURE 8.2 ■ Results From the Russell et al. (2018) Experiment (Study 1—Sexual Orientation Known Conditions)

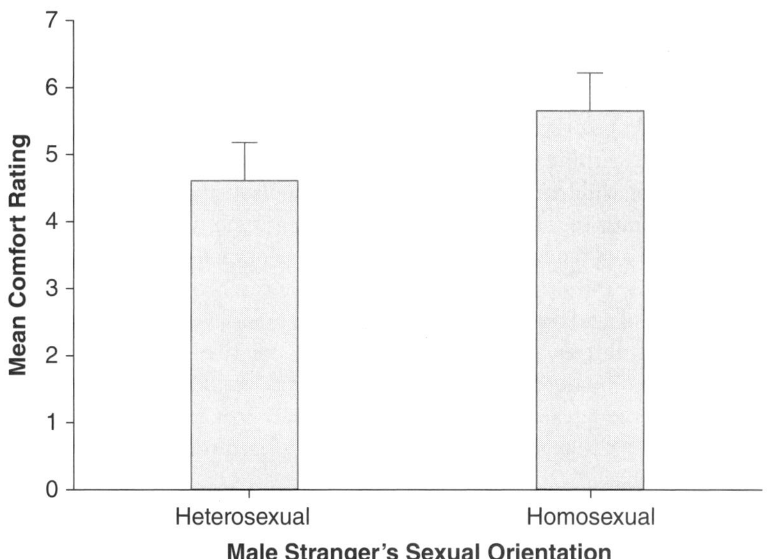

Source: Russell et al. (2018).

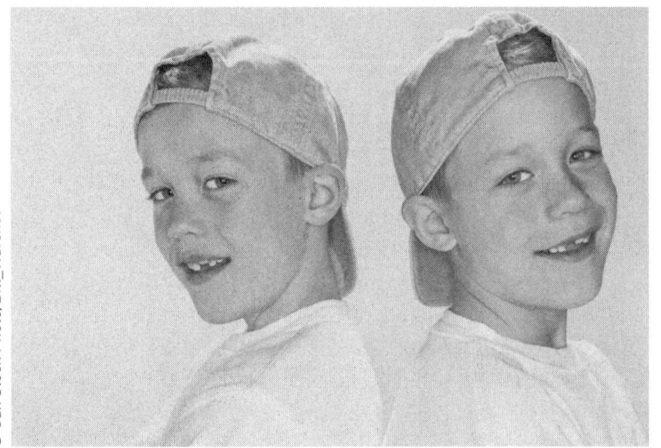

Photo 8.3 Identical twins can serve as participants in a matched design where they share the same genetics and, in some cases, the same upbringing.

may appear as if this condition has the worst effect on memory because of the inclusion of the poor students in this group. This would result in a source of bias in the study from the memory ability confounding variable that is not part of the independent variable.

In fact, the presence of individual differences across groups is the greatest concern for between-subjects experiments. In experiments where individual differences are likely to be present (such as the example about background music) and a small sample size is used, random assignment may not be sufficient to control for these differences. In this case, the researcher has two additional means of controlling for individual differences. The first is to manipulate the independent variable in a within-subjects experiment. This allows participants to serve as their own controls so that individual differences across groups are no longer of concern. However, for some variables, order effects may be more problematic and make between-subjects experiments preferable. If this is the case, a researcher could instead use a **matched design**. In a matched design, participants are matched on a characteristic that may contribute to group differences, but then each participant within a matched set is randomly assigned to different groups, making this a between-subjects experiment. See Figure 8.3 for an illustration of this design. In some cases, researchers use twins to create a matched set of participants based on genetics (see Photo 8.3).

matched design: A between-subjects experiment that involves sets of participants matched on a specific characteristic with each member of the set randomly assigned to a different level of the independent variable

To illustrate the matched design, consider a study conducted by O'Hanlon and Roberson (2006). They completed a series of experiments to investigate causes of the difficulties young children encounter when learning color words. Different groups of children were taught color words under different feedback conditions to compare effects of feedback type on learning of the color words. However, the researchers were concerned about the effects of children's age and current vocabulary abilities on the learning of the color words. Thus, they created sets of participants who were matched on age and vocabulary abilities and randomly assigned one member of each matched set to a different feedback condition. The matched sets allowed the researchers to control for the confounding variables of age and vocabulary abilities that otherwise may have differed across groups and caused differences in the learning scores for the feedback groups—effects that were not caused by the feedback conditions themselves. Because of this control for group differences, the researchers were able to conclude that feedback that corrects the child's errors in using color words allows the child to learn the color words faster than other forms of feedback.

Another way to ensure that participants in the groups are matched on some characteristic is to measure that characteristic (e.g., years of education, socioeconomic status, language abilities) during the experiment and then compare the groups in an additional analysis. This comparison indicates whether the groups are similar or different on that characteristic. However, if the groups are different, you are then left with the possibility that this difference affected your results. Thus, if you are concerned that a group

FIGURE 8.3 ■ Illustration of Matched Design, Counterbalancing, and Latin Square Design

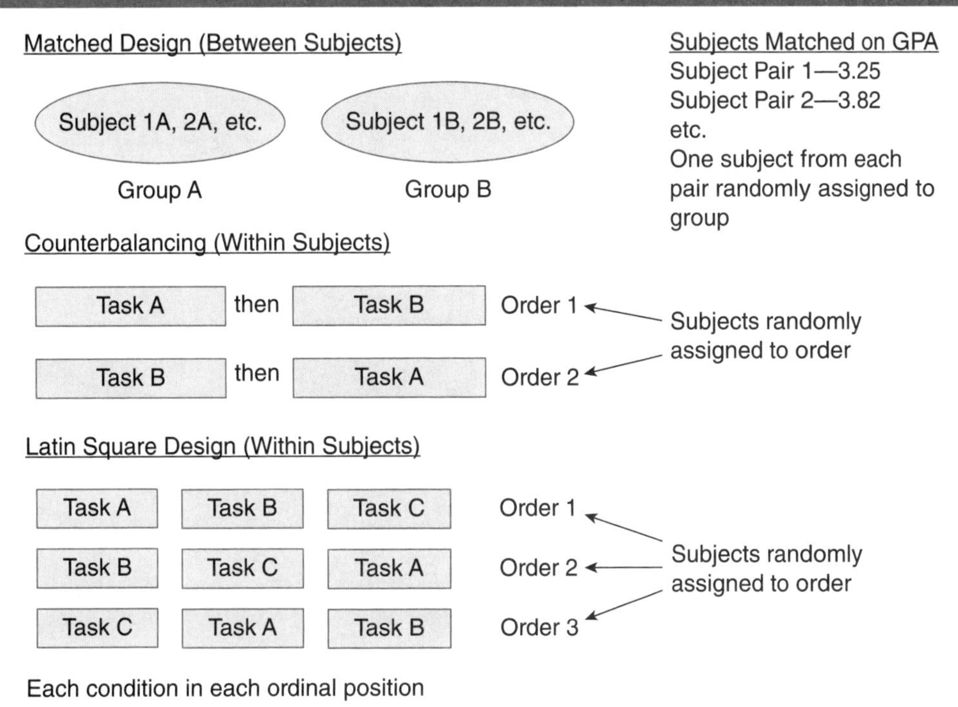

difference is likely to affect your results, it is best either to use a within-subjects manipulation or to match your participants before you assign them to the groups. Alternatively, if a between-subjects design is preferred, statistical tools can be used to account for group differences in the analysis of the data (e.g., covariate analysis).

Within-Subjects Experiments

The primary concern with within-subjects experiments is the order in which the participants receive the different levels of the independent variable. Because the participants receive all levels of the independent variable, it is possible that the order of the levels can affect the dependent variable measure. Consider the example from the previous section, where a within-subjects experiment involves a task difficulty manipulation such that all participants receive both an easy task and a difficult task (see Photos 8.4 and 8.5). The order in which they receive these tasks can certainly affect the outcome of the study. If participants receive an easy task first and then a difficult task, they are likely to view the difficult task as more difficult than they would if they had received it before the easy task. The opposite situation likely occurs for how they view the easy task, depending on whether the easy task is first or second (i.e., they may view it as "easier" if they complete the difficult task first than if they complete the difficult task second).

To solve the problem of order effects for within-subjects manipulations, a researcher typically uses counterbalancing of the order of the levels within the study. This means

Photos 8.4 and 8.5
In a within-subjects design, each participant completes the task in all of the conditions the researcher sets up with the independent variable. For example, a researcher might compare task performance when the task is easy versus when it is difficult. Each participant's performance is compared for the two conditions.

that different groups of participants receive different orders of the levels of the independent variable. For example, in the experiment described earlier, half of the participants would receive the easy task first, and half would receive the difficult task first with participants assigned in equal numbers to the two different orders. Random assignment to orders should be used. See Figure 8.3 for an illustration of counterbalancing. Using different orders of the levels counterbalances the order effects across the participants. The different orders can also be compared to determine if order effects exist, which is likely for this example. This can help a researcher determine if the effect of the independent variable depends on the order of the conditions the subjects receive.

Counterbalancing is relatively easy when there are only two conditions that participants experience in an experiment. However, many experimental designs involve more than two conditions, making counterbalancing a little more difficult for within-subjects manipulations because all the orders must be included in a full counterbalancing. To illustrate this issue, consider a within-subjects experiment with three conditions: A, B, and C. There are six possible orders in which participants can experience these three conditions: ABC, BCA, ACB, CBA, CAB, and BAC. To fully counterbalance these three conditions, you would need six different orders of the conditions and numbers of participants in multiples of six in order to make an equal number of participants randomly assigned to each of the six possible orders of conditions. Already, the counterbalancing is becoming rather complicated. What happens when you have four conditions in the experiment? The counterbalancing of four conditions is even more complicated. To simplify the counterbalancing in such a case, a partial counterbalancing technique, called a **Latin square**, can be used instead. In a Latin square, the number of orders used in the experiment is equal to the number of conditions in the design, and each condition is in each ordinal position (i.e., first, second, third, fourth) exactly once. See Figure 8.3 for an illustration of this design. Latin squares can be useful for within-subjects designs where independent variables have a number of levels.

Latin square: Partial counterbalancing technique where the number of orders of conditions used is equal to the number of conditions in the study

For example, an experiment with four conditions (A, B, C, and D) can use a Latin square to include four different orders of the conditions. Each of these conditions is positioned first once, second once, and so on within the order structure. Thus, the order for a Latin square would be ABDC, BCAD, CDBA, and DACB (see Grant, 1948, for the procedure to create a Latin square for a design with any number of conditions). In this order structure, you can see that each condition serves in each ordinal position once. The researcher then randomly assigns each participant to one of these orders, requiring fewer orders of conditions in the experiment and fewer multiples of participants to run in the experiment.

STOP AND THINK

8.1. Describe one advantage and one disadvantage of a between-subjects design.

8.2. Describe one advantage and one disadvantage of a within-subjects design.

8.3. For each of the following research descriptions, decide if you think a within-subjects or between-subjects design is better. Explain your choice in each case:

- Effect of teaching technique (comparing three different techniques) on exam scores
- Effect of social inclusion or exclusion on reading comprehension
- Effect of face familiarity on brain activity

EXPERIMENT EXAMPLES

Although any area of psychological research may include experiments, there are areas of psychology where experiments are used more often than in others. In cognitive, biological, social, and (in some cases) developmental research, one is most likely to encounter the experimental research design. Other areas of psychological research do include experiments, but manipulation can be difficult or impossible for some factors of interest (e.g., clinical conditions or personality types). Thus, the following examples come from areas where experiments are more likely to be used and illustrate how experiments are used in different areas of psychology as well as some of the experimental concepts that are described in this chapter.

Cognitive Example

Cognitive psychology includes the study of basic processing of information from the world around us. Cognitive psychologists study memory, perception, language processes, and decision making. Much of the research in these areas is focused on understanding factors that influence these processes and how they operate. Thus, experiments are a very common research design for cognitive psychologists.

Storm and Stone (2015) conducted a simple cognitive experiment to investigate the effects of saving studied information in a computer file on one's ability to learn new information. They suggested that because a saved file can be accessed later for further study, saving a file of studied words (as compared with not saving the file) would free up cognitive resources to learn new information. On each trial of the experiment, subjects in the study were asked to study two PDF files of words on a flash drive. Subjects were told that they would study the first file, then study the second file, and then be tested on the second file and the first file—in that order. For half of the trials, subjects were asked to save the first PDF list file before closing it and were told that, whenever they saved the file, they would be able to go back to it later to study it before testing. On the other trials, subjects were instructed to simply close the first PDF file without saving it. Thus, the independent variable was whether the first list was saved or not. The variable was manipulated within subjects because all the subjects received three "save" and three "no save" trials. The "save" or "no save" instruction appeared after the subjects had studied the first list. Then, after a short delay, the subjects were tested on the second word list. If the first word list had been saved on that trial, they were able to restudy it before the test on that list. If it was not saved, they were tested on the first list right after the test on the second list (see Figure 8.4 for a diagram of the procedure of the experiment). Lists were counterbalanced across "save" and "no save" conditions to remove any bias that might be caused by the difficulty of the lists. The researchers then compared recall on the second list (the one that was never saved) for trials in which the first list was saved and trials in which the first list was not saved. The results of the experiment supported the researchers' hypothesis: Subjects recalled more words from the second list when the first list had been saved than when the first list had not been saved. They concluded that saving a file that can be accessed later frees up cognitive resources for other tasks, showing benefits of reliable technology on cognition.

FIGURE 8.4 ■ Diagram of the Procedure Used in Storm and Stone's (2015) Experiment 1

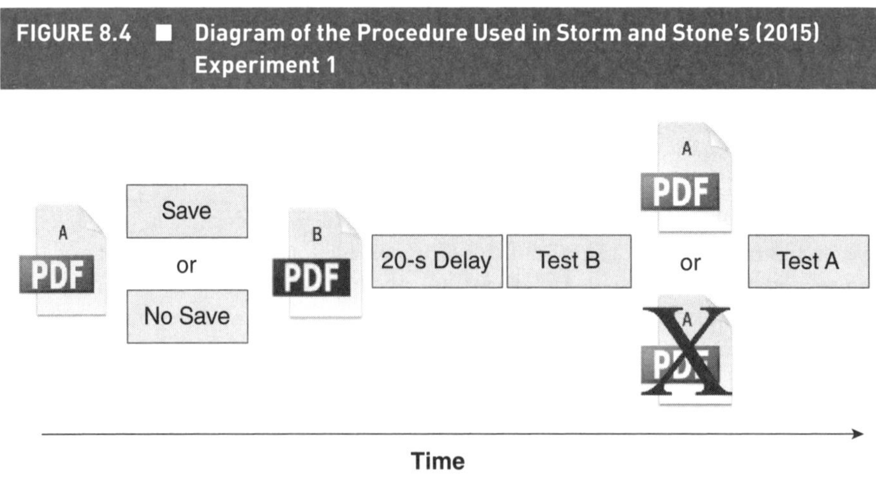

Source: Storm and Stone (2015).

Biological Example

Biological psychology (also called neuropsychology if it involves brain function) investigates the role of biological factors in behavior. Thus, experiments are often employed in this area of psychology to determine causal relationships between biology and behavior. In many cases, participants are asked to perform different tasks while brain function that corresponds to these tasks is recorded to better understand where brain activity occurs for different behaviors. Or stimulation of a biological system (e.g., the brain) may occur, and resultant behaviors are recorded. In other types of studies, brain function in animals is manipulated to observe the causal effect of the manipulation on a behavior of interest. In other words, the brain (or other biological) activity can be either the dependent variable or the independent variable in the experiment.

Ferrè, Lopez, and Haggard (2014) conducted an experiment to examine the link between the vestibular system (the system that controls our sense of balance) and one's perspective (i.e., one's own perspective vs. another person's perspective). In their study, stimulation electrodes were placed on the subjects' head below the ears (experimental trials) or neck (control trials). For the experimental trials, subjects received the stimulation, and during the control trials, subjects did not receive stimulation. One second after stimulation began (for experimental trials) or at the start of the trial (for control trials), a reversible letter (e.g., *b* or *d*) was traced by the experimenter on the subject's forehead (see Figure 8.5). After 4 s of stimulation, a tone sounded, and the subject was asked to name the letter. If the subject named the letter traced (e.g., *b*), it showed the experimenter's perspective. If the subject named the letter reversed (e.g., *d*), it showed the subject's perspective.

Figure 8.6 shows the results for the percentage of trials the subjects showed their own perspective. The percentage was higher for experimental trials (for both left and right stimulation) than for the control trials (labeled *sham* because they had fake electrodes attached for these trials). These results show that stimulation of the vestibular system increases first-person perspective, suggesting that this system is involved in our sense of self.

FIGURE 8.5 ■ Diagram of the Procedure Used in Ferrè et al.'s (2014) Experiment

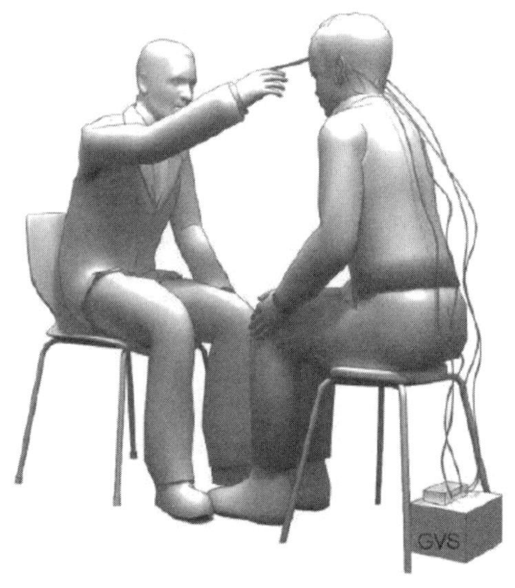

Source: Ferré et al. (2014).

Social Example

Social psychologists examine the effects of social factors on different types of behaviors. In one study from this field, Bastian, Jetten, and Ferris (2014) tested the effects of experiencing pain on social bonding. In one of their experiments, subjects were randomly assigned to "pain" and "no pain" groups. The subjects in the pain group were asked to submerge their hand in icy water for as long as possible to complete a task sorting metal balls from the bowl of water into containers and then to hold a squat position against the wall for as long as possible (see Photo 8.6). The subjects in the no pain group completed the ball-sorting task from a bowl of room temperature water and were asked to balance on one leg for 60 s and to switch legs when one leg got tired (see Photo 8.7). Thus,

FIGURE 8.6 ■ Results From Ferrè et al.'s (2014) Experiment

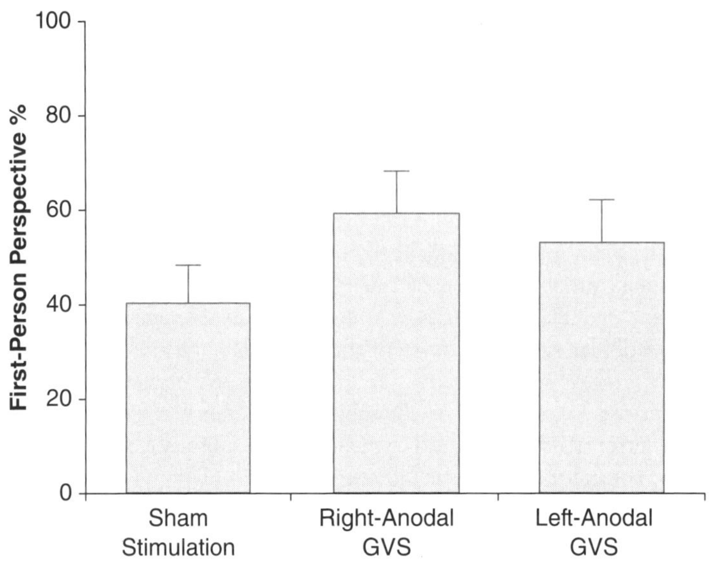

Source: Ferré et al. (2014).

Photos 8.6 and 8.7

In Bastian et al.'s (2014) experiment, they compared "pain" and "no pain" groups' feelings of bonding with others in the experiment. The pain group completed a ball-sorting task from a bowl of icy water and then had to hold a squat position for as long as possible (Photo 8.6). The no pain group completed the ball-sorting task from a bowl of room temperature water and then balanced on one leg for 60 s but could switch legs when they tired (Photo 8.7).

both groups performed the same types of tasks, but these tasks were painful for the subjects in the pain group. All subjects completed the experiment with other subjects (between one and four other people). After the tasks, subjects completed a survey measuring their feelings of bonding toward the other participants in the study. Figure 8.7 shows the mean bonding scores for the two groups. Subjects in the pain group rated their bonding higher than the subjects in the no pain group.

FIGURE 8.7 ■ Results From the Bastian et al. (2014) Study for the "Pain" and "No Pain" Groups

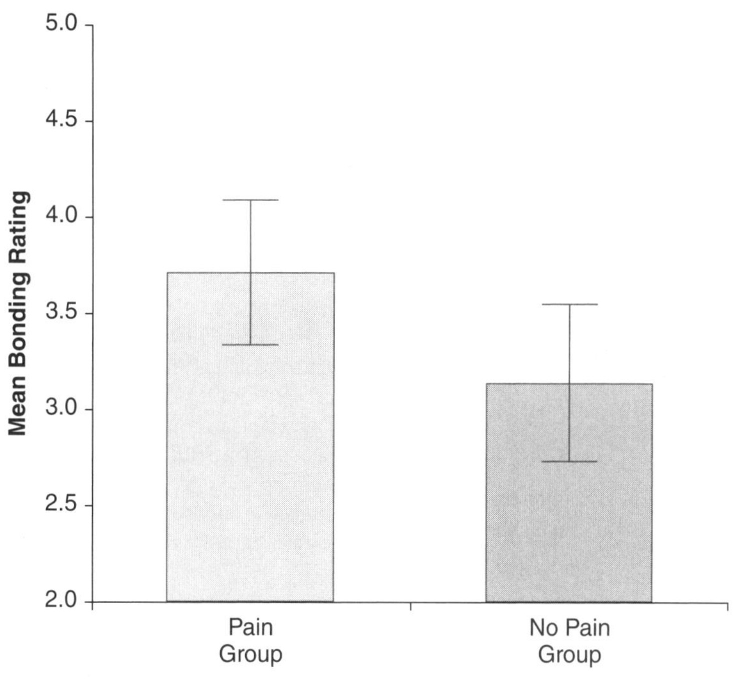

Source: Bastian et al. (2014).

STOP AND THINK

8.4. For the experiments described in the earlier Biological Example and Social Example sections, identify the independent and dependent variables.

8.5. For each of the experimental examples in this chapter (Bastian et al., 2014; Ferrè et al., 2014; Storm & Stone, 2015), identify one possible source of bias in the study.

8.6. In the Bastian et al. (2014) experiment described in the Social Example section, why do you think the researchers made sure the "no pain" group did similar tasks to the "pain" group instead of just having that group talk to the subjects they were tested with?

THINKING ABOUT RESEARCH

A summary of a research study in psychology is given here. As you read the summary, think about the following questions:

1. What aspects of this study allow us to define it as an experiment?
2. What is the independent variable? What are the levels of the independent variable? What is the dependent variable?
3. Was the independent variable in this experiment manipulated between subjects or within subjects? How do you know?
4. Do you think this study could have been conducted as the other type of design (i.e., the opposite of your answer to Question 3)? Why or why not?
5. What possible sources of bias can you identify in this study?

Research Study. Brown-Iannuzzi, J. L., Lundberg, K. B., Kay, A. C., & Payne, B. K. (2015). Subjective status shapes political preferences. *Psychological Science, 26*, 15–26.

Note: Study 2 of this article is described here.

Purpose of the Study. How does a person's perception of his or her wealth in reference to others' wealth influence his or her ideas about the redistribution of wealth as a political concept? The authors conducted four studies to answer this question. We will examine Study 2 here. In this experiment, the effect of subjective wealth status on wealth redistribution agreement was tested. The authors hypothesized that subjects who believed they were wealthier than their peers would more strongly oppose the redistribution of wealth as measured by survey score.

Method of the Study. There were 153 participants in the experiment. They were recruited through the Amazon site Mechanical Turk (MTurk). Participants were first given false feedback to a questionnaire about their subjective wealth status. They were randomly assigned to either the high status group (where they were given a positive score on a false "Composite Discretionary Index" scale) or the low status group (where they were given a negative score on the false "Composite Discretionary Index" scale). Participants were told to interpret positive scores as their having more discretionary (i.e., extra) income than their peers and negative scores as their having less discretionary income than their peers. Thus, participants' actual income did not change, but their perception of their comparison in wealth to others was manipulated. An 11-item survey about the redistribution of wealth (e.g., "In general, the wealthy should be taxed to provide benefits to the poor.") was used to measure their attitude about redistribution of wealth from the total score on the survey.

Results of the Study. The results indicated a difference between the high and low status groups in redistribution attitudes. The low status group had a higher mean score on the survey, indicating that they were more strongly in favor of redistribution of wealth.

Conclusions of the Study. The results from the study indicate that one's subjective sense of wealth compared with others influences one's political attitude toward redistribution of wealth independent of actual wealth.

Chapter Summary

Reconsider the questions from the beginning of the chapter:

- **What aspects of an experiment make it different from other research designs?** Experiments contain an independent variable that is manipulated and allows for control of alternative explanations of the results. Thus, experiments are the best research design for testing causal relationships.
- **What aspects of experiments allow for greater internal validity than other research designs?** The manipulation of a variable (independent variable) and the additional controls for confounding variables allow for greater internal validity in experiments than other types of research designs.
- **What are the different ways that independent variables can be manipulated to allow comparisons of conditions?** Independent variables can be manipulated by type of something, amount of something, or the presence or absence of something (see Chapter 7 for more discussion of this aspect of independent variables). They can also be manipulated between subjects, where each participant receives only one level of the independent variable, or within subjects, where each participant receives all levels of the independent variable.
- **What are the limitations of testing a single factor in an experiment?** With a single independent variable in an experiment, you can examine only the effects of that one independent variable on the dependent variable in your study. In addition, you cannot examine the combined effects of the independent variables on the dependent variable.

Applying Your Knowledge

The TV show *MythBusters* on the Discovery Channel often illustrates simple experiments designed to test a hypothesis from a common myth. Consider an episode I use for a class activity involving the myth that elephants are afraid of mice. The MythBusters tested this myth in a simple experiment. View the experiment at https://youtu.be/7oA77tVNKtc and then answer the following questions.

- What hypothesis were the MythBusters testing?
- What was their dependent variable?
- What was their independent variable?
- How did replicating their results make their conclusions stronger?

Test Yourself

A researcher decided to test whether the presence of another person affects participants' task performance. He asks participants to complete a maze puzzle as quickly as they can. Participants complete two puzzles: once on their own and once with a research confederate present who seems to also be working on the puzzle. Half of the participants complete the puzzle alone first, and half complete the puzzle with the confederate present first. Time to complete the puzzle is recorded for each participant for the two puzzles they complete. Use this description to answer Questions 1 to 4.

1. The dependent variable in this study is ______________.
   a. completing the maze alone
   b. completing the maze with the confederate present
   c. whether or not someone was present when they completed the maze
   d. the time to complete the maze
2. The independent variable in this study is ______________.
   a. completing the maze alone
   b. completing the maze with the confederate present
   c. whether or not someone was present when they completed the maze
   d. the time to complete the maze
3. This experiment is a ______________ design.
   a. between-subjects
   b. within-subjects
   c. mixed
4. Having half the participants complete the maze alone first and half complete it with the confederate present first is an example of ______________.
   a. using a between-subjects design
   b. using a small-*n* design
   c. using counterbalancing
5. What aspects of an experiment allow tests of causal relationships?
6. What is the advantage of using a Latin square over full counterbalancing when counterbalancing the order of conditions in a within-subjects design? How many orders are used in a Latin square?
7. Reread the sample experiment about our dog Daphne presented at the beginning of the chapter to answer the following questions:
   a. What is the independent variable, and what are the levels of this variable in the experiment?
   b. Was the independent variable manipulated between subjects or within subjects?
   c. What controls for confounding variables are described for this experiment?
   d. If you were interested in testing the effectiveness of the "treatments" for the population of all dogs, how would you conduct such an experiment?
8. A researcher conducted a study to investigate the effects of smiling on helping behavior. Participants completed a survey that they thought was the purpose of the study, but in reality, the experiment took place after they completed the survey. At the end of the survey session, half of the subjects

were thanked with a smile and half were thanked without a smile. Whether the subject received a smile or not was randomly determined. The subjects were on their way out of the lab in the hallway when they then passed a confederate who had just dropped a large stack of books. The number of subjects who helped the confederate pick up his books for the smile and no smile groups was compared.

a. What is the independent variable in this experiment? Is the independent variable manipulated between subjects or within subjects?
b. Can you think of an important ethical issue for this experiment and how to handle it in the procedure of the experiment?

A study is conducted to examine the effects of office layout on work productivity. Employees in a company are currently organized into cubicles. Their current work productivity (number of e-mails sent, number of reports completed) per day is measured for each day in 1 week. Then the layout is reorganized with employees grouped at small tables set around a large open room according to unit of the company. After getting used to this new layout for a month, their work productivity is again measured for each day in 1 week. Use this description to answer Questions 9 to 11:

9. This is a ____________ experiment.
   a. between-subjects
   b. within-subjects
10. The independent variable in this experiment is ____________.
    a. the day of week that productivity was measured on
    b. 1 week
    c. number of e-mails sent
    d. the office layout
11. A possible confounding variable in this experiment is ____________.
    a. group differences in work productivity
    b. which day of the week productivity is measured on
    c. order effects

9

HYPOTHESIS-TESTING LOGIC

CONSIDER THE FOLLOWING QUESTIONS AS YOU READ CHAPTER 9

- What is a standardized score?
- What is the standard error?
- How can we use a population mean and the standard error to test a hypothesis?
- What are the steps in hypothesis testing?
- What is statistical significance, and what does it tell us about our hypothesis?
- What types of errors exist in our hypothesis-testing procedure?
- How can I reduce the chance of an error in testing hypotheses?

LEARNING OBJECTIVES FOR CHAPTER 9

- Identify the five basic steps in hypothesis testing.
- Use a *z* score to test a simple hypothesis.
- State null and alternative hypotheses.
- Identify the types of errors that can occur in hypothesis testing.

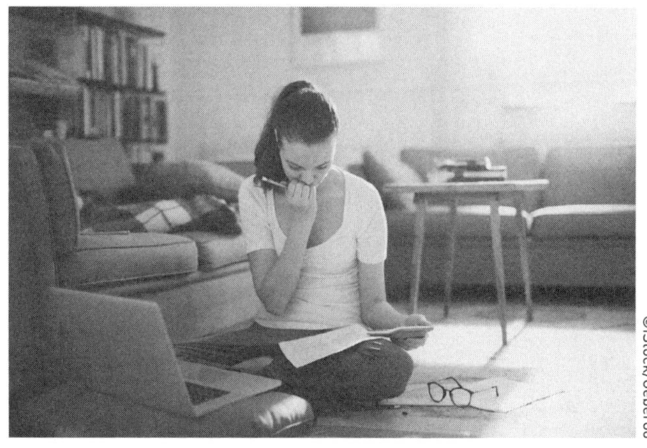

©iStock/Geber86

Photo 9.1
Research question: Does taking online quizzes help students prepare for exams?

In this chapter, we will begin to examine how we test hypotheses about populations using statistics. To help you understand the goals of hypothesis testing, consider this example: You want to know if taking the online quizzes your instructor has assigned this semester helps students in your course prepare for exams (see Photo 9.1). To answer this research question, you conduct a study to compare the mean final exam score in your course for students who took the online quizzes this semester with the mean final exam score for all the previous semesters for which online quizzes were not available for students to take. In other words, you want to compare the current class exam mean with the exam mean for the population of all classes who have taken the final exam in the past without the aid of online quizzes. Your instructor tells you that the mean score for all past classes is 75 (she has taught this course many times in her career). She also tells you that the mean for the students who took the online quizzes this semester is 82. Is 82 significantly higher than the population mean of 75, showing that the online quizzes helped raise exam scores, or is 82 just a slightly higher value by chance because the current sample of students happened to score a bit higher than the population mean? Figure 9.1 shows the comparison of these values in the population distribution of exam scores. How can you determine whether 82 is significantly higher than 75 or not in terms of a comparison to the population of all past classes? The answer is to use a standardized score known as a ***z* score**!

***z* score:** A standardized score that indicates the location of a score within a population distribution

FIGURE 9.1 ■ Distribution of Final Exam Scores in the Population of Students Who Have Taken the Course in the Past

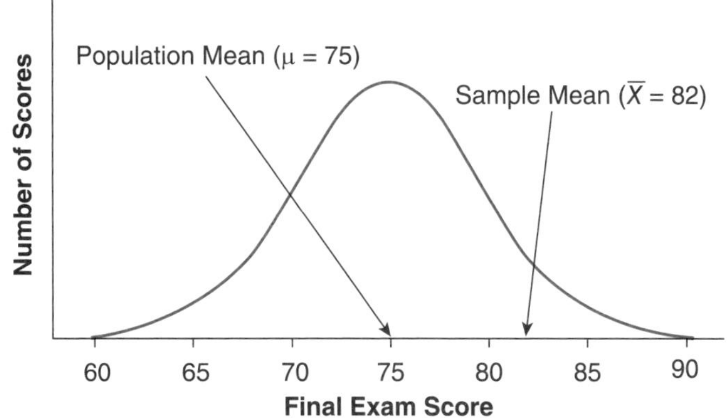

THE *z* SCORE TRANSFORMATION

Transforming data to *z* scores provides a way of locating a score in a standardized distribution. This transformation can be useful in cases where we want to compare two scores that come from two different populations. Here's a classic example: Do you weigh more than your dog? Unless you have a very large dog, in absolute measurement of weight, you probably weigh more. But if we consider how heavy your dog is compared with other dogs and how heavy you are compared with other humans (male or female), then the comparison would be more informative in terms of your relative weights. We can do this by transforming your weight and your dog's weight into *z* scores. Figure 9.2 shows these weight distributions in the relevant populations. The top graph shows the distribution of dog weights for the population of all dogs, the bottom left graph shows the distribution of human male weights for the population of adult males at all ages, and the bottom right graph shows the distribution of human female weights for the population of adult females at all ages. Notice that both the mean and standard deviation (in this chapter, the abbreviation of *SD* will be used with numerical values) for each distribution are given (the standard deviation units are marked on the distributions) and that the means and standard deviations are different across the distributions. With *z* scores, we can compare scores that come from very different distributions on the same measurement scale.

FIGURE 9.2 ■ Distribution of Weights (in Pounds) for Dog, Human Male, and Human Female Populations

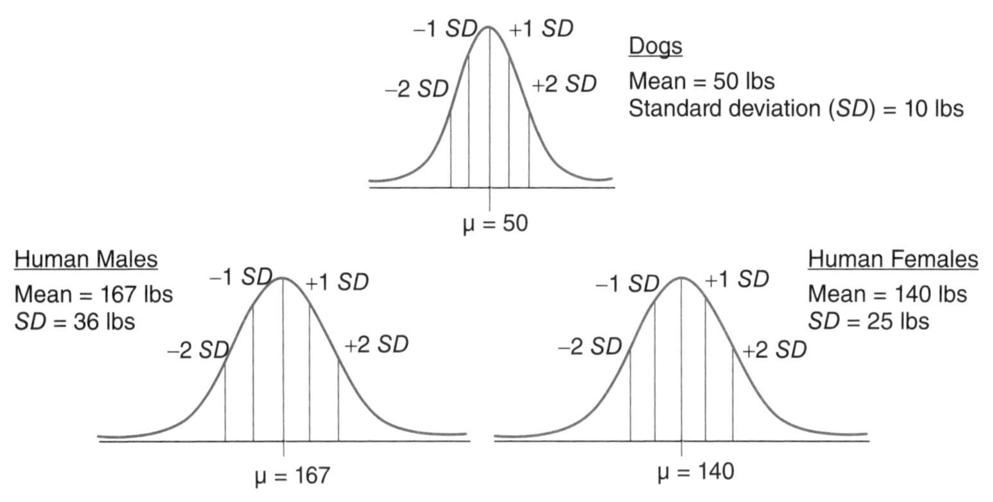

Note: Dog weights are hypothetical; source for human weights is Ogden, Fryar, Carroll, and Flegal (2004).

Photo 9.2 My dog, Daphne; she is 53 pounds.

Locate your weight on the male or female distribution graph. Are you above or below the mean? How many standard deviations are you away from the mean (e.g., less than 1 *SD*, more than 1 *SD*, more than 2 *SD*s)? Now, locate your dog's weight on the dog distribution graph (if you do not have a dog, you can borrow my dog, Daphne, who is 53 pounds; see Photo 9.2). Is your dog within 1 *SD* of the mean? (If you're using Daphne, she's less than 1 *SD* above the mean.) Next, compare the location of your weight in the appropriate weight distribution (human male or female) and your dog's weight in the dog distribution. How do these locations compare relative to the means of the distributions? This will help you answer the question of whether or not you are heavier than your dog. If, for example, you are 1 *SD* below the mean in your weight distribution, but your dog (or Daphne) is less than 1 *SD* above the mean in the dog weight distribution, then your dog (or Daphne) is heavier than you are in terms of relative weights. That's how we use *z* scores to compare scores from different distributions.

A *z* score transformation for an entire distribution of scores works the same way as the dog and human weight example I just described. Using a *z* score transformation standardizes the scores according to the population they come from to allow us to compare the scores—a *z* score gives us the location of the scores in their distribution. Thus, a *z* score is a value that represents the distance of a score from the population mean in terms of how many standard deviations the distance is in that distribution. A score can be 1 *SD* above the mean, 1.5 *SD*s below the mean, 3 *SD*s above the mean, and so on. The *z* score will tell us the distance from the mean in standard deviation units. And the sign of the score (positive or negative) tells us whether the score is above or below the population mean.

For any distribution, we can transform all the scores in the distribution to create a *z* score distribution for the original distribution. Figure 9.3 shows an example *z* score distribution. In other words, we could standardize all the scores in a distribution to create a *z* score distribution for those scores. In all cases, the mean of the *z* score distribution will be zero, because the *z* scores represent the distance from the mean, so the mean distance in a *z* score distribution should be zero (i.e., the mean minus the mean equals zero). The standard deviation will always be 1.0, because the transformed scores will be in standard deviation units once we've converted the scores to values that represent how many standard deviations there are from the mean of zero in our new distribution. The shape of the standardized (i.e., *z* score) distribution, however, will be the same as the original distribution. If the original distribution is symmetrical, the *z* score transformed distribution will be symmetrical.

FIGURE 9.3 ■ An Example *z* Score Distribution

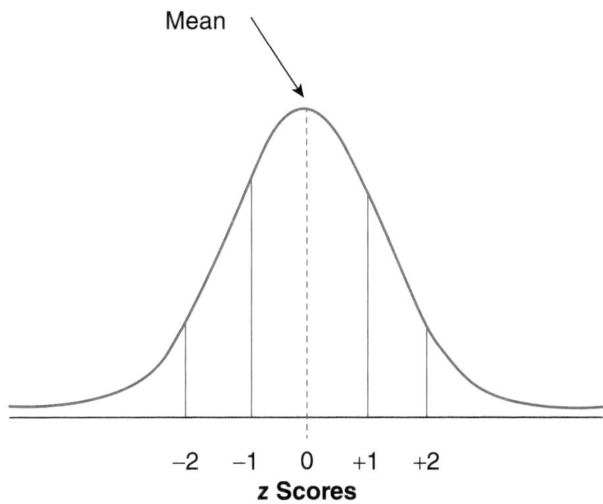

Calculating a *z* Score by Hand

Now, let's look at how we transform our data scores to *z* scores. I'll begin with how to calculate *z* scores by hand and the formula notations for *z* scores using Daphne's weight. As described in the previous section, a *z* score represents a score's distance from the mean in standard deviation units. Therefore, we need to know the mean for the population (μ) and the population standard deviation (σ). If you take a look at Figure 9.2, you will see that both the μ and σ are given for each distribution. Daphne's weight is 53 pounds. Remember that this weight score is less than 1 *SD* above the mean because it falls between the mean and the first line in the graph (marking the score that is 1 *SD* above the mean). The μ for the dog weight distribution is given as 50. We need to know how far Daphne's weight is from the mean (μ) and in which direction, so we need to calculate a difference score between her weight (53) and the mean (50). That will be the first part of our calculation (53 – 50 = +3). The next part is to put that difference score into standard deviation units by dividing it by the population standard deviation (σ). The standard deviation of the dog weight distribution is given as 10 pounds, so we will divide the difference score (+3) by the σ of 10 $\left(\frac{+3}{10} = +.3\right)$. This is the *z* score for Daphne's weight: +.3. In other words, her weight is .3 *SD*s above the mean in the population distribution of dog weights.

The calculation we just completed gives us this formula:

$$z = \frac{(X - \mu)}{\sigma}$$

X is the score we want to transform, μ is the population mean, and σ is the population standard deviation. Let's try another example using this formula and my weight of 150 pounds. Am I heavier or lighter than Daphne? The *z* score comparison will tell us. We will use the μ of 140 pounds and μ of 25 pounds from the female weight distribution in Figure 9.2. Thus, the *z* score for my weight is as follows:

$$z = \frac{(150 - 140)}{25} = \frac{+10}{25} = +.4$$

If we compare my weight *z* score of +.4 and Daphne's weight *z* score of +.3, we see that I am, in fact, heavier than Daphne for our relative weight distributions (but not by much!).

STOP AND THINK

9.1. Let's try another example: Compare the weight of my husband, Jeff (135 pounds) with another dog I know named Rafiki (7.5 pounds; see Photo 9.3). First calculate the *z* scores for Jeff's weight and Rafiki's weight using the correct means and standard deviations (Jeff is male) presented in Figure 9.2. Compare the two *z* scores. Who is heavier: Jeff or Rafiki?

9.2. Now try the *z* score transformation for your own weight using the distributions presented in Figure 9.2. If you have a dog (and know its weight), you can also calculate the *z* score for your dog's weight. Compare the two *z* scores (or use Daphne's *z* score; see the text in this section showing the calculation). Are you heavier or lighter than your dog (or Daphne)? How about compared with Rafiki?

9.3. What does a *z* score of −1.5 tell you about the location of that score in the distribution?

Calculating a *z* Score Using Excel

Calculating a *z* score using Excel is simply a matter of typing the *z* score formula into a cell in the data window. If you have your score (X) typed into a single cell, you can use that cell in the formula. Or you can simply put the score into the formula itself. The formula to type into a cell in Excel for calculating Daphne's weight is this:

$$=(53-50)/10$$

Using this formula, you will see the same value we calculated earlier (.3) appear in that cell in the spreadsheet. If you have all the population scores entered into Excel before your *z* score calculation, you can calculate the population mean (μ) and standard deviation (σ) using the AVERAGE formula to determine these values ahead of time if you do not already have them.

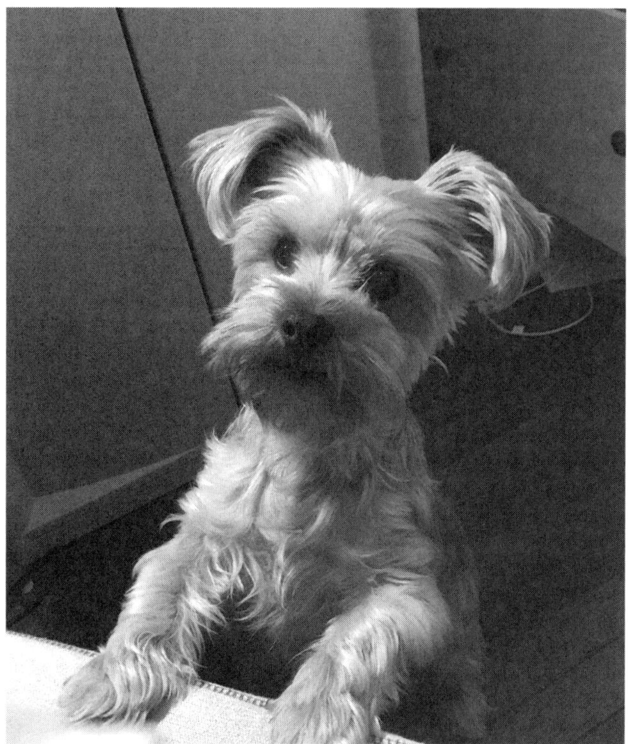

Diana M. Steakley-Freeman

Photo 9.3
Rafiki the dog; he is 7.5 pounds.

Calculating a *z* Score Using SPSS

The procedure for calculating z scores in SPSS is also fairly simple. You first need to have the score(s) you want to use in the calculation in a column in the data window. Once you have the scores entered, you can choose the Compute Variable function from the Transform menu at the top. This will open the window shown in Figure 9.4. In the Target Variable box, you will need to name the new variable that contains the z score(s) (e.g., z score). Then in the Numeric Expression box, you can create the z score equation using the column containing your score(s) and the known population μ and σ. Figure 9.4 shows how this equation might look for Daphne's weight as a z score. When you click on OK, the z score(s) will appear in a new column in the data window with the label you have given to the new variable that contains the z scores.

FIGURE 9.4 ■ Compute Variable Window in SPSS Showing the Equation for Calculating a *z* Score for Scores in the First Column of the Data Window

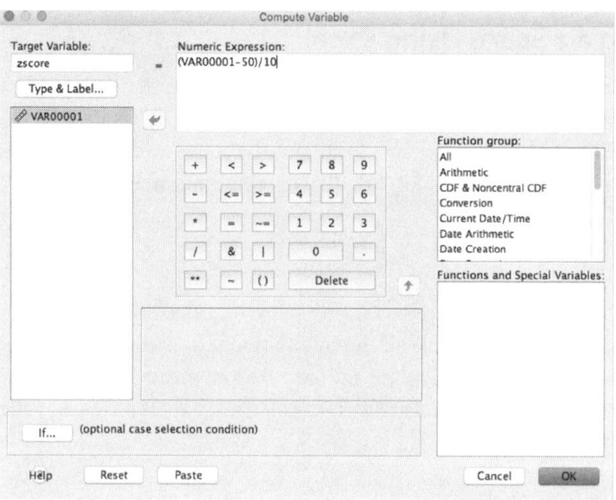

SUMMARY OF STEPS

- Type data into a column in the data window.
- Choose Compute Variable from the Transform menu at the top.
- In the Compute Variable window (see Figure 9.4), name your new *z* score variable in the Target Variable box.
- Type in the formula for the *z* score (see Figure 9.4). You can click your data variable into the Numeric Expression box by highlighting it and clicking on the arrow.
- When you click OK, the calculated *z* scores will appear in a new column in the data window.

THE NORMAL DISTRIBUTION

Now that you know how to calculate a *z* score and what it tells you about a score's location in a distribution, let's look at how this information can be useful in testing hypotheses. Knowing the location of a score in the population can help us do this. Let's go back to the example we started the chapter with: You want to determine if the online quizzes in your course help students prepare for the final exam. You know the score you want to compare with the distribution (the current class mean of 82) and the population mean for the distribution ($\mu = 75$) from your instructor. What else do you need in order to calculate the *z* score for the current class mean? (If you need a hint, look back at the formula for the *z* score to see what is missing.) What's missing is the population standard deviation (σ). Let's suppose your instructor gives you that—it's the standard deviation from the set of all past final exam mean scores for the course without online quizzes: $\sigma = 3$. Now you have all the information needed to find the location of the current class's mean score in the population distribution of all past mean exam scores without online quizzes. We can calculate the *z* score using the following formula:

$$z = \frac{(82-75)}{3} = \frac{7}{3} = +2.33$$

This *z* score tells us that the current class mean with online quizzes is 2.33 *SD*s above the population mean of exam scores without online quizzes. Does this tell us whether the online quizzes increased the score? It will help us with this, but we need more information before we know whether the quizzes increased the mean score or not.

What we need to know now is the shape of the population distribution of mean scores without online quizzes. Suppose that this distribution looks similar to the one shown in Figure 9.5. You can see from the graph that the distribution is symmetrical. But it is also a special type of symmetrical distribution known as the **normal distribution**. You've probably heard about normal distributions before, but you may not have known what makes them different from other distributions. Not only are normal distributions symmetrical, but the proportion of scores in each part of the distribution is already known. In other words, a specific portion of the scores in the distribution falls between the mean and one standard deviation in the distribution, both above and below the mean (i.e., 68%). You can see this portion in the normal distribution shown in Figure 9.6 (34% above the mean

normal distribution: A symmetrical distribution in which the percentage of scores in each portion of the distribution is known and 34% below the mean). In fact, the percentage of scores that falls in each part of the distribution for the segments marked by the standard deviation units is already known. Thus, we know how likely it is that a score will fall into different parts of the normal distribution. For example, we know that 68% of the scores fall within 1 *SD* of the mean and that 95% of the scores will fall within 2 *SD*s of the mean (you can verify this by adding up the percentages for the portions above and below the mean within 2 *SD*s in Figure 9.6).

FIGURE 9.5 ■ The Population Distribution of Exam Scores Without Online Quizzes—a Normal Distribution

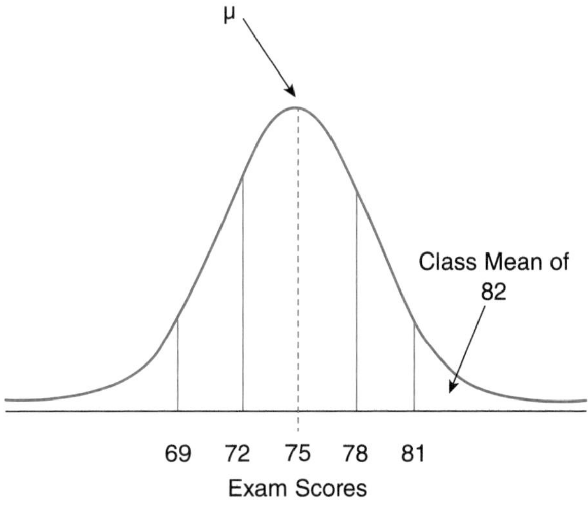

FIGURE 9.6 ■ The Normal Distribution

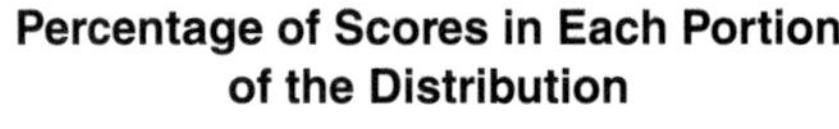

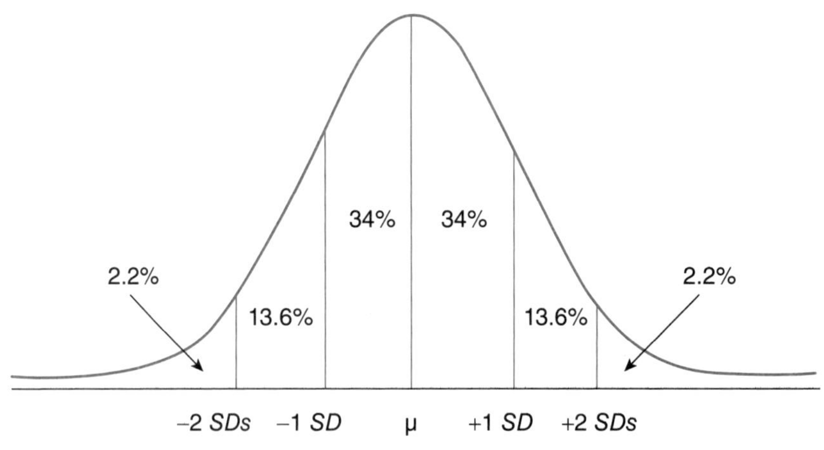

Locating a *z* Score in the Normal Distribution

Knowing the percentage of scores in different portions of the normal distribution is useful because it can help us determine the likelihood of getting a specific range of scores (e.g., the *z* score we calculated for Daphne's weight [+.3] or a score higher or lower than that score) in the distribution. In other words, it can tell us how common a score is for that distribution. The percentage values shown in Figure 9.6 are useful for determining the likelihood of obtaining a *z* score that falls within 1 or 2 *SD*s from the mean, but how do we determine the likelihood of obtaining a score that is in between these values, such as Daphne's weight *z* score of +.3? The answer is to use the **Unit Normal Table** that contains the proportion of scores for different sections of the normal distribution for many *z* score values. Appendix C of this text contains a Unit Normal Table that you can use to find the proportion value for the *z* score you are looking for. Let's look at the columns of this table: Column A contains the *z* scores, and Columns B and C contain the proportion in body and proportion in tail for the normal distribution. Columns B and C are related such that Column C contains the part of the distribution that is not in Column B (i.e., Column C = 1 − Column B). Table 9.1 shows a small part of the Unit Normal Table where the *z* score of .30 is located (one of the rows marked in color).

Unit Normal Table: A table of the proportion of scores in a normal distribution for many different *z* score values

If you read across the table to Columns B and C for a *z* score of .30, it shows a proportion of .6179 for the proportion in body and .3821 for the proportion in tail. This means that 61.79% of the scores in the normal distribution are at a *z* score of +.30 or lower and 38.21% of the scores in the distribution are at a *z* score of +.30 or higher. This also tells us that Daphne's weight score is a fairly common score in the dog weight distribution because, although it's not right at the 50/50 point in the middle where the mean is (and where the most common scores are), it's still pretty close to the mean with many scores both above and below this value. Thus, the Unit Normal Table can help us determine the likelihood of a range of scores in the normal distribution when we want to know how likely it is that we would obtain a *z* score at or above or below a specific value. We're not at the point where we can test a hypothesis yet, but as you'll see in the next section, knowing the likelihood of obtaining specific *z* score values is the first step.

But before we look further at how we can use the Unit Normal Table to test our hypothesis, let's practice using this table a bit more. Let's go back to my weight *z* score of +.40 and see if we can determine what the likelihood of getting this score or lower is using the table in Appendix C. Look again at Table 9.1. The row with the *z* score of .4 is marked in color as well. If you read across the table to Columns B and C, you will see that the chance of getting a *z* score of +.40 or lower is 65.54% (Column B) and +.40 or higher is 34.46%. If we compare these percentages with the ones given for a *z* score of +.30, we see that the score of +.40 is a little less common because there is a lower percentage of scores at that value or higher in the distribution.

Let's now consider how the table works for negative *z* scores: Suppose we want to know the likelihood of obtaining a *z* score of −.40 and lower. In this case, the percentages are the same, but now Column C contains the chance of getting this score or lower in the distribution. This is because Column C is the percentage of scores in the tail of the distribution, which is the portion that does not contain the mean of the distribution. Because negative *z* scores are below the mean, the tail part is now the part that is lower than that score. Column B, the body of the distribution, shows the percentage for the portion of the distribution that does contain the mean. For negative *z* scores, Column B will be the

TABLE 9.1 ■ A Section of the Unit Normal Table

Column A *z* score	Column B Proportion in body	Column C Proportion in tail
.25	.5987	.4013
.26	.6026	.3974
.27	.6064	.3936
.28	.6103	.3897
.29	.6141	.3859
.30	.6179	.3821
.31	.6217	.3783
.32	.6255	.3745
.33	.6293	.3707
.34	.6331	.3669
.35	.6368	.3632
.36	.6406	.3594
.37	.6443	.3557
.38	.6480	.3520
.39	.6517	.3483
.40	.6554	.3446

Note: The entire table is shown in Appendix C.

percentage of scores higher than that score. Thus, you will need to pay attention to the sign (+ or −) of the *z* score when you decide which column of the table to use in determining the correct percentage for scores you are looking for.

USING THE NORMAL DISTRIBUTION TO DETERMINE THE PROBABILITY OF A SAMPLE MEAN

Now we can use the Unit Normal Table to figure out the likelihood of a range of scores. Let's consider how this information is useful in determining whether online quizzes increased the final exam mean in your course compared with final exam means from past courses when the online quizzes were not available (the example we started the chapter with). To answer this question, we need to go back to a concept discussed in Chapter 4: the distribution of sample means. Remember from that chapter that the distribution of sample means is the distribution of means from all possible samples of a specific size from the population. In other words, if we are looking at a sample size of 30 students (the number who take your course each semester) and the entire population of students were to take that course (without online quizzes) at some point in their college career, the distribution of sample means would contain the final exam means for all of those classes. We can then use the mean from the distribution of sample means along with its standard deviation to determine the current class's mean exam score using the *z* score we calculated earlier. The mean and standard deviation from your instructor were $\sigma = 75$, $\sigma = 3$, and the *z* score we calculated for your class mean of 82 was +2.33 (see Figure 9.7).

If we also know that the population for the class final exam mean scores is a normal distribution, we can use the Unit Normal Table to determine how likely it is that we would get a mean score of 82 or higher in the population of means for courses without online quizzes. If you look at Appendix C at the end of the text using the method we followed in the previous section, you'll find that the percentage of scores in the distribution with *z* score +2.33 or higher is less than 1%. Figure 9.7 shows the location of the *z* score and the percentage of scores in the tail of the distribution of sample means. This value is listed in Column C of the Unit Normal Table (we are looking at a positive *z* score, so we need the value from the proportion in tail from the table). This is a pretty unlikely score from the set of all exam means for this course. This tells us there's a very low chance that our mean score of 82 came from this population because it is a very uncommon score for this distribution. However, in order to determine if the class mean of 82 is really higher than the overall mean of 75 (i.e., if the online quizzes really helped), we need to compare our class mean of 82 with scores in the distribution of sample means. We will consider how to do this in the next section, but our goal will be to determine the location of our

FIGURE 9.7 ■ Distribution of Sample Means for Course Final Exam Mean *z* Scores

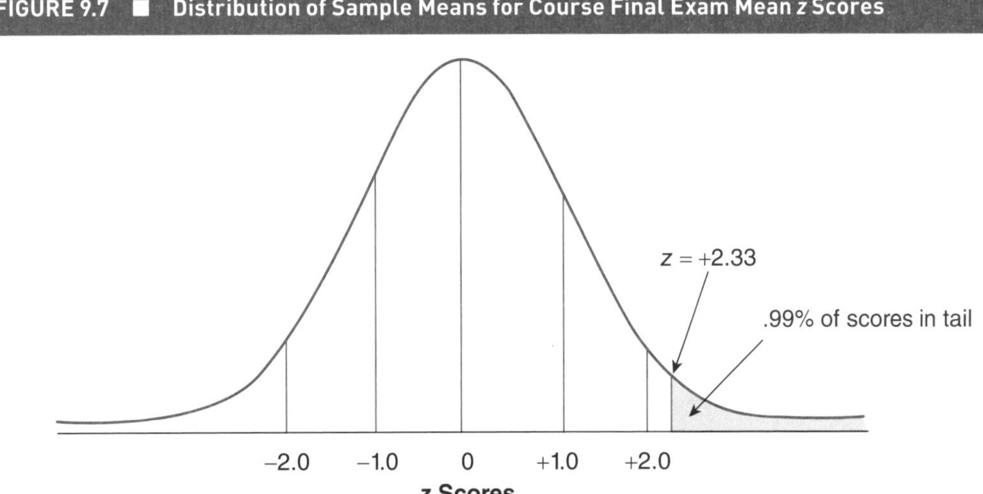

class mean in the distribution of sample means using a z score calculation. This is how z scores can help us test our hypotheses, but we would need to know the population mean and standard deviation to calculate the z score and that the population is a normal distribution to use this method. Otherwise, the proportion values in the Unit Normal Table are not accurate. In the next chapter, we will also consider how we decide if a mean score is unlikely enough to decide it probably does not come from the distribution of sample means.

Used in this way, the z score can be used in a one-sample z test as an inferential statistic that can help us test hypotheses. Figure 9.8 shows the full flowchart for choosing an inferential statistic for your study. In the next section, we will discuss the process of hypothesis testing in more detail.

FIGURE 9.8 ■ Statistical Test Decision Flowchart

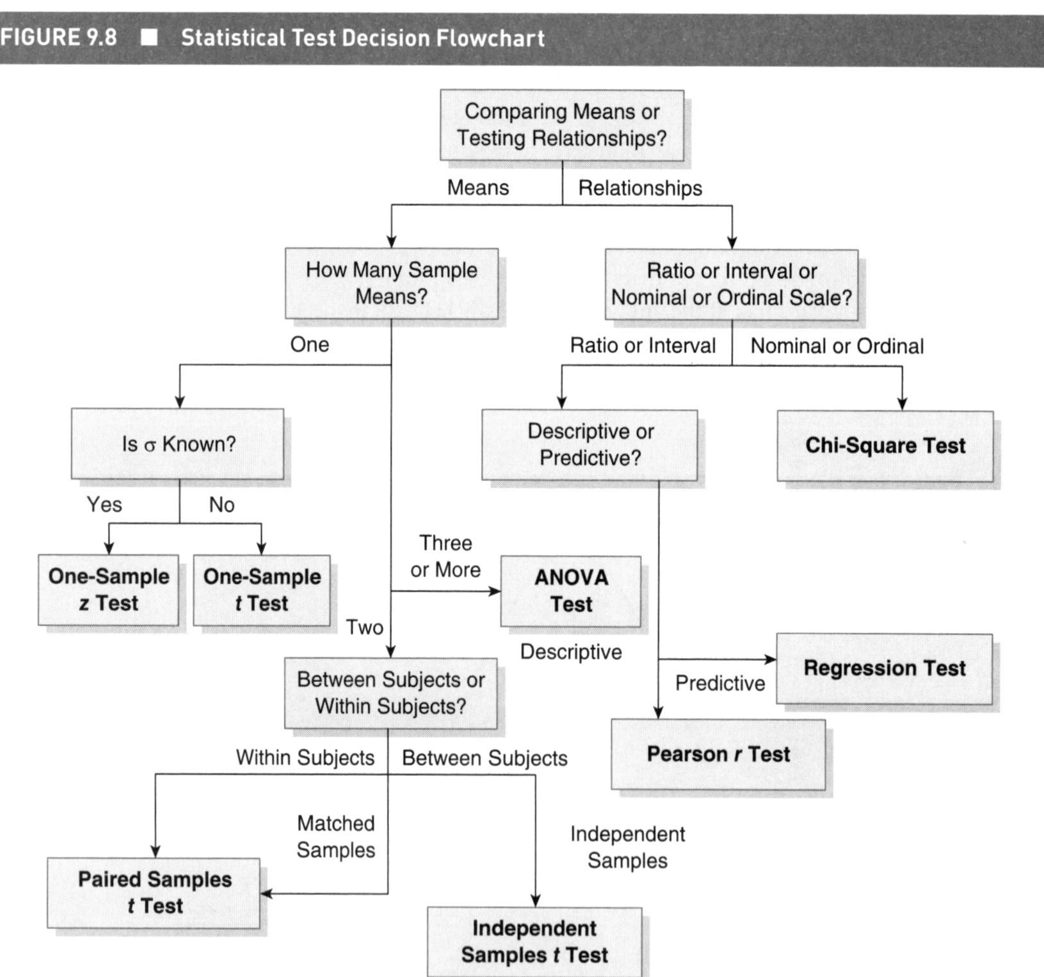

STOP AND THINK

9.4. Using the Unit Normal Table, find the percentage of scores in the normal distribution that are at the value or above in the distribution:

a. +1.25

b. −.08

c. −2.17

9.5. Explain what is meant by the column descriptions of proportion in body and proportion in tail from the Unit Normal Table.

9.6. Suppose you wanted to know whether caffeine reduces sleep. You conduct a simple study on yourself in which you record the number of hours you slept on nights when you've had caffeine after 7:00 p.m. and calculate a mean number of sleep hours of 7.25. Suppose that you also know that for all nights when you haven't had caffeine, you sleep an average of 8.5 hr with a standard deviation of .5 hr and that your number of hours slept distribution is a normal distribution. Use the *z* score transformation and Unit Normal Table procedures discussed in this chapter to determine how likely it is that your mean sleep time with caffeine is a score (based on the proportion in the tail) in your population distribution of mean sleep times without caffeine.

USING THE NORMAL DISTRIBUTION TO TEST HYPOTHESES

Recall the online quiz example from the last section—we are looking at a normal population of final exam scores to compare with your class mean of 82. Although we were able to find the location of this score in the population of final exam scores, this did not quite tell us what we want to know—whether this is a likely mean from the distribution of sample means for the class size of 30. This will tell us (with a certain probability) that the online quiz class mean is different from the mean scores without the online quizzes. Thus, we need to figure out how likely a mean this is in the distribution of sample means. In order to find out how likely this mean is in the distribution of sample means, we will need to look more closely at that distribution.

The Distribution of Sample Means Revisited

As I have discussed in this chapter, the distribution of sample means is a special distribution that contains all the sample means we would get if we were to draw all the possible samples of a specific size from the population and determine each sample's mean score. In other words, the distribution of sample means' scores are the sample means from all possible samples of a specific size drawn at random from the population. Recall that a *z* score is calculated based on the distance of the score from the mean divided by the standard deviation of the distribution (i.e., $z = \frac{(X - \mu)}{\sigma}$). Thus, if we want to calculate a *z* score for a sample mean to determine how likely it is that it came from the distribution of sample means for that population, we will need to know the mean and standard deviation for this distribution. If we were to calculate the mean of all the sample means from samples drawn from the population, we would end up with the population mean μ; thus, the mean of the distribution of samples is equal to the population mean μ. So, if we know the population mean, we will also know the mean of the distribution of sample means.

Things get a bit trickier in determining the standard deviation for the distribution of sample means. Recall from the discussion of sampling that the larger our sample is, the closer we will get to the actual population values in our sample. Thus, sample size will influence the spread of the scores in our distribution of sample means. The larger the sample size (n), the lower the variability in the distribution of sample means because we're getting a better estimate of the population mean with each sample. Thus, the standard deviation for the distribution of sample means is based on σ and n. If we know these values, we can calculate the standard deviation of the distribution of sample means, known as the **standard error**. The standard error represents the sampling error present in our samples (i.e., how much we expect the sample to differ from the population). We can calculate the standard error using the following formula:

standard error: The estimate of sampling error that is determined from the standard deviation of the distribution of sample means

$$\sigma_{\bar{X}} = \frac{\sigma}{\sqrt{n}}$$

where $\sigma_{\bar{X}}$ is the standard error, σ is the population standard deviation, and n is the sample size for the sample we are looking at. In other words, $\sigma_{\bar{X}}$ is the standard deviation of the distribution of sample means we want to locate our sample mean in.

central limit theorem: The mathematical description of the shape of the distribution of sample means that states that for a population with mean μ and standard deviation σ, the distribution of sample means for sample size *n* will have a mean equal to μ, a standard deviation equal to the standard error, and a shape approaching a normal distribution as *n* becomes very large

Finally, we need to consider the shape of the distribution of sample means. If the population is normal, then the distribution of sample means is also normal. This means we can use the Unit Normal Table to find the proportion of scores in different parts of the distribution of sample means, as we did in the previous section. However, even if the population distribution's shape is unknown (or known to be something other than normal), we can still determine the shape of the distribution of sample means using the **central limit theorem**. The central limit theorem is a mathematical description of the shape of the distribution of sample means that will allow us to determine if the distribution of sample means is normal in shape. This turns out to be very important in inferential statistics because, in many cases, we do not know the shape of the population. The central limit theorem states that for a population with mean μ and standard deviation σ, the distribution of sample means for sample size n will have a mean equal to μ, a standard deviation equal to the standard error, and a shape approaching a normal distribution as n becomes very large (i.e., approaches infinity). In practical terms, the shape of the distribution of sample means is almost exactly normal anytime n is greater than 30. Thus, we can use the Unit Normal Table to determine the proportion of scores in different sections of the distribution of sample means whenever our sample size is greater than 30.

Conducting a One-Sample *z* Test

Based on the description of the distribution of sample means in the previous section, you should be able to see how we can use a known population μ and σ to calculate a *z* score for a sample mean to determine its location in the distribution of sample means. We will need to adjust our *z* score formula a bit to fit the distribution of sample means:

$$z_{\bar{X}} = \frac{\left(\bar{X} - \mu\right)}{\frac{\sigma}{\sqrt{n}}}$$

The new *z* score ($z_{\bar{X}}$) for the distribution of sample means will tell us the location of our sample mean within this distribution. If our population is a normal distribution or our sample size is greater than 30, we can then use the Unit Normal Table to determine how extreme a score this is in the distribution of sample means. For our example with $\mu = 75$, $\sigma = 3$, and $\bar{X} = 82$, we can calculate $z_{\bar{X}}$:

$$z_{\bar{X}} = \frac{\left(82 - 75\right)}{\frac{3}{\sqrt{30}}} = \frac{7}{3/5.48} = \frac{7}{.55} = +12.73$$

This is a different value than the *z* score of +2.33 that we calculated earlier in this chapter for the location of the score in the population of final exam scores. That is because we have calculated the location of the sample mean in the distribution of sample means here that has a smaller standard deviation than the population of scores.

If you look in a Unit Normal Table, you will see that a *z* score of 12.73 is very large—in fact, the table given in Appendix C only goes up to a *z* score of +3.51, where only .02% of the scores in the distribution are at this *z* score or higher. Thus, there will be less than .02% of the scores in the distribution of sample means at +12.73 or higher. This tells us that our class mean of 82 is a very rare sample mean in the distribution of sample means for final exam means in classes without online quizzes. But how rare does it have to be before we can decide that it probably doesn't belong in this distribution of means? The standard we use in the behavioral sciences for determining this is 5% (i.e., a proportion of 0.05 in the distribution), meaning there's only a 5% chance (or less) that our sample mean came from this distribution. If the percentage of scores for a sample mean *z* score is at 5% or less for that score or higher (or lower for negative *z* scores), then we can conclude that it is rare enough for us to decide that it is different from the means in this distribution. In other words, our class mean of 82 is higher (with less than .02% probability) than what is expected for the final exam mean from a class that did not have online quizzes. Therefore, we can conclude that the online quizzes did help students score higher on the final exam. This is the general process we use in inferential statistics. In the next section, we will consider this process as a series of steps to follow to test our hypothesis.

STOP AND THINK

9.7. Using the standard cutoff probability of 0.05 or lower, find the *z* score in the Unit Normal Table that corresponds to this probability value (*Hint:* Look for the closest value to 0.05 without going over in the proportion in *Tail* column). Using the *z* score you found as a comparison, if your sample mean had a *z* score of +4.5u for the distribution of sample means, what would this tell you about your hypothesis?

9.8. The Graduate Record Exam (GRE) Verbal test is reported to have a mean score of about 150 and a standard deviation of about 8 (Educational Testing Service, 2016). The GRE prep course you are thinking of taking advertises that it can improve scores on this test. They report that the mean score for this year's class of 100 students scored a mean of 160 on the test. Based on these values, is it worth it to take the class?

LOGIC OF HYPOTHESIS TESTING

As you saw in the example in the previous section, the starting place for our hypothesis-testing procedure is a research question we want to answer. For the example I have been using in this chapter, the question was whether or not online quizzes helped students achieve a higher score on the course's final exam. The one-sample z test we conducted helped us determine an answer to this question. Now let's consider another research question: Does memory ability change as one ages? A reasonable hypothesis is that memory ability does change with age. How can we test this hypothesis? One way is to conduct a study (a quasi-experiment) comparing memory for older and younger adults and compare their memory scores. A hypothesis-testing procedure using inferential statistics can help us.

The hypothesis-testing procedure can be summarized in five steps:

Step 1: State your research question and make hypotheses about the answer.

Step 2: Set a decision criterion for making a decision about the hypotheses.

Step 3: Collect your sample data.

Step 4: Calculate statistics.

Step 5: Make a decision about the hypotheses.

Table 9.2 provides an overview of these steps that you can refer to as I discuss them further in this chapter. In the next few sections, we will go through each step for our memory and aging research question.

Step 1: State Hypotheses

For this example, we have already stated our research question: Does memory ability change with age? We have also stated our hypothesis about the answer to this question: Memory does change with age. Thus, part of this step is already complete. One thing to note is that the hypothesis we are making is about the population of people, not about our sample. It is the population we want to learn about when we conduct our study. We are only using the

TABLE 9.2 ■ Overview of the Hypothesis-Testing Steps

Step 1: State hypotheses.	State the research question, and develop the null and alternative hypotheses using literature in the research area.
Step 2: Set decision criterion.	Set the decision criterion alpha (α) as a probability that the sample mean is a score in the distribution of sample means; consider how your alpha level will influence the chance of Type I and Type II errors in your test.
Step 3: Collect sample data.	Design your study to test your hypotheses, recruit sample participants or subjects, and collect data on the dependent variables of interest.
Step 4: Calculate statistics.	Summarize data with descriptive statistics; choose an appropriate inferential statistics test and calculate the inferential statistic and corresponding probability (p) value for that statistic.
Step 5: Make a decision.	Compare the statistic p value with α; make a decision to either reject or retain the null hypothesis based on this comparison and then decide if you can accept the alternative hypothesis.

sample to represent this population because we cannot test the entire population. Thus, the hypotheses we make are always about a population we want to learn about. We could state our hypothesis as "In the population of people, memory changes with age."

In the hypothesis-testing procedure, the hypothesis made by the researcher is usually the **scientific or alternative hypothesis** (it is the alternative hypothesis to an important hypothesis that you will read about next). The scientific or alternative hypothesis is that an effect of the independent or subject variable exists (for an experiment or quasi-experiment) or a relationship between the variables exists (for a correlational study). For our example, the hypothesis that memory changes with age in the population of people is the scientific or alternative hypothesis that is consistent with predicting that aging causes a change in memory ability for individuals in the population. However, we also must consider a second hypothesis in our test: the **null hypothesis**. The null hypothesis is the opposite hypothesis to the scientific or alternative hypothesis: that an effect or relationship does not exist in the population. The null hypothesis is also important to state in Step 1 of our procedure because, as you will see later in this chapter, it is the null hypothesis we are directly learning about when we calculate our inferential statistics in Step 4 and make a decision about in Step 5.

scientific or alternative hypothesis: The hypothesis that an effect or relationship exists (or exists in a specific direction) in the population

null hypothesis: The hypothesis that an effect or relationship does not exist (or exists in the opposite direction of the alternative hypothesis) in the population

For our example, then, we will have two hypotheses to state to complete Step 1: the scientific or alternative hypothesis (denoted by H_1 or sometimes as H_a for *alternative*) and the null hypothesis (denoted by H_0). We can state these hypotheses as follows:

H_0: *In the general population, memory abilities do not change with age* or *In the general population, different age groups have the same mean memory scores.*

The null hypothesis makes the opposite prediction from the alternative hypothesis: *Memory abilities do not change with age.*

H_1: *In the general population, memory abilities change with age* or *In the general population, different age groups have different mean memory scores.*

two-tailed hypothesis: Both directions of an effect or relationship are considered in the alternative hypothesis of the test

one-tailed hypothesis: Only one direction of an effect or relationship is predicted in the alternative hypothesis of the test

What we have considered previously is called a **two-tailed hypothesis** because we are considering both possible directions of the difference between means in the hypothesis. In other words, our alternative hypothesis does not predict whether younger or older individuals will have higher memory scores; it simply states that the mean scores for younger and older individuals in the population will be *different.* It does not include a prediction about which population will have higher scores. However, for this study, you might find previous studies that indicate that as people age their memory abilities decline. Thus, you could make a directional or **one-tailed hypothesis**. As a one-tailed hypothesis, our alternative hypothesis could be stated as follows:

H_1: *In the general population, older individuals have lower memory scores than younger individuals.*

We could also make the opposite prediction (e.g., H_1: *In the general population, older individuals have higher memory scores than younger individuals*), but the first hypothesis stated previously is more likely to be consistent with the results of previous studies. For this alternative hypothesis, our null hypothesis must include any other possible outcomes, so our null hypothesis is as follows:

H_0: *In the general population, older individuals have higher memory scores than younger individuals or the memory scores of the two age groups are the same.*

For a one-tailed hypothesis, the null hypothesis contains the predictions of no effect or relationship *and* the effect or relationship in the direction opposite to that predicted in the alternative hypothesis. See the top portion of the flowchart in Figure 9.9 for a comparison of one-tailed and two-tailed hypotheses for this study.

One-tailed hypotheses are typically made only when a researcher has a logical reason to believe that one particular direction of the effect will occur. Thus, one-tailed hypotheses are often made when the other direction of the effect logically should not occur or does not answer the research question. They may also be made when the literature review of an area indicates that one direction of the effect has been shown consistently over a number of research studies.

STOP AND THINK

9.9. For each of the following statements, indicate if a one- or two-tailed test is most appropriate:

   a. Taking aspirin reduces the chance of a heart attack.

   b. Quizzing yourself before a test will increase your test score compared with simply rereading your notes.

   c. Completing a puzzle under a time constraint will affect your accuracy.

   d. Sleep affects depression.

9.10. For each of the previously given statements in 9.9, state the alternative and null hypotheses.

FIGURE 9.9 ■ Flowchart of the Steps in Hypothesis Testing for Memory and Aging Example

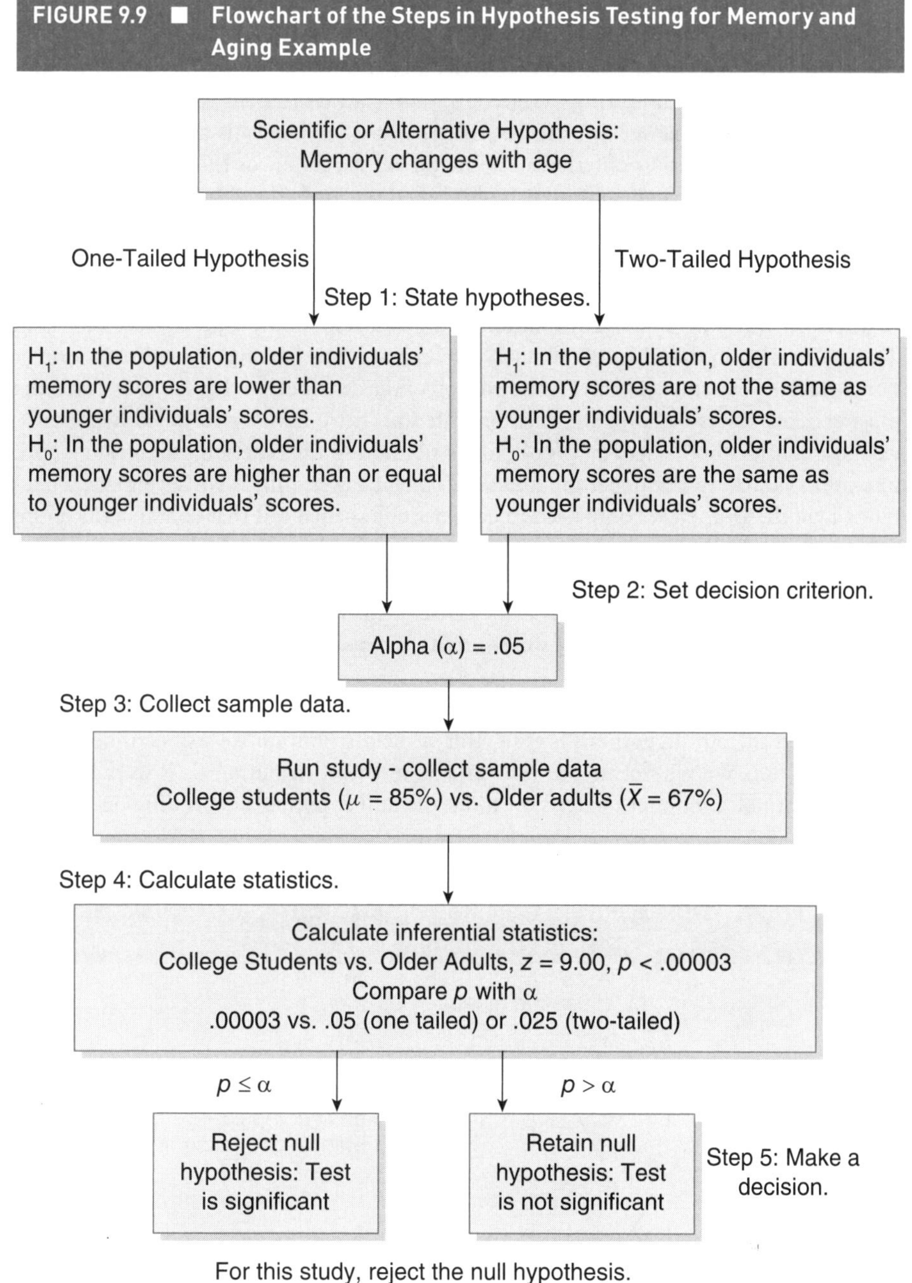
Scientific or Alternative Hypothesis:
Memory changes with age
One-Tailed Hypothesis
Two-Tailed Hypothesis
Step 1: State hypotheses.
H1: In the population, older individuals' memory scores are lower than younger individuals' scores.
H0: In the population, older individuals' memory scores are higher than or equal to younger individuals' scores.
H1: In the population, older individuals' memory scores are not the same as younger individuals' scores.
H0: In the population, older individuals' memory scores are the same as younger individuals' scores.
Step 2: Set decision criterion.
Alpha (α) = .05
Step 3: Collect sample data.
Run study - collect sample data
College students (μ = 85%) vs. Older adults (X̄ = 67%)
Step 4: Calculate statistics.
Calculate inferential statistics:
College Students vs. Older Adults, z = 9.00, p < .00003
Compare p with α
.00003 vs. .05 (one tailed) or .025 (two-tailed)
p ≤ α
p > α
Reject null hypothesis: Test is significant
Retain null hypothesis: Test is not significant
Step 5: Make a decision.
For this study, reject the null hypothesis.

Step 2: Set Decision Criterion

Now that we have completed Step 1 and have stated our alternative and null hypotheses, we can move on to Step 2 and set our decision criterion. Let's consider what we are doing when we set this value.

In inferential statistics tests, we are calculating a value that tells us the location of the sample mean in a distribution, just as we did with z scores in the last section. But the values we have from the sample are descriptive statistics in the form of a mean score (or, in some cases, a value indicating the strength of a relationship). Thus, we are looking at the location of a sample mean in the distribution of sample means as we did earlier in this chapter. The decision criterion value marks off a portion of this distribution that represents the most extreme scores. It is also called the **alpha level** because the criterion probability is denoted by the Greek letter α. As described earlier, the criterion is typically set at 0.05 (i.e., 5% of the most extreme scores) in research in the behavioral sciences. This means that we want to look at the proportion in tail from the Unit Normal Table that sets off this part of the distribution (and its corresponding z score—see Stop and Think 9.7 earlier in this chapter). Figure 9.10 illustrates this portion of the distribution of sample means. The shaded areas are the portion of the distribution that are considered the most extreme scores equal to the decision criterion. If we have a two-tailed hypothesis, we must consider both shaded tails of the distribution so the criterion proportion is split in two (i.e., 0.025 in the upper tail and 0.025 in the lower tail). If we have made a one-tailed hypothesis, then we only need to consider one shaded tail that contains the entire proportion—which tail depends on the direction we have predicted: the upper tail if we predict the mean will be higher and the lower tail if we predict that the mean will be lower. The shaded portion is known as the **critical region** of the distribution because it is the part we are looking at to see if we can reject the null hypothesis (one of our possible decisions in Step 5).

alpha level: The probability level used by researchers to indicate the cutoff probability level (highest value) that allows them to reject the null hypothesis

critical region: The most extreme portion of a distribution of statistical values for the null hypothesis determined by the decision criterion (i.e., alpha level—typically 5%)

Notice in Figure 9.10 that the distribution of sample means corresponds to the sample means when the null hypothesis is true. This is the distribution we will consider in our hypothesis test. We will locate our test statistic in this distribution (is it in the shaded portion(s) or not?) and make a decision about the null hypothesis depending on whether

FIGURE 9.10 ■ Distribution of Sample Means When the Null Hypothesis Is True

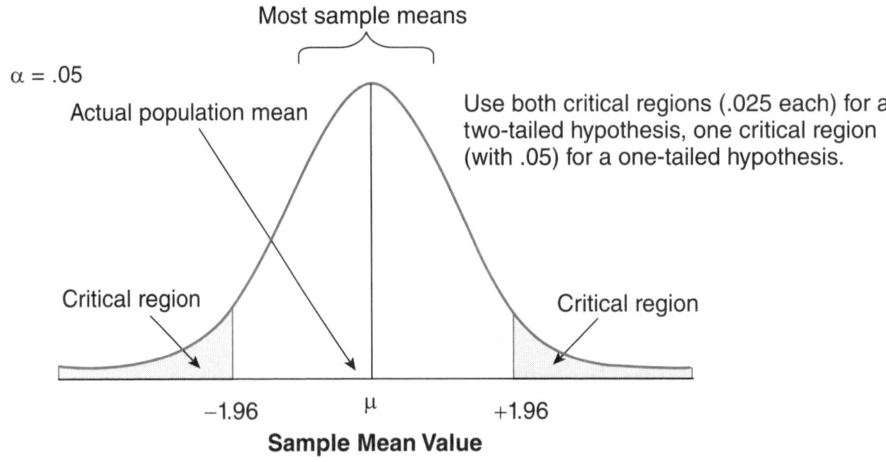

our sample mean is extreme for this distribution or not. This is because the evidence provided by the inferential test is the likelihood of obtaining the data in the study if we assume the null hypothesis is, in fact, true. That is what the inferential test focuses on: What is the chance of obtaining the data in this study when the null hypothesis is true? If the chance is fairly high, then there is no evidence to reject the null hypothesis. If the chance is very low, then the researcher takes that as evidence against the null hypothesis, rejects it, and supports the alternative hypothesis that there is an effect or relationship. It is important to set your decision criterion before you begin the study so that you have a clear basis for making a decision when you get to Step 5. If we wait to choose our alpha level, we might be tempted to make the wrong decision because our probability value seems low enough. This could result in an error in our hypothesis-testing procedure. I will discuss these errors and how we use our decision criterion to make a decision further as we consider Step 5: Make a decision.

Step 3: Collect Sample Data

In Step 3, we are ready to design our study to test our hypothesis, recruit a sample, and collect our data. For our example (looking at whether memory changes with age), we might design a study looking at memory abilities for college students and older adults. For example, suppose we know the population mean and standard deviation of a standardized memory test for college students because many of them have taken it as they participated in research studies. We might then design a study where we recruit a sample of 100 older adults to complete the memory test to see how their mean score on the test compares. Our sample of older adults represents the population of all older adults (e.g., over the age of 60). We can then consider where our sample mean falls in the distribution of sample means for college students to see if the older adults' mean score is an extreme score in this distribution based on our decision criterion. If it is, we can decide to reject the null hypothesis (H_0: memory does not change with age) and conclude that the older adults' memory scores appear to be part of a different distribution with a lower (or higher) mean. See Figure 9.9 for an overview of this study.

Step 4: Calculate Statistics

As Figure 9.9 shows, the known population mean μ for the standardized memory test in our study is 85% and our sample mean $\overline{X}$ is 67%. What we want to know from our hypothesis test is whether 67% is different enough from 85% to conclude that older adults show different memory abilities from the young adults. To determine this, we will need to calculate an inferential statistic. If we know the standard deviation for the memory test for the population of college students, we can use our one-sample z test. Figure 9.11 shows the relevant portion of the inferential statistics flowchart for a one-sample z test. Suppose we know that the standard deviation is $\sigma = 20$ and that the population of memory scores is a normal distribution. With this information, we're ready to calculate the $z_{\overline{X}}$. For this example, the calculation is as follows:

$$z_{\overline{X}} = \frac{(85-67)}{\frac{20}{\sqrt{100}}} = \frac{18}{20/10} = \frac{18}{2} = +9.00$$

***p* value:** Probability value associated with an inferential test that indicates the likelihood of obtaining the data in a study when the null hypothesis is true

We can use the Unit Normal Table in Appendix C to find the probability value (also known as a ***p* value**) associated with this *z* score. We have already seen earlier in this chapter that the highest value in the table is 3.51 with a *p* value of .0002. So, we know that the *p* value for 9.00 will be lower than .0002. This *p* value is what we need before we move on to Step 5 and make a decision.

However, before we move on to our last step, let's consider what would happen if we did not know the population standard deviation value, as is often the case in a research study. Without the σ value, we cannot calculate the standard error as we have done for our one-sample *z* test. Instead, our standard error will need to be calculated from an estimate of the population σ. The best guess we can make for this value is the standard deviation in our sample because the sample values are meant to represent the ones we would find in the population. Thus, our standard error formula would be as follows:

$$s_{\bar{X}} = \frac{s}{\sqrt{n}}$$

***t* test:** Significance test used to compare means

This calculation of the standard error changes the test statistic calculation and becomes a new statistic known as *t* (instead of *z*). We could then conduct a one-sample ***t* test** instead of a *z* test to test our hypothesis. We will discuss this test in the next chapter.

Things get even more complicated if we don't know the population μ either. In this case, we would have to represent both age groups' populations in our study with separate

FIGURE 9.11 ■ Portion of the Statistical Test Decision Flowchart for a One-Sample *z* Test

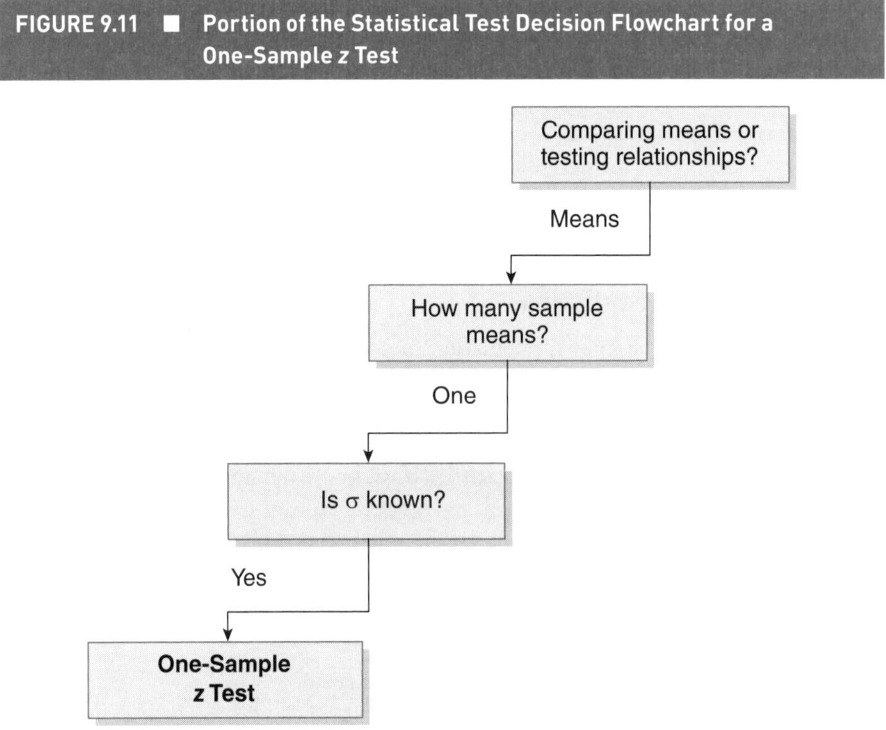

samples: a sample of college students and a sample of older adults. We can still calculate a t statistic, but it will be a new inferential test called an independent samples t test. This test is discussed in the next chapter. Later chapters in this text will also consider cases where there are more than two samples in a study with an inferential test known as analysis of variance (ANOVA). However, in each inferential test, we are using the same hypothesis-testing procedure with the five steps described in this chapter.

All the inferential statistics described in this text use a calculation that relies on differences or relationships seen in the data with an estimate of sampling error divided out of these differences or relationships. Thus, the test statistic is a value representing the differences or relationships seen in the sample data corrected for chance differences or relationships that could be seen due to relying on samples (instead of whole populations). If the test statistic is a low value, then the differences or relationships seen in the sample are likely due to chance sampling factors. If the test statistic is a high value, then the differences or relationships seen in the sample are likely due to actual differences or relationships that exist in the population. These outcomes correspond to the decisions we can make in the test.

Step 5: Make a Decision

In our last step, we need to make a decision about the null hypothesis based on how unlikely our sample mean is in the distribution of sample means that would exist when the null hypothesis is true. We will either find evidence against the null hypothesis and reject it or fail to find this evidence and retain it. How unlikely does a sample mean have to be before we decide it did not come from this distribution of sample means and reject the null hypothesis? This is where our alpha level comes into play. It is the proportion of our distribution of sample means that falls into the critical regions. Figure 9.10 shows these regions for $\alpha = 0.05$, our standard alpha level (bounded by the z scores of ± 1.96). It is the highest probability that a sample mean came from this distribution of sample means that we will accept as evidence against the null hypothesis. It is set by the researcher at a low value (such as 0.05) to allow rejection of the null hypothesis only when it is very unlikely that the sample mean came from the distribution of sample means for the null hypothesis. *In other words, the decision to reject or not reject the null hypothesis is based on the probability of obtaining the data in the sample when the null hypothesis is true.* A low alpha level helps us avoid an error in our hypothesis-testing procedure.

The probability of a sample mean appearing in the distribution of sample means is compared with the alpha level in an inferential test. Remember that most sample means occur near the actual population mean, so if the probability is high that the sample mean came from this distribution, then it is more likely that the null hypothesis is true, given the data we collected. If the p value is equal to or lower than the alpha level, then we can reject the null hypothesis as unlikely to be true. If the p value is higher than the alpha level, we cannot reject the null hypothesis, as it might be true (however, the test does *not* provide evidence *for* the null hypothesis, only against it).

Now, consider our example once again. Figure 9.9 shows the z and p values we determined in the previous section for our sample data. In Step 5, we compare the p value with our α level. For this example, we compare 0.0003 versus half of 0.05, which is 0.025 (we have two critical regions with a two-tailed test, so we divide α in half here). If our p value is lower than α, as it is here, we can reject the null hypothesis that memory does not change with age. If we reject this hypothesis, then we will have supported the alternative hypothesis that it does change with age. Looking back at the means, the older adults showed a lower mean score than the population of college students. Thus, we can conclude for this study that memory declines with age.

STOP AND THINK

9.11. Suppose the z score we had calculated for our example in this chapter was +2.30. In this case, what would our p value be? With an $\alpha = 0.05$, what decision would you make for this example?

9.12. Consider another example: An anxiety questionnaire is known to have $\mu = 50$ and $\sigma = 5$ in the general population. A sample of 50 college students is given the questionnaire after being asked to prepare a 5-min speech on a topic of their choosing to see if this task elevates their anxiety level from what is expected based on the population mean score on the questionnaire. The sample mean is $\bar{X} = 58$.

a. State the alternative and null hypotheses for this study. Is the alternative hypothesis a one-tailed hypothesis or two-tailed hypothesis?

b. Calculate the one-sample z score for this sample. What is the probability of obtaining this z score when the null hypothesis is true?

c. For an alpha level of 0.05, what decision would you make for this study? What can you conclude about the speech preparation task and its effect on anxiety level?

TYPES OF HYPOTHESIS-TESTING ERRORS

One thing that is important to keep in mind is that we are using probability to make our decision in the hypothesis-testing procedure. The test statistic's p value tells us the chance of obtaining that statistical value (using the sample data to calculate it) when the null hypothesis is true. Even if we reject the null hypothesis as our decision in the test, there is still a small chance that it is, in fact, true. Likewise, if we retain the null hypothesis as our decision, it is still possible that it is false. These are the kinds of errors that can be made in our hypothesis test, and they are always possible because we are relying on a probability (not a certainty) to make a decision.

Table 9.3 illustrates the different possible outcomes of a hypothesis test. The columns represent the reality for the population being studied: Either the null hypothesis is true and there is no effect or relationship (e.g., older adults do not have different memory scores and their mean memory score is the same as the population mean for the younger adults), or the null hypothesis is false and there is an effect or relationship (e.g., older adults do have different memory scores and their mean memory score is not the same as the population mean for the younger adults). When a hypothesis test is conducted, the researcher does not know whether the null hypothesis is true or false. However, as described in the previous section, the inferential test is conducted to look for evidence that the null hypothesis is not true. If that evidence is found, the researcher decides that the null hypothesis is false and rejects it. This is the outcome represented in the first row of Table 9.3. If, in fact, the null hypothesis is false, the researcher has made a correct decision in the test, because the decision matches the reality about the null hypothesis. However, it is possible to make the wrong decision. Thus, the outcome to reject the null hypothesis in the first row under the column where the null hypothesis is actually true is an error. The researcher's decision does not match the reality for the null hypothesis. This is called a **Type I error** and indicates that the researcher has rejected the null hypothesis when it is really true (e.g., we find in our study that older adults have a different memory score mean from the young adults, but in the population of older adults, they do not have a different mean score). The chance of making a Type I error is determined ahead of time by the researcher when an alpha level is chosen. Thus, in tests with $\alpha = 0.05$, there is a 5% chance of making a Type I error.

Type I error: An error made in a hypothesis test when the researcher rejects the null hypothesis when it is actually true

The second row in Table 9.3 illustrates test outcomes for the other decision that can be made in the significance test: retaining or failing to reject the null hypothesis, which occurs when evidence against it is not found in the test. A correct decision is made in the test when the decision is to fail to reject the null hypothesis and this hypothesis is really false (bottom right box). However, another type of error, called a **Type II error**, can be made when the null hypothesis is not rejected but is actually false (e.g., we find in our study that older adults do not have a different mean memory score than young adults, but in the population, older adults do have a different mean score from the younger adults). This means that an effect or relationship exists in the population but was not detected in the data for the sample. The chance of a Type II error is more difficult to determine. There are several factors that can influence the probability of a Type II error, including the alpha level chosen, the size of the effect or relationship, and the sample size in the study. The researcher can lower the chance of a Type II error by using an optimal sample size and making sure that the study is designed to maximize the effect or relationship being studied. By keeping the Type II error rate low, you are increasing the **power** of your hypothesis test to detect an effect or relationship that actually exists. Thus, it is important to keep Type II errors in mind as you design your study to conduct a powerful test of the hypothesis.

Type II error: An error made in a hypothesis test when the researcher fails to reject the null hypothesis when it is actually false

power: The ability of a hypothesis test to detect an effect or relationship when one exists (equal to 1 minus the probability of a Type II error)

TABLE 9.3 ■ Possible Outcomes of a Statistical Test

Decisions	Null hypothesis is actually false	Null hypothesis is actually true
Reject the null hypothesis	Correct decision!	Type I error
Fail to reject the null hypothesis	Type II error	Correct decision!

Predicting the Null Hypothesis

As mentioned previously, in many cases, the alternative hypothesis is also the researcher's hypothesis. The researcher predicts that an effect or relationship exists in the population. However, in some cases, the researcher may wish to predict that an effect or relationship does not exist in the population. Is this an appropriate thing for a researcher to do when using inferential statistics? Many would argue that it is not appropriate for a researcher to predict the null hypothesis because significance tests do not provide evidence for the null hypothesis. In fact, most papers that are published in psychological journals describe studies that showed significant results (Francis, 2013) because it can be difficult to draw strong conclusions from studies that do not show significant results. However, power analyses can be used to estimate the chance of a Type II error occurring and the null hypothesis being falsely retained. While any single study with nonsignificant results is not sufficient to provide support for the null hypothesis, a series of studies that have a reasonable level of power to detect effects (80% or higher is the generally accepted level; Cohen, 1988) that all show the same nonsignificant results may provide some support for the null hypothesis. Thus, if researchers want to predict the null hypothesis, they must be prepared to conduct several studies in order to obtain some support for their hypothesis. Many researchers (e.g., Francis, 2013; Greenwald, 1975) also argued that a bias against the null hypothesis can result in researchers ignoring studies that do not find significant effects (which can be caused by the bias against publishing them). In addition, because it is important that theories of behavior can be falsified, it is sometimes necessary to predict the null hypothesis in order to truly test a theory. Finally, in order to get around this issue, several researchers (e.g., Cohen, 1990; Loftus, 1993) have suggested alternatives to the hypothesis-testing procedure described in this chapter as a means of interpreting data.

STATISTICAL SIGNIFICANCE

significant test: *p* value is less than or equal to the alpha level in an inferential test and the null hypothesis can be rejected

One concept not yet discussed in this chapter is what it means for a hypothesis test to be a **significant test**. If the p value for the test statistic is less than or equal to the alpha level, the test is said to be significant. In other words, a significant inferential test means that the null hypothesis can be rejected, the alternative hypothesis has been supported, and the researcher can conclude that there is an effect or relationship for the data in the current study. This means that hypothesis tests where the decision is to reject the null hypothesis are reported as *significant* tests.

Note that this term does not mean *important* in the way this term is typically used outside of statistics. A hypothesis test can be significant in the statistical sense without being very important at all. In fact, with a large enough sample size, it is often easy to obtain a significant difference between groups that is based on subject differences unrelated to the study or a significant statistical relationship between factors that are not related in any meaningful or causal way (e.g., amount of rainfall in a month and number of people buying soda in that month). So be aware that statistical significance may not mean that a result tells us something important about behavior.

Calculation Summary

standard error: Population standard deviation divided by the square root of the sample size

one-sample z test: Sample mean minus the population mean, divided by the standard error

STOP AND THINK

9.13. For each description that follows, indicate the situation: correct decision, Type I error, or Type II error.

a. An effect of amount of sleep on mood exists, but the results of the study were not significant.

b. A relationship between early reading and later academic achievement exists, and the results of the study were significant.

c. An effect of caffeine on work productivity does not exist, but the results of the study were significant.

THINKING ABOUT RESEARCH

A summary of a research study in psychology is given here. As you read the summary, think about the following questions:

1. Identify the five steps of hypothesis testing in this article description. Indicate what was determined at each step. State what you think are the null and alternative hypotheses for this study.
2. Why do you think the participants were blindfolded in this this study? What source of possible bias does this control for?
3. What is the likely reason the authors used a one-sample *t* test instead of a *z* test to analyze their results?
4. Based on the description of this study, what population mean μ do you think the authors compared their sample mean with?
5. Based on the information in this chapter, what formula do you think they used to calculate standard error in their inferential test?

Research Study. Wagman, J. B., Zimmerman, C., & Sorric, C. (2007). "Which feels heavier—a pound of lead or a pound of feathers?" A potential perceptual basis of a cognitive riddle. *Perception, 36,* 1709–1711.

Purpose of the Study. Wagman et al. investigated the perceptual causes of why people answer the riddle about the respective heaviness of equal masses of lead and feathers as if one feels heavier. In their study, participants were asked to hold a box of lead bearings and a box of feathers of equal

(Continued)

(Continued)

weight and indicate which box felt heavier. Based on the size and weight illusion (where larger objects are expected to be heavier regardless of actual mass) as applied to mass distribution of objects, the researchers predicted that participants would select the box of lead at a different rate than chance due to the different mass distributions of lead and feathers within the boxes.

Method of the Study. Participants included 23 blindfolded students. Each participant completed 20 trials in which they held one box in their palm and then a second box in the same palm. One box held lead pellets, and one box held feathers. The objects were secured within the box to keep them from creating any sound stimuli that could be used to make judgments. Participants were then asked to indicate which box felt heavier, the first box or the second box. Lead and feather boxes were presented in a random order on each trial. If participants could not determine a difference in heaviness between the boxes, chance performance (10 responses for the first box and 10 responses for the second box) was expected.

Results of the Study. To test their hypothesis that the boxes did not feel equally heavy to the participants, the researchers conducted a one-sample *t* test on the number of trials (out of 20) that each participant reported the box of lead felt heavier. The mean number of times participants reported the box of lead felt heavier was 11.12 times out of the 20 trials. They found that this sample differed significantly from chance with a calculated *t* value of 2.64 with a *p* value of 0.015. APA style for reporting the statistic is $t(22) = 2.64$, $p = 0.015$.

Conclusions of the Study. The results of the study suggest that objects with equal mass can be perceived at different heaviness due to the difference in mass distribution within a held box of lead and feathers.

Chapter Summary

- **What is a standardized score?**
  A standardized score is a score that has been transformed based on its location from the population mean and put in standard deviation units. It is also called a *z* score and can be used to compare the location of scores in their different distributions.

- **What is the standard error?**
  Standard error is a measure of variability in the distribution of sample means that takes sample size into account. It provides an estimate of sampling error for our hypothesis test.

- **How can we use a population mean and the standard error to test a hypothesis?**
  The one-sample *z* test and *t* test both consider the difference between a measured sample mean and a known population mean with our estimate of sampling error in the form of the standard error removed in the calculation of the test statistic. This statistical value is then used to determine the probability (*p*) value of getting our sample mean in the distribution of sample means for the population. A low *p* value indicates an extreme score for the distribution, making it possible to reject the

null hypothesis that the sample mean is from this distribution.

- **What are the steps in hypothesis testing?**
  The five steps of hypothesis testing take us through the procedure described (see Table 9.2 for an overview of the procedures by step):
  Step 1: State hypotheses.
  Step 2: Set decision criterion.
  Step 3: Collect sample data.
  Step 4: Calculate statistics.
  Step 5: Make a decision.
- **What is statistical significance, and what does it tell us about our hypothesis?**
  A statistically significant hypothesis test is one where we have decided to reject the null hypothesis based on the evidence found in the sample data against it. If we reject the null hypothesis, we can accept the alternative hypothesis, which is typically the hypothesis we have made as researchers.
- **What types of errors exist in our hypothesis-testing procedure?**
  Hypothesis-testing procedures can result in either Type I or Type II errors, depending on the decision we make in Step 5. If we reject the null hypothesis in error (i.e., the null hypothesis is actually true), then we are making a Type I error. If we retain the null hypothesis in error (i.e., the null hypothesis is actually false), then we are making a Type II error.
- **How can I reduce the chance of an error in testing hypotheses?**
  Setting our decision criterion alpha to a low value will reduce the chance of a Type I error. Increasing our sample size and/or effect size will increase power, which is the same as reducing the chance of a Type II error.

Test Yourself

1. A standardized score is __________.
   a. a *z* score
   b. a score that has been transformed to allow comparisons across distributions
   c. a new score that represents the original score's distance from the distribution mean in standard deviation units
   d. all of the above
2. A *z* score of −1.45 indicates that __________.
   a. the original score is between 1 and 2 *SDs* above the mean
   b. the original score is between 1 and 2 *SDs* below the mean
   c. the original score is not in the population distribution because it is negative
   d. the original score cannot be transformed into a standardized score
3. The Unit Normal Table can tell us __________.
   a. the *z* score for a score in a distribution
   b. the *z* scores for all the scores in a distribution
   c. the percentage of scores at a specific *z* score or higher in the normal distribution
   d. the percentage of scores at a specific *z* score or higher in a skewed distribution

(Continued)

(Continued)

4. For a population with $\mu = 100$ and $\sigma = 10$, what is the *z* score for a score of 90?
   a. +10
   b. −10
   c. +1.0
   d. −1.0
5. For the population described in Question 4, what is the *z* score for a score of 120?
   a. +20
   b. −20
   c. +2.0
   d. −2.0
6. Calculating a *z* score can help us test a hypothesis about a population.
   a. True
   b. False
7. A *z* score will tell us the distance from the mean of a score in a distribution but not the direction of that location from the mean.
   a. True
   b. False
8. The Unit Normal Table will tell us the exact probability of a *z* score in any distribution.
   a. True
   b. False
9. You are taking two psychology courses: Cognition and Research Methods. On the same day, you take an exam in both courses. In Cognition, you score a 78 on the exam ($\mu = 75$ and $\sigma = 3$). In Research Methods, you score an 82 ($\mu = 78$ and $\sigma = 5$). In which class did you actually do better on the exam (relative to the population)?
10. Some intelligence tests have a $\mu = 100$ and $\sigma = 10$. If you score a 110 on an intelligence test with this distribution, what is the *z* score for your score?
11. Explain why a *z* score is called a standardized score.
12. For each *z* score that follows, find the percentage of scores at that value or higher in the normal distribution:
    a. +1.67
    b. −2.02
    c. −.80
    d. +.08
13. Your score on a course exam was 95, and your *z* score on this exam was +2.0. The distribution of exam scores had a $\sigma = 5$. What was the mean on the exam?
14. A standardized math test for 5th graders has a $\mu = 50$. A student scores 60 on this exam, and their z score is +1.50. What is the σ for the standardized test?
15. The standard error is __________.
    a. determined from the population standard deviation and the sample size
    b. an estimate of the sampling error
    c. the variability of the distribution of sample means
    d. all of the above
16. The alpha level is the __________.
    a. chance that the null hypothesis is true
    b. chance that the null hypothesis is false
    c. decision criterion for rejecting the null hypothesis set by the researcher
17. The researcher's hypothesis is typically the opposite of the _________ hypothesis.
    a. alternative
    b. null
    c. population

18. The hypothesis-testing procedure can provide evidence against the __________.
    a. null hypothesis
    b. alternative hypothesis
    c. distribution of sample means standard error

19. The possible decision(s) in Step 5 of the hypothesis-testing procedure are to __________.
    a. reject the null hypothesis
    b. accept the null hypothesis
    c. retain the null hypothesis
    d. only a and b
    e. only a and c

20. The hypothesis-testing procedure will tell us the probability that the null hypothesis is true.
    a. True
    b. False

21. The best estimates of the population mean and standard deviation when these values are not known are the mean and standard deviation values in the sample.
    a. True
    b. False

22. The inferential test statistic represents the difference between means with sampling error removed.
    a. True
    b. False

23. Explain why errors are always possible during hypothesis testing.

You pulled several all-nighters last semester to study for your final exams. You want to know if staying up all night hurt your exam performance so you will know if it is worth it to stay up all night to study. You calculate the mean score for all of the finals you have ever taken in college (your exam population μ) and find that $\mu = 87\%$ with $\sigma = 5\%$. Assume you know that this population of scores has a normal distribution. You use as your sample the mean score on all five of the final exams you took last semester, $X = 83\%$.

24. What are the null and alternative hypotheses for this example? Is this a one- or two-tailed test?

25. Use a one-sample *z* test to determine if your all-nighters hurt your performance.

26. Suppose that in reality, all-nighters do hurt your performance on exams. In this case, what type of decision has occurred in your test: correct decision, Type I error, or Type II error?

27. What is the easiest way to reduce Type II errors? What problem does this method of reducing Type II errors create? (*Hint:* Consider statistical significance vs. practical significance.)

SAGE edge™

Visit **edge.sagepub.com/mcbridermstats** to find the answers to the Test Yourself questions above, as well as quizzes, flashcards, and other resources to help you accomplish your coursework goals.

10

t TESTS

CONSIDER THE FOLLOWING QUESTIONS AS YOU READ CHAPTER 10

- How does the distribution of *t* scores differ from the distribution of *z* scores?
- How can we use the *t* Table to make a hypothesis-testing decision?
- How do standard error and estimated standard error differ?
- How can we conduct *t* tests using statistical software?
- How does our hypothesis-testing procedure differ across *t* tests?

LEARNING OBJECTIVES FOR CHAPTER 10

- Correctly calculate estimated standard error for the three different *t* tests.
- Conduct a hypothesis test using each of the three different *t* tests.
- Identify the correct *t* test for different study designs.

Imagine this scenario: You do not believe in extrasensory perception (ESP), but you have a friend who is a fervent believer and is spending large amounts of money going to psychics (see Photo 10.1). You and your friend decide to design a study to test if individuals who advertise as psychics can, in fact, predict the future to determine if data can be found to support your friend's argument. (Remember that supporting your argument would be more difficult and require multiple studies because you can only provide evidence against the null hypothesis of no ability in a single research study. You cannot provide evidence in a study for the null hypothesis using the hypothesis-testing procedure.) There are many ways you could design such a study, but in this chapter, let's consider a design where you use a simple card prediction task with a sample of psychics. In your study, you recruit a sample of 50 psychics to perform this task. Each psychic participant is asked to perform 100 trials in which a researcher selects a card at random from a deck of 52 playing cards; the psychic's task is to predict the suit (i.e., hearts, clubs, spades, or diamonds; see Photo 10.2) of the card selected. Thus, if the participants are guessing, their average accuracy rate should be about 25 correct trials out of the 100 total trials (or 25%). The guess rate tells us the population mean μ (i.e., $\mu = 25\%$) for people with no ESP, but it does not tell us the population σ, so we cannot use the one-sample z test we discussed in the last chapter because we cannot calculate the standard error ($\sigma_{\bar{X}}$) needed for the denominator of the z score calculation. However, we can estimate it using the sample standard deviation to calculate an **estimated standard error** and then use a one-sample t test instead to look for evidence against the null hypothesis.

estimated standard error: An estimate of sampling error that is determined from the standard deviation of the distribution of sample means using the sample standard deviation to represent the population standard deviation

©iStock/logoff

Photo 10.1
Research question: Can psychics really predict the future?

Before we consider the t test, let's briefly review the process of hypothesis testing with this example. Using hypothesis testing, we can look for evidence in our sample data that counters the null hypothesis that the population of psychics has no ESP (i.e., this population has an accuracy rate in the card prediction task equal to or lower than 25%). We will do this, as we did with the z test, by comparing our sample mean with the distribution of sample means for the general population of nonpsychics, which has a mean equal to the population μ of 25%. If we find that our sample mean is an extreme score in this distribution, there is a good chance that a distribution of sample means exists for psychics with a different population μ (e.g., a μ that is higher than our guessing rate of 25%). Figure 10.1 illustrates this comparison for these distributions. Calculating an inferential statistic (for our example, a t score) will provide the location of our sample mean in the population distribution of sample means for the null hypothesis (i.e., the general population of nonpsychics). This is shown in the distribution on the left in Figure 10.1. However, if the statistical value is an extreme score in this distribution, there is a good chance that it comes from a different distribution—one for a population of psychics, shown on the right in Figure 10.1. Remember that these are hypothetical distributions

©iStock/Rob_Heber

Photo 10.2
Your study includes a card prediction task in which psychics are asked to predict the suit of a card chosen at random from a deck of cards.

because we cannot test the entire population of individuals, psychics or nonpsychics. Thus, we are proposing that the distribution on the right exists only if we find an extreme enough score in our test to suggest it does not belong in the distribution on the left (the population of people with no ESP). The *p* value for our inferential statistic indicates the probability of getting our *t* score in the distribution of sample means shown on the left for the null hypothesis. We did this in the last chapter with *z* scores by looking at the distribution of sample means after a *z* score transformation and then finding the *p* value for our *z* score in the new distribution. A comparison of the *p* value to our alpha level helps us make the decision to reject the null hypothesis (i.e., our sample mean likely belongs to the distribution on the right in Figure 10.1) or to retain the null hypothesis (i.e., our sample mean could belong to the distribution on the left; we do not have evidence supporting the existence of the distribution on the right). This comparison will tell us whether our sample mean is in the critical region(s) or not for null hypothesis distribution (the shaded potion of the distribution on the left labeled *extreme scores*). In the next section, we will look at the *t* score distribution a bit more to better understand why a one-sample *t* test is the appropriate test for our study before we work through the hypothesis-testing steps to make a decision for our psychic study.

FIGURE 10.1 ■ Hypothetical Distributions for the Null and Alternative Hypotheses

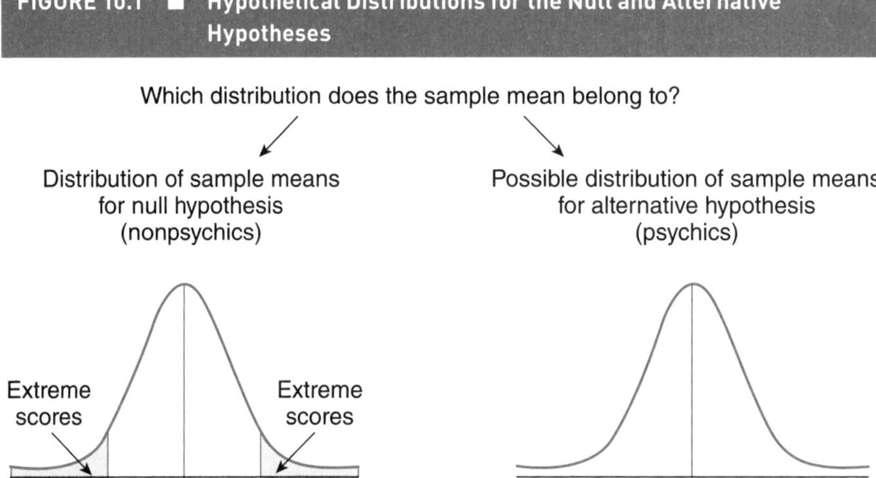

STOP AND THINK

10.1. For our psychic study, write out the alternative and null hypotheses. Is this a one-tailed or two-tailed test?

10.2. In order to use a one-sample *z* test in our psychic study, what else would we need to know?

10.3. Can you identify any sources of bias in the psychic study that might influence the results? How could we control for these biases in the study?

THE *t* DISTRIBUTION

As you read in Chapter 9, when we do not know the population σ, we cannot use the z test because the standard error cannot be calculated exactly. Instead, we must estimate the population σ from the sample standard deviation. The chart in Figure 10.2 shows the portion of the inferential statistics flowchart for the one-sample t test when the σ is not known (look back at Figure 9.8 for the complete flowchart). What we will use instead is the estimated standard error with the following formula:

$$s_{\bar{X}} = \frac{s}{\sqrt{n}}$$

The estimated standard error is then substituted into the original z test formula to calculate the statistic t:

$$t = \frac{\left(\bar{X} - \mu\right)}{\frac{s}{\sqrt{n}}}$$

The statistic t distribution differs slightly from the statistic z distribution. As also described in Chapter 9, the central limit theorem states that the distribution of sample means will approach a normal distribution with a very large sample size. Thus, the larger the sample size, the closer t is to the value of z. Figure 10.3 illustrates this using degrees of freedom ($df = n - 1$) as the indication of sample size. The larger the df, the closer the distribution of t scores is to a normal distribution. For very large df, the t distribution will be the same as the z distribution. However, it will be slightly different from normal anytime the df are less than infinity, so it's best to use the t test when we must estimate the population σ with the sample s. As you can see in Figure 10.3, the variability of the distribution increases with a smaller sample size. As I have discussed previously, this is what we expect because a smaller sample size makes it less likely that we are close to the population σ. Thus, the critical region(s) associated with our alpha level will change with the degrees of freedom. The t score that is the boundary of the critical region(s) will be higher as the sample size decreases. In other words, as the sample size increases, we will find that a smaller difference between the sample and population means results in a t score that falls in the critical region(s) for our sample.

In using t as an inferential statistic, we follow the same procedure covered in Chapter 9 for the z test: We will calculate the t score for our sample and then consider where that t score falls in the distribution of t scores for the distribution of sample means when the null hypothesis is true. We will find the critical region(s) that denote the most extreme scores in the distribution. However, because the t distribution is a slightly different shape from the normal distribution, the p values will be different, and we must now use the t Table instead of the Unit Normal Table. You will find a t Distribution Table in Appendix D of this text. As we begin to use the t Table in the next section to conduct a one-sample t test, you will see that the table has a different structure from the Unit Normal Table. Instead of looking up a p value in the table, we will be looking up the t score(s) that borders the critical region(s) and comparing it to our calculated t score for our sample.

FIGURE 10.2 ■ Portion of the Statistical Test Decision Flowchart for a One-Sample *t* Test

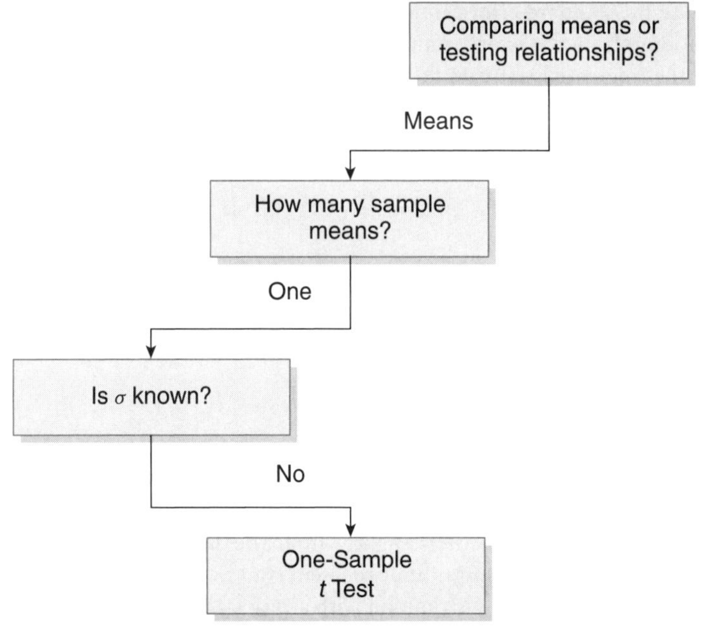

FIGURE 10.3 ■ The Shape of the *t* Score Distribution Will Change as the Sample Size (Measured in Degrees of Freedom) Changes—It Becomes More Normal With Large *df*

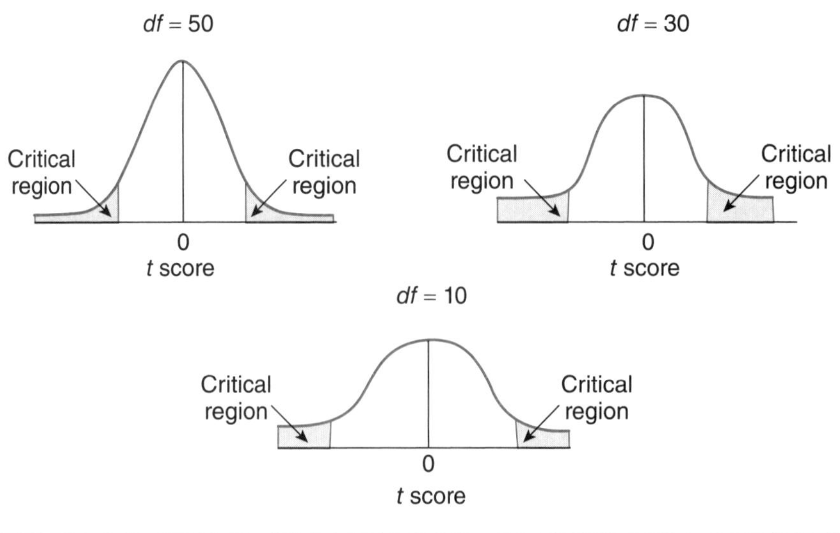

ONE-SAMPLE *t* TEST

Now that we understand the *t* distribution a bit more and how it differs from the normal distribution of *z* scores, let's use the one-sample *t* test to conduct a hypothesis test for our psychic study. We will go through each of the steps of hypothesis testing to review the steps and see how they differ for the one-sample *t* test as compared with the *z* test we conducted in Chapter 9. You can follow the chart in Figure 10.4 as we go through the steps.

Step 1: State Hypotheses

In the Stop and Think section, 10.1 asks you to state the null and alternative hypotheses. Are you able to do this using the process covered in Chapter 9? Try it now; you can check your answers in the next paragraph.

For the alternative hypothesis for our psychic study, we will predict that the population of psychics has a mean score on the card prediction task higher than 25%. Including scores lower than 25% in this hypothesis does not make sense because a lower-than-chance accuracy rate would not indicate predictive ability and that is what we are testing here. Thus, we are conducting a one-tailed test with a specific direction of the effect of psychic ability on task performance. This means our null hypothesis will include the prediction that the population of psychics has an accuracy equal to *or* lower than 25%. Both of these results would indicate no ESP in our population.

Step 2: Set Decision Criterion

As is typical for behavioral research, we will set our alpha level at 0.05 (remember that this sets our chance of making a Type I error at 5% or less). Thus, our one critical region will be above the mean and contain 5% of the scores in the distribution.

Step 3: Collect Sample Data

In Step 3, we collect our sample data. Remember that for this example, our sample contains 50 psychics to represent the population of all psychics. See Figure 10.4, Step 3, for sample mean and standard deviation.

Step 4: Calculate Statistics

Let's now consider the hypothetical data that we might have collected in our psychic study. Figure 10.4 shows the sample mean we obtained of 27% accuracy on the card prediction task. The standard deviation in the sample was 10%. Now we can calculate our estimated standard error and sample *t*. Our estimated standard error will be this:

$$s_{\bar{X}} = \frac{10}{\sqrt{50}} = \frac{10}{7.07} = 1.41$$

We can include this value as the denominator of our *t* calculation:

$$t = \frac{(27 - 25)}{1.41} = 1.42$$

FIGURE 10.4 ■ Flowchart of the Steps of Hypothesis Testing for the Psychic Study Example

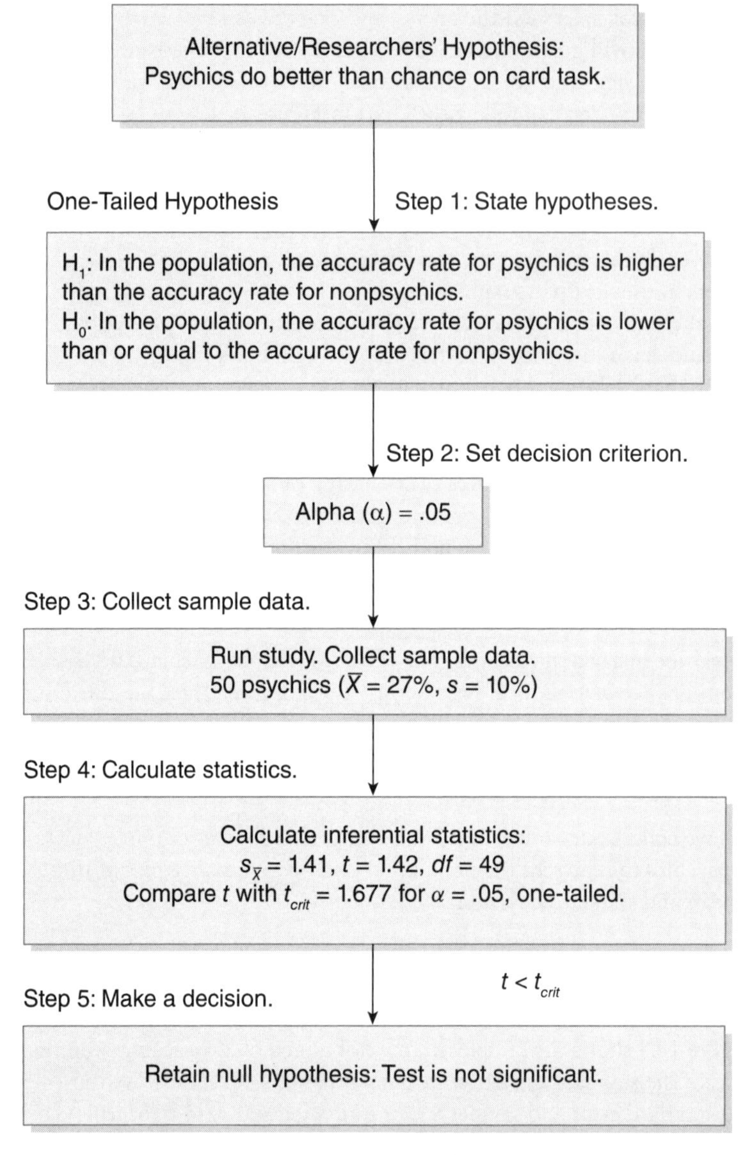
Alternative/Researchers' Hypothesis:
Psychics do better than chance on card task.
One-Tailed Hypothesis
Step 1: State hypotheses.
H_1: In the population, the accuracy rate for psychics is higher than the accuracy rate for nonpsychics.
H_0: In the population, the accuracy rate for psychics is lower than or equal to the accuracy rate for nonpsychics.
Step 2: Set decision criterion.
Alpha (α) = .05
Step 3: Collect sample data.
Run study. Collect sample data.
50 psychics ($\overline{X}$ = 27%, s = 10%)
Step 4: Calculate statistics.
Calculate inferential statistics:
$s_{\overline{X}} = 1.41$, $t = 1.42$, $df = 49$
Compare t with $t_{crit} = 1.677$ for $\alpha = .05$, one-tailed.
Step 5: Make a decision.
$t < t_{crit}$
Retain null hypothesis: Test is not significant.
For this study, retain the null hypothesis.

We now just need the degrees of freedom term:

$$df = n - 1 = 50 - 1 = 49$$

With these values, we can use the *t* Table in Appendix D to look up the critical *t* value (t_{crit}) for a one-tailed test: $df = 49$, and $\alpha = 0.05$. A portion of the table appears in Table 10.1. You must first choose the correct column based on your alpha level and whether you are conducting a one- or two-tailed test. Then you can find the correct row for your degrees of freedom. Looking at Table 10.1, you can see in the highlighted portion that our t_{crit} is 1.677 for our one-tailed test. Figure 10.5 shows where this t_{crit} value falls relative to our sample *t* score. Notice that it does not fall in the critical region.

TABLE 10.1 ■ A Section of the *t* Distribution Table

One-tailed	.05	.025	.01
Two-tailed	.10	.05	.02
df			
35	1.690	2.030	2.438
36	1.688	2.028	2.435
37	1.687	2.026	2.431
38	1.686	2.024	2.429
39	1.685	2.023	2.426
40	1.684	2.021	2.423
41	1.683	2.020	2.421
42	1.682	2.018	2.419
43	1.681	2.017	2.416
44	1.680	2.015	2.414
45	1.679	2.014	2.412
46	1.679	2.013	2.410
47	1.678	2.012	2.408
48	1.678	2.011	2.407
49	1.677	2.010	2.405
50	1.677	2.009	2.404

Note: The entire table is shown in Appendix D, but not all degrees of freedom rows are shown in this appendix.

FIGURE 10.5 ■ Distribution of t Scores for $df = 49$

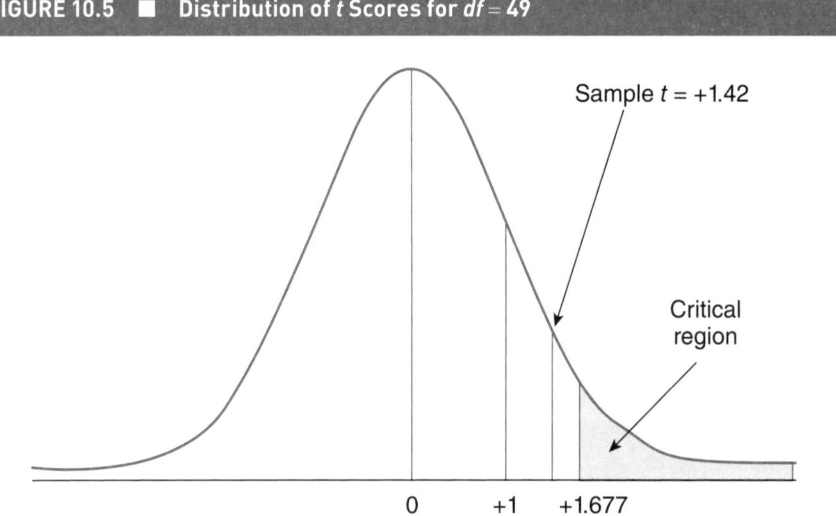

Step 5: Make a Decision

When we use the t Table to conduct a t test, we must make a decision to reject or retain the null hypothesis by comparing our sample t score with the t_{crit} value from the table. The table does not provide exact p values as the Unit Normal Table does. However, if we use a software package (such as SPSS) to conduct our test, we can determine an exact p value to compare with α as we did in Chapter 9 (I will discuss using SPSS for this test in the next section). However, our completion of the t test by hand in this section using the t Table requires a comparison of our calculated t score and the t_{crit} from the table to determine if our t score falls in the critical region as shown in Figure 10.5. Note that when df equals infinity, the t_{crit} is the same as the z_{crit} that border the critical region(s) in the z distribution.

Figure 10.4 shows this comparison in Step 5 and the corresponding decision to retain the null hypothesis because our sample t score does not exceed the t_{crit} value from the table. This means that our sample t score does not fall in the critical region of the most extreme scores in the distribution (as shown in Figure 10.5). Thus, it is still fairly likely that the sample mean came from the distribution of sample means for the null hypothesis. Our test does not support the alternative hypothesis that psychics have the ability to predict the suit of a card drawn from the deck at random, but it also does not provide evidence for the null hypothesis. We can say that the test is not significant because it failed to provide evidence against the null hypothesis. The best thing to do in this case would be to continue testing our hypothesis with additional samples and possibly some additional tasks to further test the null hypothesis.

STOP AND THINK

10.4. Suppose 36 participants complete an experiment where ads are presented subliminally during a task (e.g., Coke ads are flashed at very fast rates during movie ads). Participants are then given a recognition test for images of the ads, where two images are presented and participants must choose which of the two was presented earlier. If participants are able to process the subliminal ads when they are first presented, then their performance should be above chance (50%). This is what the researcher predicts. However, if the ads were not processed and the participants are only guessing, then their performance should be similar to chance.

a. State the alternative and null hypotheses for this study.

b. The sample mean for this study was 67% with a standard deviation of 12%. Calculate the sample *t* score for this study.

c. What decision should the researcher make about the null hypothesis in this study? (You can use Table 10.1 to find the t_{crit}.) What can the researcher conclude about their prediction from this decision?

10.5. Without looking at the table, for which sample size will there be a higher t_{crit}: $n = 30$ or $n = 50$? Explain your answer.

CONDUCTING A ONE-SAMPLE *t* TEST USING SPSS

As mentioned in the previous section, statistical software packages will calculate the estimated standard error and sample *t* score for us. Most software packages also provide the exact *p* value that corresponds to the sample *t* score, allowing researchers to compare the *p* value with their alpha level to make their decision. In this section, we will consider the process of using SPSS to conduct a one-sample *t* test.

Consider the example in Stop and Think 10.4. Suppose that this study had only 10 participants with the mean recognition accuracy rates shown in Table 10.2 (we will assume that the scores in the population are normally distributed so that we can use a *t* test even though our sample size is small). How would these data look if we entered them into the data window in SPSS? Figure 10.6 shows the data window for these data. To conduct the one-sample *t* test for these data, choose Compare Means from the Analyze menu at the top. Select the One-Sample *t* Test option in the menu of tests. The window that opens will allow you to click the data column (labeled *accuracy* in Figure 10.6) into the Test Variable box on the right to indicate that this column contains the dependent variable to be analyzed. You also need to indicate the known mean for comparison in the Test Value box by typing it in. For this example, the test value is 50 (for the chance value of 50%). When you click the OK button, the analysis begins automatically, and the output will appear in the Output Window.

TABLE 10.2 ■ Data for 10 Participants for the Subliminal Ad Example Study (See Stop and Think 10.4 for Details)

Participant 1	56
Participant 2	60
Participant 3	49
Participant 4	35
Participant 5	51
Participant 6	65
Participant 7	70
Participant 8	44
Participant 9	58
Participant 10	47

FIGURE 10.6 ■ View of Data Window in SPSS With Subliminal Ad Study Data

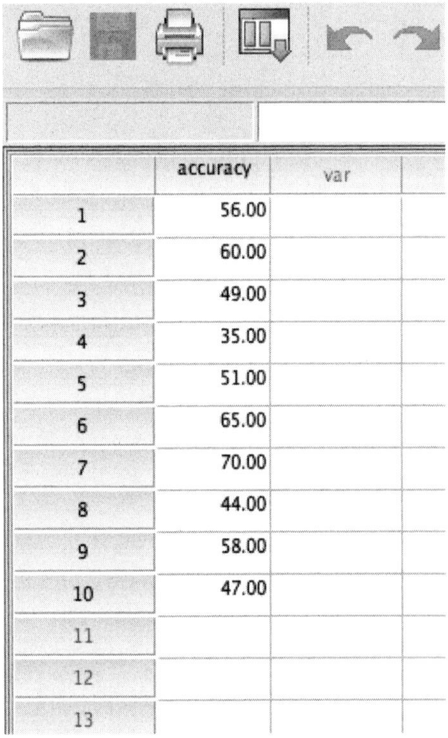

	accuracy	var
1	56.00	
2	60.00	
3	49.00	
4	35.00	
5	51.00	
6	65.00	
7	70.00	
8	44.00	
9	58.00	
10	47.00	
11		
12		
13		

A view of the output window can be seen in Figure 10.7. The output from the test contains several important values. The sample mean can be seen in the first box along with the standard deviation and estimated standard error. These are the standard descriptive statistics included in the output for a *t* test. The *t* test values are included in the second box in the output. The *t* value (1.064 for this example), the *df*, and the *p* value listed in the Sig. (for significance) column are shown in this box. Thus, unlike our hand calculation of the *t* score in the previous section, with SPSS, we can compare *p* to α as we did in Chapter 9. The default test in SPSS is a two-tailed test, but you can convert the value to a one-tailed test by dividing the *p* value in half if the means differ in the predicted direction (remember that the one-tailed test has a critical region at one end of the *t* distribution that is twice the size of the critical region for a two-tailed test—thus, the one-tailed test has a *p* value that is half the *p* value for the two-tailed test).

The *p* value in the output for this example is 0.315. If there was an effect of the ads, we expected the mean recognition score to be higher than 50%. In other words, a one-tailed test is warranted. Thus, we must divide the given *p* value in half to obtain a $p = 0.1575$ for this one-tailed *t* test. As this value is *not* equal to or lower than our alpha of 0.05 (our chosen alpha level for this example), the null hypothesis cannot be rejected and must be retained. In other words, there is no evidence that

FIGURE 10.7 ■ Output Window From the One-Sample *t* Test for the Subliminal Ad Study

T-Test

One-Sample Statistics

	N	Mean	Std. Deviation	Std. Error Mean
accuracy	10	53.5000	10.40566	3.29056

One-Sample Test

	Test Value = 50					
					95% Confidence Interval of the Difference	
	t	*df*	Sig. (2-tailed)	Mean Difference	Lower	Upper
accuracy	1.064	9	.315	3.50000	-3.9438	10.9438

participants in this experiment remembered the subliminal ads because their performance was not better than what is expected by chance.

If you were asked to report the outcome of this test in APA style, you might include a statement such as "The mean recognition score for subliminal ads ($M = 53.50$) was not significantly higher than the chance value of 50%, $t(9) = 1.06$, $p = 0.16$, one-tailed." The statistical values (rounded here to two significant digits) are given as support for a statement about the results of the study. If a two-tailed hypothesis had been made for this study, then the result would be reported as "not significantly different" instead of "not significantly higher" because we would expect a difference in either direction for a two-tailed hypothesis.

SUMMARY OF STEPS

- Type the data into a column in the data window.
- Choose Compare Means from the Analyze menu at the top.
- Choose One-Sample *t* Test from the list of tests.
- In the Variable window, click your data column into the Test Variable box.
- Enter your known population mean (μ) into the Test Value box.
- Click OK; your statistics will appear in the Output window as shown in Figure 10.7.
- Compare the *p* value from the Sig. column to your alpha level.

STOP AND THINK

10.6. Use the following data to conduct a one-sample *t* test (with $\alpha = 0.05$) to determine if the score on a standardized test (for scores that are normally distributed) with a known population mean of 100 is influenced by a new instructional method: 95, 105, 110, 90, 120, 110, 100, 95, 105, 125, 80, 100, 120, 115, 115, 120, 120, 105

10.7. Use the output shown in Figure 10.8 for a new data set to decide which decision is appropriate for a two-tailed test with an alpha level of 0.05: to reject or retain the null hypothesis.

FIGURE 10.8 ■ SPSS Output for Stop and Think 10.7

T-Test

One-Sample Statistics

	N	Mean	Std. Deviation	Std. Error Mean
Rating	20	5.0500	2.08945	.46721

One-Sample Test

	Test Value = 4					
	t	*df*	Sig. (2-tailed)	Mean Difference	95% Confidence Interval of the Difference	
					Lower	Upper
Rating	2.247	19	.037	1.05000	.0721	2.0279

ONE-SAMPLE *t* TEST ASSUMPTIONS

Each of the inferential tests that we will discuss in this text will have some assumptions that must be met in order to use the test. I will present these assumptions for each new statistic at the ends of the sections that introduce that statistic. In this chapter, I will list the assumptions for the *t* statistic that our study must meet so that we can use a *t* test.

There are two assumptions that a researcher must know to be true in order to use a *t* test:

1. The population the sample is drawn from must be normally distributed. This assumption is necessary in order to ensure that the values in the *t* Table are

accurate. However, when the sample size n is larger than 30 and the sample was selected at random from the population, violating this assumption does not change the critical t values enough to change the outcome of the hypothesis test because the distribution will be normal. Thus, this assumption is not very important if your sample size is large enough. However, if you use a small sample size in your study and you analyze the data with a t test, this will be an important assumption to verify for your population.

2. The scores in your sample must be independent observations. This means that the scores cannot be related in some systematic way to each other. If, for example, the data of one subject affects the data you collect for another subject, then the scores in your data are no longer independent. Thus, your sample must be chosen such that the scores do not affect each other. An extreme example of how this assumption could be violated in our psychic study would be if we tested more than one psychic at the same time in different rooms. If the rooms were not soundproof, the participants might be able to hear each other's responses and change their response based on what they heard the other person say. If we set up our study this way (a very bad idea), then our observations would no longer be independent because the responses of one participant depend on the responses of other participants.

It is important to be aware of these assumptions whenever you choose a t test to analyze your data.

SAMPLES WITH RELATED OR PAIRED DATA

Let's consider once again the psychic study example. Recall that you are testing the hypothesis that the population of psychics has ESP and can predict the suit of a randomly drawn playing card at a rate higher than chance (i.e., 25%). In the last section, we looked at a study testing this hypothesis in which a sample of psychics was tested with the card prediction task. No evidence was found in that study to reject the null hypothesis, which states that the population of psychics can predict the card suit no better than chance (which is the rate expected in the population of people who are not psychics). Thus, we found no evidence for the hypothesis that psychics have ESP, but we also could not find evidence against this hypothesis in our hypothesis-testing procedure. Therefore, we need to continue testing the hypothesis.

Suppose that after seeing the results of the first study, your friend who believes that psychics have ESP suggests to you that perhaps psychics need their normal fortune-telling environments (e.g., low lighting, candles, a crystal ball) in order to accurately predict the card suit (see Photo 10.3). To test this idea, you decide to do another study with a sample of psychics tested both in a fortune-telling environment and in the lab environment you used in the previous study. In this new study, a new sample of 50 psychics will each perform the card prediction task in both the fortune-telling environment and the lab

Photo 10.3 Research question: Does psychics' ESP depend on the environment they are in?

environment. They will complete 100 trials of the task in each environment, and their accuracy rate will be measured for each environment. This study is considered a within-subjects design because all the psychic participants will complete the same task in two different environments. This type of design is different from the design we used in our first psychic study in the last section. In this new study, we are no longer comparing a single sample with a known population mean. Instead, we are collecting data twice—once in the original environment and once in the fortune-telling environment—from a single sample to see if there is a difference between their average scores in the two environments. This will provide another test of the hypothesis that they have ESP—in this case, we expect a difference between the environments because the hypothesis is that they have ESP only in the fortune-telling environment.

In this section, we will consider how to test hypotheses with a single sample under different conditions. For our new psychic study, we will compare data on the card prediction tasks for two environments: a lab environment and a fortune-telling environment for this one sample. This will be done using a within-subjects design. In this design, each participant in the study will give you two accuracy rates—one in the lab room and one in the fortune-telling room. Other common within-subjects designs include comparisons of data before and after some event or treatment has occurred. In this way, we can determine if the scores on a measure have changed from before and after some treatment of interest (e.g., a new teaching method). This is known as a pretest–posttest design because you are comparing scores for a sample from before the treatment (the pretest) to after the treatment (the posttest).

Another way to examine related or paired data is using a matched design. In a matched design, participants are paired across the treatment conditions on some variable of interest. For example, suppose an instructor wants to compare the use of online quizzes to help students learn the material in her course. To test this hypothesis, she might decide to compare final exam scores in two sections of her course—one that is given the online quizzes and one that is not given the quizzes. However, she might be concerned that there are more students in one section who already know more of the material than the students in the other section. To control for this source of bias across the sections, she could use a matched design in which students are matched in pairs across the two sections based on their preexisting knowledge of the course material before they start the course. This can be accomplished by giving a test to all the students at the start of the semester and matching the students into pairs who have the same or similar scores on the test—with one member of each pair in each section. Figure 10.9 shows how this can be done. Matched designs can also be done with twins to match genetics and/or upbringing in a study or couples to examine differences across members of the couple while matching the dynamics of the relationship within each couple.

FIGURE 10.9 ■ A Matched Design Comparing Two Sections' Final Exam Scores—One Section Given Online Quizzes and the Other Section Not Given the Quizzes

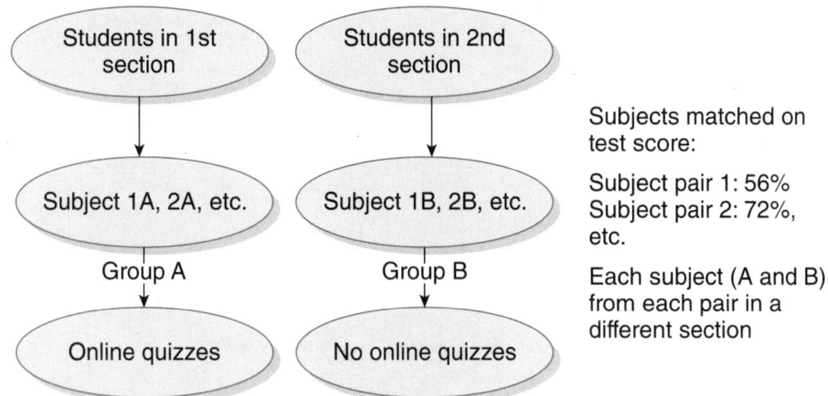

In a related or paired samples *t* test, we compare scores that are related in some way (i.e., the same subjects or pairs of subjects matched on some characteristic), conducting the test in a very similar way to the one-sample *t* test case covered in the previous section. In the case of related samples, we will use the difference scores between the pairs of scores for each match as our dependent variable and compare the difference score mean with the difference expected if there is no difference: $\mu = 0$ (or with a specific difference that is expected in the population). In other words, we combine the two sets of scores into a single score (i.e., the difference score) so that we have a single sample mean to compare with a population mean. Our new test conducted this way is the related or paired samples *t* test (both labels are given because *related* and *paired* labels are used frequently).

Let's consider our new psychic study to see how this is done. Imagine that we have conducted our study. Our new sample of 50 psychics has participated in the study in which each psychic has completed the card prediction task in a lab room and in a room set up as a fortune-telling environment (see Photo 10.3). Which room they use first is decided randomly such that half of the psychics complete the task in the lab room first and half of them complete the task in the fortune-telling room first. This is done to ensure that room order does not affect the results. Figure 10.10 shows the design of this study. You can see in this figure that each participant has an accuracy score for each room. However, in order to test our hypothesis about whether there is a difference in accuracy across the room types, we need to calculate the difference scores between the rooms for each participant.

FIGURE 10.10 ■ Design of the Within-Subjects Psychic Study

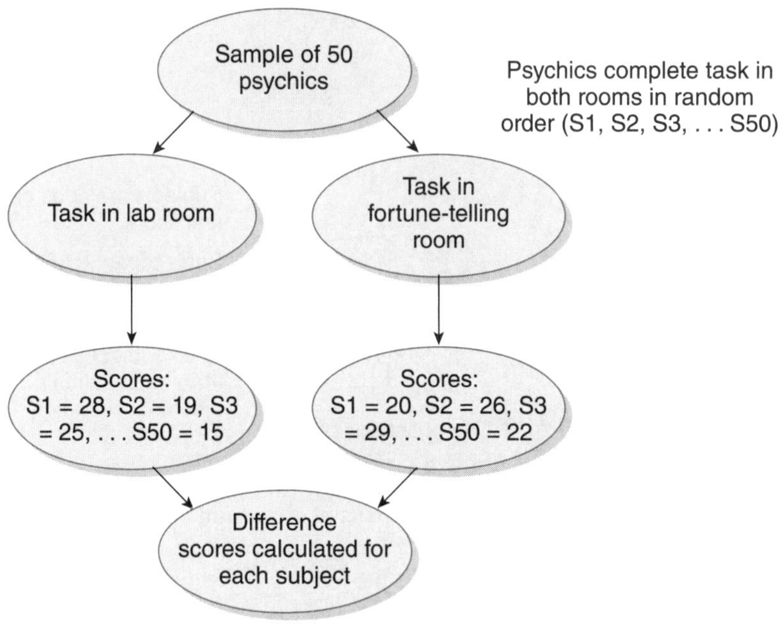

To calculate our difference scores, we simply need to subtract the score for each psychic while in the fortune-telling room from their score while in the lab room. In other words, the difference score will equal $X_{\text{fortune-telling}} - X_{\text{lab}}$. We will need to calculate this difference score (D) for each participant. Thus, from Figure 10.10, for S1 = (20–28) = −8, S2 = (26–19) = 7, S3 = (29–25) = 4, . . . S50 = (22–15) = 7. We can then calculate the mean of the difference scores, $\bar{D}$, by adding up all the difference scores and dividing by the total number of subjects, as we have done in calculating the mean for any set of scores. In the next section, we will work through all of the hypothesis-testing steps for our related samples t test and consider a new formula for t.

STOP AND THINK

10.8. For the online quizzes study shown in Figure 10.9, is this an experiment? Why or why not? How about our new psychic study shown in Figure 10.10? Is this an experiment? What are the differences between the designs of these studies?

10.9. What are the null and alternative hypotheses for our new psychic study? Be sure to state these hypotheses in terms of populations of difference scores.

CALCULATING A RELATED OR PAIRED SAMPLES *t* TEST

Let's continue with our new within-subjects psychic study to work through our hypothesis-testing process and see how the process will change for our new *t* test.

Step 1: State Hypotheses

Were you able to state the hypotheses for the study in Stop and Think 10.9? If so, they should match the hypotheses listed here:

H_1: *In the population, the mean difference score should be greater than zero.*

H_0: *In the population, the mean difference score should be less than or equal to zero.*

Why did we compare our sample mean for difference scores to zero? We compare the sample mean to zero because if there is no effect of room type on prediction accuracy, then we expect no difference between the scores the participants provide in the two rooms. Thus, on average, the difference scores will be zero. Why did we include *less than . . . zero* as part of the null hypothesis? We include *less than . . . zero* in the null hypothesis because a negative difference score would indicate higher accuracy in the lab room than in the fortune-telling room. This is not what we expect for our psychics. We specifically predicted higher accuracy for the fortune-telling room as our researcher's hypothesis; thus, our alternative hypothesis is one-tailed with a *greater than zero* predicted direction. To understand what the positive and negative difference scores tell us about our prediction, we must pay attention to the order in which we do our subtraction when calculating the difference scores. In our psychic study, we calculated difference scores as $X_{\text{fortune-telling}} - X_{\text{lab}}$. This means we expect a positive difference score mean if our hypothesis is correct. However, it is also possible that we would be expecting a negative difference if we expected the lab setting to show higher accuracy in the task and we considered this mean difference in our study. Thus, it is important to consider which condition we expect will be higher in our study and set up our mean comparison to reflect the difference score (positive or negative) that we expect in our hypothesis.

Step 2: Set Decision Criterion

Once again, we will set our alpha level at .05. Thus, our one critical region will contain positive mean difference scores and contain 5% of the scores in the distribution.

Step 3: Collect Sample Data

In Step 3, we collect our sample data. Our sample contains 50 psychics that represent the population of all psychics. Each of the psychics in our sample will provide two accuracy scores: one for the lab room and one for the fortune-telling room. However, our test relies on an analysis of the difference scores, so our difference scores will be our dependent variable of interest in this study, calculated as $X_{\text{fortune-telling}} - X_{\text{lab}}$.

Step 4: Calculate Statistics

Once we have the difference score data from our sample, we are ready to calculate the statistics for our sample. We first need to calculate the sample mean for the difference scores, $\bar{D}$. We will also need to calculate the standard deviation for our difference scores, s_D, in order to calculate the estimated standard error, which will serve as the estimate of sampling error in our t calculation. Figure 10.11 shows the portion of the inferential statistics flowchart for the paired samples t test. Let's assume that our descriptive statistics for the psychic sample are $\bar{D} = 1.0$ and $s_D = 2.9$. With these values and our sample size, n, we are ready to calculate the estimated standard error:

$$s_{\bar{D}} = \frac{s_D}{\sqrt{n}} = \frac{2.9}{\sqrt{50}} = \frac{2.9}{7.07} = .41$$

We can then insert the $s_{\bar{D}}$ value into our t formula:

$$t = \frac{\bar{D} - \mu_{\bar{D}}}{s_{\bar{D}}} = \frac{1-0}{.41} = 2.44$$

Now, we can use the t Distribution Table in Appendix D to find our t_{crit} value. But we'll need the *df* in order to find the correct value for our sample size:

$$df = n - 1 = 50 - 1 = 49$$

Because our alpha and *df* are the same as in our psychic study from earlier in the chapter and we are again conducting a one-tailed test, our t_{crit} will be the same (t_{crit} = 1.677). Thus, our critical region is the same as the one shown in Figure 10.5. However, our sample t value is higher here and falls in a different place in our t distribution. Let's see how this changes our decision.

Step 5: Make a Decision

Remember that with a hand-calculated t test, we must compare our sample t score with the t_{crit} value from the table to decide if we have evidence against our null hypothesis. If our sample t score falls in the critical region, we can reject the null hypothesis. For this study, our sample t is greater than the t_{crit}, and because our alternative hypothesis predicts a positive t score (which is what we have from our sample), we have enough evidence here to reject the null hypothesis and conclude that accuracy is higher for our psychics in the fortune-telling room than in the lab room. Our study provides evidence that the room does have an effect on psychics' accuracy rates. However, we will still need more testing of our hypothesis that their accuracy is higher than chance because we did not yet find evidence for this hypothesis. We only know that it is higher in one type of room than another type. And, of course, there is a chance that we made a Type I error here and rejected the null hypothesis when it is actually true. So further testing is warranted (we will consider one more study for this hypothesis later in this chapter).

FIGURE 10.11 ■ Portion of the Statistical Test Decision Flowchart for a Paired Samples *t* Test

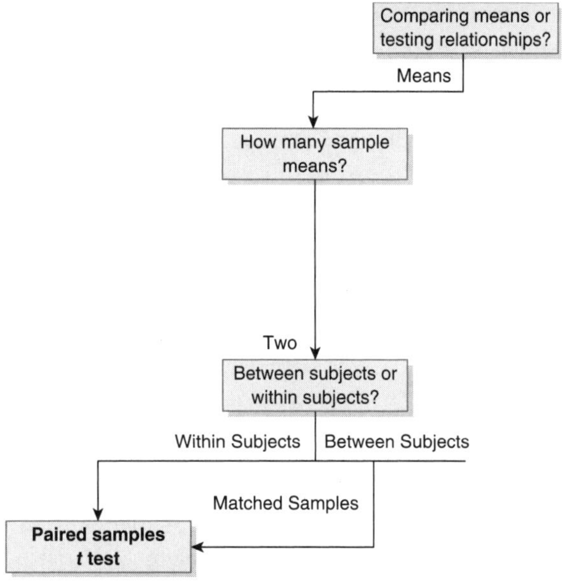

STOP AND THINK

10.10. Suppose 36 participants complete an experiment where ads are presented subliminally during a task (e.g., Coke ads are flashed at very fast rates during movie ads). Participants are then given a recognition test for images in the ads in which two images are presented and participants must choose which one of the two was presented earlier. However, the researcher wants to know if standard ads (e.g., a glass of Coke being poured over ice) are remembered differently than emotional ads (e.g., a person drinking a Coke is tightly hugging another person). To test this, each of the 36 participants completes the recognition task for both types of ads (i.e., when first presented, both types of ads are shown in a random order and recognition trials are included for both types of ads). Thus, each participant will have a separate recognition score for standard and emotional ads.

a. State the alternative and null hypotheses for this study.
b. The sample mean for the difference scores in this study was 15% with a standard deviation of 5%. Calculate the sample *t* score for this study.
c. What decision should the researcher make about the null hypothesis in this study? What can the researcher conclude about their prediction from this decision?

10.11. Suppose the study described in 10.10 was conducted with two separate samples of participants—one that received standard ads and one that received emotional ads. Describe how this study might be conducted with a matched pairs design.

CONDUCTING A RELATED OR PAIRED SAMPLES *t* TEST USING SPSS

As with the one-sample *t* test, SPSS will also calculate a related or paired samples *t* test for you, providing the exact *p* value for your sample *t* score. Consider the example study described in Stop and Think 10.10. This is a within-subjects design comparing recognition performance for two types of subliminal ads: standard and emotional. Suppose you conducted this study with 10 participants. If you had done so, you might have obtained the data shown in Figure 10.12. Notice how the data are organized in this window: There is a row for each subject in the study and separate columns for the recognition scores for the two types of ads. This is how you would enter data for a within-subjects or matched design into SPSS. Because the scores come from either the same subjects or pair of subjects, each score from that subject or pair goes in the same row with separate columns for scores from each condition.

FIGURE 10.12 ■ SPSS Data Window for the Subliminal Ad Study With 10 Participants

	Standard	Emotional	va
1	56.00	71.00	
2	60.00	59.00	
3	49.00	66.00	
4	35.00	78.00	
5	51.00	49.00	
6	65.00	82.00	
7	70.00	77.00	
8	44.00	52.00	
9	58.00	51.00	
10	47.00	78.00	
11			
12			
13			

To run the test, choose the Paired Samples *t* test in the Compare Means portion of the Analyze menu. To compare the two types of ads, click the Standard column to add it as Variable 1 and then the Emotional column as Variable 2. Then, click the arrow to add them as a Paired Variable. When you click OK, the test runs, and the output appears in the Output window.

The output indicates descriptive statistics in the first box and the test statistic and *p* value in the third box labeled *Paired Samples Test* (see Figure 10.13). For this study, the *t* value is −2.624 with a *p* value of .028. In this case, the *p* value is lower than alpha of .05. Therefore, the null hypothesis (that there is no difference between the ad types) can be rejected and the alternative hypothesis (that there is a difference between the ad types) is supported. The means indicate which ad type was remembered better: In this study, the emotional ads ($M = 66.3$) were remembered better than the standard ads ($M = 53.5$), $t(9) = -2.62$, $p = .03$. The second box of the output provides a test of the relationship between the two sets of scores (see Chapter 12 for more information about tests for relationships).

FIGURE 10.13 ■ SPSS Output for the Paired Samples *t* Test on the Ad Study Data

***t* Test**

Paired Samples Statistics

		Mean	*N*	Std. Deviation	Std. Error Mean
Pair 1	Standard Ads	53.5000	10	10.40566	3.29056
	Emotional Ads	66.3000	10	12.68464	4.01123

Paired Samples Correlations

		N	Correlation	Sig.
Pair 1	Standard Ads and Emotional Ads	10	.118	.745

		Paired Differences							
		95% Confidence Interval of the Difference							
		Mean	Std. Deviation	Std. Error Mean	Lower	Upper	*t*	*df*	Sig. (two-tailed)
Pair 1	Standard Ads and Emotional Ads	−12.800	15.42581	4.87807	−23.835	−1.7650	−2.624	9	.028

SUMMARY OF STEPS

- Type data for each condition in separate columns in the data window: one row per subject or matched pair of subjects.
- Choose Compare Means in the Analyze menu.
- Choose Paired Samples *t* test from the list of tests.
- Click on each column in the window to add them as Variable 1 and Variable 2.
- After the two conditions are indicated as the variables, click the arrow to add them as a Paired Variable.
- Click OK to run the test and look for the *p* value in the Sig column under Paired Samples Test in the Output window to compare with your alpha level.

STOP AND THINK

10.12. You are trying to decide whether you should purchase paper copies of the textbooks required for your courses next semester or purchase the online copies of the texts that are much cheaper. You are concerned that with the online texts, staring at the computer screen may be too distracting because you also receive texts and instant or chat messages on your computer. To help you make this decision, you look at the research done on paper versus computer text reading. You find a study that had participants read two passages about two different topics. Each participant read both passages—one as a paper copy and one on the computer screen. After a distractor task lasting 30 min, the participants were tested for their comprehension of the passages with a multiple-choice test containing 10 questions about each passage. Their scores were then input into SPSS, and a paired samples *t* test was conducted. Use the SPSS output in Figure 10.14 to answer the following questions:

a. What is the sample *t* score for the difference scores?

b. What is the *p* value for the sample *t* score?

c. Assuming the researchers used an $\alpha = .05$, what does this test tell you about comprehension of paper versus computer text? Does this help you decide which types of texts you should buy? Why or why not?

PAIRED SAMPLES *t* TEST ASSUMPTIONS

The assumptions that must be satisfied to use the related or paired samples *t* test are similar to those of the one-sample *t* test:

1. The population of difference scores must be a normal distribution. Recall that this assumption is needed to ensure the accuracy of the t_{crit} values in the *t* Table.

FIGURE 10.14 ■ SPSS Output for the Paired Samples *t* Test Run for the Study Described in Stop and Think 10.12

Paired Samples Statistics

		Mean	*N*	Std. Deviation	Std. Error Mean
Pair 1	Paper Text	6.3000	10	1.41814	.44845
	Computer Text	5.8000	10	1.87380	.59255

Paired Samples Correlations

		N	Correlation	Sig.
Pair 1	Paper Text and Computer Text	10	.109	.765

Paired Samples Test

	Paired Differences					*t*	*df*	Sig. (two-tailed)
	Mean	Std. Deviation	Std. Error Mean	95% Confidence Interval of the Difference: Lower	95% Confidence Interval of the Difference: Upper			
Pair 1 Paper Text Computer Text	.50000	2.22361	.70317	−1.09068	2.09068	.711	9	.495

However, as was the case with the one-sample *t* test, violating this assumption will not change the outcome of the test for sample sizes greater than 30 (i.e., $df = 30$ or higher).

2. The scores from different participants or pairs of participants must be independent. This means that across the subjects (or across the pairs of subjects for matched designs), the scores cannot depend on the scores of the other participants (or pairs). However, because scores will be related for the same or pairs of subjects by definition, this assumption does not apply to scores within subjects or pairs of subjects.

INDEPENDENT SAMPLES

In the last section, we considered a study where we found evidence for a difference in psychics' prediction abilities in lab and fortune-telling environments. However, we are still lacking evidence for our original prediction from the beginning of the chapter that psychics do have ESP that allows them to predict the suit of a randomly drawn card in our card prediction task. Earlier in the chapter, we tested this hypothesis with a single sample of psychics who performed our card prediction task, but our sample did not show an accuracy rate significantly greater than the chance guessing rate of 25%. Thus, we still need to conduct further tests of our hypothesis because a nonsignificant result provides evidence neither for nor against the alternative hypothesis. In this chapter, we will consider a more common design used to test hypotheses in behavioral research in which two samples are compared for two possible populations that differ on the factor of interest in the study.

In the new study to test our hypothesis, we will test both self-proclaimed psychics in our card prediction task and a sample of nonpsychics. The sample of psychics will represent the population of psychics, and the sample of nonpsychics will represent the population of nonpsychics. We will compare the mean accuracy rates for the two samples to test the hypothesis that the two populations (psychics and nonpsychics) have different population means for card suit prediction accuracy. Figure 10.15 illustrates the design of this study. Our null and alternative hypotheses will be stated as comparisons of the population means for these two populations with the sample means and sample variability used to calculate our sample t score. With two samples to compare, we will use the independent samples t test to complete our hypothesis-testing process for this new study.

Our new study design is a between-subjects design because it involves the comparison of two separate and independent samples. The samples may be drawn from different populations, as in our new psychic study, or come from the same population but be exposed to different treatment conditions.

For example, suppose you wanted to know whether rereading one's notes from lectures or taking quizzes is a better study technique for exams (a two-tailed test would be used here because there is no prediction about which one is better). To answer this question, you might conduct a study in which you recruit a sample from the population of students at your school to participate in the study. The students in the sample might then be randomly assigned to one of two conditions: (1) a condition in which they read a paragraph of text about a topic and then reread the paragraph before a multiple choice test about the topic or (2) a condition in which they read the paragraph of text and then attempt to recall the main ideas from the paragraph before taking the topic test. In this study, the group of students that reread the paragraph represents the population of students who use this study technique, and the group of students that recall the ideas from the paragraph represents the population of students who use this study technique (see Figure 10.16). The mean and variability for the multiple-choice test scores for each sample can then be calculated to compare them using an independent samples t test. The top part of the t score calculation will contain the mean difference observed between the samples, and the bottom part of the t score calculation will contain the mean difference expected by chance due to sampling error (i.e., these are different samples drawn from the population of students, so we wouldn't expect the two samples to always have the same mean test score even if they used the same study technique). The *t* test is then completed in the same way we have done in the previous two chapters: finding the t_{crit} value in the *t* Table and deciding if our sample *t* score is in the critical region(s) for the *t* distribution based on the distribution of sample means. If it is, we have evidence against the null hypothesis and can conclude that the populations in the different treatment conditions have different mean scores. If our sample *t* score is not in the critical region(s), we cannot conclude that the population means are different and must retain the null hypothesis.

Consider the mean data shown in Figure 10.17. These data show the mean memory score on a final memory test after two groups of participants used the two study techniques described here (rereading the paragraphs or recalling the main ideas from the paragraphs) before taking a final memory test on the paragraph topic. These data came from a study conducted by Roediger and Karpicke (2006) in an experiment in which they waited 2 days (a realistic amount of time between the study time and the time of the test) before giving a final memory test after the participants studied the paragraph information using one of these two techniques. These researchers directly compared these two conditions using an independent samples *t* test and found that the difference was significant, meaning that the *t* score for their sample was within the critical regions of the *t* distribution for an alpha level of .05.

FIGURE 10.15 ■ New Study Design for the Comparison of Two Samples: Psychics and Nonpsychics

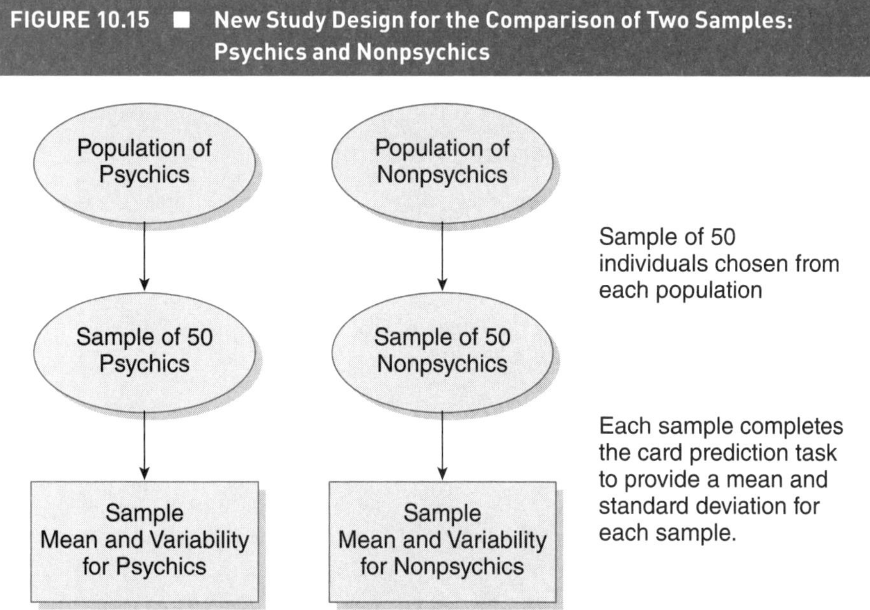

FIGURE 10.16 ■ Comparison of Populations of Students Using Two Different Study Techniques in a Two-Tailed Test

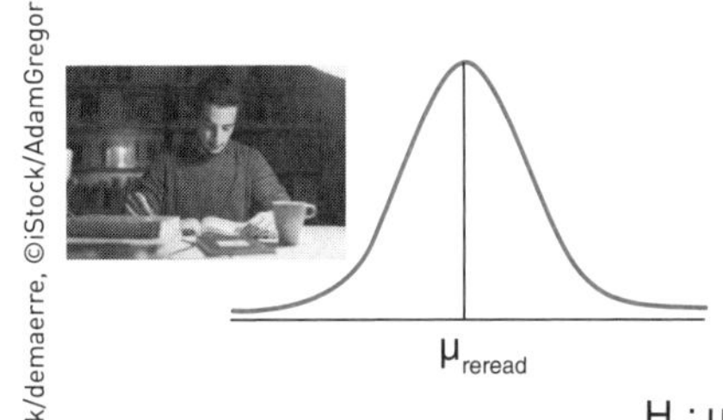

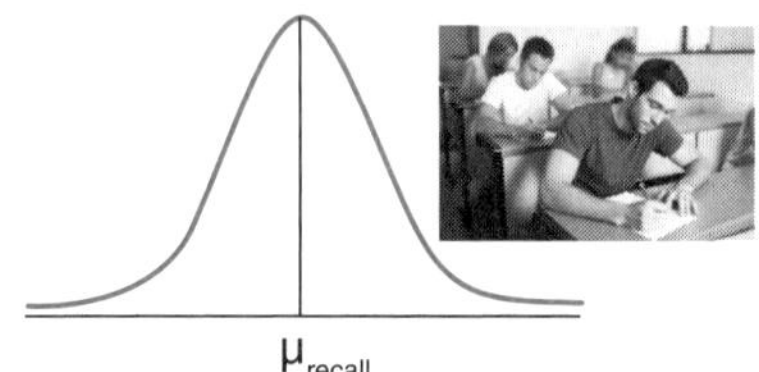

H_0: $\mu_{reread} = \mu_{recall}$
H_1: μ_{reread} not equal to μ_{recall}

STOP AND THINK

10.13. For our new psychic study with psychic and nonpsychic samples, is this an experiment? Why or why not?

10.14. For the study technique example just described, is this an experiment? Why or why not?

Estimating Sampling Error for Two Samples

One important difference between the way we calculate the sample t score for a between-subjects design and the one-sample and related samples designs is the way we estimate sampling error with the estimated standard error. Up to this point, we have calculated the estimated standard error with the standard deviation (from the one sample or the difference scores) divided by the square root of the sample size n. In formula form, for one-sample designs it is this:

$$s_{\bar{X}} = \frac{s}{\sqrt{n}}$$

For difference scores from the same sample of participants or a matched pair of participants, the formula is as follows:

$$s_{\bar{D}} = \frac{s_D}{\sqrt{n}}$$

You could also write this formula using the variance instead of the standard deviation (remember that the variance is just the standard deviation squared):

$$s_{\bar{X}} = \sqrt{\frac{s^2}{n}} \text{ and } s_{\bar{D}} = \sqrt{\frac{s_D^2}{n}}$$

This works because taking the top part of this formula is the same (algebraically) as the top part of the first set of formulas we've been using (i.e., the square root of a squared number is just the number itself). And how do we calculate the variance for a sample? If you review how we calculated the standard deviation in Chapter 6, you will find this formula:

$$s = \sqrt{\frac{SS}{n-1}}$$

SS is the sum of squared deviations of the scores from the mean. The variance is the square of the standard deviation, so if we remove the square root symbol, our formula for the variance of a sample is as follows:

$$s^2 = \frac{SS}{n-1}$$

It is also the *SS* divided by the *df* (remember, $df = n - 1$).

FIGURE 10.17 ■ Comparison of Mean Memory Scores for Two Study Techniques Tested by Roediger and Karpicke (2006) With a Two-Day Delay Between Study and Final Test

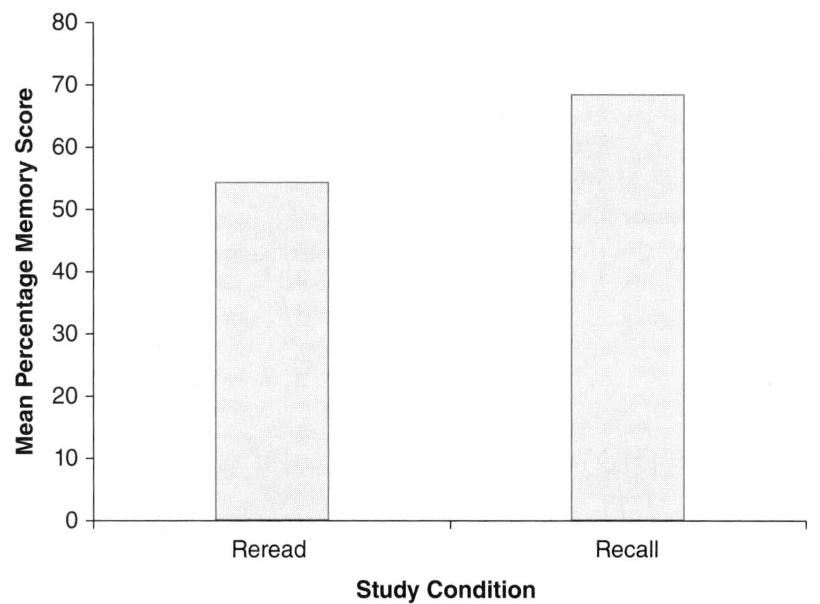

Source: Roediger and Karpicke (2006).

FIGURE 10.18 ■ Portion of the Statistical Test Decision Flowchart for an Independent Samples *t* Test

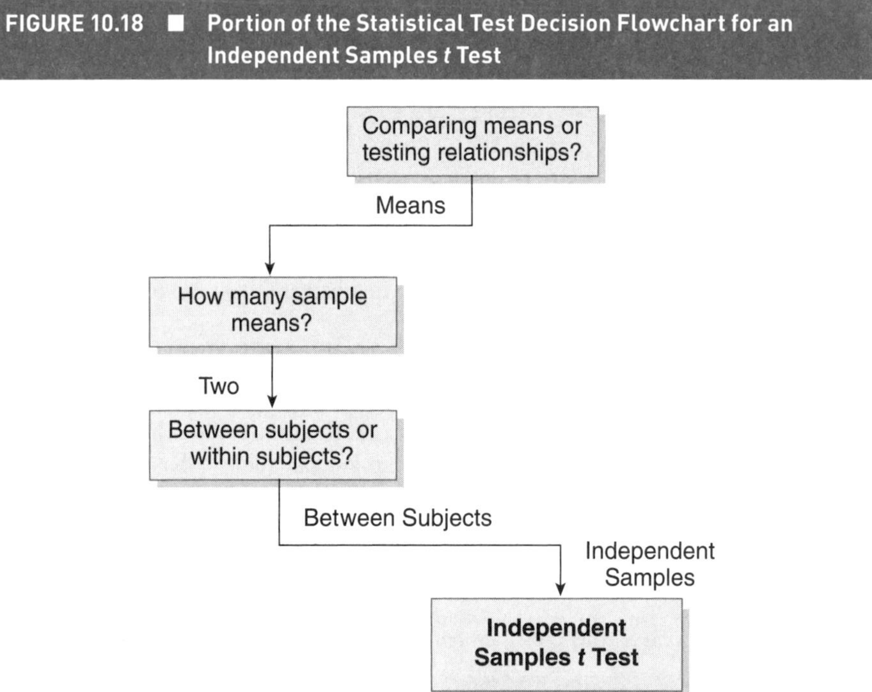

Why am I showing you all these different ways to write the same formula? Well, in order to calculate the estimated standard error for two samples, we'll need to use these terms (SS, s^2, df) in order to first calculate the **pooled variance** for the samples. This is a value that is the variance for two samples with the size of the sample considered in the calculation. This is important because in some cases, the sample sizes will be different across groups (e.g., $n = 25$ for one group and $n = 28$ for the other group), and we need to determine one standard error term for both groups. The pooled variance is denoted by s_p^2 and is used to calculate the estimated standard error, $s_{\bar{X}_1 - \bar{X}_2}$ for the bottom of our sample *t* score calculation. This will serve as the estimate of sampling error in our independent samples *t* test and is based on the variability from the two samples in the study. We will examine how to conduct the independent samples *t* test for our new psychic study in the next section.

pooled variance: The combined variance terms for two samples weighted by the sample size of each sample

CALCULATING THE INDEPENDENT SAMPLES *t* TEST

Let's go back now to our new psychic study and consider how we can compare mean accuracy scores on the card prediction task for our two samples (see Figure 10.16).

We can follow the same steps for hypothesis testing as we have done in previous sections of this chapter. The step that will change a bit is the calculation of statistics step.

Step 1: State Hypotheses

What are our hypotheses for the new study? Remember that we will state these as differences between populations. Our prediction is that the psychics will have a higher accuracy score than the nonpsychics, so we can state our alternative hypothesis as follows:

> H_1: *The population mean for psychics will be higher than the mean for the population of nonpsychics* or $\mu_{psychics} > \mu_{nonpsychics}$.

This means that our null hypothesis will state that the means are equal or that the nonpsychics' mean will be higher:

> H_0: *The population mean for psychics will be less than or equal to the mean for the population of nonpsychics* or $\mu_{psychics} \leq \mu_{nonpsychics}$.

Step 2: Set Decision Criterion

Once again, we will set our alpha level at .05. Thus, our one critical region will be above the mean difference score (i.e., $\mu_{psychics} - \mu_{nonpsychics}$) of zero and contain 5% of the scores in the distribution.

Step 3: Collect Sample Data

In the current study, we are looking at two samples of data. Let's suppose that although we recruited 50 psychics and 50 nonpsychics, only 45 of the psychics showed up (the other 5 had clients that day). Thus, our samples have different sizes, $n_{\text{psychics}} = 45$ and $n_{\text{nonpsychics}} = 50$. For each sample, we will need to determine the mean accuracy score and the variance to determine the pooled variance in Step 4.

Step 4: Calculate Statistics

Now, let's calculate our descriptive and inferential statistics. Figure 10.18 shows the portion of the inferential statistics flowchart for the independent samples *t* test. Let's suppose the mean accuracy score for the psychics was 26% and the mean accuracy score for the nonpsychics was 25%. We also need to calculate the variance from the individual scores in each sample using the formula given earlier in the chapter that includes the *SS* and *df* values. Let's use these values: $SS_{psychics} = 550$, $SS_{nonpsychics} = 350$ and $df_{psychics} = 45 - 1 = 44$, $df_{nonpsychics} = 50 - 1 = 49$. We can now calculate the pooled variance using the following formula:

$$s_p^2 = \frac{SS_{psychics} + SS_{nonpsychics}}{df_{psychics} + df_{nonpsychics}}$$

This formula will take into account the variability in each sample using the sum of squares (*SS*) and the sample size of each sample (using *df*). Remember that the variance for one sample is the *SS* divided by the *df*, so here we have a formula that combines these values for the two samples. So, for our study, we have the following:

$$s_p^2 = \frac{550 + 350}{44 + 49} = \frac{900}{93} = 9.68$$

Thus, our pooled variance is 20.93. This is a variance term that combines the variability from our two samples. This value will be used to calculate the estimated standard error for our sample *t* score with the formula

$$s_{\bar{X}_1 - \bar{X}_2} = \sqrt{\frac{s_p^2}{n_{psychics}} + \frac{s_p^2}{n_{nonpsychics}}}$$

In other words, the estimated standard error is the square root of the sum of the pooled variance divided by each sample size. This is analogous to the estimated standard error from our single sample in which we had the standard deviation divided by the square root of *n*. Because we have a variance term, the top part is also under the square root, and because we have two samples, we need to add in the value separately for each sample based on its sample size. Thus, our estimated standard error for the current study is this:

$$s_{\bar{X}_1 - \bar{X}_2} = \sqrt{\frac{9.68}{45} + \frac{9.68}{50}} = \sqrt{.215 + .194} = .64$$

Our sample *t* score is also calculated using the values for each sample. The actual mean difference minus the expected mean difference is the top of the equation and the estimated standard error representing the mean difference expected by chance (i.e., sampling error) is the bottom of the equation:

$$t = \frac{(\bar{X}_1 - \bar{X}_2) - (\mu_1 - \mu_2)}{s_{\bar{X}_1 - \bar{X}_2}}$$

The $(\mu_1 - \mu_2)$ difference is the mean population difference expected under the null hypothesis, just as it was for our related or paired samples *t* test (typically, zero). We can now substitute in our sample statistics:

$$t = \frac{\left(\bar{X}_{psychics} - \bar{X}_{nonpsychics}\right) - \left(\mu_{psychics} - \mu_{nonpsychics}\right)}{s_{X_{psychics} - X_{nonpsychics}}}$$

$$t = \frac{(26 - 25) - 0}{.64} = \frac{1}{.64} = 1.56$$

We now have our sample *t* score and can move on to Step 5 to make a decision.

Step 5: Make a Decision

In Step 5, we need to compare our sample *t* score with the t_{crit} value from the *t* Distribution Table. We will need to know our alpha level (.05), our total *df*: $df_{1+2} = df_1 + df_2 = [(45 - 1) + (50 - 1)] = 44 + 49 = 93$, and whether we have a one- or two-tailed test (one-tailed). Using this information, our t_{crit} from the table is $t_{crit} = 1.658$ (this is the more conservative value from the table for $df = 120$, the closest value to $df = 93$). Comparing our sample *t* score with this t_{crit}, we find that $t_{sample} < t_{crit}$. Thus, our sample *t* is not in the critical region, and we cannot reject the null hypothesis. Although we still cannot use this as evidence for the null hypothesis, the results from this study provide one additional set of data that is inconsistent with our hypothesis that psychics have ESP. We are slowly building a case against the idea that psychics have ESP that helps them predict the suit of a card chosen from a deck of cards.

STOP AND THINK

10.15. Suppose 36 participants complete an experiment where ads are presented subliminally during a task (e.g., Coke ads are flashed at very fast rates during movie ads). Participants are then given a recognition test for images of the ads, where two images are presented and participants must choose which one of the two was presented earlier. Both men and women (18 of each gender) participate in the study, and the researcher predicts that the recognition accuracy will differ across gender.

a. State the alternative and null hypotheses for this study.

b. The difference between the sample means in this study was 6%. The *SS* for the men was 250, and the *SS* for the women was 150. Calculate the sample *t* score for this study (remember to start with the pooled variance before you calculate the estimated standard error).

c. What decision should the researcher make about the null hypothesis in this study? What can the researcher conclude about their prediction from this decision?

10.16. Calculate the pooled variance for these two samples' scores:

Sample 1: 45, 59, 65, 26, 70, 52, 55

Sample 2: 81, 72, 69, 59, 75, 71, 62

CONDUCTING AN INDEPENDENT SAMPLES *t* TEST USING SPSS

Data for the comparison of gender study described in Stop and Think 10.15 are shown in the SPSS window in Figure 10.19. Notice that the data for all participants are typed into a single column. In the next column, code numbers indicate which sample the data belong to. The men were coded in Rows 1 through 10 with a *1*, and the women were

FIGURE 10.19 ■ Data for Stop and Think 10.15 Shown in the SPSS Data Window

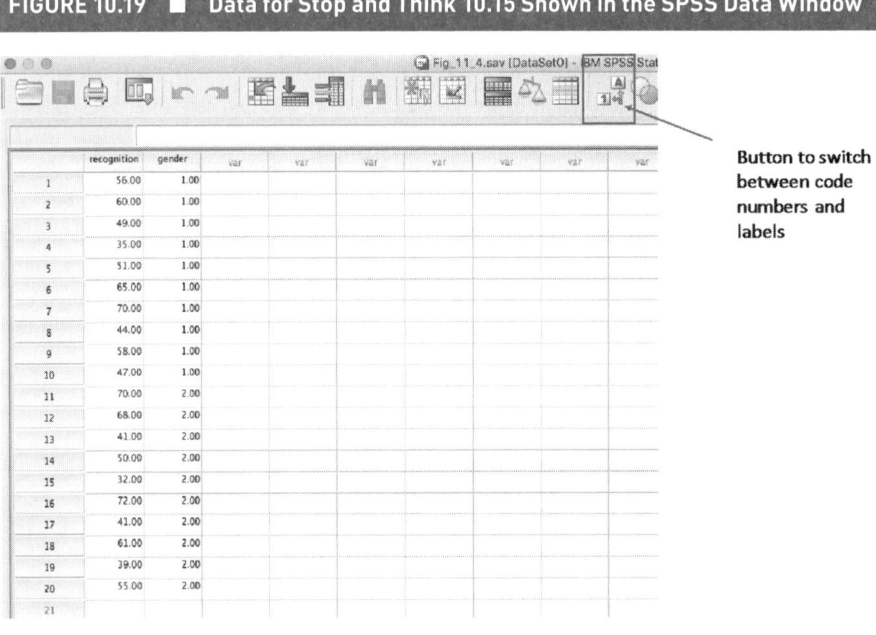

	recognition	gender	var	var	var	var	var	var	var
1	56.00	1.00							
2	60.00	1.00							
3	49.00	1.00							
4	35.00	1.00							
5	51.00	1.00							
6	65.00	1.00							
7	70.00	1.00							
8	44.00	1.00							
9	58.00	1.00							
10	47.00	1.00							
11	70.00	2.00							
12	68.00	2.00							
13	41.00	2.00							
14	50.00	2.00							
15	32.00	2.00							
16	72.00	2.00							
17	41.00	2.00							
18	61.00	2.00							
19	39.00	2.00							
20	55.00	2.00							
21									

coded in Rows 11 through 20 with a *2*. In the Variable View, the codes were defined for these groups by indicating labels for each number in the Values column for this variable. A button appears in the menu at the top, allowing you to switch back and forth between the code numbers and code labels.

To conduct the independent samples t test for these data, go to the Compare Means tab in the Analyze menu and choose the Independent Samples t Test option. The test window allows you to click over the recognition score column as the Test Variable and the gender codes as the Grouping Variable. You must then choose Define Groups to indicate that the values in this column range from 1 to 2. When you click OK, the test automatically runs and the output appears in the Output window (see Figure 10.20). The first box in the output provides descriptive statistics for each group. The second box contains the test statistic and p value. For this study, the t value is .107 and the p value (see the Sig. column) is .916. This is a two-tailed test (it is possible that either men or women could have higher recognition scores), so the p value given can be directly compared with alpha. In this analysis, the p value is greater than the alpha of .05, so the null hypothesis cannot be rejected. Therefore, there is no evidence in these data that men and women differ in their recognition of subliminally presented ads.

SUMMARY OF STEPS

- Type data into a column in the data window.
- Add number codes for the groups in another column in the data window.
- Define codes in the Values column in the Variable View tab.
- Choose Compare Means from the Analyze menu.
- Choose Independent Samples *t* Test option from the list of tests.
- Click your data variable into the Test Variable box using the arrow.
- Click Define Groups to type in the range of codes used for your groups (e.g., 1 and 2).
- Click OK and view the *p* value in the Sig. column in the Output window to compare with your alpha level.

FIGURE 10.20 ■ Output Window for Data From Stop and Think 10.15 for an Independent Samples *t* Test

➜ **T-Test**

Group Statistics

	gender	*N*	Mean	Std. Deviation	Std. Error Mean
recognition	Men	10	53.5000	10.40566	3.29056
	Women	10	52.9000	14.44107	4.56667

Independent Samples Test

		Levene's Test for Equality of Variances		t-test for Equality of Means						
									95% Confidence Interval of the Difference	
		F	Sig.	*t*	*df*	Sig. (2-tailed)	Mean Difference	Std. Error Difference	Lower	Upper
recognition	Equal variances assumed	2.217	.154	.107	18	.916	.60000	5.62870	-11.22545	12.42545
	Equal variances not assumed			.107	16.361	.916	.60000	5.62870	-11.31092	12.51092

STOP AND THINK

10.17. For the following set of data from two independent samples, conduct an independent samples *t* test (by hand or using SPSS) to determine if the mean scores for each sample are significantly different.

Sample 1: 5, 7, 4, 7, 2, 6, 7, 3, 4, 5

Sample 2: 3, 4, 3, 4, 3, 3, 3, 4, 5, 4, 3

INDEPENDENT SAMPLES *t* TEST ASSUMPTIONS

The assumptions that must be satisfied to use the independent samples *t* test are the same as those of the other *t* tests, but there is also a third assumption regarding the variability in the two populations:

1. The population of difference scores must be a normal distribution. This allows us to use the *t* Distribution Table to find our t_{crit} value.
2. The scores from different participants within each sample must be independent. Thus, the scores from the different individuals within each sample cannot be related in some way.
3. The populations that the samples represent must have equal variance. This means that the two populations being compared in the study must have the same variability. This assumption is known as **homogeneity of variances**. Meeting this assumption allows for good estimates of the sampling errors using the pooled variance term. However, an adjustment can be made (see next paragraph) if this assumption has been violated. You will see in later chapters that all tests (*t* tests and analyses of variance [ANOVAs]) that involve between-subjects variables include the homogeneity of variances assumption.

homogeneity of variances: The assumption of independent samples *t* tests and analyses of variance (ANOVAs) that the variance in the scores in the populations is equal across groups

The new assumption regarding equal variance across the two populations being compared can be tested when SPSS is used to conduct the independent samples *t* test. Take another look at Figure 10.20. Notice that there are two rows of values for the *t* statistic for the independent samples test. The first row is labeled *equal variances assumed*, and the second row is labeled *equal variances not assumed*. These statements refer to the homogeneity of variances assumption of between-subjects tests (*t* tests and ANOVAs). If this assumption is violated, the *t* test may be inaccurate. Thus, Levene's test for this assumption is provided in the SPSS output (left side of the second box) for the test. If this test is significant (comparing *p* to alpha), then the statistical values need to be adjusted, and the second row of values in this box should be used. The two rows in this box are given to allow for both possibilities.

Calculation Summary

estimated standard error: Sample standard deviation divided by the square root of the sample size

one-sample t *test:* Sample mean minus the population mean, divided by the estimated standard error

related or paired samples t *test:* Sample mean of the difference scores minus the population mean for difference scores, divided by the estimated standard error

pooled variance: Sum of the sum of squares of each sample divided by the sum of the degrees of freedom for each sample

independent samples t *test:* Difference between sample means minus the expected population mean difference for the null hypothesis, divided by the estimated standard error

THINKING ABOUT RESEARCH

A summary of a research study in psychology is given here. As you read the summary, think about the following questions:

1. Is this study an experiment? Explain your answer.
2. What are the null and alternative hypotheses for these experiments?
3. Which *t* test is the appropriate test to use to test the hypothesis for this study?
4. If the mean difference between younger and older adults had not been significant in Experiment 2, do you think the researchers' conclusions for the study overall would have changed? Why or why not?
5. Suppose the researchers had created pairs of younger and older adults (one of each age group per pair) based on a pretest score before they conducted the study. With this design, which *t* test would be the appropriate test to use to test their hypotheses?

Research Study. Worthy, D. A., Gorlick, M. A., Pacheco, J. L., Schnyer, D. M., & Maddox, W. T. (2011). With age comes wisdom: Decision making in younger and older adults. *Psychological Science, 22,* 1375–1380.

Purpose of the Study. To compare decision making in different age groups, the researchers recruited samples of younger and older adults to complete tasks where rewards were either dependent on their previous choices or independent of their previous choices. According to the authors, most previous studies had examined younger and older adult decision making in response-independent tasks, finding that younger adults outperform older adults. However, the authors argue that many decisions in life depend on previous choices (e.g., the type of career one has chosen affects one's retirement options, the type of student one is in high school affects one's college options) and that these types of decisions may involve different processes. Thus, the researchers predicted that the younger adult advantage in decision making may not hold for response-dependent tasks.

Method of the Study. The current study involved two experiments. In Experiment 1, younger and older adults performed a decision-making task where the rewards (points) for their responses (choosing one of four decks of cards shown on the screen) were independent of their previous choices. In this task, the rewards were always higher for one type of deck than the others. In Experiment 2, samples of younger and older adults performed the same decision-making task, but the rewards in Experiment 2 depended on their responses on previous trials. In each experiment, the participants completed 100 trials of the decision-making task. The number of reward points each participant earned in the task was measured as their performance on the task.

Results of the Study. In Experiment 1 (the response-independent task), younger adults showed the performance advantage found in previous studies. However, in Experiment 2, older adults earned more points on average than the younger adults with the response-dependent task. Both of these differences were significant. Figure 10.21 shows the comparison of younger and older adults' performance in the two experiments.

Conclusions of the Study. The results of the study showed that the difference in younger and older adults' decision-making performance depends on the type of task being performed: Younger adults

(Continued)

(Continued)

FIGURE 10.21 ■ Data From the Experiments Conducted by Worthy et al. (2011)

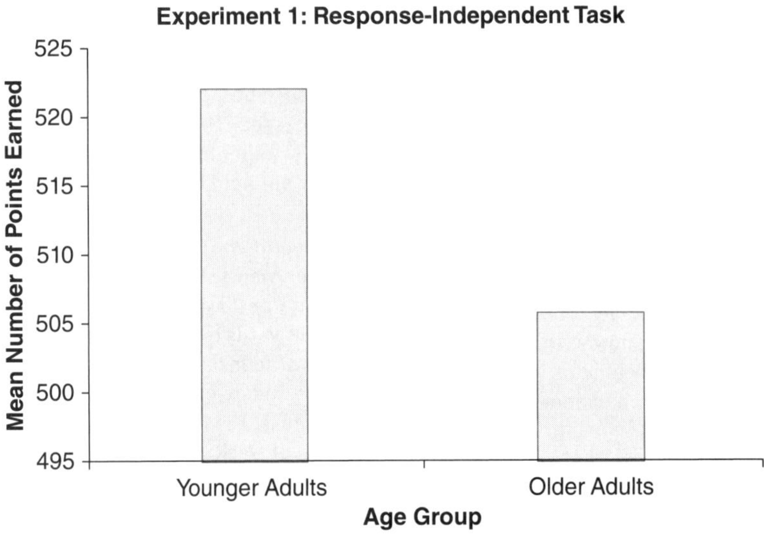

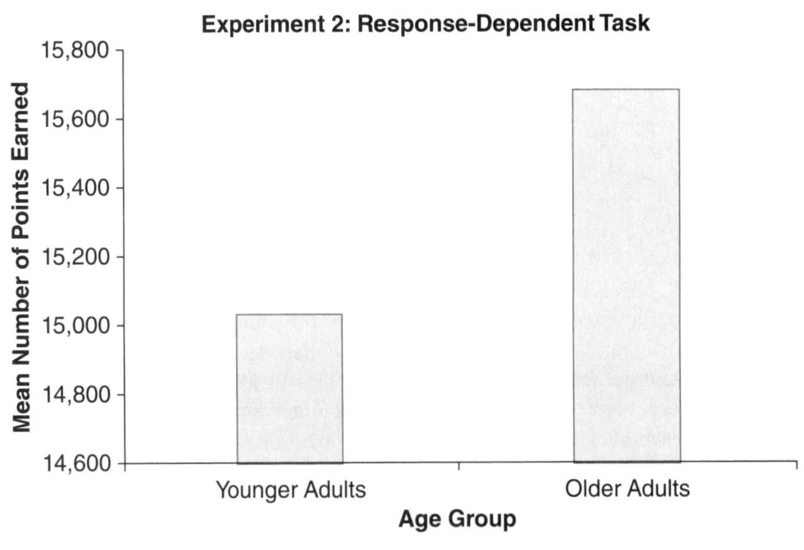

performed better with the response-independent task, but older adults performed better with the response-dependent task. The researchers concluded from these results that younger and older adults approach decision-making tasks in different ways.

Chapter Summary

- **How does the distribution of *t* scores differ from the distribution of *z* scores?**
  Unlike the distribution of *z* scores, the shape of the distribution of *t* scores changes as sample size increases. The larger the sample size, the closer the *t* value will be to the *z* score for that sample. This is due to the use of estimated standard error (from the sample standard deviation) instead of the standard error calculated from a known population σ.

- **How can we use the *t* Table to make a hypothesis-testing decision?**
  As with the Unit Normal Table, we can use the *t* Table to figure out if our sample mean is in the critical region(s) of the distribution of sample means when the null hypothesis is true. However, instead of obtaining a *p* value from the table, the *t* Table provides the t_{crit} value that borders the critical region(s). We must then compare the t_{crit} with our sample *t* score in order to make a decision about the null hypothesis.

- **How do standard error and estimated standard error differ?**
  Estimated standard error is used when we do not know the population σ. In this case, we estimate σ with the sample *s* and calculate the estimated standard error as our measure of the sampling error in our calculation of *t*.

- **How can we conduct a *t* test using statistical software?**
  When we use statistical software such as SPSS to conduct *t* tests, the output provides the exact *p* value for our *t* score. We can then compare the *p* with our α to make a decision about the null hypothesis.

- **How does our hypothesis-testing procedure differ across *t* tests?**
  The hypothesis-testing procedure is very similar across the one-sample and paired samples *t* tests. The main difference is that the paired samples test uses difference scores across the two scores for each participant as the data. However, the independent samples *t* test requires a pooled variance term in order to calculate estimated standard error.

Test Yourself

1. When we do not know the population σ, we use the ______________ to calculate estimated standard error.
   a. population mean
   b. sample mean
   c. sample standard deviation
   d. sampling error

2. With a sample size of 25, our degrees of freedom would be ______________.
   a. 26
   b. 25
   c. 24
   d. 20

3. In the calculation of a *t* score, the estimated standard error is an estimate of ______________.
   a. the population mean
   b. the population standard deviation
   c. the difference between the sample mean and the population mean

4. When we calculate an inferential statistic looking at mean differences, the numerator

(Continued)

(Continued)

is the ___________________ and the denominator is the ___________________.

a. actual mean difference, mean difference expected by chance due to sampling
b. mean difference expected by chance due to sampling, actual mean difference
c. population mean, sample mean
d. sample mean, population mean

5. For a sample of 36 participants and sample standard deviation of 3, the estimated standard error would be _______________.
   a. 0.08
   b. 0.50
   c. 1.0
   d. 3.0
6. The shape of the *t* distribution will be normal whenever the population is normal.
   a. True
   b. False
7. An assumption of the *t* test is that the scores must be independent observations.
   a. True
   b. False
8. The *t* Table provides the *p* value for each *t* score to allow the researcher to compare *p* with α.
   a. True
   b. False
9. In the related or paired samples *t* test, the difference scores typically predicted by the null hypothesis _________.
   a. equal 0
   b. equal 1
   c. equal −1
   d. depend on the alternative hypothesis
10. For a sample size of _________, we do not need to be worried about violating the assumption of a normal distribution for the population.
    a. 10
    b. 25
    c. 30
    d. 31 or higher
11. The dependent variable for a within-subjects design is _______________.
    a. accuracy
    b. speed
    c. difference scores across conditions
    d. difference scores across participants
12. A matched design might involve _______________.
    a. couples
    b. twins
    c. the same participants completing all the conditions
    d. both a and b
13. The estimated standard error in a related or paired samples *t* test is based on the standard deviation of the difference scores.
    a. True
    b. False
14. The *df* for a matched pairs design is based on the total number of participants instead of the number of pairs.
    a. True
    b. False
15. An assumption of the related or paired samples *t* test is that all scores across conditions are independent.
    a. True
    b. False

16. The pooled variance is_______________.
    a. the estimated standard error in an independent samples *t* test
    b. the combined variance for two independent samples
    c. the variance in the populations the samples were drawn from in a study
17. The variance of a sample depends on _______________ and _______________.
    a. the mean of the sample, the sample degrees of freedom
    b. the mean of the sample, the sum of squares for the sample
    c. the sum of squares for the sample, the sample degrees of freedom
18. With an independent samples *t* test, a researcher can draw conclusions about _______________.
    a. a comparison of two population means
    b. a comparison of two population variances
    c. the importance of sample size to the sampling error in a test
19. Levene's test in SPSS will help a researcher know if the assumption of _______________ for the independent samples *t* test holds for their study.
    a. a normal population of scores
    b. the homogeneity of variances
    c. the independent observations
20. The homogeneity of variances assumption states that the variance in the two samples must be equal.
    a. True
    b. False
21. A between-subjects study with results showing no significant mean difference between conditions supports the null hypothesis that no difference exists between the populations the samples represent.
    a. True
    b. False
22. Like other *t* tests, the independent samples *t* test assumes that the scores between participants are independent.
    a. True
    b. False
23. A researcher wants to know if using videos to illustrate concepts in class improves exam scores. He uses the videos before the first exam in his course and collects exam scores from the 62 students in his class. On average, they score 78% with a standard deviation of 5%. Use this description to answer the following questions.
    a. What else does the researcher need to know in order to use a one-sample *t* test to test his hypothesis?
    b. What is the null hypothesis for this study?
    c. What t_{crit} should the researcher use in this study if his $\alpha = 0.05$?
24. Your instructor tells you that his exam scores always show a 75% average score. But he thinks the class you're in seems to be grasping the material better than his previous classes. You decide to test this. The reported mean on the exam for your class is 80% with a 10% standard deviation. There are 49 people in your class. Assuming $\alpha = 0.05$, is he right about your class understanding better than previous classes (using the exam score as a measure of this)?
25. A researcher wants to know if using videos to illustrate concepts in class improves exam scores. He uses the videos after the first exam in his course and then collects exam scores from the 62 students in his class

(Continued)

(Continued)

for the second exam. He wants to compare scores on the first exam and the second exam to see if the scores increased after he started using the videos. On average, the difference in scores between the first exam and the second exam was 5% with a standard deviation of 8%. Use this description to answer the following questions.

a. What is the alternative hypothesis for this study?

b. What is the null hypothesis for this study?

c. What t_{crit} should the researcher use in this study if his $\alpha = .05$?

d. Do the videos seem to help? Explain your answer.

26. A group of students is tested on their driving ability in a research study that was done to investigate the effect of cell phone use on driving performance. A sample of 25 students drive a test course in a driving simulator to measure their driving accuracy (based on how often they deviate from the course, miss a red light, etc.). Then, all 25 students are tested on the driving course again while holding a conversation on their cell phone with a researcher. The mean difference score in driving accuracy shows that, on average, accuracy decreases by 25% while talking on the cell phone with a standard deviation of 15%. Does cell phone use cause a significant decrease in driving performance?

27. Suppose you conducted a study to test the hypothesis that social pressure affects memory accuracy. You set up a study in which participants view a video of a person robbing a convenience store. Then, half of the participants watch a video of other participants discussing the crime. In reality, the participants in the video are part of the experiment, and some of the details of the crime that are discussed are inaccurate. The actual participants are told that they should consider other people's perspectives on the crime because it is difficult for any one person to accurately remember all the details. The other half of the participants do not view the video discussion of the crime but are also told that it is difficult for any one person to accurately remember all the details of the crime. Thirty minutes after viewing the original crime video, all participants are given a recognition memory test about details of the crime. For this study, answer the following questions:

a. What are the alternative and null hypotheses for this study?

b. Suppose that 10 participants participated in each group in the study. For the recognition accuracy data provided here, conduct an independent samples *t* test to analyze these data.

Video Discussion Group: 67, 80, 69, 72, 75, 79, 66, 71, 69, 79

No Video Discussion Group: 78, 65, 79, 84, 88, 79, 89, 90, 85, 87

c. From the test result you obtained, what can be concluded about the null hypothesis you stated?

SAGE edge™

Visit **edge.sagepub.com/mcbridermstats** to find the answers to the Test Yourself questions above, as well as quizzes, flashcards, and other resources to help you accomplish your coursework goals.

11

ONE-WAY ANALYSIS OF VARIANCE

CONSIDER THE FOLLOWING QUESTIONS AS YOU READ CHAPTER 11

- How do we test hypotheses about populations for three or more groups?
- Why does analysis of variance (ANOVA) use variance instead of mean differences in its calculation?
- What is an *F* ratio, and how is it calculated?
- How do between-groups and within-groups variance terms differ?
- How do we use the *F* Table to conduct a one-way ANOVA?

LEARNING OBJECTIVES FOR CHAPTER 11

- Correctly calculate between- and within-groups variance terms for an *F* ratio.
- Understand why variance terms are used to calculate an *F* ratio.
- Apply ANOVA to data from a study.

In the last chapter, we examined *t* tests that allow us to compare two means: a sample mean with the population mean (one-sample *t* test), two means from the same sample under two different conditions (paired or related samples *t* test), and two means from different samples (paired or related samples t test for matched samples and independent samples t test for independent samples). But what if there are more than two conditions or samples that we want to compare in our study? It would be inefficient to make this comparison in multiple studies if we can compare three or more conditions or samples all at once in a single study. But if we compare three or more groups in our study, how do we calculate an inferential statistic based on mean differences? This is when **analysis of variance (ANOVA)** can help us.

analysis of variance (ANOVA): Inferential test used for designs with three or more sample means

Let's consider a new example. Text publishers are often trying to figure out in which format they should release a text that will help students the most in learning course material. Is a traditional paper text the best type of text for students to use, or is an electronic text preferable? And if an electronic text is better, should it be interactive to allow students to take quizzes and complete activities on specific concepts as they go, or should an electronic text be set up as a paper text (but in electronic form) with the activities at the ends of the chapters? Can we answer these questions with a single study? Yes, we can. To answer these questions, our study would have a single independent variable of *text format* with three conditions: paper text, standard electronic text, and interactive electronic text. Figure 11.1 illustrates this design. To compare these three text formats, we could conduct a study with 90 students in which 30 students are randomly assigned a format to use in a course. We might ask students to rate their satisfaction with the text at the end of the course on a 1 to 10 scale and then compare the ratings across text formats to determine which format received the highest rating.

To compare the sample means for our text format study, we will use an ANOVA with the hypothesis-testing procedure. ANOVA is an inferential test that examines mean differences as a variance term instead of looking at the mean difference between two

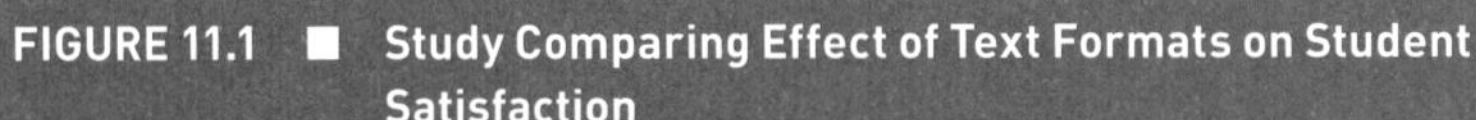

FIGURE 11.1 ■ Study Comparing Effect of Text Formats on Student Satisfaction

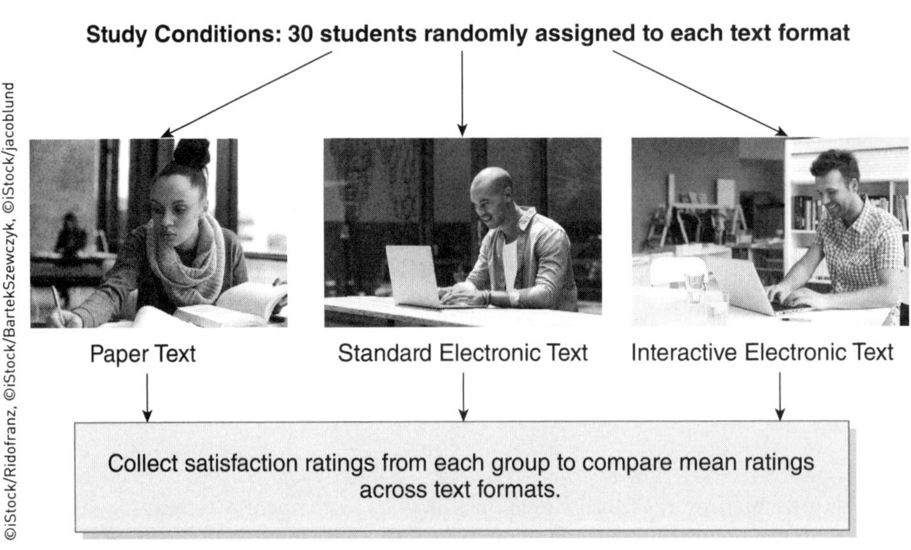
Study Conditions: 30 students randomly assigned to each text format
Paper Text
Standard Electronic Text
Interactive Electronic Text
Collect satisfaction ratings from each group to compare mean ratings across text formats.
©iStock/Ridofranz, ©iStock/BartekSzewczyk, ©iStock/jacoblund

sample means. Because it uses variance terms, ANOVA allows us to compare more than two means at once in a ratio value that represents the mean differences observed in the samples over the mean differences expected due to sampling error. As we go through this chapter, you will see how the variance terms are calculated to create the statistic known as an *F* value that can be compared with the distribution of *F* values, as we did with the *t* distribution.

MORE THAN TWO INDEPENDENT SAMPLES

Our example study shown in Figure 11.1 uses a design that includes three sample means from different groups of participants. Studies that compare more than two samples or conditions within a single study are common in psychology. If you begin reading journal articles in psychology, you will notice that ANOVA is a common inferential test used by researchers to test their hypotheses. Although ANOVA can be used with both between-subjects and within-subjects designs, we will focus in this chapter on between-subjects designs with one independent variable that has three or more levels. Between-subjects designs with more than one independent variable and within-subjects designs are discussed in later chapters.

Between-Subjects Designs With Three or More Groups

When we compare scores across three or more groups, we are using a between-subjects design in which the individuals in the sample either come from different populations (e.g., children, young adults, and older adults; different ethnic groups) or are randomly assigned to different conditions within the study. The goal in both cases is for the groups created in the study to represent the population that group comes from—the different populations they are drawn from or the population under those conditions. Figure 11.2 illustrates this comparison for our example study looking at text formats. The groups in the text format conditions represent the population of students using each format. Thus, we will make hypotheses comparing these three grouped populations in our hypothesis-testing procedure.

Hypotheses With Three or More Groups

To state our hypotheses for a study with three or more groups, we will need to consider all the groups in stating both the null and alternative hypotheses. Our null hypothesis will always predict that all the population means are equal to each other. However, there are many possibilities for our alternative hypothesis. For example, we could predict that just one population mean is greater (or less) than the others but that the rest are equal to one another. Or we could predict that all the population means are different from one another. Or we could simply predict that at least one of the population means will be different from the others. This is the alternative hypothesis we will make for our text format study (see Figure 11.2) because we do not know which text format is the most preferred format. The number of ways the alternative hypothesis can be stated for a design with

FIGURE 11.2 ■ Comparison of Populations in the Text Format Study

Comparison of populations under three different treatment conditions

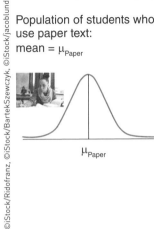

Population of students who use paper text: mean = μ_{Paper}

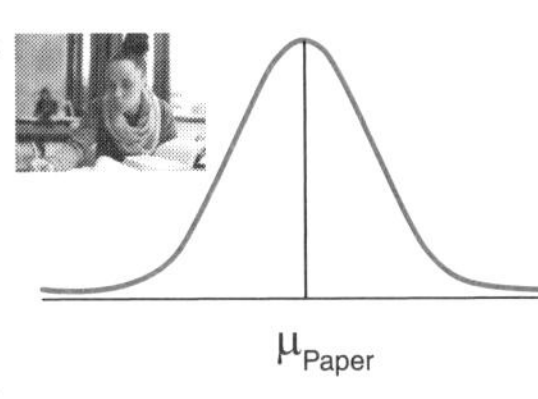

μ_{Paper}

Population of students who use standard electronic text: mean = $\mu_{StdElec}$

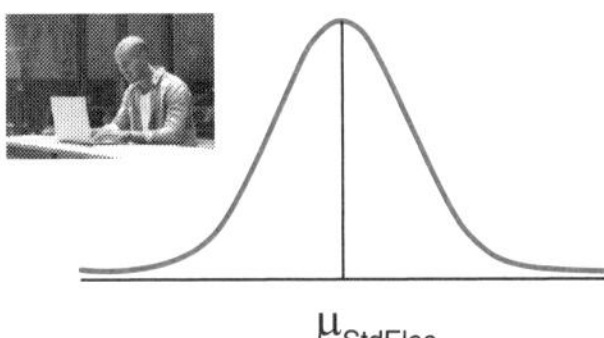

$\mu_{StdElec}$

Population of students who use interactive electronic text: mean = $\mu_{IntElec}$

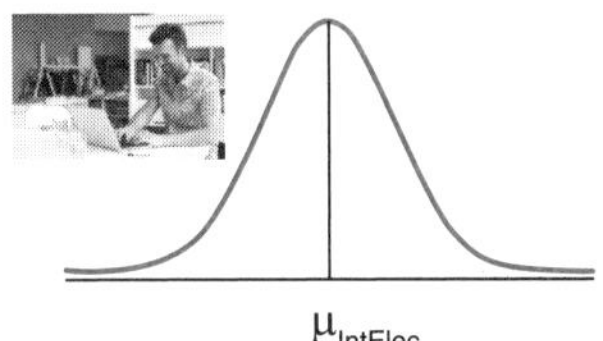

$\mu_{IntElec}$

H_0: $\mu_{Paper} = \mu_{StdElec} = \mu_{IntElec}$

H_1: At least one population mean is different from the others.

more than two samples will depend on how many samples we are comparing in our study. We no longer have a choice between one- and two-tailed tests when we compare three or more sample means. In fact, you will see later in this chapter that the F distribution only has one tail because it can never be a negative value. Therefore, you should state your alternative hypothesis according to the design of your study and how you expect the different sample means to be ordered in comparing the groups. But regardless of how we state our hypotheses, we should always make predictions about the *population* means (not the sample means) that our groups represent in our study.

Using Variance Instead of Mean Differences

In fact, the reason that our F value will always be a positive value is that we use variance terms in the F ratio instead of sample mean differences in our calculations. As mentioned earlier, with three or more means to compare, we cannot simply use the difference between sample means in the top portion of our F ratio. We would have multiple mean differences (e.g., the difference between the first and second groups, the difference between the second and third groups) to consider with three or more groups to compare. To get around this issue, we will use a variance term in our F ratio to represent the mean differences. Remember that the variance is simply the standard deviation squared. So, in looking at mean differences, we will be looking at the sum of the squared differences between each sample mean and the overall mean (called the *grand mean*) for all of the groups in our study. This is called the **between-groups variance**. It is calculated from the average squared difference between the sample mean and the overall mean for all the groups in our study. The between-groups variance term makes up the top (numerator) of the F ratio because it tells us how much our sample means differ from the average of all the sample means.

between-groups variance: The average squared difference between the sample means and the overall (grand) mean

The bottom (denominator) of the F ratio is still an estimate of sampling error—how much of a mean difference we expect by chance. This is called the **within-groups variance** because it is based on the average difference between the scores within each group and the group mean. This is similar to what we calculated in the pooled variance term for the independent samples t test, but for an ANOVA, we have to calculate this term for all of our groups and then add the terms together. It is also sometimes called the *error term* in the F ratio because it is our estimate of sampling error. Thus, the F ratio is as follows:

within-groups variance: The average squared difference between the scores in each group and the group mean

$$F = \frac{Between\text{-}Groups\ Variance}{Within\text{-}Groups\ Variance}$$

Just as in our t score calculation, the F value is a ratio of the treatment (i.e., independent variable) effect plus error over the estimate of error:

$$F = \frac{Treatment\ Effect + Error}{Error}$$

The F value then represents the average mean difference across groups due to the treatment with sampling error divided out. Later in this chapter, we will examine how we calculate these variance terms from our data.

The between- and within-groups variance terms divide the total variance in the data in two (not equally, though). The total variance in the data can be determined from the sum of the squared differences of each individual score from the overall (grand) mean, regardless of which group the score came from. When we calculate between- and within-groups variance, we are adding together two parts of the total variance such that the between- and within-groups variances added together equal the total variance in the data.

The between- and within-groups variance terms separate the total variance into two parts—one that shows us the differences due to the treatment and the error (between groups) and one that shows us the differences due to sampling error (within groups).

The *F* Distribution

The F distribution is similar to the distribution of t scores except that because we are using variance terms that are squared, F can never be less than zero. In fact, the F ratio can never equal zero unless there is no variability in the data (i.e., everyone has the same score in the data set), and this will never happen in real data collected from a sample. You should also consider that the F ratio will equal 1.0 if there is no effect of the treatment or independent variable because in this case, you will have a ratio of error divided by error. Thus, the closer the F value gets to 1.0, the less of an effect there is of the independent variable in the data.

Because of these characteristics of the ratio, the shape of the F distribution is positively skewed with a tail of extreme values at the positive end. Figure 11.3 shows the F distribution shape with the critical region indicated in the tail. However, the exact shape of the distribution will depend on the sample size and the number of groups in our study

FIGURE 11.3 ■ The *F* Distribution

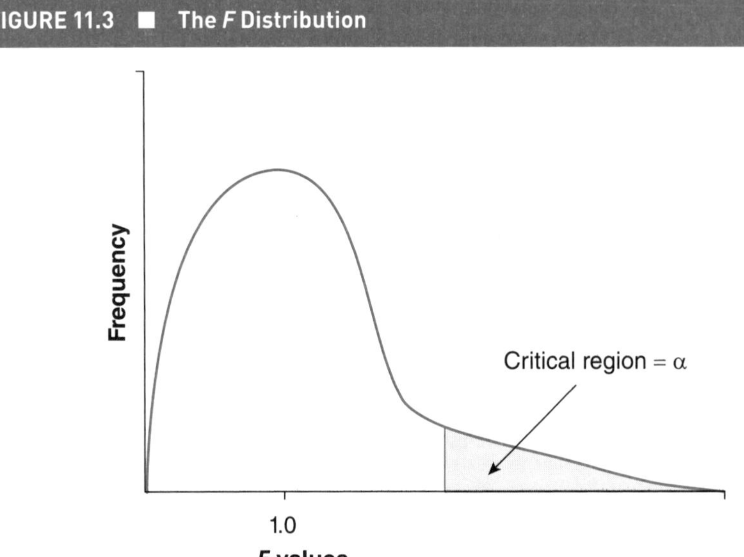

represented by degrees of freedom (*df*) terms in the between- and within-groups variance. Therefore, for an ANOVA, we will have two *df* terms: $df_{between}$ and df_{within}. The between-groups *df* is one less than the number of groups in the study because this term is the average of mean differences for the groups (i.e., the sample size in this term is the number of groups). The within-groups *df* is one less than the number of subjects in each group times the number of groups because this term comes from the average of the differences between the scores in each group and the group means (i.e., the sample size in this term is the sum of the *df*s for each group).

STOP AND THINK

11.1. Thinking about what you know about how to calculate the variance and the description of the between and within groups variance terms in this last section, how do you think we will calculate these terms in our *F* ratio? (*Hint:* Review the formula for the pooled variance from Chapter 10, and think about which difference scores will contribute to each term.)

11.2. A researcher is interested in differences in spatial abilities that might exist between individuals with different hand dominance because she suspects that left-handed individuals have superior spatial abilities, as suggested by results from past studies. She designs a study to compare spatial abilities for three groups: right-hand dominant, left-hand dominant, and ambidextrous (i.e., neither hand is dominant). Hand dominance is determined from a questionnaire given at the start of the study asking participants which hand they prefer to use (right, left, or either) for different tasks (e.g., writing, throwing). Each group then completes a spatial ability task in which they have to navigate a dot on the computer screen through a maze using a map that they study ahead of time. Time to complete the maze is measured. State the alternative and null hypotheses for this study.

CALCULATING THE *F* SCORE IN AN ANALYSIS OF VARIANCE

The preceding sections in this chapter described the concepts that make up the *F* ratio and the distribution of *F* values. In this section, I will focus on how we actually calculate the between- and within-groups variance terms that make up the ratio as we work through the process of hypothesis testing for our text format study using a one-way between-subjects ANOVA as our inferential statistics test (see Figure 11.4 for the portion of the test flowchart for this test).

Step 1: State Hypotheses

As described previously, the null hypothesis for a one-way ANOVA will always predict that the population means across groups are equal. Consistent with this, our null hypothesis for the text format study is this:

H_0: *The population means for students using paper, standard electronic, and interactive electronic texts are equal* or H_0: $\mu_{Paper} = \mu_{StdElec} = \mu_{IntElec}$.

FIGURE 11.4 ■ Portion of the Statistical Test Decision Flowchart for a Between-Subjects One-Way ANOVA

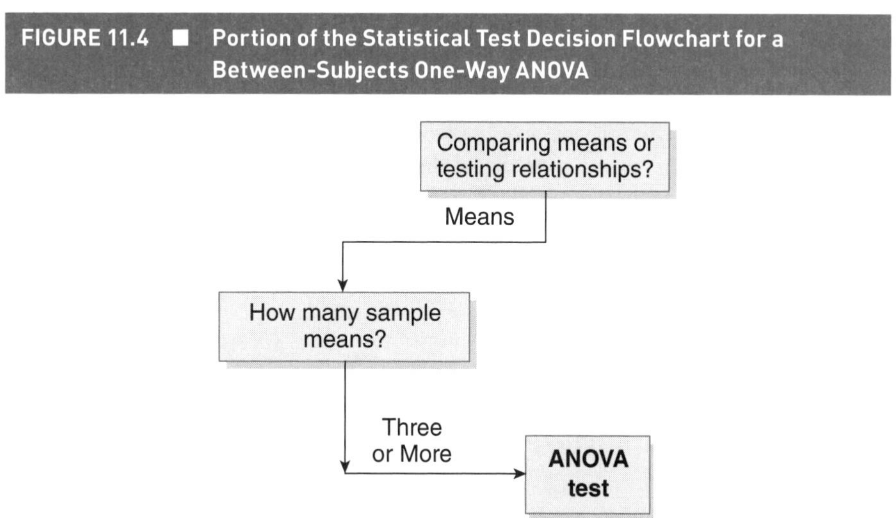

The alternative hypothesis could be stated in several ways (examples were given earlier in the chapter), but for this example, we'll assume that we do not have a specific prediction about which text format is preferred. Thus, our alternative hypothesis is this:

H_1: *At least one population mean is different from the rest for the text format populations.*

When you state the alternative hypothesis, carefully consider what prediction you can reasonably make for the population means for all the groups in your study.

Step 2: Set Decision Criterion

As we have done in previous chapters, we will set our alpha level at 0.05. This will give us one critical region in the *F* distribution (see Figure 11.3) that contains 5% of the *F* scores in the distribution.

Step 3: Collect Sample Data

We are now ready to consider the sample data for our study. Let's assume that we ran this study with three randomly selected groups from the sample of students we recruited. The data for this study showed the means for the satisfaction ratings to be as follows:

$$\bar{X}_{Paper} = 4.17, \bar{X}_{StdElec} = 5.33, \bar{X}_{IntElec} = 7.83$$

We will also need to know the overall mean, also called the *grand mean*, in order to calculate the between-groups variance term. This is the mean of the group means. The grand mean for our data is as follows:

$$\bar{X}_{Total} = 5.78$$

For the within-groups variance term, we will need to determine the sum of squared deviations of each score from its sample mean. We calculated the sum of squares for each sample in Chapter 10 when we calculated the pooled variance, and you have already seen several examples in previous chapters of how to calculate the sum of squares, so this term should be familiar. Here, we have calculated the sum of squared deviations for the scores in each group from the group mean. For our data, we have the following:

$$SS_{Paper} = 53, SS_{StdElec} = 75, SS_{IntElec} = 75$$

Also recall that we have n = 30 per group in our study. We will use the n when we calculate our variance terms in the next step.

Step 4: Calculate Statistics

Now, we can begin to calculate our sample *F* value using the between- and within-groups variance terms. As described earlier in this chapter, the *F* value is a ratio of the between- and within-groups variance terms:

$$F = \frac{\textit{Between-Groups Variance}}{\textit{Within-Groups Variance}}$$

The between-groups variance is based on the effect of the treatment + error, and the within-groups variance is based on the sampling error estimate from our data. Recall that the general formula for the variance is $\frac{SS}{df}$. Thus, for the between-groups variance term, we use the following formula:

$$\textit{Between-Groups Variance (also called Mean Square Between)} = \frac{SS_{Between}}{df_{Between}}$$

For our within-groups variance term, we use this formula:

$$\textit{Within-Groups Variance (also called Mean Square Within)} = \frac{SS_{Within}}{df_{Within}}$$

Note that the variance terms are also known as mean square (*MS*) terms because they represent the average (i.e., mean) sum of squared deviations for that term.

Let's break each of these formulas into the parts we will calculate separately. For the $SS_{Between}$ term, we will consider the group means' squared deviations from the grand mean:

$$SS_{Between} = n\Sigma\left(\bar{X}_{Group} - \bar{X}_{Total}\right)^2$$

This formula shows the sum of the squared differences between each group mean ($\bar{X}_{Group}$) and the grand mean ($\bar{X}_{Total}$) times the number of scores per group (n). We can use the sample means we determined in Step 3 to calculate the $SS_{Between}$:

$$\begin{aligned} SS_{Between} &= 30\left[(4.17-5.78)^2 + (5.33-5.78)^2 + (7.83-5.78)^2\right] \\ &= 30(2.59 + .20 + 4.20) = 30(6.99) = 209.7 \end{aligned}$$

We will also need the $df_{Between}$ term that is one less than the number of groups (a) to complete the between-groups variance calculation:

$$df_{Between} = a - 1 = 3 - 1 = 2$$

Thus, the between-groups variance ($MS_{Between}$) is this:

$$MS_{Between} = \frac{SS_{Between}}{df_{Between}} = \frac{209.7}{2} = 104.9$$

This will be the top (numerator) of our F ratio.

Next, we need to calculate the MS_{Within} term to determine the bottom (denominator) of our F ratio. We'll begin with the SS_{Within} term. Here is the formula for the within SS term:

$$SS_{Within} = \Sigma\left(X - \bar{X}_{Group}\right)^2$$

This is the sum of squared deviations of each score from its group mean. This is the same as follows or the sum of the sum of squares for each group.

$$SS_{Within} = \Sigma\left(SS_{Group}\right)$$

Each SS_{Group} term was given in Step 3:

$$SS_{Within} = (53 + 75 + 75) = 203$$

We also need the df_{Within} term, which is the number of groups (a) times n minus 1 (the same as adding together the *df*s for each group). For our study, we have the following:

$$df_{Within} = a(n-1) = 3(30-1) = 87$$

So our MS_{Within} term is this:

$$MS_{Within} = \frac{SS_{Within}}{df_{Within}} = \frac{203}{87} = 2.33$$

Now, we can calculate our F ratio:

$$F = \frac{Between\text{-}Groups\ Variance}{Within\text{-}Groups\ Variance} = \frac{MS_{Between}}{MS_{Within}} = \frac{104.9}{2.33} = 45.02$$

With this value, we can move on to Step 5, where we will determine the F_{crit} and make a decision about the null hypothesis.

Step 5: Make a Decision

As described in an earlier section of this chapter, the shape of the F distribution depends on both the $df_{Between}$ and df_{Within}. In addition to our alpha level (determined in Step 2), we need to use the df terms to find the F_{crit} value to compare with the F value we calculated from our data. Table 11.1 shows a portion of the F Distribution Table provided in Appendix E. Because the standard alpha level used in behavioral research is 0.05 in most cases, the table provides F_{crit} values for this alpha level. The columns represent the different values of the $df_{Between}$ term and the rows represent the different values of df_{Within}. Table 11.1 shows the portion of the table for df_{Within} in the range of 60 to 100.

The closest value for df_{Within} without going over is 80, so that's the row we'll use to find our F_{crit}. Moving over to the column for $df_{Between} = 2$, we see that $F_{crit} = 3.11$. This value is highlighted in Table 11.1.

Compared with the $F_{crit} = 3.11$, is our calculated F value in the critical region for the F distribution? Yes, it is: 45.02 is larger than 3.11. Figure 11.5 shows this distribution and the critical region. Thus, we have enough evidence to reject the null hypothesis and conclude that there is at least one difference across the population means for the different text formats. But which ones are different? Our one-way ANOVA cannot tell us this. It only tells us about the **main effect**—the overall effect of our independent variable. In other words, a main effect will indicate that a difference exists across the conditions but

main effect: Test of the differences between all means for each level of an independent variable in an ANOVA

TABLE 11.1 ■ A Section of the *F* Distribution Table

$df_{Between}$ →			
df_{Within} ↓	1	2	3
60	4.00	3.15	2.76
65	3.99	3.14	2.75
70	3.98	3.13	2.74
80	3.96	3.11	2.72
100	3.94	3.09	2.70

FIGURE 11.5 ■ *F* Distribution and Critical Region for Text Format Study ($df_{Between} = 2$, $df_{Within} = 80$)

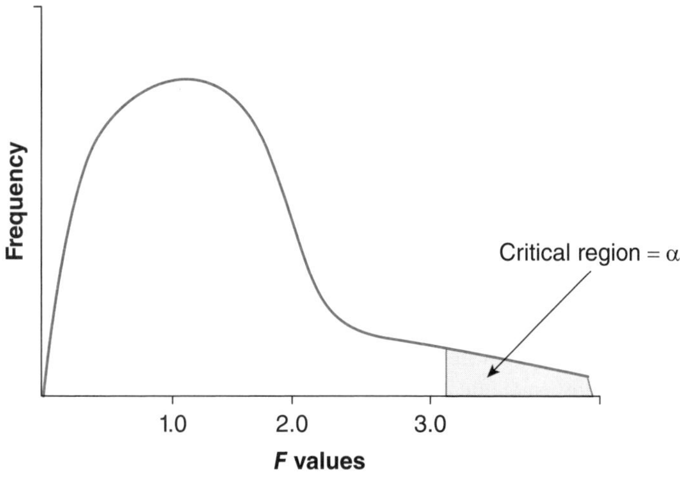

post hoc tests: Additional significance tests conducted to determine which means are significantly different for a main effect

not which conditions are significantly different. Instead, we will need to conduct **post hoc tests** to determine which means are significantly different from one another.

Post hoc tests are *t* tests that compare pairs of sample means to determine where a difference found in an ANOVA is across the conditions. In most cases, we will want to use a post hoc test that controls for the increase in alpha that will occur each time we conduct a paired *t* test on the same set of data. Because each additional test is done with the same set of data, the chance of making at least one Type I error increases with each test. In other words, with each test we run on our data set, we increase the Type I error rate, so we must correct for this increase. In fact, this is one of the reasons to use an ANOVA for studies with three or more conditions instead of multiple *t* tests: An ANOVA does not increase the Type I error rates across the tests.

The most common post hoc test used to correct for this increase in Type I error (and also the post hoc test that controls for the increase in Type I error most conservatively) is a Bonferroni test, where our chosen alpha level is divided by the number of tests we are doing. If we want to compare each of the three means in our text format study with each other, we would need three extra *t* tests, so our alpha level for these tests would be $\frac{.05}{3} = .017$. However, conducting a post hoc test is *only* appropriate if the overall effect (the main effect) is significant. *Do not* conduct post hoc tests for nonsignificant main effects. In addition, post hoc tests are only needed for main effects with three or more levels to compare. With only two levels of an independent variable, a significant main effect indicates that the means for those two levels are different. We will consider post hoc tests further in the next section.

CONDUCTING A ONE-WAY BETWEEN-SUBJECTS ANALYSIS OF VARIANCE USING SPSS

Let's now look at how we can conduct the one-way ANOVA for our text format study using SPSS. Our data come from the satisfaction ratings on a 1 to 10 scale that were collected from the 90 participants at the end of the study (30 participants per group). A portion of these data are shown in the SPSS data window in Figure 11.6. Notice that these data are entered as they would be for an independent samples *t* test, but there are three groups coded in the second column instead of two groups. The group labels were entered for the code numbers in the Variable View tab for the data window.

To run an ANOVA on the satisfaction ratings data with the text format variable, you can choose the Compare Means option in the Analyze menu. Then, select the One-Way ANOVA test. The Variable Definition window appears. Click the Ratings column into the Dependent List window to define the dependent variable. Then click the Format column into the Factor window to define it as the independent variable. You must also choose the Options button and select Descriptives if you want to view the descriptive statistics for the samples. In the Options window, you will also see a box you can check to conduct the test for homogeneity of variances (see Test Assumptions section).

FIGURE 11.6 ■ SPSS Data Window for the Text Format Study Data

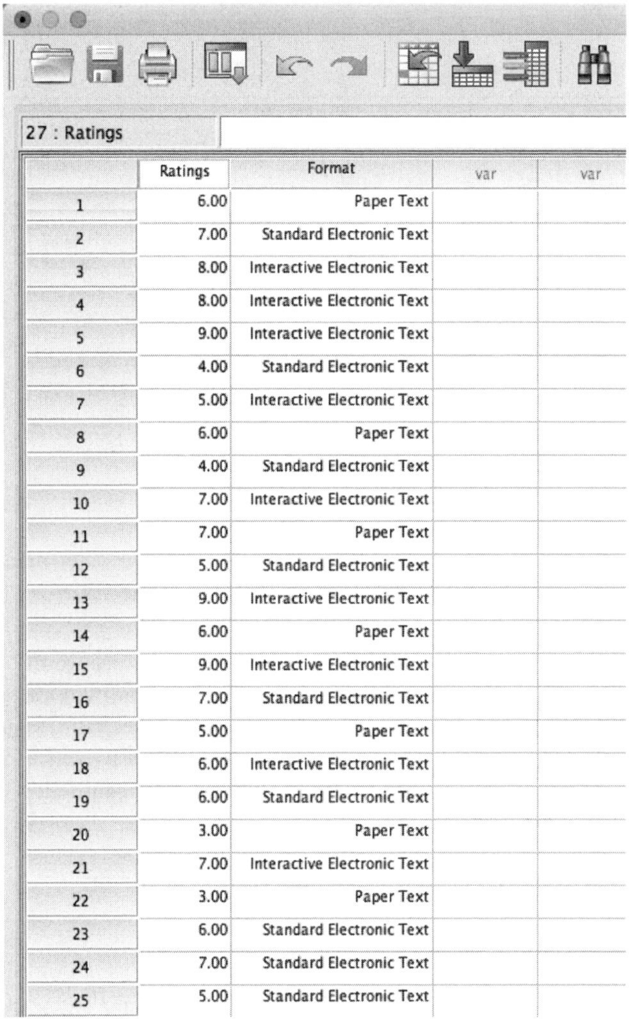

27 : Ratings

	Ratings	Format	var	var
1	6.00	Paper Text		
2	7.00	Standard Electronic Text		
3	8.00	Interactive Electronic Text		
4	8.00	Interactive Electronic Text		
5	9.00	Interactive Electronic Text		
6	4.00	Standard Electronic Text		
7	5.00	Interactive Electronic Text		
8	6.00	Paper Text		
9	4.00	Standard Electronic Text		
10	7.00	Interactive Electronic Text		
11	7.00	Paper Text		
12	5.00	Standard Electronic Text		
13	9.00	Interactive Electronic Text		
14	6.00	Paper Text		
15	9.00	Interactive Electronic Text		
16	7.00	Standard Electronic Text		
17	5.00	Paper Text		
18	6.00	Interactive Electronic Text		
19	6.00	Standard Electronic Text		
20	3.00	Paper Text		
21	7.00	Interactive Electronic Text		
22	3.00	Paper Text		
23	6.00	Standard Electronic Text		
24	7.00	Standard Electronic Text		
25	5.00	Standard Electronic Text		

The Output window contains a box with descriptive statistics (if you chose that option) and a box with the F statistic and p value (see Figure 11.7). The between-groups row of the statistics box shows the between-groups variance terms (Sum of Squares, *df*, and Mean Square). This row also contains the calculated F and p values. The within-groups row contains the values for the within-groups variance (i.e., error) term. For our text format data, we have an F value of 45.12 and a p value less than 0.001 (the value is low enough that the rounded p is shown as 0.000, but remember that p can never equal zero, so you should report this value as $p < 0.001$). The test is significant because the p value

FIGURE 11.7 ■ SPSS Output for the Text Format Study Data

Oneway

Descriptives

Satisfaction Ratings

	N	Mean	Std. Deviation	Std. Error	95% Confidence Interval for Mean		Minimum	Maximum
					Lower Bound	Upper Bound		
Paper Text	30	4.1667	1.64177	.29974	3.5536	4.7797	1.00	8.00
Standard Electronic Text	30	5.3333	1.62594	.29685	4.7262	5.9405	1.00	8.00
Interactive Electronic Text	30	7.8333	1.28877	.23530	7.3521	8.3146	5.00	10.00
Total	90	5.7778	2.15562	.22722	5.3263	6.2293	1.00	10.00

ANOVA

Satisfaction Ratings

	Sum of Squares	*df*	Mean Square	*F*	Sig.
Between Groups	210.556	2	105.278	45.119	.000
Within Groups	203.000	87	2.333		
Total	413.556	89			

Note: These values are slightly different from those on pp. 307–308 due to rounding.

(less than 0.001) is lower than our alpha level of 0.05. In other words, we can reject the null hypothesis that there is no difference between the condition means. This result might be reported as "The effect of text format on satisfaction ratings was significant, $F(2,87) = 45.12$, $p < 0.001$." However, this test does not tell us which conditions are different from one another. To learn which means are significantly different from the others, we need to conduct post hoc tests.

SUMMARY OF STEPS

Type the data into each data window. Add codes for condition in a separate column.

- Choose Compare Means from the Analyze menu.
- Choose the One-Way ANOVA test from the options.
- Click the data column into the Dependent List box.
- Click the codes column into the Factor box.
- Click the Options button and choose Descriptive if you would like the means and variability statistics printed into the Output (you can also choose Homogeneity of Variance Test under Options to check this assumption).

Note: A one-way ANOVA can also be run using the General Linear Model function from the Univariate options in the Analyze menu; this method will be discussed in Chapter 15.

Post Hoc Tests

The post hoc button allows you to run post hoc tests along with the ANOVA. These tests are useful if the main effect of your independent variable is significant (as it is for our example here), indicating a difference between at least two of the groups. Selecting the post hoc button brings up a list of different post hoc tests. These tests vary according to how conservatively they control for Type I errors across the set of post hoc tests. SPSS provides options for the three most common post hoc tests used in psychological studies, which are the least significant difference (LSD), Bonferroni, and Tukey tests. The LSD test does not provide any correction for Type I errors across tests. The Bonferroni test provides the strongest control for Type I errors across tests. The Tukey test falls somewhere between these two tests in control for Type I errors. For our example, we will use the Bonferroni test that was described in the section on calculating the ANOVA by hand. Click on the Bonferroni box to conduct this test. Then click Continue and OK to begin the ANOVA.

The post hoc tests indicate which pairs of means are significantly different from one another. These tests are shown in the Post Hoc Tests box in the SPSS Output window (see Figure 11.8). The Bonferroni test chosen for this example is listed above the box. The box shows p values (in the Sig. column) lower than 0.05 for all the comparisons. If we examine the means shown in the first box of Figure 11.7, we find that the Interactive Electronic text was the most preferred format followed by the Standard Electronic format and then the Paper format as the least preferred with significant differences for each pair.

Although all the differences were significant in this example, you may conduct tests in which only some of the differences are significant. In these cases, you can conclude that there is a significant mean difference between the conditions where the p value given is lower than your alpha level, but you cannot conclude that there is a difference if the p value is higher than the alpha level. In those cases, you must retain

FIGURE 11.8 ■ SPSS Output for the Text Format Study Data With Bonferroni Post Hoc Tests

Post Hoc Tests

Multiple Comparisons

Dependent Variable: Satisfaction Ratings
Bonferroni

(I) Text Format	(J) Text Format	Mean Difference (I-J)	Std. Error	Sig.	95% Confidence Interval	
					Lower Bound	Upper Bound
Paper Text	Standard Electronic Text	-1.16667*	.39441	.012	-2.1295	-.2039
	Interactive Electronic Text	-3.66667*	.39441	.000	-4.6295	-2.7039
Standard Electronic Text	Paper Text	1.16667*	.39441	.012	.2039	2.1295
	Interactive Electronic Text	-2.50000*	.39441	.000	-3.4628	-1.5372
Interactive Electronic Text	Paper Text	3.66667*	.39441	.000	2.7039	4.6295
	Standard Electronic Text	2.50000*	.39441	.000	1.5372	3.4628

Note: *The mean difference is significant at the 0.05 level.

the null hypothesis that there is no difference between groups until further testing can be done.

STOP AND THINK

11.3. Use the following terms to calculate the *F* ratio and determine if the main effect is significant:

$SS_{Between} = 150$, $df_{Between} = 3$, $SS_{Within} = 900$, $df_{Within} = 57$

11.4. Based on what you know about the component parts of the *F* ratio, approximately what value should *F* equal if there is no treatment (i.e., independent variable) effect on the data? Explain why.

11.5. What is the purpose of a post hoc test? What does it tell us? Explain why we do not need a post hoc test if there are only two groups in our study.

TEST ASSUMPTIONS

The test assumptions for a one-way between-subjects ANOVA are the same as those for the independent samples *t* test because the test is doing the same thing as a *t* test but with additional groups. Thus, the assumptions include the following:

1. The population of scores must be a normal distribution. As you have seen in previous chapters, this is a standard assumption for inferential tests that compare means.
2. The scores from different participants within each sample must be independent. Thus, the scores from the different individuals within each sample cannot be related.
3. The populations that the samples represent must have equal variance. In other words, the assumption of homogeneity of variances must hold. This assumption was introduced in Chapter 10 along with Levene's test for this assumption in SPSS.

Calculation Summary

between-groups sum of squares: The sum of the sum of squared deviations for each group mean from the grand mean times the group sample size

within-groups sum of squares: The sum of the sum of squared deviations for each score from its group mean

between-groups degrees of freedom: The number of groups minus one

within-groups degrees of freedom: The sample size minus one times the number of groups *or* the sum of the degrees of freedom (sample size minus one) for all the groups *between-groups mean squares:* The between-groups sum of squares divided by the between-groups degrees of freedom

within-groups mean squares: The within-groups sum of squares divided by the within-groups degrees of freedom

F *ratio:* The between-groups mean square divided by the within-groups mean square

THINKING ABOUT RESEARCH

A summary of a research study in psychology is given here. As you read the summary, think about the following questions:

1. Is this study an experiment? Explain your answer.
2. Explain why an ANOVA is needed for this study instead of a *t* test.
3. What factor would have been included in the ANOVA analysis for comparison of the switch–stay scores?
4. How do you know that the one-way ANOVA was significant in this study?
5. Explain why these researchers used post hoc tests as part of their analyses.

Research Study. Haun, D. B. M., Rekers, Y., & Tomasello, M. (2014). Children conform to the behavior of peers; other great apes stick with what they know. *Psychological Science, 25,* 2160–2167.

Note: Study 1 from this article is described next.

Purpose of the Study. The study examined social learning behaviors in order to compare human social learning to social learning in nonhuman primates. Past studies (e.g., Laland & Galef, 2009) have shown that, similar to humans, many different animal species show evidence of social groups with behavioral differences. In addition, both humans and animals have shown evidence of social learning. In the current study, the researchers were interested in examining whether nonhuman primates show the same level of conformity to peer behavior that humans show. Study 1 was conducted to examine how often human children, chimpanzees, and orangutans change their current problem-solving strategy after watching peers perform a different strategy for the problem. Study 2 was conducted to examine whether the presence and number of peers during the strategy test phase would influence the children's strategy-switching behavior.

Method of the Study. In this study, 18 children, 12 chimpanzees, and 12 orangutans participated. Participants completed a task of dropping balls into one of three slots in boxes presented to them on a display (see Figure 11.9 for a diagram of the task). One of the boxes dispensed a reward (chocolate for children, peanuts for animals) when a ball was dropped into its top slot. Participants completed the task until they received the reward on 8 of 10 consecutive trials. They then watched three familiar peers (one at a time) perform the task for two trials each using a different box than the one the participant had used in the initial phase. Peers were rewarded on both of their trials. Participants were then tested on the task again while the peers watched. They performed three trials in the test phase. Each of the three trials was recorded as a *stay* response (they used their same box from the initial phase),

(Continued)

(Continued)

a *switch* response (they used the box they had seen their peers use), or an *other* response (they used a different box from both the initial phase and their peers).

FIGURE 11.9 ■ Task Performed by Participants in the Haun et al. (2014) Study

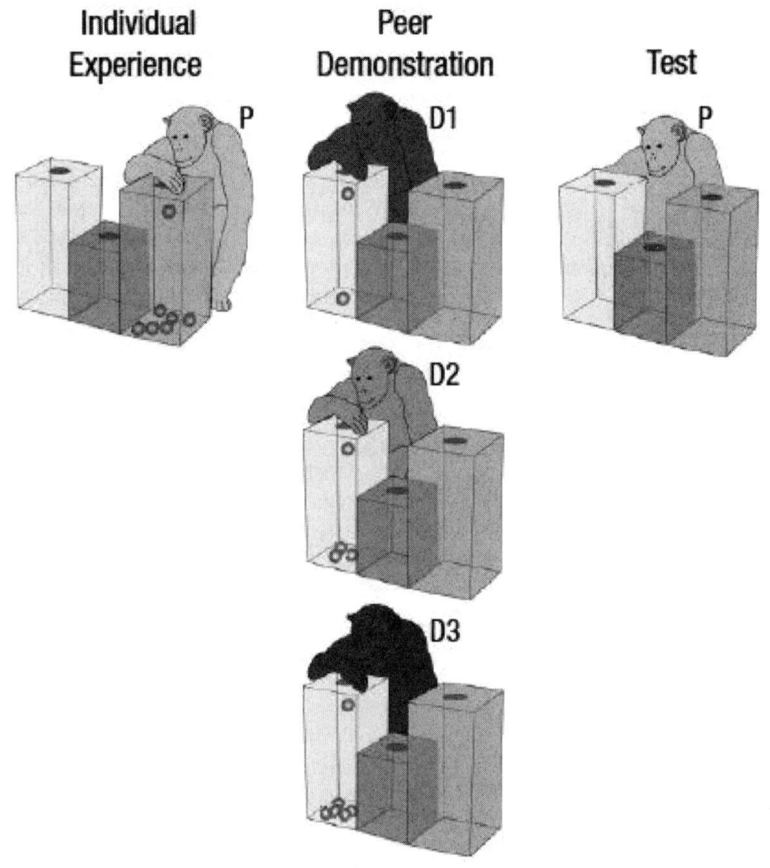

Source: Haun, Rekers, and Tomasello (2014).

Note: P = Participant, D = Demonstration (D1, D2, and D3).

Results of the Study. A switch–stay score was calculated for each participant for the three trials they performed in the test phase. Positive scores indicate more *switch* responses, and negative scores indicate more *stay* responses. Figure 11.10 illustrates the results for the three participant groups. The graph shows that, on average, children switched their responses to those shown by their peers, whereas animals stayed with their original responses, showing less influence of the peer demonstrations.

FIGURE 11.10 ■ Mean Switch–Stay Scores for the Haun et al. (2014) Study

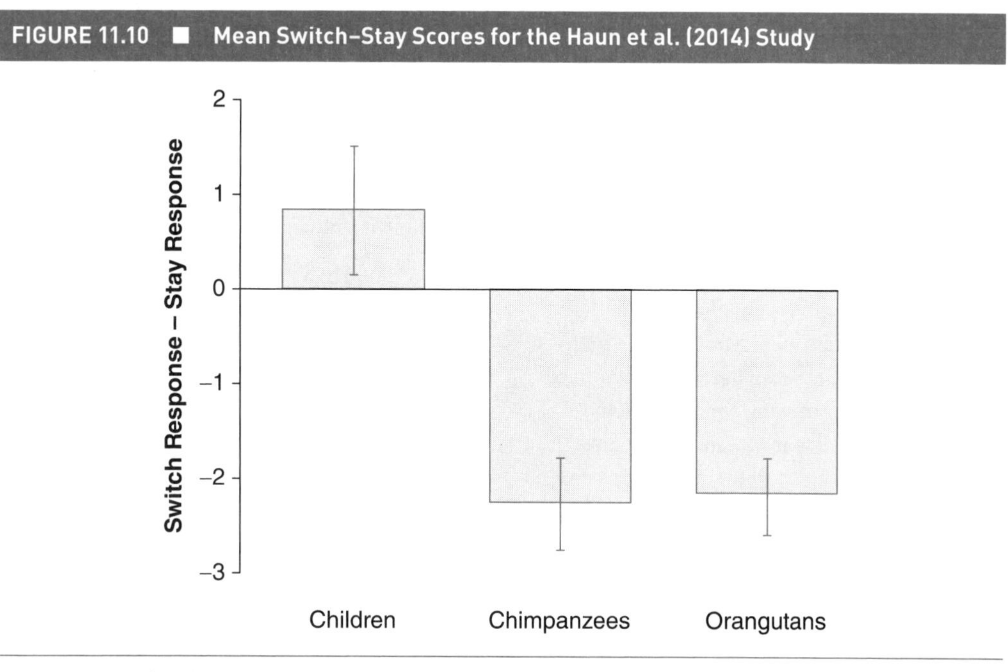

Source: Haun et al. (2014).

Conclusions of the Study. From the results of the study, the researchers concluded that humans are more willing to adjust their behavior to match peers' behavior than are nonhuman primates. From their studies, the researchers concluded that nonhuman primates are not influenced socially by peers' behavior as much as humans are.

Chapter Summary

- **How do we test hypotheses about populations for three or more groups?**
  We can test hypotheses about populations for three or more groups in a similar way as with two groups. We can represent each population (different types of individuals or the same individuals under different conditions) with a different group in our study and then compare the sample means on our dependent variable using a one-way between-subjects ANOVA. The ANOVA will tell us if there is a difference among the means, and post hoc tests can tell us which means are significantly different if the ANOVA is significant.

- **Why does ANOVA use variance instead of mean differences in its calculation?**
  We cannot use mean differences when we have more than two groups because there would be more than one mean difference to

(Continued)

(Continued)

consider. Thus, ANOVA uses variance terms based on the sum of squared differences between the sample means and the overall (grand) mean to give us a value in the numerator of our statistic representing the effect of the treatment plus error.

- **What is an *F* ratio, and how is it calculated?**
  The *F* ratio represents the treatment plus error over error. It is calculated from the between-groups mean variance (the sum of squared differences between the groups divided by degrees of freedom) over the within-groups mean variance (the sum of squared differences within the groups divided by the degrees of freedom).

- **How do between-groups and within-groups variance terms differ?**
  The between-groups variance term is based on how much the groups differ from each other, whereas the within-groups variance term is based on how much the scores differ from each other within each group.

- **How do we use the *F* Table to conduct a one-way ANOVA?**
  We use the *F* Table the same way we used the *t* Table to find a critical value that tells us where the critical region is in the *F* distribution. However, the F_{crit} is based on both degrees of freedom terms: $df_{Between}$ and df_{Within}.

Test Yourself

1. Instead of the estimated standard error, the *F* ratio uses the ________________ as the estimate of sampling error in its calculation.
   a. pooled variance
   b. between-groups variance
   c. within-groups variance
2. With more than two groups in a study, the appropriate statistical test to use is a ______________.
   a. one-way between-subjects ANOVA
   b. one-way within-subjects ANOVA
   c. independent samples *t* test
   d. multi-sample *t* test
3. To find F_{crit} in the *F* Table, you need to know ______________.
   a. $df_{Between}$
   b. df_{Within}
   c. your alpha level
   d. all of the above
4. An ANOVA can tell you ______________.
   a. if your null hypothesis is true
   b. if there is at least one mean difference across your sample means
   c. which of your sample means are different from each other
   d. both b and c
5. An ANOVA should always be followed with a post hoc test.
   a. True
   b. False
6. A post hoc test can tell you which of your sample means is different from the others.
   a. True
   b. False

7. Conducting multiple tests to determine if multiple pairs of means from the same data are different will increase your chance of making at least one Type I error.
   a. True
   b. False

8. A researcher tested the effect of type of music (classical, country, and rock) on subjects' mood. An alpha level of 0.05 was used in the test. The outcome of the ANOVA was $F(2,65) = 16.91$, $p < 0.001$.
   a. What is the null hypothesis for this study?
   b. Is there evidence to reject the null hypothesis? How do you know?
   c. What can the researcher conclude from the outcome of this test?

9. Using the sample data that follows, conduct an ANOVA to determine if there is a significant main effect:
   a. Group 1: 74, 62, 59, 78, 65, 90, 45, 51, 67, 71
   b. Group 2: 88, 90, 54, 79, 85, 78, 92, 74, 89, 77
   c. Group 3: 72, 86, 93, 91, 80, 79, 84, 75, 78, 92

10. Explain why the mean of the *F* distribution for the null hypothesis is 1.0.

11. Suppose that a new drug was found to reduce depression. A study was conducted to try to find the best dosage in reducing symptoms. Three dosage levels of the drug (10 mg, 25 mg, and control–placebo) were given to different groups of subjects. The data represent mood level from a standardized mood questionnaire (where high scores indicate better mood and less depression). The data from the study are given here:

10 mg	25 mg	Control–Placebo
16	4	2
18	6	10
10	8	9
12	10	13
19	2	11

   a. Create a line or bar graph (using whatever software you wish) for the means from this data set (paste the graph into your lab write-up). After looking at the graph, does the dosage of the drug appear to have an effect on depression score?
   b. Based on the ANOVA results, does dosage affect mood? Present the statistical values in American Psychological Association (APA) style.
   c. Conduct the ANOVA using SPSS, and choose the post hoc button. Click the Bonferroni test. The output will indicate for each pair of conditions whether the difference between the means is significant. Use the *p* values provided to make statements about how the different dosage conditions compared.

12. There have been a number of studies on the adjustment problems people experience when traveling across time zones (i.e., "jet lag"; e.g., see Moore-Ede, Sulzman, & Fuller, 1982). Jet lag always seems to be worse when traveling east. Consider this hypothetical experiment. A researcher obtained volunteers willing to travel to various locations and then examined how many days it takes a person to adjust after taking a long flight. One group flew east across time zones (e.g., California to New York). A second group traveled west

(Continued)

(Continued)

(e.g., New York to California). A third group took a long flight within one time zone (e.g., San Diego to Vancouver). The number of days it took each subject to adjust to daily activities in the new city is reported here.

Westbound	Eastbound	Same time zone
2	6	1
1	4	0
3	6	1
3	8	1
2	5	0
4	7	0

13. Conduct the one-way ANOVA for the travel-type variable. Be sure to label the values for the four levels in the Variable view. Do long plane flights (in general) cause jet lag? Give the appropriate statistical and *p* values that tell you this. Mean values for conditions should be included.

12

CORRELATION TESTS AND SIMPLE LINEAR REGRESSION

CONSIDER THE FOLLOWING QUESTIONS AS YOU READ CHAPTER 12

- How do hypothesis tests differ across experiments and correlational studies?
- What can you learn from testing relationships between measures?
- What can you learn from conducting a regression analysis?
- What does it mean to find the best-fit line for a set of data?
- How much causal information can be gained from correlation and regression hypothesis tests?

LEARNING OBJECTIVES FOR CHAPTER 12

- State hypotheses for correlational studies.
- Choose the appropriate statistical tests for hypotheses about relationships.
- Calculate Pearson *r* and simple linear regression statistics.

So far in this text, I have described some hypothesis tests (*t* tests and analyses of variance [ANOVAs]) that are appropriate for experiments and quasi-experiments in which a researcher is comparing measures for different groups of participants or for two sets of scores from the same participants. In this chapter, we will consider how to test hypotheses for another type of research study: correlational studies. Recall that in correlational studies, the goal is to examine the relationship between two (or more) measures of behavior to determine whether the measures change together or whether one can predict the other. For example, colleges and universities use test scores from high school students (e.g., the SAT or ACT) to predict how well those students will perform in college to decide whom to admit. This prediction can be made because test scores and college grade point average (GPA) were found to be related in studies looking at the relationship between these measures. I do something similar when I am recruiting students to serve as teaching assistants for my courses: I assume that the scores on exams in my course are related to how much knowledge a student has of the material in the course (an important quality in a teaching assistant) and ask students who have earned high exam scores to be teaching assistants. Correlational studies can test whether these relationships exist and examine what kind of relationship (positive or negative, predictive) is present.

CORRELATION VERSUS CAUSATION

Correlational studies can help us test hypotheses about relationships between measured variables and whether the value for one measure can predict a value on another measure. However, we must be cautious about the conclusions we make from data collected in correlational studies. Experiments are designed to minimize other possible explanations for the results of the study besides the causal factor(s) tested in the study. In correlational studies, we cannot control for these other explanations as well as we can in experiments; thus, we cannot draw causal conclusions in correlational studies as well as we can in experiments. Correlational studies are designed to test if a relationship exists and, if so, what type of relationship. They can also tell us how we can predict one measure from another if a relationship exists. If we find evidence that a relationship exists, we must be careful not to conclude that one factor *caused* another to change, as we do when we conduct experiments. Causation from one factor to another may not exist or may be in a different direction than we think it is. This sort of error is easy to make from research results presented in the media. If we hear that a study showed a link between a lot of coffee drinking and certain types of cancers, we might be tempted to conclude that drinking a lot of coffee can cause cancer. However, there are other types of relationships that could exist to produce the relationship reported in the study. It's possible that people who are developing cancer already drink a lot of coffee because it eases their symptoms. This would mean that the causal relationship is in the opposite direction to what we first concluded: Developing cancer causes one to drink a lot of coffee, not the other way around. It could also be that something else causes both things to happen. Perhaps people who are generally anxious drink a lot of coffee and are also more likely to develop certain types of cancer (e.g., due to chronic inflammation). In this case, it is the high level of anxiety that causes both the drinking of a lot of coffee and cancer, meaning that these factors are not directly related in a causal way. Instead, they are both related to a third factor that causes

FIGURE 12.1 ■ Some Possible Relationships Between Drinking Coffee and Developing Cancer

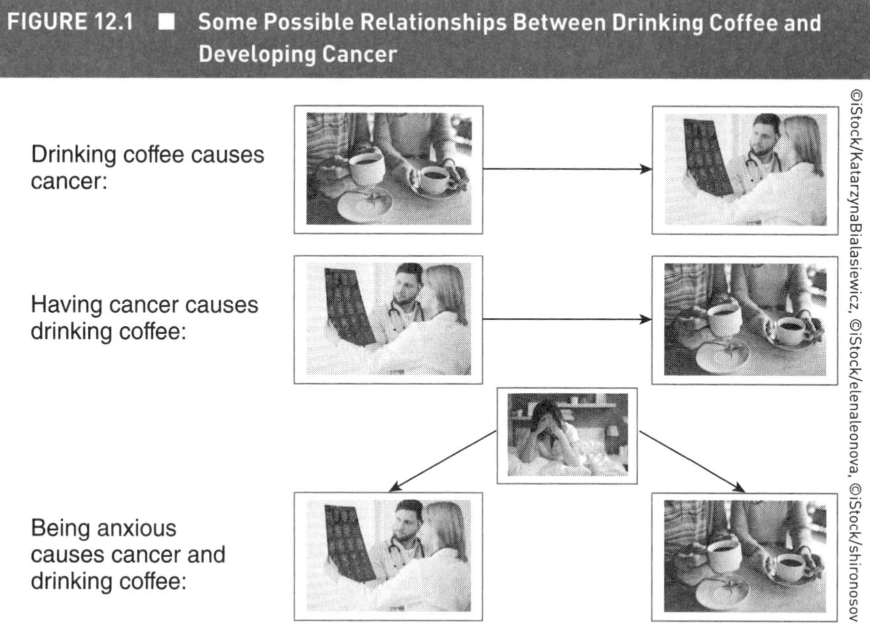
Drinking coffee causes cancer:
Having cancer causes drinking coffee:
Being anxious causes cancer and drinking coffee:
©iStock/KatarzynaBialasiewicz, ©iStock/elenaleonova, ©iStock/shironosov

both of them. Figure 12.1 illustrates these different types of relationships, showing that correlations do not always mean causation.

Statistical Relationships

In Chapter 9, we first examined a flowchart for statistical test decisions in inferential tests (see Figure 9.8). In the past several chapters, we focused on tests that compared means in the left portion of this chart. In this chapter, we are focusing on tests for relationships in the right portion of the chart. Figure 12.2 shows the right portion from Figure 9.8 for tests designed to examine relationships between variables. This section of the chart is separated according to the type of scale the data for a study are measured on: ratio or interval or nominal or ordinal. This chapter will examine tests used for ratio or interval data. Chapter 13 will examine a common test that can be used for nominal or ordinal data.

Recall that ratio or interval data involve numerical responses or measures that are equally spaced on the scale. In many cases, these scales are also continuous scales of measurement in which the units of measure can be divided into smaller and smaller units (e.g., distance can be in yards or meters and then divided into feet and further divided into inches or centimeters). The *t* tests and ANOVAs used for comparing means are also appropriate for ratio or interval data, as discussed in the previous chapters in this section of the text, but when testing relationships with ratio or interval data, a common inferential test used is the **Pearson *r* test**. You will see this test listed in the chart in Figure 12.2 if you follow the decision tree down through the ratio or interval data to the descriptive

Pearson *r* test: A significance test used to determine whether a linear relationship exists between two variables measured on ratio or interval scales

FIGURE 12.2 ■ Portion of the Statistical Test Decision Flowchart for Testing Relationships

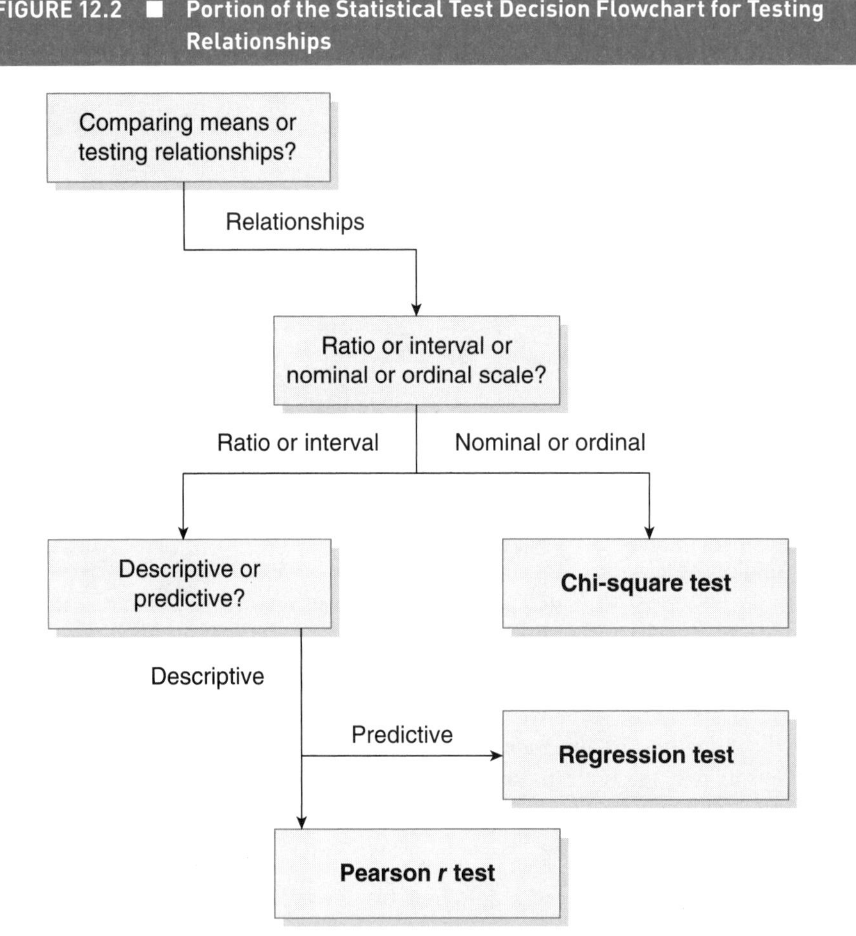

branch. The Pearson r is a value between −1.0 and +1.0 that indicates the size and direction of a relationship between two numerical measures. The larger the numerical value of the Pearson r, the stronger the relationship. The sign of the Pearson r value indicates the direction of the relationship, where +1.0 is the strongest possible positive relationship and −1.0 is the strongest possible negative relationship. A Pearson r of zero indicates no relationship between the variables. Note that the relationship we are considering with a Pearson r is a linear relationship.

Figure 12.3 presents example graphs of three different relationships. A graph of data points that can show the relationship between two variables is presented with one measure on the x-axis and the other measure on the y-axis and is called a *scatterplot*. Scatterplots were first introduced in Chapter 6. The scatterplots in Figure 12.3 show relationships with the Pearson rs of −1.0, 0, and +1.0. Each scatterplot shows a different possible relationship between two measures. The first is a perfect negative relationship. It shows that each data point (a data point represents the scores on the two measures for

FIGURE 12.3 ■ Three Types of Relationships Between Measures

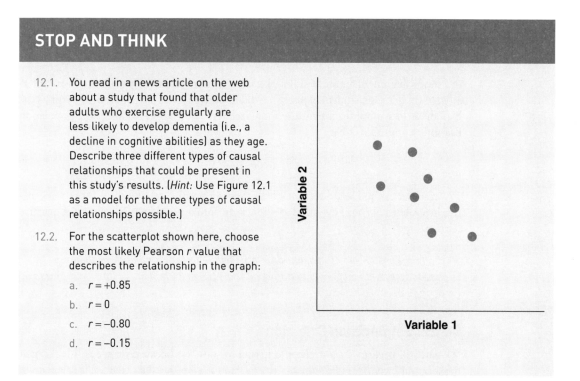

$r = -1.0$	$r = 0.0$	$r = 1.0$
Perfect negative correlation	No relationship	Perfect positive correlation

an individual in the sample) follows a straight line descending down from the top left of the graph. The middle graph shows no relationship. The data points do not cluster in any systematic way; they are spread across the whole graph. The last graph shows a perfect positive relationship. It is similar to the first graph, but the straight line ascends from the bottom left to the top right. Most data sets, however, will look like something in between these graphs—either on the positive or negative side of $r = 0$.

STOP AND THINK

12.1. You read in a news article on the web about a study that found that older adults who exercise regularly are less likely to develop dementia (i.e., a decline in cognitive abilities) as they age. Describe three different types of causal relationships that could be present in this study's results. (*Hint:* Use Figure 12.1 as a model for the three types of causal relationships possible.)

12.2. For the scatterplot shown here, choose the most likely Pearson *r* value that describes the relationship in the graph:

a. $r = +0.85$

b. $r = 0$

c. $r = -0.80$

d. $r = -0.15$

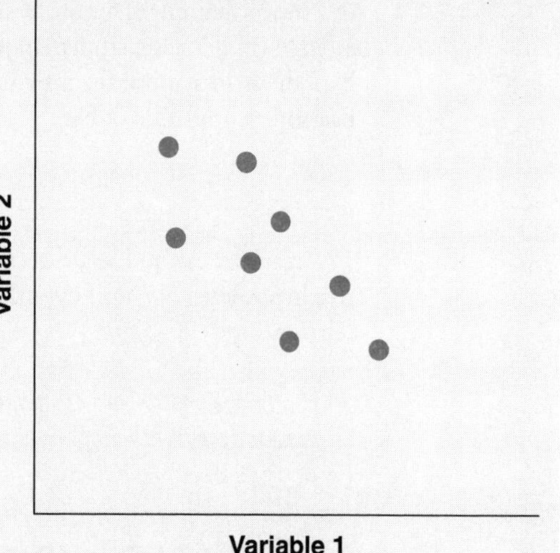

HYPOTHESIS TESTING WITH PEARSON *r*

Like the previous inferential statistics we have discussed, we can use Pearson *r* correlations to test hypotheses, but in this case the hypotheses will be about relationships between dependent variables. We can complete our hypothesis-testing steps for hypotheses about relationships just as we did for hypotheses about mean differences. But for a correlational study, we will predict a relationship (and perhaps its direction) for our alternative hypothesis and no relationship (and possibly one in the opposite direction from the alternative hypothesis) for our null hypothesis. The data collected in our study will involve two measured variables collected from a group of individuals. A Pearson *r* test will be the inferential statistic calculated in Step 4, and it is based on a ratio of how much our two measured variables of interest change together versus how much they change in total. In other words, a Pearson *r* is a ratio of two different variability measures calculated from the two dependent variables in our data.

Let's begin our hypothesis testing with a hypothetical study looking at the relationship between the number of hours that students study for a final exam and their final exam scores.

Step 1: State Hypotheses

In Step 1, we will state our hypotheses for the relationship between hours of study and final exam scores. Our alternative hypothesis for this relationship will be one-tailed, because we will predict that the relationship is positive—the more hours of study, the higher the exam score:

H_1: *In the population of students, there is a positive relationship between the number of hours that students study for an exam and the score on the exam.*

Notice that our hypothesis still makes a prediction about the population we're interested in (in this case, students), just as we did in previous chapters. We can also express the hypothesis in symbol form by using the Greek letter ρ (rho) to stand for the population Pearson *r* correlation value:

$$\rho_{students} > 0$$

Because we've made a directional hypothesis (a positive relationship) for our alternative hypothesis, our null hypothesis will include both a correlation of zero and a negative relationship:

H_0: *In the population of students, there is no relationship or a negative relationship between the number of hours that students study for an exam and the score on the exam* or $\rho_{students} \leq 0$.

Step 2: Set Decision Criterion

We will still need to set a decision criterion for our test because we are still looking at the location of our sample statistic (the Pearson *r* from our data that we'll calculate in

Step 4) within the distribution of Pearson *r* values expected when the null hypothesis is true. As we did with the *t* test, we will consider the most extreme scores in this distribution as evidence against the null hypothesis (within both positive and negative tails for a nondirectional hypothesis and within either the positive or negative tail for a directional hypothesis). If our alpha level is set at 0.05, this will create critical regions in this distribution for rejecting the null hypothesis. However, unlike the distribution of sample means, the distribution of *r* values will stop at values of +1.0 on the high end and −1.0 on the low end because *r* cannot be a value beyond +1.0 or −1.0. Thus, the shape will be a bit different but will still depend on the sample size in our study. We will still use a table of critical values (see Appendix F) to compare with our calculated Pearson *r* in Step 5.

Remember that the logic of our hypothesis test is to consider the probability of obtaining the data in our study if the null hypothesis is true (i.e., there is no relationship between the variables). That is what we are measuring with the *p* value that comes from the test. A Pearson *r* test will provide the same kind of *p* value that our previous tests provided, giving us the probability of obtaining our data when the null hypothesis is true. If this *p* value is low enough (i.e., at our chosen alpha level or lower), we will use that as evidence against the null hypothesis.

Step 3: Collect Sample Data

To make the calculations for this example easier to understand, let's consider a sample size of only $n = 5$ for this study. It would certainly be better to test our hypothesis with a larger sample size, but for our hand calculations, we will look at five data points. The measures for the number of hours studied and exam score variables from our five study participants are as follows:

	Number of hours studied	Final exam score
Subject #1	6	96
Subject #2	1	72
Subject #3	5	88
Subject #4	3	72
Subject #5	3	78

To calculate the Pearson *r* statistic in Step 4, we will need to know some of the descriptive statistics for this data set. Specifically, we will need the means for each variable so that we can calculate the sum of squared deviations for the variables and a new measure known as the **sum of products**. The sum of products is the product (i.e., multiplication) of the deviations from the mean for each measure, summed across all the participants in the study. We will calculate these values in Step 4, but for now, we just need the means for the two measures:

sum of products: The sum of the products of the squared deviations from the mean of the scores for each variable

$$M_{HoursStudied} = 3.6 \text{ hr}; M_{ExamScore} = 81.2$$

Figure 12.4 shows a scatterplot of these data. In this figure, the data points are closely clustered together and slope up toward the top right of the graph, indicating a strong positive relationship between the variables.

Step 4: Calculate Statistics

As with the other inferential statistics, the Pearson *r* value is a ratio of variance terms. It is the calculation of the sum of products (*SP*) divided by the square root of the product of the individual sums of squares for each variable (SS_X and SS_Y):

$$r = \frac{SP}{\sqrt{SS_X SS_Y}}$$

SP is the sum of products, SS_X is the sum of squared deviations for one of the dependent variables (the one that appears on the x-axis of a scatterplot), and SS_Y is the sum of squared deviations for the other dependent variable (the one that appears on the y-axis of a scatterplot). If we are interested in predicting one variable from the other (e.g., predicting the final exam score using the number of hours studied score), then the variable that predicts is our *X* variable (also called the *predictor variable*) and the one being predicted is our *Y* variable (also called the *response variable*).

FIGURE 12.4 ■ Scatterplot of Data for Number of Hours Studied and Final Exam Score

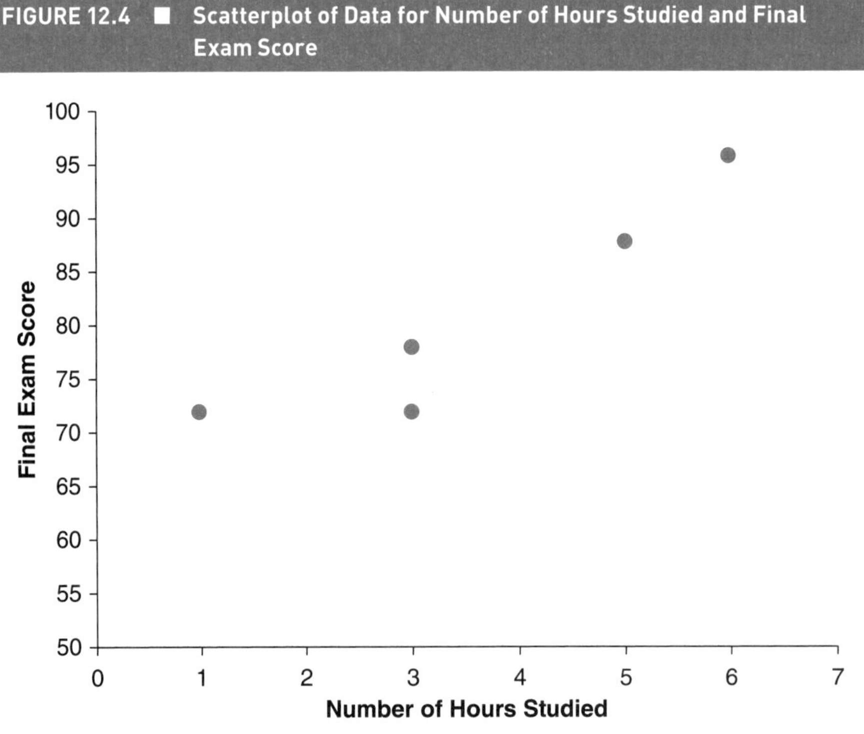

Now, let's begin our calculations using the data and means presented in Step 3. We will start with the SS_X and SS_Y terms because these are values we have calculated in past chapters, and they should be familiar to you. SS_X is the sum of squared deviations for our X variable: number of hours studied.

$$SS_X = \left[(6-3.6)^2 + (1-3.6)^2 + (5-3.6)^2 + (3-3.6)^2 + (3-3.6)^2\right]$$
$$= [5.76 + 6.76 + 1.96 + .36 + .36] = 15.2$$

and

$$SS_Y = \left[(96-81.2)^2 + (72-81.2)^2 + (88-81.2)^2 + (72-81.2)^2 + (78-81.2)^2\right]$$
$$= [219.04 + 84.64 + 46.24 + 84.64 + 10.24] = 444.8$$

These terms will make up the denominator of the Pearson r value. Now we just need our sum of products term. We will also use the deviations from the mean for SP, but we will multiply these for each subject across the variables instead of squaring them as we did in the sum of squares.

$$SP = \begin{bmatrix}(6-3.6)(96-81.2)+(1-3.6)(72-81.2)+(5-3.6)(88-81.2)+\\(3-3.6)(72-81.2)+(3-3.6)(78-81.2)\end{bmatrix}$$
$$= [(2.4)(14.8)+(-2.6)(-9.2)+(1.4)(6.8)+(-.6)(-9.2)+(-.6)(-3.2)]$$
$$= [35.52 + 23.92 + 9.52 + 5.52 + 1.92] = 76.4$$

Notice that the SP term is positive in this case. If you examine the details of the calculation that was just given, you may notice that the individual terms can also be negative (they are products, not squares). Because we are calculating products for SP, it can be a negative value. Thus, the SP term will determine whether the Pearson r is a positive value, representing a positive relationship, or a negative value, representing a negative relationship.

Now we are ready to calculate the Pearson r using our SP, SS_X, and SS_Y values.

$$r = \frac{SP}{\sqrt{SS_X SS_X}} = \frac{+76.4}{\sqrt{(15.2)(444.8)}} = \frac{+76.4}{\sqrt{6760.96}} = \frac{+76.4}{82.22} = +.93$$

The Pearson $r = +0.93$ indicates a rather strong positive relationship between number of hours studied and final exam score. But we still need to complete Step 5 to decide if we have evidence against the null hypothesis that the relationship between these variables is negative or does not exist in the population of students. The last value we need to calculate in Step 4 to assist us in Step 5 is the degrees of freedom. For a Pearson r correlation, $df = n - 2$. This is because we use up one degree of freedom for each variable in the calculation of its mean. For this calculation, remember that n refers to the number of subjects per group. We have only one group of subjects in this study; each dependent variable is measured once from each subject. Thus, $N = n = 5$ so $df = 5 - 2 = 3$. Now we are ready for Step 5 in which we will make the decision to reject or retain the null hypothesis.

Step 5: Make a Decision

To complete our test, we need to find the Pearson r critical value for our one-tailed test with $\alpha = 0.05$. Appendix F contains the critical values for a Pearson r with separate columns for different alpha levels and whether we are conducting a one- or two-tailed test. Rows in this appendix indicate critical values based on degrees of freedom. With a one-tailed test and $\alpha = 0.05$, we will look in the first column of the appendix. The row for $df = 3$ shows a critical r value of ± 0.805. Our calculated r of $+0.93$ is higher than this critical value, indicating that our calculated r is in the critical region. Thus, we can reject the null hypothesis and conclude that there is a positive relationship between number of hours studied and final exam score, as we predicted.

CONDUCTING A PEARSON *r* TEST USING SPSS

We can also use SPSS to conduct a Pearson r hypothesis test. Let's consider a new example in this section. Suppose we were interested in the relationship between age and memory ability. To measure this relationship, we give a sample of participants a task to mail a postcard back to us in exactly 5 days. We measure the age in years for each participant and then measure the number of days late that the postcard was mailed based on the postmark on the postcards we receive (with a score of zero days late if the card is mailed on time). These data are shown in Table 12.1. To conduct a Pearson r test using SPSS, we will enter the age and memory data into the data window as they appear in Table 12.1. Thus, the data window should contain two columns of data: age in years and number of days the postcard was late for each participant.

TABLE 12.1 ■ Data for Age or Memory Example

Participant number	Age	Number of days
1	81	1
2	77	0
3	69	0
4	73	2
5	89	0
6	67	1
7	65	1
8	70	0
9	78	2
10	75	0
11	21	3

Participant number	Age	Number of days
12	18	10
13	19	8
14	24	7
15	20	5
16	21	8
17	22	7
18	18	6
19	19	7
20	20	9

To run the Pearson *r* test, choose the Bivariate test in the Correlate option of the Analyze menu. Click the two variables into the Variables box. The Pearson *r* test box should be clicked. You can also choose to conduct either a two-tailed test (either a positive or negative relationship is predicted) or a one-tailed test if the prediction is for a specific type (positive or negative) of relationship. Two-tailed tests are the default, so you will need to click the other box to change to a one-tailed test in those cases. We will conduct a two-tailed test for these data to consider both a positive and a negative relationship that might exist between age and this memory ability, so no change is needed for this example. Click OK to run the test. The Correlations box in the output (see Figure 12.5) indicates

FIGURE 12.5 ■ SPSS Output for a Pearson *r* Test

Correlations

Correlations

		Age in Years	Number of Days Late
Age in Years	Pearson Correlation	1	-.900**
	Sig. (two-tailed)		.000
	N	20	20
Number of Days Late	Pearson Correlation	-.900**	1
	Sig. (two-tailed)	.000	
	N	20	20

** Correlation is significant at the 0.01 level (2-tailed).

SUMMARY OF STEPS

- Enter the data in the data window with each measure in a separate column.
- Choose the Correlate option from the Analyze menu.
- Select the Bivariate test from the test choices.
- Click each of your measured variables over to the Variables box (you can click more than two variables at once if you have more than two to analyze).
- Click the Pearson test box to select this test.
- The default is a two-tailed test, so if you have a one-tailed test, click that option in the window.
- Click OK to run the test; the Pearson *r* and associated *p* value will appear in the Output window.

STOP AND THINK

12.3. For a correlational study looking at the relationship between mood score and outside high temperature recorded on a particular day, we find $r(58) = -0.75$, $p = 0.002$. With this test result, what can we conclude about the relationship between mood and weather temperature? Looking at the statistics reported, from how many subjects was mood measured in this study?

12.4. For the data that follows, conduct a Pearson *r* test to determine if a significant relationship exists between the variables. If there is a significant relationship, indicate if the relationship is positive or negative.

Student's GPA: 3.56, 2.79, 3.01, 3.95, 4.00, 2.90, 3.35, 3.67, 3.77, 3.30, 2.75, 3.04

Number of Hours Spent Playing Video Games per Week: 12, 25, 45, 15, 20, 50, 16, 25, 40, 15, 40, 20

the Pearson *r* value (the sign indicates the direction of relationship) in the first row and the *p* value in the second row. For our example, the variables are significantly related (negatively) with $r = -0.90$ and $p < 0.001$. In other words, in this study as age increased, the number of days it took participants to remember to mail the card decreased. Thus, the older the participant was, the closer they remembered to mail the postcard to the date requested.

REGRESSION ANALYSES

If your goal is to predict a score on one variable from the score on another, regression will help you do that (see Figure 12.2 for predictive relationships). Regression analyses will provide the equation for the line that best fits the data. If you consider the data presented in the scatterplot in Figure 12.4, you can imagine a straight line passing through these data points that is as close as possible to all the data points in the graph. A regression analysis will give us the equation for that line.

We will use some of the same calculations we conducted for our Pearson *r* calculation to find the equation for the best-fit line to our data. Our equation is based on the equation of a line, which is $Y = X\,(slope) + intercept$, where *Y* is a score on the *Y* variable, *X* is a score on the *X* variable, *slope* is the amount of slant of the line (steeper slant = higher slope value), and the *intercept* is the value of *Y* where the line crosses the *y*-axis. This equation is often expressed as $Y = Xb + a$, such that *a* is the intercept and *b* is the slope. Because the *X* and *Y* values are the scores on the variables we measured, we do not need to calculate these values for our equation, but we do need to calculate values for *a* and *b* using our data to find the equation. The values for both *a* and *b* will depend on the strength and direction of the linear relationship between the two measured variables. As an example of how to calculate these values, we will go back to the example looking at number of hours studied and final exam score.

Slope

The first part of the equation we will calculate is the slope. This calculation is based on the ratio of the sum of products term and sum of squared deviations for the *X* variable (our predictor variable). Thus, the slope for the best-fit line equation to predict final exam score from the number of hours studied is as follows:

$$b = \frac{SP}{SS_x} = \frac{+76.4}{15.2} = 5.03$$

Note that if the *SP* term is positive, the slope will be positive and the line will slant up to the right, but if the *SP* term is negative, the slope will be negative and the line will slant down to the right.

Intercept

Now that we have calculated the slope value, we can use it and the means of the *X* and *Y* variables to calculate the intercept where the line will cross the y-axis. We will use this equation:

$$a = \overline{Y} - b\overline{X} = 81.2 - (5.03)(3.6) = 81.2 - 18.11 = 63.09$$

This means the line equation for the best-fit line to our data is this:

$$Y = 5.03X + 63.09$$

This line will pass through the means for the *X* and *Y* variables on our scatterplot and show the line that best describes the linear relationship between number of hours studied and final exam score (see Figure 12.6).

To show you how this is useful, suppose you wanted to use this equation to predict our exam based on how many hours you planned to study for the exam. You want to do well on the exam, but you need time to study for two other exams that same week, so you want to make sure your planned study time is optimal. Your plan is to study for 6 hr for the exam; what score do you expect to receive with this amount of study? We can

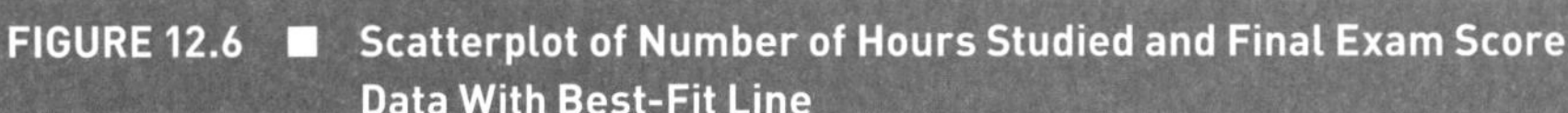

FIGURE 12.6 ■ Scatterplot of Number of Hours Studied and Final Exam Score Data With Best-Fit Line

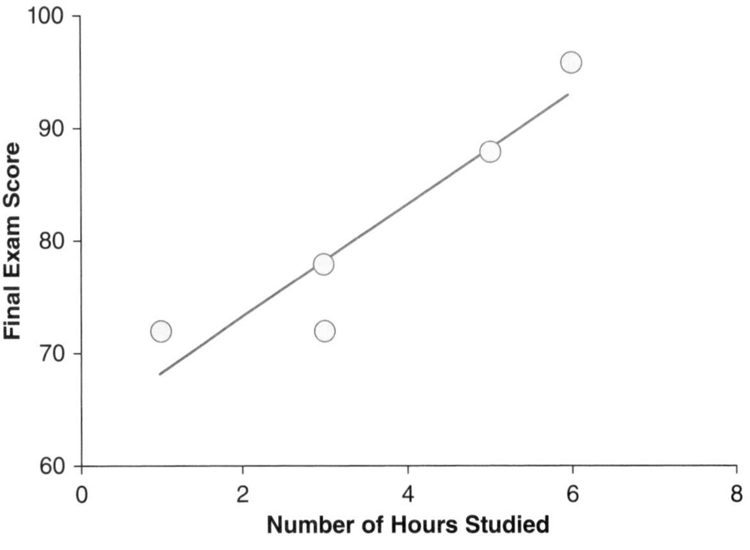

calculate a predicted score using the equation we found: $Y = 5.03X + 63.09$. To make the prediction, you need to enter in the hours you plan to study as X in the equation (this is the predictor variable):

$$Y = 5.03(6) + 63.09 = 30.18 + 63.09 = 93.27$$

Using this equation, you can predict you will get about 93% on the exam, so 6 hr of study should be enough for you to get an A.

R^2 Fit Statistic

linear regression: A statistical technique that determines the best fit line to a set of data to allow prediction of the score on one variable from the score on the other variable

R^2: Fit statistic indicating how well an equation fits the data

We have the equation for the best-fit line that we can use to predict the value of our Y variable (the response variable) from a value of our X variable (the predictor variable). But how accurate will our prediction be? This depends on how well the best-fit line fits (gets close to) the data points. If the line gets very close to the data points, our prediction will be good, but if the data points are spread out across the graph and our line does not get very close to all of them, then our prediction may not be very accurate. Thus, when we conduct a **linear regression**, it is important to look at an accuracy measure of how well the best-fit line fits the data so we will know how accurate our predictions will be. A fit statistic can help us determine the accuracy of our best-fit line. For linear regression, we can use R^2 as the fit statistic. R^2 is a measure of how much of the variability in one measure is explained by the value of the other measure. In other words, it represents how much of the change in the Y variable is related to the change in the X variable.

R^2 is easy to determine for a linear regression if we know the Pearson r value—it is simply r^2. However, R^2 can be used as a fit statistic for other kinds of relationships as well (e.g., nonlinear relationships; see the last section in this chapter) and is calculated in a different way for those relationships.

R^2: Fit Statistic Indicating How Well an Equation Fits the Data

For our example for predicting exam score from the number of hours studied using linear regression,

$$R^2 = (.93)^2 = .86$$

This tells us that 86% of the variability in final exam scores is explained by the number of hours that students studied for the exam. This represents a good fit to the data and tells us that our predictions will be fairly accurate.

Conducting a Linear Regression Using SPSS

SPSS can be used to conduct a linear regression for measured variables as well. We will once again use the age and days late in mailing the postcard data in Table 12.1 as our example. To determine the best-fit line for these data using SPSS, we will use the Regression option in the Analyze menu. We will choose the Linear option from Regression and then define our X and Y variables by clicking them over to the boxes. In this example, we want to use age to predict the number of days late the postcard was mailed, so age will be the X or independent variable (predictor variable), and number of days late will be the Y or dependent variable (response variable) for this analysis. We can click these variables into the boxes and then click OK to run the analysis.

Several sets of boxes appear in the Output window for our linear regression (see Figure 12.7), so we will need to find the pieces we need to build our linear equation. Remember that our line equation is $Y = Xb + a$, so we need to find the slope (b) and the intercept (a) in the output. Both values are listed in the last box under B for Unstandardized Coefficients. The slope is listed in the line with the variable Age in Years (−0.113), and the intercept is listed in the row labeled *Constant* (9.209). With these values, we can state our best-fit line equation as this:

$$Y = -.113X + 9.209$$

This equation will allow us to predict the number of days late for the postcard mailing using the subject's age in years. However, we do not yet know how accurate our prediction will be—we need to also look at the R^2 value to know how much of the variability in days late is explained by the subject's age. We can find the R^2 value in the Model Summary box at the top of the Output under R Square: 0.811. This value is quite high, so our prediction will be fairly accurate, although R^2 values of 0.90 and higher are generally preferred to ensure good accuracy in our predictions.

FIGURE 12.7 ■ SPSS Output for Linear Regression

Model Summary

Model	R	R Square	Adjusted R Square	Std. Error of the Estimate
1	.900[a]	.811	.800	1.59066

a. Predictors: (Constant), Age in Years

ANOVA[a]

Model		Sum of Squares	df	Mean Square	F	Sig.
1	Regression	195.006	1	195.006	77.071	.000[b]
	Residual	45.544	18	2.530		
	Total	240.550	19			

a. Dependent Variable: Number of Days Late

b. Predictors: (Constant), Age in Years

Coefficients[a]

Model		Unstandardized Coefficients		Standardized Coefficients	t	Sig.
		B	Std. Error	Beta		
1	(Constant)	9.209	.707		13.035	.000
	Age in Years	-.113	.013	-.900	-8.779	.000

a. Dependent Variable: Number of Days Late

SUMMARY OF STEPS

- Enter the data in the data window with each measured variable in a separate column.
- Choose the Regression option in the Analyze menu.
- Select the Linear type of relationship from the list.
- Click your predictor (*X*) variable into the Independent variable box.
- Click your response (*Y*) variable into the Dependent variable box.
- Click OK to run the analysis.
- Find the intercept labeled *Constant* and the slope labeled with the predictor variable in the Coefficients table of the Output window; the R^2 will appear in the Model Summary table.

NONLINEAR RELATIONSHIPS

The analyses presented in this chapter examine linear relationships between measured variables. However, relationships between variables can exist that are not functionally linear. For example, suppose that in our study looking at the relationship between number of hours studied and final exam score, we had also measured the students' anxiety level with a 1 to 10 rating scale just before they took their final exam (higher ratings indicate more anxiety). With this additional variable of anxiety score, we can examine the relationship between anxiety level and final exam score to see if there is a relationship. Our data might look something like this:

	Anxiety rating	Final exam score
Subject #1	5	96
Subject #2	1	72
Subject #3	7	88
Subject #4	10	72
Subject #5	2	78

You might notice in looking at these values that anxiety rating is not consistently increasing or decreasing with final score. Instead, it might look like there is no relationship. But let's look at a scatterplot of these data points shown in Figure 12.8. These data points look more like an inverted U shape than a straight line. Thus, a quadratic equation is likely a better fit to these data than a linear equation. In this case, a nonlinear regression would be better to conduct than a linear regression to examine the possibility of a nonlinear relationship. Looking at a scatterplot of your data is a good idea before deciding

FIGURE 12.8 ■ Scatterplot of Anxiety Ratings and Final Exam Score Data

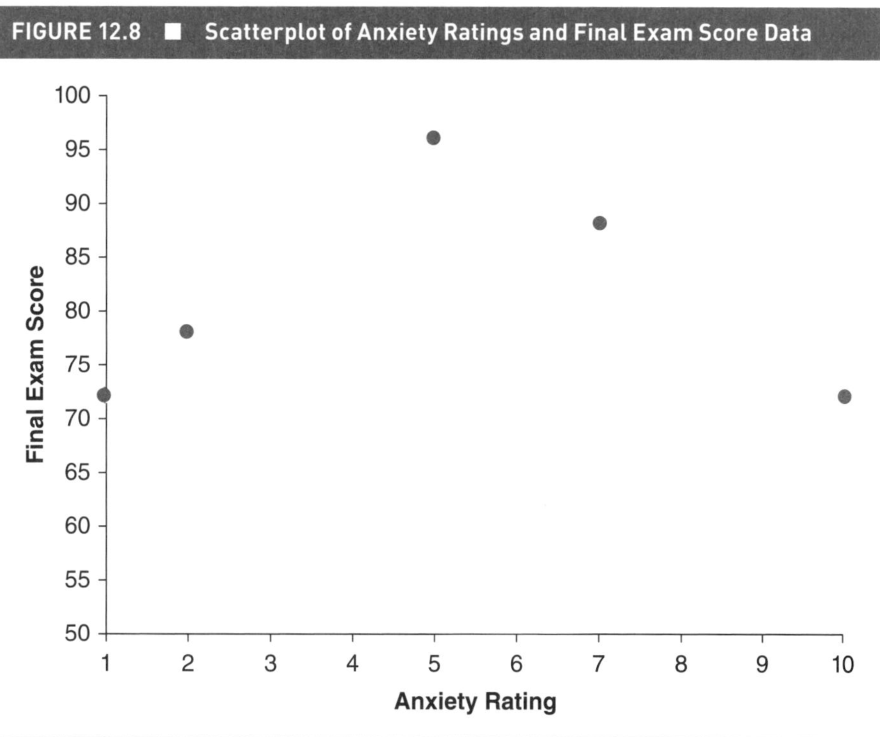

what kind of equation you want to fit to your data if you do not have a theoretical prediction about the form of the relationship before you start your study. However, this is only a starting place: You should not draw conclusions about the relationship or how well a function fits your data without first conducting a regression analysis and examining a fit statistic.

Calculation Summary

sum of products: The sum of the products of the squared deviations from the mean of the scores for each variable

Pearson r*:* The sum of products divided by the square root of the product of the sum of squares of the *X* variable and the sum of squares of the *Y* variable

slope: The sum of products divided by the sum of squares for the *X* variable

intercept: The mean of the *Y* variable minus the slope times the mean of the *X* variable

THINKING ABOUT RESEARCH

A summary of a research study in psychology is given here. As you read the summary, think about the following questions:

1. Identify the dependent variables in this study that provided a test of the researchers' hypothesis.
2. What are the advantages and disadvantages of conducting this study as a correlational study instead of an experiment?
3. Based on the scatterplot and the Pearson *r* shown in Figure 12.9, is the relationship between the measures positive or negative? How do you know?
4. Using the reported sample size, an alpha level of 0.05, and Appendix F, determine if the Pearson *r* value shown in Figure 12.9 is significant or not.
5. Both of the measures in this study were based on self-reports from the participants. What are the disadvantages of using self-report measures in research?

Research Study. Inzlicht, M., McKay, L., & Aronson, J. (2006). Stigma as ego depletion: How being the target of prejudice affects self-control. *Psychological Science, 17,* 262–269.

Note: Study 1 from this article is described here.

Purpose of the Study. This study was designed to examine the relationship between stigma and one's sense of their own self-control. In Study 1, the researchers examined the correlation between one's sensitivity to race-based prejudice and self-reported self-regulation abilities in Black college students. They predicted that higher sensitivity to prejudice would be related to lower self-regulation ability.

Method of the Study. Black university students ($N = 38$) completed two surveys to measure

FIGURE 12.9 ■ Scatterplot From the Inzlicht et al. (2006) Study

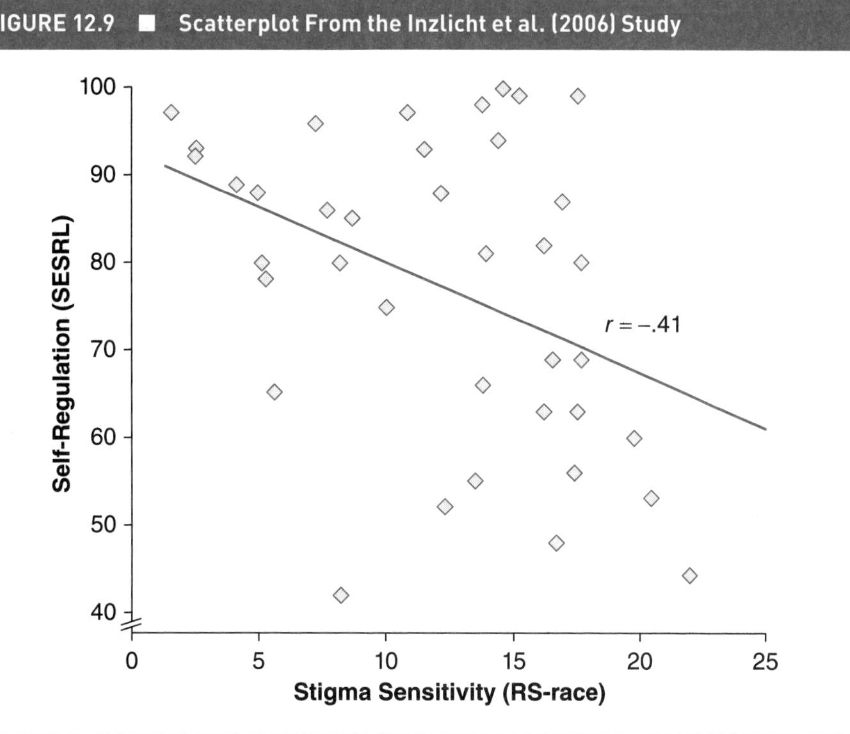

Source: Inzlicht, McKay, and Aronson (2006).

sensitivity to race-based stigma and self-regulation abilities. The stigma sensitivity measure contained 12 scenarios describing situations with a negative outcome. Participants read each scenario and imagined themselves in the situation. They then rated how concerned they were and how likely it was that the outcome was due to their race. The self-regulation measure contained 11 items for participants to rate concerning the confidence they had in their abilities (e.g., motivating themselves to do schoolwork, studying when there were other things to do).

Results of the Study. Figure 12.9 shows a scatterplot of the stigma sensitivity and self-regulation scores with the calculated Pearson *r* score.

Conclusions of the Study. The researchers concluded that Black college students who are more sensitive to race-based stigma also reported lower self-regulation abilities. Follow-up studies in this article also showed that students who had the race-based stigma activated showed reduced self-control in cognitive and motor control tasks.

Chapter Summary

- **How do hypothesis tests differ across experiments and correlational studies?**
Hypothesis tests differ for experiments and correlational studies in the way hypotheses are made and the inferential statistics that are calculated. In correlational studies, we make hypotheses about relationships and whether they are positive or negative instead of about mean differences. We then test the null hypothesis by using tests designed to tell us about the strength and direction of the relationship that exists between two measured variables, such as a Pearson *r* test.
- **What can you learn from testing relationships between measures?**
When we look for relationships between measures, we can determine the strength and direction of those relationships and if they are significant. We can also determine the equation that will allow us to predict the value of one variable from the value on the other variable using regression analysis.
- **What can you learn from conducting a regression analysis?**
Regression analyses provide the best equation for predicting the value of one variable from the value on the other variable. We can also find a fit statistic that can tell us how accurate those predictions will be.
- **What does it mean to find the best-fit line for a set of data?**
The best-fit line for a set of data is the line that comes the closest to the most data points in a scatterplot of the data. The closer the line comes to the data points overall, the better the linear equation will describe the data.
- **How much causal information can be gained from correlation and regression hypothesis tests?**
We cannot determine causation from correlation and regression tests. The best we can do is use regression to predict the value of one variable from the value on the other variable with a specific level of accuracy. However, this does not tell us that one variable is *causing* the value of the other variable.

Test Yourself

1. In correlational studies, ________________ is not as well-tested as it is in experiments.
    a. a relationship
    b. a linear relationship
    c. causation
    d. a scatterplot
2. Creating a ________________ is a good way to view the type of relationship that exists between two measured variables.
    a. scatterplot
    b. linear regression
    c. bar graph
    d. sum of squares

3. A Pearson r correlation is a ratio of the _______________ and the _______________.
   a. difference between variable means, sum of products
   b. sum of products, scatterplot
   c. change in variables together, total variability
   d. both a and c
4. A _______________ analysis can help you predict the value of one variable from the value of the other variable.
   a. scatterplot
   b. regression
   c. Pearson r
   d. sum of products
5. Which of the following is an appropriate null hypothesis for a Pearson r test?
   a. The means of the two variables do not differ in the population.
   b. There is no relationship between the two variables in the population.
   c. There is a negative relationship between the two variables in the sample.
   d. Both b and c.
6. In a linear regression, the X variable is the _______________ variable, and the Y variable is the _______________ variable.
   a. predictor, response
   b. response, predictor
7. Finding a significant relationship between two variables in a correlational study tells you that one of the variables caused the change in the other variable, even though you do not know which variable was the causal factor.
   a. True
   b. False
8. A Pearson r of +0.85 indicates a strong, positive relationship between the dependent variables.
   a. True
   b. False
9. A linear regression can determine the best-fit line to the data.
   a. True
   b. False
10. Regression analyses can only determine if a relationship between variables is linear.
    a. True
    b. False
11. For the following data sets, determine if there is a significant correlation between the following variables.

    Number of Books in One's Office: 155, 67, 25, 3, 80, 75, 15, 200, 67, 85, 55, 30

    Extraversion Score: 57, 97, 89, 40, 36, 98, 68, 75, 80, 43, 55, 85
12. A study reported $r(98) = 0.32$. Is this a significant correlation? How do you know?
    a. Determine if there is a relationship between the following measures:

       Number of Texts Sent Per Hour: 12, 5, 18, 3, 0, 22, 10, 7, 16, 7, 2, 1, 8

(Continued)

(Continued)

Score on an Extraversion Questionnaire:
18, 7, 22, 6, 6, 29, 15, 10, 19, 17, 11, 9, 13

b. Using these data, find the best fit regression line equation that allows you to predict number of texts sent from extraversion score.

Visit **edge.sagepub.com/mcbridermstats** to find the answers to the Test Yourself questions above, as well as quizzes, flashcards, and other resources to help you accomplish your coursework goals.

13

CHI-SQUARE TESTS

CONSIDER THE FOLLOWING QUESTIONS AS YOU READ CHAPTER 13

- What is the difference between a parametric and a nonparametric test?
- What does it mean that a nonparametric test is less powerful than a parametric test?
- How can we test relationships across categorical variables?
- What is the expected frequency?
- What does a chi-square test tell us about relationships between categorical variables?

LEARNING OBJECTIVES FOR CHAPTER 13

- Conduct a hypothesis test for relationships between categorical variables.
- Calculate crosstabs for expected frequencies.
- Calculate a chi-square statistic.
- Understand how power is affected when using a nonparametric test.

Imagine that we are interested in whether class standing and grade in a class are related. This could be helpful in knowing which year it is best to take a specific required course. If, for example, juniors and seniors get higher grades than freshmen and sophomores, perhaps it is best to take the class in later years in college. But in this case, class standing and grade (i.e., A, B, C, D, F) are not continuous variables measured in numbers. Instead,

FIGURE 13.1 ■ Portion of the Statistical Test Decision Flowchart for Testing Relationships

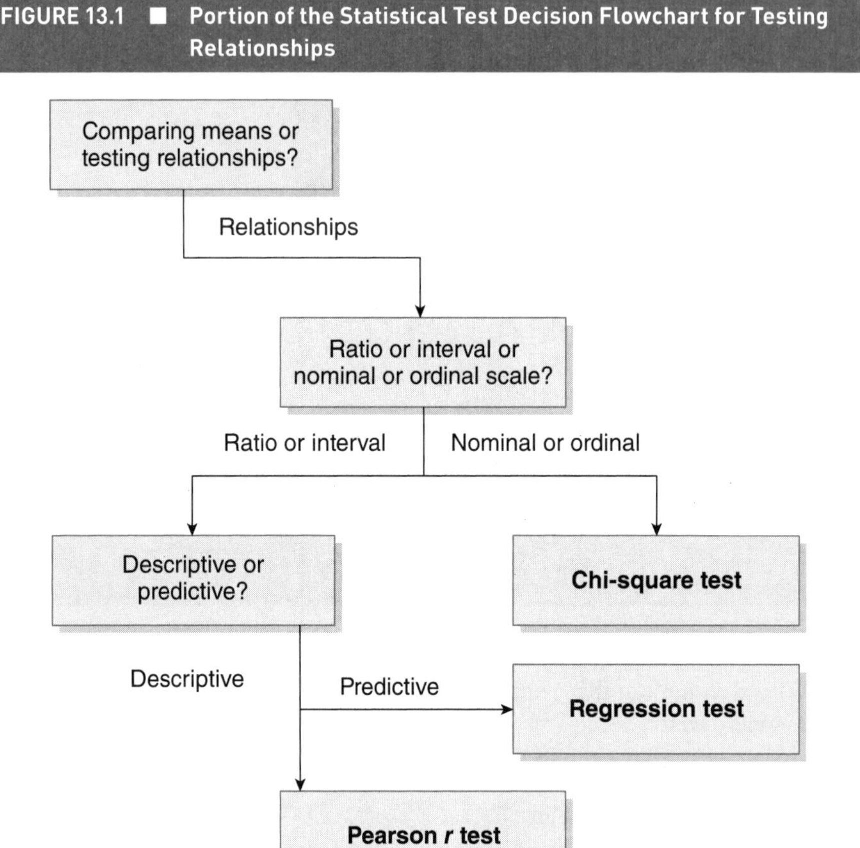

chi-square (χ^2) test: A significance test used to determine whether a relationship exists between two variables measured on nominal or ordinal scales

nonparametric test: An inferential statistics test that can be used to test hypotheses about categorical variables

parametric test: An inferential statistics test that can be used to test hypotheses about continuous variables

they are ordinal variables with categorical levels. Thus, the Pearson *r* and linear regression tests we discussed in Chapter 12 will not be the best tests to examine the relationship we want to know about. Figure 13.1 once again shows the portion of the flowchart (first seen in Figure 9.8) for testing relationships. A quick look at Figure 13.1 shows that a chi-square test is one we can use to test relationships between these variables.

In Chapter 12, we discussed the tests designed for descriptive and predictive relationships between variables measured on ratio and interval scales of measurement. In this chapter, we will examine a common test used for relationships between categorical variables measured on nominal and ordinal scales: a **chi-square** (χ^2) **test**.

PARAMETRIC VERSUS NONPARAMETRIC TESTS

The chi-square test is what is known as a **nonparametric test** to set it apart from the type of test used for continuous variables (called a **parametric test**). Parametric tests are the tests we have discussed in this text so far that involve calculations for numerical data. If data are not in numerical form but instead involve categories, these calculations cannot be computed (primarily because the distributions will not be normal in shape, as required by the assumptions for these tests). Thus, for categorical variables, we need a different kind of test—a nonparametric test. For nonparametric tests, the data are typically in the form of frequencies for different categories on a variable, such as how many students in the class were juniors and how many students earned an A grade. They are useful when we want to test hypotheses about categorical variables. However, they are not as powerful as parametric tests, so they should only be used when necessary. Recall that *power* is the ability to detect an effect or relationship when one exists in the population. In other words, when the power of a test is reduced, we are less likely to obtain a significant relationship, even if the relationship exists. This means our Type II error (the chance of retaining the null hypothesis when it is false) is higher for nonparametric tests. Therefore, we may need to conduct several studies to detect a relationship that exists for categorical variables.

STOP AND THINK

13.1. For each of the following sets of variables, indicate if a parametric or a nonparametric test is more appropriate to examine the relationship between the variables:

a. Percentage grade on final exam and number of hours of sleep the night before the exam
b. Students' expected letter grade in a course and the actual grade in the course
c. Preference rank of five different campus activities (e.g., 1st, 2nd, 3rd) and major in college
d. Score on a depression questionnaire (out of 100) and course satisfaction ratings (on a scale of 1 to 5)

13.2. Explain why we cannot calculate the mean and standard deviation for scores on a categorical variable.

OBSERVED VERSUS EXPECTED FREQUENCIES

The chi-square test will examine the relationship between categorical variables in terms of what frequencies are expected if there is no relationship between the variables (i.e., the null hypothesis). These expected frequencies are then compared with the frequencies observed in the data collected from the sample in our study to determine if the expected and observed frequencies differ significantly. If they do, then the null hypothesis is rejected, and you can conclude that a relationship exists between the variables.

Let's consider the expected frequencies for the class standing and grade example. Table 13.1 shows the cells for each possible combination of these two variables. We will fill in each cell with the frequency we would expect if there is no relationship between class standing and grade in the class. To calculate the expected frequencies ($f_{Expected}$), we first need to examine the data collected. Suppose there are 200 people in the course, and

TABLE 13.1 ■ Table of Cells for Class Standing and Grade in the Class

Grade or class standing	Freshman	Sophomore	Junior	Senior
A				
B				
C				
D				
F				

we obtain their class standing and course grades from the registrar's office on campus (with identifying information removed, of course).

To calculate the expected frequencies, we will use this formula:

$$f_{Expected} = \frac{f_{column} f_{row}}{n}$$

Here, f_{column} is the column total for that cell, and f_{row} is the row total for that cell. With this formula, we can calculate the expected frequency for each cell in Table 13.1. For example, the $f_{Expected}$ for Freshman and A is as follows:

$$f_{Expected} = \frac{50(30)}{200} = \frac{1500}{200} = 7.5$$

The data in the form of observed frequencies ($f_{Observed}$) are shown in the cells in Table 13.2. We will need the row and columns total frequencies for the calculations of expected frequencies; these totals are also shown in Table 13.2.

TABLE 13.2 ■ Table of Observed Frequencies for Class Standing and Grade in the Class in the Sample

Grade or class standing	Freshman	Sophomore	Junior	Senior	Row totals
A	3	6	10	11	30
B	21	20	25	4	70
C	12	15	15	18	60
D	8	6	6	5	25
F	6	3	4	2	15
Column totals	50	50	60	40	200

This $f_{Expected}$ will be placed in the first cell of the expected frequency table (see Table 13.3). Using this formula, we can calculate the rest of the $f_{Expected}$ values to complete Table 13.3. Note that the expected frequencies for the Freshman and Sophomore columns are identical because the column totals for these columns are the same. We will use the observed and expected frequencies to calculate the chi-square statistic in Step 4 of our hypothesis test in the next section.

TABLE 13.3 ■ Table of Expected Frequencies for Class Standing and Grade in the Class If There Is No Relationship Between These Variables

Grade or class standing	Freshman	Sophomore	Junior	Senior
A	7.5	7.5	9	6
B	17.5	17.5	21	14
C	15	15	18	12
D	6.25	6.25	7.5	5
F	3.75	3.75	4.5	3

CALCULATING A CHI-SQUARE BY HAND

Even though the chi-square test is a nonparametric test, we can still conduct a hypothesis test by using this statistic. The five steps of hypothesis testing will still apply. However, we will not consider a population parameter (e.g., μ, ρ) in our hypotheses because there are no parameters to estimate from our sample (e.g., sample means) in a nonparametric test. Instead, the hypotheses will simply be stated in terms of whether a relationship exists between the variables or not.

Step 1: State Hypotheses

As I mentioned in the previous section, the null hypothesis will predict no relationship between the variables. The alternative hypothesis will predict a relationship. If we find a significant difference between the expected and observed frequencies (calculated using the chi-square statistic), we can reject the null hypothesis. Thus, our null hypothesis is as follows:

H_0: *In the population of students, there is no relationship between class standing and the letter grade in the course.*

Our alternative hypothesis is this:

H_1: *In the population of students, there is a relationship between class standing and the letter grade in the course.*

Step 2: Set Decision Criterion

Like the other inferential statistics, the chi-square statistic has a distribution of values when the null hypothesis is true with a different shape based on the degrees of freedom. It cannot be negative; therefore, there is only a tail of extreme values on the positive end of the distribution, as with the F statistic. The critical region will be located in this positive tail bounded by the critical chi-square value determined by the degrees of freedom in our study. The size of this region is still based on the chosen alpha level. As with our previous tests, we will choose an alpha level of 0.05, setting the size of the critical region at 5% of the chi-square distribution.

Step 3: Collect Sample Data

We have already completed Step 3 for our example in the previous section (looking at expected versus observed frequencies). Our observed frequencies (i.e., our data) are shown in Table 13.2, and our calculated expected frequencies are shown in Table 13.3. We will use these frequencies to calculate our chi-square statistic in Step 4.

Step 4: Calculate Statistics

The chi-square statistic is calculated from the sum of the squared differences between the observed and expected frequencies divided by the expected frequencies. In other words, it uses the squared deviations between the frequencies divided by the frequency expected by chance when the null hypothesis is true. This is very similar to the ratios we calculated in our parametric tests, so it is based on the same logic as those tests. The formula is as follows:

$$\chi^2 = \Sigma \frac{\left(f_{Observed} - f_{Expected}\right)^2}{f_{Expected}}$$

From Tables 13.2 and 13.3, we can insert the frequencies for each cell.

$$\begin{aligned}
\chi^2 &= \Sigma \frac{\left(f_{Observed} - f_{Expected}\right)^2}{f_{Expected}} \\
&= \left[\frac{(3-7.5)^2}{7.5}\right] + \left[\frac{(21-17.5)^2}{17.5}\right] + \left[\frac{(12-15)^2}{15}\right] + \left[\frac{(8-6.25)^2}{6.25}\right] \\
&\quad + \left[\frac{(6-3.75)^2}{3.75}\right] + \left[\frac{(6-7.5)^2}{7.5}\right] + \left[\frac{(20-17.5)^2}{17.5}\right] + \left[\frac{(15-15)^2}{15}\right] \\
&\quad + \left[\frac{(6-6.25)^2}{6.25}\right] + \left[\frac{(3-3.75)^2}{3.75}\right] + \left[\frac{(10-9)^2}{9}\right] + \left[\frac{(25-21)^2}{21}\right] \\
&\quad + \left[\frac{(15-18)^2}{18}\right] + \left[\frac{(6-7.5)^2}{7.5}\right] + \left[\frac{(4-4.5)^2}{4.5}\right] + \left[\frac{(11-6)^2}{6}\right] \\
&\quad + \left[\frac{(4-14)^2}{14}\right] + \left[\frac{(18-12)^2}{12}\right] + \left[\frac{(5-5)^2}{5}\right] + \left[\frac{(2-3)^2}{3}\right] \\
&= 2.7 + .7 + .6 + .49 + 1.35 + .3 + .36 + 0 + .01 + .15 + .11 + .76 \\
&\quad + .5 + .3 + .06 + 4.17 + 7.14 + 3 + 0 + .33 \\
&= 23.03
\end{aligned}$$

We also need to calculate degrees of freedom to find the $\chi^2_{critical}$ value in Step 5. The degrees of freedom for a chi-square test depend on the number of columns and rows:

$$df = (\#Columns - 1)(\#Rows - 1) = (4-1)(5-1) = 3(4) = 12$$

With $df = 12$ and our $\alpha = 0.05$, we can move on to Step 5 to find the critical value and make a decision.

Step 5: Make a Decision

To complete our chi-square test, we need to find the $\chi^2_{critical}$ for 12 degrees of freedom and alpha level of 0.05. We will compare our calculated χ^2 to the $\chi^2_{critical}$. Appendix G contains the chi-square critical values. In this case, $\chi^2_{critical} = 21.03$, and our calculated $\chi^2 = 23.03$—for American Psychological Association (APA) style, include the *df* and *N* as well: $\chi^2(1, N = 200) = 23.03$. This means our calculated χ^2 is in the critical region (our calculated value is larger), and we can reject the null hypothesis. For this example, we can conclude that class standing and grade in the class are related. If we look back at Tables 13.2 and 13.3, we can examine where the observed and expected frequencies differ to determine the characteristics of the relationship: More As were earned by seniors, and fewer were earned by freshmen and sophomores than expected if there is no relationship between class standing and grade. This tells us that students taking the class as a senior tended to earn As more often than students who were freshmen and sophomores. But remember, this is a correlation and does not tell us that class standing has a causal relationship to grade earned. Other characteristics of the students may have cause them to take the class later in their college careers and earn higher grades.

CALCULATING A CHI-SQUARE TEST USING SPSS

Like the other tests conducted in previous chapters, SPSS can calculate a chi-square test for you. Because the data are category frequencies, you need to enter those categories in as your data in the data window to run the test. If you have two variables to compare, each row will contain two category labels, one for each variable. Consider the example included in Chapter 12 (see Table 12.1) that examined the variables of age and days late returning a postcard. Suppose that instead of continuous variables of age in years, we simply grouped the participants into two groups: younger and older adults. We could also consider accuracy of returning the postcard as a categorical variable—either they mailed the postcard on time or they did not (see Table 13.4). With these categorical variables, we can use a chi-square test to examine the relationship.

The data window in SPSS would be organized by variable columns with these categories. Table 13.4 shows the categorical data for this example. To run the chi-square analysis, choose the Crosstabs option in the Descriptive Statistics portion of the Analyze menu. Click one variable into the Row box and the other variable into the Column box. Choose the statistics tab to click the chi-square test from the list. Click Continue and then OK to begin the analysis.

TABLE 13.4 ■ Categorical Data for Chi-Square Analysis With Age and Postcard Mailing Accuracy Variables

Participant 1	Older	Yes	Participant 11	Younger	No
Participant 2	Older	Yes	Participant 12	Younger	No
Participant 3	Older	No	Participant 13	Younger	Yes
Participant 4	Older	Yes	Participant 14	Younger	Yes
Participant 5	Older	Yes	Participant 15	Younger	No
Participant 6	Older	No	Participant 16	Younger	No
Participant 7	Older	Yes	Participant 17	Younger	No
Participant 8	Older	Yes	Participant 18	Younger	Yes
Participant 9	Older	Yes	Participant 19	Younger	No
Participant 10	Older	Yes	Participant 20	Younger	Yes

The Output window from the test is shown in Figure 13.2. The second box in the output shows the observed frequencies from the data. The χ^2 value is shown in the box labeled *Chi-Square Tests*. The chi-square value of 3.333 is shown in the first row with its p value of 0.068. For this example, the relationship is not significant because the p value is larger than our alpha level of 0.05. In other words, the accuracy of returning the postcard on time did not depend on the age group of the participant when these variables were categorical.

Recall from Chapter 12 that the Pearson r correlation we conducted on these data was significant. In that case, we used continuous variables of age in years and number of days late and found that these variables were significantly related. This comparison across the tests illustrates the issue of power with nonparametric tests. With the categorical variables and nonparametric test used in this chapter, the power to detect a relationship is lower than the example in Chapter 12, and we failed to find a significant relationship. This illustrates how the use of continuous variables and a parametric test is a more powerful way to test hypotheses about populations.

SUMMARY OF STEPS

- Enter the categorical data in separate columns in the data window—be sure to define the values in the Variable View tab.
- Choose Descriptive Statistics from the Analyze menu.
- Select Crosstabs from the Descriptive Statistics options.
- Click one variable in the Row box and the other variable into the Column box.
- Click the Statistics tab, and check the Chi-Square box in the window.
- Click OK to run the test; the test and p values will appear in the Output window.

FIGURE 13.2 ■ SPSS Output From the Chi-Square Analysis

Crosstabs

Case Processing Summary

	Cases					
	Valid		Missing		Total	
	N	Percentage	*N*	Percentage	*N*	Percentage
Age* Response	20	100.0%	0	.0%	20	100.0%

Age* Response Crosstabulation

Count

		Response		Total
		Yes	No	
Age	Older	8	2	10
	Younger	4	6	10
Total		12	8	20

Chi-square Tests

	Value	*df*	Asymp. Sig. (2-sided)	Exact Sig. (2-sided)	Exact Sig. (1-sided)
Pearson chi-square	3.333[a]	1	.068		
Continuity correction[b]	1.875	1	.171		
Likelihood ratio	3.452	1	.063		
Fisher's exact test				.170	.085
N of valid cases	20				

a. 2 cells (50.0%) have expected count less than 5. The minimum expected count is 4.00

b. Computed only for a 2x2 table

Calculation Summary

expected frequency: The frequency total for the column times the frequency total for the row divided by the sample size

chi-square: The sum of the squared differences between the observed and expected frequencies divided by the expected frequencies

STOP AND THINK

13.3. Using the row and column frequencies given, calculate the expected frequencies for each cell in the following table.

Smoking status or gender	Men	Women	Row totals
Smoker			30
Nonsmoker			170
Column totals	100	100	200

13.4. For the observed frequencies in the following table, conduct a chi-square test to determine if there is a relationship between the variables.

Sleep or exam outcome	Slept	Did not sleep
Pass	40	20
Fail	5	10

THINKING ABOUT RESEARCH

A summary of a research study in psychology is given here. As you read the summary, think about the following questions:

1. What were the variables included in this study? Were these variables categorical or continuous? How do you know?
2. Why was the chi-square test appropriate to test the researchers' hypothesis? Include all possible reasons for the use of this test.
3. Based on the results given in the description that follows, was the chi-square test significant? How do you know? Using the information given for the study, what is the appropriate $\chi^2_{critical}$ for this study?
4. Based on the information presented in the Results of the Study section, what type of relationship was present for the variables you described earlier? Describe this relationship in your own words.

Research Study. Converse, B. A., Risen, J. L., & Carter, T. J. (2012). Investing in karma: When wanting promotes helping. *Psychological Science, 23,* 923–930.

Note: Experiment 1a from this article is described here.

Purpose of the Study. The researchers conducted an experiment to investigate whether desiring an outcome that someone has no control over (e.g., getting a job you applied for) is related to helping behavior (e.g., donating to a charity). Desiring an outcome was expected to relate to subsequent helping behavior.

Method of the Study. Undergraduate students ($N = 95$) were asked to participate for $3.00 compensation. Participants were assigned to either a wanting or routine condition using instructions for an essay they were to write. Those in the wanting condition were asked to write about a current event from their lives in which they wanted a specific outcome that was important to them. Those in the routine condition were asked to write about one of their daily routines. After being compensated for the study, an experimenter asked if the participant would be willing to sign up to work on a boring task for monetary compensation that would be donated to a local food bank. The researchers recorded how many participants agreed to do the task for charity.

Results of the Study. A chi-square test was conducted to examine the relationship between assigned essay condition (wanting or routine) and the number of participants who said yes and no to completing the boring task for charity. The calculated χ^2 was 4.90 and p value was 0.027. Overall, 94% from the wanting condition and 78% from the routine condition agreed to complete the boring task.

Conclusions of the Study. The researchers concluded that the essay condition assigned to the participants in the experiment was related to their helping behavior.

Chapter Summary

- **What is the difference between a parametric and a nonparametric test?**
  A parametric test is used with continuous variables, and a nonparametric test is used with categorical variables. Nonparametric tests are needed when sample statistics cannot be calculated to estimate population parameters. They are less powerful than a parametric test.
- **What does it mean that a nonparametric test is less powerful than a parametric test?**
  Nonparametric tests are less powerful than parametric tests, which means that they are less able to detect relationships between variables that exist in the population. In other words, a Type II error is more likely with a nonparametric test than with a parametric test.

(Continued)

(Continued)

- **How can we test relationships across categorical variables?**
  Nonparametric tests can be used to test relationships across categorical variables. For example, a chi-square test compares the observed category frequencies on the variables with the expected category frequencies on the variables when the null hypothesis is true.
- **What is the expected frequency?**
  The expected frequency is the number of participants expected in a cell category when there is no relationship between the variables (i.e., the null hypothesis is true).
- **What does a chi-square test tell us about relationships between categorical variables?**
  A chi-square test can tell us if there is evidence to reject the null hypothesis (that there is no relationship between two categorical variables). In other words, we can find evidence that there is a relationship between the variables.

Test Yourself

1. Parametric tests are used with ____________________ variables; nonparametric tests are used with ____________________ variables.
   a. nominal, ordinal
   b. ratio, interval
   c. nominal and ordinal, ratio and interval
   d. ratio and interval, nominal and ordinal
2. The chi-square test is a(n) ____________________ test.
   a. inferential
   b. parametric
   c. nonparametric
   d. both a and b
   e. both a and c
3. The chi-square statistic is based on __________.
   a. expected frequencies divided by the degrees of freedom
   b. the difference between the observed and expected frequencies
   c. the difference between the means of the two variables
4. Expected frequencies are the frequencies we would expect if __________.
   a. the null hypothesis is true
   b. the null hypothesis is false
   c. the alternative hypothesis is true
   d. both b and c
5. If we want to determine if there is a relationship between grade point average (GPA; on a 4-point scale) and ACT score, it would be best to use a chi-square test.
   a. True
   b. False
6. We cannot calculate the expected frequencies until we collect the categorical data from our sample.
   a. True
   b. False
7. The chi-square hypothesis test does not rely on a critical region of a distribution.
   a. True
   b. False

8. When conducting a chi-square test using SPSS, the data must be entered into the data window as categories for the variables.
   a. True
   b. False
9. The chi-square test can be conducted as a one-tailed or two-tailed test.
   a. True
   b. False
10. Using the row and column frequencies given, calculate the expected frequencies for each cell in the table that follows.

Voting status or supports candidate	Voted	Did not vote	Row totals
Yes			300
No			200
Column Totals	200	300	500

11. For the observed frequencies in the table that follows, conduct a chi-square test to determine if there is a relationship between the variables.

Class section or grade outcome	Live class	Online class
Pass	50	130
Fail	10	20

12. For the data that follows, conduct a hypothesis test to determine if the variables are related.

Female and Dog Owners: 25

Male and Dog Owners: 40

Female and Cat Owners: 60

Male and Cat Owners: 25

SAGE edge™

Visit **edge.sagepub.com/mcbridermstats** to find the answers to the Test Yourself questions above, as well as quizzes, flashcards, and other resources to help you accomplish your coursework goals.

14

MULTIFACTOR EXPERIMENTS

CONSIDER THE FOLLOWING QUESTIONS AS YOU READ CHAPTER 14

- How do factorial experiments differ from single-factor experiments?
- What are the advantages of conducting experiments with more than one independent variable?
- What is an interaction, and what can we learn from testing interactions?

LEARNING OBJECTIVES FOR CHAPTER 14

- Understand how crossing levels of independent variables creates conditions in an experiment.
- Identify an interaction in an experiment.
- Design a multifactor experiment.

Recall the story at the beginning of Chapter 8 about my dog Daphne and her "bad behavior." We conducted a single-factor experiment in that situation to compare different "treatments" to help Daphne's separation anxiety. Now suppose that the chew toys that contained treats had only helped reduce her bad behaviors on some occasions—sometimes she stopped these behaviors with the chew toy and sometimes she did not. In addition, suppose that giving her our worn clothes had also helped reduce her bad behaviors on some occasions but not others. It may be that different situations called for different treatments—one treatment did not help in every case.

If this had happened, we may have considered what factors went along with the differences in the effectiveness of the treatments and conducted a second, more complex, experiment. For example, suppose that we noticed that some of the times we tried the treatments, we were gone all day at work and school, whereas other trials with the treatments were with shorter trips (to the grocery store, etc.). We might hypothesize that the effectiveness of the different treatments *depends* on the length of our outing. To test this hypothesis, we might conduct an experiment with a **factorial design** to examine both the effects of the two treatments (our worn clothing and the chew toy) and the length of outing (1–2 hr and all day) on the reduction of bad behavior. Figure 14.1 illustrates the design of this experiment. This more complex experiment with two independent variables would allow us to learn whether the worn clothing works best for one of the outing lengths and the chew toy works best for the other outing length. We can also test overall effects of the treatments (does one treatment work better than the other regardless of outing length?) and the outing length (are more bad behaviors exhibited on longer outings overall regardless of the treatment we try?). This is the main advantage of factorial designs: You can examine the effects of each independent variable on its own as well as the combined effects of the independent variables and answer this question: Does the effect of one independent variable depend on the level of the other independent variable?

factorial design: An experiment or quasi-experiment that includes more than one independent variable

Figure 14.2 shows a possible outcome of our experiment with Daphne. In this case, our hypothesis that different treatments are effective for different outing lengths is supported. The graph shows that when we leave for short outings, the chew toy is better at reducing her bad behaviors, but when we are gone all day for a long outing, the worn clothing is better at reducing her bad behaviors.

FIGURE 14.1 ■ Design of the Factorial Experiment With Daphne

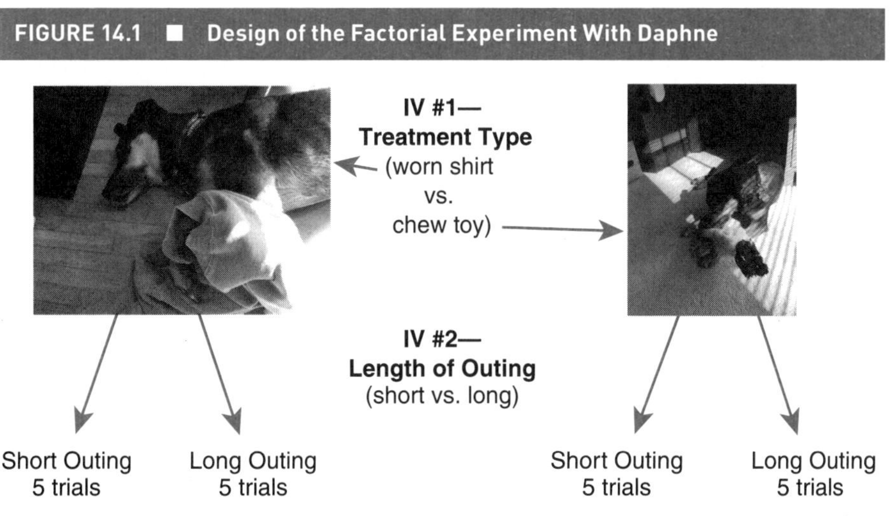

Source: © Dawn McBride

FIGURE 14.2 ■ Results From the Experiment With Daphne

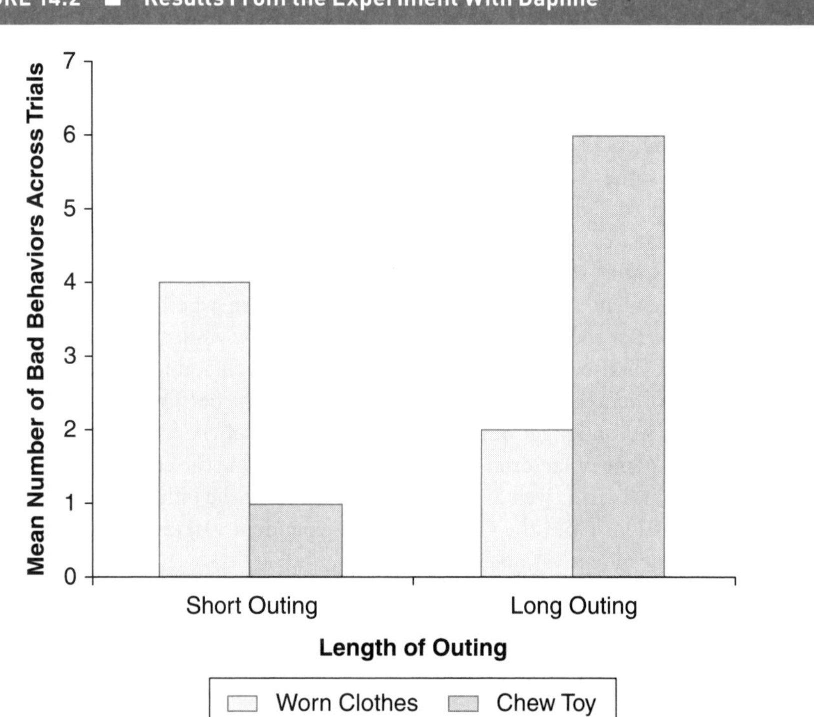

FACTORIAL DESIGNS

Many of the experimental examples we discuss in this and other chapters of the text involve a single independent variable, where the goal of the experiment is to compare the observations for the different levels of the independent variable. However, many experiments conducted by researchers are factorial designs, meaning they contain more than one independent variable. The primary advantages of a factorial design over simpler experiments are that a researcher can be more efficient in testing the effects of multiple independent variables in a single experiment and can also examine the combined effects of those independent variables on the dependent variable. Thus, many experiments conducted by psychologists are factorial designs because of these benefits of factorial designs.

Testing the combined effects of the independent variables is the unique feature of factorial designs. Without including multiple independent variables in a single experiment, we would not be able to detect the different effects a factor might have on behavior in different situations. For example, if we compare the outcomes of the two experiments with Daphne, we would come to different conclusions about the best treatment for her bad behaviors. In the single-factor experiment described in Chapter 8, we decided that the chew toy was the best treatment. But what if we had more short outing trials in that experiment than long outing trials? This would lead us to believe that the chew toy was best when, in reality, it was best only for short outings. By including the length of outing as a second independent variable in our factorial experiment, we are able to determine that, overall, the chew toy and the worn clothes are both effective but for different outing lengths. If we're gone all day, the worn clothing is actually better at keeping her on her best behavior. When the effect of one independent variable (e.g., treatment type) depends on the levels of another independent variable (e.g., short or long outing), it is called an **interaction effect**.

interaction effect: The effect of one independent variable depends on the level of the other independent variable

In factorial designs, the comparison of the mean scores for the levels of one independent variable is the test of the main effect of that independent variable. Remember that the levels of the independent variable are the different conditions that are part of the independent variable. For example, the chew toy and the worn clothes are the levels of the independent variable of treatment type in our experiment with Daphne. The main effects provide a test of the separate effect of each independent variable on the dependent variable in a factorial design. The main effect is one type of effect tested in an analysis of variance (ANOVA), which is the type of statistical analysis used most often for a factorial experiment (one-way ANOVA was introduced in Chapter 11).

Let's consider main effects on their own before we move on. Main effects examine the independent effect of each independent variable. In the experiment with Daphne, we would test a main effect for type of treatment (worn clothes versus chew toy) on the number of bad behaviors and a main effect for length of outing on number of bad behaviors. Suppose the mean number of bad behaviors in this experiment were as shown in the boxes in Table 14.1. These are the means for each condition (or crossing of the independent variable levels) in my experiment. These are the means graphed in Figure 14.2. If we want to look at the main effects, we need to examine the average means (i.e., **marginal means**) for each level of the independent variables. These means are shown in the table in the shaded areas. They are determined by averaging the condition means for each row and column. For example, the overall mean number of bad behaviors from Daphne when we gave her worn clothing for all outing lengths was the average of 4 (for the short outing) and 2 (for the long outing), giving us a marginal mean of 3 for this level of treatment type. If we compare the marginal means for all levels of an independent variable, we can determine if the independent variable has its own effect on the dependent variable separate from any other independent variables in the design. If we look again at Table 14.1, it looks like there is a main effect of outing length with more bad behaviors for long outings ($M = 4$) than for short outings ($M = 2.5$) but no main effect for treatment type because these marginal means (3 and 3.5) are very similar.

marginal means: Average mean scores for each level of an independent variable

TABLE 14.1 ■ Condition and Marginal Means for the Experiment With Daphne

	Short outing	Long outing	Treatment type marginal means
Worn clothes	4	2	3
Chew toy	1	6	3.5
Outing length marginal means	2.5	4	

The other type of effect tested in an ANOVA is an interaction effect. Thus, a test for an interaction effect compares the differences between the levels of one independent variable across the levels of another independent variable. This will determine whether the effects of one independent variable *depend* on the level of the other independent variable the scores were measured under.

To make the concept of an interaction more concrete, consider the factorial design in Figure 14.3. This design contains two independent variables, IVA and IVB, each with two levels. The columns indicate levels of IVA, and the rows indicate levels of IVB. The cells indicate the conditions created by combining the levels of the two independent variables. To determine the overall means for a level of an independent variable (i.e., the means compared in a main effect), the researcher averages the means for the cells in the columns and the rows. Main effects are determined by comparing the level means for each independent variable (i.e., comparing means for the rows and comparing means for the columns). To examine the interaction effect, the researcher must consider the differences between rows or columns. For example, one way to look at an interaction effect would be to consider the difference between *A*1*B*1 and *A*1*B*2 and compare it with the difference between *A*2*B*1 and *A*2*B*2. If those differences are not the same, then there is an interaction effect. In other words, the effect of IVB depends on whether you are looking at the *A*1 level or the *A*2 level of IVA.

It may take some time to understand interactions, so let's consider an example to further illustrate the concept. Suppose that the design illustrated in Figure 14.3 corresponds to independent variables of type of therapy (IVA) and length of therapy (IVB) in an experiment comparing the effects of therapy on depression symptoms. Figure 14.4 presents the variables and the levels of each variable as well as the conditions created by the combination of these levels. In addition, means for each level of the independent

FIGURE 14.3 ■ Diagram of a General Factorial Design With Two Independent Variables, Each With Two Levels

IVB:	IVA: *A*1	*A*2	
*B*1	*A*1*B*1	*A*2*B*1	Average the means for *A*1*B*1 and *A*2*B*1 to determine the overall mean for *B*1.
*B*2	*A*1*B*2	*A*2*B*2	Average the means for *A*1*B*2 and *A*2*B*2 to determine the overall mean for *B*2.
	Average the means for *A*1*B*1 and *A*1*B*2 to determine the overall mean for *A*1.	Average the means for *A*2*B*1 and *A*2*B*2 to determine the overall mean for *A*2.	

variables and conditions are included. These are the mean scores on the depression questionnaire (higher numbers indicate more depression symptoms). To determine main effects for therapy type, the condition means for each of the conditions that involve individual therapy are averaged and compared with the average of the condition means that involve group therapy (i.e., column averages). In other words, the main effect of therapy type involves a comparison of 62.5 (for individual) and 67.5 (for group). This procedure is similarly followed to determine if there is a main effect of therapy length by averaging the means for the conditions in each row. The main effect for therapy length involves a comparison of 67.5 (1 week) and 62.5 (6 weeks).

There are several ways by which the means for the conditions may create an interaction between therapy type and therapy length. Often, creating a graph of the condition means illustrates an interaction best. If the lines in a line graph are not parallel, this can indicate an interaction between the independent variables (the effect also needs to be confirmed by inferential statistics—Chapter 15 will describe how to conduct a two-way ANOVA). One scenario for the results from this experiment is that depression symptoms depend on both therapy type and length. This means that the independent variables interact. Panel 1 in Figure 14.5 illustrates the interaction shown in the condition means in Figure 14.4. You can see in this graph that the mean depression score is lowest for 6 weeks of individual therapy. Panels 2 and 3 in Figure 14.5 show some additional ways that an interaction could occur in this experiment.

FIGURE 14.4 ■ Diagram of a Specific Factorial Design With Two Independent Variables, Each With Two Levels

Therapy Type:	Individual $M = 62.5$	Group $M = 67.5$	
Therapy Length: 1 week $M = 67.5$	1 week of individual therapy $M = 75$	1 week of group therapy $M = 60$	Average the means for the two 1-week therapy conditions to determine the marginal mean for 1 week of therapy.
6 weeks $M = 62.5$	6 weeks of individual therapy $M = 50$	6 weeks of group therapy $M = 75$	Average the means for the two 6-weeks therapy conditions to determine the marginal mean for 6 weeks of therapy.
	Average the means for the two individual therapy conditions to determine the marginal mean for individual therapy.	Average the means for the two group therapy conditions to determine the marginal mean for group therapy.	

Note: M stands for mean.

FIGURE 14.5 ■ Examples of Different Types of Interaction Effects

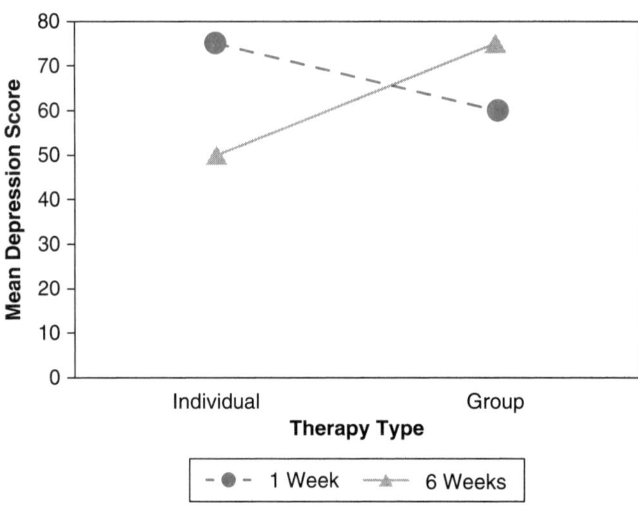

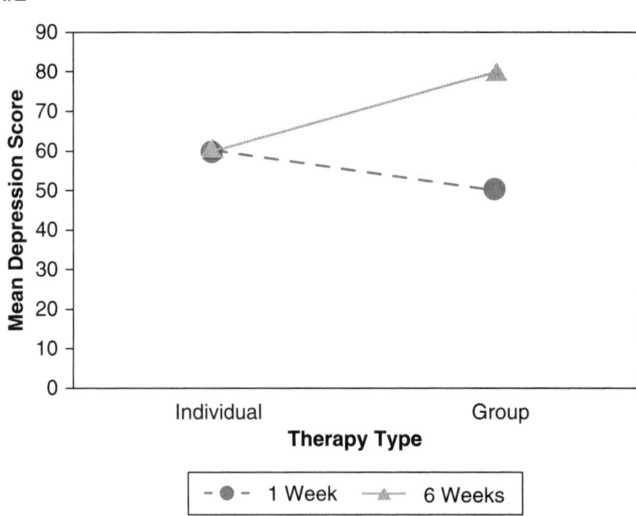

Panel #3

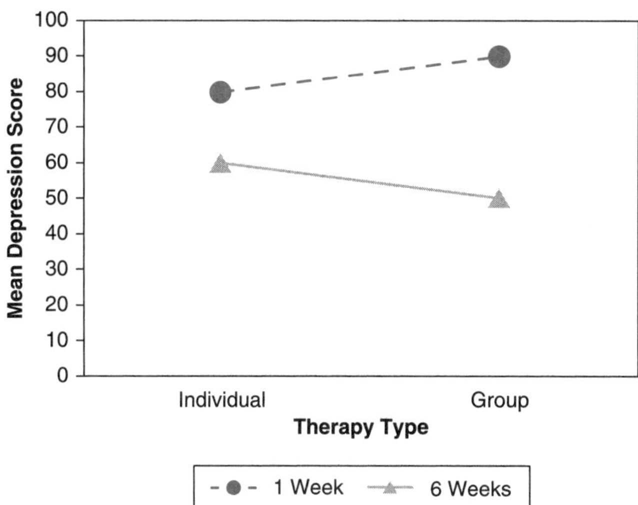

Panel #4

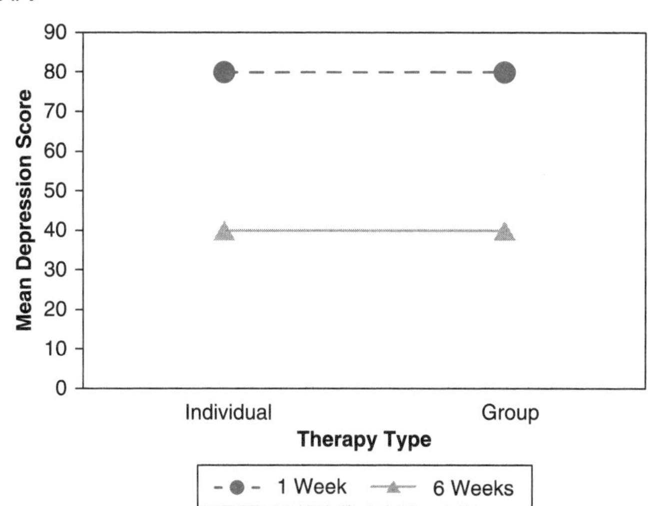

MORE ABOUT INTERACTIONS

Another way these independent variables might interact is with similar depression scores for individual therapy regardless of therapy length but different depression scores for group therapy depending on therapy length. Panel 2 in Figure 14.5 illustrates this scenario. The reverse scenario can also occur with similar scores for group therapy conditions but different scores for individual therapy conditions depending on therapy length. Finally, these independent variables can interact such that the depression scores are different for the two therapy lengths at both levels of therapy type. Panel 3 in Figure 14.5 illustrates this possibility. Each of these outcomes represents an interaction effect between therapy type and length. Panel 4 shows results with no interaction. In the graph in Panel 4, a main effect of therapy length is shown with no main effect of therapy type and no interaction. Graphs are useful in determining the type of interaction that occurred and should be followed up with additional statistical tests to determine exactly where the differences between the conditions in the interaction are in order to best describe the interaction effect. The follow-up statistical tests are called **simple effects tests**.

simple effects tests: Statistical tests conducted to characterize an interaction effect when one is found in an ANOVA

Interactions between independent variables can reveal interesting effects of the variables beyond what is seen in the main effects of each variable. For example, in the results shown in Panel 1 of Figure 14.5, there would be no main effects of the independent variables (if you average the two means for group and individual therapy, you get similar values; if you average the two means for 1 and 6 weeks of therapy, you get similar values), but there is a clear interaction of these variables. If therapy type had been the only independent variable included in the experiment with 6 weeks of therapy, the results might have led the researchers to conclude that group therapy is always superior. However, this would not be a complete picture of the effects of therapy. The addition of the therapy length independent variable provides a lot more information than either the therapy type or therapy length variables on their own. Thus, factorial experiments can provide researchers with much more information about behavior.

© Can Stock Photo/pruden

Photo 14.1 Consider an experiment designed to investigate consumer preferences for different types of ice cream.

Another example may help further illustrate the concept of an interaction. Suppose that you work for a company that makes ice cream. Your boss has tasked you with the job of finding out if two proposed changes affect ice cream sales by conducting an experiment to test the effects of these changes on consumer preferences (see Photo 14.1). One proposal is to add more chocolate chips to the chocolate chip flavor of the ice cream. The other proposal is to use real vanilla in all the ice cream flavors (currently, the company uses artificial vanilla flavoring). Both proposals cost the company money, so they want you to determine if either proposal increases consumer preference for the ice cream to decide if these additions are worthwhile. Thus, your experiment includes two independent variables: chocolate chip ice cream with (1) type of vanilla (artificial or real) manipulated and (2) amount of chips manipulated (current amount or 30% more chips). Figure 14.6 illustrates this design. You collect ratings of the ice cream from a group of 100 consumers, each of whom rates each type of ice cream on a scale of 1 to 7 for desire to purchase the ice cream. In other words, your design is a within-subjects design, as all participants rate all the ice cream conditions (in different counterbalanced orders).

Figure 14.7 includes hypothetical mean ratings for each ice cream condition. Marginal means are also included for each level of the two independent variables. Looking at the marginal means, it appears as though the two independent variables each independently affected the participants' ratings. For type of vanilla, the real vanilla received a mean rating of 4.5, whereas the artificial vanilla received a rating of only 3. The amount of chips variable shows similar results: Participants gave higher ratings to the ice cream with 30% more chips ($M = 4.5$, where M is the mean) than with the current level of chips ($M = 3.0$). Thus, if you just looked at the main effects, you might be tempted to recommend that your company implement both an increase in chocolate chips in ice cream that contains chips and use of real vanilla in all their ice cream flavors. However, looking at the condition means indicates something different. All the condition means show a rating of 3.0 for the ice cream, except in the real vanilla/30% more chips condition, where the mean rating was much higher than the other conditions ($M = 6.0$). In other words, the two variables interacted in such

FIGURE 14.6 ■ Diagram of the Ice Cream Experiment Design

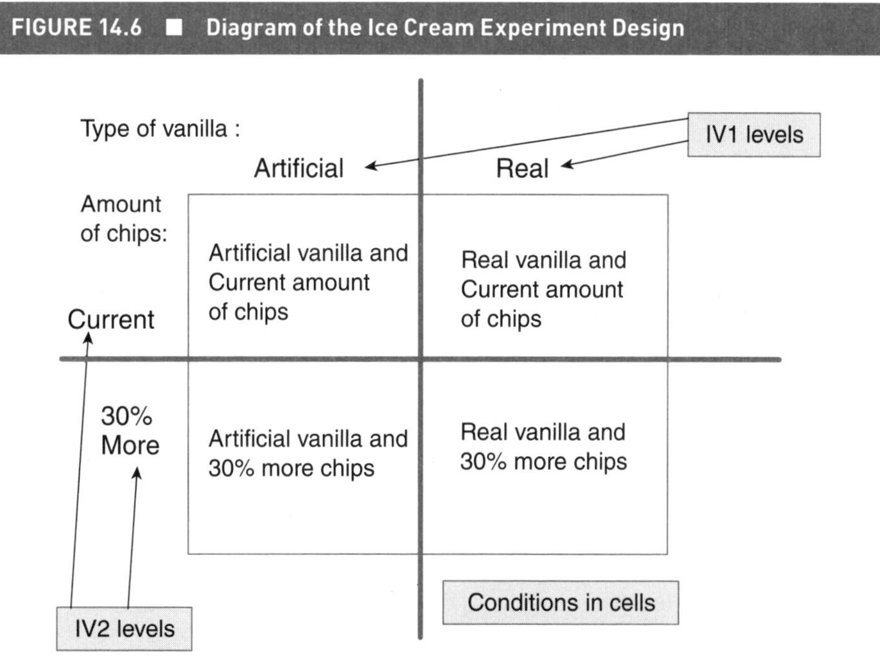

Note: IV = independent variable.

a way that this single condition seemed to result in the most preferred type of ice cream. Changing from artificial to real vanilla did not affect the ratings if the amount of chips stayed the same. Likewise, adding 30% more chips did not affect ratings if artificial vanilla was used. Only the combination of real vanilla and 30% more chips resulted in high ratings for the ice cream. This description of the interaction of the two independent variables provides the clearest picture of the results. Based on the interaction shown in the condition means, your recommendation should be to implement both proposals together only for the chocolate chip ice cream (at least until more flavors can be tested to determine how these factors affect other flavors). This example illustrates the importance of interactions in factorial designs.

FIGURE 14.7 ■ Hypothetical Means for the Ice Cream Experiment

Type of vanilla: / Amount of chips:	Artificial	Real	
Current	3	3	3
30% More	3	6	4.5
	3	4.5	

STOP AND THINK

14.1. Imagine that the results of the ice cream experiment had been different. Suppose instead that ratings for the ice cream were higher whenever more chocolate chips were used regardless of whether real or artificial vanilla was used. Would this represent an interaction? Why or why not?

14.2. Now imagine that the results from the ice cream experiment showed that ratings were higher when real vanilla was used regardless of the proportion of chocolate chips. Would this represent an interaction? Why or why not?

EXPERIMENT EXAMPLES

As in Chapter 8, some experiment examples from different areas of psychology follow. In each case, a factorial design was used. The descriptions will focus on the aspects of factorial designs discussed in this chapter: main effects and interactions.

Cognitive Example

Experiments are very common in cognitive research. The Thinking About Research section at the end of the chapter describes one cognitive experiment focused on study techniques and memory. The study example that follows here tested effects of suggestive retrieval techniques on false memories for having committed a crime. In this study by Shaw and Porter (2015), subjects were recruited who had not had previous contact with police, had not committed the crimes used in the study, and had experienced an emotional event between the ages of 11 and 14 (based on reports from caregivers). Subjects were interviewed three times with about 1 week between interviews. At the interviews, subjects were told about one real event that had occurred (an emotional event reported by the caregivers) and one false event. For half of the subjects, the false event was of them committing a crime (see Photo 14.2). For the other half, the false event was a noncriminal emotional event. After the events were described to the subjects, they were asked to recall as much as they could about each event. During the first interview, none of the subjects could recall anything about the false event, as expected. Subjects were encouraged to try to remember what they could when they reported no memory for the events. Subjects were told to imagine themselves in the scenario and were guided through an imagining of the event. They were encouraged to imagine themselves in the event and to try to remember the details each night before bed. At the two additional interviews, subjects were asked to try to remember the events. Their recall was videotaped. They were also asked to rate their anxiety level during the event, their confidence in their memories, and the vividness of their memories. During debriefing, subjects were asked if they had believed the false event had actually occurred.

Photo 14.2
Shaw and Porter (2015) used an experiment to examine creation of false memory for committing a crime in some of their participants.

Results showed that 83.3% of the subjects reported they believed the false event had actually happened. For just the criminal false event, 70% reported that they believed the event had occurred, showing that false memories for having committed a crime can be induced using imagination techniques. Figure 14.8 shows the ratings for anxiety during the event, vividness of memories, and confidence in memories for the subjects who believed the false event had occurred (i.e., had a false memory for the event). Main effects of memory type (true or false) are evident for the vividness and confidence ratings

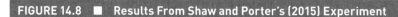

FIGURE 14.8 ■ Results From Shaw and Porter's (2015) Experiment

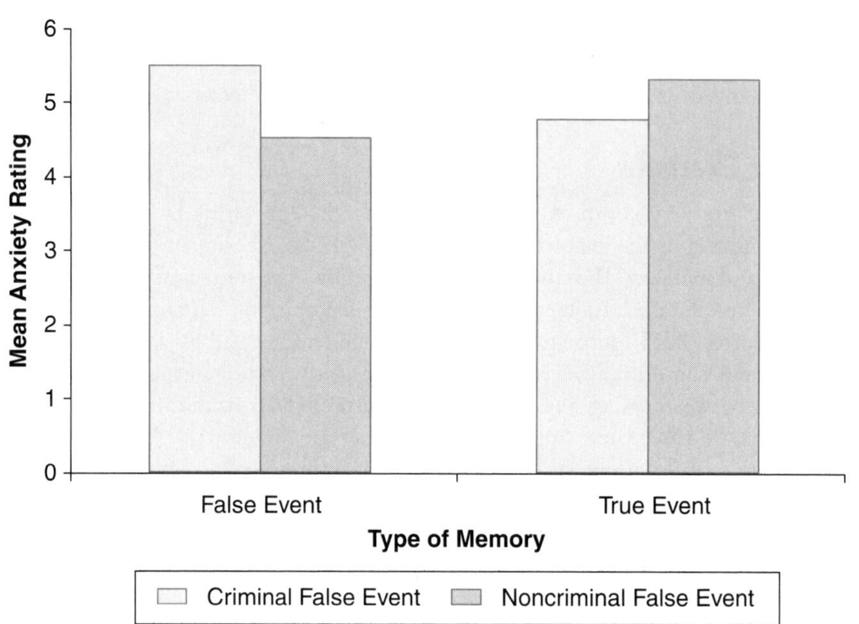

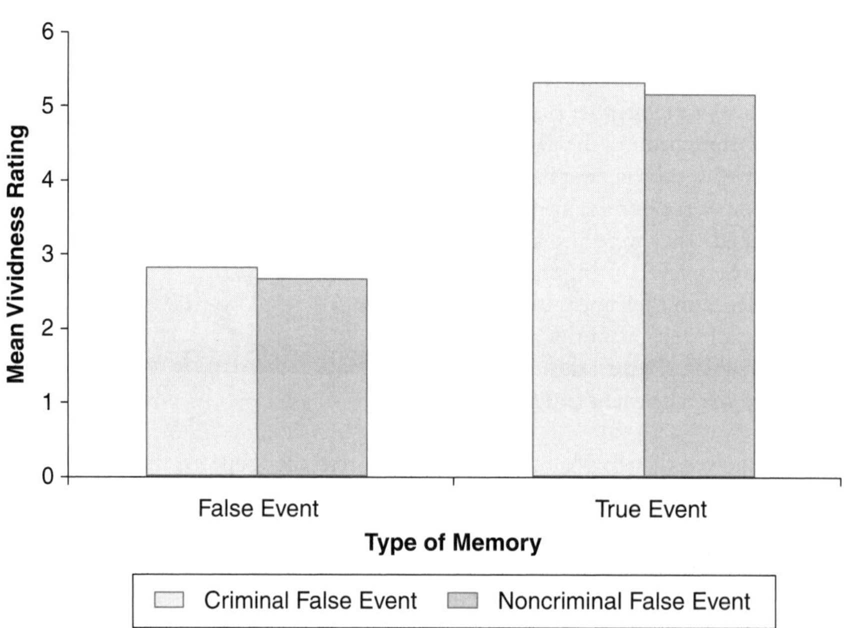

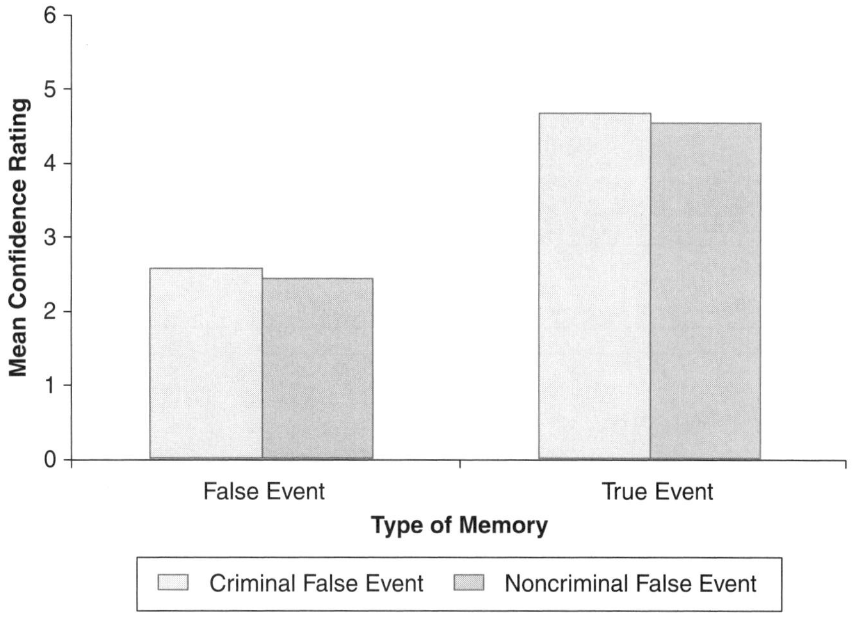

Source: Shaw and Porter (2015).

(higher ratings for true than false memories); however, an interaction may be present for the anxiety ratings. Based on the reported mean ratings, for those who received a criminal false event, anxiety seems to be higher for the false event than the true event (which was a noncriminal event), but for those who received a noncriminal (but emotional) false event, anxiety seems to be higher for the true event than for the false event. Thus, the anxiety rating difference between true and false events depended on whether the subject received a false criminal or false noncriminal event.

Biological Example

Studies in neuropsychology also sometimes involve experiments comparing brain activity for different conditions. In one such study, researchers (Silvers et al., 2014) were interested in comparing the brain activity and behavioral responses to appetizing food for children and adults. They tested the hypothesis that food craving (as measured by participants' ratings and activity in an area of the brain known as the ventral striatum) differs as a function of age. Participants were asked to consider the food shown in two conditions: a "close" condition or a "far" condition. In the close condition, subjects were asked to imagine the food in front of them and to think about the taste and smell of the food. In the far condition, subjects were asked to focus on the color and shape of the food rather than its appetitive qualities. Subjects were then shown appetizing foods (half were sweet and half were salty to reduce bias due to type of food) and to think about the foods according to the instruction (close or far) on that trial. Then they were asked to rate how much they wanted to eat the food on a 5-point scale. Figure 14.9 shows the sequence of events

FIGURE 14.9 ■ Task Used in the Silvers et al. (2014) Experiment

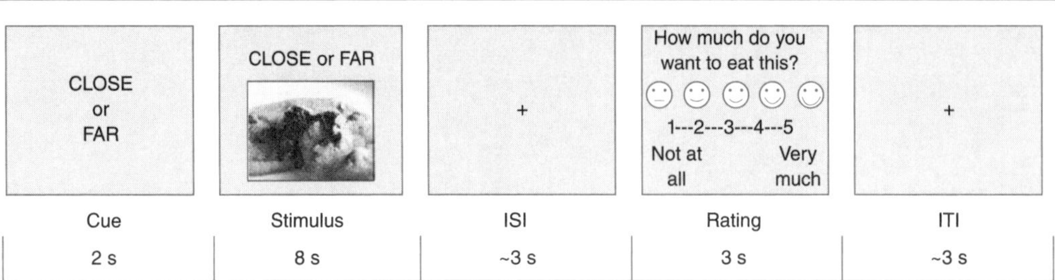

Source: Silvers et al. (2014).

Note: ISI = interstimulus interval; ITI = intertrial interval.

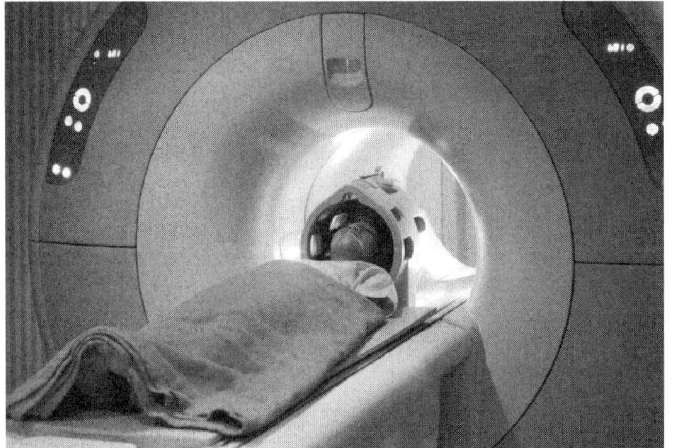

©istockphoto.com/JohnnyGreig

Photo 14.3
Silvers et al. (2014) examined brain activity using an fMRI scan while participants view food in different conditions.

in the task. Brain activity in the ventral striatum was measured using functional magnetic resonance imaging (fMRI) while subjects completed the task (see Photo 14.3).

Results showed that adults reported lower craving ratings than children. In addition, lower craving ratings were seen on "far" than "close" trials. There was no interaction of age and trial type on craving ratings. For the brain activity measure, adults showed lower activity in the ventral striatum than children, indicating there was less brain activity in adults related to craving than in children. Older adults also showed more activity than children in the prefrontal cortex where inhibition is controlled. This study shows that there is an age effect not only on craving of appetizing food but also on the brain activity that accompanies craving of food.

Social Example

Experiments in social psychology have been described in the other chapters of this text. In Chapter 3, the Zimbardo (1973) experiment, where a randomly assigned role as a prisoner or guard in a mock prison affected participants' behavior, was described as an example of a study that may have violated ethical standards. A one-factor (one independent variable) experiment about effects of pain on social bonding was described in Chapter 8. Thus, if you have read that chapter, you have already encountered some examples of the use of experiments in social psychology. Another example from social psychology looks at effects of exclusion on emotion (see Photo 14.4). In this study, researchers Wesselmann, Bagg, and Williams (2009) asked participants to watch a game of Cyberball, where three virtual players pass a ball around on the computer screen. Participants observed an "inclusion" game, where all three players were included in the ball throwing, or an "exclusion" game, where one player was systematically excluded by the other two players from the game. Half of the participants were asked to take the perspective of one of the players of the game, whereas the other half did not receive these instructions. The researchers then measured the participants' mood and basic needs satisfaction (e.g., self-esteem, how much meaning is in their lives) using a questionnaire. The results showed that observing an exclusion game produced lower scores on the questionnaire than observing an inclusion game. There was also an interaction between type of game (inclusion or exclusion) and perspective taking (taking a player's perspective or not). Questionnaire scores were lower in the perspective-taking condition when the game showed exclusion but were higher for perspective taking when the game showed inclusion. Figure 14.10 shows this interaction. In other words, watching someone be excluded lowered participants' mood but was particularly harmful when they took a player's perspective in this game.

Photo 14.4 Wesselmann et al. (2009) examined the effects of exclusion on emotion.

FIGURE 14.10 ■ Results of the Wesselmann et al. (2009) Cyberball Exclusion Study—Perspective Taking Raised Scores for the Inclusion Game but Lowered Scores for the Exclusion Game

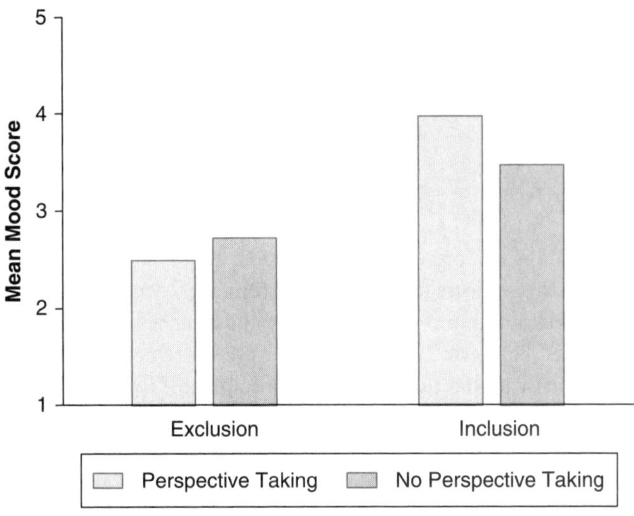

Source: Wesselmann et al. (2009).

Developmental Example

Whereas many studies in developmental psychology are quasi-experiments because of the inclusion of age as a subject variable, some developmental psychologists are also interested in exploring how causal relationships change across age groups. Thus, some researchers conduct experiments that contain a true independent variable and age as a subject variable, making them factorial in design.

An example of this type of study was conducted by Hund and Plumert (2003). These researchers were interested in how memory for the location of objects is influenced by the similarity of objects and whether this relationship is the same for different age groups. They tested 7-, 9-, and 11-year-olds and adults in an experiment that manipulated the similarity of target objects. The participants in the experiment were asked to learn the location of objects in a model house (see Photo 14.5). The objects were placed on dots in different sections of the house to help the participants learn the locations. Then the dots were removed, and the participants were asked to place the objects in the locations in which they remembered the experimenter placing them during the learning phase of the experiment. Half of the participants in each age group were shown objects in the same category (e.g., vehicles) placed in the same section of the house (i.e., location was related to object similarity). The other half of the participants in each age group were shown objects that were randomly placed in different sections of the house (i.e., location was not related to object similarity). Location errors (i.e., how far the participant placed the objects from their original positions) were recorded for the two object-type groups.

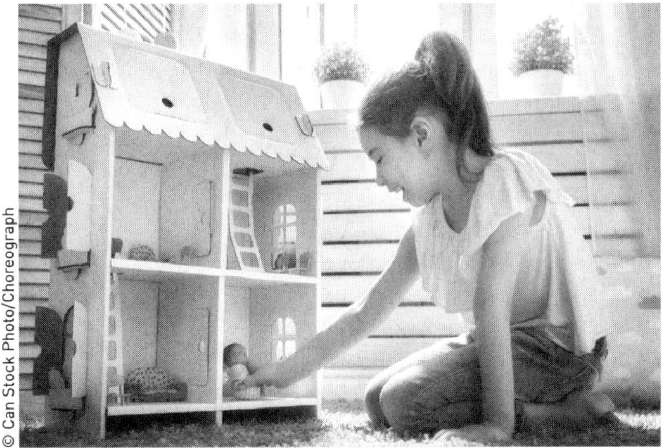

Photo 14.5 Hund and Plumert (2003) tested location memory using a model dollhouse for different age groups of children.

The researchers randomly assigned the participants to object-type groups to control possible group differences. The objects were also placed in the house in a random order to control for possible order effects in the placement of the objects.

The results of the study indicated that, although older participants made fewer errors, participants in all age groups placed related objects closer together (i.e., had greater location error) than unrelated objects. This difference across object-type groups was present for all age groups, indicating that location memory relies on the similarity of objects for individuals from age 7 years through adulthood. In other words, "information about what objects are influences memory for where objects are located" (Hund & Plumert, 2003, p. 946). However, remember that age is a subject (or quasi-independent) variable that was not manipulated. Thus, any differences found for age groups (e.g., fewer errors for older participants) cannot be fully interpreted as a causal effect because of the absence of a manipulation for this variable. This limitation exists for all developmental designs that compare age groups as a subject variable, even if another manipulated variable is included in the design, as in the Hund and Plumert experiment.

STOP AND THINK

14.3. What is a source of bias that might be present in the Shaw and Porter (2015) experiment?

14.4. What is a source of bias that might be present in the Silvers et al. (2014) experiment?

THINKING ABOUT RESEARCH

A summary of a research study in psychology is given here. As you read the summary, think about the following questions:

1. What are the independent variables in this experiment? Identify the levels of each independent variable.
2. Explain why this is a between-subjects experiment. Why was a two-way ANOVA needed to analyze the results?
3. What is the dependent variable? (*Hint:* Look at Figures 14.11 and 14.12.)
4. From what you see in Figures 14.11 and 14.12, did the results indicate an interaction effect between the independent variables? If so, describe the interaction.
5. Do the graphs in Figures 14.11 and 14.12 show main effects of either independent variable? Explain your answer.

Research Study. Roediger, H. L., III, & Karpicke, J. D. (2006). Test-enhanced learning: Taking memory tests improves long-term retention. *Psychological Science, 17,* 249–255.

Purpose of the Study. These researchers were interested in the best study technique for remembering educationally relevant information for later testing. In two experiments, they compared two study techniques: rereading the passage to be remembered and recalling the passage to be remembered. They predicted that recalling the passage would result in better memory performance on a later test than rereading the passage.

Method of the Study. College students participated in the two experiments: 100 students in Experiment 1 and 180 students in Experiment 2. In Experiment 1, participants first read a passage about the sun or about sea otters for 7 min. They were then asked to take 7 min either rereading the passage (study) or recalling the information in the passage (test). After a 2-min break, they then were asked to read the other passage (whichever they had not read in the first portion of the study) for 7 min. Then they were asked to either reread the passage or recall the passage (again, whichever task they had not done for the first passage). Thus, all participants received both types of study techniques. Finally, all participants were asked to recall the passages after 5 min, 2 days, or 1 week. Experiment 2 used the same procedure,

(Continued)

(Continued)

except that participants only read one passage and reread the passage three times, reread the passage twice and recalled it once, or recalled it three times before the final test. There was also no 2-day final test group in Experiment 2.

Results of the Study. Results from Experiments 1 and 2 are shown in Figures 14.11 and 14.12. In Experiment 1, the only group that performed better on the final test after rereading instead of recalling was the 5-min delay group. For the 2-day and 1-week delay groups, recalling the passage resulted in better scores on the final test than rereading the passage. Experiment 2 showed similar results to

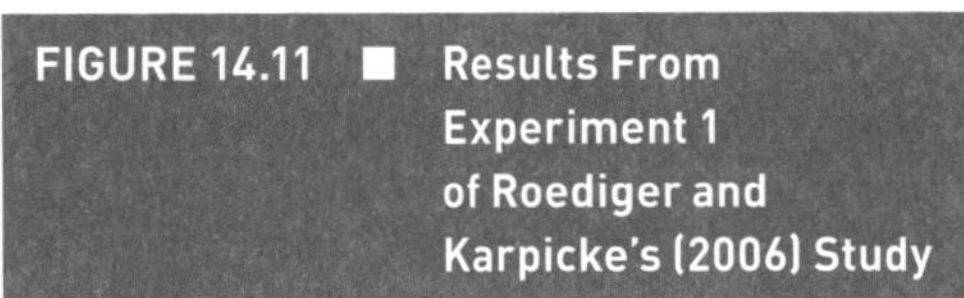

FIGURE 14.11 ■ Results From Experiment 1 of Roediger and Karpicke's (2006) Study

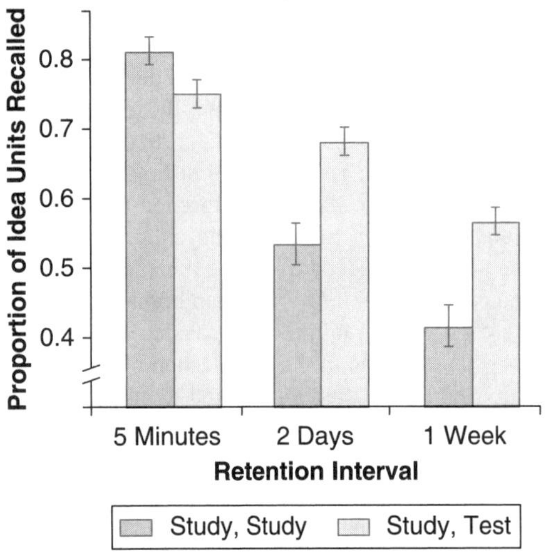

Source: Roediger and Karpicke (2006).

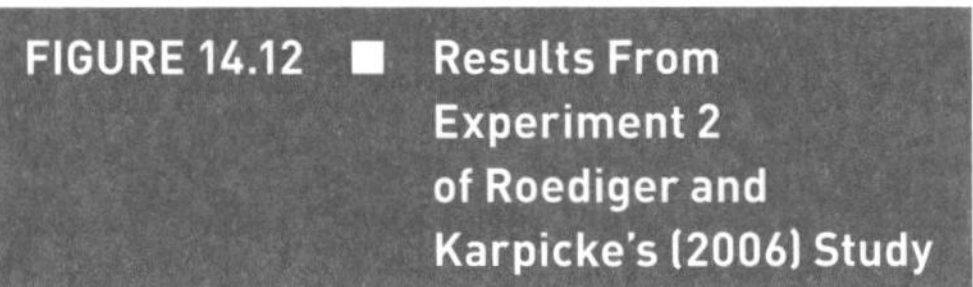

FIGURE 14.12 ■ Results From Experiment 2 of Roediger and Karpicke's (2006) Study

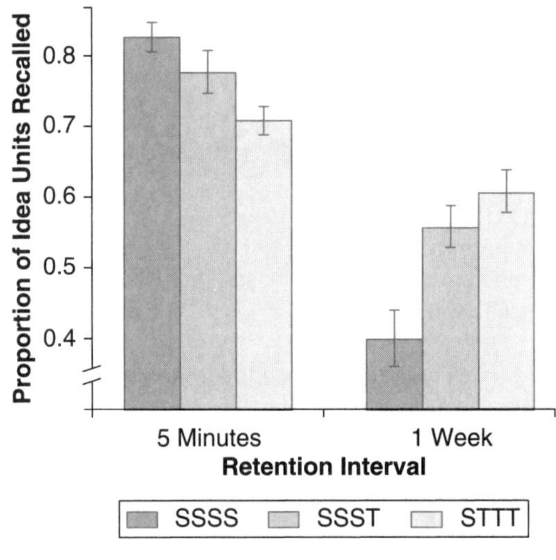

Source: Roediger and Karpicke (2006).

Experiment 1. With a 5-min delay, the group that reread the passage three times scored the highest on the final test, but with a 1-week delay, the group that recalled the passage three times scored the highest on the final test.

Conclusions of the Study. These results suggest that for delays longer than 5 min, the best study technique for remembering information is to recall that information. The more frequently the participants recalled the information, the better they did on a test 1 week after initial study. These results also suggest that recalling information can protect against forgetting.

Chapter Summary

Reconsider the questions from the beginning of the chapter:

- **How do factorial experiments differ from single-factor experiments?**
  In factorial experiments, more than one independent variable is included in the design. This means the crossing of the levels of these independent variables creates four or more conditions to consider in the experiment. The separate effects of each independent variable are seen by comparing the overall means for each level of an independent variable while ignoring the levels of the other independent variables. These are the main effects. There is also the interaction of the independent variables in a factorial experiment that can be tested.
- **What are the advantages of conducting experiments with more than one independent variable?**
  One advantage is that it is more efficient than a single-factor design. You need only one sample to collect data about multiple factors. The other main advantage is the testing of the interactions between variables. This allows you to determine whether the effects of one independent variable depend on the levels of another independent variable in your design. Single-factor designs do not allow for testing of interaction effects.
- **What is an interaction, and what can we learn from testing interactions?**
  An interaction can occur between independent variables such that the effect of one independent variable depends on which level of the other independent variable one is looking at. For example, an independent variable can show a difference between levels for the first level of another independent variable but show no difference between levels for the second level of the other independent variable. We can learn about the combined effects of multiple independent variables on the dependent variable by testing multiple independent variables in factorial designs.

Applying Your Knowledge

Imagine that you and a friend are comparing studying methods for exams. You have been using your notes and text strategy, but your friend has been taking the practice quizzes from her text and then having a study partner create additional quiz questions to test each other. You decide to conduct a small-*n* experiment with yourself as the only participant to compare your study strategy with your friend's strategy. You use both techniques in two classes you are currently taking: Psychology and Statistics. You use rereading for Exam 1 in Psychology and Exam 2 in Statistics. You use quizzing yourself for Exam 2 in Psychology and Exam 1 in Statistics. You then take a look at your exam scores in these courses:

(Continued)

(Continued)

	Psychology	Statistics
Rereading	76	72
Quizzing	88	95

- **How would you interpret these exam scores? Do you think you should stick with your study strategy or switch to your friend's strategy? Explain your answer.**

Test Yourself

FIGURE 14.13

Therapy length:	Therapy type: Talk	Drug
4 weeks	60	75
12 weeks	90	75

1. Marginal means are compared when testing a(n) ____________.
   a. main effect
   b. interaction
   c. correlation
2. To examine an interaction, one should look at the ______________ in a graph.
   a. marginal means
   b. condition means
   c. Pearson *r* correlations
   d. condition means for just one independent variable
3. Factorial experiments will always have ____________.
   a. more than one independent variable
   b. more than one dependent variable
   c. a significant interaction
   d. a significant main effect
4. Parallel lines in a line graph of condition means for a factorial experiment show that an interaction effect is present in the data.
   a. True
   b. False
5. For the table of condition means (means are mood scores), indicate which effects (main effect of type of therapy, main effect of length of therapy, interaction between type and length of therapy) are likely to be present (see Figure 14.13). If an effect is present, indicate which levels or conditions were higher.
6. Create a graph of the results in Question 5. Be sure to correctly label the axes of your graph.
7. Reread the sample factorial experiment about our dog Daphne, which was presented at the beginning of the chapter, to answer the following questions:
   a. What are the independent variables, and what are the levels of these variables in the experiment?

b. Were the independent variables manipulated between subjects or within subjects?

c. Was an interaction effect found in this experiment? If so, describe it.

8. Identify the independent and dependent variables included in the studies described in the Experiment Examples section and listed here. For any independent variable(s), also state the levels of the independent variable.

   a. Shaw and Porter (2015)

   b. Silvers et al. (2014)

   c. Wesselmann et al. (2009)

   d. Hund and Plumert (2003)

9. A researcher conducted a study to investigate the effects of smiling on helping behavior. Participants completed a survey that they thought was the purpose of the study, but in reality, the experiment took place after they completed the survey. At the end of the survey session, half of the subjects were thanked with a smile, and half were thanked without a smile. Whether the subject received a smile or not was randomly determined. The gender of the person giving the smile also varied by participant: Some subjects received the smile from a female researcher, and some subjects received the smile from a male researcher. The subjects were on their way out of the lab in the hallway when they then passed a confederate who had just dropped a large stack of books. The number of subjects who helped the confederate pick up his books was measured. The results showed that the subjects who were thanked by a male researcher showed similar helping behaviors across smile and no smile conditions. However, subjects who were thanked by a female researcher showed more helping behaviors when they received a smile than when they did not.

   a. What are the independent variables in this experiment? Identify how each independent variable was manipulated (i.e., between-subjects or within-subjects).

   b. From the description of the results, was an interaction present? Explain your answer.

10. Use the abstract from McBride, Beckner, and Abney (2011) to answer the questions that follow:

> To address mixed results reported in previous studies, the current experiments examined forgetting in prospective memory (PM) by manipulating the delay between PM instruction and cue presentation in event-based PM tasks. PM performance was measured for delays of 2 to 20 min in Experiment 1 and for delays of 1 to 10 min in Experiment 2. Experiment 2 included both focal and nonfocal PM tasks, and speed on the ongoing task was measured to examine evidence for monitoring processes across the delays tested. The results suggest that nonfocal PM performance follows a nonlinear forgetting function (i.e., rapid decline for shorter delays and slower decline for longer delays) when tested over delays from 1 to 20 min. No effect

(Continued)

(Continued)

of delay was seen for the focal task tested in Experiment 2 from 1 to 10 min. Experiment 2 also showed ongoing task costs for the first delay but not for longer delays, suggesting that monitoring was significantly reduced between 1 and 2.5 min of the ongoing task trials.

a. What are the independent and dependent variables for the experiments in this study?
b. Do you think the results described here represent an interaction between the independent variables? Why or why not?

SAGE edge™

Visit **edge.sagepub.com/mcbridermstats** to find the answers to the Test Yourself questions above, as well as quizzes, flashcards, and other resources to help you accomplish your coursework goals.

15

TWO-WAY ANALYSIS OF VARIANCE

CONSIDER THE FOLLOWING QUESTIONS AS YOU READ CHAPTER 15

- Can we examine more than one causal factor in a single study?
- How do levels of a factor and conditions differ in a factorial design?
- What is the difference between a main effect and an interaction?
- How do we calculate an *F* ratio for an interaction?
- What does a significant interaction tell us about our data?

LEARNING OBJECTIVES FOR CHAPTER 15

- Understand what it means for independent variables to interact.
- Conduct a two-way analysis of variance (ANOVA).
- Evaluate an interaction with simple effects.

In Chapter 11, we considered a study with three test format groups to compare all at once. Although this type of factor (one with more than two groups) is common in behavioral research studies, it is even more common to examine multiple causal factors in a single study. As you saw in Chapter 14, this allows a researcher to gain more information about factors that influence the behaviors of interest in one study. For example, suppose we think not only that the text format affects student satisfaction ratings with the text but also that the subject topic of the text matters as well. It is possible that satisfaction ratings are lower for chemistry texts than for psychology texts in addition to the lower ratings we saw in the last chapter for paper texts than electronic text formats. It is also possible that the difference in satisfaction between the text formats *depends* on the subject topic, such that for psychology texts, the interactive electronic format is best but for chemistry texts, it is not the best. In other words, there might be an interaction between text format and subject topic.

We can test all these possible effects in one study with two main factors: text format (with paper text, standard electronic text, and interactive electronic text) and subject topic (with a psychology text and a chemistry text). Figure 15.1 illustrates the design of this study. Different participants would be randomly assigned to each of the different conditions in the study. This means that to have the same number of participants in each condition in the study as when we only had the text format factor, we need to double the total sample size to 180 so that 60 participants can be assigned to each text format with 30 of those participants assigned to each of the subject topics in each text format (possibly dependent on which courses the participants are currently enrolled in). We can then compare satisfaction ratings for the three text formats and the two topic subjects and then determine if the difference across text formats (if any is found) depends on which topic subject the participants are studying. In the next section, we will discuss the different parts of multifactor studies and what we can learn about behavior in these studies.

FACTORIAL DESIGNS

In the previous chapter, we examined studies with more than one independent variable. These studies have a factorial design. Recall that factorial designs are studies that examine more than one independent variable to determine the separate and combined effects of the independent variables on the dependent variable. In fact, this is the primary advantage of a factorial design: You can examine multiple factors at once *and* their combined effects on the data. This design provides more information to the researcher all at once with only one sample. Because of the benefits of this design, many experiments conducted by psychologists are factorial designs.

Testing the combined effects of the independent variables is the unique feature of factorial designs. Without including multiple independent variables in a single experiment, we would not be able to detect the different effects a factor might have on behavior in different situations. For example, if we only compare satisfaction ratings for the three text formats for psychology texts, as we did in the last chapter, we might miss a different effect of text format on other subject topics, such as chemistry. In the single-factor experiment described in Chapter 11, we concluded that the interactive electronic format was most preferred by students. But what if students prefer a paper text or a standard electronic text when they are studying a different topic? Our single-factor study would lead us to believe that the interactive electronic text was best when, in fact, it is only best for one subject topic. By including the subject topic as a second independent variable in our factorial experiment, we are able to determine whether, overall, the interactive electronic

FIGURE 15.1 ■ Study Design With Two Factors: Text Format and Subject Topic

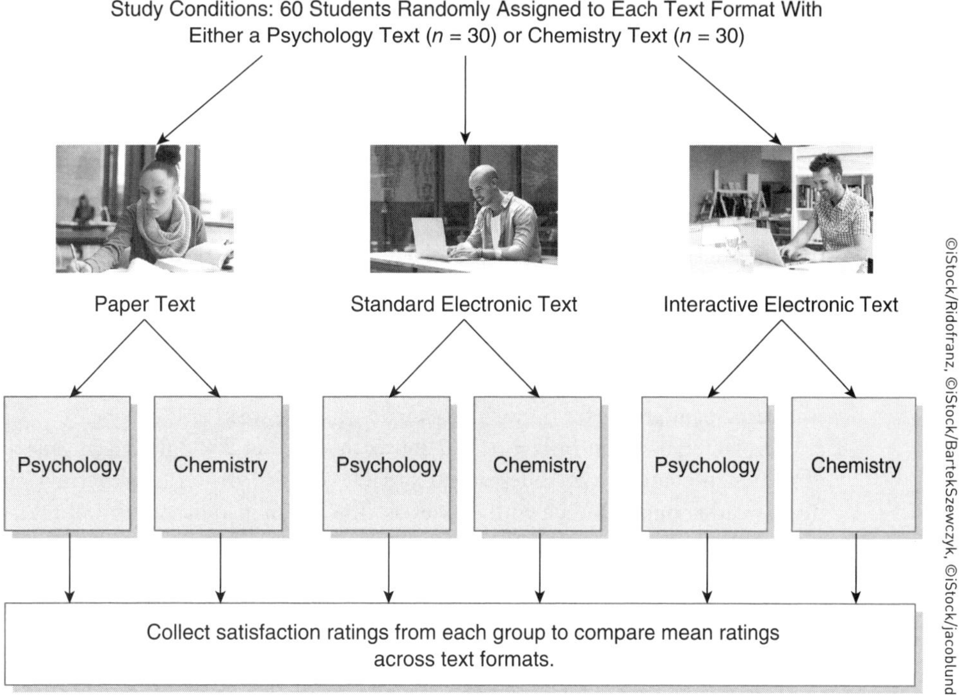
Study Conditions: 60 Students Randomly Assigned to Each Text Format With Either a Psychology Text (n = 30) or Chemistry Text (n = 30)
Paper Text
Standard Electronic Text
Interactive Electronic Text
Psychology
Chemistry
Psychology
Chemistry
Psychology
Chemistry
Collect satisfaction ratings from each group to compare mean ratings across text formats.
©iStock/Ridofranz, ©iStock/BartekSzewczyk, ©iStock/jacoblund

text format is best for both subject topics or if a different text format is preferred when the subject topic changes. When the effect of one independent variable (e.g., text format) *depends* on the levels of another independent variable (e.g., subject topic), this is called an interaction effect.

In factorial designs, the comparison of the mean scores for the levels of the independent variable is the test of the main effect of that independent variable. This is no different than the comparison of the overall test formats we made in Chapter 11. The levels of the independent variable are the different conditions that are part of the independent variable. The different types of texts we are comparing in our example study are the levels of the independent variable of text format. The main effects provide a test of the effect of each independent variable on the dependent variable. When we have more than one independent variable in a study, we can test the separate effect of each independent variable on the dependent variable by looking at the main effect for each of the independent variables. An ANOVA will provide a test for each main effect in our design.

The other type of effect tested in a factorial ANOVA is an interaction effect. The interaction effect compares the effect of one independent variable across the levels of another independent variable to determine how the independent variables *interact* to affect the dependent variable. A test for an interaction effect compares the differences between the levels of one independent variable across the levels of another independent variable. This will determine if the effects of one independent variable *depend* on the level of the other independent variable. Thus, we can make separate hypotheses in a factorial experiment about each main effect and the interaction of the factors in our hypothesis-testing procedure.

To make the concept of an interaction more concrete, consider a simple factorial design with two independent variables that investigates the effect of outdoor temperature on mood. Participants are asked to complete a simple puzzle task either inside a lab with windows or outside the lab on a patio next to the lab building. The temperature outside on the day of testing is recorded as either in the 75 to 80 °F range or in the 90 to 95 °F range (the study is only run on days with these temperature ranges) with participants randomly assigned to task setting. At the end of the testing session, participants are asked to rate on a 1 to 10 scale how much they enjoyed doing the task. In this type of study, we might find an interaction: Participants enjoy the task more in the outdoor setting than the lab setting with the 75 to 80 °F weather but enjoy the task more in the lab setting (with air conditioning) than the outdoor setting with the 90 to 95 °F weather. In other words, which setting the participant prefers for the task *depends* on what the weather is outside.

The factorial design in Figure 15.2 shows this type of 2 × 2 design in general terms. This design contains two independent variables (IVs): IVA (e.g., task setting) and IVB (e.g., weather outside), each with two levels. The columns indicate levels of IVA, and the rows indicate levels of IVB. The cells or boxes indicate the conditions (e.g., lab setting with 75–80 °F weather) in the study created by combining the levels of the two independent variables. To determine the overall means for a level of an independent variable (i.e., the means compared in a main effect), the researcher averages the means for the cells in the columns and the rows. Main effects are determined by comparing the level means for each independent variable (i.e., comparing means for the columns for the main effect

FIGURE 15.2 ■ Diagram of a General Factorial Design With Two Independent Variables, Each With Two Levels

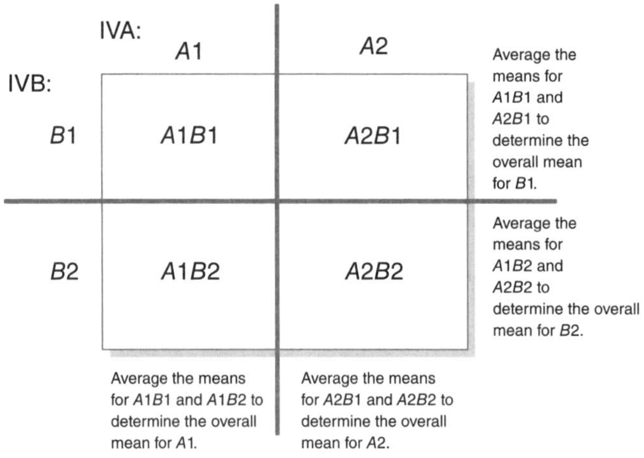

IVB: \ IVA:	*A*1	*A*2	
*B*1	*A*1*B*1	*A*2*B*1	Average the means for *A*1*B*1 and *A*2*B*1 to determine the overall mean for *B*1.
*B*2	*A*1*B*2	*A*2*B*2	Average the means for *A*1*B*2 and *A*2*B*2 to determine the overall mean for *B*2.
	Average the means for *A*1*B*1 and *A*1*B*2 to determine the overall mean for *A*1.	Average the means for *A*2*B*1 and *A*2*B*2 to determine the overall mean for *A*2.	

of IVA and comparing means for the rows for the main effect of IVB). To examine the interaction effect, the researcher must consider the differences between rows or columns. For example, one way to look at an interaction effect would be to consider the difference between *A*1*B*1 (e.g., lab setting with 75–80 °F weather) and *A*2*B*1 (e.g., outdoor setting with 75–80 °F weather) and compare it with the difference between *A*1*B*2 (e.g., lab setting with 90–95 °F weather) and *A*2*B*2 (e.g., outdoor setting with 90–95 °F weather). If those differences are not the same, then there is an interaction effect. In other words, the effect of IVA depends on whether you are looking at the *B*1 level or the *B*2 level of IVB.

STOP AND THINK

Suppose that you work for a company that makes ice cream. Your boss has tasked you with finding out if two proposed changes affect ice cream sales by conducting an experiment to test the effects of these changes on consumer preferences. One proposal is to add more chocolate chips to the chocolate chip flavor of the ice cream (i.e., compare current amount of chips with 30% more chips). The other proposal is to use real vanilla in all the ice cream flavors (currently, the company uses artificial vanilla flavoring, so you need to compare chocolate chip ice cream with real and artificial vanilla). Both changes would cost the company money, so they want you to determine if either change increases consumer preference for the ice cream to decide if these changes are worthwhile. You collect ratings of the ice cream in each condition from a group of 400 consumers, each of whom rates one type of ice cream on a scale of 1 to 7 for desire to purchase. (*Hint:* This example should look familiar—it was first described in Chapter 14.)

15.1. What are the independent and dependent variables in this study?

15.2. Describe the main effects that would be tested in this study. Which levels would be compared in each main effect test?

15.3. Describe one way that the independent variables in this study might interact to affect the dependent variable.

CALCULATING A TWO-WAY ANALYSIS OF VARIANCE

Let's look again at our factorial text format by subject topic experiment shown in Figure 15.1. To conduct our hypothesis test, we will need to calculate an *F* ratio for each main effect and for the interaction. The main effects are similar to the one-way between-subjects ANOVA we calculated in Chapter 11, but our within-groups variance term will be a bit different because we now have to consider the deviations within all of our conditions (six conditions in our 3 × 2 design). The *F* ratio for the interaction will be our new term, but it will use the same within-groups variance term as the main effects, so we need to calculate only one within-groups variance term that will be used in the denominator of all three *F* ratios. Let's begin with Step 1 of our process.

Step 1: State Hypotheses

In Step 1, we need to state hypotheses for our two main effects (for text format and for subject topic) and for the interaction. We will use the data from the one-way design in Chapter 11 to predict that the interactive electronic text will receive the highest satisfaction ratings as our alternative hypothesis for the text format main effect. Let's assume that there might be a difference in satisfaction between our psychology and chemistry texts but that no specific direction is predicted. Finally, we will predict that there will be interaction between these two factors, such that the difference across the text formats is different for psychology and chemistry texts. Therefore, our hypotheses for this study are as follows:

Main Effect of Text Format

H_0: *The population means for students using paper, standard electronic, and interactive electronic texts are equal.*

H_1: *The population mean for the interactive electronic format is higher than the rest of the population means for text format.*

Main Effect of Subject Topic

H_0: *The population means for psychology and chemistry texts are equal.*

H_1: *The population means for psychology and chemistry texts are not equal.*

Interaction Between Text Format and Subject Topic

H_0: *There is no interaction effect in the population for text format and subject topic.*

H_1: *There is an interaction effect in the population for text format and subject topic.*

Step 2: Set Decision Criterion

Our alpha level will be set at 0.05.

Step 3: Collect Sample Data

Let's look at the descriptive statistics we will need in order to calculate the between- and within-groups variance terms for our F ratios. The condition means are shown in Figure 15.3. We will also need the means for each level of our independent variables, which can be calculated by averaging across the condition means for each level. These are shown at the ends of the rows and columns in Figure 15.3 and are called marginal means. The marginal means will be used to calculate between-groups variance terms in Step 4 for our main effects. The grand mean $\overline{X}_{Grand}$ is also shown in Figure 15.3 and can be calculated by averaging either set of marginal means or the six condition means. With the descriptive statistics shown in Figure 15.3, we are ready to move on to Step 4 and calculate our F ratios.

Step 4: Calculate Statistics

To conduct our ANOVA, we have three separate F ratios to calculate: one for the main effect of text format, one for the main effect of subject topic, and one for the interaction

FIGURE 15.3 ■ Descriptive Statistics for Step 3 of Hypothesis Testing for the Format by Subject Topic Study

	IVA—Text Formats			
IVB—Subject Topic	Paper	Standard Electronic	Interactive Electronic	**Marginal Means**
Psychology	Mean = 5.4	Mean = 6.2	Mean = 8.8	Mean = 6.8
Chemistry	Mean = 5.2	Mean = 7.2	Mean = 6.4	Mean = 6.3
Marginal Means	Mean = 5.3	Mean = 6.7	Mean = 7.6	**Grand Mean** = 6.55

between these two factors. Each of the *F* ratios will use the same within-groups error in the denominator, but the between-groups terms in the numerator will differ. Let's begin with the between-groups terms.

Main Effects Between-Groups Variance Terms

For the main effect of text format, the between-groups variance term will be very similar to the one we calculated in Chapter 11. However, we have to collapse across two levels of our other factor, subject topic, so we need to add those levels (*b*) to our calculation. The between-groups *SS* term is this:

$$SS_{Text\ Format} = n(b)\Sigma\left(\bar{X}_A - \bar{X}_{Grand}\right)^2$$

Here, $\bar{X}_A$ is the marginal mean for each level of text format, and *b* is the number of levels of IVB (in this case, subject topic). Thus, the between-groups *SS* for text format is as follows:

$$SS_{Text\ Format} = 30(2)\left[(5.3-6.55)^2 + (6.7-6.55)^2 + (7.6-6.55)^2\right]$$
$$= 60[1.56 + .02 + 1.10] = 60[2.68] = 160.80$$

We next need to determine the $df_{TextFormat}$, which is $df = a - 1 = 3 - 1 = 2$. With these two terms, we can calculate the between-groups variance for text format:

$$MS_{Text\ Format} = \frac{160.80}{2} = 80.4$$

The main effect for subject topic will be calculated in the same way, collapsing across the levels of text format:

$$SS_{Subject\ Topic} = n(a)\Sigma\left(\bar{X}_B - \bar{X}_{Grand}\right)^2 =$$

$$SS_{Subject\ Topic} = 30(3)\left[(6.8 - 6.55)^2 + (6.3 - 6.55)^2\right] = 90\left[.06 + .06\right] = 10.80$$

Therefore, $df_{Subject Topic} = b - 1 = 2 - 1 = 1$. Thus, $MS_{Subject Topic} = 10.80$

Interaction Between-Groups Variance Term

The between-groups variance term for the interaction will involve the condition means, the marginal means for both factors, and the grand mean. The interaction *SS* is based on the deviation of the condition mean from the grand mean. However, this also contains the difference between the marginal means and the grand mean that we used in the terms in the previous section, so we need to subtract these differences out. With some algebra, our *SS* for the interaction becomes this:

$$SS_{Interaction} = n\Sigma\left(\bar{X}_{AB} - \bar{X}_A - \bar{X}_B + \bar{X}_{Grand}\right)^2$$

Thus, our *SS* for the interaction is this:

$$SS_{Interaction} = 30\begin{bmatrix}(5.4 - 5.3 - 6.8 + 6.55)^2 + (6.2 - 6.7 - 6.8 + 6.55)^2 \\ +(8.8 - 7.6 - 6.8 + 6.55)^2 \\ +(5.2 - 5.3 - 6.3 + 6.55)^2 + (7.2 - 6.7 - 6.3 + 6.55)^2 \\ +(6.4 - 7.6 - 6.3 + 6.55)^2\end{bmatrix}$$

$$= 30[.02 + .56 + .90 + .02 + .56 + .90] = 30[2.96] = 88.8$$

The $df_{Interaction} = (a - 1)(b - 1) = 2(1) = 2$, so the between-groups variance term is this:

$$MS_{Interaction} = \frac{88.8}{2} = 44.4$$

Within-Groups Variance Term

The within-groups variance (i.e., error term) will be the same for all three effects (the two main effects and the interaction), so we only need to calculate it once. As in the one-way ANOVA, it is based on the deviations between each score and its group mean. The within-groups *SS* term for the factorial design is calculated with this formula:

$$SS_{Within} = \Sigma(X - \bar{X}_{AB})^2$$

This means that you need to calculate the sum of the squared differences between each score and its condition mean. Remember that the *SS* is the sum of squared deviations of each score from its condition mean: $SS = \Sigma(X - \bar{X}_{AB})^2$. The $\bar{X}_{AB}$ means for this calculation are shown in Figure 15.3. Suppose that the first score in the paper text or psychology condition is a rating of 5; its deviation from the group mean is (5 – 5.4) = –0.4, and that squared is 0.16. You would do this for all 180 scores and add them together to calculate the within-groups *SS* term. Imagine that we did this for our data set and got $SS_{Within} = 1000$. We can now calculate the df_{Within} term to find the within-groups variance:

$$df_{within} = a(b)(n-1)$$

Thus, the $df_{Within} = 3(2)(30–1) = 174$ and the within-groups variance is this:

$$MS_{Within} = \frac{1000}{174} = 5.75$$

Now we are ready to calculate our *F* ratios for each effect.

F Ratios

With the values we have calculated for the between-groups variance terms and the within-groups error term, we can calculate our three *F* ratios for the ANOVA. For the main effect of text format, the *F* ratio is this:

$$F_{TextFormat} = \frac{80.4}{5.75} = 13.98$$

For the main effect of subject topic, the *F* ratio is this:

$$F_{SubjectTopic} = \frac{10.8}{5.75} = 1.88$$

For the interaction effect of text format × subject topic, the *F* ratio is this:

$$F_{Interaction} = \frac{44.4}{5.75} = 7.72$$

In Step 5, we will find the F_{crit} for each of these effects based on the *df* terms used in the calculation of the *F* ratios.

Step 5: Make a Decision

It is time to go back to our *F* Table to find the F_{crit} values for each of our *F* ratios to determine if our calculated values fall in the critical region for the *F* distribution. For the main effect of text format, we need $F_{crit}(2,174)$, where 2 is the $df_{Between}$ value and 174 is the df_{Within} value. If we use the table in Appendix E to find the F_{crit} in the column with 2 *df* and the row with 120 *df*, we find $F_{crit}(2,120) = 3.92$ (the highest df_{Within} value in the table is 120, so we can use that value from the table). Our calculated *F* value is 13.98, which is higher than 3.92, so the main effect of text format is significant, meaning there is a difference between at least two of the mean ratings for the formats. We would need to conduct a post hoc test to determine which levels of text format are different from the others.

Our next effect to test is the main effect of subject topic. We need $F_{crit}(1,174)$ for this effect. From the table in Appendix D, we find $F_{crit}(1,120) = 3.92$ (we can continue to use $df_{Within} = 120$ as the closest value to our error *df*). Our calculated *F* ratio for the main effect of subject topic was 1.88, so this effect is not significant (1.88 is lower than 3.92). This tells us that we have no evidence for an overall difference in satisfaction based on subject topic.

Finally, we can examine the interaction effect between the two factors. A significant interaction will tell us that the effect of text format on satisfaction ratings depends on which subject topic the text covers. The F_{crit} will be the same as that for the main effect of text format because the degrees of freedom for the interaction are the same. Thus, $F_{crit}(2,120) = 3.92$. Once again, our calculated *F* of 7.72 is higher than the critical value, so the interaction is significant. To fully describe the interaction effect, we should conduct follow-up tests called *simple effects*, but for now, let's just look at a graph of the condition means to see what the interaction looks like. Figure 15.4 shows the condition means for each text format grouped by subject topic. What we can see in this graph is that the most preferred text format differs for the two subject topics: For the psychology text, students prefer the interactive electronic text, but for the chemistry text, they prefer the standard electronic text. This is how the text format preference *depends* on the subject topic: A different format is rated highest across the subject topics. Because the interaction showed a different ordering of satisfaction for the text formats for the two subject topics, the main effect of text format becomes less important in our analysis. The overall differences across the text formats are no longer meaningful because the main effect pattern doesn't apply to both the psychology and chemistry texts in the same way. In the next section, we will examine interactions further to see some different ways an interaction can occur within our data.

STOP AND THINK

15.4. For each description that follows, indicate which type of effect is being tested (main effect or interaction):

a. Three groups of subjects are exposed to three different types of stories to compare the effect of type of story on reading speed.

b. Researchers examine whether the effect of note-taking method (by hand or on a computer) on test score depends on the type of class a student is taking.

c. A study tested the effects of both room color and presence or absence of plants on recovery time in a hospital. The individual effects of room color and presence or absence of plants were tested.

15.5. A study was conducted to compare effects of gender and mood on spatial abilities. Men and women participated in a study in which half of the participants of each gender were placed in a positive mood (by watching an uplifting film clip) and half of each gender were placed in a negative mood (by watching a sad film clip). Immediately after watching the film clips, the participants were asked to navigate through a maze to reach the exit point. The amount of time to navigate the maze (in seconds) was measured and is listed below for each participant by condition. Use these data to test the main effects of the gender and mood variables and the interaction between these variables.

Male and Positive Mood: 56, 36, 75, 23, 55, 70, 82, 41, 88, 52, 60, 49

Female and Positive Mood: 57, 82, 43, 59, 66, 79, 88, 71, 75, 70, 80, 69

Male and Negative Mood: 90, 102, 69, 82, 79, 95, 103, 110, 84, 90, 99, 105

Female and Negative Mood: 110, 94, 85, 66, 79, 120, 93, 97, 82, 80, 104, 95

15.6. Reread the ice cream study described for Stop and Think 15.1 through 15.3. Imagine that the results of this study had been different. Suppose instead that ratings for the ice cream were higher whenever more chocolate chips were used, regardless of whether real or artificial vanilla was used. Would this represent an interaction? Why or why not?

15.7. Now imagine that the results from the ice cream experiment showed that ratings were higher when real vanilla was used regardless of the proportion of chocolate chips. Would this represent an interaction? Why or why not?

FIGURE 15.4 ■ Mean Satisfaction Ratings for the Text Format by Subject Topic Study Showing the Interaction Between the Two Factors

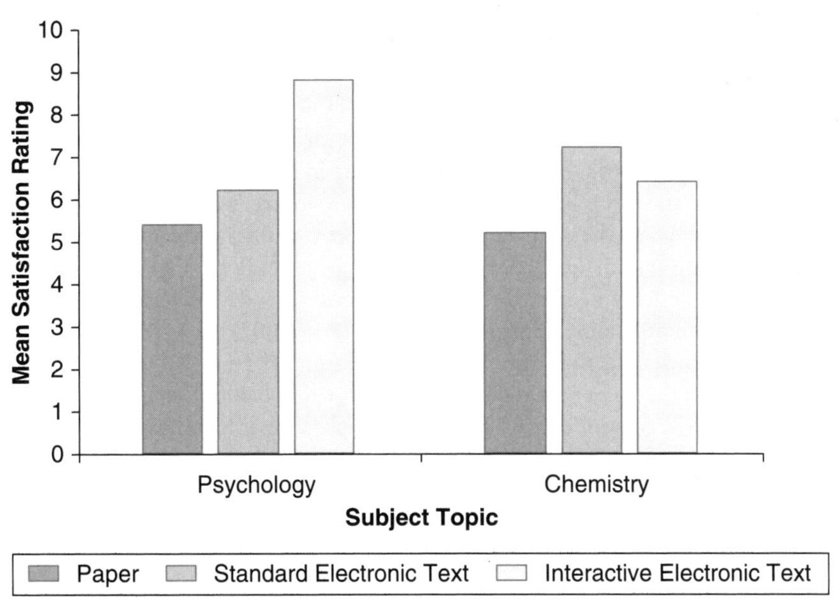

CALCULATING TWO-WAY BETWEEN-SUBJECTS ANALYSIS OF VARIANCE USING SPSS

With more than one factor in our design, we'll need to begin using the General Linear Model function in the Analyze menu in SPSS to conduct a factorial ANOVA. Consider a factorial experiment where memory is compared for different types of items. In this experiment, two factors are manipulated: the type of item studied (either pictures or words) and the type of test a participant receives for studied items (recognition of items formatted as words or pictures). In this study, we will consider whether memory performance differs for studied pictures and words (i.e., the main effect of study format) or differs for tests with pictures and words (i.e., the main effect of test format) and whether format match (picture or word) across study and test is better than when the format mismatches (i.e., the interaction of these factors). Percentage correct recognition data are presented in Table 15.1.

Recall from the examples we have already discussed for between-subjects designs that the data should all be entered into one column in the data window in SPSS because each score is from a different participant. However, you will need two additional columns to code the levels of the factors: one for the study format and one for the test format. Remember to label the columns with the variable names and to insert value labels for the codes.

To run the two-way between-subjects ANOVA, choose the Univariate test option in the General Linear Model portion of the Analyze menu. A Definition window appears for you to click over the dependent and independent (Fixed Factor box) variables. You do not need to select any post hoc tests for the main effects in this design because there are only two levels of each independent variable, but you can choose them in the Options tab if you have a design where one or more independent variables contains three or more levels. But in our 2×2 example, an examination of the means will indicate which level results in higher recognition for any significant main effects. If you select the factors in the Descriptives window, these means will appear in the output. Click OK to begin the analysis.

The output contains three tests of interest that appear in the Tests of Between-Subjects Effects box (see Figure 15.5). The two main effects are indicated in the rows with the variable labels (*Study* and *Test*). The main effect of study format was significant: $F(1,36) = 8.91$, $p = 0.005$; however, the main effect of test format was not significant: $F(1,36) = 1.32$, $p = 0.257$. The means in the Descriptive Statistics box indicate that studied pictures ($M = 80.45$) were better remembered than studied words ($M = 71.50$), regardless of test format. This is a common finding in memory studies (Paivio, 2007). However, the interaction between study format and test format was also significant: $F(1,36) = 31.96$, $p < 0.001$. Note that the p value in the output for the interaction is listed as 0.000. Remember than p can never equal zero. The convention used in reporting such values is to indicate that the p value was less than 0.001. The graph in Figure 15.6 illustrates this interaction. From the graph, we can see that the match in study and test format did affect recognition scores such that a match in format from study to test resulted in higher scores than the mismatch conditions.

TABLE 15.1 ■ Data From a 2 × 2 (Study Format × Test Format) Memory Experiment

Participant number	Picture study and picture test	Participant number	Picture study and word test
1	92	11	68
2	88	12	50
3	87	13	54
4	78	14	80
5	95	15	85
6	90	16	78
7	71	17	92
8	89	18	74
9	93	19	79
10	89	20	77
Word study and picture test		**Word study and word test**	
21	56	31	88
22	62	32	90
23	59	33	67
24	70	34	79
25	65	35	85
26	67	36	78
27	45	37	90
28	51	38	74
29	67	39	89
30	71	40	77

SUMMARY OF STEPS

- Type the data into one column of the data window; add a column of codes for levels of each independent variable.
- Choose General Linear Model from the Analyze menu.
- Choose Univariate from the choices.
- In the Definition window, click the data column over for the Dependent Variable and the columns of codes over to the Fixed Factor box.
- Under Options, choose Descriptive Statistics for means and variability and click Continue.
- Under Post Hoc, click the data variable over, and check the box of the post hoc test you wish to run. Click Continue (only appropriate if the independent variable has three or more levels and the main effect is significant).
- Click OK to run the ANOVA; results for each test appear in the Output window.

FIGURE 15.5 ■ SPSS Output for the 2 × 2 Study or Test Format Study

Univariate Analysis of Variance

Between-Subjects Factors

		Value Label	*N*
Study format	1.00	Picture	20
	2.00	Word	20
Test format	1.00	Picture	20
	2.00	Word	20

Descriptive Statistics

Dependent Variable: Recognition Score

Study Format	Test Format	Mean	Std. Deviation	*N*
Picture	Picture	87.2000	7.29992	10
	Word	73.7000	13.08986	10
	Total	80.4500	12.42440	20
Word	Picture	61.3000	8.52513	10
	Word	81.7000	7.88881	10
	Total	71.5000	13.16894	20
Total	Picture	74.2500	15.36871	20
	Word	77.7000	11.29089	20
	Total	75.9750	13.42498	40

Tests of Between-Subjects Effects

Dependent Variable: Recognition Score

Source	Type III Sum of Squares	*df*	Mean Square	*F*	Sig.
Corrected Model	3793.075[a]	3	1264.358	14.066	.000
Intercept	230888.025	1	230888.025	2568.673	.000
Study	801.025	1	801.025	8.912	.005
Test	119.025	1	119.025	1.324	.257
Study *Test	2873.025	1	2873.025	31.963	.000
Error	3235.900	36	89.886		
Total	327917.000	40			
Corrected Total	7028.975	39			

a. $r^2 = .540$ (Adjusted $r^2 = .501$).

FIGURE 15.6 ■ Line Graph of the Interaction Between Study Format and Test Format

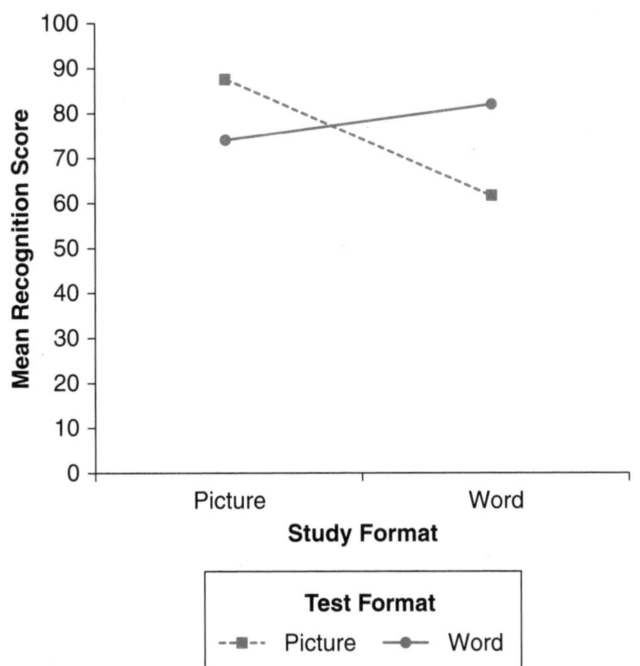

TEST ASSUMPTIONS

The test assumptions for the two-way between-subjects ANOVA are the same as those for the one-way between-subjects ANOVA.

1. The population of scores must be a normal distribution. As you have seen in previous chapters, this is a standard assumption for inferential tests.
2. The scores from different participants within each sample must be independent. Thus, the scores from the different individuals within each sample cannot be related.
3. The populations that the samples represent must have equal variance. In other words, the assumption of homogeneity of variances must hold. Levene's test can be run to test for this assumption in SPSS using the Options tab.

Calculation Summary

interaction of between-groups sum of squares: The sum of the sum of squared values for each group mean minus the two marginal means for that group plus the grand mean times the group sample size

within-groups sum of squares: The sum of the sum of squared deviations for each score from its group mean

interaction of between-groups degrees of freedom: The *df* for one factor times the *df* for the other factor

within-groups degrees of freedom: The sample size minus one times the number of levels of each factor

THINKING ABOUT RESEARCH

A summary of a research study in psychology is given here. As you read the summary, think about the following questions:

1. What are the independent variables in this experiment? Identify the levels of each independent variable.
2. What are the dependent variables? (*Hint:* Look at Figure 15.7.)
3. Does the researchers' hypothesis predict any main effects or an interaction between these independent variables? Explain your answer.
4. Describe the tests that the factorial ANOVAs for this study would conduct.
5. From what you see in Figure 15.7, did the results indicate an interaction effect between the independent variables for

either of the dependent variables? Explain your answer.

6. Does the graph in Figure 15.7 show main effects of either independent variable for either dependent variable? Why or why not?

Research Study. Wagman, J. B., Langley, M. D., & Farmer-Dougan, V. (2018). Carrying their own weight: Dogs perceive changing affordances for reaching. *Quarterly Journal of Experimental Psychology, 71*, 1040–1044.

Purpose of the Study. To show that changes in behavior based on environmental constraints are similar across species, the point at which dogs change from head-only reaches to rearing reaches was examined. Studies with humans have shown that such behavior changes occur when stability is threatened—the current study examined these behavior changes in terms of the height at which the dogs reared up on two legs to reach an object based on whether they were wearing a weighted backpack or not. The researchers hypothesized that to maintain their stability, the taller dogs would rear at a higher height than shorter dogs and that when the dogs were wearing a backpack, they would rear at a lower height than without the backpack.

Method of the Study. Subjects were 20 dogs from local owners and shelters. Upon arrival, the dog's weight was measured. For the reaching apparatus, a cup containing a hot dog treat was mounted on a horizontal crossbar that could be raised and lowered by the experimenter to change the bar heights (see Photos 15.1A and 15.1B). Each dog was shown the hot dog in the cup at eye level until they reached for the treat without prompting. The bar was then raised 5 cm on each trial until the dog reared to reach the treat cup. The bar height was then measured. Then the bar was lowered 1.25 cm until the dog no longer reared for the treat. This procedure was then repeated until the dog reared twice at the same height and did not rear at the height 1.25 cm below the height measured. This procedure was repeated with a dog backpack placed on the dog containing weight equal to 10% of the dog's weight. Finally, shoulder height was measured for each dog.

Results of the Study. Figure 15.7 shows the results for mean rearing boundary (top graph) and mean rearing boundary relative to shoulder height (bottom graph) for tall and short dogs with and without the weighted backpack. Tall dogs reared at a higher boundary height than short dogs, and on average, dogs reared at a higher boundary height without the weighted backpack. However, when the dogs' shoulder height was considered (see bottom graph of Figure 15.7), no difference was seen between short and tall dogs—only the difference between weighted and unweighted trials remained.

Conclusions of the Study. The researchers concluded from these results that dogs, like humans, change their reaching behaviors at the point at which stability is threatened, not at the absolute maximum reaching height while standing. These results show that perceptual-action behaviors are similar across dogs and humans in this way.

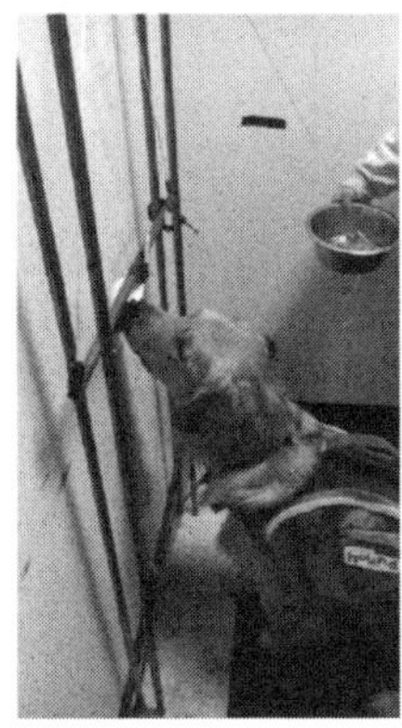

Photo 15.1A–B
This is the apparatus used by Wagman, Langley, and Farmer-Dougan (2018). Photo 15.1A shows a dog reaching with its head only. Photo 15.1B shows a dog reaching while rearing.

Source: Wagman et al. (2018).

(Continued)

(Continued)

FIGURE 15.7 ■ Results From Wagman et al.'s (2018) Experiment

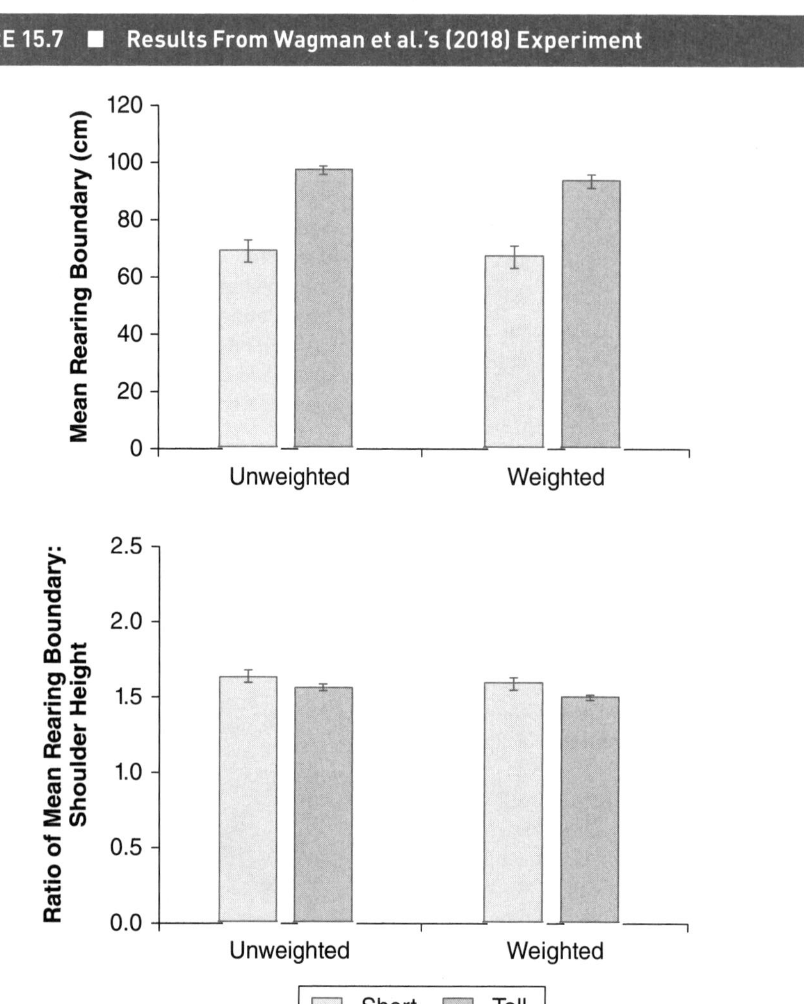

Source: Wagman et al. (2018).

Chapter Summary

- **Can we examine more than one causal factor in a single study?**
  Yes, a factorial design includes multiple factors in a single study. The main effects of each factor can be tested, along with the interaction between factors.
- **How do levels of a factor and conditions differ in a factorial design?**
  In a factorial design, the levels of a factor are the different situations compared for that factor, whereas the conditions in the study are the situations encountered by the participants that come from combining the levels of the factors.
- **What is the difference between a main effect and an interaction?**
  Main effects test differences between the overall levels of a factorial (through the marginal means) and the interaction tests whether differences across the conditions for one level differ from the condition differences for the other level(s). In other words, the interaction tests whether the effect of one factor *depends* on the level of the other factor.
- **How do we calculate an *F* ratio for an interaction?**
  The *F* ratio for an interaction is based on the sum of squared deviations of the scores in each group from their condition mean (between-groups variance term) divided by the error (within-groups variance term).
- **What does a significant interaction tell us about our data?**
  A significant interaction tells us that the effect of one factor *depends* on the level of the other factor. An interaction can occur in a number of ways, including opposite effects at each level, a smaller effect at one level than the other, or an effect at one level and no effect at the other level.

Test Yourself

1. The benefit of a factorial design that is not present in a single-factor study is that you can ________.
   a. test main effects
   b. examine effects of multiple factors in one ANOVA
   c. examine the combined effect of multiple factors on the dependent measure
   d. both b and c
2. An interaction tells you that ________.
   a. there is an overall effect of your independent variable
   b. the effect of one independent variable depends on the level of the other independent variable
   c. neither of your independent variables affects your dependent variable
   d. none of the above

(Continued)

(Continued)

3. In a factorial design, levels of an independent variable are __________.
   a. compared with marginal means
   b. the same as the conditions
   c. not defined
4. A researcher investigated the effects of color of a website background on consumer behavior. Three website colors were tested: blue, red, and yellow. In addition, the type of product being purchased was compared: The websites contained either sports equipment or books. The amount each individual purchased on the website they saw was measured. Overall, yellow websites resulted in larger purchase amounts than the other colors, but the color effect was present only for books. No color effect was present for sports equipment sites. According to this description, which of the following were significant in the ANOVA?
   a. The main effect of website color
   b. The main effect of type of product
   c. The interaction between website color and type of product
   d. Both a and b
   e. Both a and c
5. In a factorial experiment, an interaction between the independent variables will always be present.
   a. True
   b. False
6. For a factorial design, you only need to conduct one ANOVA to test all the effects.
   a. True
   b. False
7. If you find a significant interaction in your factorial design, then the main effects must also be significant.
   a. True
   b. False
8. A researcher conducted a study to investigate the effects of smiling on helping behavior. Participants completed a survey that they thought was the purpose of the study, but in reality, the experiment took place after they completed the survey. At the end of the survey session, half of the subjects were thanked with a smile and half were thanked without a smile. Whether the subject received a smile or not was randomly determined. The gender of the person giving the smile also varied by participant: Some subjects received the smile from a female researcher and some subjects received the smile from a male researcher. The subjects were on their way out of the lab in the hallway when they then passed a confederate who had just dropped a large stack of books. The number of subjects who helped the confederate pick up his books was measured. The results showed that the subjects who were thanked by a male researcher showed similar helping behaviors across smile and no-smile conditions. However, subjects who were thanked by a female researcher showed more helping behaviors when they received a smile than when they did not.
   a. What are the independent variables in this experiment? Identify how each

independent variable was manipulated (i.e., between subjects or within subjects).

b. Explain why you think the researcher decided to compare gender of the confederate in this study.

c. From the description of the results, was an interaction present? Explain your answer.

9. For the SPSS output in Figure 15.8, write a results section in American Psychological Association (APA) style.

FIGURE 15.8 ■ SPSS Output for a Factorial Design

Univariate Analysis of Variance

Between-Subjects Factors

		Value Label	N
Instruction_Type	1.00	Live Lecture	6
	2.00	Online Lectures	6
Item_Type	1.00	Multiple Choice	6
	2.00	Short Answer	6

Descriptive Statistics

Dependent Variable: Test_Score

Instruction_Type	Item_Type	Mean	Std. Deviation	N
Live Lecture	Multiple Choice	5.3333	.57735	3
	Short Answer	10.6667	1.15470	3
	Total	8.0000	3.03315	6
Online Lectures	Multiple Choice	4.6667	.57735	3
	Short Answer	21.6667	2.88675	3
	Total	13.1667	9.49561	6
Total	Multiple Choice	5.0000	.63246	6
	Short Answer	16.1667	6.33772	6
	Total	10.5833	7.24203	12

(Continued)

(Continued)

Tests of Between-Subjects Effects

Dependent Variable: Test_Score

Source	Type III Sum of Squares	df	Mean Square	F	Sig.
Corrected Model	556.250[a]	3	185.417	71.774	.000
Intercept	1344.083	1	1344.083	520.290	.000
Instruction_Type	80.083	1	80.083	31.000	.001
Item_Type	374.083	1	374.083	144.806	.000
Instruction_Type * Item_Type	102.083	1	102.083	39.516	.000
Error	20.667	8	2.583		
Total	1921.000	12			
Corrected Total	576.917	11			

a. R Squared = .964 (Adjusted R Squared = .951).

16

ONE-WAY WITHIN-SUBJECTS ANALYSIS OF VARIANCE

CONSIDER THE FOLLOWING QUESTIONS AS YOU READ CHAPTER 16

- How do within-subjects designs differ from between-subjects designs?
- What are the advantages of using a within-subjects design? What are the disadvantages?
- How does the calculation of the variance terms in an analysis of variance (ANOVA) change for within-subjects designs?
- Are there new assumptions to consider for an ANOVA with a within-subjects design?

LEARNING OBJECTIVES FOR CHAPTER 16

- Understand why we use an interaction term for the error term in within-subjects designs.
- Conduct a within-subjects ANOVA.

Remember the example presented in previous chapters about my dog, Daphne (see Photo 16.1)? In those chapters, I described an experiment we conducted to determine how to reduce separation anxiety in Daphne when we left her home alone. We varied the type of treatment (worn clothing and a chew toy) and the length of time we were gone (short outings and long outings) and measured the number of bad behaviors we found when we returned home after each combination of these factors (i.e., worn clothing for a short outing, worn clothing for a long outing). This design was first shown in Figure 14.1. One thing that was different about this experiment, though (compared with the types of experiments I had described previously), was that Daphne experienced *all* the conditions in the experiment (she was the only subject tested). This means the experiment was conducted with a within-subjects design.

WITHIN-SUBJECTS DESIGNS

The difference between within-subjects and between-subjects designs is about how the independent variable is manipulated. In between-subjects designs, each participant in the study experiences only one condition in the study. In within-subjects designs, each participant in the study experiences all of the conditions in the study. In Chapter 10, we looked at two different t tests that are used for these types of designs when two means are compared—the paired or related samples t test for within-subjects designs and the independent samples t test for between-subjects designs. For our study with Daphne, though, we are comparing more than two means in a within-subjects design. With more than two means to compare, we cannot use a t test to test our hypotheses. Instead, we will use an ANOVA as we did for the designs described in Chapters 11 and 15. However, we will need to calculate the F ratio in a different way to account for the measurement of the dependent variable from the same participants in all the conditions.

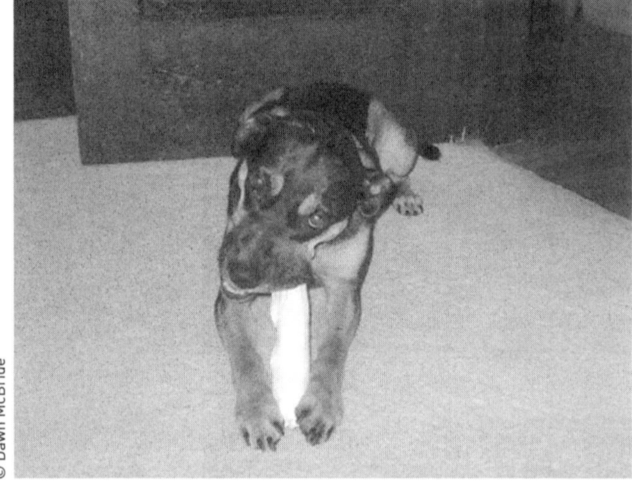

Photo 16.1
Previous chapters described a study with our dog, Daphne, in which she experienced several treatments to try to reduce her separation anxiety.

One advantage of the within-subjects design is the reduction of error in the data. Because participants are being compared with themselves (under different conditions), there are no between-group differences that contribute to the variability in the data (see Figure 16.1). There is only one group of individuals who contribute data under multiple conditions in the study. Because of this, the error term (i.e., within-groups variance) in our F ratio for this design will be lower than the error term that would be calculated for the same data if it were a between-subjects design. This allows us a better chance of detecting an effect that exists (i.e., more power). I discussed power in Chapter 9, when the basics of hypothesis testing were introduced along

FIGURE 16.1 ■ Within-Subjects Designs Reduce the Error Term in an ANOVA by Removing Between-Group Differences From the Data

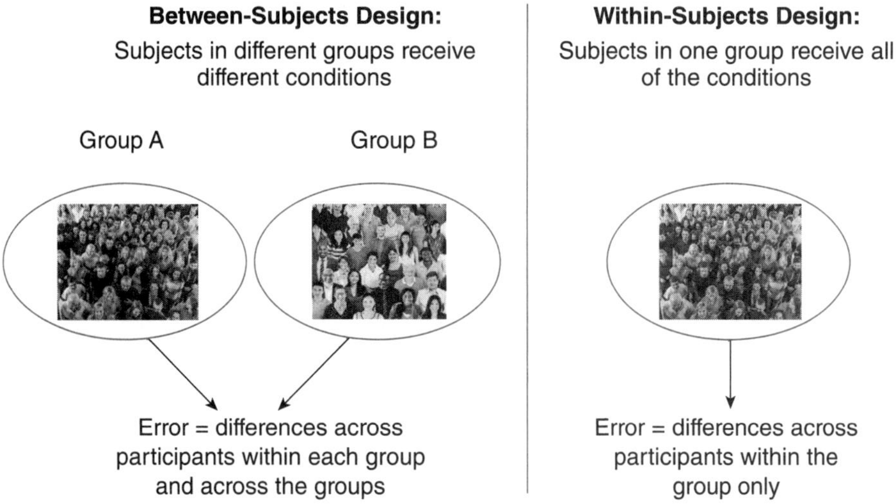

Between-Subjects Design:
Subjects in different groups receive different conditions

Group A

Group B

Error = differences across participants within each group and across the groups

Within-Subjects Design:
Subjects in one group receive all of the conditions

Error = differences across participants within the group only

Source: ©iStock/skynesher, ©iStock/Rawpixel

with the types of errors that can be made in our tests. The chance of a Type II error is 1-power, so when we increase power, we reduce our chance of a Type II error (where we do not detect an effect that exists).

Another advantage of a within-subjects design is the lower burden on the researcher to recruit participants for the study. Because the participants provide data in all conditions of the study, fewer individuals are needed in the sample. This is especially useful when sampling from smaller populations (e.g., rare clinical populations) or when a population is difficult to sample from (e.g., you have no incentive to offer participants). However, this advantage can become a disadvantage if the study procedure is long or difficult. Some participants may choose to drop out of the study (either explicitly withdrawing or indirectly withdrawing by failing to complete the task as instructed), reducing the sample size and possibly biasing the sample. The people who choose not to complete the study may be different in important ways from the people who choose to complete it, introducing a self-selection bias between our sample and the whole population.

Another issue to overcome in within-subjects designs is possible bias from the order of the conditions the participants experience. It is possible that the order in which they experience the conditions in the study will affect the behaviors or responses the participants make, biasing the data collected. Thus, order effects are a concern in a within-subjects study. This issue can be handled within the design by randomly assigning participants to different orders of the conditions to reduce this bias, a process known as counterbalancing. Counterbalancing allows the researcher to collect data in a within-subjects design using different orders of conditions. Order effects can then be tested by including the order of conditions as a factor in the data analyses. Thus, there are both advantages and disadvantages to using within-subjects designs compared with the between-subjects designs we have discussed in the previous chapters.

In this chapter, we will consider some within-subjects designs that compare more than two means. The one-way within-subjects design involves one independent variable with three or more levels. We will go through the calculation of the *F* ratio for this design both by hand and by using SPSS. However, the differences between the between-subjects and within-subjects ANOVA calculations also apply to two-way designs; I will briefly discuss two-way designs at the end of the chapter so you can see how to generalize these differences to more complex designs.

STOP AND THINK

16.1. For each study that follows, indicate whether it is a between-subjects or within-subjects design. Also indicate which type of inferential test (*t* test or ANOVA) is the correct choice for testing the hypothesis.

a. A statistics instructor is interested in the best type of quiz to use to prepare students in her course. She randomly assigns students in her course to one of three groups: no study quiz, a multiple-choice study quiz, or a short-answer study quiz. She then compares the exam scores for the three groups.

b. A statistics instructor is interested in the best type of quiz to use to prepare students in her course. She provides no quiz for the first exam, a multiple-choice quiz for the second exam, and a short-answer quiz for the third exam. She then compares the scores on the three exams for her class.

c. A neuropsychologist is treating several Alzheimer's disease patients in a clinic. He wants to determine the best time of day to discuss treatment issues with his patients, but he notices that mental state seems to vary with time of day. Thus, he designs a study to determine the time of day in which his patients seem to have the most cognitive awareness: morning or afternoon. He tests each patient at both times of day and compares scores on a cognitive screening scale for morning and afternoon.

16.2. For the study in 16.1b, explain why this study is not a true experiment. How can this study be redesigned to make it an experiment?

16.3. Explain how counterbalancing could be used in the studies described in b and c in 16.1.

CALCULATING A WITHIN-SUBJECTS ANALYSIS OF VARIANCE

Our hypothesis-testing steps will be very similar to those used with between-subjects ANOVAs. The main difference will be in the calculation of the *F* ratio in Step 4. I will describe those differences in that step.

To go through the hypothesis-testing steps, let's consider a within-subjects study that examines the effects of different distractions on driving performance. Here, we will consider a hypothetical experiment of this type that compares driving performance in terms of how quickly people can press a brake when an object suddenly appears in their path. Three conditions will be considered in this experiment: (1) driving while listening to the radio where the general topics of the songs played will need to be later recalled, (2) driving while listening to a phone conversation where the general topics of the conversation will need to be later recalled, and (3) driving with no extra task (the control condition). Because driving ability can differ from person to person, the study is conducted as a within-subjects design so that a participant's driving performance can be compared under each of the three conditions being tested. Figure 16.2 illustrates this design. This design will remove error in the data that occurs from the variability in driving performance that might exist between groups if the conditions were compared for different participants.

Step 1: State Hypotheses

In Step 1, we will state our hypothesis for the effect of driving condition—that driving with a distraction, most especially listening to a phone conversation, decreases driving performance relative to driving with no distraction. Thus, our hypotheses for the main effect in this study are as follows:

H_0: *The population means for people driving with and without distraction are equal:* $\mu_{control} = \mu_{radio} = \mu_{phone}$.

H_1: *The population means for people driving under different distraction conditions will be ordered as follows in terms of driving performance:* $\mu_{control} > \mu_{radio} > \mu_{phone}$.

FIGURE 16.2 ■ Design of a Within-Subjects Study Looking at the Effects of Different Types of Distractions on Driving Performance

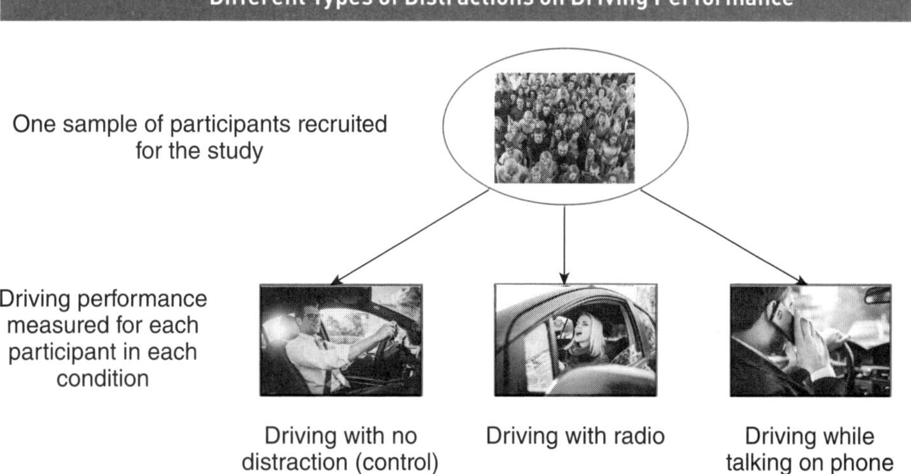
One sample of participants recruited for the study
Driving performance measured for each participant in each condition
Driving with no distraction (control)
Driving with radio
Driving while talking on phone

Source: ©iStock/skynesher, ©iStock/Geber86, ©iStock/Minerva Studio, ©iStock/Halfpoint

Step 2: Set Decision Criterion

Our alpha level will be set at 0.05.

Step 3: Collect Sample Data

To make our calculations simple for this example, we'll only consider a sample size of $n = 5$ in this study. However, note that a larger sample size would be needed (at least 20 participants) if we were to conduct this study to test our hypothesis. As in our one-way between-subjects design, we'll need to calculate the condition means from the subjects' data for each condition. But for the within-subjects design, we will also need means for each subject across the conditions to calculate our error term (how these are used to calculate our *F* ratio will be described in the next section). Thus, for each subject, we will calculate an overall mean that collapses each subject's data across the conditions in the study. The condition and subject means for our driving study are shown in Table 16.1. In the next step, we'll use these means to calculate the *F* ratios.

Step 4: Calculate Statistics

For the *F* ratio, the between-groups variance term will be calculated the same way it was for a between-subjects design: with the sum of squared differences between the condition

TABLE 16.1 ■ Data for Our Hypothetical Driving While Distracted Study—Values Represent Reaction Time for Braking When an Obstacle Appears

Subject #	A_1—No distraction	A_2—Driving with radio	A_3—Driving with phone	Subject marginal means
1	800	1200	1900	$\bar{X}_{S1} = 1300$
2	800	1300	1400	$\bar{X}_{S2} = 1167$
3	900	1500	1600	$\bar{X}_{S3} = 1333$
4	500	1800	1200	$\bar{X}_{S4} = 1167$
5	1300	1500	2200	$\bar{X}_{S5} = 1667$
Condition Marginal means	$\bar{X}_{A1} = 860$	$\bar{X}_{A2} = 1460$	$\bar{X}_{A3} = 1660$	$\bar{X}_{Grand} = 1327$

means and grand mean, multiplied by the number of subjects (n). However, the within-groups variance term will be quite different—it is the sum of squares interaction term for the interaction between the subjects and the conditions, SS_{SXA}. Recall that an interaction tells us if the differences across the levels of one factor are the same or different for each level of the other factor (i.e., does the effect of one factor *depend* on the level of the other factor?). Here, one of our factors is the subjects, where each subject is a different level. We expect the subjects as a group to differ across the conditions if the independent variable has an effect. But when the subjects show differences from one another that are not the same across the conditions (i.e., an interaction between the subjects and the conditions), this represents the error we get from subject to subject in our study. This interaction means that the subject-to-subject differences *depend* on the condition. Therefore, we will use the interaction term as the error term because the interaction between the subjects and the conditions will give us an estimate of the error that exists in our data based on differences from subject to subject across the conditions of the study. We will examine the formulas for these terms next.

Between-Groups Variance Term

For the between-groups variance term, we will use this formula:

$$SS_{Driving\ Condition} = n\Sigma\left(\bar{X}_A - \bar{X}_{Grand}\right)^2$$

Here, $\bar{X}_A$ is the marginal mean for each condition in our study, and n is the number of subjects in our sample (for within-subjects designs, N and n are the same value). Thus, the between groups SS for driving condition is as follows:

$$SS_{Driving\ Condition} = (5)\left[(860-1327)^2 + (1460-1327)^2 + (1660-1327)^2\right]$$

$$= 5\left[218089 + 17689 + 110889\right] = 5\left[346667\right] = 1733333$$

We also need the $df_{DrivingCondition}$, which is $df = a - 1 = 3 - 1 = 2$. With these two terms, we can calculate the between-groups variance for driving condition:

$$MS_{DrivingCondition} = \frac{1733333}{2} = 866667$$

Within-Groups Variance Term

As indicated at the beginning of this section, the error term for a within-subjects ANOVA is based on the interaction between the subjects and the independent variable. Recall that the general formula presented in Chapter 15 for an interaction is this:

$$SS_{Interaction} = \Sigma(\bar{X}_{AB} - \bar{X}_A - \bar{X}_B + \bar{X}_{Grand})^2$$

Here, the A term is our independent variable, but the B term is the subjects. Using this general formula, the SS for the subjects × driving condition interaction is as follows:

$$SS_{Subjects \times Driving\ Condition} = \begin{bmatrix} (800-860-1300+1327)^2 + (800-860-1167+1327)^2 \\ +\ldots+(2200-1660-1667+1327)^2 \end{bmatrix}$$
$$\begin{bmatrix}1089+10000+1156+\ldots+90000+40000\end{bmatrix} = 673333$$

Although each value in the calculation is not shown previously (only the first few and last values), this formula is calculated for each individual score (i.e., 15 scores for our example data set in Table 16.1). You can verify this by completing the formula for all 15 scores shown in the table. The $df_{Interaction} = (a - 1)\ (b - 1) = 2(4) = 8$, making the within-groups variance term as follows:

$$MS_{Subjects \times Driving\ Condition} = \frac{673333}{8} = 84167$$

F Ratio

With the values we have calculated for the between-groups variance terms and the within-groups error term, we can calculate the F ratio for the ANOVA. For the main effect of driving condition (the only effect we will test in our one-way design), the F ratio is this:

$$F_{TextFormat} = \frac{866667}{84167} = 10.30$$

In Step 5, we will find the F_{crit} for this effect by using the df terms included in its calculation.

Step 5: Make a Decision

In this step, we are looking for the F_{crit} value to determine if our calculated F ratio falls in the critical region for the F distribution. For the main effect of driving condition, we need $F_{crit}(2,10)$, where 2 is the $df_{Between}$ value and 10 is the df_{Within} value. If we use the table in Appendix D to find the F_{crit} in the column with 2 df and the row with 10 df, we find $F_{crit}(2,10) = 4.10$. Our calculated F value of 10.30 for the main effect of driving condition is higher than the F_{crit}, meaning that our test is significant—there is a mean difference between the three driving conditions. In this case, we must reject our null hypothesis.

STOP AND THINK

16.4. You are conducting a study to determine the best study technique to prepare for multiple choice exams. Your friends agree to participate in your study. Across the course of the semester, each of your friends agrees to use each of the study techniques you're interested in to prepare for one of their multiple choice exams: rereading their notes, taking the multiple choice quizzes that come with their textbooks, and working with a study partner to quiz each other. You compare exam scores (a percentage out of 100) for exams in which your friends used each of the three study techniques. Explain how you could use counterbalancing to control for order effects in this study.

16.5. You have conducted the study described previously and found the following data by condition. Conduct the within-subjects ANOVA to determine if you found an effect of study technique in your study.

Reread Notes: 67, 89, 78, 75, 77, 80

Multiple Choice Quizzes: 95, 95, 85, 100, 87, 86

Quiz With Study Partner: 75, 77, 80, 66, 85, 90

16.6. Regardless of what you found in 16.5, imagine that your ANOVA was significant. What is another possible explanation of this result (other than that study technique had an effect on exam scores)?

CALCULATING ONE-WAY WITHIN-SUBJECTS ANALYSIS OF VARIANCE USING SPSS

In this section, we will look at how to conduct the one-way within-subjects ANOVA using SPSS. In SPSS, within-subjects designs are referred to as *repeated measures*, so keep this in mind as you work through the example in this section. To illustrate the analysis in SPSS, we will go back to the SPSS example we covered in Chapter 11 for the one-way between-subjects design. This will allow us to compare how the ANOVA differs for the same data for between- and within-subjects designs. Recall that this example is for a study comparing satisfaction ratings for three different text format conditions with 30 participants per group. In our revised example here, let's assume the participants were the same individuals in each group. Thus, each participant rated each text format (perhaps for different chapters of the text). These data are shown in Figure 16.3 for the SPSS data window and correspond to the data analyzed (for a between-subjects design) in Chapter 11.

FIGURE 16.3 ■ SPSS Data Window for the Text Format Study Data

	Paper	Standard	Interactive	var	var
1	6.00	7.00	8.00		
2	6.00	4.00	8.00		
3	6.00	4.00	9.00		
4	7.00	5.00	5.00		
5	6.00	7.00	7.00		
6	5.00	6.00	9.00		
7	3.00	6.00	9.00		
8	3.00	7.00	6.00		
9	3.00	5.00	7.00		
10	5.00	6.00	5.00		
11	1.00	4.00	9.00		
12	8.00	2.00	10.00		
13	4.00	8.00	7.00		
14	2.00	7.00	7.00		
15	3.00	6.00	5.00		
16	3.00	5.00	8.00		
17	3.00	5.00	8.00		
18	3.00	5.00	8.00		
19	2.00	5.00	9.00		
20	4.00	6.00	9.00		
21	5.00	6.00	8.00		

For within-subjects designs, two things change in SPSS from the between-subjects examples described in earlier chapters: (1) The data appear in separate columns for each condition in the data window (remember that each participant or set of matched participants has data in a single row), and (2) we use the Repeated Measures test in the General Linear Model option of the Analyze menu. Each of the text format conditions is listed in a different column in the data window in SPSS with the column labeled by condition (see Figure 16.3). In addition, the within-subjects ANOVA is run by choosing the Repeated Measures test in the General Linear Model portion of the Analyze menu. This test is used to conduct an ANOVA for any design comparing three or more means that contains a within-subjects variable. The first window that appears for this test is the within-subjects variable definition window. In the top space, name the variable (e.g., Textcond), and then indicate the number of conditions for this variable (e.g., 3) by typing the number into the Number of Levels space and adding this variable to the list. Then, click Define to choose the columns for each level on the right side of the next window that appears. If your design also contains a between-subjects variable, you can define that variable here as well as in the Between-Subjects factor box. To run post hoc tests for this design (in the case that the main effect of text condition is significant in the ANOVA), you must choose the Options button (the Post Hoc button is used only for between-subjects variables), click over the text condition variable into the Display Means box, and then check the Compare Main Effects box. You can then choose a post hoc test from the drop-down bar. You may also wish to choose the Display Descriptive Statistics option in this window. Click Continue and OK to run the test.

The output (see Figure 16.4) is more complex for the repeated measures test than for the other tests we have seen. However, the output still contains the information needed to determine if the tests are significant. Figure 16.4 shows the portions of the output needed to interpret the results for this example. To evaluate the main effect of the text condition, look for the Tests of Within-Subjects Effects box. The first column of this box shows the F and p values. For this example, $F = 37.979$ and $p < 0.001$. Therefore, we can reject the null hypothesis that there is no difference in condition means because the main effect of text condition is significant.

The post hoc tests are shown in the box of the output labeled *Pairwise Comparisons*. The conditions are indicated by code value with p values listed in the Sig. column. The post hoc tests indicate that ratings for the paper text condition are lower than ratings for the interactive electronic text and that the standard electronic text had lower ratings than the interactive electronic text—both $p < 0.001$.

If you compare the sum of squares terms across the two analyses for the same data analyzed as a between-subjects design in Chapter 11, you will see that the between-groups terms (labeled *Textcond* for the within-subjects effects in Figure 16.4) are the same, but the within-groups or error sum of squares is lower for the within-subjects design than the between-subjects design. However, because we had fewer overall subjects in the within-subjects design than the between-subjects design, the error *df* is higher in the between-subjects design, giving us a higher F value.

FIGURE 16.4 ■ SPSS Output for the Text Format Study Data

General Linear Model

Within-Subjects Factors

Measure: MEASURE_1

Textcond	Dependent Variable
1	Paper
2	Standard
3	Interactive

Descriptive Statistics

	Mean	Std. Deviation	N
Paper Text	4.1667	1.64177	30
Standard Electronic Text	5.3333	1.62594	30
Interactive Electronic Text	7.8333	1.28877	30

Tests of Within-Subjects Effects

Measure: MEASURE_1

Source		Type III Sum of Squares	df	Mean Square	F	Sig.
Textcond	Sphericity Assumed	210.556	2	105.278	37.979	.000
	Greenhouse-Geisser	210.556	1.912	110.128	37.979	.000
	Huynh-Feldt	210.556	2.000	105.278	37.979	.000
	Lower-bound	210.556	1.000	210.556	37.979	.000
Error(Textcond)	Sphericity Assumed	160.778	58	2.772		
	Greenhouse-Geisser	160.778	55.446	2.900		
	Huynh-Feldt	160.778	58.000	2.772		
	Lower-bound	160.778	29.000	5.544		

Textcond

Estimates

Measure: MEASURE_1

Textcond	Mean	Std. Error	95% Confidence Interval Lower Bound	95% Confidence Interval Upper Bound
1	4.167	.300	3.554	4.780
2	5.333	.297	4.726	5.940
3	7.833	.235	7.352	8.315

Pairwise Comparisons

Measure: MEASURE_1

(I) Textcond	(J) Textcond	Mean Difference (I-J)	Std. Error	Sig.[b]	95% Confidence Interval for Difference[b] Lower Bound	Upper Bound
1	2	-1.167	.470	.057	-2.361	.028
	3	-3.667*	.391	.000	-4.659	-2.674
2	1	1.167	.470	.057	-.028	2.361
	3	-2.500*	.425	.000	-3.581	-1.419
3	1	3.667*	.391	.000	2.674	4.659
	2	2.500*	.425	.000	1.419	3.581

Based on estimated marginal means

*. The mean difference is significant at the

b. Adjustment for multiple comparisons: Bonferroni.

Multivariate Tests

	Value	F	Hypothesis df	Error df	Sig.
Pillai's trace	.769	46.518[a]	2.000	28.000	.000
Wilks' lambda	.231	46.518[a]	2.000	28.000	.000
Hotelling's trace	3.323	46.518[a]	2.000	28.000	.000
Roy's largest root	3.323	46.518[a]	2.000	28.000	.000

Each F tests the multivariate effect of Textcond. These tests are based on the linearly independent pairwise comparisons among the estimated marginal means.

a. Exact statistic

SUMMARY OF STEPS

- Enter the data into each data window—one column for each condition.
- Choose the General Linear Model from the Analyze menu.
- Choose Repeated Measures from the list of tests.
- Define conditions of within-subjects variables by typing in a name for the variable and the number of levels of this variable; click Add.
- Click Define, and then choose the columns from the left for the conditions of the within-subjects variable.
- If there are any between-subjects variables in the design, click those columns into the Between-Subjects Factor box.
- To display means and choose post hoc tests, click the Option tab.
- For means, click the Descriptive Statistics box.
- For post hoc tests, move the within-subjects variable label over to the Display Means For: box. Then click the Compare main effects box, and choose the post hoc you want to run from the drop-down menu under Confidence interval adjustment.
- Click Continue and OK to run the analyses (see Figure 16.4 for example output).

TEST ASSUMPTIONS

The first two test assumptions for the within-subjects ANOVA are the same as those for the between-subjects ANOVA:

1. The population of difference scores must be a normal distribution.
2. The scores from different participants within each sample must be independent.

However, the third assumption for the within-subjects ANOVA is a new assumption known as the **sphericity assumption**. This assumption is that pairs of scores in the population for the same individuals have similar variability.

sphericity assumption: Assumption of the repeated measures (within-subjects) ANOVA that pairs of scores in the population have equal variance

3. Sphericity: In the population of scores, the differences between pairs of scores from the same individuals are equal.

SPSS provides a test of the sphericity assumption for repeated measures (i.e., within-subjects) ANOVAs. This test for the example data analyzed in the previous section is shown in Figure 16.5. If the sphericity test is significant, the *F* statistic needs to be adjusted to retain accuracy of the test. To make these adjustments, the Tests of Within-Subjects Effects box (shown in Figure 16.4) contains a few different corrections below the Sphericity

FIGURE 16.5 ■ SPSS Output for the Sphericity Test

Mauchly's Test of Sphericity[a]

Measure: MEASURE_1

Within Subjects Effect	Mauchly's W	Approx. Chi-Square	df	Sig.	Epsilon[b]		
					Greenhouse-Geisser	Huynh-Feldt	Lower-bound
Textcond	.954	1.321	2	.517	.956	1.000	.500

Tests the null hypothesis that the error covariance matrix of the orthonormalized transformed dependent variables is proportional to an identity matrix.

a. Design: Intercept
Within Subjects Design: Textcond

b. May be used to adjust the degrees of freedom for the averaged tests of significance. Corrected tests are displayed in the Tests of Within-Subjects Effects table.

Assumed row. The sphericity assumed values are used if the sphericity test is not significant. However, if the sphericity test is significant, a correction is used because violations of this assumption can increase the chance of a Type I error (Keppel & Wickens, 2004). A common correction used in psychological research is the Greenhouse–Geisser correction. A full discussion of the correction techniques is provided in Howell's (2013) statistics text (as well as other, more advanced statistics texts).

MORE COMPLEX WITHIN-SUBJECTS DESIGNS

The analyses conducted in this chapter were done for within-subjects designs with a single independent variable. However, the analyses can also be done in a similar fashion for factorial within-subjects designs. As in between-subjects designs, the ANOVA would test the main effects for each independent variable and the interaction between the variables. As in the one-way designs considered in this chapter, the between-groups variance terms of the F ratios would be calculated the same way they are in between-subjects designs. But the within-groups variance terms will include the interaction with the subjects factor, as you saw in the calculations conducted in this chapter. Any test that involves a within-subjects factor (main effects and interactions) will use the error term calculated in this chapter. However, the calculation of the error term becomes more complicated as each independent variable is added to the design—SPSS and other software packages are helpful in conducting these analyses.

Calculation Summary

within-subjects error term: The interaction between subjects and the independent variable

THINKING ABOUT RESEARCH

A summary of a research study in psychology is given here. As you read the summary, think about the following questions:

1. What are the independent variables in this experiment? Identify the levels of each independent variable.
2. Why do you think these researchers used a within-subjects design for this study?
3. What are the dependent variables? (*Hint:* Look at Figure 16.8.)
4. From what you see in Figure 16.8, did the results indicate an interaction effect between the independent variables? If so, describe the interaction.
5. Does the graph in Figure 16.8 show main effects of either independent variable?

Research Study. Bub, D. N., Masson, M. E. J., & Lin, T. (2013). Features of planned hand actions influence identification of graspable objects. *Psychological Science, 24,* 1269–1276.

tolgart/istockphoto

Photo 16.2
Bub, Masson, and Lin (2013) hypothesized that knowing what action is appropriate for an object (e.g., holding a mug in your hand) can affect your identification of the object.

Purpose of the Study. These researchers investigated how action plans (e.g., moving your hand and arm to pick up an object) influence object identification. One might think that object identification would affect action plans (e.g., you would plan your movements differently to pick up a mug versus a frying pan). However, these researchers suggested that the causal relationship can also go

FIGURE 16.6 ■ Stimuli Used in Bub et al.'s (2013) Experiment

Source: Bub et al. (2003).

(*Continued*)

(Continued)

FIGURE 16.7 ■ Trial Sequence Used in Bub et al.'s (2013) Experiment

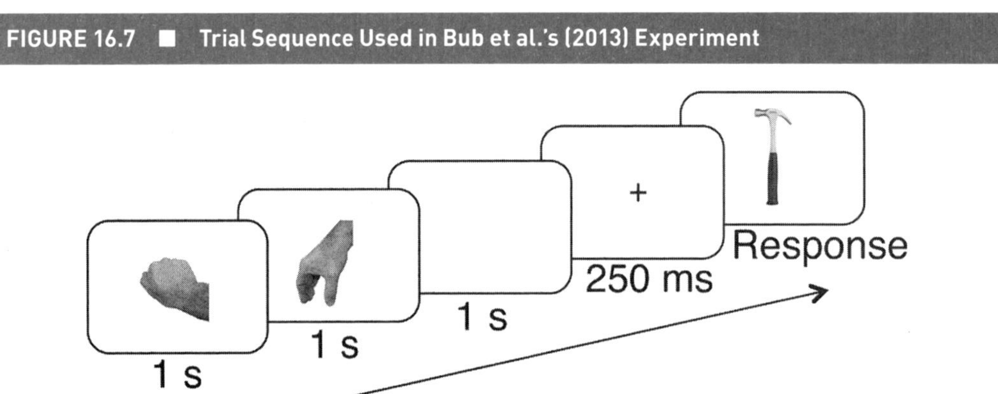

Source: Bub et al. (2003).

the other way, that the action plan made can influence how well you identify an object (see Photo 16.2). After familiarization trials, they gave subjects an action plan for their hand and then asked them to identify an object that could be held in the hand as quickly and accurately as possible. They hypothesized that when the action plan matched the way the object would be held, subjects would be faster at naming the objects.

Method of the Study. There were 20 undergraduate students in the experiment. The subjects first received familiarization trials with the action plans. They were shown pictures of hands and asked to mimic the hand posture (see Figure 16.6 for hand pictures). Subjects then received familiarization trials with the objects. Each object (see Figure 16.6 for pictures of the objects) was presented with its name and the subject read the name out loud. Then the critical trials were presented. On each trial, a hand action plan in two-hand pictures (see Figure 16.7 for the sequence of events in a trial) was shown to the subjects one at a time. Then, after a 250-ms fixation cross was shown, the object appeared and subjects were to name the object as quickly as possible. Their response was recorded by the computer's microphone with their naming time for each trial. Thus, trials were either congruent or incongruent in terms of the hand orientation (vertical or horizontal) for picking up the objects and the hand alignment (left hand or right hand) for picking up the objects.

Results of the Study. Figure 16.8 presents the results for naming time and naming errors according to the congruency of the orientation and alignment of the action plans shown before the pictures. These results show that naming time was fastest when both features (i.e., orientation and alignment) either matched or did not match the object shown for picking it up. Thus, if only one feature matched and the other feature did not, subjects were slower to name the object than when they both matched or both did not match.

Conclusions of the Study. The results of the study showed that action plans affected object identification as the authors predicted. Having one motor feature in mind that can be used to pick up the object and one motor feature that cannot be used to pick up the object interfered with naming of the objects.

FIGURE 16.8 ■ Results From Bub et al.'s (2013) Experiment

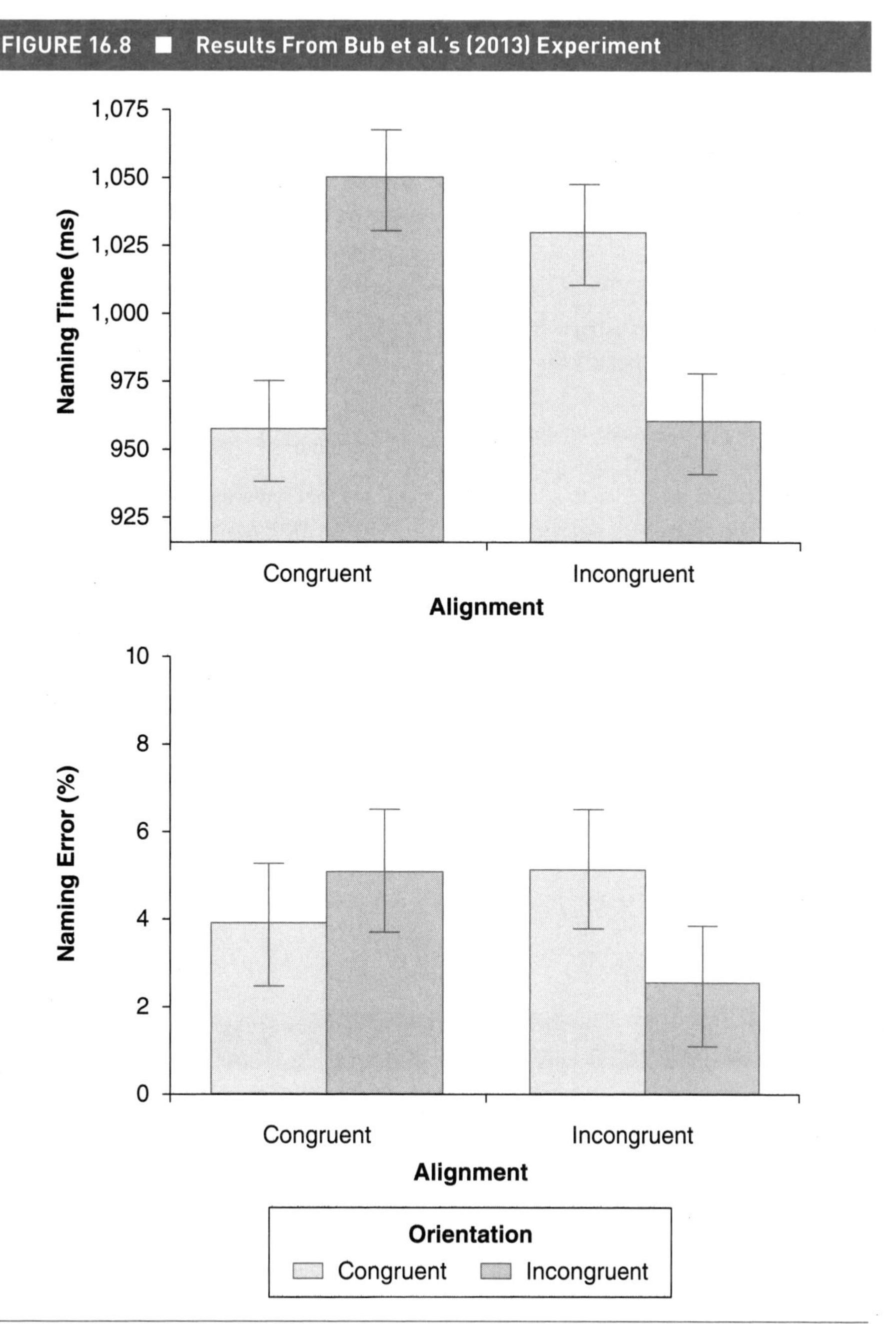

Source: Bub et al. (2003).

Chapter Summary

- **How do within-subjects designs differ from between-subjects designs?**
  The primary difference between between-subjects and within-subjects designs is that in within-subjects designs, data are collected from each participant in all the conditions of the study instead of only one condition as in between-subjects designs.

- **What are the advantages of using a within-subjects design? What are the disadvantages?**
  The advantages of within-subjects designs (relative to between-subjects designs) are that there is less error (due to a lack of between-group differences across different groups of participants), and fewer participants are needed in the study to collect the same amount of data. The disadvantages are that there may be order effects from the order of the conditions the participants receive (which can be controlled with counterbalancing) and that the participants' procedure will be longer in the study, which could result in loss of subjects across the procedure and/or fatigue effects.

- **How does the calculation of the variance terms in an ANOVA change for within-subjects designs?**
  The between-groups variance term is calculated the same way in both types of designs. However, the within-groups error term is calculated differently. For within-subjects designs, the error term is calculated from the interaction between subjects and the independent variable.

- **Are there new assumptions to consider for an ANOVA with a within-subjects design?**
  Yes, the within-subjects ANOVA has a sphericity assumption to satisfy that states that pairs of scores from the same participants in the population must have equal variance. SPSS provides a test of the sphericity assumption and some corrections if the test is significant.

Test Yourself

1. In a within-subjects ANOVA, the error term is calculated from the interaction between the independent variable and the __________.
   a. other independent variables in the study
   b. between-groups variance term
   c. subjects as a factor
   d. none of the above

2. An advantage of a within-subjects design is __________.
   a. fewer participants are needed in the study
   b. there is less error in the data
   c. that counterbalancing is not needed
   d. both a and b
   e. both b and c

3. A disadvantage of within-subjects designs is that __________.
   a. more participants are needed in the study
   b. there is more error in the data
   c. order effects can be present in the data
   d. both a and b
   e. both b and c
4. Counterbalancing is a procedural technique that helps control for __________.
   a. between-groups error
   b. within-groups error
   c. subject fatigue
   d. order effects
5. The assumption that pairs of scores from the same individuals in the population have equal variance is called the ____________________ assumption.
   a. Levene's
   b. sphericity
   c. independence
   d. pairs
6. In within-subjects analyses, $N = n$.
   a. True
   b. False
7. With the same number of participants, a between-subjects design should result in less error than a comparable within-subjects design.
   a. True
   b. False
8. In within-subjects designs, order effects can be tested by including order as a factor in the analysis.
   a. True
   b. False
9. Suppose you conducted a study to test the hypothesis that social pressure affects memory accuracy. You set up a study in which all of the participants view three different videos of a person robbing a convenience store (order of the videos is counterbalanced across participants). After one crime video, participants watch other participants discussing the crime. After another crime video, the participants read a summary of the crime written by another participant. In reality, these other participants are part of the experiment, and some of the details of the crime that are discussed or written are inaccurate. The actual participants are told that they should consider other people's perspectives on the crime because it is difficult for any one person to accurately remember all the details. After the third crime video, the participants do not view the discussion or read a summary of the crime (i.e., the control condition) but are also told that it is difficult for any one person to accurately remember all the details of the crime. Thirty minutes after viewing the crime videos, all participants are given a recognition memory test about details of the crimes. For this study, answer the following questions:
   a. What is the correct statistical test that should be used to analyze the data?
   b. What is the null hypothesis that will be tested?
   c. Suppose that 10 participants participated in the study. For the following recognition accuracy data, use SPSS to conduct the correct statistical test to analyze these data:

(Continued)

(Continued)

Video Discussion Watched: 67, 80, 69, 72, 75, 79, 66, 71, 69, 79

Video Summary Read: 80, 75, 65, 77, 60, 69, 73, 79, 71, 80

No Video Discussion or Summary Control: 78, 65, 79, 84, 88, 79, 89, 90, 85, 87

d. From the SPSS output you obtained, what can be concluded about the null hypothesis you stated?

e. Why should the researchers consider whether the order of the video conditions had an effect on recognition accuracy in this study?

SAGE edge™

Visit **edge.sagepub.com/mcbridermstats** to find the answers to the Test Yourself questions above, as well as quizzes, flashcards, and other resources to help you accomplish your coursework goals.

APPENDIX A

Sample APA Style Research Report

Does Delay Affect

Prospective Memory Accuracy?

Jackie K. Cavallo

Illinois State University

Abstract

The present experiment was designed to test the effect of delay on prospective memory. Prospective memory is remembering to complete a task in the future (Einstein & McDaniel, 2005). Previous studies that measured forgetting of prospective memory have reported mixed results. Thus, the current study tested the effect of delay in an attempt to clarify the effect. Delay between the presentation of the prospective memory instructions and the prospective memory cue was manipulated. Delays of 5 to 20 min were tested. Results indicated that prospective memory performance did not change as delay increased. Thus, there was no evidence that delay affects prospective memory for this range of delays.

Keywords: prospective memory, forgetting

Does Delay Have an Effect on Prospective Memory Accuracy?

Prospective memory (PM) is the act of remembering to perform a task at some point in the future (Einstein & McDaniel, 2005). More and more research is taking place on this topic. Researchers in this area have been examining the effect of delay on PM. In these studies, the delay between the PM instructions and the presentation of the PM cue was manipulated. Knowing how delay affects PM may indicate how similar PM is to retrospective memory (i.e., remembering something you have experienced in the past).

Previous studies have reported mixed results for the effect of delay on PM. For example, in a study by Nigro and Cicogna (2000), university students answered two standardized questionnaires. After completing the first questionnaire, participants were told to relay a message to the experimenter in charge of giving the second questionnaire. The message was the same for all participants. Random assignment was used to place the participants in one of three delay conditions: 10 min, 2 days, or 2 weeks. On seeing the second experimenter at their designated time, participants were to give the message. Results showed that PM accuracy was not affected by delay of the second session. However, Hicks, Marsh, and Russell (2000) did find an effect of delay on PM performance. They manipulated delay in a laboratory study of PM and found that PM performance increased from a delay of 2.5 min to a delay of 15 min. Thus, the effect of delay on PM is unclear.

Contrary to the results of Hicks et al. (2000), Meier, Zimmerman, and Perrig (2006) found that PM performance decreased with longer delays. In their second experiment, they administered delays of 5, 15, and 45 min using two distractor tasks. Results suggested that as the delays got longer the PM accuracy decreased.

The purpose of the current study was to find out if delays between the PM instructions and the presentation of the PM cue significantly affect PM accuracy. Delays of 5, 10, 15, and 20 min were used. Based on the results of Meier et al. (2006) for delays in this range, I hypothesized that as delay increased, PM accuracy would decrease.

Method

Participants

The participants were 80 undergraduate students from a psychology department subject pool at Illinois State University. They completed the experiment voluntarily and received extra credit in their courses for their participation. Participants were randomly assigned to one of the four conditions—5-, 10-, 15-, or 20-min delay—with 20 participants per condition.

Design

A between-subjects design was used to examine the differences between the four delay conditions and PM accuracy. The independent variable was delay between instruction of the PM task and the PM cue. The levels of the independent variable were 5-, 10-, 15-, and 20-min delays. The dependent variable in the study was PM accuracy.

Materials

The stimuli consisted of categories and items that did or did not belong to a specific category. The stimuli were drawn from Battig and Montague's (1969) category norms. There were 11 categories presented to the participants with exemplars: fruit, vegetable, human body part, metal, fish, flower, city, color, sport, musical instrument, and places to sleep. There were 280 category and exemplar pairings in the experiment, divided into four blocks of trials. Trials were numbered for participant accuracy in recording judgments on the record sheet. Half the exemplars belonged to the category presented, whereas the other half did not belong. The participants were given response sheets numbered from 1 to 280. They circled "yes" or "no" on each trial according to whether or not the exemplar belonged in the category. Four PM cues appeared in the category-judgment trials: hotel, dormitory, library, and restaurant. Two of these cues were presented with a correct category, and two were presented with an incorrect category. The trials were presented with PowerPoint. In each trial, categories and exemplars were presented in the center of the computer screen.

Procedure

Participants were run individually. Participants first read and signed an informed consent form. The ongoing task for the four conditions was to identify whether the item exemplar on the right of the screen belonged in the category presented on the left of the screen. In addition, the PM task for all participants was to mark an "X" next to the trial number when a building was displayed in the trial. Both the ongoing and PM task instructions were read to the participant by the researcher. Ten practice trials followed. At that time, if participants had any questions, they were answered before the rest of the experiment continued.

Each of the 280 trials remained on the screen for 5 s. There were three breaks of 30 s between each block of trials. The four PM cues appeared within a minute period at the delay time for each delay group. At the end of the experiment, the participants were debriefed.

Results

The effect of delay on prospective memory accuracy was tested. A one-way analysis of variance (ANOVA) was run on the accuracy data with an alpha level of .05. Means and standard deviations for PM accuracy can be found in Figure 1. PM accuracy in all conditions was relatively low. We found that the effect of delay on PM accuracy was not significant: $F(3,37) = 0.06$, $p = .98$.

In addition to PM accuracy, we analyzed the ongoing task accuracy for each delay. With an alpha level of .05, a one-way ANOVA was used to analyze these data. Means and standard deviations for the ongoing-task accuracy can be found in Table 1. The ongoing-task accuracy was high in all conditions. Results indicated that the effect of delay on the ongoing task accuracy was not significant: $F(3,37) = 1.44$, $p = .25$.

Discussion

The current study was designed to examine how the amount of time between the PM instructions and the presentation of the PM cue affects PM accuracy. The hypothesis was that as delay increased, PM accuracy would decrease. The results of the current study indicated that PM accuracy was not significantly affected by delay. The overall PM accuracy was low for all conditions. It was also found that delay did not affect the accuracy of the ongoing task. The overall ongoing-task accuracy was high in all conditions.

The present results are consistent with some previous studies that found no effect of delay on PM accuracy. An example of such a study is that of Nigro and Cicogna (2000), where they found no effect of delay for delays from 10 min to 2 weeks. In the current study, results consistent with Nigro and Cicogna's were found for delays from 5 to 20 min. However, the present results are inconsistent with those reported by Meier et al. (2006). They found significant effects of delay for delays of 5 to 45 min. The inconsistency could be due to the way delay was manipulated (e.g., no distractor task was used in the present study) or the shorter delays used in the present study.

This study examined the effects of delay on PM accuracy in the hope of better understanding factors that affect PM and how similar PM is to retrospective memory, which typically shows an effect of delay. The results of this study indicated no effect of delay on PM. Future studies should continue to explore delay as a possible factor that affects PM to allow us to fully understand how PM works.

References

Battig, W. F., & Montague, W. E. (1969). Category norms for verbal items in 56 categories: A replication and extension of the Connecticut category norms. *Journal of Experimental Psychology Monographs, 80*(3, Pt. 2). doi:10.1037/h0027577

Einstein, G. O., & McDaniel, M. A. (2005). Prospective memory: Multiple retrieval processes. *Current Directions in Psychological Science, 14,* 286-290. doi:10.111/j.0963-7214.2005.00382.x

Hicks, J. L., Marsh, R. L., & Russell, E. J. (2000). The properties of retention intervals and their affect on retaining prospective memories. *Journal of Experimental Psychology: Learning, Memory, and Cognition, 26,* 1160-1169. doi:10.1037//0278-7393.26.5.1160

Meier, B., Zimmerman, T. D., & Perrig, W. (2006). Retrieval experience in prospective memory: Strategic monitoring and spontaneous retrieval. *Memory, 14,* 872-889. doi:10.1080/09658210600783774

Nigro, G., & Cicogna, P. C. (2000). Does delay affect PM performance? *European Psychologist, 5,* 228-233. doi:10.1027//1016-9040.5.3.228

Table 1

Mean Ongoing Task Performance

Delay	Mean	Standard Deviation
5 min	.97	.05
10 min	.95	.04
15 min	.98	.04
20 min	.96	.03

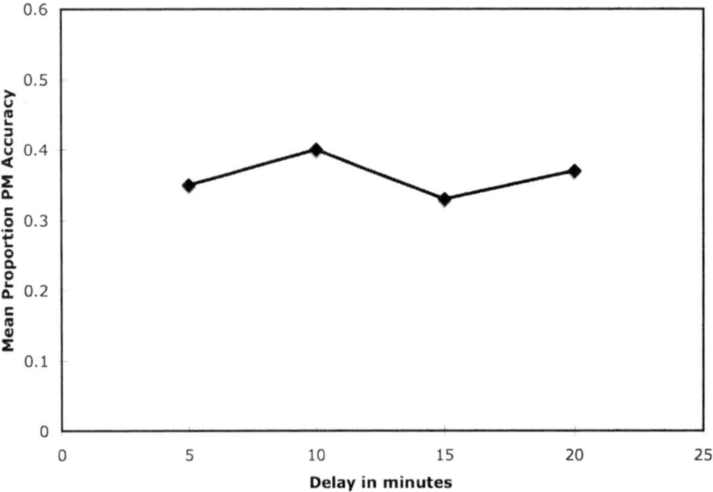

Figure 1. Mean proportion accuracy for prospective memory task as a function of delay

APPENDIX B

Answers to Stop and Think Questions

CHAPTER 1

1.1. Answers will vary but should use some of the ways of knowing: intuition, deduction, authority, and observation.

1.2. Answers will vary but should include a measure that will indicate anxiety based on some type of observation.

1.3. Psychology and biology both have research and practice areas, where the two areas inform each other.

1.4.

a. Population: Schoolchildren ages 9 and 10
   Sample: Students in a fifth-grade class at a particular elementary school
b. Population: Likely meant to be adults, possibly specifically college students
   Sample: College students recruited from a specific subject pool.
c. Population: Retirees
   Sample: Retirees at a particular retirement center
d. Population: People who have had a traumatic brain injury (TBI)
   Sample: Patients recovering from TBI at a local hospital who agree to participate

1.5.

a. interval
b. ratio
c. interval
d. ratio

1.6. A study can be designed to more directly observe behavior—for instance, by bringing subjects into the controlled environment of a lab. Doing so would increase internal validity but possibly at the sacrifice of external validity.

1.7. Symmetrical. The scores on either side of the middle score are nearly a mirror image.

1.8. Skewed. There are more scores on the high end, particularly in the B range.

1.9. Seven received an A; 13 received a D or F.

CHAPTER 2

2.1.

a. descriptive
b. causal
c. causal

2.2. A literature review helps researchers determine what the open questions still are in a field, what hypotheses they should make, and what methodologies work best in that area.

2.3. The purpose of a journal article is to report to others what was found in a research study.

2.4. Reading journal articles can help researchers determine what research questions they should ask, what hypotheses they should make, and what methodologies work best in that area.

2.5. Peer review is conducted to improve the quality of a journal article by having experts in an area provide suggestions to improve the writing, research, or conclusions of the authors. It also helps determine whether a study gets published or not.

2.6. The abstract is a short summary. The introduction provides research questions, hypotheses, and relevant background and purpose for a study. The method provides details of the methodology such that other researchers could replicate the study if they wish. The results summarize data collected in a study and provide tests of the hypotheses from the data. The discussion describes conclusions from the results of the study. The references provide full references for all sources cited in a paper.

2.7. Theory-driven hypotheses are based on a theory or description of how behavior works. Data-driven hypotheses are based on results from similar, past studies. Some hypotheses are based on both theory and past results.

2.8. Reading journal articles can help a researcher make both theory-driven and data-driven hypotheses.

2.9. A theory is a description of how behavior operates. A hypothesis is a prediction about how results will turn out in a study that might provide a test of a theory.

2.10.

a. results
b. method (materials subsection)
c. abstract (maybe), introduction, and discussion
d. discussion
e. results (also possibly a table or figure)

2.11. The goal of a method section is to provide enough detail that someone could replicate the study if they wish. This will also ensure that the reader has enough information to understand how the study was conducted in order to evaluate the conclusions made.

2.12. More detailed information is provided in a paper report than in poster and oral presentations. Poster and oral presentations typically cover main ideas about the study in bullet points for speedy understanding of the study. However, the main ideas of the study (why, how, what was found, and what was learned) are provided in all types of presentations.

CHAPTER 3

3.1. Participation is voluntary; participants cannot be coerced and must be informed about the research. Unnecessary harm or risk must be reduced, and the benefits must outweigh the risks. Participants can end their participation at any time.

3.2. Obtaining informed consent involves informing the participant about what will occur in the study, including any risks involved and the participant's right to withdraw at any time, and then obtaining their consent to participate after they have been informed about the research.

3.3. Answers will vary but may include coercion, risks outweighing the benefits, and/or not reducing unnecessary risks.

3.4. The institutional review board (IRB) reviews proposed research studies to ensure that ethical guidelines are followed.

3.5. It does not provide opportunities for information about how the drug affects women. It violates the justice principle because if only men are tested, women do not obtain the benefits of the testing.

3.6. Debriefing typically takes place to ensure that subjects understand the purpose of the research and any deception used without introducing bias from this information that might be present if debriefing occurred before the study.

3.7. Violations of ethics in reporting research occur if authors report false data or plagiarize from other sources without providing citations to those sources.

CHAPTER 4

4.1. There can be 36 outcomes. The most common value is 7. The probability is 1 in 6.

4.2. Answers will vary.

4.3. Answers will vary, but generally speaking, if you roll enough times, the distribution should be symmetrical.

4.4.

a. The population is college students at that particular school. A stratified random sample was used to make sure the proportion of men and women was that of the entire school.

b. The population is adults (or could be all humans), but a volunteer sample of psychology students is used.

4.5. Answers will vary, but here is a way this can be done:

I would probably narrow the scope to adults in the United States. I would then set salary requirements for each group ("people with more money" and "people with less money"). Through either census data or a survey, I would create equal-sized pools of people to poll. I would use a cluster sample to make sure there are the same amount of people in each group.

CHAPTER 5

5.1.

a. External validity
b. Reliability
c. Internal validity

5.2. Closed-ended responses might be poorly written such that they bias subjects toward a particular response. They also don't allow for responses that do not fit the scale chosen by the researcher.

5.3.

a. Systematic observation
b. Survey or questionnaire
c. Naturalistic observation
d. Archival data

5.4. Answers will vary. Any of the data collection techniques could be used in different ways.

5.5.

a. Correlational study
b. Experiment
c. Quasi-experiment

5.6. Case studies examine just one individual or a small group of individuals. Thus, it may be difficult to generalize the results from a case study to others because the individual(s) tested may be unique.

5.7. Answers will vary, but the most likely option is a quasi-experiment. A quasi-experiment could be used as a pretest–posttest design with productivity compared both before and after the cappuccino machine is introduced. A quasi-experiment could also be used if you observed which coworkers used the cappuccino machine and then compared productivity for those who used the machine and those who did not.

5.8. Answers will vary.

CHAPTER 6

6.1. Symmetrical

6.2.

a. 55.6

b. 60.2

The mean for the second set is nearly five points higher. The second set has an outlier at 96, which gives the distribution a positive skew.

6.3.

a. Median: 4

Mode: 4

The median and mode scores are the same, so both are representative of this distribution.

b. Median: 87

Mode: 87

The median and mode scores are the same, so both are representative of this distribution.

(In both sets of data, the median and mode are the same.)

6.4. One or two outliers will tilt the mean toward that end, whether high or low. A median score gives a more accurate figure to associate with the “average” for a particular distribution of scores.

6.5.

a. Median is best for a measure of speed because it is typically a skewed distribution.

b. Time of day is a categorical variable here, so the mode is the best measure to use.

c. Mean is likely to be used for rating scales, but if the distribution is skewed, the median can be used, or if the distribution is bimodal (e.g., mostly *1*s and *5*s), the mode can be used.

6.6. Because the last value is open-ended, calculating a mean is not accurate (a value of 4 could mean 4 siblings, 5 siblings, 6 siblings, and so on). The mode would be best here, or you can use the median to show where the midpoint of the distribution is.

6.7.

a. 1.55

b. 3.01

Answers will vary. The variability is narrower in the first set (4), so the standard deviation of those 9 data points is small. In the second set, we have more variability and the standard deviation is greater.

6.8.

a. 1.64
b. 3.28

The standard deviations will be a little larger because we're using degrees of freedom to correct for fewer scores than we would have with a whole population. We're dividing by a number that is smaller than *N*.

6.9.

a. Continuous
b. Continuous
c. Categorical
d. Categorical

6.10.

a. A bar graph to give a visual breakdown of the different majors, which is a categorical variable
b. A line graph—because the variable (amount of time) is a continuous variable
c. A line graph—because the variable (mean performance on a task—likely percentage correct) is a continuous variable

6.11. Answers will vary.

6.12. c

6.13. d

CHAPTER 7

7.1.

a. Room size (small, medium, large)
b. Game condition (inclusion, exclusion) and time of measure (before and after the game)
c. Treatment condition (current, new) and time of measure

7.2. Age of subject, subject's height (unless you have them stand on something)

7.3. In single-blind designs, the subject does not know which condition he or she receives. This design should be used when demand characteristics are of concern. In double-blind designs, the researcher also does not know which condition a subject receives. This design is used when experimenter bias is of concern.

7.4. Because subjects take the same test both times, they could remember some of the questions and do better the second time simply because they have remembered them and paid attention to or looked up the answer.

CHAPTER 8

8.1. Advantages: No order effects from one condition to another, subjects' participation is short.

Disadvantages: Group differences may be present, need more subjects.

8.2. Advantages: No group differences will be present, don't need as many subjects. Disadvantages: Order effects from one condition to another may occur, need subjects for longer period of time.

8.3. Answers will vary.

8.4. Biological Example: Type of trial (right stimulation, left stimulation, sham)

Social Example: Pain group (pain, no pain)

8.5. Answers will vary.

8.6. This reduced the possible bias due to the type of tasks used (e.g., arm in water regardless of temperature, physical activity regardless of pain).

CHAPTER 9

9.1. Jeff ($z = -0.89$) is heavier than Rafiki ($z = -4.25$).

9.2. Answers will vary.

9.3. It is to the left of (less than) the mean by 1.5 standard deviations.

9.4.

a. 11%
b. 53%
c. 99%

9.5. Proportion in *body* refers to the percentage of scores at or above the z score. Proportion in *tail* refers to the percentage of scores below the z score, or what remains of the distribution.

9.6. The probability is 0.006, or about 1%.

9.7. $z = 1.64$

The sample mean is rare enough that it is most likely different from the population mean.

9.8. Yes

9.9.

a. One-tailed
b. One-tailed
c. Two-tailed
d. Two-tailed

9.10.

a. Alternative: Aspirin decreases the chance of heart attacks in the population.

   Null: Aspirin increases or has no effect on the chance of heart attacks in the population.

b. Alternative: Quizzing oneself, rather than rereading notes, increases test scores in the population.

   Null: Quizzing oneself, rather than rereading notes, decreases or has no effect on test scores in the population.

c. Alternative: Time constraints will increase or decrease your accuracy in completing a puzzle in the population.

   Null: Time constraints will not affect your accuracy in completing a puzzle in the population.

d. Alternative: The amount of sleep one gets affects depression in the population.

   Null: The amount of sleep one gets does not affect depression in the population.

9.11. $p = .01$

We can reject the null hypothesis and accept the alternative hypothesis.

9.12.

a. Alternative: The task of preparing a 5-min speech increases anxiety among the population of college students.

   Null: The task of preparing a 5-min speech decreases or does not affect anxiety among the population of college students.

   This is a one-tailed test.

b. $z = 11.27$

   There's a less than .00003 chance that the null hypothesis is true.

c. Since the p value is less than alpha, we can reject the null hypothesis. The results suggest that preparing for a speech increases anxiety.

9.13.

a. Type II
b. Correct decision
c. Type I

CHAPTER 10

10.1. Alternative: The population of psychics will perform better than the population of nonpsychics (higher than 25% correct) when predicting the suit of individual playing cards.

Null: The population of psychics will perform the same (25% correct) or worse than the population of nonpsychics when predicting the suit of individual playing cards.

This is a one-tailed test.

10.2. The population standard deviation

10.3. Answers will vary, but some common biases for this type of study might be experimenter bias (experimenters could inadvertently indicate correct answers) and possible marks on the cards that could help participants pick the correct answer, so using a computer to present stimuli and collect responses would be best.

10.4.

a. Alternative: Those in the population shown subliminal Coke ads will choose the Coke image more than 50% of the time.

   Null: Those in the population shown subliminal Coke ads will choose the Coke image 50% of the time or at a lower rate.

b. $t = 8.5$

c. $t_{crit} = 1.69$

   Our *t* score falls into the critical region, so we can reject the null hypothesis. The results support the idea that people process subliminal ads.

10.5. $n = 30$

The smaller the sample size, the greater the variability of the distribution. It's harder to tell how close we are to the population standard deviation. So the t_{crit} score will be larger, necessitating a smaller critical area in which to hit in order to reject the null hypothesis.

10.6. $t = 2.496$

Given that it's a two-tailed experiment, the *t* score (2.496) does fall in the critical area ($t_{crit} = 2.11$). We must reject the null hypothesis. The new method does have a significant effect on test scores.

10.7. We can reject the null hypothesis because the *t* score (2.25) falls in the critical area ($t_{crit} = 2.09$).

10.8. Both the online quizzes and psychic studies are experiments. They both compare behavior between two groups in which participants are randomly assigned to groups. That is, the independent variable is not subject to their choice. The difference is that the online quizzes study uses a between-subjects design (each subject is assigned to one group) while the psychic study is a within-subjects design (each subject partakes in both groups to find a difference score).

10.9. Alternative: In the population, the mean difference score should be greater than zero.

Null: In the population, the mean difference score should be less than or equal to zero.

10.10.

a. Alternative: In the population, the mean difference score should be greater than or less than zero.

   Null: In the population, the mean difference score should be zero.

b. $t = 18.07$

c. The null hypothesis can be rejected. The *t* score falls into the critical area. There appears to be a difference in recognition between standard and emotional ads.

10.11. Group A would receive standard ads, and Group B would receive emotional ads. Pairs of subjects between groups would be assigned. Ideally, you would pair subjects based on recognition accuracy. You could give all subjects an initial trial with a different (non-Coke) subliminal ad. Based on their recognition abilities, pair one subject in Group A with one subject in Group B. After running the Coke ad trials, you would find difference scores by comparing Subject 1A to Subject 1B, Subject 2A to Subject 2B, and so on. You could then find a mean for difference scores.

10.12.

a. .711

b. .495

c. The *p* value is greater than α, so we must retain the null. There is not enough evidence to suggest there's a difference between paper or computer text. The results do not help you decide which types of textbooks to buy because comprehension appears approximately the same between texts.

10.13. It is a quasi-experiment. One group is made up of self-proclaimed psychics, and the other group is made up of nonpsychics. Because the independent variable (psychic/nonpsychic) is already a characteristic of the subjects, it cannot be randomly assigned (which would make it a true experiment). Otherwise, behavior between two conditions is being measured and compared.

10.14. Yes, it is an experiment because subjects are randomly assigned to one of two groups—the reread group or the recall group.

10.15.

a. Alternative: The population mean for men will be different than the population mean for women.

Null: The population mean for men will be the same as the population mean for women.

b. $t = 5.26$

c. The *t* score falls in the critical region, so the null hypothesis can be rejected. The results suggest that men and women recognize subliminal ads at a different rate.

10.16. $s_p^2 = 133.64$

10.17. $SS_1 = 28 \quad SS_2 = 4.73$

$X_1 = 5 \quad X_2 = 3.55$

$s_p^2 = 1.72$

$s_{\bar{X}_1 - \bar{X}_2} = 0.57$

$t = 2.55$

$t_{crit} = 2.09$

Our t score falls in the critical region, so we can reject the null hypothesis. The same mean scores are significantly different.

CHAPTER 11

11.1. Answers will vary.

We will combine the sum of squares of the groups and divide by the sum of degrees of freedom.

11.2. Alternative: The population mean time is less for left-handed individuals than right-handed or ambidextrous individuals.

Null: The population mean time is equal between left-handed, right-handed, and ambidextrous individuals.

11.3. There is a significant main effect. The F ratio (3.17) is greater than the critical score (2.79).

11.4. F would equal 1. That would indicate the ratio of between-groups and within-groups variance is balanced.

11.5. Answers will vary.

A post hoc test can help tell us if there is a significant difference between groups. Our hypothesis might state that one group sees a significant difference, but it might not identify which group. We don't need a post hoc test in a study with two groups because we can perform a two-tailed test if we don't hypothesize a specific direction for a difference between groups.

CHAPTER 12

12.1. The regular exercise could be staving off dementia.

Sharper cognitive abilities (a lack of dementia) could lead to regular exercise.

A third variable (favorable climate, for instance) could be behind both the regular exercise and avoidance of dementia.

12.2. c

12.3. There is a significant negative correlation between mood and weather temperature.

There were 60 subjects in the study.

12.4. There is not a significant relationship, though there is a negative correlation.

CHAPTER 13

13.1.

a. Parametric
b. Nonparametric
c. Nonparametric
d. Parametric

13.2. Scores on a categorical variable do not have a true numerical value.

13.3.

Smoker/Men = 15
Smoker/Women = 15
Nonsmoker/Men = 85
Nonsmoker/Women = 85

13.4. The χ^2 figure falls into the critical region, so we can reject the null hypothesis. Results suggest that there is a relationship between the variables.

$\chi^2 = 5.56$

$df = 1$

$\chi^2_{crit} = 3.84$

CHAPTER 14

14.1. No, this would be a main effect of amount of chips.

14.2. No, this would be a main effect of type of vanilla.

14.3. Answers will vary.

14.4. Answers will vary.

CHAPTER 15

15.1. Independent variables:

- Amount of chocolate chips (normal or 30% more)
- Presence of real vanilla (real vanilla or artificial vanilla)

Dependent variable:

- Ratings on desire to buy ice cream

15.2. The difference in ratings between ice cream with the normal amount of chocolate chips and 30% more chocolate chips would be affected.

The difference in ratings between ice cream with artificial vanilla and ice cream with real vanilla would be affected.

15.3. The addition of real vanilla could affect the ratings of the chocolate chip ice cream. Maybe additional chocolate chips on their own don't raise the rating, but the combination of additional chocolate chips and vanilla might.

15.4.

a. Main effect
b. Interaction
c. Main effect

15.5.

The main effect of gender was not significant ($F = 2.09$, $p = .155$).

The main effect of mood was significant ($F = 43.74$, $p < .001$).

The interaction between gender and mood was not significant ($F = 2.20$, $p = .145$).

15.6. No. It would represent a main effect. The increase in ratings is not contingent on the combination of variables, only that particular variable.

15.7. No. Again, it would represent a main effect because the increase would be dependent on that one variable.

CHAPTER 16

16.1.

a. Between-subjects, ANOVA
b. Within-subjects, ANOVA
c. Within-subjects, t test

16.2. It's not a true experiment because the grouping criteria could not be randomly assigned. The test would also need to be controlled. To make it an experiment, keep the three conditions, but randomly assign participants to each condition. Then, give each group of participants the same test.

16.3. For the quiz study, the class would need to be divided into three groups so that one third of the participants get the no-quiz condition first, one third get the multiple choice condition first, and one third get the short answer condition first. Each group would be run in different order to eliminate sequencing bias. For the Alzheimer's study, test each participant only once a day—half in the morning and half in the afternoon. After that, test again but at the alternate time of day.

16.4. Divide your friends into three groups. Tell one of the groups to try rereading notes for the first exam, quizzes for the second exam, and a study partner for the third exam. Have the second group start with the quizzes for the first exam. Have the third group start with the study partner for the first exam.

16.5. There is a significant effect on study technique.

$F = 5.310$, $p = .027$

16.6. The exam that showed the highest scores could have simply covered easier material.

APPENDIX C

Unit Normal Table (*z* Table)

A	B	C	A	B	C	A	B	C	A	B	C
z score	Body	Tail	*z* score	Body	Tail	*z* score	Body	Tail	*z* score	Body	Tail
0.00	0.5000	0.5000	0.22	0.5871	0.4129	0.44	0.6700	0.3300	0.66	0.7454	0.2546
0.01	0.5040	0.4960	0.23	0.5910	0.4090	0.45	0.6736	0.3264	0.67	0.7486	0.2514
0.02	0.5080	0.4920	0.24	0.5948	0.4052	0.46	0.6772	0.3228	0.68	0.7517	0.2483
0.03	0.5120	0.4880	0.25	0.5987	0.4013	0.47	0.6808	0.3192	0.69	0.7549	0.2451
0.04	0.5160	0.4840	0.26	0.6026	0.3974	0.48	0.6844	0.3156	0.70	0.7580	0.2420
0.05	0.5199	0.4801	0.27	0.6064	0.3936	0.49	0.6879	0.3121	0.71	0.7611	0.2389
0.06	0.5239	0.4761	0.28	0.6103	0.3897	0.50	0.6915	0.3085	0.72	0.7642	0.2358
0.07	0.5279	0.4721	0.29	0.6141	0.3859	0.51	0.6950	0.3050	0.73	0.7673	0.2327
0.08	0.5319	0.4681	0.30	0.6179	0.3821	0.52	0.6985	0.3015	0.74	0.7704	0.2296
0.09	0.5359	0.4641	0.31	0.6217	0.3783	0.53	0.7019	0.2981	0.75	0.7734	0.2266
0.10	0.5398	0.4602	0.32	0.6255	0.3745	0.54	0.7054	0.2946	0.76	0.7764	0.2236
0.11	0.5438	0.4562	0.33	0.6293	0.3707	0.55	0.7088	0.2912	0.77	0.7794	0.2206
0.12	0.5478	0.4522	0.34	0.6331	0.3669	0.56	0.7123	0.2877	0.78	0.7823	0.2177
0.13	0.5517	0.4483	0.35	0.6368	0.3632	0.57	0.7157	0.2843	0.79	0.7852	0.2148
0.14	0.5557	0.4443	0.36	0.6406	0.3594	0.58	0.7190	0.2810	0.80	0.7881	0.2119
0.15	0.5596	0.4404	0.37	0.6443	0.3557	0.59	0.7224	0.2776	0.81	0.7910	0.2090
0.16	0.5636	0.4364	0.38	0.6480	0.3520	0.60	0.7257	0.2743	0.82	0.7939	0.2061
0.17	0.5675	0.4325	0.39	0.6517	0.3483	0.61	0.7291	0.2709	0.83	0.7967	0.2033
0.18	0.5714	0.4286	0.40	0.6554	0.3446	0.62	0.7324	0.2676	0.84	0.7995	0.2005
0.19	0.5753	0.4247	0.41	0.6591	0.3409	0.63	0.7357	0.2643	0.85	0.8023	0.1977
0.20	0.5793	0.4207	0.42	0.6628	0.3372	0.64	0.7389	0.2611	0.86	0.8051	0.1949
0.21	0.5832	0.4168	0.43	0.6664	0.3336	0.65	0.7422	0.2578	0.87	0.8078	0.1922

A	B	C	A	B	C	A	B	C	A	B	C
z score	Body	Tail	*z* score	Body	Tail	*z* score	Body	Tail	*z* score	Body	Tail
0.88	0.8106	0.1894	1.22	0.8888	0.1112	1.56	0.9406	0.0594	1.90	0.9713	0.0287
0.89	0.8133	0.1867	1.23	0.8907	0.1093	1.57	0.9418	0.0582	1.91	0.9719	0.0281
0.90	0.8159	0.1841	1.24	0.8925	0.1075	1.58	0.9429	0.0571	1.92	0.9726	0.0274
0.91	0.8186	0.1814	1.25	0.8944	0.1056	1.59	0.9441	0.0559	1.93	0.9732	0.0268
0.92	0.8212	0.1788	1.26	0.8962	0.1038	1.60	0.9452	0.0548	1.94	0.9738	0.0262
0.93	0.8238	0.1762	1.27	0.8980	0.1020	1.61	0.9463	0.0537	1.95	0.9744	0.0256
0.94	0.8264	0.1736	1.28	0.8997	0.1003	1.62	0.9474	0.0526	1.96	0.9750	0.0250
0.95	0.8289	0.1711	1.29	0.9015	0.0985	1.63	0.9484	0.0516	1.97	0.9756	0.0244
0.96	0.8315	0.1685	1.30	0.9032	0.0968	1.64	0.9495	0.0505	1.98	0.9761	0.0239
0.97	0.8340	0.1660	1.31	0.9049	0.0951	1.65	0.9505	0.0495	1.99	0.9767	0.0233
0.98	0.8365	0.1635	1.32	0.9066	0.0934	1.66	0.9515	0.0485	2.00	0.9772	0.0228
0.99	0.8389	0.1611	1.33	0.9082	0.0918	1.67	0.9525	0.0475	2.01	0.9778	0.0222
1.00	0.8413	0.1587	1.34	0.9099	0.0901	1.68	0.9535	0.0465	2.02	0.9783	0.0217
1.01	0.8438	0.1562	1.35	0.9115	0.0885	1.69	0.9545	0.0455	2.03	0.9788	0.0212
1.02	0.8461	0.1539	1.36	0.9131	0.0869	1.70	0.9554	0.0446	2.04	0.9793	0.0207
1.03	0.8485	0.1515	1.37	0.9147	0.0853	1.71	0.9564	0.0436	2.05	0.9798	0.0202
1.04	0.8508	0.1492	1.38	0.9162	0.0838	1.72	0.9573	0.0427	2.06	0.9803	0.0197
1.05	0.8531	0.1469	1.39	0.9177	0.0823	1.73	0.9582	0.0418	2.07	0.9808	0.0192
1.06	0.8554	0.1446	1.40	0.9192	0.0808	1.74	0.9591	0.0409	2.08	0.9812	0.0188
1.07	0.8577	0.1423	1.41	0.9207	0.0793	1.75	0.9599	0.0401	2.09	0.9817	0.0183
1.08	0.8599	0.1401	1.42	0.9222	0.0778	1.76	0.9608	0.0392	2.10	0.9821	0.0179
1.09	0.8621	0.1379	1.43	0.9236	0.0764	1.77	0.9616	0.0384	2.11	0.9826	0.0174
1.10	0.8643	0.1357	1.44	0.9251	0.0749	1.78	0.9625	0.0375	2.12	0.9830	0.0170
1.11	0.8665	0.1335	1.45	0.9265	0.0735	1.79	0.9633	0.0367	2.13	0.9834	0.0166
1.12	0.8686	0.1314	1.46	0.9279	0.0721	1.80	0.9641	0.0359	2.14	0.9838	0.0162
1.13	0.8708	0.1292	1.47	0.9292	0.0708	1.81	0.9649	0.0351	2.15	0.9842	0.0158
1.14	0.8729	0.1271	1.48	0.9306	0.0694	1.82	0.9656	0.0344	2.16	0.9846	0.0154
1.15	0.8749	0.1251	1.49	0.9319	0.0681	1.83	0.9664	0.0336	2.17	0.9850	0.0150
1.16	0.8770	0.1230	1.50	0.9332	0.0668	1.84	0.9671	0.0329	2.18	0.9854	0.0146
1.17	0.8790	0.1210	1.51	0.9345	0.0655	1.85	0.9678	0.0322	2.19	0.9857	0.0143
1.18	0.8810	0.1190	1.52	0.9357	0.0643	1.86	0.9686	0.0314	2.20	0.9861	0.0139
1.19	0.8830	0.1170	1.53	0.9370	0.0630	1.87	0.9693	0.0307	2.21	0.9864	0.0136
1.20	0.8849	0.1151	1.54	0.9382	0.0618	1.88	0.9699	0.0301	2.22	0.9868	0.0132
1.21	0.8869	0.1131	1.55	0.9394	0.0606	1.89	0.9706	0.0294	2.23	0.9871	0.0129

(Continued)

(Continued)

A	B	C	A	B	C	A	B	C	A	B	C
z score	Body	Tail	z score	Body	Tail	z score	Body	Tail	z score	Body	Tail
2.24	0.9875	0.0125	2.56	0.9948	0.0052	2.88	0.9980	0.0020	3.20	0.9993	0.0007
2.25	0.9878	0.0122	2.57	0.9949	0.0051	2.89	0.9981	0.0019	3.21	0.9993	0.0007
2.26	0.9881	0.0119	2.58	0.9951	0.0049	2.90	0.9981	0.0019	3.22	0.9994	0.0006
2.27	0.9884	0.0116	2.59	0.9952	0.0048	2.91	0.9982	0.0018	3.23	0.9994	0.0006
2.28	0.9887	0.0113	2.60	0.9953	0.0047	2.92	0.9982	0.0018	3.24	0.9994	0.0006
2.29	0.9890	0.0110	2.61	0.9955	0.0045	2.93	0.9983	0.0017	3.25	0.9994	0.0006
2.30	0.9893	0.0107	2.62	0.9956	0.0044	2.94	0.9984	0.0016	3.26	0.9994	0.0006
2.31	0.9896	0.0104	2.63	0.9957	0.0043	2.95	0.9984	0.0016	3.27	0.9995	0.0005
2.32	0.9898	0.0102	2.64	0.9959	0.0041	2.96	0.9985	0.0015	3.28	0.9995	0.0005
2.33	0.9901	0.0099	2.65	0.9960	0.0040	2.97	0.9985	0.0015	3.29	0.9995	0.0005
2.34	0.9904	0.0096	2.66	0.9961	0.0039	2.98	0.9986	0.0014	3.30	0.9995	0.0005
2.35	0.9906	0.0094	2.67	0.9962	0.0038	2.99	0.9986	0.0014	3.31	0.9995	0.0005
2.36	0.9909	0.0091	2.68	0.9963	0.0037	3.00	0.9987	0.0013	3.32	0.9995	0.0005
2.37	0.9911	0.0089	2.69	0.9964	0.0036	3.01	0.9987	0.0013	3.33	0.9996	0.0004
2.38	0.9913	0.0087	2.70	0.9965	0.0035	3.02	0.9987	0.0013	3.34	0.9996	0.0004
2.39	0.9916	0.0084	2.71	0.9966	0.0034	3.03	0.9988	0.0012	3.35	0.9996	0.0004
2.40	0.9918	0.0082	2.72	0.9967	0.0033	3.04	0.9988	0.0012	3.36	0.9996	0.0004
2.41	0.9920	0.0080	2.73	0.9968	0.0032	3.05	0.9989	0.0011	3.37	0.9996	0.0004
2.42	0.9922	0.0078	2.74	0.9969	0.0031	3.06	0.9989	0.0011	3.38	0.9996	0.0004
2.43	0.9925	0.0075	2.75	0.9970	0.0030	3.07	0.9989	0.0011	3.39	0.9997	0.0003
2.44	0.9927	0.0073	2.76	0.9971	0.0029	3.08	0.9990	0.0010	3.40	0.9997	0.0003
2.45	0.9929	0.0071	2.77	0.9972	0.0028	3.09	0.9990	0.0010	3.41	0.9997	0.0003
2.46	0.9931	0.0069	2.78	0.9973	0.0027	3.10	0.9990	0.0010	3.42	0.9997	0.0003
2.47	0.9932	0.0068	2.79	0.9974	0.0026	3.11	0.9991	0.0009	3.43	0.9997	0.0003
2.48	0.9934	0.0066	2.80	0.9974	0.0026	3.12	0.9991	0.0009	3.44	0.9997	0.0003
2.49	0.9936	0.0064	2.81	0.9975	0.0025	3.13	0.9991	0.0009	3.45	0.9997	0.0003
2.50	0.9938	0.0062	2.82	0.9976	0.0024	3.14	0.9992	0.0008	3.46	0.9997	0.0003
2.51	0.9940	0.0060	2.83	0.9977	0.0023	3.15	0.9992	0.0008	3.47	0.9997	0.0003
2.52	0.9941	0.0059	2.84	0.9977	0.0023	3.16	0.9992	0.0008	3.48	0.9997	0.0003
2.53	0.9943	0.0057	2.85	0.9978	0.0022	3.17	0.9992	0.0008	3.49	0.9998	0.0002
2.54	0.9945	0.0055	2.86	0.9979	0.0021	3.18	0.9993	0.0007	3.50	0.9998	0.0002
2.55	0.9946	0.0054	2.87	0.9979	0.0021	3.19	0.9993	0.0007	3.51	0.9998	0.0002

APPENDIX D

t Distribution Table

TABLE D.1 ■ The *t* Distribution

Table entries are values of *t* corresponding to proportions in one tail or in two tails combined.

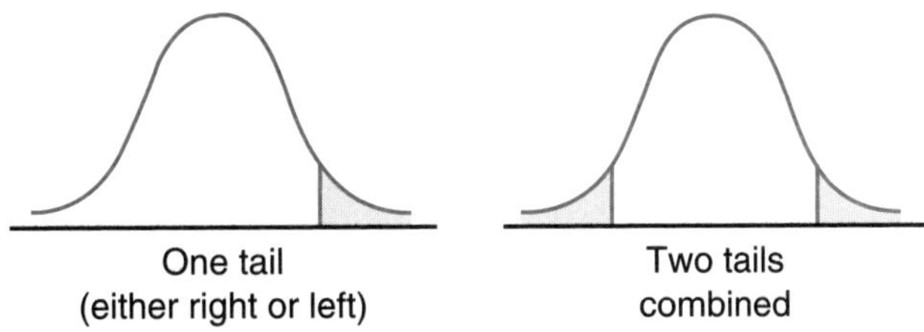

	Proportion in One Tail					
	0.25	0.10	0.05	0.025	0.01	0.005
	Proportion in Two Tails Combined					
df	0.50	0.20	0.10	0.05	0.02	0.01
1	1.000	3.078	6.314	12.706	31.821	63.657
2	0.816	1.886	2.920	4.303	6.965	9.925
3	0.765	1.638	2.353	3.182	4.541	5.841
4	0.741	1.533	2.132	2.776	3.747	4.604
5	0.727	1.476	2.015	2.571	3.365	4.032
6	0.718	1.440	1.943	2.447	3.143	3.707
7	0.711	1.415	1.895	2.365	2.998	3.499
8	0.706	1.397	1.860	2.306	2.896	3.355
9	0.703	1.383	1.833	2.282	2.821	3.250
10	0.700	1.372	1.812	2.228	2.764	3.169

(Continued)

TABLE D.1 ■ (Continued)

	Proportion in One Tail					
	0.25	0.10	0.05	0.025	0.01	0.005
	Proportion in Two Tails Combined					
df	0.50	0.20	0.10	0.05	0.02	0.01
11	0.697	1.363	1.796	2.201	2.718	3.106
12	0.695	1.356	1.782	2.179	2.681	3.055
13	0.694	1.350	1.771	2.160	2.650	3.012
14	0.692	1.345	1.761	2.145	2.624	2.977
15	0.691	1.341	1.753	2.131	2.602	2.947
16	0.690	1.337	1.746	2.120	2.583	2.921
17	0.689	1.333	1.740	2.110	2.567	2.898
18	0.688	1.330	1.734	2.101	2.552	2.878
19	0.688	1.328	1.729	2.093	2.539	2.861
20	0.687	1.325	1.725	2.086	2.528	2.845
21	0.686	1.323	1.721	2.080	2.518	2.831
22	0.686	1.321	1.717	2.074	2.508	2.819
23	0.685	1.319	1.714	2.069	2.500	2.807
24	0.685	1.318	1.711	2.064	2.492	2.797
25	0.684	1.316	1.708	2.060	2.485	2.787
26	0.684	1.315	1.706	2.056	2.479	2.779
27	0.684	1.314	1.703	2.052	2.473	2.771
28	0.683	1.313	1.701	2.048	2.467	2.763
29	0.683	1.311	1.699	2.045	2.462	2.756
30	0.683	1.310	1.697	2.042	2.457	2.750
40	0.681	1.303	1.684	2.021	2.423	2.704
60	0.679	1.296	1.671	2.000	2.390	2.660
120	0.677	1.289	1.658	1.980	2.358	2.617
∞	0.674	1.282	1.645	1.960	2.326	2.576

Source: Fisher, R. A., & Yates, F. (1974). *Statistical Tables for Biological, Agricultural and Medical Research* (6th ed., Table III). London: Longman Group Ltd. (Previously published by Oliver and Boyd Ltd., Edinburgh.) Adapted and reprinted with permission of Addison Wesley Longman.

APPENDIX E

F Distribution Table

TABLE E.1

Critical Values for the *F* Distribution

Critical values at $\alpha = 0.05$ level of significance are given in lightface type.

Critical values at $\alpha = 0.01$ level of significance are given in boldface type.

Degrees of Freedom (*df*) Denominator	Degrees of Freedom (*df*) Numerator: 1	2	3	4	5	6	7	8	9	10	20	∞
1	161	200	216	225	230	234	237	239	241	242	248	254
	4052	**5000**	**5403**	**5625**	**5764**	**5859**	**5928**	**5928**	**6023**	**6056**	**6209**	**6366**
2	18.51	19.00	19.16	19.25	19.30	19.33	19.36	19.37	19.38	19.39	19.44	19.5
	98.49	**99.00**	**99.17**	**99.25**	**99.30**	**99.33**	**99.34**	**99.36**	**99.38**	**99.40**	**99.45**	**99.5**
3	10.13	9.55	9.28	9.12	9.01	8.94	8.88	8.84	8.81	8.78	8.66	8.5
	34.12	**30.92**	**29.46**	**28.71**	**28.24**	**27.91**	**27.67**	**27.49**	**27.34**	**27.23**	**26.69**	**26.1**
4	7.71	6.94	6.59	6.39	6.26	6.16	6.09	6.04	6.00	5.96	5.80	5.6
	21.20	**18.00**	**16.69**	**15.98**	**15.52**	**15.21**	**14.98**	**14.80**	**14.66**	**14.54**	**14.02**	**13.5**
5	6.61	5.79	5.41	5.19	5.05	4.95	4.88	4.82	4.78	4.74	4.56	4.37
	16.26	**13.27**	**12.06**	**11.39**	**10.97**	**10.67**	**10.45**	**10.27**	**10.15**	**10.05**	**9.55**	**9.02**
6	5.99	5.14	4.76	4.53	4.39	4.28	4.21	4.15	4.10	4.06	3.87	3.67
	13.74	**10.92**	**9.78**	**9.15**	**8.75**	**8.47**	**8.26**	**8.10**	**7.98**	**7.87**	**7.39**	**6.88**
7	5.59	4.74	4.35	4.12	3.97	3.87	3.79	3.73	3.68	3.63	3.44	3.23
	13.74	**9.55**	**8.45**	**7.85**	**7.46**	**7.19**	**7.00**	**6.84**	**6.71**	**6.62**	**6.15**	**5.65**
8	5.32	4.46	4.07	3.84	3.69	3.58	3.50	3.44	3.39	3.34	3.15	2.93
	11.26	**8.65**	**7.59**	**7.01**	**6.63**	**6.37**	**6.19**	**6.03**	**5.91**	**5.82**	**5.36**	**4.86**
9	5.12	4.26	3.86	3.63	3.48	3.37	3.29	3.23	3.18	3.13	2.93	2.71
	10.56	**8.02**	**6.99**	**6.42**	**6.06**	**5.80**	**5.62**	**5.47**	**5.35**	**5.26**	**4.80**	**4.31**
10	4.96	4.10	3.71	3.48	3.33	3.22	3.14	3.07	3.02	2.97	2.77	2.54
	10.04	**7.56**	**6.55**	**5.99**	**5.64**	**5.39**	**5.21**	**5.06**	**4.95**	**4.85**	**4.41**	**3.91**

(Continued)

TABLE E.1 ■ (Continued)

Degrees of Freedom (*df*) Denominator	Degrees of Freedom (*df*) Numerator											
	1	2	3	4	5	6	7	8	9	10	20	∞
11	4.84	3.98	3.59	3.36	3.20	3.09	3.01	2.95	2.90	2.86	2.65	2.40
	9.65	**7.20**	**6.22**	**5.67**	**5.32**	**5.07**	**4.88**	**4.74**	**4.63**	**4.54**	**4.10**	**3.60**
12	4.75	3.89	3.49	3.26	3.11	3.00	2.92	2.85	2.80	2.76	2.54	2.30
	9.33	**6.93**	**5.95**	**5.41**	**5.06**	**4.82**	**4.65**	**4.50**	**4.39**	**4.30**	**3.86**	**3.36**
13	4.67	3.80	3.41	3.18	3.02	2.92	2.84	2.77	2.72	2.67	2.46	2.21
	9.07	**6.70**	**5.74**	**5.20**	**4.86**	**4.62**	**4.44**	**4.30**	**4.19**	**4.10**	**3.67**	**3.17**
14	4.60	3.74	3.34	3.11	2.96	2.85	2.77	2.70	2.65	2.60	2.39	2.13
	8.86	**6.51**	**5.56**	**5.03**	**4.69**	**4.46**	**4.28**	**4.14**	**4.03**	**3.94**	**3.51**	**3.00**
15	4.54	3.68	3.29	3.06	2.90	2.79	2.70	2.64	2.59	2.55	2.33	2.07
	8.68	**6.36**	**5.42**	**4.89**	**4.56**	**4.32**	**4.14**	**4.00**	**3.89**	**3.80**	**3.36**	**2.87**
16	4.49	3.63	3.24	3.01	2.85	2.74	2.66	2.59	2.54	2.49	2.28	2.01
	8.53	**6.23**	**5.29**	**4.77**	**4.44**	**4.20**	**4.03**	**3.89**	**3.78**	**3.69**	**3.25**	**2.75**
17	4.45	3.59	3.20	2.96	2.81	2.70	2.62	2.55	2.50	2.45	2.23	1.96
	8.40	**6.11**	**5.18**	**4.67**	**4.34**	**4.10**	**3.93**	**3.79**	**3.68**	**3.59**	**3.16**	**2.65**
18	4.41	3.55	3.16	2.93	2.77	2.66	2.58	2.51	2.46	2.41	2.19	1.92
	8.28	**6.01**	**5.09**	**4.58**	**4.25**	**4.01**	**3.85**	**3.71**	**3.60**	**3.51**	**3.07**	**2.57**
19	4.38	3.52	3.13	2.90	2.74	2.63	2.55	2.48	2.43	2.38	2.15	1.88
	8.18	**5.93**	**5.01**	**4.50**	**4.17**	**3.94**	**3.77**	**3.63**	**3.52**	**3.43**	**3.00**	**2.49**
20	4.35	3.49	3.10	2.87	2.71	2.60	2.52	2.45	2.40	2.35	2.12	1.84
	8.10	**5.85**	**4.94**	**4.43**	**4.10**	**3.87**	**3.71**	**3.56**	**3.45**	**3.37**	**2.94**	**2.42**
21	4.32	3.47	3.07	2.84	2.68	2.57	2.49	2.42	2.37	2.32	2.09	1.81
	8.02	**5.78**	**4.87**	**4.37**	**4.04**	**3.81**	**3.65**	**3.51**	**3.40**	**3.31**	**2.88**	**2.36**
22	4.30	3.44	3.05	2.82	2.66	2.55	2.47	2.40	2.35	2.30	2.07	1.78
	7.94	**5.72**	**4.82**	**4.31**	**3.99**	**3.76**	**3.59**	**3.45**	**3.35**	**3.26**	**2.83**	**2.31**
23	4.28	3.42	3.03	2.80	2.64	2.53	2.45	2.38	2.32	2.28	2.04	1.76
	7.88	**5.66**	**4.76**	**4.26**	**3.94**	**3.71**	**3.54**	**3.41**	**3.30**	**3.21**	**2.78**	**2.26**
24	4.26	3.40	3.01	2.78	2.62	2.51	2.43	2.36	2.30	2.26	2.02	1.73
	7.82	**5.61**	**4.72**	**4.22**	**3.90**	**3.67**	**3.50**	**3.36**	**3.25**	**3.17**	**2.74**	**2.21**
25	4.24	3.38	2.99	2.76	2.60	2.49	2.41	2.34	2.28	2.24	2.00	1.71
	7.77	**5.57**	**4.68**	**4.18**	**3.86**	**3.63**	**3.46**	**3.32**	**3.21**	**3.13**	**2.70**	**2.17**

Degrees of Freedom (*df*) Denominator	Degrees of Freedom (*df*) Numerator											
	1	2	3	4	5	6	7	8	9	10	20	∞
26	4.22	3.37	2.98	2.74	2.59	2.47	2.39	2.32	2.27	2.22	1.99	1.69
	7.72	**5.53**	**4.64**	**4.14**	**3.82**	**3.59**	**3.42**	**3.29**	**3.17**	**3.09**	**2.66**	**2.13**
27	4.21	3.35	2.96	2.73	2.57	2.46	2.37	2.30	2.25	2.20	1.97	1.67
	7.68	**5.49**	**4.60**	**4.11**	**3.79**	**3.56**	**3.39**	**3.26**	**3.14**	**3.06**	**2.63**	**2.10**
28	4.20	3.34	2.95	2.71	2.56	2.44	2.36	2.29	2.24	2.19	1.96	1.65
	7.64	**5.45**	**4.57**	**4.07**	**3.76**	**3.53**	**3.36**	**3.23**	**3.11**	**3.03**	**2.60**	**2.07**
29	4.18	3.33	2.93	2.70	2.54	2.43	2.35	2.28	2.22	2.18	1.94	1.63
	7.60	**5.42**	**4.54**	**4.04**	**3.73**	**3.50**	**3.33**	**3.20**	**3.08**	**3.00**	**2.57**	**2.04**
30	4.17	3.32	2.92	2.69	2.53	2.42	2.34	2.27	2.21	2.16	1.93	1.61
	7.56	**5.39**	**4.51**	**4.02**	**3.70**	**3.47**	**3.30**	**3.17**	**3.06**	**2.98**	**2.55**	**2.01**
31	4.16	3.30	2.91	2.68	2.52	2.41	2.32	2.25	2.20	2.15	1.92	1.60
	7.53	**5.36**	**4.48**	**3.99**	**3.67**	**3.45**	**3.28**	**3.15**	**3.04**	**2.96**	**2.53**	**1.89**
32	4.15	3.29	2.90	2.67	2.51	2.40	2.31	2.24	2.19	2.14	1.91	1.59
	7.50	**5.34**	**4.46**	**3.97**	**3.65**	**3.43**	**3.26**	**3.13**	**3.02**	**2.93**	**2.51**	**1.88**
33	4.14	3.28	2.89	2.66	2.50	2.39	2.30	2.23	2.18	2.13	1.90	1.58
	7.47	**5.31**	**4.44**	**3.95**	**3.63**	**3.41**	**3.24**	**3.11**	**3.00**	**2.91**	**2.49**	**1.87**
34	4.13	3.28	2.88	2.65	2.49	2.38	2.29	2.23	2.17	2.12	1.89	1.57
	7.44	**5.29**	**4.42**	**3.93**	**3.61**	**3.39**	**3.22**	**3.09**	**2.98**	**2.89**	**2.47**	**1.86**
35	4.12	3.27	2.87	2.64	2.49	2.37	2.29	2.22	2.16	2.11	1.88	1.56
	7.42	**5.27**	**4.40**	**3.91**	**3.59**	**3.37**	**3.20**	**3.07**	**2.96**	**2.88**	**2.45**	**1.85**
36	4.11	3.26	2.87	2.63	2.48	2.36	2.28	2.21	2.15	2.11	1.87	1.55
	7.40	**5.25**	**4.38**	**3.89**	**3.57**	**3.35**	**3.18**	**3.05**	**2.95**	**2.86**	**2.43**	**1.84**
37	4.11	3.25	2.86	2.63	2.47	2.36	2.27	2.20	2.14	2.10	1.86	1.54
	7.37	**5.23**	**4.36**	**3.87**	**3.56**	**3.33**	**3.17**	**3.04**	**2.93**	**2.84**	**2.42**	**1.83**
38	4.10	3.24	2.85	2.62	2.46	2.35	2.26	2.19	2.14	2.09	1.85	1.53
	7.35	**5.21**	**4.34**	**3.86**	**3.54**	**3.32**	**3.15**	**3.02**	**2.92**	**2.83**	**2.40**	**1.82**
39	4.09	3.24	2.85	2.61	2.46	2.34	2.26	2.19	2.13	2.08	1.84	1.52
	7.33	**5.19**	**4.33**	**3.84**	**3.53**	**3.30**	**3.14**	**3.01**	**2.90**	**2.81**	**2.39**	**1.81**
40	4.08	3.23	2.84	2.61	2.45	2.34	2.25	2.18	2.12	2.07	1.84	1.51
	7.31	**5.18**	**4.31**	**3.83**	**3.51**	**3.29**	**3.12**	**2.99**	**2.88**	**2.80**	**2.37**	**1.80**

(Continued)

TABLE E.1 ■ (Continued)

Degrees of Freedom (*df*) Denominator		Degrees of Freedom (*df*) Numerator											
		1	2	3	4	5	6	7	8	9	10	20	∞
	42	4.07	3.22	2.83	2.59	2.44	2.32	2.24	2.17	2.11	2.06	1.82	1.50
		7.27	**5.15**	**4.29**	**3.80**	**3.49**	**3.26**	**3.10**	**2.96**	**2.86**	**2.77**	**2.35**	**1.78**
	44	4.06	3.21	2.82	2.58	2.43	2.31	2.23	2.16	2.10	2.05	1.81	1.49
		7.24	**5.12**	**4.26**	**3.78**	**3.46**	**3.24**	**3.07**	**2.94**	**2.84**	**2.75**	**2.32**	**1.76**
	60	4.00	3.15	2.76	2.53	2.37	2.25	2.17	2.10	2.04	1.99	1.75	1.39
		7.08	**4.98**	**4.13**	**3.65**	**3.34**	**3.12**	**2.95**	**2.82**	**2.72**	**2.63**	**2.20**	**1.60**
	120	3.92	3.07	2.68	2.45	2.29	2.18	2.09	2.02	1.96	1.91	1.66	1.25
		6.85	**4.79**	**3.95**	**3.48**	**3.17**	**2.96**	**2.79**	**2.66**	**2.56**	**2.47**	**2.03**	**1.38**
	∞	3.84	3.00	2.60	2.37	2.21	2.10	2.01	1.94	1.88	1.83	1.57	1.00
		6.63	**4.61**	**3.78**	**3.32**	**3.02**	**2.80**	**2.64**	**2.51**	**2.41**	**2.32**	**1.88**	**1.00**

APPENDIX F

Pearson *r* Critical Values Table

TABLE F.1

Critical Values for the Pearson *r* Correlation*

*To be significant, the sample correlation (*r*) must be greater than or equal to the critical value in the table.

	Level of Significance for One-Tailed Test			
	0.05	0.025	0.01	0.005
	Level of Significance for Two-Tailed Test			
$df = n - 2$	0.10	0.05	0.02	0.01
1	0.988	0.997	0.9995	0.99999
2	0.900	0.950	0.980	0.990
3	0.805	0.878	0.934	0.959
4	0.729	0.811	0.882	0.917
5	0.669	0.754	0.833	0.874
6	0.622	0.707	0.789	0.834
7	0.582	0.666	0.750	0.798
8	0.549	0.632	0.716	0.765
9	0.521	0.602	0.685	0.735
10	0.497	0.576	0.658	0.708
11	0.476	0.553	0.634	0.684
12	0.458	0.532	0.612	0.661
13	0.441	0.514	0.592	0.641
14	0.426	0.497	0.574	0.623
15	0.412	0.482	0.558	0.606
16	0.400	0.468	0.542	0.590

(Continued)

TABLE F.1 ■ (Continued)

	Level of Significance for One-Tailed Test			
	0.05	0.025	0.01	0.005
	Level of Significance for Two-Tailed Test			
df = *n* − 2	0.10	0.05	0.02	0.01
17	0.389	0.456	0.528	0.575
18	0.378	0.444	0.516	0.561
19	0.369	0.433	0.503	0.549
20	0.360	0.423	0.492	0.537
21	0.352	0.413	0.482	0.526
22	0.344	0.404	0.472	0.515
23	0.337	0.396	0.462	0.505
24	0.330	0.388	0.453	0.496
25	0.323	0.381	0.445	0.487
26	0.317	0.374	0.437	0.479
27	0.311	0.367	0.430	0.471
28	0.306	0.361	0.423	0.463
29	0.301	0.355	0.416	0.456
30	0.296	0.349	0.409	0.449
35	0.275	0.325	0.381	0.418
40	0.257	0.304	0.358	0.393
45	0.243	0.288	0.338	0.372
50	0.231	0.273	0.322	0.354
60	0.211	0.250	0.295	0.325
70	0.195	0.232	0.274	0.302
80	0.183	0.217	0.256	0.283
90	0.173	0.205	0.242	0.267
100	0.164	0.195	0.230	0.254

Source: Fisher, R. A., & Yates, F. (1974). *Statistical Tables for Biological, Agricultural and Medical Research* (6th ed., Table VI). London: Longman Group Ltd. (Previously published by Oliver and Boyd Ltd., Edinburgh.) Adapted and reprinted with permission of Addison Wesley Longman.

APPENDIX G

Chi-Square Critical Values Table

TABLE G.1 ■ Critical Values of Chi-Square (χ^2)

	Level of Significance	
df	.05	.01
1	3.84	6.64
2	5.99	9.21
3	7.81	11.34
4	9.49	13.28
5	11.07	15.09
6	12.59	16.81
7	14.07	18.48
8	15.51	20.09
9	16.92	21.67
10	18.31	23.21
11	19.68	24.72
12	21.03	26.22
13	22.36	27.69
14	23.68	29.14
15	25.00	30.58
16	26.30	32.00
17	27.59	33.41
18	28.87	34.80
19	30.14	36.19
20	31.41	37.47
21	32.67	38.93

(Continued)

TABLE G.1 ■ (Continued)

	Level of Significance	
df	.05	.01
22	33.92	40.29
23	35.17	41.64
24	36.42	42.98
25	37.65	44.31
26	38.88	45.64
27	40.11	46.96
28	41.34	48.28
29	42.56	49.59
30	43.77	50.89
40	55.76	63.69
50	67.50	76.15
60	79.08	88.38
70	90.53	100.42

Source: Fisher, R. A., & Yates, F. (1974). *Statistical Tables for Biological, Agricultural and Medical Research* (6th ed., Table IV). London: Longman Group Ltd. (previously published by Oliver and Boyd Ltd., Edinburgh.) Reprinted with permission of Addison Wesley Longman Ltd.

GLOSSARY

abstract: A summary of an article that appears at the beginning of the article and in searchable databases of journal articles

alpha level: The probability level used by researchers to indicate the cutoff probability level (highest value) that allows them to reject the null hypothesis

amount variable: A variable that includes levels with a different amount of the treatment changing from level to level

analysis of variance (ANOVA): Inferential test used for designs with three or more sample means

applied research: Research conducted with the goal of solving everyday problems

archival data: Data collection technique that involves analysis of preexisting data

attrition or mortality: Occurs when participants choose not to complete a study

authority: Relying on a knowledgeable person or group as a means of knowing about the world

bar graphs: Graphs of data for categorical variables where the bar height represents the size of the value (e.g., mean)

basic research: Research conducted with the goal of understanding fundamental processes of phenomena

between-groups variance: The average squared difference between the sample means and the overall (grand) mean

between-subjects variable: Participant experiences only one level of the independent variable

bivalent independent variable: An independent variable with two levels—a design is considered bivalent if it contains only one bivalent independent variable

case study: A research design that involves intensive study of particular individuals and their behaviors

categorical variables: Measures with responses as categories that cannot be divided into smaller units

causal hypothesis: A prediction about the results of a study that includes the causes of a behavior

causal research question: A research question that asks what causes specific behaviors to occur

central limit theorem: The mathematical description of the shape of the distribution of sample means that states that for a population with mean μ and standard deviation σ, the distribution of sample means for sample size n will have a mean equal to μ, a standard deviation equal to the standard error, and a shape approaching a normal distribution as n becomes very large

central tendency: Representation of a typical score in a distribution

chi-square (χ^2) test: A significance test used to determine if a relationship exists between two variables measured on nominal or ordinal scales

closed-ended response scale: Participants' responses to survey questions according to the response options provided by the researcher

cluster sample: A sample chosen randomly from clusters identified in the population

coercion: Forcing participants to participate in research without their consent

confederate: A person who is part of a research study but acts as though he or she is not to deceive the participant about the study's purpose

confidence intervals: Ranges of values that the population mean likely falls in with a specific level of certainty

confidentiality: The researcher's responsibility to protect the participants' identity and right to privacy (including participant responses) during and after the research study

confounding variable: An extraneous factor present in a study that may affect the results

consent form: A form provided to the participants at the beginning of a research study to obtain their consent for the study and explain the study's purpose and risks and the participants' rights as participants

construct validity: The degree to which a survey is an accurate measure of interest

content analysis: An archival data collection technique that involves analysis of the content of an individual's spoken or written record

continuous variables: Measures with number scores that can be divided into smaller units

control group: The group of participants in an experiment that do not experience the treatment level of the independent variable

convenience or purposive sample: A sample chosen such that the probability of an individual being chosen cannot be determined

correlational study: A type of research design that examines the relationships between multiple dependent variables without manipulating any of the variables

counterbalancing: A control used in within-subjects experiments where equal numbers of participants are randomly assigned to different orders of the conditions

critical region: The most extreme portion of a distribution of statistical values for the null hypothesis determined by the alpha level (typically 5%)

data-driven hypothesis: Hypothesis for a study that is based on the results of previous, related studies

debriefing: Discussing the purpose and benefits of a research study with participants—often done at the end of the study

deception: Misleading participants about the purpose or procedures of a research study

deduction: Using logical reasoning and current knowledge as a means of knowing about the world

degrees of freedom: The number of scores that can vary in the calculation of a statistic

demand characteristics: A source of bias that can occur in a study due to participants changing their behavior based on their perception of the study and its purpose

dependent or response variable: A variable that is measured or observed from an individual

descriptive hypothesis: A prediction about the results of a study that describes the behavior or the relationship between behaviors

descriptive research question: A research question that asks about the presence of behavior, how frequently it is exhibited, or whether there is a relationship between different behaviors

descriptive statistics: Statistics that help researchers summarize or describe data

discussion: Section of an APA-style article that compares the results of a study with the predictions and the results of previous studies

distribution: A set of scores

distribution of sample means: The distribution of all possible sample means for all possible samples of a particular size from a population

double-blind design: Procedure used to control for experimenter bias by keeping the knowledge of the group assignments from both the participants and the researchers who interact with the participants

estimated standard error: An estimate of sampling error that is determined from the standard deviation of the distribution of sample means using the sample standard deviation to represent the population standard deviation

ex post facto design: Quasi-experiment where subjects are grouped based on a characteristic they already possess (e.g., age or gender)

experiment: A type of research design that involves manipulation of an independent variable, allowing control of extraneous variables that could affect the results

experimental group: The group of participants in an experiment that experience the treatment level of the independent variable

experimenter bias: A source of bias in a study created when a researcher treats groups differently (often unknowingly) based on knowledge of the hypothesis

external validity: The degree to which the results of a study apply to individuals and realistic behaviors outside the study

face validity: A study or scale appearing to be intuitively valid on the surface

factorial design: An experiment or quasi-experiment that includes more than one independent variable

field experiment: An experiment conducted in the participants' natural environment

frequency distribution: A graph or table of a distribution showing the frequency of each score in the distribution

Hawthorne effect: A source of bias that can occur in a study due to participants changing their behavior because they are aware that they are being observed

homogeneity of variances: The assumption of independent samples *t* tests and analyses of variance (ANOVAs) that the variance in the scores in the population is equal across groups

hypothesis: Prediction regarding the results of a research study

independent variable: A variable in an experiment that is manipulated by the researcher such that the levels of the variable change across or within subjects in the experiment

inferential statistics: A set of statistical procedures used by researchers to test hypotheses about populations

informed consent: Obtaining consent from participants for participation in research after the participants have been informed about the purpose, procedure, and risks of the research

institutional review board (IRB): A committee of knowledgeable individuals who oversee the ethics of research with human participants conducted at an institution

interaction effect: The effect of one independent variable depends on the level of the other independent variable

internal validity: The degree to which a study provides causal information about behavior

Internet sample: A sample chosen from the population by recruiting on the Internet

interobserver or interrater reliability: A measure of the degree to which different observers rate behaviors in similar ways

interval scale: A scale of data measurement that involves numerical responses that are equally spaced, but scores are not ratios of each other

interviews: A data collection technique that involves direct questioning of individuals about their behaviors and attitudes

introduction: A section of an APA-style article that introduces the topic of the study, reviews relevant background studies, and presents predictions for the data

intuition: Relying on common sense as a means of knowing about the world

Latin square: Partial counterbalancing technique where the number of orders of conditions used is equal to the number of conditions in the study

levels of the independent variable: Different situations or conditions that participants experience in an experiment because of the manipulation of the independent variable

line graphs: Graphs of data for continuous variables where each value is graphed as a point and the points are connected to show differences between scores (e.g., means)

linear regression: A statistical technique that determines the best fit line to a set of data to allow prediction of the score on one variable from the score on the other variable

literature review: A process of searching for and reviewing previous studies related to a study being developed to add to the knowledge in an area and make appropriate predictions about the data

main effect: Test of the differences between all means for each level of an independent variable in an ANOVA

marginal means: Average mean scores for each level of an independent variable

matched design: A between-subjects experiment that involves sets of participants matched on a specific characteristic with each member of the set randomly assigned to a different level of the independent variable

mean: The calculated average of the scores in a distribution

median: The middle score in a distribution, such that half of the scores are above and half are below that value

method: Section of an APA-style article that describes the participants, design, stimuli, apparatus, and procedure used in the study

mode: The most common score in a distribution

multivalent variable: An independent variable that includes three or more levels—a design is considered multivalent if there is only one independent variable that contains three or more levels

naturalistic observation: A data collection technique involving noninvasive observation of individuals in their natural environments

negative relationship: Relationship between variables characterized by an increase in one variable that occurs with a decrease in the other variable

nominal scale: A scale of data measurement that involves nonordered categorical responses

nonparametric test: An inferential statistics test that can be used to test hypotheses about categorical variables

normal distribution: A symmetrical distribution in which the percentage of scores in each portion of the distribution is known

null hypothesis: The hypothesis that an effect or relationship does not exist (or exists in the opposite direction of the alternative hypothesis) in the population

Nuremberg Code: Set of ethical guidelines developed for research with human participants based on information gained during the Nuremberg trials after World War II

observation: Relying on what one observes as a means of knowing about the world

one-tailed hypothesis: Only one direction of an effect or relationship is predicted in the alternative hypothesis of the test

open-ended response scale: Participants respond to survey questions in any manner they feel appropriate for the question

operational definition: The way a behavior is defined in a research study to allow for its measurement

order effects: Occur when the order in which the participants experience conditions in an experiment affects the results of the study

ordinal scale: A scale of data measurement that involves ordered categorical responses

outcome variable: The dependent variable in a correlational study that is being predicted by the predictor variable

outlier: An extreme high or low score in a distribution

***p* value:** Probability value associated with an inferential test that indicates the likelihood of obtaining the data in a study when the null hypothesis is true

parametric test: An inferential statistics test that can be used to test hypotheses about continuous variables

Pearson *r* test: A significance test used to determine whether a linear relationship exists between two variables measured on ratio or interval scales

peer review: A process that takes place prior to publication of an article in many journals where experts make suggestions for improving an article and make recommendations about whether an article should be published in a journal

placebo: A sugar pill given to the control group in a drug study to allow all groups to believe that they are receiving a treatment

plagiarism: Claiming another's work or ideas as one's own

pooled variance: The combined variance terms for two samples weighted by the sample size of each sample

population: A group of individuals a researcher seeks to learn about from a research study

positive relationship: Relationship between variables characterized by an increase in one variable that occurs with an increase in the other variable

post hoc tests: Additional significance tests conducted to determine which means are significantly different for a main effect

power: The ability of a hypothesis test to detect an effect or relationship when one exists (equal to 1 minus the probability of a Type II error

predictor variable: The dependent variable in a correlational study that is used to predict the score on another variable

presence–absence variable: A variable that involves a manipulation with a level that involves the treatment and a level that does not involve the treatment

pretest–posttest design: A type of research design (often a quasi-experiment) where behavior is measured both before and after a treatment or condition is implemented

probability sample: A sample chosen such that individuals are chosen with a specific probability

qualitative: Nonnumerical participant responses

quantitative: Numerical data

quasi-experiment: A type of research design where a comparison is made, as in an experiment, but no random assignment of participants to groups occurs

quasi-independent or subject variable: Variable that allows comparison of groups of participants without manipulation (i.e., no random assignment)

quota sample: A sample chosen from the population such that available individuals are chosen with equivalent proportions of individuals for a specific characteristic in the population and sample

R^2: Fit statistic indicating how well an equation fits the data

random assignment: Participants are randomly assigned to levels of the independent variable in an experiment to control for individual differences as an extraneous variable

range: The difference between the highest and lowest scores in a distribution

ratio scale: A scale of data measurement that involves numerical responses in which scores are ratios of each other

reaction time: Measurement of the length of time to complete a task

regression toward the mean: Can occur when participants score higher or lower than their personal average—the next time they are tested, they are more likely to score near their personal average, making scores unreliable

reliability: The degree to which the results of a study can be replicated under similar conditions

results: Section of an APA-style article that presents a summary of the results and the statistical tests of the predictions

risk–benefit analysis: Weighing the risks against the benefits of a research study to ensure that the benefits outweigh the risks

sample: The group of individuals chosen from the population to represent it in a research study

sampling error: The difference between the observations in a population and in the sample that represents that population in a study

scatterplot: A graph showing the relationship between two dependent variables for a group of individuals

scientific or alternative hypothesis: The hypothesis that an effect or relationship exists (or exists in a specific direction) in the population

significant test: p value is less than or equal to alpha in an inferential test and the null hypothesis can be rejected

simple effects tests: Statistical tests conducted to characterize an interaction effect when one is found in an ANOVA

simple random sample: A sample chosen randomly from the population such that each individual has an equal chance of being selected

single-blind design: Procedure used to hide the group assignment from the participants in a study to prevent their beliefs about the effectiveness of a treatment from affecting the results

skewed distribution: A distribution of scores where the shape of the distribution shows a clustering of scores at the low or high end of the scale

small-*n* design: An experiment conducted with one or a few participants to better understand the behavior of those individuals

social desirability bias: Bias created in survey responses from respondents' desire to be viewed more favorably by others, typically resulting in overreporting of positive behaviors and underreporting of negative behaviors

sphericity assumption: Assumption of the repeated measures (within-subjects) ANOVA that pairs of scores in the population have equal variance

standard deviation: A measure representing the average difference between the scores and the mean of a distribution

standard error: The estimate of sampling error that is determined from the standard deviation of the distribution of sample means

stratified random sample: A sample chosen from the population such that the proportion of individuals with a particular characteristic is equivalent in the population and the sample

sum of products: The sum of the products of the squared deviations from the mean of the scores for each variable

survey research: A research study that uses the survey observational technique to measure behavior

symmetrical distribution: A distribution of scores where the shape of the distribution shows a mirror image on either side of the middle score

systematic observation: Data collection technique in which control is exerted over the conditions under which the behavior is observed

***t* test:** Significance test used to compare means

testing effects: Occur when participants are tested more than once in a study—with early testing affecting later testing

theory: An explanation of behavior that can be tested through research studies

theory-driven hypothesis: Hypothesis for a study that is based on a theory about the behavior of interest

third-variable problem: The presence of extraneous factors in a study that affect the dependent variable and can decrease the internal validity of the study

two-tailed hypothesis: Both directions of an effect or relationship are considered in the alternative hypothesis of the test

Type I error: An error made in a significance test when the researcher rejects the null hypothesis that is actually true

Type II error: An error made in a significance test when the researcher fails to reject the null hypothesis that is actually false

type variable: A variable that involves a manipulation of types of a treatment

Unit Normal Table: A table of the proportion of scores in a normal distribution for many different *z* score values

validity: The accuracy of the results of a study

variability: The spread of scores in a distribution

variable: An attribute that can vary across individuals

variance: The standard deviation of a distribution squared

volunteer sample: A sample chosen from the population such that available individuals are chosen based on who volunteers to participate

within-groups variance: The average squared difference between the scores in each group and the group mean

within-subjects variable: Participant experiences all levels of the independent variable

***z* score:** A standardized score that indicates the location of a score within a population distribution

REFERENCES

Abramson, P. R. (1984). *Sarah: A sexual biography.* Albany: State University of New York Press.

Adair, J. G. (1984). The Hawthorne effect: A reconsideration of the methodological artifact. *Journal of Applied Psychology, 69,* 334–345.

Adolph, K. E., Cole, W. C., Komati, M., Garciaguirre, J. S., Badaly, D., Lingeman, J. M., . . . Sotsky, R. B. (2012). How do you learn to walk? Thousands of steps and dozens of falls per day. *Psychological Science, 23,* 1387–1394. doi:10.1177/0956797612446346

American Psychological Association. (2003). *1999 Doctorate Employment Survey.* Retrieved January 11, 2008, from http://research.apa.org/des99report.html#patterms

American Psychological Association. (2010). *Publication manual of the American Psychological Association* (6th ed.). Washington, DC: Author.

American Psychological Association. (2017). *Ethical principles of psychologists and code of conduct.* Retrieved August 10, 2018, from http://www.apa.org/ethics/code

Anderson, B., & Harvey, T. (1996). Alterations in cortical thickness and neuronal density in the frontal cortex of Albert Einstein. *Neuroscience Letters, 21,* 161–164.

Anderson, C. A., Shibuya, A., Ihori, N., Swing, E. L., Bushman, B. J., Sakamoto, A., . . . Saleem, M. (2010). Violent video game effects on aggression, empathy, and prosocial behavior in Eastern and Western countries: A meta-analytic review. *Psychological Bulletin, 136,* 151–173.

Ashe, S. E. (1955). Opinions and social pressure. *Scientific American, 193,* 31–35.

Ban, S. W., Lee, M., & Yang, H. S. (2004). A face detection using biologically motivated bottom-up saliency map model and top-down perception model. *Neurocomputing: An International Journal, 56,* 475–480.

Bartecchi, C., Aldever, R. N., Nevin-Woods, C., Thomas, W. M., Estacio, R. M., Bartelson, B. B., & Krantz, M. J. (2006). Reduction in the incidence of acute myocardial infarction associated with a citywide smoking ordinance. *Circulation, 114,* 1490–1496.

Bastian, B., Jetten, J., & Ferris, L. J. (2014). Pain as social glue: Shared pain increases cooperation. *Psychological Science, 25,* 2079–2085.

Beck, A. T., & Steer, R. A. (1993). *Beck Anxiety Inventory manual.* San Antonio, TX: PsychCorp.

Beck, A. T., Steer, R. A., & Brown, G. K. (1996). *Manual for the Beck Depression Inventory–II.* San Antonio, TX: PsychCorp.

Birnbaum, M. H. (2001). *Introduction to behavioral research on the Internet.* Upper Saddle River, NJ: Prentice Hall.

Bohbot, V. D., & Corkin, S. (2007). Posterior parahippocampal place learning in H.M. *Hippocampus, 17,* 863–872.

Boothby, E. J., Clark, M. S., & Bargh, J. A. (2014). Shared experiences are amplified. *Psychological Science, 25,* 2209–2216.

Bramel, D., & Friend, R. (1981). Hawthorne, the myth of the docile worker, and class bias in psychology. *American Psychologist, 36,* 867–868.

Brandt, A. (2000). Racism and research: The case of the Tuskegee syphilis experiment. In S. M. Reverby (Ed.), *Tuskegee's truths: Rethinking the Tuskegee syphilis study* (pp. 15–33). Chapel Hill: University of North Carolina Press.

Brown-Iannuzzi, J. L., Lundberg, K. B., Kay, A. C., & Payne, B. K. (2015). Subjective status shapes political preferences. *Psychological Science, 26,* 15–26.

Broyles, L. M., Tate, J. A., & Happ, M. B. (2008). Videorecording in clinical research. *Nursing Research, 57,* 59–63.

Bub, D. N., Masson, M. E. J., & Lin, T. (2013). Features of planned hand actions influence identification of graspable objects. *Psychological Science*, *24*, 1269–1276.

Burger, J. M. (2009). Replicating Milgram: Would people still obey today? *American Psychologist*, *64*, 1–11.

Chiang, H. (2008). Communicative spontaneity of children with autism: A preliminary analysis. *Autism*, *12*, 9–21.

Coane, J. H., & McBride, D. M. (2006). The role of test structure in creating false memories. *Memory & Cognition*, *34*, 1026–1036.

Coane, J. H., McBride, D. M, Termonen, M.-L., & Cutting, J. C. (2016). Categorical and associative relations increase false memory relative to purely associative relations. *Memory & Cognition*, *44*, 37–49.

Cohen, J. (1988). *Statistical power analysis for the behavioral sciences* (2nd ed.). Hillsdale, NJ: Lawrence Erlbaum.

Cohen, J. (1990). Things I have learned (so far). *American Psychologist*, *45*, 1304–1312.

Compton, M. T., Goulding, S. M., & Walker, E. F. (2007). Cannabis use, first-episode psychosis, and schizotypy: A summary and synthesis of recent literature. *Current Psychiatry Review*, *3*, 161–171.

Conte, A. M., & McBride, D. M. (2018). Comparing time-based and event-based prospective memory over short delays. *Memory*, *26*, 936–945.

Converse, B. A., Risen, J. L., & Carter, T. J. (2012). Investing in karma: When wanting promotes helping. *Psychological Science*, *23*, 923–930.

Corneille, O., Monin, B., & Pleyers, G. (2005). Is positivity a cue or a response option? Warm glow vs evaluative matching in the familiarity for attractive and not-so-attractive faces. *Journal of Experimental Social Psychology*, *41*, 431–437.

DeSouza, E., & Fansler, A. G. (2003). Contrapower sexual harassment: A survey of students and faculty members. *Sex Roles*, *48*, 519–542.

Educational Testing Service. (2016). 2016–2017 interpreting your GRE® scores. Retrieved May 15, 2017, from https://www.ets.org/s/gre/pdr

Einstein, G. O., & McDaniel, M. A. (2005). Prospective memory: Multiple retrieval processes. *Current Directions in Psychological Science*, *14*, 286–290.

Ferrè, E. R., Lopez, C., & Haggard, P. (2014). Anchoring the self to the body: Vestibular contribution to the sense of self. *Psychological Science*, *25*, 2106–2108.

Francis, G. (2013). Replication, statistical consistency, and publication bias. *Journal of Mathematical Psychology*, *57*, 153–169.

Fromkin, V., Krashen, S., Curtiss, S., Rigler, D., & Rigler, M. (1974). The development of language in Genie: A case of language acquisition beyond the "critical period." *Brain and Language*, *1*, 81–107.

Geraerts, E., Bernstein, D. M., Merekelbach, H., Linders, C., Raymaekers, L., & Loftus, E. F. (2008). Lasting false beliefs and their behavioral consequences. *Psychological Science*, *19*, 749–753.

Grant, D. A. (1948). The Latin square principle in the design and analysis of psychological experiments. *Psychological Bulletin*, *45*, 427–442.

Green, S. M., Hadjistavropoulos, T., & Sharpe, D. (2008). Client personality characteristics predict satisfaction with cognitive behavior therapy. *Journal of Clinical Psychology*, *64*, 40–51.

Greenwald, A. G. (1975). Consequences of prejudice against the null hypothesis. *Psychological Bulletin*, *82*, 1–20.

Griggs, R. A., & Whitehead, G. I. III (2015). Coverage of recent criticisms of Milgram's obedience experiments in introductory social psychology textbooks. *Theory & Psychology*, *25*, 564–580.

Haun, D. B. M., Rekers, Y., & Tomasello, M. (2014). Children conform to the behavior of peers; other great apes stick with what they know. *Psychological Science*, *25*, 2160–2167.

Heidenreich, B. A. (1993). Investigations into the effects of repeated amphetamine administration and crus cerebri lesions on the electrophysiology of midbrain dopamine neurons in the rat. *Dissertation Abstracts International*, *53*, 4522.

Hilts, P. J. (1996). *Memory's ghost: The nature of memory and the strange tale of Mr. M.* New York, NY: Touchstone.

Howell, D. C. (2013). *Statistical methods for psychology.* Belmont, CA: Wadsworth.

Hund, A. M., & Plumert, J. M. (2003). Does information about what things are influence children's memory for where things are? *Developmental Psychology, 39*, 939–948.

Inzlicht, M., McKay, L., & Aronson, J. (2006). How being the target of prejudice affects self-control. *Psychological Science, 17*, 262–269.

Kahn, J. H., & Hessling, R. M. (2001). Measuring the tendency to conceal versus disclose psychological distress. *Journal of Social and Clinical Psychology, 20*, 41–65.

Kane, J. (2012). Top 10 myths of heart health. *PBS Newshour.* Retrieved January 20, 2016, from http://www.pbs.org/newshour/rundown/the-top-10-myths-of-heart-health

Keppel, G., & Wickens, T. D. (2004). *Design and analysis: A researcher's handbook.* Upper Saddle River, NJ: Pearson.

Krantz, J. H., & Dalal, R. (2000). Validity of web-based psychological research. In M. H. Birnbaum (Ed.), *Psychological experiments on the Internet* (pp. 35–60). San Diego, CA: Academic Press.

Laland, K. N., & Galef, B. G. (2009). *The question of animal culture.* Cambridge, MA: Harvard University Press.

Landsberger, H. (1955). Interaction process analysis of professional behavior: A study of labor mediators in twelve labor-management disputes. *American Sociological Review, 20*, 566–575.

Lester, D. (2006). Understanding suicide through studies of diaries: The case of Cesare Pavese. *Archives of Suicide Research, 10*, 295–302.

Lipman, P. D., & Caplan, L. J. (1992). Adult age differences in memory for routes: Effects of instruction and spatial diagram. *Psychology and Aging, 7*, 435–442.

Loftus, E. F. (1993). Psychologists in the eyewitness world. *American Psychologist, 48*, 550–552.

McBride, D. M., Beckner, J. K., & Abney, D. H. (2011). Effects of delay of prospective memory cues in an ongoing task on prospective memory task performance. *Memory & Cognition, 39*, 1222–1231.

McBride, D. M., Coane, J. H., & Raulerson, B. (2006). An investigation of false memory in perceptual implicit tasks. *Acta Psychologica, 123*, 240–260.

Metcalfe, J., Casal-Roscum, L., Radin, A., & Friedman, D. (2015). On teaching old dogs new tricks. *Psychological Science, 26*, 1833–1842.

Middlemist, D. R., Knowles, E. S., & Matter, C. F. (1976). Personal space invasions in the lavatory: Suggestive evidence for arousal. *Journal of Personality and Social Psychology, 33*, 541–546.

Mihai, A., Damsa, C., Allen, M., Baleydier, B., Lazignac, C., & Heinz, A. (2007). Viewing videotape of themselves while experiencing delirium tremens could reduce the relapse rate in alcohol-dependent patients. *Addiction, 102*, 226–231.

Milgram, S. (1963). Behavioral study of obedience. *Journal of Abnormal and Social Psychology, 67*, 371–378.

Moore, D. W. (2004). *Sweet dreams go with a good night's sleep.* Retrieved January 11, 2008, from http://www.gallup.com/poll/14380/Sweet-Dreams-Good-Nights-Sleep.aspx

Moore-Ede, M. C., Sulzman, F. M., & Fuller, C. A. (1982). *The clocks that time us: Physiology of the circadian timing system.* Cambridge, MA: Harvard University Press.

Mueller, C. M., & Dweck, C. S. (1998). Praise for intelligence can undermine children's motivation and performance. *Journal of Personality and Social Psychology, 75*, 33–52.

Nairne, J. S. (2009). *Psychology.* Belmont, CA: Thompson Wadsworth.

Nairne, J. S., VanArsdall, J. E., Pandeirada, J. N. S., Cogdill, M., & LeBreton, J. M. (2013). Adaptive memory: The mnemonic value of animacy. *Psychological Science, 24*, 2099–2105.

National Commission for the Protection of Human Subjects of Biomedical and Behavioral Research. (1979). *Belmont report.* Washington, DC: Department of Health and Human Services.

Oaklander, M. (2015). Here's what happens when you drink wine every night. *Time.* Retrieved January 20, 2016, from http://time.com/4070762/red-wine- resveratrol-diabetes

Ogden, C. L., Fryar, C. D., Carroll, M. D., & Flegal, K. M. (2004). Mean body weight, height, and body mass index, United States 1960–2002. *Centers for Disease Control, 347*, 1–18.

O'Hanlon, C. G., & Roberson, D. (2006). Learning in context: Linguistic and attentional constraints on children's color term learning. *Journal of Experimental Child Psychology, 94*, 275–300.

Olzmann, J. A. (2007). Pathogenic mechanisms of DJ-1 in Parkinson's disease. *Dissertation Abstracts International: Section B: The Sciences and Engineering, 68*, 2857.

Paivio, A. (2007). *Mind and its evolution: A dual coding theoretical approach*. London, England: Psychology Press.

Pal, S., & Saksvik, P. O. (2008). Work-family conflict and psychosocial work environment stressors as predictors of job stress in a cross-cultural study. *International Journal of Stress Management, 15*, 22–42.

Reiniger, H. (Producer). (2001). *Discovering psychology* (Updated ed.) [Television series]. Burlington, VT: Annenberg.

Retrospection: Social sciences' problematic interfaces with the social order. (2008). *PsycCRITIQUES, 53*. Retrieved June 9, 2009, from http://psych.hanover.edu/research/exponnet.html

Roediger, H. L., III, & Karpicke, J. D. (2006). Test-enhanced learning: Taking memory tests improves long-term retention. *Psychological Science, 17*, 249–255.

Roediger, H. L., III, & McDermott, K. B. (1993). Implicit memory in normal human subjects. In F. Boller & J. Grafman (Eds.), *Handbook of neuropsychology* (Vol. 8, pp. 63–131). Amsterdam, The Netherlands: Elsevier.

Rubin, D. C., & Friendly, M. (1986). Predicting which words get recalled: Measures of free recall, availability, goodness, emotionality, and pronunciability for 925 nouns. *Memory & Cognition, 14*, 79–94.

Russell, E. M., Ickes, W., & Ta, V. P. (2018). Women interact more comfortably and intimately with gay men—but not straight men—after learning their sexual orientation. *Psychological Science, 29*, 288–303.

Schnall, S., Benton, J., & Harvey, S. (2008). With a clean conscience: Cleanliness reduces the severity of moral judgments. *Psychological Science, 19*, 1219–1222.

Schnall, S., Haidt, J., Clore, G. L., & Jordan, A. H. (2008). Disgust as embodied moral judgment. *Personality and Social Psychology Bulletin, 34*, 1096–1109.

Schuler, H. (1982). *Ethical problems in psychological research*. New York, NY: Academic Press.

Scutti, S. (2018). Do video games lead to violence? CNN.com. Retrieved April 19, 2018, from https://www.cnn.com/2016/07/25/health/video-games-and-violence/index.html

Seli, P., Carriere, J. S. A., Wammes, J. D., Risko, E. F., Schacter, D. L., & Smilek, D. (2018). On the clock: Evidence for the rapid and strategic modulation of mind wandering. *Psychological Science, 29*, 1247–1256. doi:10.1177/0956797618761039

Shadish, W. R., Cook, T. D., & Campbell, D. T. (2002). *Experimental and quasi-experimental designs for generalized causal inference*. Boston, MA: Houghton Mifflin.

Shaw, J., & Porter, S. (2015). Constructing rich false memories of committing crime. *Psychological Science, 26*, 291–301.

Shea, C. (2011, November 13). Fraud scandal fuels debate over practices of social psychology. *Chronicle of Higher Education*. Retrieved July 12, 2015, from http://chronicle.com/article/As-Dutch-Research-Scandal/129746

Silvers, J. A., Insel, C., Powers, A., Franz, P., Weber, J., Mischel, W., . . . Ochsner, K. N. (2014). Curbing craving: Behavioral and brain evidence that children regulate craving when instructed to do so but have higher baseline craving than adults. *Psychological Science, 25*, 1932–1942.

Sofer, C., Dotsch, R., Wigboldus, D. H. J., & Todorov, A. (2015). What is typical is good: The influence of face typicality on perceived trustworthiness. *Psychological Science, 26*, 39–47.

Storm, B. C., & Stone, S. M. (2015). Saving-enhanced memory: The benefits of saving on the learning and remembering of new information. *Psychological Science, 26*, 182–188.

Strayer, D. L., & Johnston, W. A. (2001). Driven to distraction: Dual-task studies of simulated driving and conversing on a cellular phone. *Psychological Science, 12*, 462–466.

U.S. Department of Health and Human Services. (2005). *Code of federal regulations*. Retrieved June 15, 2008, from http://www.hhs.gov/ohrp/humansubjects/guidance/45cfr46.html

Vohs, K. D., & Schooler, J. W. (2008). The value of believing in free will: Encouraging a belief in determinism increases cheating. *Psychological Science*, *19*, 49–54.

von Hippel, W., Ronay, R., Baker, E., Kjelsaas, K., & Murphy, S. C. (2016). Quick thinkers are smooth talkers: Mental speed facili-tates charisma. *Psychological Science, 27*, 119–122.

Wagman, J. B., Langley, M. D., & Farmer-Dougan, V. (2018). Carrying their own weight: Dogs perceive changing affordances for reaching. *Quarterly Journal of Experimental Psychology*, *71*, 1040–1044.

Wagman, J. B., Zimmerman, C., & Sorric, C. (2007). "Which feels heavier—a pound of lead or a pound of feather?" A potential perceptual basis of a cognitive riddle. *Perception, 36,* 1709–1711.

Wakefield, A. J., Murch, S. H., Anthony, A., Linnell, J., Casson, D. M., Mali, M., . . . Walker-Smith, J. A. (1998). Ileal-lymphoid-nodular hyperplasia, non-specific colitis, and pervasive developmental disorder in children. *The Lancet*, *351*, 637–641. (retracted)

Wesselmann, E. D., Bagg, D., & Williams, K. D. (2009). "I feel your pain": The effects of observing ostracism on the ostracism detection system. *Journal of Experimental Social Psychology*, *45*, 1308–1311.

Witelson, S., Kigar, D. L., & Harvey, T. (1999). The exceptional brain of Albert Einstein. *Lancet*, *353*, 2149–2153.

Worthy, D. A., Gorlick, M. A., Pacheco, J. L., Schnyer, D. M., & Maddox, W. T. (2011). With age comes wisdom: Decision making in younger and older adults. *Psychological Science*, *22*, 1375–1380.

Wynn, K. (1992). Addition and subtraction by human infants. *Nature*, *358*, 749–750.

Zimbardo, P. G. (1973). On the ethics of intervention in human psychological research: With special reference to the Stanford prison experiment. *Cognition*, *2*, 243–256.

Zimbardo, P. G. (1974). On "Obedience to authority." *American Psychologist*, *29*, 566–567.

INDEX